KENNEDY

KENNEDY

By Theodore C. Sorensen

Special Counsel to the Late President

KONECKY&KONECKY

Konecky & Konecky
72 Ayers Point Rd.
Old Saybrook, CT 06475

This edition published by special arrangement with
HarperCollins Publishers, Inc.

ISBN: 1-56852-035-2

Printed in the United States of America

The lines of verse appearing on page 64 are a paraphrase of the Robert Frost poem
"Stopping by Woods on a Snowy Evening" from *Complete Poems of Robert Frost.*
Copyright 1923 by Holt, Rinehart and Winston, Inc. Copyright 1951 by Robert Frost.
By permission of Holt, Rinehart and Winston, Inc.

The poem on page 336 is a translation by Robert Graves of a Domingo Ortega poem
from Mr. Graves' volume of lectures *Oxford Addresses on Poetry.* (c) International
Authors, N.V. 1962, published by Doubleday & Co., Inc., and Cassell & Co. Ltd. Reprinted
by permission of International Authors, N. V.

The Edna St. Vincent Millay poem, entitled "Second Fig," quoted on page 381 is from *Collected
Poems,* Harper & Row, Publishers. Copyright 1922, 1950 by Edna St. Vincent Millay. Reprinted by
permission of Norma Millay Ellis.

The lines of verse quoted on page 748 are from a poem especially composed by the Irish poet
D.L. Kelleher for the christening of Dr. Thomas Kiernan's son. Grateful acknowledgment is made
to Dr. Kiernan for permission to reprint.

For my father
C. A. SORENSEN (1890–1959)
who showed me the way

CONTENTS

[vii]

CONTENTS

KENNEDY

PROLOGUE

Across the muddy Potomac from the Lincoln Memorial a green and gentle slope rises gradually to what was once the home of Robert E. Lee. From halfway up that hill one can see on a clear autumn day most of the majesty that is Washington. The three marble monuments and memorials—to the men who forged in the Presidency an instrument of power and compassion—remind a grateful nation that it has been blessed in its gravest trials with its greatest leaders. In the distance the dome of the Capitol covers a milieu of wisdom and folly, Presidential ambitions and antagonisms, political ideals and ideologies. To the right is the stark and labyrinthian Pentagon, guiding under Presidential command the massive armed might on which hinge our security and survival. On the grassy slope itself, reminding us that "since this country was founded, each generation of Americans has been summoned to give testimony to its national loyalty," are marked with simple stones "the graves of young Americans who answered the call to service." And away to the left, its white sandstone hidden behind a screen of greenery, is the seat of executive power, the scene of more heroic dramas, comedies and tragedies than any stage in the world.

It was on just such a clear autumn afternoon, on October 20, 1962, that President John Fitzgerald Kennedy stood on the second-story back porch of the White House, gazing at this same panorama, and talked—as he almost never talked—of life and death. His brother, the Attorney General, was with us, as were others from time to time. In the oval study on the other side of that porch door, the President had moments earlier concluded an historic meeting. The two great nuclear powers, the United States and the Soviet Union, were faced with their first direct military confrontation since acquiring the capacity to destroy each other. Soviet ships were to be stopped by an American naval barricade in the Caribbean. The cause was Soviet missiles on the island of Cuba, and the effect was certain to be world-wide.

Our talk on that cool and sunlit back porch was not all somber. Only three weeks earlier we had been up all night with a civil rights battle at the University of Mississippi, a battle termed the most serious constitutional crisis of the century—and presumably with reference to this and his other burdens, the President's first comment upon reaching the privacy of the porch was: "Well, we earned our pay this month."

We talked quietly about his decision, and about the meeting that had just ended. "You have to admire Adlai," he said. "He sticks to his position even when everyone is jumping on him." We talked about the political consequences of the crisis on the coming Congressional elections. The President was canceling the remainder of the most intensive mid-term campaign ever conducted by a Chief Executive, and he guessed (wrongly, as it turned out) that the crisis would benefit those Republicans who had been urging military action against Cuba. "Would you believe it?" he said sardonically. "Homer Capehart is the Winston Churchill of our time!"

In more serious tones we talked calmly of the possibility of nuclear war. As was true some sixteen months earlier in the Berlin crisis, his most solemn feelings concerned the killing of children—his children and all children, children who bore no hate and no responsibility for the errors of men, but who would bear the burden of devastation and death more heavily than anyone else. Less than two years earlier, after the birth of his son John, he had mused aloud over Bacon's words: "He that hath wife and children hath given hostages to fortune." Now he was talking not only about his own but all children, including those yet unborn. "If it weren't for them," he said, "for those who haven't even lived yet, these decisions would be easier."

John Kennedy wanted no war. It was no longer "a rational alternative," he had said a year earlier. He had devoted more time in the White House to deterring and preventing it than to all other subjects combined. Now war loomed large on the horizon. Weakness would only insure it, and strength was not certain to avoid it. A single misstep on his part could extinguish the lights of civilization, but even all the right steps could turn out wrong. Inwardly I recalled his words accepting the Presidential nomination:

All mankind waits upon our decision. A whole world looks to see what we will do. We cannot fail their trust. We cannot fail to try.

Then abruptly he lightened the atmosphere once again. "I hope you realize," he said with a grin, "that there's not enough room for everybody in the White House bomb shelter"; and we joked back and forth about who was on the list.

A few instructions followed: on keeping his decision open until he had one last talk with the Air Force—on keeping his decision secret until he announced it on Monday night—on redrafting his address to the nation and the world. He showed no signs of either frenzy or despair, retaining the same confident calm I had seen in him always. Despite the fatiguing pace of conferences and travels that had crowded his week, his voice exuded vitality and his commands were crisp and clear. Finally, to work on the new speech draft, I returned to my office in the West Wing of the White House, immeasurably cheered by his good humor, warmed by his deep feeling, inspired by his quiet strength.

A few minutes later the President called me on the telephone. "Did you notice what Doug Dillon said about the Jupiters?" he asked. I had. Talk in the meeting that afternoon had turned to the vulnerability to Soviet attack of the American Jupiter missiles which the previous administration had placed in Italy and Turkey, and which the Soviets seemed likely to equate with their new emplacements in Cuba. Dillon, Kennedy's Secretary of Treasury, had been Eisenhower's Under Secretary of State; and he had interjected at that point the information that the Jupiters had practically been forced on Italy and Turkey by an administration unable to find any worthwhile use for them.

"I just wanted to make sure you got that down for the book we're going to write," said John Kennedy. And I replied, as I had on other occasions, "You mean the book *you're* going to write, Mr. President."

This is my substitute for the book he was going to write. It reflects, to the extent possible, his views during his last eleven years. It employs, to the extent possible, his words and his thoughts. It explains, to the extent possible, his reasons.

I have no doubt that he would have written such a book. "It has recently been suggested," he said during his first month in the White House, "that, whether I serve one or two terms in the Presidency, I will find myself at what might be called the awkward age—too old to begin a new career and too young to write my memoirs." But in several conversations he made clear to me his intention to write his memoirs as soon as he left the White House—at least the story of his Presidency, which might well have been only a first installment.

It would have been a remarkable book. Few American Presidents who made so much history possessed his sense of history—or his talent as a writer, or his willingness to be so candid. Far more than most politicians, he not only could objectively measure his own performance but also cared deeply about how that performance would be measured by future historians as well as contemporary voters. His own recollections of public service would have made a memorable volume—carefully factual, amazingly frank, witty and wise—and none of his biographers or chroniclers can hope to do as well.

Anyone aspiring to that task, moreover, must begin with the knowledge that Kennedy was not only a scholar of history but a severe judge of historical and biographical works. He was a Pulitzer Prize winner in biography in his own right, and during his research on *Profiles in Courage* he expressed surprise at the paucity of good biographies. During his years as President he remarked more than once that history depends on who writes it. The consistent inaccuracy of contemporary press accounts caused him to wonder how much credence they would someday be given by those researching his era; and when the Mississippi legislature prepared an official report on the 1962 clash at its state university, placing all blame on the hapless Federal marshals directed by the Kennedys, the President remarked that this was the kind of local document that scholars a generation from now would carefully weigh—and "it makes me wonder," he said, "whether everything I learned about the evils of Reconstruction was really true."

The sternest tests of all, not surprisingly, he applied to works about himself. Before he was President, when he had some choice in the matter, he was very particular about who wrote his biography. Most of the books and magazine articles about him, he noted, inevitably copied each other, repeating the same myths, mistakes, quotations out of context and allegations previously disproven. (A particularly flagrant example was the constant repetition of charges concerning statements Kennedy had allegedly made as a young Congressman to a Harvard seminar, charges still being circulated a decade after they had been thoroughly discredited.) In 1958 he waged an intensive effort with his contacts in the publishing world to prevent a projected biography by a writer inaccurately representing himself to potential publishers as a Kennedy intimate—a man whom Senator Kennedy in fact regarded as uninformed, unobjective and unsound.

Part of this reaction was an oversensitivity to criticism. But an equally large motivation was his concern as an historian that history portray him accurately. Thus he agreed in 1959 to make all files and facts available without condition or limitation to Professor James MacGregor Burns for the only serious pre-Presidential biography published—not because he assumed that Burns would write a panegyric (which Burns didn't) but because he believed that Burns's ability, and his standing in the liberal intellectual community, would give the book stature among the audience we hoped it would reach.

His concern for history continued once he entered the White House. He gave considerable attention to the library which would preserve his papers. He was accessible to the press and other writers, candid and articulate in public and private, and determined to elucidate, educate and explain. At the urging of the eminent historian on his staff, Arthur Schlesinger, Jr., he agreed that procedures should be established to record the firsthand recollections of participants in crucial events while our memories were still fresh.

But he never found time to do it. He arranged for the comprehensive transcription of major deliberations, and at times he dictated memoranda of conversations for the files. But he communicated many of his key decisions by voice instead of in writing, by telephone instead of letter and to one instead of many. Of the record he did leave in writing—his speeches, messages, cables, letters and memoranda—comparatively few were based on first drafts he had dictated or written out himself.

He was, moreover, in some ways deliberately elusive in his approach. While those on the inside knew far more than those on the outside, no one—no single aide, friend or member of his family—knew all his thoughts or actions on any single subject. My particular responsibilities in his Senate and White House office enabled me to know a little bit about a lot of things, but by no means everything about anything. His motives were often unknown or unclear to others, for he resisted the obvious and the easy; and he was usually too busy with the next decision to take time to explain the last.

At times he talked as if he wanted us to be preserving important conversations through memoranda in our files. His rule against future "backstairs" memoirs (which stemmed from a friendly warning offered by Margaret Truman) applied to the household staff, not his professional aides. Yet at other times he made it clear that he would not feel comfortable in confidential talks if he thought one or more participants would be rushing to record their interpretations of his views.

He was the kind of President who would want a great book written about his administration—but he was also the kind who would want to write it himself. He assumed Schlesinger would be writing a solid book —but he otherwise expressed disdain for the reliability of most government memoirs and diaries. He thought that Emmet Hughes, a part-time speech-writer for Eisenhower, had betrayed the trust of Republican officials by quoting their private conversations against them. "I hope," said Kennedy, "that no one around here is writing that kind of book."

This is not that kind of book. It is not even a neutral account. An impassioned participant cannot be an objective observer. Having formed a strong attachment for John Kennedy, I cannot now pretend an attitude of complete detachment. Having devoted nearly eleven years to advancing his interests and explaining his views, I cannot now cloak my partisanship as disinterested scholarship. This book, let it be clear at the outset, praises John Kennedy and what he has done, not merely out of loyalty and affection, but out of deep pride and conviction.

Nevertheless he both deserves and would have desired something better than a portrait that painted him as more herculean than human. In life he did not want his counsel to be a courtier, and in death he would not want his biography confined to eulogies. Making no claims of omniscience or infallibility, he freely admitted imperfections and ignorance in many areas. He credited luck with many of his achievements, and he would have willingly applied to himself what he said of Winston Churchill: "Accustomed to the hardships of battle, he [had] no distaste for pleasure."

While legend recalls our martyred heroes as beloved by all and defeated by none, John Kennedy had enemies as well as friends, and disappointments as well as achievements. He recognized these facts more openly and more clearly than either his admirers or his detractors. His delight in poking fun at the pompous and the preposterous included a refusal to take himself too seriously. It included an ability to laugh at exaggerated claims that were made on his behalf—including some he made himself.

"You are obliged to tell our story in a truthful way," he said to his Voice of America employees, "to tell it, as Oliver Cromwell said about his portrait, with all our blemishes and warts, all those things about us that may not be so immediately attractive." He said the same to a group of foreign students. I believe he would have said the same to me. Proud of his work, he would be pleased to have this book or any book admire it, but he would want it to be admired with the same candor and objectivity with which he admired it himself.

This book does not purport to be a full-scale biography of John Kennedy or a comprehensive history of his era. Yet it is more than a personal memoir. I have attempted to put into context and perspective my observations and association with an extraordinary man during an extraordinary period, relying primarily on what I know rather than on what others have written. I have not interviewed those whose memories may have been shaded by subsequent events, but have depended principally on my files and recollections—for which there can be no footnotes.

As a result, in addition to certain facts omitted for reasons of security or propriety, those episodes in John Kennedy's life in which I did not participate—including all that took place before 1953 and many thereafter—are not reported here in intimate detail. I do not claim that those included were necessarily the most important, only that none has been deliberately excluded and that the real John Kennedy can be more clearly sketched through firsthand recollections.

Many lesser issues, events and personalities have also been omitted for reasons of space. In time, a painstaking scholarly study must systematically analyze each document and day of the Kennedy administration, but I am able to write here only of the peaks, and not of the tortuous paths which led up to them. This is a book, moreover, about one man—not his family, his friends or his foes, not Washington or the world he inhabited, and those in search or need of further facts on those subjects will find them here only as they pertain to John Kennedy.

If some passages seem politically partisan, it is because he was a Democrat and proud of it. My purpose is neither to condemn nor condone the actions of others, nor to substitute my judgment for my subject's. My only obligation is to the truth about Kennedy.

Historical truths, to be sure, are rarely the object of unanimity. Recollections differ, opinions differ, even the same facts appear different to different people. John Kennedy's own role will be recalled in wholly different fashion, I am certain, by those in different relationships with him. To the politicians, he was first and last a politician. To the intellectuals, his qualities of mind were most memorable. Differing traits and trade-marks are recalled by his friends and by his family.

Most regrettable, in my view, are those memorials and tributes which speak more of his style than of his substance. The Kennedy style *was* special—the grace, the wit, the elegance, the youthful looks will rightly long be remembered. But what mattered most to him, and what in my opinion will matter most to history, was the substance—the strength of his ideas and ideals, his courage and judgment. These were the pith and purpose of his Presidency, of which style was but an overtone. I would be the last to diminish the value of his speeches. But their significance lay not in the splendor of their rhetoric but in the principles and policies they conveyed.

During his days at the White House he became weary of hearing the cynics say that his personality was more popular than his program. In his view the two were mutually reinforcing and inseparable. Now the same people—unwilling or unable to perceive the changes he wrought —are writing that his legacy was more one of manner than of meaning.

For still others the tragedy of his death has obscured the reality of his achievements. In emphasizing the youthful promise left unfulfilled, they overlook the promises he kept. His death, to be sure—symbolic though senseless—should never be forgotten. But I think it more important that John Kennedy be remembered not for how he died but for how he lived.

PART ONE

The Emerging Kennedy

CHAPTER I

THE MAN

THE TRULY EXTRAORDINARY MAN," it has been written, "is truly the ordinary man." The first time I met John Kennedy I was immediately impressed by his "ordinary" demeanor—a quality that in itself is extraordinary among politicians. He spoke easily but almost shyly, without the customary verbosity and pomposity. The tailor-made suit that clothed a tall, lean frame was quietly stylish. A thatch of chestnut hair was not as bushy as cartoonists had portrayed it. He did not try to impress me, as office-holders so often do on first meetings, with the strength of his handshake, or with the importance of his office, or with the sound of his voice.

We talked briefly on that morning in early January, 1953, about my application for a job in his new Senate office. I had come to that meeting with more hope than expectation. A month earlier, when I had reviewed with a knowledgeable Washington attorney the list of new Senators for whom I might work, he had snorted at the name of Kennedy. "Jack Kennedy," he said, "wouldn't hire anyone Joe Kennedy wouldn't tell him to hire—and, with the exception of Jim Landis, Joe Kennedy hasn't hired a non-Catholic in fifty years!"

Both of these suppositions turned out to be false. But it was true that Congressman Kennedy's election to the Senate from Massachusetts, after three elections to the House, had not inspired any predictions of greatness in the national press or in Democratic Party circles. The intellectual journals of opinion had doubts about his credentials as a liberal, about his religion and, above all, about his father. The more popular press emphasized the financial cost of his campaign, the participation of his family, his new tea-party technique of electioneering and the sympathy evoked in female hearts by his tousled hair and boyish looks.

No one stopped to think that more than tea and sympathy must have been required for Kennedy, in the face of Eisenhower's sweep of Massachusetts, to oust Eisenhower's campaign manager, the well-known Henry Cabot Lodge, who had first been elected to the Senate when Kennedy was a freshman in college. Kennedy was, in fact, only the third Democrat elected to the Senate in the history of Massachusetts, but the solid significance of his narrow victory (51.5 percent of the vote) had largely been obscured by the glamour and glitter of his publicity.

Except for the Palm Beach tan on a handsome, youthful face, I saw few signs of glamour and glitter in the Senator-elect that winter morning. His Senate offices were not yet available—a new Congressman was moving into his old House suite—and it was in the latter's outer office, sitting almost in the doorway amidst the clutter and confusion of two staffs, that we talked very briefly—about the salary, my experience and his needs in the office. He spoke with a clear and natural voice, listened attentively and promised an early decision. The occasional tapping of his fingers on his teeth and knee, I later learned, was a habitual sign of his restless energy, not impatient irritation.

A few days later we talked briefly again. This time I raised a few questions of my own to satisfy myself about his convictions (he was not pro-McCarthy, he said, but he did doubt Owen Lattimore) and my role (I would report directly to him and could supplement my salary assisting him with published articles). Then, on the basis of these two hurried conversations of some five minutes each, he offered me the position of No. 2 Legislative Assistant in his Senate office, for a "trial" period of one year.

I accepted. The Temporary Committee of the Congress on Railroad Retirement Legislation, for which I had been working some eight months, had completed its report; and the Executive Branch, for which I had previously worked briefly as a lowly attorney, had imposed a job "freeze" in advance of the Eisenhower inauguration. Senator Paul Douglas of Illinois, the committee chairman, aided by his Legislative Assistant Bob Wallace, had kindly recommended me to a host of Democratic Senators and Senators-elect; and among the latter was Jack Kennedy, who had worked with and admired Douglas. (Kennedy had, in fact, expressed an interest a year earlier in Senator Douglas for the Presidency.)

Another Senator-elect—with a more liberal image and a more sympathetic press—had also considered employing me, emphasizing his desire to secure an assistant to help get his name in the news. Kennedy, I felt, had offered a more challenging assignment. The textile mill towns and other depressed areas of Massachusetts had neither responded to the growing competition of other regions and fibers nor made the most of postwar industrial development. Kennedy's campaign slogan in 1952 had been "He can do more for Massachusetts,"[1] and he wanted a man to help him translate the slogan, the problems and the repeated studies made of those problems into a legislative program—a man who could meet that very month, he said, with Professor Seymour Harris of Harvard, John Harriman of the Boston *Globe,* Alfred Neal of the Boston Federal Reserve Bank and other experts on boosting the New England economy. Having never been to New England or studied much economics, but sharing his concern for the unemployed, I started to work.

I cannot single out any one day as the time I began to understand John Kennedy as a human being. Gradually I discovered that the simplicity of this man's tastes and demeanor was, while genuine, deceptive as well as disarming. Although he possessed unusual empathy, and a remarkable sense of what was fitting and appropriate for every kind of occasion, he never "put on an act," feigning anger or joy when he did not feel it. Nevertheless his hidden qualities outnumbered the apparent. The freshman Senator from Massachusetts, with all his "ordinary" ways, was an enormously complex and extraordinarily competent man.

I came to marvel at his ability to look at his own strengths and weaknesses with utter detachment, his candid and objective responses to public questions, and his insistence on cutting through prevailing bias and myths to the heart of a problem. He had a disciplined and analytical mind. Even his instincts, which were sound, came from his reason rather than his hunches. He hated no enemy, he wept at no adversity. He was neither willing nor able to be flamboyant or melodramatic.

But I also learned in time that this cool, analytical mind was stimulated by a warm, compassionate heart. Beneath the careful pragmatic approach lay increasingly deep convictions on basic goals and unusual determination to achieve them. "Once you say you're going to settle for second," he said in 1960 regarding the Vice Presidency, "that's what happens to you in life, I find." Jack Kennedy never settled for second if first was available.

Many who knew him only casually mistook his refusal to display emotion as a lack of concern or commitment. James McGregor Burns, whose pre-Presidential Kennedy biography and subsequent public statements made much of this same point, irritated the Senator (and his wife) considerably. "Burns seems to feel," he told me, "that unless somebody overstates or shouts to the top of their voice they are not concerned about a matter."

[1] A slogan subsequently adapted by the Democratic Senatorial Campaign Committee for many states, and more recently used, without change but this time with considerable criticism, by Edward Kennedy in his 1962 race for the same Senate seat.

The more one knew John Kennedy, the more one liked him. And those of us who came to know him well—though we rarely heard him discuss his personal feelings—came to know the strength and warmth of his dedication as well as his logic. As John Buchan wrote of a friend in John Kennedy's favorite book, *Pilgrim's Way*, "He disliked emotion, not because he felt lightly but because he felt deeply." John Kennedy could always look at himself objectively and laugh at himself whole-heartedly—and those two rare gifts enabled him to talk lightly while feeling deeply. As he said himself about Robert Frost, "His sense of the human tragedy fortified him against self-deception and easy consolation."

There were other qualities beneath the surface. Under that seemingly fortunate and gay exterior lay an acute awareness of the most sobering kinds of tragedy. He lived with the memory of a much admired older brother killed in the war and the memory of a sister killed in a plane crash overseas. Add to this a history of illness, pain and injury since childhood, and the fact that another sister was confined to a home for the mentally retarded, and one understands his human sensitivity. No mention was ever made of any of these subjects by the Senator. But his familiarity with tragedy had produced in him both a desire to enjoy the world and a desire to improve it; and these two desires, particularly in the years preceding 1953, had sometimes been in conflict.

His mental processes—so direct and clear-cut in conversation—were not uncomplicated either. He was at that time considered with some disdain to be an intellectual by most Massachusetts politicians and considered with equal disdain to be a politician by most Massachusetts intellectuals. As an undergraduate at Harvard, particularly during his early years, he was thought by one of his tutors (Professor, later Ambassador, Galbraith) to be "gay, charming, irreverent, good-looking and far from diligent." Yet he graduated *cum laude,* and his Professor of Government, Arthur Holcombe, found him "a very promising pupil. An interest in ideas and in their practical uses . . . came naturally to him."

At the age of twenty-three he had expanded his highly regarded senior thesis—representing, he wrote his father, "more *work* than I've ever done in my life"—into a distinguished book on *Why England Slept,* a well-reasoned and well-regarded analysis of that nation's lack of preparedness for the Second World War. At the age of thirty-five he continued to be widely read in history, biography and politics. But he had little interest in abstract theories. He primarily sought truths upon which he could act and ideas he could use in his office.

His reasons for seeking political office were mixed. In subsequent years he would scoff at the magazine writers who explained his career in terms of some single psychological motivation—to prove himself to his father, or to outdo his late older brother, or to preserve an old family custom, or to be the instrument of Irish revenge. He had, in fact, assumed as a youth that politics was barred to him so long as his older brother Joe—more robust and extroverted and nearer to the traditional image of a Massachusetts politician—aspired to that profession. (Perhaps young Jack foresaw the charge that he and his two younger brothers would later hear of "too many Kennedys.") Early in our acquaintance he told me that he had considered careers as a lawyer, a journalist, a professor of history or political science, or an officer in the Foreign Service. (A brief try at Stanford Business School apparently persuaded him to seek more interesting fields.) But after Joe's death, he entered the political arena—*not* to take Joe's place, as is often alleged, not to compete subconsciously with him, but as an expression of his own ideals and interests in an arena thereby opened to him.

His entry was neither involuntary nor illogical. "Everything seemed to point to it in 1946," he said. Both his grandfathers had held elective office, and as a boy he had accompanied his Grandfather Fitzgerald to political rallies, heard him sing "Sweet Adeline," and watched him, he once told me, waste too much time afterward with hangers-on while his grandmother waited patiently in the car. An old-time Boston chronicler, Clem Norton, believes young Jack's first speech was to a group of Fitzgerald's cronies at a Parker House Hotel gathering. After the boy had been waiting outside for an hour or so, he was brought in, and old John F. picked him up and placed him on a table with the words: "Here's my grandson, here's the finest grandson in the world." To which young John F. responded, "My Grandpa is the finest grandpa in the world." And the crowd cheered Jack Kennedy's first public speech.

But, as always, he was listening and learning more than speaking. He listened to his father discuss his own high appointive offices and Roosevelt and the New Deal at the dinner table. At Harvard, on an assignment from Professor Holcombe, he had spent a year reading every utterance of an obscure Republican Congressman. ("The thought," he later wrote, "that some zealous and critical sophomore is now dissecting my own record in a similar class often causes me some concern.") As a student and assistant to his father, he had met politicians in England, France and elsewhere.

In the South Pacific he had debated politics with his companions amid the grim toll of international political disorder. In a brief fling at journalism he had observed power politics at Potsdam and the San Francisco UN Conference and covered the British elections.

All this had sharpened his interest in public affairs and public service. "I never would have run for office if Joe had lived," he said. But, Joe had died, a seat was open, and Jack Kennedy knew he wanted to be a participant, not an observer. He was, in many ways, an old-fashioned patriot—not in the narrow nationalistic sense but in his deep devotion to the national interest. He had compared firsthand the political and economic systems of many countries on several continents, and he greatly preferred our own. He shared Buchan's belief that "democracy . . . was primarily an attitude of mind, a spiritual testament" and that "politics is still the greatest and the most honorable adventure."

Although by the time we met in 1953 he had achieved considerable success as a politician, he had no grandiose picture of himself as a chosen savior of mankind from any specific evil. But he did recognize, with his customary objectivity that put both modesty and ego aside, that he possessed abilities, ideals and public appeal which could be combined to help the nation with whatever problems it faced. In all the years that followed, however the problems and his public image may have changed, that private vision of himself and his role never altered.

DIFFERENCES AND SIMILARITIES

When I first began to work for him, it seemed we had nothing in common.

He was worth an estimated ten million dollars, owing primarily to the vast trust funds his father had established many years earlier for each of the nine Kennedy children, and he had been accustomed to the social circles of Palm Beach, New York and the French Riviera. My own background was typical of a middle-income family in a Middle Western city, Lincoln, Nebraska.

I had never been out of the United States and rarely out of the Middle West. But the Senator, as a student, tourist, assistant to his Ambassador father (1938), naval officer (1941-1945), journalist (1941 and 1945) and Congressman (1947-1953), had traveled to every major continent and talked with the presidents and prime ministers, the shopkeepers and scholars, of some thirty-seven countries.

I had been seventeen years old when the Second World War ended. He had been one of its genuine combat heroes. Having pulled strings to be accepted for active duty, when his back might have excused him from service altogether, he inspired and assisted his shipmates to safety when the torpedo boat he commanded, the PT-109, was rammed in two by an enemy destroyer during a night operation in the Solomons. An expert swimmer from his days at Cape Cod and on the Harvard swimming team, he had towed one injured sailor three dark and freezing miles, grasping the man's life-belt strap in his teeth, although his own back and health had been shattered.

He had attended the exclusive Choate Preparatory School for boys, graduated with honors from Harvard, and studied briefly at Princeton,

Stanford and the London School of Economics. My total tuition in six years at the University of Nebraska, from which I received my degree in law, could not have paid for a single year at Harvard.

He was a Catholic—by heritage, habit and conviction—and a friend of Cardinals. I was a Unitarian, a denomination whose absence of dogma and ritual places it at the opposite end of the religious spectrum.

He had never been to the prairie states; I had never been to the New England states. He was thirty-five (born May 29, 1917), and I was twenty-four—although I carefully kept my age a secret from him at the time, and he seemed more amused than astonished when he learned it two years later.

His two grandfathers, the sons of Irish immigrants, had both been prominent and successful politicians in their native Boston; mine were poor immigrants from Denmark and Russia. (He once sent me a postcard from Copenhagen, admiring its beauty and wondering "why the Danes ever emigrated.")

His father had gained fame and power through skillful, sometimes cynical, operations in the worlds of finance and commerce; and Joseph Kennedy's 1940 break with the administration of Franklin Roosevelt after holding a series of appointive offices in it had been followed by an increasingly outspoken conservatism, although he remained a registered Democrat. My father, on the other hand, had been a crusading lawyer and reformer—a student on Henry Ford's "peace ship," a pioneer for human rights and woman suffrage, the draftsman of Nebraska's unique unicameral legislature, the founder of its all-public power system, an insurgent Republican Attorney General, an associate of the independent Senator George Norris and a supporter of Franklin Roosevelt —although remaining a registered Republican.

As a Congressman and candidate for the Senate, Jack Kennedy had been privately scornful of what he called the "real liberals," and he knew and cared comparatively little about the problems of civil rights and civil liberties. He never joined the Americans for Democratic Action and was skeptical of the liberal American Veterans Committee. I had helped organize a Lincoln chapter of the ADA and a local race relations organization, lobbied the Nebraska legislature for a fair employment practices bill and joined in a Supreme Court brief *amicus curiae* on the school desegregation cases.

Although he came to know and understand from his constituents, as a Congressman and candidate, the problems of poor housing and unemployment he had never experienced as a Kennedy, his chief interests were in foreign affairs. Mine were domestic. He asked me one day in 1953—long before national politics was on our horizon—what Cabinet posts would interest me most, if I ever had a choice; and I replied, "Justice, Labor and Health-Education-Welfare." "I wouldn't have any interest in any of those," he said emphatically, "only Secretary of State or Defense."

Yet all these differences made very little difference in his attitude. He was not simply a sum of all the elements in his background—a Catholic war veteran from a wealthy Boston family who had graduated from Harvard. His most important qualities he had acquired and developed on his own, and those who attempted to pigeonhole him according to the categories in his case history were sadly mistaken.

Clearly he was proud of his military service, his Purple Heart and his Navy and Marine Corps Medal. As a constant reminder of that brush with death, he kept on his desk preserved in plastic the coconut shell on which he had scratched his message of rescue from that far-off Pacific island. As a young Congressman he had been a leader in the postwar efforts of the more progressive veterans' organizations to secure passage of a Veterans' Housing Bill. But he was neither a professional warrior nor a professional veteran. He never boasted or even reminisced about his wartime experiences. He never complained about his wounds. When a flippant high school youth asked him, as we walked down a street in Ashland, Wisconsin, in 1959, how he came to be a hero, he gaily replied, "It was easy—they sank my boat."

He was unawed by generals and admirals (even more so once he was President) and had grave doubts about military indoctrination. When still hospitalized by the Navy in 1944, he had written to a friend concerning the "super-human ability of the Navy to screw up everything they touch."

> Even the simple delivery of a letter frequently overburdens this heaving puffing war machine of ours. God save this country of ours from those patriots whose war cry is "what this country needs is to be run with military efficiency."

He had also achieved some notice in 1949 when he stated on the floor of the House that "the leadership of the American Legion has not had a constructive thought for the benefit of this country since 1918." (Some insist that his original retort was somewhat more sweeping and bitter than this *Congressional Record* version.)

He was proud of his academic training but did not believe that all wisdom resided in Harvard or other Eastern schools. (As President, upon receiving an honorary degree at Yale, he observed, "Now I have the best of both worlds—a Yale degree and a Harvard education.") And he was proud to have been elected to the Harvard Board of Overseers, for few Catholics had ever been elected. His defeat for that post in 1955 was a new and disappointing experience for a man accustomed to winning.

But he selected his Senate and White House aides without regard to the source of their education, and he recognized that his own Ivy League background was not always a political asset. When I included in the first draft of an article for his alumni magazine the statement:

A Harvard diploma is considered by most Massachusetts voters to be evidence of devotion to the public,

the Senator changed it to read:

A Harvard diploma is considered by *many* Massachusetts voters, *although not all I hasten to add,* to be evidence of *some talent and ability.*

He did not believe that all virtue resided in the Catholic Church, nor did he believe that all non-Catholics would (or should) go to hell. He felt neither self-conscious nor superior about his religion but simply accepted it as part of his life. He resented the attempt of an earlier biographer to label him as "not deeply religious"; he faithfully attended Mass each Sunday, even in the midst of fatiguing out-of-state travels when no voter would know whether he attended services or not. But not once in eleven years—despite all our discussions of church-state affairs—did he ever disclose his personal views on man's relation to God.

He did not require or prefer Catholics on his staff and neither knew nor cared about our religious beliefs. Many of his close friends were not Catholics. While he was both a Catholic and a scholar, he could not be called a Catholic scholar. He cared not a whit for theology, sprinkled quotations from the Protestant version of the Bible throughout his speeches, and once startled and amused his wife by reading his favorite passage from Ecclesiastes (". . . a time to weep and a time to laugh; a time to mourn and a time to dance . . .") with his own irreverent addition from the political world: "a time to fish and a time to cut bait." During the eleven years I knew him, I never heard him pray aloud in the presence of others, never saw him kiss a bishop's ring and never knew him to alter his religious practices for political convenience.

"There is an old saying in Boston," he said, "that 'we get our religion from Rome and our politics at home.' " He showed no awe of the Catholic hierarchy and no reservations about the wisdom of separating church and state. "There is nothing inconsistent," he wrote me in 1959, "about believing in the separation of church and state and being a good Catholic —quite the reverse. . . . I don't believe there is . . . [any] conflict between being a Catholic and fulfilling your constitutional duties." A priest, angered by his answer at a Catholic girls' school that "recognition of Red China was not a moral issue," asked him, "Senator Kennedy, do you not believe that all law comes from God?" The Senator snapped back, "I'm a Catholic, so of course I believe it—but that has nothing to do with international law."

Although he was born to money and did not hesitate to spend it, he had no special interest in accumulating more of it. He had nothing in common with those wealthy individuals who were indifferent to the needs of others. He consistently voted—on oil and gas issues, for example—against his own (and his father's) pocketbook. His father had never pressed him or any of the Kennedy brothers to follow in his financial footsteps. Having never had to think about money, the Senator often left Washington without it, and would reimburse me for tabs I picked up in our travels. It is said that in his first campaign for Congress his mother, relating her son's talents to a Boston cab driver, found herself presented with a $1.85 fare bill he had run up in that very cab earlier in the campaign because he had no cash with him. Instead of assuming the life of ease which was clearly open to him, Jack Kennedy forced himself physically and mentally to enter successively more difficult levels of political and governmental activity.

His closest friends covered a wide social range, and no one ever thought him a snob. Although he once expressed astonishment that I would ride a streetcar home, he never drove the most expensive car, and returned, with regrets, to the dealer a flashy white Jaguar his wife gave him for Christmas in 1957. They lived in a fashionable but unpretentious house and avoided the Washington cocktail circuit to an unusual degree. Both strongly preferred small groups of friends to large crowds.

The Senator never wore a ring, a diamond stickpin or any jewelry other than an ordinary watch and tie clasp. All his government salaries— as Congressman, Senator and President—he donated to charity, roughly half a million dollars. His political campaigns, while costly, avoided the kind of lavish display (such as billboards, full-page advertisements or telethons) that might provoke charges of excess. But he was not ashamed of the fact that his father's wealth had enabled him to present himself for public office without being financially dependent on powerful pressure groups. On the contrary, he regarded his own good fortune as an obligation: "Of those to whom much is given, much is required." And he asked his wife to save for his files this passage from Albert Einstein:

> A hundred times every day I remind myself that my inner and outer life depend on the labors of other men, living and dead, and that I must exert myself in order to give in the same measure as I have received.

Jack Kennedy loved Boston and Boston loved Jack Kennedy, but he was always more than a Bostonian. Like many lovers they rarely lived together. He was born in the Boston suburb of Brookline. He was brought up in his more formative years in Bronxville, New York, where his father had moved the entire family in the belief that an Irish Catholic businessman and his children would have less opportunity in Boston. The Senator's parents had voted in Florida since he was a child. He spent his summers at Hyannis Port on Cape Cod. When he launched his first campaign in 1946 as a shy, skinny, twenty-eight-year-old candidate for Congress in Boston's hard-boiled Eleventh District, from which James Michael Curley was retiring, he knew almost no one in the city except his grandfather; and he relied on friends from his student and Navy days, whether residents of Massachusetts or not, to supplement the efforts of his family and their political contacts. Except for two very brief stints as a newspaperman, his entire working career was centered largely in Washington, D.C.

Even during those years in the House and Senate when he was concentrating on service to Massachusetts, he was more of a national figure. He never owned a house in Boston as he did in Washington. Although as a Congressman and Senator he maintained a voting residence in a somewhat plain and faded apartment building at 122 Bowdoin Street across from the Massachusetts State House, he was rarely there when not campaigning. The fact that several other Kennedys—and their families—for a time claimed the same three-room apartment (No. 36) as their voting address was a source of some amusement and sometimes irritation to local politicians. "If he's elected President," one was reported to have said, "he'll be the first carpetbagger voter to get to the White House." From time to time, prior to his 1958 re-election, the Senator considered buying a house in Boston, but since his winters were spent in Washington, New York and Palm Beach, he settled instead for a summer home on Cape Cod.

As a Senator from Massachusetts, he did not insist that his professional staff members come from the state they would be serving and studying. In fact, he preferred that they did not. "That way," he told me, "if they don't work out, I'm under no political pressure or obligation to retain them." He was, however, amused that his assistant on New England's economic problems came from Nebraska; and he once suggested, when I was to represent him at a Massachusetts businessmen's dinner, that I tell anyone who asked that I came "from West Hyannis Port. No one at the dinner will be from there."

We had different ideological backgrounds, and most of the professional liberals were slow to warm to him. But I found that he was the truest and oldest kind of liberal: the free man with the free mind. He entered Congress, he freely admitted, with little or no political philosophy. The aggressive attitudes of many "professional liberals" made him "uncomfortable." But he was not opposed, as he wrote me in the fall of 1959,

> to the liberal credo as it is generally assumed. You are certainly regarded as a liberal and I hope I am in the general sense, but we both speak disparagingly of those doctrinaire "liberals" . . . who are so opposed to me. . . . The word "conservative" has many implications with which I do not want to be identified. "Restrained" is more exact. I know too many conservatives in politics with whom I have nothing in common.

Kennedy had seen that many devotees of the left as well as the right could be rigid and dogmatic in their views, parroting the opinions of their respective political and intellectual leaders without reflection or re-examination. His own vote, in contrast, was not tied to the vote of any other Senator or group of Senators or to the wishes of any private individual or group.

The most formal statement of his political credo was in his 1960 address to the Liberal Party of New York:

> I believe in human dignity as the source of national purpose, in human liberty as the source of national action, in the human heart as the source of national compassion and in the human mind as the source of our invention and our ideas. . . . Liberalism . . . faith in man's ability . . . reason and judgment . . . is our best and our only hope in the world today.

He said this and he believed it. But he had not written it and did not naturally speak of his philosophical outlook in such grandiloquent terms. He usually summed up his place on the political spectrum in simpler ways:

> A Northern Democrat with some sense of restraint.

> A moderate Democrat who seeks to follow the national interest as his conscience directs him to see it.

> A practical liberal . . . a pragmatic liberal.

When asked which kind of President he hoped to be, liberal or conservative, he replied, "I hope to be responsible." Perhaps his wife summed him up best as "an idealist without illusions."

As Senator, candidate and President, his tests were: Can it work? Can it help? And, often but not always: Can it pass? He could grasp the essence of a complex subject with amazing speed, and his natural instincts were almost always on the progressive side of an issue. But his natural caution required him to test those instincts against evidence and experience. This realistic emphasis on the possible induced critics and commentators to describe him as a pragmatist, which for the most part he was. But he had a strong streak of idealism and optimism as well. To be reminded by daily disappointments that he lived in an imperfect world did not surprise or depress him, but he cared enough about the future of that world never to be satisfied with the present. Indeed, in his campaign and in the White House, his analyses of conditions in his country and planet consistently began with those four words: "I am not satisfied . . ."

HIS GROWTH

For the most part, all the foregoing would serve to describe him in 1963 as well as 1953. But he was not the same man. For no attribute he possessed in 1953 was more pronounced or more important than his capacity for growth, his willingness to learn, his determination to explore and to inquire and to profit by experience. He was always interested in a new challenge or competition. He had a limitless curiosity about nearly everything—people, places, the past, the future. Those who had nothing to say made him impatient. He hated to bore or be bored. But he enjoyed listening at length to anyone with new information or ideas on almost any subject, and he never forgot what he heard. He read constantly and rapidly—magazines, newspapers, biography and history (as well as fiction both good and bad). At times, on a plane or by a pool, he would read aloud to me a paragraph he found particularly forceful. After taking the time while a Senator to enroll in a speed-reading course in Baltimore with his friend Lem Billings and brother Bob, he could read twelve hundred words a minute. More amazing was the accuracy with which he remembered and applied what he read.

Consequently he was always learning and growing. When one of his grammar school teachers retired in 1963, he sent her a wire stating that he had thought of returning for a refresher course in mathematics, "but the rigors of self-education in Washington" made it impossible. In my daily contacts with him, the many changes which this growth and self-education produced rarely seemed pronounced; but looking back over the little less than eleven years in which we worked together, I can see that he changed in many ways—and that he was more than eleven years older.

Least important were the outward changes. He became handsomer as he grew grayer, the full face and broad shoulders of maturity providing a more striking and appealing presence than the earlier, more slender boyishness. He looked much older in person than he did on television or in photographs, but that was always true. He still looked younger than his years. His face became more lined, but the ready smile, the thoughtful eyes and the lack of affectation all remained. He had his hair cut (by the same House Office Building barber, whatever his office) a little less fully in later years, but it was always thicker than anyone else's. In fact, when chided by staff members on the regular scalp massages a succession of secretaries were trained to give him—a habit acquired from his father—he observed that he was the only one in the room who received such special hair treatment "and the only one with all his hair."

His clothes continued to be expensive but always conservative and—once he became a Senator and a married man—always neat. In his office he rarely worked in his shirt sleeves and never with his tie loosened, though he would sometimes jerk out the tail of his monogrammed shirt to clean the glasses he occasionally wore for reading. From time to time he would try wearing a hat or a vest to lessen talk about his youth, but it never lasted. And he never tried to appear more "folksy" by wearing, in either work or play, an informal bow tie, a gaudy shirt, a light-colored or odd-colored suit or a multicolored handkerchief in his breast pocket. He changed clothes frequently and knew his large wardrobe intimately. When I needed a necktie in the midst of the campaign, Dave Powers handed me one he was sure the Senator never wore. But the candidate's first words on entering the room were: "Is that my tie you're wearing?"

His speaking changed. Except for an occasional "Cubar" and "vigah," his Boston-Harvard accent became less pronounced, though still noticeable. His self-confidence on the platform grew, and his ability to read— and, at the right time, to discard—a prepared text increased. The Congressman and freshman Senator whose private conversations were always informed and articulate but whose public speeches were rarely inspired or inspiring became the candidate and President whose addresses stirred the hearts of the world. While his spelling also improved, his handwriting became even worse.

These outward changes over the years were pale in comparison to the more profound changes in his personality and philosophy.

He became less shy and more poised in his public appearances. The youthful aspirant for Congress who had reluctantly toured taverns and textile mills in search of Massachusetts voters—who even as a Presidential hopeful felt he might impose upon, or be rejected by, each new group of voters—became in time the President who welcomed every opportunity to get away from his desk and get back to the people. While most of the shyness in public disappeared, a well-bred deference in private did not. No one was ever addressed as "fellow," "son," "old man" or "old boy." The wives of his associates were always addressed as "Mrs.," and most office-holders, particularly his elders, by their titles, or as "Mr."

He became, if not less demanding of his staff, at least more apologetic about disrupting their lives and schedules, and the same was true of the general public. In 1953, as he parked his car in front of a "No Parking" sign in downtown Washington, he smilingly told me, "This is what Hamlet means by 'the insolence of office.' " But little more than ten years later, in November, 1963, he insisted in New York on dismissing the usual Presidential police escort on his ride from the airport to the city, accepting the delays of traffic and traffic lights because of the inconvenience his rush-hour arrival would otherwise create for New Yorkers.

Though his mind had more and more with which to be preoccupied, he became less absent-minded and better organized, with an amazing ability to compartmentalize different dates and duties. Even as his schedule tightened and his burdens grew, he acquired more respect for punctuality. He was still always in a hurry and often behind in his appointments, but he less often kept other officials waiting unnecessarily, or asked airlines to hold their flights, or drove dangerously fast on public highways. In his last-minute dashes to the airport during the early Senate days, he would take me along to talk business as he drove, and an aide, "Muggsy" O'Leary, to handle parking and luggage. Muggsy refused the front seat on these high-speed trips, calling it the "death seat," and I acceded to Muggsy's preference only for fear that, if I were in the back seat, the Senator would turn around as he drove.

He also grew more accustomed to disappointment in his plans and to criticism in print. In 1954 he was deeply disturbed by Boston *Post* editorials accusing him of "sacrificing the best interests of the people who elected him." But in 1963 when right-wing author Victor Lasky printed out of context every unfavorable rumor or report that could be collected about the Kennedys under the title of *JFK: The Man and the Myth*, JFK dismissed both book and author as more pitifully ridiculous than dangerous.

The fact that Lasky and other critics could discover inconsistencies between his Congressional, Senatorial and Presidential positions did not surprise or dismay him. "We all learn," he observed in 1960, "from the time you are born to the time you die. . . . Events change . . . conditions change, and . . . you would be extremely unwise . . . to pursue policies that are unsuccessful."

He did not feel bound for life by his views as a Boston Congressman on the promotion of farm income, for example, or the expansion of world trade. When a Republican Congressman in 1961 quoted against him a fiery speech of 1949 in which Congressman Kennedy had criticized the Truman China policy, President Kennedy, though not retreating from the thrust of his earlier policy view, had no hesitation in stating to questioning newsmen, "In my speech in 1949 I placed more emphasis on personalities than I would today. . . . I would say that my view today is more in accordance with the facts than my view in 1949."

Clearly in later years he was more liberal than he had been as a young Congressman who had, in his words, "just come out of my father's house." He still refused to think with accepted stereotypes or to talk with sweeping generalities or to act with dogmatic solutions. He still refused to embrace change for the sake of change or to oppose compromise when compromise was required. But he cared more about ideas and ideals where once he had cared chiefly about winning. He had talked to me with concern but calm in our first meeting about the statistics of unemployment in Lawrence, Massachusetts. But as we drove through West Virginia in 1960, he climbed back into the car after a visit to a jobless miner's shack visibly moved. He shook his head in dismay and said nothing. Unlike those liberals who start out with all the answers, he had started out asking questions. And more than most "self-made" men, the deep convictions he had developed were not inherited from his parents or imposed by his environment but were instead the product of his own reasoning and learning.

In the early stages of his public career his foreign policy speeches had a militant ring. Defense, in his view, was the bulk of diplomacy and disarmament was only a dream. But with increased perspective and responsibility came a renewed commitment to peace. Nothing gave him greater satisfaction in the White House than signing the Nuclear Test Ban Treaty.

The Senator who in 1954 paid little attention to the historic Supreme Court desegregation decision became less than a decade later the first President in history to invoke all the executive, legislative and moral powers of his office on behalf of equal rights.

The young Congressman who voted for the McCarran Internal Security Act, and who was—by his own admission—insufficiently sensitive to the ruin of reputations by McCarthyism, became the President who awarded the Enrico Fermi prize to the much abused J. Robert Oppenheimer, pardoned Communist leader Junius Scales, halted the postal interception of Communist propaganda, welcomed the controversial Linus Pauling into the White House, and appointed to his administration several of McCarthy's favorite targets.

In 1953 he knew little and cared less about agriculture, conservation and natural resources. His views on basic economic, fiscal and monetary policies were either unformed or uninformed. He had seen comparatively little of his own country, its land and its inhabitants. He had never toured a mining town or viewed a cotton field or visited a national forest.

He had never, as he later admitted in a Farm Belt speech, "plowed a furrow, straight or crooked."

But by 1961 it could be said that no President had ever seen so often and known so well the people and the problems of every part of the country. During the preconvention campaign days, after a rainy day inspection of a farm near Columbus, Nebraska, he told his luncheon audience that the town banker had informed him of the bank's basic rule: Lend no money to a man who's never had mud on his face and manure on his shoes. "Today," said the Senator from Boston, "I can qualify for a loan."

He was fully aware of his own growth and evolution. He was, in fact, disappointed that the Burns biography of 1959 had not emphasized "a far greater evolution than he suggests. He could contrast my indifferent record at school with my present intensity." The Senator candidly compared his political development with his scholastic performance. "The fact of the matter is," he told me, "that I fiddled around at Choate and really didn't become interested until the end of my sophomore year at Harvard."

Some might say that he fiddled around as a Congressman and really didn't become interested until his sophomore year in the Senate. It seemed to me in 1953 that an inner struggle was being waged for the spirit of John Kennedy—a struggle between the political dilettante and the statesman, between the lure of luxury and lawmaking. His performance in the House of Representatives had been considered by most observers to be largely undistinguished—except for a record of absentee-ism which had been heightened by indifference as well as ill health and by unofficial as well as official travels.

Having won a Senate seat and a satisfactory measure of glory, he had proved his worth in his chosen profession of politics. It was six years until re-election, and the responsibilities of a freshman Democratic Senator under a Republican Congress and administration were neither weighty nor exciting. Having borne more pain and gloom than he liked to remember, he enjoyed in his bachelor days carefree parties and companions on both sides of the Atlantic Ocean. There was a natural temptation to spend the limited number of days in which he could count on enjoying full health in pursuit of pleasure as well as duty.

But gradually the statesman won out, as his convictions deepened, his concerns broadened and Washington and the world occupied more and more of his time. And as clear as the fact of John Kennedy's extraordinary growth is the fact that many factors contributed to it: his reading, his traveling, and the widening scope of his associates, experiences and responsibilities.

In 1952 he was elected to the United States Senate, broadening his concerns as well as his constituency.

In 1953 he was married, ending the carefree life of the bachelor and establishing a home of his own.

In 1954 a spinal operation brought him close to death, and the long months of immobile recuperation were spent in sober reflection.

In 1955 he learned, as he researched and wrote a book, about the essence of democracy, the public office-holder's relations with his public.

In 1956 he narrowly missed the Vice Presidential nomination of his party, emerging as a national figure in wide demand.

In 1957-1959 he crisscrossed the country constantly, campaigning in areas wholly unlike his own, observing as well as orating, learning as well as teaching.

In 1960 he was successively Presidential candidate, Presidential nominee and President-elect, and the increased horizons and responsibilities of each role increased the breadth and depth of his perception.

In 1961 the Presidency altered his outlook and insight even more.

Fortunately, however, the gaiety and laughter within him never subsided. As Senator and President, in his home or on a boat, in the pool or private quarters of the White House, and particularly at Cape Cod and Palm Beach, he was always able to relax as intensively as he worked, to catch up on his sleep or his sun or his golf, and to laugh at his children and the world and himself.

Nor did he, in his moments of utmost pride and solemnity, ever pretend to be free from human vices and imperfections; and he would not want me to so record him. Like Lincoln's a hundred years earlier, his language and humor could be as coarse in private conversation as they were correct on the public platform. He followed Franklin's advice of "early to bed, early to rise" only when he could not otherwise arrange his schedule.

He had no passion for cards, dice or professional gambling—he never played poker, tried bridge only briefly and grew bored with backgammon—but he would briefly try his luck on campaign stops at Las Vegas, liked to bet on his golf games and did consistently well in our office World Series betting pools. Attending a Boston Red Sox game with aide Dave Powers, a baseball statistician without peer, he asked Powers how often slugger Ted Williams hit a home run, and Powers immediately calculated "one out of every fifteen times at bat." "All right," said Kennedy, "I'll bet you ten dollars to one he doesn't hit one this time." Powers accepted the bet—Williams hit a home run—and Kennedy, who would later defy all the odds in politics, was more careful thereafter not to challenge them in baseball against Powers.

In eleven years I did not see him smoke a total of eleven cigarettes, but with increasing frequency he enjoyed an expensive cigar after a meal or during a conference. (His decision as President to exclude Cuban tobacco was clearly a "sacrifice" for him.)

Along with the vast quantities of milk he usually drank with his campaign plane meals, he sometimes liked a bottle of beer. He had, in fact, revealed the drinking of a bottle of beer or two when his father was about to present him with the thousand-dollar check given to all Kennedy boys who did not smoke or drink before the age of twenty-one. When relaxing, he enjoyed a daiquiri, a scotch and water or a vodka and tomato juice before dinner and a brandy stinger afterward. He rarely drank in any quantity, and it rarely had any detectable effect on him. But he once told me with some gusto of his rather flippant remarks to a pompous couple one night in the West Indies when too much sun and rum had dissolved his customary reserve.

He was not free from vanity about his appearance. He knew that good pictures were the lifeblood of politics, and he resented photographers who waited to snap him brushing perspiration from his brow during a speech. He would not pose in honorary Indian headdresses or marshal's hats, and could avoid putting them on or take them off faster than most photographers could raise their cameras. As a Senator he often recoiled at the sight of the pale, gaunt, early Congressional pictures still in use by some Massachusetts newspapers, and he always ordered his Administrative Assistant Ted Reardon to make certain more timely portraits were submitted.

His only brushes with the law arose from his earlier tendencies as a driver to ignore both traffic signs and traffic. The only occasion he was stopped when I was with him was when he sped to a mere forty-five MPH in order to pass a car in a sparsely settled area of Washington. Unfortunately it was a thirty-five-mile zone, and the car was a police car. Inasmuch as the Senator was not recognized by the two officers, was without his wallet and driver's license, could not find the auto's registration and decided not to claim the privileges of his office, they were prepared to take him for booking to the nearest precinct station (with me driving) until I walked back to their car and gave his name and occupation. "Why didn't he say so?" the officer demanded; and, after peering once again into the Kennedy station wagon window, proclaimed, "Yep, it's him all right," and waved us on our way.

Through all these years, as John Kennedy learned and grew, it was my unique privilege to learn from him and to grow with him. Our relationship grew as well. After I had worked with him a month he increased my pay. Three months later, when his other legislative assistant moved out, he increased my responsibilities. In the next few years, our working together on legislation, speeches, Massachusetts politics and *Profiles in Courage* brought us closer together.

Before his back flared up, we played touch football. We went to the movies in Palm Beach, in Washington and in his father's basement at Hyannis Port, the low quality of some of the films in no way diminishing his enjoyment. We swam in his pool at Palm Beach while discussing politics and personalities. In 1956 I attended my first National Convention with him. From that summer of 1956 through November, 1960, we traveled together constantly, and long hours of conversation and observation in airplanes, airports and hotels forged a bond of intimacy in which there were few secrets and no illusions.

Some say that in time I talked and gestured, as well as thought and wrote, like the Senator. I doubt that he ever thought so, but occasionally, for reasons of time more often than mischief, he would have me assume his identity on the telephone.

It took me a few years to address him as "Jack" instead of "Senator," and we agreed in 1957 that the decorum befitting a national political aspirant required that I return to calling him "Senator" in the presence of others. But "Jack" was still the accepted salutation in private until January 20, 1961.

HIS FAMILY

The most important people in his life, however, were the members of his family, and particularly his father, his brother Bob and his wife Jacqueline.

The roles of Bob and Jacqueline emerge throughout the pages that follow. The role of Joseph P. Kennedy in his son's undertakings was neither so large as the father sometimes liked to claim nor so small as he sometimes preferred to pretend. The usual areas of parental influence were often exaggerated by the detractors of both father and son into a Svengali-puppet relationship. Those who knew Jack Kennedy as a strong and self-sufficient person, with drive and desire and independence since early manhood, agreed with the thoughts Jacqueline Kennedy expressed to a 1959 biographer who had overstated the influence of both Joe, Sr.'s wishes and Joe, Jr.'s death: "No matter how many older brothers and fathers my husband had had, he would have been what he is today—or the equivalent in another field."

Even in campaigns the father concerned himself almost entirely with tactics, almost never with substance. He knew that Jack disagreed with him sharply on most matters of public policy, and that they spoke for two different generations. Although the Ambassador seldom refrained from pronouncing his own views, he rarely tried to change Jack's, and never sought to influence his vote. Jack, in turn, never in my experience argued with his father. "I don't attempt to convert him and he doesn't attempt to convert me," he said. Both agreed they could disagree agreeably. "You couldn't write speeches for me," Joseph Kennedy said to me at our first meeting at Hyannis Port in the fall of 1953, in tones I later learned were friendly. "You're too much of a liberal. But writing for Jack is different."

Father and son could scarcely have been more different. The "very few" members of the National Association of Manufacturers who supported his election, the President smilingly remarked to their 1961 convention, must have been "under the impression that I was my father's son." Both had a natural charm—but the father, though very emotional underneath, was often dour ar.d gruff while his son kept outwardly calm. Both had a winning Irish smile—but the father was capable of more angry outbursts than his infinitely patient son. Both had a tough inner core, capable of making hard decisions and sticking to them—but the father had a more aggressive exterior compared to his son's consistently gentle composure. The father's normal conversation was often filled with hyperbole—his son's speech, in private as in public, was more often characterized by quiet understatement.

Both had a hatred of war, but the father leaned more to the concept of a Fortress America while his son felt our concern must be global. On domestic matters, while preferring the simpler machinery and lower taxes of an earlier era, the father emphasized personalities as much as issues. "Do you realize," his son said to me in 1953, "that his first choice for the Presidency last year was Senator [Robert A.] Taft and his second was Justice [William O.] Douglas?"

Father and son also had much in common: a delightful sense of humor, a fierce family loyalty, a concern for the state of the nation, endless vitality and a constant air of confidence no matter how great the odds or the pressures. ("I still don't know how I did," the candidate said after getting the usual cheery word by telephone from his father after the second Nixon-Kennedy debate. "If I had slipped and fallen flat on the floor, he would have said, 'The graceful way you picked yourself up was terrific.'")

They also admired, with good reason, each other's political judgment, and it was in this area that they most often collaborated. The senior Kennedy understood the inner workings of politics and politicians. He enjoyed talking to the older professionals, getting progress reports on his son and suggesting the right emphasis for campaign advertising and television. In the 1958 re-election campaign a slogan in which considerable funds had already been invested was discarded because he felt, with some justification, that "Be proud of your vote" might be misunderstood and resented by the opponent's fellow Italian-Americans.

During that same campaign, perhaps stepping over the fine line between tactics and substance, the Ambassador, as he was known, talked

to me at length about the gist of a proposed television speech, in effect
delivering such a talk to me by telephone. Finally he subsided with the
comment: "At least that's what I would like to hear." And I, more in daring than in disagreement, said, "But, Mr. Kennedy, maybe you don't reflect what the typical voter would like to hear." "Hell," the man whose
fortune ran to hundreds of millions exploded, with more feeling than
logic, "I'm the only typical man around here!"

He could be, I observed, exceedingly warm and gentle, despite the
legends which emphasized only a fierce temper, a curt manner and a
cynical outlook. Yet Mr. Kennedy often contributed to his own legend
with elaborate claims about himself and his children. Even his son
Jack did on occasion. When a newspaper story on Eunice Kennedy's
wedding stated that a Kennedy business associate had smilingly acknowledged that its cost would run into six figures, the Senator
exclaimed, "Now I know that story is a phony—no one in my father's
office smiles."

But leaving the legend aside, the Ambassador at home was a likable
man. I saw him only at his home, for he almost never came to his
son's office, though they talked frequently by telephone. I had no difficulty in getting along well with him. I admired the spirit of public
service he had helped implant in his sons, after his own service as
Chairman of the Securities and Exchange Commission, Chairman of
the Maritime Commission and Ambassador to Great Britain.[2]

I also admired his devotion to his children, to their education, happiness and success. However domineering his manner may have seemed,
he had instilled in them a will to win without ever breaking their spirits.
"I grew up in a very strict house," said the Senator, "where there were no
free riders." His father had sent his sons to secular public and private, not
parochial, schools and taught them to learn from Harold Laski as well as
Herbert Hoover. He permitted each child to choose his own career, companions and political philosophy, however they may have differed from
his own. He never discussed business or money at the dinner table, but he
did talk about politics and personalities. He took pride in his children's
educational and literary achievements ("Although," the Senator told me
of this successful, well-informed man, "I've almost never seen him read
a serious book").

To assist his son's fight to the top, he was willing to do anything—
even stay out of the fight. He was not "banished," as rumored in the fall
of 1960, but took the same summer trip to Europe he had taken for

[2] "And in those days," the Senator told me, "an Ambassador was really on his
own. Today, if there is any flap, Dulles can fly to London in a few hours, but
when I decided to fly back to Harvard from the Embassy in 1938, there was no
nonstop plane, and it took both a train ride and a boat ride to reach what plane
there was."

many years. "He is not going to participate actively in the campaign," the Senator said, "but he never has. But I will be talking with him frequently. . . . His interest is constant."

The Ambassador knew that he was a controversial figure and that in his son's Presidential campaign his own opinions were better left unsaid and his participation unseen. He knew he had endowed his sons with enemies as well as friends. Much of the liberal suspicion of the Ambassador was in fact unfounded. While it is true that his conversation at times reflected the ethnic antagonisms and epithets that had long characterized East Boston and Massachusetts, this hardly made him an anti-Semite; and when he took a group of us to lunch at his country club in Palm Beach, he boasted that he was the only Gentile member.

His son Jack, who was singularly immune to prejudices of any kind (although he, too, would refer in private political discussions to "the Italians" or "the Jews" or "the Irish" in the same way he talked about "the farmers" or "the veterans"), resented the manner in which his father's views on race and religion were both overstated in the press and attributed to his sons. More than one group of voters had to be reassured in 1960 that Jack Kennedy was independent of his father's policies and positions. Harris Wofford, who worked on race relations in the 1960 campaign, tells of Kennedy's reaction to the news that Negro leader Martin Luther King's father had announced his support—after the Senator's phone call to Mrs. King—stating he had previously planned to vote against Kennedy on religious grounds. "That was a hell of an intolerant statement, wasn't it?" said Kennedy. "Imagine Martin Luther King having a father like that." Then a pause, a grin and a final word: "Well, we all have our fathers, don't we?"

But Jack Kennedy knew that his father was no bigot, whatever his enemies might say; and far from regarding him as a handicap or embarrassment, he had strong filial feelings of loyalty and love. Once, lunching with a noted radical's son who was involved in a complicated altercation with the senior Kennedy, he asked, "Do you always agree with your father? No? But you love him?" Smiling with pleasure at his companion's affirmative answer, he leaned back and said simply, "Same here." At times he was annoyed by exaggerated statements in the press about his father's forcing him into politics or masterminding his campaign (particularly when it was the Ambassador himself who was both directly and correctly quoted). But he never disowned, disclaimed or apologized for his father or his father's money. He was grateful that Joseph Kennedy's many successes—in such diverse industries as banking, shipbuilding, investments, movies, liquor, real estate and oil—had made possible for his sons the financial independence which assists political success. At our first strategy meeting on the Presidential campaign

in 1959, the Ambassador made clear that the family's full financial resources were available, if needed. ("Not all of them, Dad," said Bob in
mock horror. "Don't forget Teddy and me.")

Until his stroke in December, 1961, Joseph P. Kennedy was the
vibrant center of Kennedy family life—a constant source of praise and
criticism, advice and commands, laughter and wrath. With each successive tragedy that befell the family, he showed the others how to
close ranks and march ahead—though some say he never got over the
loss of his oldest son Joe.

Joseph P. Kennedy, Jr. had been a young man of many qualities—
handsome, husky, gregarious, talented, aggressive, and adored by his
eight younger brothers and sisters as well as by his parents. He talked
openly of someday reaching the Presidency. Jack, the next oldest, often
fought with him but also sought to be his intimate and, for a time, his
imitator. They attended the same schools, traveled together in Europe,
participated in similar sports. Both enlisted in the Navy before Pearl
Harbor and both preferred hazardous duty.

Rejecting the rotation home that two tours of combat duty and some
fifty missions over European waters had earned him, Joe volunteered
for an experimental mission—flying a Liberator bomber loaded with
explosives from which he would bail out once a control plane had
directed it on target. With an earth-shaking blast that was never explained, his plane disintegrated in the air while still over England.

In a private book of tributes which he edited, Jack wrote:

> I think that if the Kennedy children . . . ever amount to any-
> thing, it will be due more to Joe's behavior and his constant ex-
> ample than to any other factor.

And to a friend he wrote:

> Joe's loss has been a great shock to us all. He did everything
> well and with a great enthusiasm, and even in a family as large
> as ours, his place can't ever be filled.

It never was, but in some ways brother Bob came closest to filling
it for both Jack and his father. Bob, nine years younger than Jack,
was not so close to him in their youth. "The first time I remember
meeting Bobby," his older brother said, "was when he was three and a
half, one summer on the Cape." The first time I remember meeting Bob,
in 1953, he had not yet developed the degree of patience and perspective
which would later make him so valuable a member of the Cabinet. At the
invitation of his friend, Staff Director Francis Flanagan, he had accepted
a position on the staff of the Senate Permanent Investigations Subcommittee, then about to run rampant under the fanatical chairmanship of

Senator Joseph McCarthy. Senator Kennedy told me he opposed his brother's acceptance but would not stand in his way. It was not long before Bob left McCarthy and his chief counsel, Roy Cohn, who, he said, paid scant attention to the facts.

In those days Bob, when crossed, could be as rough and rugged as his physique (and as his brother Joe had apparently been before him). He also tended then toward the more militant views that endeared him to his father. But his absolute loyalty and hardheaded judgment made him a valuable confidant of his less argumentative older brother. In Jack's 1952 race for the Senate, as in the 1960 race for the Presidency, Bobby was the logical choice for campaign manager. He could be trusted more implicitly, say "no" more emphatically and speak for the candidate more authoritatively than any professional politician. "Just as I went into politics when Joe died," said the Senator to an interviewer, "if anything happened to me tomorrow my brother Bobby would run for my seat." Bob's unique role is implicit in nearly every chapter that follows.

Another brother, Teddy, showed increasing signs of possessing Jack's warmhearted popular appeal and natural political instincts. In September, 1957, a *Saturday Evening Post* article concluded:

> Fervent admirers of the Kennedys . . . confidently look forward to the day when Jack will be in the White House, Bobby will serve in the Cabinet as Attorney General and Teddy will be the Senator from Massachusetts.

But even fervent admirers thought that day, if it ever came, was still far away.

Jack had replaced brother Joe as leader of the Kennedy offspring, a source of advice and assistance and an object of their affection. He, in turn, cared more deeply about the approval of his parents and siblings than that of anyone except his wife. He took a genuine interest in their travels, their spouses, their schooling, their careers, their appearance, antics and ideas, even taking time out in the White House, for example, to talk with sister Pat's husband Peter Lawford about his acting career and unknown to Peter making some efforts on his behalf.

Family gatherings at Hyannis Port or Palm Beach—to which I was an infrequent visitor—were occasions of great merriment, athletic and intellectual competition, exchanges of banter and bouquets, and relaxation in sailing, swimming, softball, football, tennis, golf, reading and the nightly movie. One afternoon, playing softball despite a sore back, the Senator hit safely in each appearance at bat, but sent his cousin Ann Gargan to run for him. On another occasion Mrs. John F. Kennedy and Mrs. Joseph P. Kennedy were induced by the others to put on a fashion show of their latest Paris purchases.

Despite many similarities, each of the Kennedys differed from the Senator and from each other. But they were bound by ties of genuine filial and fraternal affection, ties that were strengthened by family tragedy and pride. They were all intensely competitive and at home vied with each other. But when it came to competing with the rest of the world, the warmth of their solidarity strengthened Jack and awed his adversaries.

Most of their wealthy neighbors in Republican Hyannis Port—for Nixon three to two in 1960—had little to do with the Kennedys. ("They never showed such interest," Eunice observed to me sardonically the day after the 1960 election as we watched the friendly waves of one family that lived nearby.) But the Kennedys were content with their own company. Outside companionship, when desired, was imported from among their own circle of friends. Jack's friends and those of the family were largely indistinguishable to an outsider—some had known one first and some another. Others had known Joe, Jr. or Kathleen.

For the most part the Senator's "social" friends had little to do with the serious side of his life, and his working associates and staff were not involved in his social life. He liked the companionship of such men as K. Lemoyne "Lem" Billings, Charles F. "Chuck" Spalding and Paul B. "Red" Fay, Jr., not because of their success in the world of business, but because they were amusing, easygoing companions. His college room-mates Torby Macdonald and Ben Smith, newsmen Charlie Bartlett and Ben Bradlee, writer-artist Bill Walton and Congressional chum George Smathers could all discuss politics with the Senator from their own experiences, but they were rarely invited on a trip or a holiday for that purpose. Even as President, while boating with his old friend the British Ambassador, Kennedy was more likely to discuss raising children than NATO.

His closest friends differed from him and from each other in background and interests—and not all of them liked each other. But they were all normal, healthy, intelligent and affable men, and they were all loyal to Jack Kennedy. He in turn was loyal to them—one expressed surprise to me after the Presidential election that "Jack still has time to bother with me." But the President said later at a news conference, "The Presidency is not a very good place to make new friends. I'm going to keep my old friends."

Both friends and family volunteered (or were drafted) for Jack's political campaigns. Sisters Eunice, Pat and Jean helped organize the famous 1952 tea parties. But at those gatherings the star attraction, next to the candidate, was the articulate, intelligent and elegant Mrs. Joseph P. Kennedy, Sr., always looking amazingly younger than her years.

Although her father, Mayor John F. "Honey Fitz" Fitzgerald, had been a more ebullient and colorful politician than Patrick J. Kennedy, her husband's father, Rose Kennedy was more quietly devout and less outwardly combative than her husband and sons. From her the latter inherited much of their shy but appealing warmth and spiritual depth. But the mother was no less proud of their success and no less determined to help. Often after she had watched her son on television she would telephone me with a suggestion about some word he had misused or mispronounced. "She's a natural politician," the President remarked to me in 1957 with mingled pride and astonishment, after a long-distance call from his mother. "She wanted to know the political situation and nationalities in each of the states she's visiting this fall."

Jacqueline Bouvier Kennedy, on the other hand, was not a natural politician—but, exquisitely beautiful, highly intelligent and irresistibly charming, she was a natural political asset. She had been an apolitical newspaper girl when they met at the home of their friends, the Charles Bartletts, "who had been shamelessly matchmaking for a year," she said. On her first visit to the Senator's office (as his fiancée) in the summer of 1953, she seemed awestruck by the complexities of his work. After their marriage in Newport on September 12 of that year, she interested him slightly in art and he interested her slightly in politics.

Reared in a world of social graces far from the clamor of political wars, she at first found little to attract her in either the profession or its practitioners. Politics kept her husband away too much. Politicians invaded their privacy too often. "It was like being married to a whirl-wind," she was quoted by one reporter in speaking about their early life. "Politics was sort of my enemy as far as seeing Jack was concerned." She had no desire to write speeches or right wrongs, though her interest in her husband's concerns gradually grew. She had been, she admitted in a brief 1960 talk, "born and reared a Republican. But you have to be a Republican to realize how nice it is to be a Democrat."

Campaigning, moreover, was a fatiguing experience. She was an active horsewoman, water skier and swimmer, but in some ways as deli-cate in health as in manner. Touch football on the Kennedy Hyannis Port lawn was a novel undertaking (in one huddle she said to me, "Just tell me one thing: when I get the ball, which way do I run?"), and she once broke her ankle while being pursued across the goal by two of Teddy Kennedy's "giant" Harvard teammates. Of greater concern to both the Senator and Jacqueline (as she preferred being known, or Jackie, as everyone called her) was the fact that she suffered a miscarriage and a stillbirth before Caroline's birth in 1957.

Understandably, she was slow to accept, and he was reluctant to impose, the rigors of campaigning and handshaking. Her shy beauty and smile intensified crowd interest in the candidate whenever she could travel with him. But in the early years of their marriage she preferred to find quieter ways to assist the husband who was twelve years her senior: translating French works on Indochina, learning history to keep up with his reading ("He's much more serious than I thought he was before I married him," she said) and, above all, providing him with a relaxing home life in which he could shed the worries of the world.

HIS HEALTH

For much of their first two years of married life, home to John Kennedy meant a sickbed, and through most of the years of his life with Jacqueline he suffered sharp physical pain. The chief cause of his hospitalization and discomfort was his back; but the cause of his near death in the fall of 1954 was the shock of a spinal operation upon his inadequate adrenal system.

It was this same adrenal insufficiency that gave rise to all the health rumors that plagued him for years. Before his nomination politicians whispered about it—at least one, Governor Pat Brown of California, asked him about it. In my liaison role between reporters and doctors, I realized how concerned he was that the public not consider him too sickly for the burdens of the campaign and the Presidency or too un- likely to live out his first term if elected. Aside from his 1954-1955 spinal surgery, his confinements in the hospital for any cause, however minor, were never publicized during his career as Senator, even though it often meant my offering other excuses for canceling or rearranging speaking dates (one of the tasks I disliked the most). On one occasion he checked into the New England Baptist Hospital in Boston simply as "Mr. K."— although his special back-supporting mattress was later carried by an easily recognizable brother Teddy through the crowded hospital lobby.

The Senator had no wish to falsify the facts concerning his adrenals, but he did insist that whatever had to be published be precise. Thus he avoided the term Addison's disease, which, though it was no longer a barrier to a full life, had a frightening sound to most laymen and was interpreted differently by different physicians. Originally, before the newer adrenal hormones were available, Addison's disease carried implications wholly absent in the Senator's case—including tubercular glands, a brownish pallor, progressive anemia and, in most cases, progressive deterioration and death. (The year-round sun tan which he maintained through visits to Palm Beach and use of a sun lamp caused one suspicious reporter to question whether this wasn't a symptom, whereupon the usually modest Senator exposed a part of his anatomy that had not been browned by the sun.)

Instead of the term Addison's disease, he preferred to refer to the "partial mild insufficiency" or "malfunctioning" of the adrenal glands which had accompanied the malaria, water exposure, shock and stress he had undergone during his wartime ordeal. He also preferred, rather than giving the impression that his life depended on cortisone (which he had taken in earlier years and to which his later drugs were related), to refer to the fact that the insufficiency was completely compensated for and controlled through "simple medication taken by mouth."

Though he was troubled for a time by high fevers, and any major operation was a risk, the insufficiency caused no other illness, and was regularly and routinely checked. In fact a December, 1958, examination (ACTH stimulation test) showed satisfactory adrenal function. In 1960, however, the rumors were rampant; and two lieutenants of his chief rival for the nomination, Lyndon Johnson—Mrs. India Edwards and John Connally, later Governor of Texas—chose to highlight a convention press conference with doubts about Kennedy's life expectancy based on the assertion that he had Addison's disease. Their subsequent explanation was that Kennedy's spirited defense of his youth and vigor on television that day (in reply to a Truman attack) had by implication cast doubt on the health of other candidates, including heart patient Johnson. Johnson disowned the attack, and a subsequent explicit statement from Kennedy headquarters and a full exposition in the press put an end to all rumors and doubts—although the Republicans, not surprisingly, raised the issue again forty-eight hours before the election, with Congressman Walter Judd (a physician) attempting to cast doubt on Addisonians', and thus Kennedy's, "physical and mental health."

Addison's disease sounds ominous, but a bad back is commonplace. Consequently Kennedy's chronically painful back caused him less trouble politically, though it continued to cause him more trouble physically. Injured in 1939 playing football at Harvard, and reinjured when his PT boat was rammed, his back underwent a disc operation by Naval surgeons in 1944 which had no lasting benefit. He frequently needed crutches to ease the pain during the 1952 campaign. When the crutches reappeared in the summer of 1954, he complained to me about their awkwardness but not about his agonizing pain. When he then decided that an extremely dangerous double spinal fusion operation in October would be better than life as a cripple, he did not hint at the risks of which he had been warned and made plans with me for resuming work in November.

But the effect of surgery on his adrenal shortage caused, as he had been told might happen, severe postoperative complications. Twice he was placed on the critical list and his family summoned. Twice the last rites of his church were administered. Twice he fought his way back to life, as he had once before in the Pacific.

But he obviously could do no work, in November or for weeks thereafter. He was totally out of touch with our office from mid-September, 1954, to mid-January, 1955, having in the meantime been taken by stretcher to Palm Beach for Christmas. In February, 1955, suffering from a nearly fatal infection, he underwent still another dangerous operation to remove a metal plate that had been inserted in the preceding surgery. Back in Palm Beach, he worked on *Profiles in Courage,* but was bedridden most of the time. He was finally able to return to Washington in May, 1955.

Even then he was required for some months to remain in bed as much as possible. And always thereafter he kept a rocking chair in his office, wore a cloth brace and corrective shoes, and slept with a bed board under his mattress, no matter where he traveled. In hotels where no board was available we would move his mattress onto the floor.

Still hobbled by pain until the Novocain injections and other treatments of Dr. Janet Travell gave him new hope for a life free from crutches if not from backache, he bitterly doubted the value of the operation which had nearly ended his life. With several individual exceptions—such as Dr. Travell and the Lahey Clinic's Sara Jordan, who had treated him since he was eleven—he had never been impressed by the medical profession, remaining skeptical of its skills and critical of its fees. After his health had been shattered during the war, while still on duty in the South Pacific, he wrote his brother Bobby:

> Keep in contact with your old broken down brother. . . . Out here, if you can breathe, you're one A and "good for active duty anywhere"; and by anywhere they don't mean El Morocco or the Bath and Tennis Club.

After his first back operation in 1944 he had written to an inquiring friend:

> In regard to the fascinating subject of my operation, I should naturally like to go on for several pages . . . but will confine myself to saying that I think the doc should have read just one more book before picking up the saw.

After his 1954-1955 operations he once showed me the gaping hole in his back—not to complain about the pain but to curse a job which he found wholly unsatisfactory.

When my own back went bad in the midst of the 1956 campaign, he recommended a series of steps to relieve and remedy the discomfort. And when I replied that I would do so as soon as a "medical back expert" so advised me, he said ruefully, "Let me tell you, on the basis of fourteen years' experience, that there is no such thing!"

He knew the medical profession well. For all his vitality and endurance, John Kennedy had suffered since childhood from a multitude of physical ailments. "We used to laugh," his brother Bob has written, "about the great risk a mosquito took in biting Jack Kennedy—with some of his blood the mosquito was almost sure to die." Never complaining about his pains or imagining new ones, he used (and carried with him about the country) more pills, potions, poultices and other paraphernalia than would be found in a small dispensary. As a boy he had required twenty-eight stitches after a bike collision with Joe. He had serious cases of scarlet fever and appendicitis and almost died of diphtheria. He had to stop school temporarily when he was fourteen on account of illness and underwent the same experience at Princeton and the London School of Economics. In the Navy he apparently suffered from malaria, and spent considerable time in the Chelsea, Massachusetts, Naval Hospital because of his back.

As a Congressman he was so pale and thin his colleagues feared for his life, and in a round-the-world trip in 1951 he was taken to a military hospital in Okinawa with a temperature of over 106 degrees and little hope for his survival. Looking back, it is impossible to say which of these bouts was due to his adrenals, which was jaundice, hepatitis or malaria, or which of these may have helped bring on the other.

His eyes required glasses for heavy reading, worn rarely for published pictures and never in public appearances. (In the fall of 1963, he told me his eyesight was weaker and that the use of large type for his prepared speech texts was all the more important.) The state of his hearing obliged him to ask me, during one debate on the Senate floor, to feed facts and figures into his right ear instead of his left. Years of injections were required to lessen his stomach's allergic sensitivity to dogs, which he loved. A variety of other allergies remained. A youthful football injury to his right knee brought him pain from time to time and often caused a slight limp even in the White House.

His stomach was always sensitive—at one point it was suspected he had ulcers—and though he did not faithfully follow his diet (which did not, for instance, include a drink of vodka and tomato juice), he usually ate carefully and often. In the Senate his lunches were for a time prepared at home and brought by Jacqueline or "Muggsy" O'Leary to his office. On the campaign circuit he avoided the mass cooking at most banquets and ate in his hotel room or elsewhere. To keep something in his stomach, he ate frequently during the day—on the plane, at airport stops, before and after speeches, at every meal and between meals—great quantities of milk, creamed soups or chowder, sirloin steak, baked potatoes, ice cream and hot chocolate made with milk.[3]

[3] In early 1955 he joshed Jacqueline that her expensive course in French cooking had taught her some imaginative recipes but not how to make him hot chocolate.

But it would be wrong to assume that he was a sickly man. "Vigah," as he supposedly pronounced it, became a humorous byword during his administration—but it was accurate. He had astounding vitality, stamina and endurance, and this made him resent all the more the fact that he had to give up tennis and touch football and at times proceed gingerly with his children and golf. Many reporters and staff members fell weary or ill at his campaign pace, and he invited all those who had doubts about his health to accompany him on his grueling travels.

He made no pretense of ever having been a star athlete, despite his prowess in many sports. "Politics is an astonishing profession," he told a banquet as President. "It has enabled me to go from being an obscure member of the Junior Varsity at Harvard to being an honorary member of the Football Hall of Fame." But he had a strong, agile and nimble physique for a man over thirty-five years old, six feet tall and over 165 pounds. He rarely had a cold and never a headache. Though he drove himself too hard for too long, he looked out for his health in most other ways ("Better than 99 percent of my patients," said Dr. Travell in 1960). He took his pills, watched his posture (after his operation, for previously he had been a sprawler), exercised regularly and bathed at least three times a day to relax and heat his aching back muscles. He managed to nap under the severest pressures and on the shortest notice, in planes, in cars and in his hotel room before a speech. He was never a confirmed hunter or fisherman, but he liked to be outdoors, and he inevitably seemed to feel better in good weather.

Yet pain was almost always with him—"at least one-half of the days that he spent on this earth," according to his brother. "Those who knew him well," said Bob Kennedy, "would know he was suffering only because his face was a little whiter, the lines around his eyes were a little deeper, his words a little sharper. Those who did not know him well detected nothing." But Kennedy accepted it all with grace. His philosophy was summed up midway in his Presidential term in a news conference answer on the Reservists:

> . . . there is always inequity in life. Some men are killed in a war, and some men are wounded, and some men never leave the country. . . . It's very hard in military *or in personal* life to assure complete equality. Life is unfair. Some people are sick and others are well.

Life was unfair in many ways to John Kennedy. But he never complained. He loved life too much.

CHAPTER II

❦

THE SENATOR

JOHN KENNEDY WAS NOT one of the Senate's great leaders. Few laws of national importance bear his name. And after he graduated in November, 1958, from the traditionally inactive freshman class, his opportunities for major contributions to the Senate—except for his battle for fair labor reform and against rackets—were increasingly eroded by the demands of his Presidential campaign.

During his first four years Kennedy's two committees—Labor and Government Operations—handled comparatively little legislation of importance. He was frustrated in his efforts both to obtain major assignments (e.g., an investigation of lobbying) for the Government Operations Committee and to exchange his seat on that committee for another on a more important one. In 1957 Majority Leader Lyndon Johnson named him to the prestigious Foreign Relations Committee, but in 1955 I had had occasion to write to Senator Kennedy while he was in Europe:

> Lyndon Johnson has finally come through, making up for his failure to appoint you to the Foreign Relations or Finance Committees. He had recommended that you be appointed to the Boston National Historic Sites Commission!

Nevertheless, considering his eight years as a whole, the Senator could take some pride in his less spectacular work in committee, in his participation in major debates, in the dubious measures he had helped defeat and in the smaller bills, amendments and modifications for which he could take some credit. Not all were widely known or controversial. He originated, for example, the resolution leading to the "Three Wise

Men" study of Western aid levels to India and Pakistan. It was highly important, but rarely mentioned. A review of his voting record, and the bills and amendments he sponsored that were enacted, reflects his widening horizons, his deepening convictions and his growing interest in ideas as well as voters. Except for absences due to illness, his attendance record on roll-call votes improved—although his 1959-1960 campaign efforts coincided and at times conflicted with a sharp increase in his committee responsibilities. (When Kennedy reminded Nikita Khrushchev at Vienna in 1961 that they had met during the Chairman's 1959 American tour at a Senate Foreign Relations Committee meeting, the latter replied, "I remember . . . you were late.")

RELATIONS WITH OTHER SENATORS

Senator Kennedy was never a full-fledged member of the Senate's inner circle, the "club" whose influence has been exaggerated by both its defenders and its detractors. He was too young, too liberal and too outspoken. Early in his first term, his participation in a floor debate caused him to move closer to the front from his seat in the back row, and he found himself temporarily sitting next to Senate "Dean" Carl Hayden, who had entered Congress more than forty years earlier. Ever interested in history, he asked Senator Hayden what changes, if any, had occurred in that time, and the reply was: "New members did not speak in those days."

Nevertheless, even in the early years the older members of the Senate would have agreed with Kennedy's first Naval promotion report: "Very willing and conscientious." He was liked and respected by nearly all Senators. Fellow Democrats appreciated his never-ending willingness to speak at their fund-raising dinners and to appear on their televised reports. His close friends included liberal Republicans such as John Sherman Cooper and conservative Democrats such as George Smathers. His contributions to floor debate were well regarded for their careful facts and cool logic. His independent votes in committee and on the floor were appreciated as the product of intelligence, courage and restraint. "My crowd listens when your man gets up to speak," Senator Lister Hill of Alabama told me. "They know he's done his homework and they know no one else can deliver his vote."

His independent ways, however, also disgruntled a few colleagues. Because he voted with the Democratic leadership on committee assignments, Wayne Morse—whose fiery logic Senator Kennedy admired ("The only man," he told me, "who speaks in precise paragraphs without a text")—denounced him in Massachusetts and opposed his participation in the 1954 Neuberger campaign in Oregon. Because he was the only

Democrat voting against the Democratic leadership on the 1955 Interstate Highway Bill on the day he returned from his convalescence, one Democratic Senator grumbled that Kennedy might have stayed away one more day. When he voted to give flexible farm price supports a chance to prove their merit (they didn't, he later concluded), Minnesota's Democrats under Hubert Humphrey canceled their invitation to Kennedy to speak.[1]

He also found that economy in government was a principle in the Senate but not always a practice. In the House Kennedy had taken pride in being one of a handful of Democrats who had upheld President Truman's vetoes of unjustified veterans' pensions. In the Senate he had led the fight for the reform measures recommended by the Second Hoover Commission (on which his father served), though it was under fire from the Democratic National Committee. When a New England business group which had badgered him mercilessly about reducing Federal spending insisted that he vote more funds for airport construction, he voted against the increase partly for that reason. But when, after careful study, he openly attacked "pork barrel" river and reclamation projects, their sponsors resented his role and overrode his protests. When he exposed a Congressional pension plan as actuarially unsound, a few veteran staff members hoping for windfalls spoke sarcastically about his wealth.

He refused to adopt the practice of most liberal Senators of cosponsoring every measure circulated by every other liberal regardless of its effect on the budget, and his refusal was sometimes interpreted as rudeness. When we left the Capitol at the close of the 1954 session, he was racked by the pain in his back and discouraged over the opposition to his efforts to save money on the Colorado and Delaware rivers. "We made a lot of enemies for nothing," he said, in one of his rare moments of discouragement.

But Senators are accustomed to divisions and debate, and he had no real "enemies" among his colleagues—with two possible exceptions. One was the lady from Maine, Senator Margaret Chase Smith—"a very formidable political figure," he termed her in 1963. She was, during all the years of his travels for new Senatorial candidates, the only Republican Senator who regarded it as a personal affront that he had campaigned for a Democratic opponent.

The other "enemy" was Senator Joseph McCarthy of Wisconsin. There were many reasons for McCarthy and Kennedy to be close. No state had a

[1] The aging but mentally agile Senator Theodore Francis Green from industrialized Rhode Island voted with Kennedy on this issue, for all New England farmers thought high grain supports increased their feed costs; and when Kennedy asked Green if the farmers in Rhode Island were backing him up in this controversy, the old Senator replied, "Oh my, yes—*both* of them."

higher proportion of McCarthy supporters than Massachusetts. No news-paper was more devoted to his every cause than the Boston *Post*. Mc-Carthy had not spoken in Massachusetts in the 1952 Senate campaign, and neither Kennedy nor Lodge, uncertain of the impact, had raised the issue of his methods. McCarthy had Bob Kennedy on his committee staff in 1953. Earlier he had visited the Kennedy girls at Cape Cod, and for some time he had basked in the admiration of the Ambassador. (In 1954, however, Senator Kennedy put down the phone after a chat with Hyannis Port and remarked, "McCarthy's really gone now—even my father is down on him!")

But McCarthy's rough and wide-ranging hunts for Reds, "pinks" and headlines had often trampled on the liberties and sensibilities of those who had committed no crime, and John Kennedy was too rational and reasonable a man to remain indifferent to the extremism known as McCarthyism. After he voted against the confirmation to the Federal Communications Commission of McCarthy's friend Robert Lee—a vote which had been converted into a test of McCarthy strength and senti-ment—McCarthy would pass Kennedy in the hall without a nod. McCarthy was also disappointed that Kennedy had supported Charles "Chip" Bohlen to be Ambassador to the Soviet Union—supported former President of Harvard James B. Conant to be Ambassador to West Ger-many, despite a personal plea from McCarthy to Kennedy—supported a Hatch Act amendment barring political speeches by McCarthy friend Scott McLeod, then Security Chief at the Department of State—and later opposed McLeod's nomination as Ambassador to Ireland. ("I sympathize with their wanting to get rid of McLeod," Kennedy told me, "but why pick on poor old Ireland?")

In addition, Kennedy was a thorn in McCarthy's side in the full Government Operations Committee of which McCarthy was chairman (as he was of its Investigations Subcommittee). When McCarthy sought to name former Senator Owen Brewster as chief counsel to the full com-mittee, Kennedy, fearing the tactics for which Brewster was noted would transfer to the full committee all the sins of the subcommittee, was responsible for delaying and defeating the appointment. When McCarthy sought a contempt citation of Corliss Lamont for refusing to answer questions on his books, Kennedy blocked its approval in committee until the Department of Justice certified its constitutionality (and the Supreme Court, he later noted, ruled the Department wrong).

Except for the Boston *Post*, however, most of his constituents and the nation still regarded the junior Senator from Massachusetts as neutral or equivocal on McCarthy. Kennedy made no speeches which appeased the passions of the multitudes of McCarthyites among the Massachusetts Irish, but, like most of his colleagues from sensitive states, he made no speeches against him. That was wrong. On a television interview in February of 1954, he stated that McCarthy and his associates were guilty of partisan excesses in calling Democrats "the party of treason." Any specific vote found him on the side of civil liberties—he opposed, for example, looser restrictions on wiretapping and a bill to compel the waiver of a witness' rights under the Fifth Amendment. He led the fight against loyalty oaths for students and labor leaders, and he supported changes in the rules to prevent the abuse of witnesses. But on the broader and vaguer issue of "McCarthyism" he preferred, like the Supreme Court, not to decide a case which was not actually before him. He answered constituent mail on the question with caution, stating candidly his views on specific issues but avoiding a commitment on the man.

Many thoughtful Americans believed that McCarthy's conduct *was* an issue before the Senate as a whole. His name had become symbolic of an atmosphere which was increasingly intimidating many civil servants, teachers and others suspected of unorthodox beliefs. Within the strangely isolated walls of the Senate, however, a different atmosphere prevailed—an atmosphere in which, as Kennedy said later, "Most members are reluctant to judge personally the conduct of another. Perhaps that was wrong in McCarthy's case—perhaps we were not as sensitive as some and should have acted sooner. That is a reasonable indictment that falls on me as well."

In any event, the case of McCarthy was soon formally before the Senate—less for the damage he had done to the reputation of loyal citizens than for the damage he had done to the reputation of the Senate. Senator Kennedy was not enthusiastic about the approach of Vermont Senator Ralph Flanders, whose rather loosely worded motion for a Senate censure of McCarthy initiated his downfall. McCarthy's violations of due process, Kennedy reasoned, made it all the more important that due process be strictly followed in any proceeding against him. "Flanders had supported McCarthy wholeheartedly in the '52 campaign when his talks were irrational," he told me. "He only got mad at him when he went to work on the Republican Party." And in the speech Kennedy had been planning to give in support of censure, he pointed out:

Although [the Senator from Vermont] has cited incidents stretching back as far as 1949 in support of his resolution, he has since that date voted to seat the Senator from Wisconsin as Chairman of the Government Operations Committee, voted funds for his investigations and failed—until recently—to protest publicly these past acts. . . . Indeed, as recently as last March, after Senator McCarthy had described in a speech the conduct of the

Democratic Party as "twenty years of treason" or at best "criminal stupidity," the Senator from Vermont . . . called this speech "magnificent for the Republican Party" and . . . stated that "all would be forgiven if he will only take the position and perform the way he did" the previous night.

The Kennedy speech had been carefully based on Senatorial and legal precedents. As a devotee of civil liberties I was proud of my participation in drafting it and the Senator's plan to deliver it. It cast aside, as any court would, all the specious, emotion-tinged charges that surrounded the case. "Nor do I agree," he had written, "with those who would override our basic concepts of due process by censuring an individual without reference to any single act deserving of censure."

Instead, the Kennedy speech emphasized the need to identify concrete censurable practices which had occurred since the Senate had seated—and thus implicitly approved—McCarthy in 1953. He suggested that the record of hearings on the dispute between McCarthy and the Army provided ample grounds within the precedents of previous Senate censures. He later told me, "I think the grounds we picked were far superior to the ones the Watkins Committee picked." His text, which covered more than twelve double-spaced pages, concluded with a quotation from the Bingham censure case by my boyhood hero, Senator Norris, urging censure "for the welfare of the country . . . and for the honor and dignity of the United States Senate."

But this speech was never given and never released. On the night of July 31, 1954, I stood in the back of a crowded Senate chamber, holding in my hand copies prepared for distribution, as the first censure debate began. That afternoon at a strategy meeting called by Senator Herbert Lehman of New York, agreement on the need for more specific charges had been reached by Kennedy and other liberal Senators, most of whom had also previously avoided antagonizing the vocal McCarthy supporters in their states. Now Senator Kennedy was in his seat, speech in hand, crutches by his side. Senator Flanders made a vague and ineffective plea for action. Then a brilliant speech by Senator Morse, who had attended the afternoon meeting, turned the debate into one over proper procedure, and the Senate wisely voted to refer the whole matter to a Select Committee.

That committee, under Senator Arthur Watkins of Utah, at first hoped to file its report in late summer before the Senate went home. When it did not, Senator Kennedy, desperate for relief from his back, hoped that he would be out of the hospital before the Senate reconvened to consider the report in November. Instead, he was near death's door in November, remaining incommunicado even when carried by stretcher to Palm Beach in December. In constant pain, under heavy sedation, almost wholly immobile, he could not use the telephone, read the *Congressional Record* or consider serious memoranda; and it was not until mid-January, 1955, when we discussed the Formosa Resolution and then later his book, that he and I could be in touch.

The responsibility for recording or not recording him on the censure vote in November, 1954, thus fell on me. I knew, had he been present, that he would have voted for censure along with every other Democrat. (He subsequently stated his approval of the action taken.) I guessed that my failure to record him would plague him for years to come. But I had been trained in the discipline of due process and civil liberties. An absent juror, who had not been present for the trial or even heard the indictment (which in this case was amended in the course of debate), should not have his predetermined position recorded. In all conscience I could not ask the Secretary of the Senate to pair or record Kennedy for censure.

Without question, as the Senator himself later admitted, he could have been more outspoken against McCarthy and his methods before the censure vote, had he not felt inhibited by his family's friendship; and he could have more clearly stated his position after he returned to the Senate, although that struck him as cheap and hypocritical inasmuch as McCarthyism, and not long thereafter McCarthy, were dead. But his failure to be recorded at the time of the vote, which was persistently raised against him in some quarters, was due to my adherence to basic principles of civil liberties and not to his indifference to them.

CIVIL RIGHTS IN THE SENATE

However, those who were seeking excuses to doubt John Kennedy's liberalism found new grounds in 1957. Although civil rights had not been a major issue in Massachusetts, where righteous laws against discrimination and persistent acts of discrimination had coexisted comfortably for years, Kennedy as Congressman and Senator had identified himself with the small civil rights bloc in both houses. He had supported a strong FEPC, abolition of the poll tax, antilynching legislation and amendment of the rule on filibusters. He had been the first member of Congress from New England to appoint a Negro to his staff.

In 1957 he supported the administration's mild but precedent-setting voting rights bill, endorsing the effort to extend under Title III the Attorney General's injunctive powers to cases on schooling and other rights. He asked me, however, to examine whether there was any legal basis in Vice President Richard Nixon's proposed ruling to by-pass committee consideration of the bill. When I reported that I could find no such basis in either the Senate's rules and precedents or the Constitution, and that similar manipulation could be employed by conservative Senators on right-to-work and other House bills, he supported the unsuccessful Morse request that the civil rights bill proceed normally to committee, subject to discharge in one week.

Many of the civil rights Democrats privately agreed with Morse that the ill-feeling engendered by abandoning traditional procedures would make passage of a strong bill more difficult. But fearful of being outmaneuvered politically by Nixon and the Republicans, most of them voted to uphold the Vice President's ruling; and Kennedy's vote for orderly procedure was condemned by civil rights leaders as a bid for Southern Presidential support. At a convention of the National Association for the Advancement of Colored People, in mail from Boston Negro leaders, in editorials and columns, Kennedy's vote was assailed.

The full force of their fury, however, was yet to come. Majority Leader Lyndon Johnson, whose own star had been rising on the national horizon, was determined to obtain passage of the first civil rights bill since Reconstruction. A careful counter of Senate heads, he knew that he did not have the votes to break a Southern filibuster, that adoption of the "jury trial amendment" might avoid a full-scale filibuster, and that the votes of Kennedy and his friend John Pastore were needed for the adoption of that amendment.

The question dealt with by this amendment was whether local voting officials who had defied court orders on the registration of Negroes could be tried for criminal as well as civil contempt of court without a jury trial. The amendment required a jury trial in both kinds of cases. Both sides exaggerated its importance, with some Northerners calling the bill meaningless with such an amendment and some Southerners calling the bill monstrous without it. Enforcement of the bill could not, in fact, depend upon criminal (as opposed to civil) contempt proceedings. But emotion and oversimplification made the amendment a symbol at the expense of the facts. And although some three dozen other non-Southern Senators supported it, Kennedy's vote was regarded as crucial.

He turned for advice to two Harvard professors of law, both noted for their devotion to civil rights, Mark DeWolfe Howe and Paul Freund. Both answered that acceptance of the amendment to pass the bill involved no betrayal of principle. Kennedy, followed by Pastore, supported the "jury trial amendment." It passed. The bill passed. "It would be a heavy blow," the Senator said to his critics, to abandon "a bill of real merit for the doubtful satisfaction of standing dogmatically by a provision which does not . . . add significantly to the substantive effect of the measure."

But his critics would not be stilled. His vote for broad injunctive powers under Title III was dismissed as "playing both sides." His other votes and statements on behalf of the bill were ignored. NAACP Executive Secretary Roy Wilkins told New England members that Kennedy had not earned their support.[2]

That storm eventually passed; Wilkins in fact praised Kennedy's civil rights record during his 1958 Senate re-election campaign as "one of the best . . . of any Senator in Congress." But the Senator would always marvel at the comparative public inattention paid, except by its enemies in the South, to his more important vote on Title III—which was later largely incorporated in the Kennedy Civil Rights Bill of 1963. In more than one speech he would quote, with understanding as well as amusement, a legendary verse said to have been found among the papers of a deceased legislator:

> *Among life's dying embers*
> *These are my regrets:*
> *When I'm "right" no one remembers,*
> *When I'm "wrong" no one forgets.*

LABOR RACKETEERING AND REFORM

But Negroes and Southerners were not the only members of the traditional Democratic coalition whose disfavor he would risk in the Senate. Organized labor had long been a powerful Kennedy ally. Throughout his House and Senate tenures, he had served on the Labor Committees of each body. Labor leaders admired his opposition in the House to the Taft-Hartley Bill and his leadership in the Senate for higher minimum wages, improved Social Security with medical care, aid to depressed areas and nationwide unemployment compensation standards. His labor record was, in the inflated parlance of politics, "a thousand percent." The Massachusetts Teamsters (who were never linked with the corrupt practices of their national leaders) had been consistent Kennedy supporters. But between 1957 and 1959 the relationship between Kennedy and his labor friends underwent a severe strain.

To pursue information on corrupt labor practices initially uncovered by the Permanent Investigations Subcommittee (then chaired by Senator John McClellan, with Robert Kennedy as Chief Counsel), the Senate in 1957 established a special investigating committee on labor rackets,

---

2 Wilkins linked Kennedy's vote with a supposed newspaper picture showing the Senator with his arm around the Governor of Georgia. Most gregarious politicians would assume such a picture existed. But the restrained Senator from Massachusetts knew that he had never posed, as he wrote Wilkins, with his "arm around the Governor *or anyone else*," and Wilkins later admitted that he had intended only "a figure of speech."

with members from both the McClellan Subcommittee and the Senate Labor Committee. McClellan and Bob Kennedy carried over their roles; John Kennedy was asked to join.

He knew it meant risking his good relations with organized labor—and that at least two other Senators with national ambitions, Henry Jackson and Stuart Symington, had declined to serve. There had also been hints of National Teamster support for his Presidential candidacy if only Bob Kennedy would "play smart."[3]

But whatever the political pitfalls, Kennedy was interested. Internal union safeguards had intrigued him since his Taft-Hartley studies in the House. As chairman of the Senate Labor Committee's Subcommittee on Labor Legislation, he knew he could hardly avoid involvement in any legislative proposals growing out of the hearings (although he also declined an opportunity to leave the Labor Committee for a position on another committee). The well-known antilabor views of many of the Rackets Committee members already selected, and particularly those of South Carolina's Strom Thurmond, who would eagerly take his place if he declined, underlined both the difficulty and the necessity of his accepting.

He decided to join the committee. He sponsored the resulting labor reform legislation. For the first time in his Congressional career, he concentrated intensively and almost exclusively for a period of years on a single piece of legislation. He was, said the *Christian Science Monitor,* "burning his bridges" to labor support for the Presidency. And the Senator, in one of those subsequent moments of detached self-appraisal which reflected neither boasting nor complaining, noted that it was "certainly the toughest political job any Presidential candidate could ever take on."

Labor leaders were coolly suspicious, then hotly opposed. AFL-CIO President George Meany, at a hearing called by Kennedy on his proposed reform bill, cried out, "God save us from our friends!"—to which Kennedy quietly replied: "I say that, too, Mr. Meany." Machinists President Al Hayes compared Kennedy to Argentine dictator Perón. Others sought to have him denounced in their national conventions. But then Senate Republican Leader William Knowland unleashed and nearly passed a parcel of antilabor amendments to a welfare and pension fund bill. Gradually and somewhat grudgingly, Meany and most of the top union leaders realized that some legislation was unavoidable—and that the alternatives were a Kennedy labor-management reform bill to

[3] Presumably this meant that Teamster President Jimmy Hoffa considered himself a power in the Democratic Party, but once the investigation began, Hoffa, forgetting his 1953 claim that a Republican committee in the House was persecuting him because he was a Democrat, claimed that the Kennedys were out to get him because he was a Republican.

clean up rackets they could neither deny nor condone or a Knowland labor-management relations bill to curb their collective bargaining.

The ensuing struggle, in which most AFL-CIO leaders supported both a constructive bill and their own voluntary code, gave the Senator his most intimate glimpse into the quality of labor's leadership. Men of the ilk of Beck, Hoffa and their hoodlum friends were quickly isolated from the rest. But not all the honest leaders, he found, could wield power as effectively as Hoffa. Some, he remarked to me on a trip, had grown flabby through long years in power and were out of touch or out of tune with their members. Some were sterile in their thinking and relied on subordinates and attorneys. Some were mere figureheads not effectively in control of their own unions. Some, such as the leaders of the building trades and Railroad Brotherhoods, were effective because they concentrated solely on issues affecting their members and rewarded their friends in both parties. Some were idealists and reformers who rallied to every liberal banner and were often taken for granted by the Democrats. Some were great talkers and some were great "doers"—and some, like Walter Reuther, were both.

At the same time that many labor backers were down on "the Kennedys" for their antiracketeering efforts, the labor baiters in business and Republican circles—many of whom had close ties with Beck or Hoffa—were charging the Kennedys with favoritism to Walter Reuther. When a thorough investigation showed no wrongdoing on Mr. Reuther's part, they next charged the Senator with ignoring the real issue of labor's "monopoly power," and they pushed through the House of Representatives the Landrum-Griffin restrictions on boycotts and picketing.

Businessmen also resented the Kennedys for their exposure of management's collusion with racketeers—through "fake unions and welfare funds [and] so-called sweetheart contracts to keep wages low and responsible unions out," as the Senator described it to one business audience. The President of the American Bar Association resented the Senator's statements of concern over the organized Bar's "apparent indifference" to those members who participated with the racketeers in raiding union funds. A variety of Democratic politicians also brought pressure on both Kennedys. When Jake Arvey, famed as Illinois' National Committeeman and a Stevenson confidant, asked him to intercede on behalf of a client, Senator Kennedy told him only Chief Counsel Kennedy could halt an investigation. When Arvey and his associate then left for the committee office, the Senator called Bob and told him he thought the request "smelled."

As these opposing pressures grew, Kennedy's determination grew. Aided by Ralph Dungan, Harvard labor law expert Archibald Cox and a panel of six other scholars, he drafted a labor reform bill, mastered the intricacies of labor law and, for the first time, truly mastered the legislative process. In 1958 the Kennedy-Ives bill passed the Senate by a vote of 88 to 1, only to be buried in the House. In 1959, after a long and difficult floor battle, the Kennedy-Ervin bill was passed by a vote of 90 to 1.

Interestingly enough, one crucial roll call in 1959 involved the political fortunes of most of the Presidential aspirants. Kennedy, with vigorous help from Johnson and the support of Symington, fought a high-sounding but harmful "Labor Bill of Rights" amendment offered by John McClellan. To his dismay, it passed by one vote, with Hubert Humphrey out of town. As Johnson maneuvered for reconsideration, a tie-breaking vote in its favor was cast by Vice President Nixon. Later Kennedy and Johnson succeeded in getting this decision modified, causing Barry Goldwater to cast the only vote against the bill, and causing Kennedy to remark that it was "obvious that Senator Goldwater would be satisfied with no bill that did not destroy the organized trade union movement in the United States."

The bill went to conference with the House-passed Landrum-Griffin bill. Preferring a compromise to no bill at all, Kennedy was able to eliminate fifteen restrictions on normal union activity from the House bill while retaining his own curbs on racketeering. But although the final version was on balance closer to the Senate bill, he thought it politic that it not bear his name.

Throughout the long legislative effort the investigative probe continued. Some national and Massachusetts labor leaders were angered when he signed the McClellan Committee report. Not to have done so, he replied, would have cost him his credibility on the issue in the Senate. But there were political gains as well as losses. The television public was becoming increasingly familiar with the Kennedy brothers grilling dishonest union leaders or lecturing racketeers who had misused the funds of honest members. The committee, unlike McCarthy's operation, gave all witnesses the right to offer prepared statements, to submit questions for cross-examination, to receive a transcript of the testimony, to refuse a one-man hearing and to exercise the full protection against self-incrimination. Although a large portion of the Senator's mail was from those incensed by the refusal of many witnesses to give testimony, he understood both the fairness of the Fifth Amendment and the fairness of confronting all witnesses with the evidence against them, whether they desired to respond to it or not. (He could not, however, refrain from commenting to his banquet audiences on the racketeer, wholly fictional, "who took the First, Fifth, Sixth and Sixteenth Amendments—and deeply regretted the repeal of the Eighteenth.")

HIS SENATE OFFICE

Meanwhile, in Room 362 in the Senate Office Building, where the door was always open, the Kennedy Senatorial operation was satisfying both the Senator and his Massachusetts constituents.

From the beginning, the pace was frantic and the hours were long. His staff worked hard because the Senator worked hard and because his vitality and enthusiasm were infectious. Barry Goldwater remarked to a friend that the only office still active when he left at night was inevitably the Kennedy office. Vice President Nixon's office, directly across the hall, often worked in two secretarial shifts, but the girls in the Kennedy office, with no overtime or compensatory time off, consistently worked ten, twelve or more hours with surprisingly little turnover. (Nixon and Kennedy had entered Congress together and were friendly. Guests at a 1953 Kennedy cocktail party had included all his staff, including stenographers, and the Richard Nixons. The Vice President would occasionally look in on our office and in 1955 sent a basket of fruit to welcome the Senator's return from convalescence. Earlier, when the Democrats in the 1954 elections appeared to have regained control of the Senate by a one-vote margin, the Vice President called me in to say that he had no intention of permitting the Republicans to organize the Senate by taking advantage of Kennedy's hospitalization.)

Official staff allowances were insufficient for a state with as many letter-writers as Massachusetts and a Senator with as many interests as Kennedy. He consequently supplemented the payroll out of his own pocket. His Administrative Assistant Ted Reardon, who had been with him since his first campaign for the House, oversaw the handling of constituent requests. The Senator would personally intervene in the most important problems, ranging from Agricultural Department funds for spraying gypsy moths to expediting the Marine Corps discharge of Boston Red Sox slugger Ted Williams (who, to Kennedy's chagrin, endorsed Nixon in 1960). The always affable and thoughtful Reardon also administered, to the disappointment of some Massachusetts politicians, a merit system for the selection of Senatorial West Point and Annapolis appointees which made any prejudice or partisanship impossible.

The Senator's personal secretary was my fellow Nebraskan, Mrs. Evelyn Lincoln, whose unfailing devotion and good nature more than compensated for a sometimes overly possessive attitude. ("Whatever I do or say," President Kennedy said to me one afternoon in his White House bedroom, after an urgent telephone request to his secretary, "Mrs. Lincoln [in eleven years he never called her Evelyn] will be sweet and unsurprised. If I had said just now, 'Mrs. Lincoln, I have cut off Jackie's head, would you please send over a box?' she still would have replied, 'That's wonderful, Mr. President, I'll send it right away. . . . Did you get your nap?' ")

In 1954 I recruited another Nebraskan, my law college classmate, Lee White, to assist us on legislation. Lee and the two men I secured to follow him, Ralph Dungan and Myer Feldman, were indispensable assets. The office was always overcrowded, with desks or corners for student "interns," academic advisers and temporary consultants.

The Senator was not always satisfied with his staff's work. He disliked complainers and procrastinators. He wanted the truth and both sides of an argument, but he had a special distaste for those who brought him only bad news. He always wanted more details and documentation, at the same time always seeing the larger picture into which each action or idea could fit.

The employer, like the man, was patient with his employees, but impatient with any inefficiency or incompetence. He was always accessible and ready to listen, quick to grasp a recommendation and disappointed only when there was none. He never raised his voice when expressing disagreement or dissatisfaction with our work. Indeed, he was rarely and then only briefly angry at any staff member. But he possessed, as a Senator, one serious weakness as an administrator: he could not bring himself to fire anyone. "I keep calling her in for that purpose," he said of one inefficient female assistant, "but when she comes in looking so hopeful and vulnerable, I give her another assignment. . . . You do it."

(The only serious case of office nonfeasance occurred during his convalescence away from the office. While the Senator's position was never decided by the amount or nature of his mail—it was not, in his opinion, representative and much of it was not spontaneous—he was anxious that each letter be answered promptly and with as much specific information as possible. A new girl in charge of legislative mail in 1955 found that the volume of letters, despite the Senator's absence, was greater than she could handle. Lee White, searching for an unanswered letter about which an angry constituent had telephoned him, found, stuffed in the bottom drawer of her desk, over thirteen hundred unanswered letters and postcards. She couldn't bring herself to throw them away, she confessed, with some relief that her ordeal was over. All the girls in the office joined forces to help, all the mail was answered, and the unlucky lady found another position—in a bank!)

Mail was always a burden in the office, and constituent complaints and demands were sometimes an irritant. "All of us," the Senator wrote in the introductory chapter to *Profiles in Courage,* "occasionally have the urge to follow the example of Congressman John Steven McGroarty of California, who wrote a constituent in 1934:

> One of the countless drawbacks of being in Congress is that I am compelled to receive impertinent letters from a jackass like you in which you say I promised to have the Sierra Madre mountains reforested and I have been in Congress two months and haven't done it. Will you please take two running jumps and go to hell."

Senator Kennedy signed very little of the correspondence he approved for his signature and dictated even less of it. Staff members composed letters in accordance with his thinking. Mass mailings employed a mechanical signature pen. Most of his individual letters—and sometimes even autographed books or pictures—were signed by secretaries so skillful in imitating his handwriting that even he could not detect the difference. He once complained to Ted Reardon that the signature affixed that year for his Senatorial mailing frank—which appeared on all his envelopes—was a poor, illegible imitation, and Ted respectfully pointed out that that year the Senator had submitted his own signature for the frank.

On the other hand he sometimes answered mail not worthy of his time or not even addressed to him. This resulted from his habit of picking up and leafing through whatever was lying on top of whatever desk he was passing. Whenever the number of items I had to bring to his attention was uncomfortably long, I found that some progress could be achieved by leaving many of them on the corner of my desk.

My original assignment in 1953 had been the preparation of a legislative program for the New England economy, and this led that year to a series of three comprehensive speeches on the Senate floor, a number of bills, related speeches and national magazine articles and a formal organization of the New England Senators' Conference (with a Nebraskan as secretary).

Initiation of the conference, which had been suggested in his series of Senate speeches, was shared with his Massachusetts colleague, courtly Leverett Saltonstall. Thereafter both offices worked closely together on Massachusetts problems, holding a number of joint meetings and issuing joint releases.

Though Saltonstall and Kennedy usually voted differently on national policy, they retained affection and respect for each other. Each enjoyed the additional political support gained by being associated with the other, and each privately preferred sharing Senatorial prerogatives with a colleague from the opposite party rather than with a competitor from his own. They took turns taking the lead on joint measures for Massachusetts, with the wholly unspoken understanding that they would all be known as Saltonstall-Kennedy bills in the senior Senator's 1954 and 1960 campaigns and as Kennedy-Saltonstall bills in 1958.

At a 1963 party dinner Kennedy noted that Saltonstall, at a Republican gathering earlier in the week, had introduced Senator Barry Goldwater with the less-than-ringing endorsement: "He and I have differed on many problems, but we like and respect one another." Kennedy paused as he repeated the words and then added, "I used to get a better introduction than that from Senator Saltonstall when I was in the Senate!"

On election night, 1960, the early returns indicated that Kennedy had won the Presidency and carried Saltonstall's opponent in with him. Kennedy evinced genuine regret, and expressed in the midst of all his other cares a desire to make use of his old friend's talents. "What about Ambassador to Canada?" I asked, and he replied, "He'd be perfect for it"—but Saltonstall's final victorious vote abruptly ended his ambassadorial career.

On the Senate floor, in a Tennessee speech and in a national magazine article, Kennedy emphasized in 1953 that his efforts for New England were not directed against competition from the South or any other area, so long as that competition was fair. Substandard wages were unfair competition, and he wanted the minimum raised. But the TVA and public power were fair competition, and he wanted New England's resources developed.

He took a similar approach to foreign competition. While assisting many Massachusetts industries in their applications for tariff relief, he was often the only Senator from New England voting for liberal trade programs.

But the severest test of whether his approach was provincial or national came early in 1954 when the St. Lawrence Seaway was once again before the Senate. For twenty years it had failed of passage, and for twenty years every Massachusetts Senator and Congressman, regardless of party or district, had voted against it. Kennedy had opposed it in his 1952 campaign. Saltonstall, in one of his rare disagreements with President Eisenhower, was opposing it in 1954. Massachusetts port and railroad interests were among the leading lobbyists against it. The Boston longshoremen, who had been faithful Kennedy supporters, condemned it as a threat to their jobs.

But the Senator characteristically asked me to collect for him an objective compilation of the facts—and the facts showed that the Seaway would not do the harm alleged, was needed in the national interest

and would in all probability (which was not clear in 1952) be built by
Canada alone if the United States delayed any longer. He ordered a
speech drafted in support of the project, but withheld a final decision
until the next day so he could "sleep on it."

He did not, he admitted the next day, do much sleeping. Years later
he would make far more difficult and dangerous decisions without any
loss of sleep, but this was in many ways a turning point for the thirty-
six-year-old Senator. He had no obligation to vote for the Seaway and
endanger his political base. He was not required to speak on either side.
A quiet vote of opposition would have received no attention. But he
was determined to represent the national interest, and he had told his
constituents that a provincial outlook would only continue their neglect
by the rest of the country. Still he hesitated. Then, with a shake of his
head—a shake I would often see, meaning "Well, this is what I must
do, for better or worse"—he walked over to the Senate floor and delivered
the speech.

Citing his state's traditional opposition, he declared, "I am unable
to accept such a narrow view of my function as United States Senator."
Standing proudly at the back of the chamber, I was instantly besieged
for copies. The speech was regarded as a turning point in the Seaway
debate as well as in the Senator's career. The Seaway at last became
law. The Boston *Post* accused Kennedy of "ruining New England." His
opponent in 1958 charged that it was all designed to help Joseph Kennedy's Merchandise Mart in Chicago. A friend on the Boston City Council
warned him not to walk in the 1954 St. Patrick's Day parade, lest catcalls and worse be hurled at him in the dockworkers' district. But he
marched—and there were no incidents. Throughout his career he refused to shrink from the possibilities of hostility in his audience—
whether it was in Boston, Jackson, Houston, Caracas or Dallas.

HIS SPEECH-WRITING

St. Patrick's Day 1954 also marked a change in my role in the office.
My duties as Legislative Assistant had gradually expanded over the
whole scope of his legislative activities, committees and mail. The New
England economy was still the focal point of my efforts, however. While
I worked on any outside speeches or articles concerning his New Eng-
land program, I had little to do with the few other speeches he gave.
But when he approved my suggested draft of his speech for a 1954 St.
Patrick's Day Dinner (a phenomenon unknown in my background),
my role as speech collaborator on any and all subjects was fixed for
nearly ten years.

It became my most taxing role. Although I had previously done some writing and public speaking—as a high school and college debater and as editor of the *Nebraska Law Review*—my pen (for I drafted anything of importance in longhand) was not always sufficiently fast or facile to keep pace with the Senator's varied and increasing demands. But the long, tedious hours of writing were rewarded both by the additional bond they forged between us and by his approval and use of my efforts. The morning after a particularly successful speech he would frequently call and thank me for my part.

He would never blindly accept or blandly deliver a text he had not seen and edited. We always discussed the topic, the approach and the conclusions in advance. He always had quotations or historical allusions to include. Sometimes he would review an outline. And he always, upon receiving my draft, altered, deleted or added phrases, paragraphs or pages. Some drafts he rejected entirely.

As the years went on, and I came to know what he thought on each subject as well as how he wished to say it, our style and standard became increasingly one. When the volume of both his speaking and my duties increased in the years before 1960, we tried repeatedly but unsuccessfully to find other wordsmiths who could write for him in the style to which he was accustomed. The style of those whom we tried may have been very good. It may have been superior. But it was not his.

The very fact that I was involved in his other activities and decisions, and constantly present to hear his public and private utterances, made it increasingly easy for me to fulfill the speech-writing role—and increasingly difficult to shed or even share it. "I know you wish you could get out of writing so many speeches," he said to me one weary night in an Indianapolis hotel room in 1959. "I wish I could get out of giving so many, but that's the situation we're both in for the present."

In that situation we turned out hundreds of speeches, some good, some bad, some mediocre. The poorer speeches, in my view, occurred for the most part in the early days when we were learning and in later days when we were rushed. Invariably the more time he had to edit and rewrite, the better the speech would be.

The Kennedy style of speech-writing—our style, I am not reluctant to say, for he never pretended that he had time to prepare first drafts for all his speeches—evolved gradually over the years. Prepared texts were carefully designed for an orderly presentation of their substance but with no deliberate affectation of any certain style. We were not conscious of following the elaborate techniques later ascribed to these speeches by literary analysts. Neither of us had any special training in composition, linguistics or semantics. Our chief criterion was always audience comprehension and comfort, and this meant: (1) short speeches, short clauses and short words, wherever possible; (2) a series of points or propositions in numbered or logical sequence, wherever appropriate; and (3) the construction of sentences, phrases and paragraphs in such a manner as to simplify, clarify and emphasize.

The test of a text was not how it appeared to the eye but how it sounded to the ear. His best paragraphs, when read aloud, often had a cadence not unlike blank verse—indeed at times key words would rhyme. He was fond of alliterative sentences, not solely for reasons of rhetoric but to reinforce the audience's recollection of his reasoning. Sentences began, however incorrect some may have regarded it, with "And" or "But" whenever that simplified and shortened the text. His frequent use of dashes as a means of separating clauses was of doubtful grammatical standing—but it simplified the delivery and even the publication of a speech in a manner no comma, parenthesis or semicolon could match.

Words were regarded as tools of precision, to be chosen and applied with a craftsman's care to whatever the situation required. He liked to be exact. But if the situation required a certain vagueness, he would deliberately choose a word of varying interpretations rather than bury his imprecision in ponderous prose.

For he disliked verbosity and pomposity in his own remarks as much as he disliked them in others. He wanted both his message and his language to be plain and unpretentious, but never patronizing. He wanted his major policy statements to be positive, specific and definite, avoiding the use of "suggest," "perhaps" and "possible alternatives for consideration." At the same time, his emphasis on a course of reason—rejecting the extremes of either side—helped produce the parallel construction and use of contrasts with which he later became identified. He had a weakness for one unnecessary phrase: "The harsh facts of the matter are . . ."—but, with few other exceptions, his sentences were lean and crisp.

No speech was more than twenty to thirty minutes in duration. They were all too short and too crowded with facts to permit any excess of generalities and sentimentalities. His texts wasted no words and his delivery wasted no time. Frequently he moved from one solid fact or argument to another, without the usual repetition and elaboration, far too quickly for his audiences to digest or even applaud his conclusions. Nor would he always pause for applause when it came.

He spoke at first with no gestures, though he gradually developed a short jab to emphasize his points. Often his tone was monotonous. Often his emphasis was on the wrong word. But often when his audiences were large and enthusiastic—particularly indoors, if the hall was not too vast—an almost electric charge would transmit vitality back and forth between speaker and listeners.

He used little or no slang, dialect, legalistic terms, contractions, clichés, elaborate metaphors or ornate figures of speech. He refused to be folksy or to include any phrase or image he considered corny, tasteless or trite.[4] He rarely used words he considered hackneyed: "humble," "dynamic," "glorious." He used none of the customary word fillers (e.g., "And I say to you that is a legitimate question and here is my answer"). And he did not hesitate to depart from strict rules of English usage when he thought adherence to them (e.g., "Our agenda *are* long") would grate on the listener's ear.

The intellectual level of his speeches showed erudition but not arrogance. Though he knew a little French ("very little," he commented in 1957 after a somewhat halting telephone conversation with the King of Morocco on the North African situation), he was most reluctant to include any foreign words in his addresses.

He was not reluctant, however, particularly in those pre-1960 days, to pack his speeches with statistics and quotations—frequently too many for audiences unaccustomed to his rapid-fire delivery. While I learned to keep a *Bartlett's* and similar works handy, the Senator was the chief source of his own best quotations. Some were in the black notebooks he had kept since college—some were in favorite reference books on his desk, such as Agar's *The Price of Union*—most were in his head.

He would not always be certain of the exact wording or even the author of a quotation he wanted, but he could suggest enough for his staff or the Library of Congress to find it. Preparing his brief, effective statement against the isolationist Bricker Amendment to the Constitution, for example, he told me, "Someone—was it Falkland?—gave the classic definition of conservatism which went something like 'When it is not necessary to change, it is necessary not to change.' Let's include the exact quotation and author."[5]

He also liked on occasion—especially with college audiences which he enjoyed—to include humorous illustrations and quotations in the body of his speeches. An excerpt from a particularly abusive debate

[4] When he learned that a noted political analyst claimed his opposition to Kennedy's Presidential candidacy was based on the latter's statement that Western Europe "would be flushed down the drain," the Senator could assert without hesitation that he had never used such a phrase in his life.

[5] That particular "definition" exemplified the caution with which he approached any tinkering with the Constitution, leading him to oppose not only the Bricker Amendment and the Mundt-Daniel Electoral College Amendment but a reduction in the voting age as well. He favored the latter on its merits, he said, and would support it on the ballot in Massachusetts. But he felt that his stand against needless or hasty Congressional action on Constitutional amendments required him to oppose it in the absence of more widespread action by the states or further evidence of its necessity. Had the national voting age been eighteen in 1960, polls indicate that Kennedy's margin would not have been so narrow.

between earlier Senators and statesmen always delighted him, possibly because it contrasted so vividly with his own style of understatement.

Humor in the *body* of a prepared speech, however, was rare compared to its use at the *beginning* of almost every speech he made off the Senate floor. While here, too, he preferred historical or political anecdotes, both the quality and the sources of this introductory material varied widely. He believed topical, tasteful, pertinent, pointed humor at the beginning of his remarks to be a major means of establishing audience rapport; and he would work with me as diligently for the right opening witticism, or take as much pride the next day in some spontaneous barb he had flung, as he would on the more substantive paragraphs in his text.

Successful stories told by a toastmaster or by another speaker would be jotted down for future reference. Collections of Finley Peter Dunne and Will Rogers, current newspaper columns and quotations, the works of writers who liberally sprinkled their thoughts on history and government with amusing expressions or examples (such as Denis Brogan and T. V. Smith) were all carefully mined. Standard jokebooks were never used, nor would he ever say, "That reminds me of the story of . . ." as a bridge to some irrelevant and lengthy anecdote, but many an old saw was adapted to modern politics and to a particular audience.

No laugh-getter once used or even considered was ever discarded. A large "humor folder" in my files grew continuously. Omitting all anecdotes from the texts that were distributed to the press usually avoided their being publicized, and thus made possible their use in another speech in another part of the country. Audiences watching him scribbling away during dinner often thought he was rewriting his speech, as at times he was. More often he was jotting down the opening lines most appropriate to that audience, working in many cases from a typewritten "humor list" of one-line reminders.

Except for joking about the political liabilities of his own religion, he avoided all ethnic references as well as all off-color remarks in public (although not in private). The only joke which backfired was told early in his Senate career. "The cab driver did such a good job rushing me to this luncheon," he told a Washington audience, "that I was going to give him a big tip and and tell him to vote Democratic. Then I remembered the advice of Senator Green, so I gave him no tip and told him to vote Republican." The Associated Press solemnly reported the story as though it had actually happened, and a storm of letters from cab drivers and their wives caused the Senator to think twice about his choice of humor in the future.

He liked to poke fun at politics and politicians, his party, his colleagues and himself. He liked humor that was both topical and original, irreverent but gentle. In his eight years in the Senate no speech assignment worried him longer or more deeply than his role as Democratic jester for the Washington Gridiron Club Dinner in 1958. His successful ten-minute talk on that occasion was drawn from several hours of material gathered from many sources and tried on many "experts." Thereafter he tended more and more, except perhaps on the 1960 campaign circuit, to use that kind of political, more subtle and self-belittling humor, for it was naturally consistent with his own personality and private wit.

His best humor, of course, was spontaneous, and his increasing confidence on the platform brought increasing numbers of spur-of-the-moment gibes. Candor and humor, when combined, can be dangerous weapons politically, and at times he had to restrain his natural instincts in this direction.

In addition to the humor file, we kept a collection of appropriate speech endings—usually quotations from famous figures or incidents from history which, coupled with a brief peroration of his own, could conclude almost any speech on any subject with a dramatic flourish. On many of the hectic precampaign trips of 1957-1959, he would leave one community for the next with a paraphrase from a favorite Robert Frost poem:

> Iowa City is lovely, dark and deep
> But I have promises to keep
> And miles to go before I sleep."[6]

He soon knew all these closings by heart; and while the standard closings, like the humorous openings, were almost always omitted from his released texts in order to facilitate their continued use elsewhere, his own reading copy (prepared in extra-large type) would have merely a word or a phrase to indicate the appropriate close: e.g., "Candles," "General Marshall," "Rising or Setting Sun."

Obviously the Senator was capable of selecting and remembering his own peroration without the help of these few words. But he looked upon his text and each part of it as insurance. Should the pressures of the moment or the fatigue of the trip benumb his brain as he stood on his feet, he wanted a complete text in his hands which he could follow or at least take off from. He would often deviate from his text or delete passages previously approved and sometimes discard it entirely. But—particularly in earlier days, when he knew his extemporaneous remarks were likely to be less organized, precise and grammatical than a more

---

[6] Until his wife corrected him, he at first confused two poems by using instead of the first line quoted above the words "I'll hitch my wagon to a star."

carefully prepared text—he wanted the reassurance a manuscript gave him.

HIS SENATE SPEECHES

A tremendous amount of staff research preceded every Kennedy talk. He was known in the Library of Congress as the heaviest borrower of their reference works. He did not make as many major Senate speeches as some of his more vocal colleagues, nor did he measure his—or their —effectiveness by the publicity a speech was given.

One of the most carefully researched, widely publicized and officially ignored speeches Senator Kennedy ever delivered was his address in 1957 outlining the interest of America and the West in a negotiated solution for eventual self-determination in Algeria. The speech proved to be substantially and in some ways distressingly prophetic in subsequent years, but it was bitterly criticized at the time in Washington as well as Paris. His name and speech, he later discovered, were hailed throughout North Africa—and an American correspondent who visited the Algerian camp related to the Senator his surprise at being interviewed by weary, grimy rebels on Kennedy's chances for the Presidency. There was, however, no Algerian vote in this country, and reporters looked hard for political motives.

In retrospect, Kennedy never agreed with critics who felt he should not have spoken on the subject—though perhaps "independence" sounded too precise for his purposes, he admitted—nor with those who felt he was insincerely searching for headlines. As a junior Senator, he could do no more than raise his voice, and Secretary of State Dulles told him privately that he used Kennedy's speech to advantage in putting quiet heat on the French. Moderates in Paris also welcomed the speech as support for their futile attempts to prevent extremists from taking over both sides.

The Algerian speech was consistent with the Senator's long-standing convictions about the dangers of Western colonialism and with two earlier speeches he had given on French Indochina. The longer the independence of the Vietnamese people was postponed, he said in 1953 and 1954, and the longer we believed repeated French and American predictions of an imminent French military victory, the more difficult the future would be for Vietnam and her sister states once they were fully free. He could not then have foreseen how deeply he would be involved in those correctly predicted difficulties. Indeed, on many subjects—Algeria, Indochina, India, Poland, Latin America and defense— Kennedy's speeches were well ahead of both his colleagues and the headlines.

When a major Kennedy speech on the Senate floor led to debate with the opposition, he usually held his own against more senior Republican Senators—whether it was Homer Ferguson defending Eisenhower's "new look" cut in Army strength, Styles Bridges opposing Kennedy's request for increased aid to India, William Knowland defeating by one vote a Kennedy measure to encourage Polish nationalism, or Homer Capehart demanding a secret session of the Senate to debate Kennedy's complaints about the complacent pace of our strategic forces.

Outside the labor area, his most successful effort on the Senate floor was in leading the opposition to constitutional changes in the Electoral College aimed at splitting up the strength of the more populous two-party states. (Interestingly enough, had one proposal been in effect in 1960, Nixon would have been elected President. Had the other proposal been in effect, it is likely that no candidate would have had an electoral vote majority, thus throwing the vote into the House of Representatives with no certainty of the result, inasmuch as each state delegation is given only one vote and Nixon carried twenty-six of the fifty states.)

The Kennedy Senate staff, even when supplemented in later years by the part-time or full-time efforts of Fred Holborn, Harris Wofford and Richard Goodwin, could not keep pace with his demand for new speech ideas and material. Professor Archibald Cox of the Harvard Law School (later Solicitor General) headed a team of outside experts on labor reform. Professors Max Millikan and Walt Rostow of the Massachusetts Institute of Technology (the latter was later Assistant Secretary of State) were among many advisers on foreign policy. For material on a speech on nuclear tests, he directed me to call his friend Sir David Ormsby-Gore (later U.K. Ambassador to the U.S.) in the British UN delegation. His 1954 speech on Indochina was checked with Ed Gullion of the Foreign Service (later his Ambassador to the Congo) and with an old family friend, Arthur Krock of the *New York Times* (later the chief critic of his policy in the Congo). Columnist Joe Alsop helped on a defense speech. Jacqueline translated French documents for his Vietnam speech. Law professors Freund and Howe were consulted on civil rights. Occasionally he would turn to his father's associate, New Dealer James Landis. In short, while the Senator was a brainy man, his intelligence included the ability to know his own limitations of time and knowledge and to draw on the brains of others.

HIS WRITINGS

In addition to speeches, he began in mid-term to produce a large number of magazine articles—on legislation, politics, foreign policy, economic issues and history. He asked me to help on these also. Early in 1954 he asked me to read a passage in Agar's *The Price of Union*, which had long intrigued him. It told of John Quincy Adams' independence as a Federalist Senator from Massachusetts. If we could find more such examples of Senators defying constituent pressures, he said, he would have the raw material for a worthwhile magazine essay. He wanted to remind people that politics was—or could be—the noblest profession.

Sporadically over the next few months we talked about the proposed article. I suggested Senator Norris from my home state of Nebraska, with whom my father had been associated. Arthur Krock suggested the late Senator Taft's opposition to the Nuremberg Trials. An article in the *American Bar Association Journal* told of Edmund G. Ross and the Andrew Johnson impeachment. In a book of great orations was Daniel Webster's "Seventh of March" speech and the Abolitionist attack on it. Slowly the Kennedy file of examples and material grew during 1954, but he had no time to do anything with it.

Then, in mid-January, 1955, the Senator had nothing but time. Convalescing from his back operation, he was confined to bed in his father's house in Palm Beach. At times listless, at times restless, he knew his mind required an absorbing activity to compensate for his body's painful inactivity. By telephone and letter, the "political courage" project was resurrected, a draft article completed and a copy dispatched for consideration by *Harper's Magazine*. It was tentatively entitled "Patterns of Political Courage"—and the thought was already growing in the Senator's mind that there was enough material of this kind to produce a book instead of an article.

Harper was interested in a book, and there then began a steady stream of material to the Senator's bedside stand. I did not see him until the middle of March when I traveled to Palm Beach to work with him for ten days. But I received instructions almost daily by letter and sometimes telephone—books to ship down, memoranda to prepare, sources to check, materials to assemble. More than two hundred books, journals, magazines, *Congressional Records* and old newspaper files were scanned, as well as my father's correspondence with Norris and other sources.

The Senator dictated into a machine, to local stenographers in Palm Beach and to the stenographers I brought down on my two visits. He reshaped, rewrote and coordinated historical memoranda prepared by Professor Jules Davids of George Washington University, whom Jacqueline had recommended, by James Landis and by me. He considered, and mostly rejected, new examples which our research produced, such as Senators Humphrey Marshall and Thomas Corwin. He decided to exclude the story of John Tyler's resignation from the Senate, which had been included in the original magazine article.

He insisted on knowing the full historical background of each chap-

ter. And he developed, as he read and wrote, a far keener insight into his
own political philosophy as well as the obligations of the office-holder
in a democracy. Many assumed that the book was intended as a "personal
catharsis," a justification or substitute for his role in the McCarthy
censure. In truth this was never mentioned, and the theme of the book
predated the censure controversy.

The work was a tonic to his spirits and a distraction from his pain.
A return to the hospital for another dangerous operation in February
of 1955 slowed him down only temporarily. Even there, where his survival was again in doubt, he wrote on a board propped up before him
as he lay flat on his back. Returning to Palm Beach, he resumed as
quickly as possible his steady pace of research and dictation. At first
he worked lying in bed, then propped up on the porch or patio and later
sitting in the sun near the Atlantic beach or pool.

Except for the introductory and concluding chapters, the bulk of the
manuscript was finished by the time he returned to the Senate on June 1.
Several crates of books, mostly the property of the Library of Congress,
were shipped from Palm Beach back to Washington. Still the work continued, in his office and home, day and night. Finally a title was selected
—*Profiles in Courage*—a selection he made after a long debate in which
he successively considered and rejected "Patterns of Political Courage"
(the magazine article title), "Call the Roll" (my favorite at the time),
"Eight Were Courageous" (one of the publisher's suggestions), "The
Patriots" and "Courage in the Senate."

With publication of *Profiles in Courage* on January 1, 1956, John
Kennedy became more than "just another freshman Senator." The book
was an instant and consistent best-seller. It was favorably reviewed. It
was translated into dozens of languages, from Persian to Gujrati. Although, with the exception of one chapter, attempts to convert it into
a television or film presentation fell through until 1963, most of its
chapters were reprinted in mass circulation magazines and newspapers.
Book luncheons and universities invited the author to speak. A rain of
honorary degrees began to fall.

But of all honors he would receive throughout his life, none would
make him more happy than his receipt in 1957 of the Pulitzer Prize
for biography. And of all the abuse he would receive throughout his life,
none would make him more angry than the charge a few months later
that he had not written his own book.

The charge was long rumored in private, despite the fact that the
Senator had written a best-selling book years earlier. Finally it was made
publicly by columnist Drew Pearson on the ABC television *Mike Wallace
Show* on Saturday night, December 7, 1957. When then asked by Wallace

"Who wrote the book for him?" Mr. Pearson replied, "I don't recall at the present moment."

On Sunday afternoon the Senator called me in an unusual state of high agitation and anger. He talked, as he had never done before, of lawyers and lawsuits. "We might as well quit if we let this stand," he said when I counseled caution. "This challenges my ability to write the book, my honesty in signing it and my integrity in accepting the Pulitzer Prize."

Room 362 in the Senate Office Building was as gloomy that week as the weather. We rounded up samples of the manuscript in the Senator's handwriting. We prepared a list of possible witnesses who had seen him at work on *Profiles*—secretaries who had taken dictation, visitors to Palm Beach, publishers and others. The services of Washington attorney Clark Clifford were obtained. After further conferences in Washington and New York, a direct confrontation with ABC executives was arranged.

There followed an unpleasant day. Mr. Pearson, when telephoned by ABC in the presence of the Senator and Clifford, said that Ted Sorensen had "written" the book—not merely worked on the assembly and preparation of the materials upon which much of the book was based, as the Senator had fully acknowledged in the Preface, but had actually been its author.

The ABC executives, after privately cross-examining me at length, finally agreed that the Senator was clearly the author of *Profiles in Courage* with sole responsibility for its concept and contents, and with such assistance, during his convalescence, as his Preface acknowledged. But they sought to avoid their own responsibility for publishing an untrue rumor by making a new and equally untrue charge—namely, that I had privately boasted of being the author.

More examination and argument ensued. The conversations upon which this latest charge were based proved fictitious, an invention of ABC staff members too eager to please.

"Perhaps," said an ABC vice president to the Senator, as I waited in another room, "Sorensen made the statement when drinking."

"He doesn't drink!" snapped the Senator.

"Perhaps he said it when he was mad at you."

"He's never been mad at me," said the Senator.

Finally I was called back into the room. It was agreed that I would furnish a sworn statement that I was not the author and had never claimed authorship of *Profiles in Courage*, and that ABC would make a complete statement of retraction and apology at the opening of the next *Mike Wallace Show*.

The speed as well as the tone of this retraction was gratifying. Two months later, after a talk with the Senator and a review of the evidence,

Drew Pearson—though the Senator felt no further retraction was needed —included in his column the small parenthetical note that the "author of 'Profiles in Courage' is Senator Jack Kennedy of Massachusetts."

Flying back to Washington that night in December, Clark Clifford and I could laugh over one aspect of the day's dismal, though necessary, proceedings. I was not the author of Jack Kennedy's book—but I had "ghost-written" ABC's statement of retraction and regret.

CHAPTER III

THE POLITICIAN

IN 1956 HARVARD UNIVERSITY awarded John Kennedy an honorary degree with a citation as brief and balanced as the best of his speeches: "Brave officer, able Senator, son of Harvard; loyal to party, he remains steadfast to principle."

The second clause was an admirable summary of the Senator's politics. Loyal to party, he remained steadfast to principle. His votes in the Senate were independently determined but consistently with the progressives in his party. He had not always cast a straight Democratic ballot at the polls, but had long worked at speech-making and fund-raising for fellow Democrats both inside and outside Massachusetts. He did not conceal his party label, as many do, in his campaign media, but he also successfully appealed for independent and Republican votes. He was rarely personal about politics—even though in private he talked more about personalities than issues—and did not dislike those who opposed or even attacked him so long as they were open and impersonal in their stand.

In *Profiles in Courage* he wrote: "We cannot permit the pressures of party responsibility to submerge on every issue the call of personal responsibility." But he was a partisan Democrat. He told me midway through his first Senate term that, had he arrived from outer space wholly ignorant of the issues, he would, "after listening a while to Mundt, Curtis and that group, gladly be a Democrat." Democrats, he said, generally had more heart, more foresight and more energy. They were not satisfied with things as they were and believed they could make them better.

But his partisanship had not been sufficiently blind or bitter to en-

dear him to some of the "professional" party leaders, "pols," hacks and
hangers-on in Massachusetts. He was of Irish descent, like most of them,
but he was "Harvard Irish." Despite the fact that he consistently ran
ahead of other Democrats in the state, he did not, in their judgment,
look or talk like the traditional Massachusetts politician. It was a judgment with which he might have agreed. "I hadn't considered myself
a political type," he wrote in 1960, explaining why he had assumed in
college that his older brother would be the family politician. Nevertheless this product of an unusually political family, representing the most
political of cities, liked politics more each year, and became in time
a far better practitioner of that profession than any of the so-called
"professionals."

The professionals thought he had shown his party unreliability early
as a young Congressman. He had been the only member of the Massachusetts Democratic delegation in 1947 unwilling to sign a petition to
President Truman seeking clemency for James Michael Curley. Curley,
onetime Mayor of Boston, Congressman and Governor of Massachusetts,
was regarded as the "elder statesman" of the old-style Democratic politics,
with which Kennedy had no wish to be associated. More importantly, he
later told me, Curley's term in prison for a mail fraud conviction had
barely started, and a check with the authorities showed no grounds for a
medical plea. Despite Curley's popularity in his old district, despite a
request from delegation leader John McCormack, the young Congressman could not be persuaded that the party image would be helped by
the "Purple Shamrock's" premature release.

The Senator enjoyed Edwin O'Connor's novel of urban politics, *The
Last Hurrah,* but he regretted the resulting reglorification of Curley, upon
whose career it seemed to be based. When Curley died late in 1958, the
Senator was reached in an Anchorage hotel room by a Massachusetts
radio reporter who was apparently unaware that it was 5 A.M. in Alaska.
After struggling briefly with a cautious, telephone-recorded statement
about Curley's "colorful" career which would surely be "missed," Kennedy
gave up with his own somewhat colorful—and presumably recorded—
oath and went back to sleep.

The old-line politicians grumbled also that Kennedy had always
relied on a personal organization instead of the party and on amateurs
instead of "pros." He used a self-proclaimed "pol" named Francis X.
Morrissey as a political confidence man and buffer in Boston—but
depended on his brothers and others of whom the "pros" had barely
heard to run his Massachusetts campaigns. As a Senator, they complained, he voted too independently, spent too much time courting
Republican voters and was not helping the party (i.e., themselves) sufficiently by dispensing patronage. They overlooked the fact that a fresh-

man Democratic Senator under a Republican administration has very little Federal patronage to dispense; and that his influence on state government patronage was limited during his eight years in the Senate by the two occupants of the governor's office—Republican Christian Herter, and then a Democrat, Foster Furcolo, who was not on friendly terms with the Senator.

In 1954, when Furcolo sought election to the Senate against the incumbent Republican Leverett Saltonstall, Kennedy agreed to make a major television appearance with the two state-wide Democratic candidates on October 7, the night before he entered the hospital. The Senator, resting at Hyannis Port, sent me to Boston in advance to help work out the script. On the afternoon of the broadcast, harmony prevailed. The three representatives agreed on the final script and their principals agreed by telephone to review it at the studio some ninety minutes before air time.

Senator Kennedy arrived at the studio that night in considerable pain. That pain increased as he waited with gubernatorial candidate Robert Murphy for over an hour without any sign of Furcolo. "Five minutes before we were to go on the air," as Kennedy later described it, "he arrived—and asked that the script be changed." He wanted a stronger endorsement. The Senator, who had encountered constant trouble with Furcolo in the 1952 campaign, was furious. For a moment the whole telecast was in doubt. When it proceeded, Kennedy's closing endorsement pointedly refrained from mentioning Furcolo by name.

Afterward, in the car outside the studio, his fury remained. The Murphy camp had earlier asked him to lend them my speech-writing services. The Senator asked me to stay in Boston, living in his apartment at 122 Bowdoin Street while he was in the hospital. In addition to my completing some voter surveys for him, he gave me two assignments: (1) help Democrat Murphy; (2) help Republican Saltonstall.

I did what I could in this latter vein—primarily suggesting means of Saltonstall's attracting Kennedy supporters and using Kennedy's name. Nor was any friendly newspaper left in doubt about Kennedy's failure to mention Furcolo in the telecast. Saltonstall won, and Kennedy, when asked on television two years later why he was supporting Furcolo as the then Democratic nominee for Governor, refused to go beyond a carefully worded reply:

Q: Why are you endorsing him this year when you failed to endorse him two years ago?

JFK: I think he is *superior* to his *present* opponent.

Q: Do you mean that he is a better man now?

JFK: I think he is superior to the man he is running against. . . .

The Kennedy-Saltonstall cooperation continued, to the personal pleasure and political benefit of both men, as noted earlier. Another Republican for whom Kennedy publicly expressed respect if not agreement was the late Senator Robert A. Taft of Ohio. Kennedy nominated him for "man of the year" in 1953—devoted a chapter to him in *Profiles in Courage*—and was chairman of a Special Senate Committee which selected Taft as one of five outstanding Senators of the past whose portraits were to hang in the Senate lobby.

The selection of these five was a fascinating exercise. After a poll by Kennedy of scholars and Senators, Webster, Clay and Calhoun had been obvious choices. The committee, operating under a self-imposed rule of unanimity, decided the other two slots should be divided between a liberal and a conservative. Taft was the "conservative" selection over an Ohio predecessor, John Sherman. Robert LaFollette, Sr., was the "liberal" choice after the leading candidate, Nebraska's George Norris, was blocked by Republican committee member Styles Bridges (either because he had tangled with Norris many years earlier, as he admitted, or because he was acting for Nebraska's conservative Senator Carl Curtis—whose earlier request that each state's current Senators be permitted to block the selection of any previous Senator from their state had been politely rejected by Kennedy).

John Kennedy's expressions of respect for Bob Taft pleased not only Joseph P. Kennedy but a key supporter and friend, Basil Brewer. Publisher of the influential New Bedford, Massachusetts, *Standard Times*, Brewer was a conservative Massachusetts Republican, an old friend of the senior Kennedy and an old foe of Henry Cabot Lodge. After Lodge had helped Eisenhower obtain the Republican nomination over Taft in 1952, the *Standard Times* endorsed Kennedy over Lodge for the Senate, and the 22,000 extra votes Kennedy piled up in the New Bedford area had helped provide his winning margin of only 70,000 votes.

RE-ELECTION TO THE SENATE

That margin was sufficiently narrow that "anybody in the state can come into this office," Kennedy told me, "and claim credit for my winning." With this margin in mind, his 1958 Senate campaign began the day after his 1952 campaign ended.[1] During the nearly six years that preceded the official opening of his re-election campaign, no preoccupa-

[1] Since the 1958 campaign and the Kennedy pre-eminence in Massachusetts state politics must be seen as a whole, I shall tell the '58 story before going back to the relatively brief bid for the Vice Presidential nomination in 1956.

tion with other matters and no prediction of easy victory were permitted
to interfere with five fundamental approaches to 1958:

1. Contact was maintained with the personal organization he had
carefully nurtured in every corner of the state. The chief Kennedy
men in each community were called "secretaries," thus avoiding both
offense to the local party "chairman" and a hierarchy of titles within
the Kennedy camp.

2. Each year a comprehensive report was mailed throughout the
state on what legislative and administrative actions he was seeking
by way of doing "more for Massachusetts." We justified the use of
Congressional franking privileges for this document on the legislator's
historic responsibility to account for his stewardship to his constituents;
and when we were unable to find a sufficiently brief quotation from an
early American statesman to this effect, Lee White and I invented one
and attributed it to "one of our founding fathers."

3. The Senator spent an increasing number of weekends speaking
throughout the state—to the Sons of Italy one night and an American
Legion post the next—to the Massachusetts Farm Bureau and the
United Polish Societies—to the Council of Catholic Nurses and a Bonds
for Israel dinner—to chambers of commerce, labor unions, Rotary
luncheons, and conventions, clubs and conferences of every imaginable
kind. Most of his speeches, particularly in the small towns, were nonpartisan and moderate in flavor.

4. The favor of the Massachusetts newspapers, largely Republican
and almost entirely Lodge-oriented in 1952, was carefully cultivated.
Reporters, editors and publishers were always welcome in the Senator's
office. Newspaper executives who needed a speaker, a guest editorial or
a helping hand with some governmental problem found their Senator
eager to be of service. As a result, in sharp contrast with 1952, not a
single Massachusetts newspaper opposed Kennedy's re-election in 1958,
and nearly all of them, including such consistently Republican spokesmen as the Boston *Herald*, openly endorsed him (the *Herald*'s endorsement following right on the heels of a Kennedy endorsement by the
Massachusetts ADA).

5. Never forgetting his supporters, the Senator constantly wooed
his opponents. He was always willing to forget differences and forgive
detractors. He bore no lasting grudges and thought politics no place
for revenge. Republicans were frequently reminded of his cooperation
with Senator Saltonstall, his support of Eisenhower foreign policy
measures and his independent voting record. Businessmen were kept
informed of his efforts to boost the state's economy and to curb labor
rackets. Budget-cutting advocates were told of his Senate leadership
on behalf of the Second Hoover Commission Report, and given the re-

prints of a warm letter of appreciation from another old friend of his father's, Herbert Hoover. Italo-Americans who were offended by his feud with Furcolo, longshoremen disgruntled by his support of the St. Lawrence Seaway, Teamsters and other union members upset by his efforts for labor reform, Negroes suspicious of his voting for the jury trial amendment—all these and other groups received material which emphasized his efforts on their behalf, his friendship for their causes and his endorsement by their leaders. In addition, of course, he made certain all mail was answered promptly, all visitors were greeted cordially and as many state problems as possible were handled by him personally.

The Kennedy approach to campaigning, which would later be applied to the Presidential primaries and then on a nationwide scale, was unique in many ways. While remembering to stir up the faithful, he concentrated on the uncommitted. Running even with his party in the urban Democratic strongholds, he won by running far ahead of his party in the suburbs and towns. Remaining deferential to local party organizations, he sought new and attractive faces for his "secretaries." Soliciting support from wealthy contributors and prominent names, he knew that hard, routine, usually boring work by large numbers of lesser known, less busy and less opinionated adherents was more important to win elections. He sought to get a little work from a lot of people. An endless number of committees was formed, giving more and more voters an opportunity to feel a part of the Kennedy organization.

He turned for a campaign manager, not to an experienced professional ("Most of them are available," he said, "only because they are experienced in losing"), but to one of his own brothers, enabling the Senator to trust completely the campaign manager's loyalty and judgment.

In March of 1959 I summed up the Kennedy approach in a talk to the Midwest Democratic Conference by suggesting eight "modern clichés" to replace the standard campaign myths:

1. One devoted volunteer like Paul Revere is worth ten hired Hessians.
2. Personal letters count more than prestige letterheads.
3. Fifty $1 contributors are better than one $100 contributor.
4. A nonpolitical talk to the unconvinced is better than a political talk to the already convinced.
5. One session in a vote-filled poolroom is worth two sessions in a smoke-filled hotel room.
6. (Regarding issues) It is better to rock the boat than to sail it under false colors.
7. No one's vote can be delivered with the possible exception of your mother's—and make sure she's registered.
8. One hour of work in 1957 is worth two hours of work in 1958.

This last "cliché" struck at the oldest and best-entrenched political myth that Kennedy challenged. "In every campaign I've ever been in," he told me in 1959, "they've said I was starting too early—that I would peak too soon or get too much exposure or run out of gas or be too easy a target. I would never have won any race following that advice."

Between 1952 and 1958 he did not follow it, and in 1958 the Massachusetts Republicans could not find a significant candidate willing to oppose him. Some Republican strategists counseled no opposition in order to keep down the Democratic turnout for Kennedy. One Boston *Herald* columnist even suggested that both parties endorse him. The Republicans "can't possibly lick him," wrote the late Bill Cunningham. "They couldn't borrow a better man and they surely haven't any like him. . . . Why not make it unanimous?"

It nearly was. In the end, his opponent was an unknown lawyer named Vincent Celeste. Vinnie, as his friends called him, was a fiery orator when making sweeping charges against the Kennedys in public. But he was more subdued in the one private conversation I had with him, after he had walked out on a League of Women Voters–sponsored public debate in which I had represented the Senator, shouting as he left a series of protests at the speech I had half-completed.

Understandably the Kennedy campaign workers at the outset had an air of overconfident lethargy. But we were shocked by a light primary turnout in which Furcolo received a larger Democratic vote seeking re-election as Governor than Kennedy did as Senator. "I'm glad it happened and got everyone off their backs," said the Senator, and he launched an intensive handshaking, speech-making, nonstop automobile tour of the state of several weeks' duration, which took him and Jacqueline within six miles of every Massachusetts voter. On occasion she would speak a few words in French or Italian to audiences of those extractions.

Every hand in sight was shaken; ever since 1946, when Dave Powers had spirited him up the back stairs of the "three-decker" apartments in Charlestown ("so we could catch them in the kitchen," said Dave), he had known there was no substitute for personal contact. Aides marveled at his stopping the car on the fatigue-ridden last night of the campaign to shake one more hand, that of an elderly woman alone on the street.

John Kennedy rolled to his fifth straight political victory by a margin of more than 873,000 votes, a record three-to-one ratio. It was the largest margin and largest total vote ever accorded any candidate in the history of Massachusetts.

He carried in with him the entire state Democratic ticket and the state's first Democratic legislature as well. With the 1960 Presidential election in mind, Kennedy had made the desired impression on politicians around the nation. He had won bigger than any other contested candidate for major office in the country.

He was also the first office-seeker in Massachusetts history to carry every city and county in the state regardless of its political, economic or ethnic complexion. Instead of losing ground among Negro voters, as predicted a year earlier, he ran ahead of Negro legislator Lincoln Pope in the latter's own ward.

In Massachusetts Kennedy was no longer regarded by the professionals as a political amateur and upstart. No one in the state could match or fault his performance; no one could doubt or challenge his leadership; and no one remembered that two years earlier the former Democratic State Committee chairman had vowed to run against Kennedy in the 1958 primary.

MASSACHUSETTS DEMOCRATIC CONTROL

Any explanation of the Senator's involvement in that 1956 State Committee fight must revolve around three names: Adlai Stevenson, William H. Burke and John Fox.

Adlai Stevenson was not the most popular figure in Massachusetts in those days, and Democratic politicians in that state traditionally kept apart from other candidates. But Kennedy was a warm Stevenson supporter for the Democratic Presidential nomination in 1956 as in 1952. Stevenson's leading opponents were Senator Estes Kefauver of Tennessee and Governor Averell Harriman of New York, and it was generally believed that House Majority Leader John McCormack was seeking a Massachusetts favorite-son designation to aid Harriman, block Stevenson and show the nation that he spoke for Massachusetts Democrats.

William H. "Onions" Burke was a rotund former tavern owner and onion farmer from the old Curley school of politics. The Eisenhower victory of 1952 having deprived him of his patronage plum as Collector of the Port of Boston, he had wrested control of the State Democratic Committee and was firmly allied with McCormack against Stevenson.

Publisher John Fox of the Boston *Post* was an erratic financier who had converted the once-respected *Post* into a shrill and bitter outlet for his extremist personal views. After giving Kennedy a backhanded endorsement in 1952, in order to justify the *Post's* nominal Democratic affiliation at a time when he was endorsing Eisenhower, he turned on the Senator shortly thereafter for not standing by Joseph McCarthy and for not attacking Harvard's President Pusey. McCarthy and Fox were angry that Pusey had failed to take stronger action against professors suspected of Communist tendencies, and Fox wanted Kennedy to join an alumni boycott of Harvard fund-raising in retaliation. When Kennedy refused, and his Senate votes continued to displease, Fox personally wrote one mean anti-Kennedy front-page editorial after another.

At the Senator's instructions—the only time he ever requested such a dossier to my knowledge—I quietly began gathering material for a possible speech on Mr. Fox, on the eminent leaders of both parties he had maligned, on his difficulties with the law and on his curious financial arrangements. That file was never used, for the *Post* in later years went bankrupt under Fox and he largely disappeared from public view. But in 1956, desperate to salvage his paper's solvency, he was hoping by his support of McCormack and Burke to further not only his dislike of Kennedy and Stevenson but also his ambition to be the most politically powerful publisher in the state of Massachusetts.

Matters came to a head in the early spring of 1956. Burke, increasingly cocky with the support of Fox, castigated all Stevenson supporters in general and the members of the ADA in particular. Senator Kennedy, though he knew his own seat was surely secure, foresaw destruction by Burke and Fox of all his efforts to make the Massachusetts Democratic Party a less shabby, more respected and more cohesive organization. Too many former Democratic followers, having acquired a little affluence and a home in the suburbs, were becoming Republicans in their search for respectability. They would never return to the party of the Burkes and the Curleys.

More importantly, Kennedy had announced for Stevenson. He had no objection to John McCormack as a token "favorite son" and made no effort to obtain write-in votes for Stevenson against McCormack in the state's nonbinding Presidential primary. But he foresaw his own standing in the state and nation being discredited if his emphatic endorsement of Stevenson was largely ignored at the convention by a Massachusetts delegation looking to Burke, McCormack and Fox for leadership. Although some assumed that talk of his being nominated as Stevenson's running mate also influenced his decision, he later wrote me in a memorandum with respect to this charge:

> I was not fighting for the Massachusetts delegation in order to have "chips" for the Vice Presidential race. I was fighting for it because I had publicly endorsed Stevenson and I wanted to make good on my commitment.

Already many members of Kennedy's personal campaign organization, as well as other "reformers," ADA members and Stevenson supporters, had battled with some success in the April, 1956, primary for seats on the State Committee. Now in May, contrary to his own strong preference to steer clear of state politics, and contrary to the counsel of those whose advice he respected, Senator Kennedy plunged into the fray. The election of a new State Committee chairman was the key objective.

Winning that election was important only because losing it would be harmful.

The eighty little-known members of the State Committee, an organization Kennedy had previously done well to ignore, suddenly found themselves important for the first time, the object of all kinds of political pressure and press inquiries. The Senator quietly rallied his forces, working principally through two key aides from his 1952 race, Lawrence O'Brien and Kenneth O'Donnell. He visited every uncommitted State Committee member and sought out Burke followers as well. At the same time the Burke forces were equally busy and far more noisy.

Kennedy dispatched me to Boston to help plan the statutory and parliamentary procedures by which control of the committee could be gained from a hostile chairman and secretary who claimed pledges from a majority of the members. The Burke forces called a State Committee meeting in Springfield for May 19 at 2 P.M. The Kennedy forces then called an official meeting of the committee to be held in the Hotel Bradford in Boston on the same day at 3 P.M. The Burke forces then rescinded their first call and said *they* were calling a meeting in the Hotel Bradford at 3 P.M.

After two intensive weeks, which concerned the Senator as much as any political fight in his career, the climax was a stormy meeting—complete with booing, shoving, name-calling, contests for the gavel and near fist fights. In the end, the Burke forces were ousted by exactly the vote Kennedy had predicted. The Senator, who had not attended the meeting, called for a new era of unity for Massachusetts Democrats.

THE VICE PRESIDENTIAL RACE

It was not really a new era. But Kennedy, who was shortly thereafter elected chairman of the state's convention delegation, and delivered four-fifths of its votes for Stevenson on the first ballot, was thus able to honor his pledge.

Earlier that year he had called me into his office with a mixed air of mystery and glee. "I'm considering," he said, "running as a New England favorite son in the New Hampshire Presidential primary." It was an appealing idea at first sight. Kefauver was otherwise certain to get a head start on Stevenson by winning in New Hampshire as he had in 1952. As a stalking horse for Stevenson, Kennedy thought he could carry New Hampshire and help unite the six New England states behind the Illinoisan. He had no illusions about himself as a serious Presidential possibility in 1956. He was not even motivated by a serious interest in the Vice Presidential nomination at that time. Nor did he think New Hampshire to be of critical importance. But he was a man of action; and, in a remark which revealed much about his activist nature, he was contemplating running for President in New Hampshire, he said, "because that's where the action is now."

In the end, Stevenson campaign manager James Finnegan preferred a Kennedy endorsement of Stevenson immediately before the New Hampshire primary. There Kefauver won, but by the time the Massachusetts State Committee fight was over, Stevenson's gains elsewhere had caused increased speculation on his choice of a running mate.

Kennedy's name had often been mentioned as a Vice Presidential possibility. In a letter to the Senator on November 22, 1955, I referred to this talk in suggesting he dispel the rumors about his health. We first heard that Stevenson was considering Kennedy early in 1956 from Theodore H. White, then writing a feature article on the Democratic Party for a national magazine. Stevenson's camp had told him, he said, that under consideration for the second spot were two Southerners (Gore and Clement, both of Tennessee) and two Catholics (Kennedy of Massachusetts and Wagner of New York). The other three names seemed obviously to have been mentioned as a means of undercutting Presidential candidates Kefauver in Tennessee and Harriman in New York, and we thus suspected that the whole item was a "plant."

But the seed, once planted, grew steadily in the thinking of Kennedy fans if not in the Senator's own mind. Governor Abraham Ribicoff of Connecticut was the first to endorse him, followed by Governor Dennis Roberts of Rhode Island. Governor Luther Hodges of North Carolina said Kennedy would be acceptable to the South. While the Senator continued to view the whole subject with more curiosity than concern, a surprising flurry of newspaper and magazine stories and editorials pointed up his assets with enthusiasm.

Why was Kennedy mentioned at all? His best-selling book and growing number of speeches had made him more widely known than most Democratic office-holders. His youthful, clean-cut demeanor, his candid, low-key approach and his heroic war record gave him a special appeal to both new and uncommitted voters. His television appearances and Harvard commencement address drew national attention (although a few disgruntled Harvardites were certain that his use of the word "campus" instead of "Yard" proved he had not written his own speech). And his religion, it was said, would help defend the ticket against Republican "soft-on-Communism" charges and help counter the effects of Stevenson's divorce.

But it became increasingly clear that his religion was not an asset in all eyes. Stevenson himself was said to be expressing some doubts on its effect (along with doubts about Kennedy's health and devotion to civil liberties). The mail to Stevenson's office on the Vice Presidency was heavily anti-Catholic anti-Kennedy. Mayor David Lawrence of Pittsburgh told Stevenson that a Catholic on the ticket meant certain defeat. Speaker Sam Rayburn held a similar view, and it was widely reported that, among many others, former President Harry Truman and former National Chairman Frank McKinney (like Lawrence and several other opponents to the idea, a Catholic himself) were equally negative on this ground. A *Look Magazine* poll of thirty-one Democratic officials in thirteen Southern states found eighteen who thought a Catholic on the ticket would be a liability in their states, only three who thought he would be an asset.

Earlier in the year, in connection with a newspaper story, the author of this *Look* article, Fletcher Knebel, had brought a similar report to the Kennedy office. The Senator, wholly willing to be rejected for the Vice Presidency but not on grounds of his religion, asked me to turn over to Knebel some material I had been gathering showing potential "Catholic vote" gains that might help offset any losses. Knebel asked me to develop the material further for his *Look Magazine* piece—and the result some months later was a sixteen-page memorandum of statistics, quotations, analysis and argument summarizing Stevenson's need to recapture those strategically located Catholic voters who normally voted Democratic.

It was, I wrote in an accompanying letter to Knebel, a "personal" document which I was "extremely reluctant to let out of my hands." But gradually and inevitably the memorandum and its subsequent refinements were shown on a limited basis to key newsmen and politicians.

Word of its existence spread. Two magazines reprinted it in full and a half-dozen presented summaries. Political leaders sought copies. The Stevenson camp asked for more. The backers of Senator Hubert Humphrey of Minnesota issued a scornful attack on these claims for the "Catholic vote" and put forward a much longer and less documented memorandum of their own making equally broad claims about the "anti-Catholic vote" and the "farm vote."

No candidates were mentioned in my document. But Senator Kennedy disliked the growing focus on his religion, and disliked even more the danger that his own assistant would be publicized as promoting this issue. We arranged with Connecticut State Chairman John Bailey, a strong supporter, to assert responsibility for the memorandum. I kept Bailey supplied with copies. He kept me entertained with tales of gullible inquiries. Most newspapers at the time accepted Bailey's statement of sponsorship; but when a more skeptical politician such as Jim Finnegan telephoned me to request six copies for Stevenson headquarters, I successively and unsuccessfully feigned ignorance, surprise, reluctance and the hope that I could "get hold of some" for him.

Like most political-statistical analyses aimed at laymen, the "Bailey Memorandum," as it became known, oversimplified, overgeneralized and overextended its premises in order to reach an impressive conclusion. That conclusion was both more sweeping than the evidence supported and more valid than its critics alleged. The document did not purport to be original research but applied existing studies and surveys to particular states and elections. It sought to answer Democratic fears of an "anti-Catholic vote" by raising hopes of recapturing a greater share of the "Catholic vote"—and while neither phenomenon can be measured with the precision this memorandum attempted, their existence and importance had long been assumed by most political and public opinion analysts.

The "Bailey Memorandum" made no pretense at being a comprehensive and objective study. It was a political answer to the sweeping assertions made against nominating a Catholic for Vice President. While I acknowledge its limitations as a scientific analysis, its political impact would surely have been somewhat more limited if, instead of discussing the "Catholic vote," I had followed the advice more recently offered by one professorial critic and referred to "situations in which Catholicism is an independent variable of fluctuating salience with respect to the voting choice."

The politicians who read the document were more concerned with probabilities than with certainties—and, whatever the memorandum's faults, the widespread attention accorded its contents at least reopened the previously closed assumption that a Catholic on the ticket spelled defeat. By the summer of 1956, as the result of President Eisenhower's poor health and Stevenson's commanding lead for the nomination, the Vice Presidency was being discussed more each day, and Kennedy's name was no longer automatically dismissed in those discussions.

The Senator's own interest in the nomination was growing, more out of a sense of competition than of conviction. While his father and wife were willing, as always, to back whatever course he chose, the latter preferred that her husband's first full year since convalescence be spent in the quiet of his home, and the former (who did not even interrupt his customary summer vacation in the South of France for the convention) saw no merit in second place on a ticket still certain to lose. But with the Senator's skeptical encouragement, I made a quick trip to New England to seek support from friendly Democrats in Maine, advice from Stevenson speech-writer Arthur Schlesinger, Jr. and counsel from Ribicoff and Bailey. It was generally agreed that Stevenson would surely consult with his political associates and advisers before selecting his running mates, and our chief task was to make certain that these men were informed of John F. Kennedy's qualities.

Assets other than his religion were being stressed once again, to the Senator's relief. "The Senator feels," I wrote Schlesinger on August 1, 1956, "that if he is to be chosen, he would prefer that it be on this basis [his other qualifications] and not because of his religion." And on the same day I had written to John Bailey:

> The Senator feels that the Catholic aspect may have been over-sold and is likely to backfire. He was somewhat disturbed by the recent newspaper reports on your use of this issue, although understanding the reasons you felt it was desirable.

A day earlier Kennedy told a reporter he was flatly not interested in a nomination that was due to his religion.

An opportunity to stress these other qualifications was presented by a letter to me from Stevenson's research director (later Congressman) Ken Hechler, requesting that I prepare for that camp's consideration "the strongest case for Kennedy." My reply stressed those qualities which I thought distinguished him from other possibilities and politicians "regardless of Governor Stevenson's need to rewin the Catholic vote"—as a contrast to Nixon, as a campaigner and vote-getter, as an author, television personality, family man, war hero, experienced legislator, friend of labor, champion of minorities, political moderate and complement to Stevenson. (At the Senator's request I struck from this list the advantages of having a wealthy running mate.) But I also emphasized that "Senator Kennedy is not pushing this matter—and whatever the final decision may be, it will in no way diminish his support and enthusiasm for Governor Stevenson."

While Kennedy's other assets were being stressed, so were his other liabilities. Kennedy was "unacceptable" to the Midwest, said Minnesota's Governor Orville Freeman, because of his votes on farm legislation.

Minnesota's Senator Humphrey, whose name led the list of some two dozen possibilities, declared himself an open candidate for the Vice Presidency. With what he thought was Stevenson's blessing, he initiated a nationwide campaign for the job. Estes Kefauver, after his Presidential hopes were ended by Stevenson in the primaries, was also angling for second spot. Kennedy, while interested and available, refused to consider himself a candidate or to permit a "campaign" worthy of the name.

While I was more eager, I had never been to a convention and knew no delegates. John Bailey talked to a few party leaders, as did the Senator. But no public endorsements were sought. Plans for a Hyannis Port meeting of all New England delegates with Stevenson were abandoned lest some pressure or preference be read into it. We stimulated a few meetings and mailings, but most of the Kennedy endorsements received by the Stevenson circle were made without our knowledge.

Most of the analyses of the situation I drew up—the comparative qualifications of the candidates, for example, and possible plans for convention action—were for my own guidance only, enabling me to respond to friendly inquiries and to talk concretely with the Senator.

In one of these talks—which occurred as he drove me home one summer evening—we discussed a letter from Schlesinger, who was then working in Stevenson's office, saying "Things look good." Said Kennedy in effect, "After all this I may actually be disappointed if I don't get the nomination." His statement was contrary to all we had previously assumed and I so remarked. "Yes," he went on, "and that disappointment will be deep enough to last from the day they ballot on the Vice Presidency until I leave for Europe two days later."

We left for Chicago and the convention in August with stacks of material—reprints of favorable editorials and stories, one-sided summaries of Kennedy's shaky farm record, the Midwest response to his Seaway support and biographical data sheets—but with very few lists of names on whom we could count. At the suggestion of Schlesinger, who had quietly kept us informed of thinking within the Stevenson camp, I went out several days in advance to test the water. Among the Stevenson aides (aside from Arthur), I found Newt Minow enthusiastic, Bill Blair friendly, the rest noncommittal. With the help of Kennedy brother-in-law Sargent Shriver and the Chicago Merchandise Mart (a Joseph Kennedy establishment which he helped direct), I was able to make arrangements for our accommodations and credentials—but very little political headway. I also encountered and refuted rumors about the Senator's health, about a financial contribution he had supposedly made to Nixon and about a tremendous campaign for the Vice Presidency being masterminded by his father.

Our far-from-tremendous campaign began in Chicago the Sunday before the convention opened. It consisted of a few friends meeting in our hotel suite. "You call them," the Senator had said to me with a smile. "You're responsible for this whole thing." "No," I said, "I'm responsible only if you lose. If you win, you will be known as the greatest political strategist in convention history."

Circumstances, more than political strategy, enabled the Kennedy face and name to be brought favorably to the attention of the convention. Many delegates who had served with Kennedy in Congress were willing to work within their own states. Massachusetts delegates spread the word in convivial get-togethers with those from other areas. The Chicago *Sun-Times* gave Kennedy an editorial boost widely read in the convention. With the exception of the Kefauver delegation from New Hampshire, most of the New England delegates who gathered each morning for breakfast (a Roberts-Ribicoff-Kennedy innovation) liked Kennedy and wanted to help. A luncheon for a local Illinois candidate, attended by key Stevenson leaders, featured Kennedy as a speaker. Several delegations invited Kennedy to address them.

On opening night Kennedy's assets were favorably displayed in his previously filmed role as narrator of the "keynote" motion picture—a documentary history of the Democratic Party which outshone the fiery, flourishing keynote speech of Frank Clement. At its close, Kennedy was introduced from the floor, and our friends around the hall had no difficulty in getting others to join in prolonged applause.

With all these boosts, Kennedy banners, buttons and volunteers began to appear from New England and Chicago sources. One Massachusetts delegate in a big Stetson hat and cowboy boots carried a sign reading "Texans for Kennedy." But buttons and banners were not the equivalent of a Stevenson endorsement. A visit to Governor Stevenson by Ribicoff, Roberts and Massachusetts Governor Paul Dever had no visible results. The plan of a mutual friend to obtain backing from a key Stevenson supporter, Mrs. Eleanor Roosevelt, collapsed, for she used the occasion to chastise the Senator in a roomful of people for being insufficiently anti-McCarthy.

Finally, on Wednesday noon, word came by a circuitous route that Kennedy was no longer under consideration. After consultation with his brother Bob, whose cool judgment and organizational skills were once again available and invaluable, the Senator sought and received a direct talk with Stevenson. Stevenson did not answer the Vice Presidential question with finality, but asked Kennedy's views on all those considered (Kennedy liked Humphrey). He then asked the Senator if he was willing to make the principal Presidential nominating speech. "I assumed," the Senator later told me of his feelings at that time, "that when I was given the opportunity to nominate Stevenson they had decided on another candidate [for Vice President]. . . . I thought the matter was closed and was not especially unhappy."

The Stevenson staff had hinted the previous week that Kennedy was a possible choice for nominator. Delaying the decision, they assured me, was no problem inasmuch as a fine speech had already been written. That afternoon—less than twenty-four hours before nominations opened —a speech draft was brought to us by Stevenson aide Willard Wirtz. From a brief conversation with Wirtz I mistakenly inferred that Kennedy had been definitely ruled out for Vice President. I also learned that even his role as Stevenson's nominator could not be final until (1) a courtesy clearance was received from Stevenson's fellow Illinoisan, Senator Douglas, and (2) that evening's fight on the party platform was over, should any schism require a Southerner in the slot of chief nominator.

The Senator asked me to review the speech and to rework it in his style while he attended the convention. It was an impossible assignment. The draft we were handed was a wordy, corny, lackluster committee product. I finally caught up with the Senator well after midnight, when the platform fight was over and he had been told definitely he would speak the next day. He looked at the original draft, then at my redraft, and said, "We'll have to start over."

He talked about a fresh opening, the points to make in a new draft and the length he desired, and asked me to bring it to his room by 8 A.M. the next morning. I did. There he reworked it further, sitting in bed. I rushed back to my room to get it retyped, and then we hurried out to Convention Hall.

Owing to our haste, one page from his copy was missing, and the Senator refused (wisely, it turned out) to rely on the teleprompter. I snatched the missing page from the teleprompter office, promising to return it as soon as it was copied. A helpful reporter, Tom Winship of the Boston *Globe*, borrowed a typewriter at the press table and banged it out.

The teleprompter failed but the speech was a success. Its reference to the two different types of campaigners on the Eisenhower-Nixon ticket—one who took the high road and one who took the low—was picked up by subsequent speakers and became a part of that year's campaign vocabulary. Illinois leader Richard Daley later said this speech helped convince him that Kennedy was needed on the ticket.

Stevenson won the nomination, and then dramatically announced that he would leave to an open convention the selection of his Vice Presidential running mate. Despite the bitter arguments of several party leaders who thought it a dangerous experiment and certain to aid Kefauver, he regarded it as a stimulant to a dull convention, as a contrast with the Republican selection of Nixon, and as a way out of the conflicting political pressures on him created by the number of friendly candidates.

His late night announcement that a genuine balloting on the Vice Presidency would be held the next day set off twelve hours of feverish political activity. Bob Kennedy and John Bailey held a hectic meeting of family and friends in our suite. Assignments were handed out. Efforts were made to reach key leaders. But we acted largely in a state of confusion and ignorance. We had no plans, no facilities, no communication, no organization, little know-how and very few contacts.

There have been many sensational stories about that Vice Presidential race: that Kennedy backers pressured Stevenson into throwing the convention open—that Kennedy was furious with Stevenson for throwing the convention open—that Kennedy decided to try for it only when Georgia announced for him—that Chicago's Dick Daley and New York's

Carmine DeSapio were both slighted because no one in the Kennedy camp recognized them—that Joseph P. Kennedy lined up several delegates by transatlantic phone—that John McCormack deliberately aided Kefauver over Kennedy—and that the Senator was stunned, tearful or deeply hurt when he failed to secure the nomination. Not one of those stories is accurate. There have also been many conflicting claims about which Kennedy friend lined up which delegation. I do not know which of those claims is accurate. I could not line up one delegate, even in my own state of Nebraska, which was solidly for Kefauver.

As always, the Senator was his own best campaigner, seeing state leaders and visiting several state caucuses. He still had doubts about the desirability of the nomination—but this was where the action was, and his combative spirit would not let him run away from a fight or run out on his friends. His brother Bob and sister Eunice toured other delegations. A handful of Congressmen—including Edward Boland and Torbert Macdonald of Massachusetts and Frank Smith, a Mississippi progressive—never rested.

I rounded up material for the nominating and seconding speeches, but it was of little use. Abe Ribicoff gave a ringing, largely extemporaneous, nominating speech. George Smathers, who could give us very little help in the Florida delegation, gave a hasty seconding speech (sample: "Jack Kennedy's name is magic in Ohio, Cincinnati, Akron, California and other areas. It will be great for us to have him on the ticket"). And John McCormack, literally propelled toward the platform at the last minute by Bob Kennedy, gave a politically oriented seconding speech ("It is time to go East") that was identifiable as a Kennedy speech only by its closing lines.

With surprising speed, the nominations closed and the balloting opened. Kefauver, Kennedy, Humphrey, Wagner, Gore and others were all in contention. I sat alone with the Senator as he lay on his bed in the Stockyards Inn, behind Convention Hall, watching the race on television. He shook his head in amazement at his unexpected strength in Georgia, Louisiana, Nevada and Virginia. "This thing is really worth winning now," he said.

Illinois' 46 (of their 64) votes gave him a boost. Maine disappointed him by splitting their 14 votes. He muttered something unprintable when Ohio's Mike DiSalle and Pennsylvania's David Lawrence, both fearful of a fellow Catholic on the ticket, delivered more than 100 of their 132 combined votes to Kefauver. "You better hustle over to the platform and find out what I do to make Kefauver's nomination unanimous," he said.

At the end of the first ballot, it appeared that Humphrey, Gore and Wagner would not make it, though the first two still hoped for a deadlock. On the next ballot many of their votes, as well as some favorite-son votes, would in all probability start switching to the leaders—either to Kefauver, who led Kennedy by a ratio greater than three to two, or to Kennedy. From our television set came the report that Humphrey was on his way to Kefauver's suite in the Stockyards Inn, presumably to switch his votes to the Tennessean. "Get up there and intercept Hubert," the Senator said. "Tell him I'd like to see him, too."

Outside Kefauver's door I found nothing but the chaos of competing cameramen and newsmen. No one knew who was inside, coming in or coming out. Hurrying to the speaker's platform, I checked briefly on the procedures for making Kefauver's nomination unanimous and raced back to the inn. En route I met Humphrey's manager, Eugene McCarthy, and delivered Kennedy's invitation (which assumed Humphrey was visiting Kefauver). Congressman McCarthy sadly shook his head. "All we have are Protestants and farmers," he said, negating any get-together. Kefauver, it later turned out, had personally come to plead with the distraught Humphrey, as had Michigan's Governor Mennen Williams, on Kefauver's behalf. McCarthy was quoted as feeling slighted that Kennedy, instead of coming himself, had sent a callow youth to offer Humphrey an "audience."

Meanwhile, the second ballot was already under way and a Kennedy trend had set in. The South was anxious to stop Kefauver, and Kennedy was picking up most of the Gore and Southern favorite-son votes. He was also getting the Wagner votes. Kefauver was gaining more slowly, but hardly a handful of his delegates had left him. Bob Kennedy, John Bailey and their lieutenants were all over the floor shouting to delegations to come with Kennedy.

When New Jersey and New York in rapid succession gave Kennedy 126½ votes he had not received on the first ballot, the press chaos was transferred from Kefauver's corridor to ours. Our television set showed wild confusion on the convention floor and a climbing Kennedy total. But the Senator was as calm as ever. He bathed, then again reclined on the bed. Finally we moved, through a back exit, to a larger and more isolated room.

The race was still neck and neck, and Kennedy knew that no lead was enough if it could not produce a majority. Oklahoma stayed with Gore ("He's not our kind of folks," the Governor of Oklahoma said to a Kennedy pleader, summing up in six words the Senator's inability to dent the Western Protestant farm and ranch areas). Wagner's votes in Pennsylvania went to Kefauver instead of Kennedy. "Lawrence," muttered the Senator. Puerto Rico stayed with Wagner, despite his withdrawal. "They didn't get the word," said the Senator somewhat ruefully.

Tennessee, torn by the conflicting ambitions of its two Senators and Governor, stayed with Gore. Then Lyndon Johnson rose for Texas. With the help of several Congressmen, he had beaten down the anti-Catholic sentiment within his delegation, including that of Sam Rayburn, and he announced the full 56 votes of Texas "for that fighting Senator who wears the scars of battle . . . the next Vice President of the United States, John Kennedy of Massachusetts."

I stretched out a hand of congratulation. "Not yet," said the Senator. But as his total grew, he finished dressing and, between glances at the television, began to discuss what he should say to the convention if nominated. North Carolina, which had passed on the second ballot, now switched half its votes to Kennedy. Kentucky's chairman announced that his delegation, "which has consistently been with the minority all through this convention, enthusiastically joins the majority and changes its vote to John Kennedy."

It almost was a majority—but not quite. In the entire nineteen-state West-Midwest area between Illinois and California, excepting Nevada, Kennedy could get no more than 20 of their 384 convention votes. Suddenly the tide turned again.

Albert Gore earlier in the year had seemed to endorse Kennedy ("I would like to see Jack Kennedy in either the first or second place on the Democratic ticket in either 1956, 1960 or 1964"). But now he released his Tennessee delegates to Kefauver. Oklahoma switched from Gore to Kefauver. Minnesota and Missouri switched their Humphrey votes to Kefauver. Illinois and South Carolina tried to stem the avalanche by switching a few more votes to Kennedy. But it was to no avail. The Kennedy current had run its course. More Kefauver votes followed.

The Senator remained silent until the television screen showed Kefauver with a majority. "Let's go," he said and plunged through the maelstrom outside his door to walk to the convention platform. Brushing aside those officials who wished him to wait until it was all over, he strode to the rostrum with a tired grin. Speaking briefly and movingly without notes, he thanked those who had supported him, congratulated Stevenson on his open-convention decision and moved to make Kefauver's nomination unanimous.

Afterward, we reviewed the accidents of chance that prevented a few dozen more delegates from putting Kennedy over the top:

• If the large electric tote board in the back of the hall had not been dismantled the night before, so that all delegates could have seen Kennedy nearing a majority . . .

• If Convention Chairman Sam Rayburn had called for a recess and a third ballot instead of second-ballot switches . . .

• If some of our friends had not unknowingly left town the day before . . .

• If Kennedy had possessed an organized campaign machine with a communications and control center . . .

• If South Carolina, Illinois and Alabama, which wished to announce switches favoring Kennedy, had been recognized by Mr. Rayburn before Tennessee, Oklahoma, Minnesota and Missouri . . .

• If additional Kennedy supporters in the California, Indiana and other delegations had not been prevented from switching their votes to the Senator when his "bandwagon" was still rolling . . .

• If there had been time for the television viewers back home to make their views known to the delegates . . .

But Jack Kennedy paid little attention to the "ifs." The basic fact was that he had run out of potential votes and could get no more in the Midwest or West. Back in his room at the inn, joined by Jacqueline and members of his family, the Senator was quiet. He was neither angry like Bob nor crying like Ben Smith. He had a few caustic comments on supposed friends who had let him down, and he composed with more sarcasm than hurt an imaginary wire to David Lawrence, who had earlier asked him to Pittsburgh. But his disappointment did not even last until his departure for Europe—it was vanquished that evening in a noisy, joking dinner with family and friends.

The convention adjourned that night on a note of intergroup harmony, with Negro soprano Mahalia Jackson singing "The Lord's Prayer" accompanied by the Chicago Swedish Glee Club. The Senator flew off to Europe with no foolish claims, charges, tears or promises to retract or regret. He was content.

Perhaps he already realized that his prominent role in the convention, his tense race with Kefauver and his graceful acceptance of defeat had made him overnight a nationally acclaimed figure. Perhaps he knew that his showing among Southern delegates—even if many of them had been motivated by their opposition to Kefauver—was the first chink in the Al Smith myth that no Catholic could win national office. And, more importantly, perhaps he already knew that were he to occupy second place on a losing Stevenson ticket in 1956, neither he nor any other Catholic would be considered again for several decades.

In later years, weary of the myth that he had entered politics as an involuntary substitute for his deceased brother Joe, he commented that Joe was more of a winner, that he, too, would have won the Congressional and Senatorial elections Jack did, that he, too, would have sought the Vice Presidency, but that he would have won the nomination—"And today Joe's political career would be a shambles." Certainly there was far more truth than humor in his quip at the Gridiron Dinner two years later:

I am grateful . . . to "Mr. Sam" Rayburn. At the last Democratic Convention, if he had not recognized the Tennessee and
Oklahoma delegations when he did, I might have won that race
with Senator Kefauver—and my political career would now be
over.

PART TWO

The Kennedy Candidacy

CHAPTER IV

❦

THE CONTENDER

JOHN F. KENNEDY WANTED SOMEDAY to be President of the United States.

This wish did not suddenly seize him at some particular time. It was not an obsession to which all other interests were subordinated. It was not inherited from his brother, imposed by his father or inspired by his illness. He was not dissatisfied with his life as a Senator, had no fascination with power for the sake of power and needed no glory for his ego. He would not have felt cheated and frustrated had the office never been his; and, prior to the events of 1956 which thrust it within the realm of possibility, he had no timetable or plans for obtaining it. Nor did he seek the job in the belief that he was fulfilling his nation's destiny or because he had some grand design for the future.

John Kennedy wanted to be President simply because, as he told a newsman early in 1956 when he had no specific intentions toward the office, "I suppose anybody in politics would like to be President"—because, as he said so often in 1960, "that is the center of action, the mainspring, the wellspring of the American system"—because, as he said in 1962, "at least you have an opportunity to do something about all the problems which . . . I would be concerned about [anyway] as a father or as a citizen . . . and if what you do is useful and successful, then . . . that is a great satisfaction."

As a Democrat he believed four more years of Republican rule would be ruinous. As a citizen he feared for the course of his country in the sixties. As a politician and public servant he aspired, as many men do, to reach the top of his profession. As a member of both houses of

Congress he was daily more aware of how limited was their power to improve our nation and society. Nothing could better sum up his reasons for seeking the Presidency than seven words he used constantly in the campaign: "because I want to get things done."

To his father, who warned that its pressures could make it "the worst job in the world," he said these problems still had to be solved by human beings. He knew the responsibilities of the office would be lonely and demanding. But he had confidence in himself, in his judgment, his courage, his knowledge of public affairs, his years of experience in the House and Senate, his background of world travel and his conversations with chief executives in this country and many others. With his usual candor he told one interviewer before the 1960 convention, "The burden is heavy . . . [but] this job is going to be done. I am one of the four or five candidates who will be considered to do it. I approach it with a feeling that I can meet the responsibilities of the office."

In private he could be even more explicit, listing the men who in his lifetime had held, sought or were among the four or five then seeking the job—men whose talents were at best not superior to his own. Of the other possible contenders he regarded Johnson as the ablest and Symington as the most likely compromise choice. He liked and respected both of them and Stevenson and Humphrey also. But Stevenson, having twice been his party's standard-bearer, said flatly he would not run again; and Kennedy objectively considered his own ability to be nominated *and* elected *and* to lead the nation through a perilous period superior to that of all four men.

Kefauver, whom he bested in a competition for a seat on the Senate Foreign Relations Committee early in 1957, appeared likely to be a candidate in 1960 only for re-election to the Senate. Governors Brown of California, Williams of Michigan, Collins of Florida, Chandler of Kentucky and Meyner of New Jersey, all of whom were mentioned by local boosters, had no visible nationwide following, although Meyner tried hard to acquire one.

Neither Republican candidate, in the Senator's opinion, was unbeatable. Richard Nixon, he wrote in 1957, would be a "tough, skillful, shrewd opponent. . . . It will take more than abusive statements to beat Mr. Nixon—those he can read riding in the 1961 Inaugural parade." But he felt that Nixon's ambitions exceeded his ability and that neither his platform presence nor his past inspired confidence among the voters.

He did not know Nelson Rockefeller prior to his election as Governor of New York. When the two were paired as speakers at the annual Al Smith Dinner in 1959, the Senator regarded it as a competition. Throughout the dinner, as he anxiously worked over his own speech, he worried all the more watching the Governor confidently smiling and talking, never glancing at his text. But the contrast could not have been greater as Rockefeller stumbled through a long and listless speech followed by Kennedy's brief, humorous and more pertinent remarks. "I'd like to appear with him every night of the week!" he exclaimed to me on the phone the next morning.

These were the men, then, Republicans and Democrats, from whose ranks the next President would be picked; and the Senator said, in effect, that someone has to do it, these are the men considered, therefore "Why not me?"

All this was not vanity but objectivity. He was as objective about his liabilities as he was about his assets. Often, to the incredulity of newsmen and to the dismay of his followers, he would objectively list those liabilities in public. He knew that no Catholic had ever been elected President of the United States, where church membership was more than two to one Protestant—that no forty-three-year-old had ever been elected President—and that for these reasons in particular his party was unlikely to pick him. On the other hand, he knew that both his religion and his youthful appearance, while mistrusted by some, had also set him apart from most politicians and helped attract a nucleus of followers.

Perhaps, if he could have been guaranteed the Democratic Presidential nomination for any future year he chose, he would not have chosen 1960. Eight or twelve more years would have removed the age handicap, softened the religious handicap and possibly weakened the Republicans. But he had no such guarantee and was not in that respect free to choose. Circumstances, events and his own competitive instincts propelled him toward making the race in 1960, and once that die was cast, he felt, it was 1960 or never. Many advised him to wait, to step aside, to settle for second place—columnists, competitors, friends and strangers. As he campaigned one day early in 1960 on the streets of Eau Claire, Wisconsin, an elderly lady whose hand he grasped said, "Not now, young man, it's too soon, it's too soon." And he replied gently but almost teasingly, "No, Mother, this is it. The time is now." And she left him with a smiling "God bless you."

Jack Kennedy did not accept—or publicly pretend to profess—the familiar fiction that this office seeks the man. "Nobody is going to hand me the nomination," he told a reporter in 1957. "If I were governor of a large state, Protestant and fifty-five, I could sit back and let it come to me."

He could not change his age. He would not change his religion. And he paid no heed to a suggestion that he seek the governorship of Massachusetts in 1958 as a safer steppingstone to the Presidency. Moreover, the governors of large states—whose offices traditionally supplied both parties with a large share of their Presidential nominees—were less prominently mentioned than Senators in the 1960 Democratic lists. This was partly due to chance. Many of the large states had Republican governors. Many of the Democratic governors were too old or too young, or their talents were not well enough known (or too well known). But it was also due to the elevation of the Senate as a forum for Presidential candidates. The once-touted executive experience of most governors was confined in large part to the problems of providing state and local services; and although rising costs and populations required unpopular tax increases to finance those services, governors, unlike Senators, had comparatively little opportunity to demonstrate their mastery of the far different national and particularly international issues with which Presidential campaigns were concerned.

It was not surprising, therefore, that at least four Senators—Kennedy, Johnson, Humphrey and Symington—were regarded as the leading contenders for the Democratic Presidential nomination in 1960; and Senators Kefauver, Gore, Lausche and Morse were also frequently mentioned. In 1958, when there were still forty-eight states and ninety-six Senators, Kennedy told the Washington Gridiron Club of a supposed press "survey" of each Senator's preference for the Presidency, in which, he claimed, "ninety-six Senators each received one vote."

The one Protestant-big-state governor whom Kennedy regarded as most likely to block him never became governor. Mayor Richardson Dilworth of Philadelphia, a friend of the Senator's, had none of Kennedy's liabilities and many of his assets—a photogenic appearance, a heroic war record, a name for idealism and integrity, and a background of wealth and education. The Senator was certain that Dilworth, if elected Governor of Pennsylvania in 1958, would be in 1960 an obvious choice for the Presidency in the same Northern and Eastern states to which Kennedy appealed and would also be more acceptable to Westerners and Southerners. But a candid reply by Dilworth to a Washington luncheon question on the recognition of Communist China gave his opponents within Pennsylvania's Democratic hierarchy an excuse to discard him; and David Lawrence, who was not a Presidential contender, was elected Governor instead.

In that same crucial election of 1958, in which Kennedy won so overwhelmingly, three other Northern liberals—who, had they been in a position to bid for the Presidency, might well have cut deeply into Kennedy's strength—all fared poorly: Averell Harriman lost his race for re-election as Governor of New York; Mennen Williams barely won re-election as Governor of Michigan; and Chester Bowles was denied the Senatorial nomination by the Connecticut State Democratic Convention. Bowles's defeat was unfairly blamed by some on Kennedy, who actually took no part in any of these contests and would have favored all four men.

This assessment of the Presidential campaign scene, I should make clear, did not take place until after 1956. In earlier years the possibility of a Kennedy Presidential candidacy sometime in the future was frequently on my mind but never on his tongue. When I suggested to him on the Senate floor in 1954 that his support of a minor economy move "might look bad in some future national campaign," he replied emphatically, "I can't start basing my life on that or I'd be no good in this job or to myself." Two years later, as he lay on his sickbed in Palm Beach, his worried wife asked me if he would someday be in the White House, and I told her what I had told Evelyn Lincoln after only one month's work in his office: that someday he should be and could be President, but he would more likely be Vice President first.

The events of 1956 did not infect the Senator with the "Presidential bug," altering his over-all ambitions and habits. But they did transform him almost instantly into a national leader of his party to whom the Presidency was no longer an impossibility.

He still did not talk in those terms. There was no single time and place at which he decided to try for the Presidency in 1960. As always, he was simply determined, in the new situation in which he found himself, to master the tides of time and events and see how far they could carry him. It was clear to me after the 1956 convention that the Presidency had become his primary goal, in politics and indeed in life. But he deliberately refrained from committing himself to the 1960 race—even privately, even in his own mind—until he was certain his nomination was possible. Volunteers requesting material or permission to form "Kennedy-for-President" clubs were asked to hold up (although their names and addresses were carefully saved in a "grass-roots support" file).

It was in an Evansville, Indiana, hotel room in October, 1959, that he said, as we chatted late one night about the nomination, "I think now I can make it"—a surprising statement to me since I had never thought he thought otherwise. Even then a final public decision was withheld until he felt it was both necessary and appropriate. A questioner in Wichita, Kansas, in November, 1959, asked him at least to name his favorite candidate. "I do have a favorite candidate," replied the Senator, refusing to be trapped. "But until he has the guts to declare he's a candidate, I'm not going to announce my support of him." For "there is," he told a reporter who pretended to be puzzled over Kennedy's refusal to announce, "a time and place for everything."

PRE-1960 TRAVELS

Autumn, 1956, was a time of campaigning for the Stevenson-Kefauver ticket. The Massachusetts Senator emerged from the spectacular Vice Presidential balloting more sought after by party members than any

Democrat other than the two nominees. Covering more than thirty thousand miles in twenty-four states, he made over 150 speeches and appearances in the course of six weeks. As we worked one night that summer on his schedule, he suddenly said, "Why don't you come along?" And on September 18, 1956, we began a series of two-man travels which over the next few years would take us into every state—most of them several times—seeking votes for Stevenson in 1956, seeking votes for Senatorial, state and local candidates in 1957-1958-1959, and seeking friends for Kennedy at every stop.

During these years, with the exception of a few overnight trips by train, we traveled exclusively by plane. The acquisition by the Kennedy family in 1959 of a private plane—later called the *Caroline* after his daughter, born in 1957—made this mode of travel more comfortable and convenient. The *Caroline* was a converted Convair complete with desk, galley and bedroom. But for more than two years, although many of the short hops and a few of the longer trips were by private plane, we relied primarily on the regular commercial carriers. In time we composed our own private rating of all the major airlines. He deplored the fact that one airline assigned its most senior stewardesses to transcontinental flights, that another used three-across seats on first-class flights and that another served invariably tasteless food. We flew from coast to coast in the prejet days when each trip was more than eight hours, the Senator working, napping, talking, reviewing his speeches and schedule, and reading newspapers, magazines and books of all kinds. Franklin's *Autobiography*, I recall, occupied most of one trip.

We rarely missed a plane and barely caught most of them. He canceled more appearances on the basis of his Senate duties or poor health than as a result of bad flying weather, but I was grateful that no large commercial airline could be induced to risk flying its planes in storms by the most persuasive United States Senator. The pilots of private planes, on the other hand, were often more willing to be daring—although I appreciated one captain who told me with some fervor, "Listen, there's only one life on this plane that's important to me—mine—and I'm not risking it for the Senator or anyone else!"

We flew in all kinds of little planes, in all kinds of weather, with all kinds of pilots—experienced and inexperienced, professional and amateur, rested and fatigued. On a flight from Phoenix to Denver, I had to hold the plane door closed. On a flight to Rockport, Maine, the pilot could not find the landing strip, and we circled over the area as he peered out one side and the Senator, sitting in the copilot's seat, looked out the other. In order to appear on time at a corn-picking contest, we landed in an Iowa cornfield. After a flight over the Green Mountains of Vermont, our pilot confided that his compass was broken. We were tossed for hours in a snowstorm over the Rockies and in a fog over Lake Michigan. In pelting rain we took off in an amphibious plane from a choppy, timber-filled bay in Alaska, with the Senator working the windshield wiper by hand.

The only moment of real danger occurred on a 1956 flight to Reno, Nevada, from Twin Falls, Idaho. Our pilot, an Idaho politician who enjoyed flying his little single-engine plane as a hobby, was confessing openly to fatigue, having picked us up that morning in Salt Lake City. With high mountains and darkness ahead, he decided to land at Elko, Nevada, and find a professional pilot who could take us the rest of the way. Just as we were approaching the Elko landing strip ("We were coming in with the wind instead of against it," the Senator later insisted), the little plane veered over on one side. The Senator gave me a swift, half-serious, half-humorous glance, and then the plane righted itself for a somewhat bumpy landing. Another pilot in another single-engine plane took us over the mountains by moonlight, all the time assuring us that one engine was really as safe as two. We landed at one end of the Reno Airport and trudged in with our bags, just as the Democratic dignitaries and brass band awaiting us marched out to meet a more dignified twin-engine plane at the other end of the field bearing two surprised industrialists.

We had stormy flights in the *Caroline* as well, but the Senator was always relaxed—working, eating or napping in its comfortable cabin, and demonstrating complete and well-placed confidence in the competence of his pilot, Howard Baer. A rough ride in the *Caroline* bore no resemblance to rough rides of earlier years, and this also made it possible for Jacqueline to join us more often.

The locations in which the Senator spoke varied as widely as the transportation. He addressed crowds on noisy street corners, at airports, on fairgrounds, in theaters, armories, high schools, state capitols, restaurants, gambling casinos, hotels, pool halls, union halls, lodge halls and convention halls of every size and shape. He learned the art of swiftly getting down from the speaker's stand into a crowd for hand-shaking instead of being trapped by a few eager voters behind the head table. He learned to pause when trains whistled or airplanes flew over— to laugh when a tray of dishes crashed (or, as in one hall, when the flag fell practically on him)—and to shout when the amplifying system broke down (once bellowing into the microphone just as it became operative again).

In addition to Democratic meetings, he addressed state legislatures, labor conventions, bar associations, civic groups and many colleges and universities. One occasion in 1960 was, he said, "the first time in fourteen years of politics that I have ever heard of a Democratic meeting and the Rotary Club joining together. I don't know whether it means the Democrats are broad-minded or the Rotary Club is broad-minded, but I am all for it." An earlier civic group had required him to abide by their tradition of each honored guest's signing the record in his own blood. He complied without protest—it was not the worst foolishness our Presidential candidates must endure.

On a national level he spoke to farmer, labor, Young Democratic, ethnic, civic and business conventions. His Senate duties enabled him to accept less than 4 percent of the hundreds of invitations that poured into his office, many of them from important Democratic candidates or fund-raising dinner chairmen. But all were carefully screened—or generated—to make certain that no state or major city was neglected. As my Christmas present to him in 1956, I had constructed a map of the United States shaded to show his strength in the Vice Presidential balloting. The almost totally blank areas west of the Mississippi made clear the task confronting him if he was to become a national figure and explained the frequency of his visits to small Western and Midwestern states.

While he approached with great caution the home states of other potential candidates, he undertook to get himself invited to any area not covered by spontaneous invitations. Friends associated with the labor movement, colleges and state leagues of municipalities could usually make the right contact whenever politicians could not.

He also approached Southern states with some caution. He wanted to acknowledge their support for him at the 1956 convention and to demonstrate that his religion would not frighten Southern voters away. But to avoid charges of segregated audiences or auspices, he spoke in the South primarily to universities and nonpolitical organizations. He could not and did not dodge the race issue, however. In Georgia to deliver a 1957 commencement address, he was asked during a state-wide telecast with the two Georgia Senators, contrary to a previous understanding, about his views on the Supreme Court's school desegregation decision. He promptly replied that he had endorsed it as the law of the land.

That fall, shortly after he had upheld President Eisenhower's use of Federal forces in Little Rock, Arkansas, to quell mob defiance of a school desegregation court order, the Senator refused to default on a commitment to Congressman Frank Smith to address the Mississippi Young Democrats. Both Northerners and Southerners warned him that he could only lose in both areas by speaking in Mississippi, and he arrived to find that Republican State Chairman Yeager had challenged him to repeat his views on the segregation issue. As he relaxed in the bathtub of his hotel room, he dictated to me an insertion in his speech, emphasizing "the same thing I told my own city of Boston."

When he delivered these lines and supported the court, I was fearful of an incident, booing or food-throwing. But his courage, if not his convictions, drew surprising applause from his audience, particularly when he added, "And now I invite Mr. Yeager to tell us his views on Eisenhower and Nixon." Afterward we talked late into the night with Mississippi's two Senators, Eastland and Stennis, and her more moderate Governor J. P. Coleman—who several years later would be attacked by his political opponents for letting a Kennedy sleep in the Mississippi Governor's Mansion. Southern Democratic loyalists were heartened by the Jackson incident, columnist Arthur Krock reported, but the tone of Kennedy's mail and editorials from the Deep South began to shift against him. His trips elsewhere in the South, however, continued.

Some weekends, up through his 1958 re-election, were saved for Massachusetts. Not enough perhaps were saved for relaxation with his family. His wife, after a miscarriage and a stillbirth expecting again in 1957, had neither the physical strength nor the political zeal to make every trip, though her frequent presence was always a major attraction and her ability to speak French, Spanish and Italian was often exploited. In time she was to visit some forty-six states with him. (In 1958 they celebrated their fifth wedding anniversary in Omaha, Nebraska, an astonishing new part of the world to Jacqueline.) In Washington the Senator often met with political leaders for lunch in his office but tried to save dinners for his wife. When the National Committee or a Democratic Women's Conference met in Washington, both Kennedys would hold a reception in their Georgetown home for friendly or influential figures. Yet his wife's inability to make every trip led to false ugly rumors about their marriage which disturbed and discouraged the Senator.

His own health bore up surprisingly well under the strain. On a few occasions his brother Bob substituted for him—on one occasion I filled in —a few meetings were postponed or canceled—but these were rare. The rest of the time he plunged ahead, standing for hours with his bad back and overworking his supposedly deficient adrenal glands. He went hatless in the below-zero clime of Fairbanks, Alaska, where most of his audience wore fur hats and parkas, hatless in a driving rain in Wisconsin and hatless in a scorching sun in Arizona—although in one downpour in West Virginia he did accept a rain hat from a Boston reporter. He was coatless in the coldest open-car motorcades. "He's got some ratty old trench coat," said his wife to a friend, "but he throws it in the trunk and never wears it." He learned to grasp a big man's hand deep in and hard before his own was crushed. But there was no way to avoid the bruised discoloration that hours of steady handshaking always produced.

He slept in countless hotels and motels, some shiny, some shabby, in governors' mansions and private homes, and frequently all night on a plane. During the day he napped whenever he could—once falling asleep in his tuxedo in Governor Ribicoff's bedroom while the leading Democrats of Connecticut waited in reception below. He always insisted that my advance arrangements include two separate bedrooms so that his slumbers would not be disturbed—but on the one occasion when this proved impossible, at the home of the University of Florida President, he fidgeted so much at my every move that my slumbers were disturbed more than his.

Other advance arrangements included a bed board under his mattress; a lectern sufficiently high that he would not have to stoop to read his text; maximum television and press coverage; an opportunity to meet local Democratic leaders, with additional meetings with editors, students, labor or farm leaders where possible; and time to rest before his speech.

Motorcycle escorts were never requested but usually provided. The Senator often asked them to keep their sirens off, convinced that motorists forced off the road were not likely to vote Democratic thereafter. But he always thanked each of his police escorts in person and had me get their names for our file. Some cities also provided detectives to watch over the Senator's suite, although in one case the two men on duty drank so much of the free beverages provided by the hotel manager that the Senator had to watch over them.

At hundred-dollar, fifty-dollar, five-dollar and one-dollar Democratic dinners, luncheons, picnics, barbecues, bean feeds, ox roasts, luaus and covered-dish, cold-plate and potluck suppers, he tasted an amazing variety of mass-produced food. Inasmuch as he could never depend on its quality, and could always depend on devoting most of his mealtime to shaking hands, signing autographs and reworking his speech, he usually tried to have a steak and baked potato in his room before dinner. Sometimes we sought out an all-night café in the late hours after his speech. Each morning I ordered the same breakfast for his room: milk, coffee, fresh (not frozen) orange juice, broiled (not fried) bacon, two soft-boiled (four-minute) eggs, buttered toast and jelly.

He met the press in every community, formally and informally— once, when his bags were lost, swathed only in bath towels in his hotel room. He became accustomed to provocative questions on his religion and to badgering on his political intentions. He learned to end a press conference before all relevant topics were exhausted and the questions became merely irritants, although he would patiently answer some questions over and over for reporters who came in late. He discovered that his speeches and press conference answers were reported only locally, never nationally, enabling him to use the same material many places.

He became an expert at packing his suitcase and preparing for all kinds of weather. Laundry was often a problem. He was probably the first man in history to wash out his own shirts and socks in the luxurious Presidential suite of a Louisville hotel. Presented at many stops with the wares for which the locality was famous, he usually returned with more baggage than he started. He told one group of sombrero donors he would wear the hat in the next St. Patrick's Day parade in Boston, but he had to leave a bushel of sweet potatoes behind in Opelousas, Louisiana, and was not certain what to do with the "worming-out medicine" he was given in Winston-Salem, North Carolina.

To save time for rest and the strain on his back, he avoided the cocktail receptions held in his honor preceding dinner until only enough time was left to meet everyone personally without getting bogged down in small talk while constantly standing. His shyness was gradually shed, although many local politicians mistook his reserve and restraint for arrogance or aloofness. He acceded to all requests for autographs and answered all questions he was asked. He learned to listen to name after name in a receiving line, to have a new smile and a few words for each individual, whether politically important or unimportant. In the South and West he was often surprised at the upper-class background of those who came through the receiving line. "Back in Massachusetts," he remarked to me more than once, "all these people would be Republicans." As he became increasingly at ease himself, he learned to put others at ease. He was good on his feet; he had a mental versatility that was clearly not superficial. His speech-making was often not as relaxed as his social presence or his question-and-answer sessions, but he learned to slow down and improved constantly.

He grew tired of hearing over and over again his own speeches—and particularly his own jokes—and grew respectful of those politicians barnstorming a state with him who each time could applaud and laugh anew. One of these was Lyndon Johnson, with whom we traveled through Texas in 1956 at a feverish pace. He particularly enjoyed listening between stops to the Majority Leader's homely mixture of political wisdom and humor (sample: Senator X's somewhat bumbling tour of the state that fall was a great success "because he made the poorest, most ignorant white man in Texas feel superior").

As 1957 became 1958 and then 1959, the Senator gave speeches, speeches and more speeches. We continually searched for new topics, themes and writers. "I can't afford to sound just like any Senator," he said. We prepared a large number of "speech sections" on different subjects, put mimeographed stacks of each on his plane and put together new combinations and cover sheets for each stop. In addition to his travels and Senate duties, he became a prolific source and subject of magazine articles. His by-line appeared on articles in more than three dozen magazines, ranging from *Foreign Affairs Quarterly* ("A Democrat Looks at Foreign Policy") to *Living for Young Homemakers* ("Young Men in Politics") to *Life* ("Where the Democrats Should Go from Here") to the *Progressive* ("If India Falls"). His face became familiar through a dozen cover stories.

Gradually the evidence became clearer that his hard work was paying off. Kennedy's audiences became larger and more enthusiastic. His presence in an airport or hotel lobby brought crowds of handshakers and autograph-seekers that no other Democrat could arouse, and the increasingly frequent presence of his wife after the birth of their daughter always augmented the crowds.

POLLS AND PUBLICITY

National and state polls of public opinion, moreover, showed rising Kennedy strength as his travels, writings, publicity and labor reform fight drew growing attention to his qualities. Whether matched against other Democrats or against the two Republican hopefuls, he ran ahead of the field. Other Democratic contenders showed strength in their own areas—Kennedy showed strength in all areas. Newspaper polls of past delegates and local party leaders produced a similar result, and pains were taken to make certain that all publicly conducted polls, by Gallup and others, were properly called to the attention of those we hoped to sway.

Equally important, however, were the results of polls privately financed and conducted, polls which were primarily taken for the Senator's information though given to friendly politicians and columnists at his discretion. More than any previous candidate in history, Kennedy sought help from the science of opinion polling—not because he felt he must slavishly adhere to the whims of public opinion but because he sought modern tools of instruction about new and unfamiliar battle-grounds. Tens of dozens of private polls were commissioned at great expense to probe areas of weakness and strength, to evaluate opponents and issues, and to help decide on schedules and tactics. Showings of strength in a particular state were often shared with the leaders of that state. States with Presidential primaries were polled more than once before he would decide on his entry, and usually many times once he entered.

More than one pollster was used. Kennedy questions were sometimes included in surveys taken by various firms for many state and local candidates. But the chief Kennedy pollster during 1959-1960—following my meeting with him in New York on December 19, 1958, an exchange of memoranda and a $100,000 guarantee—was Louis Harris, an ambitious but idealistic veteran of the opinion survey business.

All polls have their limitations. They can be most helpful in determining a rough comparison of relative strength between two well-known candidates as of the day of the survey. They can indicate how well and how favorably a candidate and his opponent are known among various voter groups. But they cannot be as precise as they pretend, provide protection against wide fluctuations or predict the final choice of the undecided. The weight of their answers often varies with the wording of their questions. They did not show us the true depth and volatility of religious bias. They told us very little about issues—except to report such profound conclusions as the fact that many voters were in favor of greater Federal spending in their own state, lower taxes and a balanced budget, and were opposed to Communism, war and foreign aid. The Senator also felt that a pollster's desire to please a client and influence strategy sometimes unintentionally colored his analyses.

Senator Kennedy never lost his interest in polls, but his skepticism grew. He blamed his loss of one Wisconsin primary district—a crucial loss—on a last-minute Harris Poll. It showed that district as already certain for Kennedy and urged more effort in an upstate district which was supposedly close but actually hopeless. The religious divisions emphasized by those Wisconsin primary results then focused attention on the religious issue in West Virginia, causing Kennedy to tumble almost overnight in Harris' poll from the 70-30 lead over Humphrey which had induced him to enter the state to a 40-60 minority position which seemed certain to wreck his candidacy. More will be said about the West Virginia primary later, but Kennedy aides O'Brien and O'Donnell grew suspicious of the whole process when they began to suspect that the county-by-county figures forecast by the poll were influenced by their own reports on local political leaders.

Republican front-runner Nixon was also a believer in polls. He also selectively released or "leaked" particular results to his political advantage. Inasmuch as his private polls included considerable findings on Kennedy, as ours did on him, the two principals arranged for a swap of several of their own private surveys, which their administrative assistants surreptitiously exchanged. (Although this occurred long before they were formally opponents, I compared it with Eisenhower's "open skies" proposal to exchange military information with the Soviets.) When the two candidates met in Florida after the 1960 election, both agreed that their pollsters—Louis Harris for Kennedy and Claude Robinson for Nixon—had been overly optimistic about the final result but on the whole highly accurate and valuable, as had the published polls of Dr. George Gallup. The same could not be said of the other pollsters and experts.

In any event, both private and public polls from 1957 to 1959 were increasingly reassuring to Kennedy and increasingly discouraging to his opponents. There were disadvantages in being the "front-runner." The Senator's critics became more open and vocal and his every word was politically interpreted. The Republican administration, in one forty-eight-hour period, turned suddenly against three Kennedy proposals it had earlier appeared to favor: aid to India, economic relations with Poland and labor reform. Veteran politicians warned that he was starting too soon, was pressing too hard and would burn himself out. One suggested no more speeches outside of Massachusetts. More than one columnist said Kennedy would not be ready for the Presidency in 1960 in terms of age and maturity and would do better to "slow down." Public relations experts warned of overexposure in the press.

At times the Senator did severely limit his out-of-state speaking engagements to concentrate on Senate duties and on his Massachusetts re-election. He also tried to ration his nationwide television appearances and to shift the publicity away from his family and personality to more emphasis on his convictions and accomplishments. But he was skeptical of the "don't start too early" adage. He preferred cooperating with interested newsmen to seeking in vain a postponement of their interest.

Moreover, his pace had several advantages. It answered all doubts about his health. It helped voters disregard his appearance of immaturity. It emphasized qualities other than his religion. And it produced a self-generating momentum which other contenders would be hard put to stop or catch. A candidate with his handicaps, Kennedy knew, had to be a front-runner and win early or not at all. And "At least," he said to me in 1958, "they've stopped talking about me only in terms of the Vice Presidency." To another friend who remarked that summer that it looked as though the Vice Presidency could be his for the asking, he replied with a grin, "Let's not talk so much about vice. I'm against vice in any form."

THE RELIGIOUS ISSUE

The Vice Presidential talk was promoted by those Democrats—including all other potential nominees—who hoped thereby to gain the Catholics while not losing the anti-Catholics. Even so wise a man as Walter Lippmann, terming religion "the problem which Senator Kennedy has posed," proposed second place on the ticket as the solution. "It is ever so," a leading Jesuit intellectual was reported to have remarked. "A Catholic is fine as a member of the board but not as chairman."

Senator Kennedy was less philosophical. "I find that suggestion highly distasteful," he said. "It assumes that Catholics are pawns on the political chessboard, moved hither and yon." It also assumed that the top spot had been permanently closed to all Catholics by the overwhelming defeat of Catholic Al Smith in 1928. Kennedy set out to challenge that assumption—and to challenge it early in the hope that the issue would lose some of its mystery and heat by 1960. Smith in 1928 had defended his church, quoting clerics and encyclicals. Kennedy defended himself, and quoted his own record and views. He spoke only of legislative, not theological, issues, and he spoke only for himself. "I think," he told me regarding this general strategy, that "we should just stick to the general principle of a determination to meet our constitutional obligations."

In March, 1959, the publication in *Look Magazine* of his views on church and state—especially his denial of any conflict between his conscience and the Constitution—aroused a storm of protest in the Catholic press. Some editors disagreed with the wording of his statement. ("Whatever one's religion in his private life may be, for the office-holder nothing takes precedence over his oath to uphold the Constitution and all its parts.") Others felt he was too defensive. Some felt he should not have submitted to a religious test, "a loyalty test for Catholics only," "bowing to bigotry." Others felt impelled to criticize him to prove that Catholics did not all think alike. His reasoning was compared by the Kansas City *Register* to that used by accused Nazi war criminals. "He appears to have gone overboard in an effort to placate the bigots," said the *Catholic Review* in Baltimore. He was termed a poor Catholic, a poor politician, a poor moralist and a poor wordsmith.

Finally his closest friend in the hierarchy, Richard Cardinal Cushing, Archbishop of Boston—a man in whom the seeds of liberalism had been richly nourished through association with and pride in the Senator—came publicly to his defense, stating that Kennedy's "simple candor . . . has given way to other people's interpretations." In an effort to allay suspicions about Church doctrine, the Cardinal prepared for publication and submitted to the Senator for approval an article entitled "Should a Catholic Be President?" Concerned about its effect on those most in need of reassurance, the Senator confidentially submitted the article to some of the most outspoken Protestant critics of Catholic doctrine in the country, with whom he or I were in touch. All agreed that publication of the article would be unwise.

Senator Kennedy asked the Cardinal to defer the article, without mentioning that he had submitted it to men with whom the Cardinal had frequently clashed. But he refused to retract a word of his *Look* interview. "I gave this interview on my own initiative," he had written in a form letter to that portion of his heavy mail which favored his stand, "because I felt that the questions which were raised were matters which reflect honest doubts among many citizens." To his critics, another form letter pointed out that his comments had not pretended to be "an exhaustive statement of Catholic thought . . . since I am trained neither in philosophy, theology nor church history," nor an exhaustive statement of

> my views on conscience, religion and public office. . . . I was simply stating candidly my firmly held belief that a Catholic can serve as President of the United States and fulfill his oath of office with complete fidelity and with no reservations. I see no cause to amend that statement now.

Nor did he feel he was appeasing bigotry merely by agreeing to answer such questions. He knew that Catholics were under suspicion by Americans of goodwill as well as by bigots. To end those suspicions, and to end the tradition against a Catholic President, he knew he had to answer not only all reasonable questions but many unreasonable questions as well. He knew he could not afford to be defensive, angry, impatient or silent, no matter how many times he heard the same insulting, foolish or discriminatory questions.

Privately, he felt it unfair that none of the other Presidential contenders in either party was so questioned. While he realized that their churches, rightly or wrongly, had less often been accused of accepting foreign control or seeking public funds and influence, his own record of votes and statements was actually more in support of church-state separation than that of any other candidate. Those Protestants who arbitrarily refused, solely because of his religion, to listen to his answers and to accept his devotion to the First Amendment, he said, were in effect violating a second, but unfortunately generally overlooked, constitutional provision, the prohibition in Article VI against any religious test for office. He discovered a widely and deeply held belief that the United States, because it is predominantly Protestant in church membership, is traditionally and even semiofficially a Protestant nation—and that the President, as spokesman, symbol and leader of the nation, is expected to attend a Protestant church. Catholics and Jews had long served with distinction as members of the Cabinet and the Congress, in a growing number of governors' mansions, and even on that arbiter of the Constitution, the Supreme Court. But the White House was "For Protestants Only," and mere consideration of a Catholic for President revived old fears and passions in states which had elected Catholics to other offices without blinking. Throughout the fall of 1959 state Southern Baptist conventions passed almost identically worded resolutions opposing the election of a Catholic and deploring religion as a campaign issue.

Kennedy believed that both Article VI and Amendment I should be scrupulously followed by all candidates and their interrogators. Thus he willingly submitted to questions on constitutional and legislative issues asked by *Look Magazine* and the Methodist Council of Bishops, but he resented a questionnaire from the POAU (Protestants and Other Americans United for the Separation of Church and State) addressed to "every Catholic candidate" and excusing non-Catholic candidates unless "they reveal any inclination" toward less church-state separation. When asked at a Los Angeles Press Club Dinner in 1959 whether a Protestant could be elected President in 1960, he replied in good humor, "If he is willing to be questioned on his views concerning the separation of church and state, I don't see why we should discriminate against him."

Of all the church-state issues of public policy on which leading Catholic ecclesiastics differed from most Protestants, the most important was education. Kennedy, who had attended public as well as non-parochial private schools, introduced in 1958 a Federal aid to education bill limited to the public schools, and later was alone among the Presidential hopefuls in the Senate in opposing Senator Morse's amendment authorizing funds for nonpublic schools. The use of Federal funds to support parochial schools, he said, was "unconstitutional under the First Amendment as interpreted by the Supreme Court."

He was "flatly opposed" to the appointment of a U.S. Ambassador to the Vatican: "Whatever advantages it might have in Rome—and I'm not convinced of those—they would be more than offset by the divisive effect at home."

He also disagreed with various Catholic clerics, conventions and publications on aid to Yugoslavia and Poland; was never found among those Catholic legislators who called for keeping Khrushchev out of the country or for more censorship of literature; and dismissed as dangerous folly all talk of a "Holy War" against atheistic Communism. Confronted late in 1959 by the most sensitive of all Catholic issues—population control—he opposed making birth control programs a condition of our foreign aid, on the grounds that this would add still another controversial burden to an already unpopular program ("You will get neither birth control nor foreign aid") and that it would be rightfully resented by the recipient nations as interference in the most delicate domestic matters. "Most people," he noted, "consider . . . that it is other people's families that provide the population explosion."

But he was equally opposed to any attempt to refuse or reduce our aid to a nation using public funds for such a program: "If they make a judgment that they want to limit their population . . . that is a judgment they should make, and economic assistance which we give permits them to make that judgment." He made clear that, if elected President, he would act on this matter in the light of the national interest, irrespective of religious considerations, "and not in accordance with the dictates of any ecclesiastical authority or group."

This last controversy was raised by a formal statement on population pressures by the American Catholic Bishops meeting in Washington in late 1959. The term "population explosion," they said (a term frequently used by Senator Kennedy in his speeches on the developing nations), "was a recently coined terror technique phrase." Some press and political observers thought the issue had doomed Kennedy's chances for the Presidency, and the Senator was sharply irritated that so sensitive and divisive an issue had been needlessly dragged into the headlines on the eve of his official campaign. The bishops' declaration furthered his belief that the hierarchy did not want him to be a candidate—that they had either deliberately issued this statement at that critical time or were else thoughtlessly unaware of the damage it would do to his chances. ("Does he suppose," said the author of the declaration to a Catholic cleric, "that every public statement on matters we must continue to defend or oppose is aimed at him?")

Rumors but never concrete proof of opposition within the hierarchy had frequently reached the Senator's ears. Whether they considered his political or his religious views too liberal, or feared a revival of religious controversy, or felt Protestants would be more likely to woo their support, was never clear. His only public reference to their position was to joke at the height of the controversy: "They're working on a package deal—if the Electoral College can be changed into an interdenominational school, they'll open up the College of Cardinals."

His own attitude had always been one of respectful independence, far less impressed by the political power of the church than many of his Protestant critics. "Naturally most of the hierarchy are extreme conservatives," he said to me one day while driving. "They are accustomed to everyone bowing down to them, to associating with the wealthiest men in the community. They like things as they are—they aren't going to be reformers." He was irritated by reports of local bishops' allegedly opposing interfaith activities or public school bond issues, just as later he would be furious when, in the midst of his Wisconsin campaign, a leading Catholic clergyman in that state forbade his members to join the YMCA. Still later, as President, he would say to a Catholic Youth Convention: "In my experience monsignors and bishops are all Republicans while sisters are all Democrats."

He never hesitated to joke in public about eminent churchmen as well as his church. Appearing at a dinner with a somewhat rotund monsignor, he called it an "inspiration . . . to be here with . . . one of those lean, ascetic clerics who show the effect of constant fast and prayer, and bring the message to us in the flesh." And in the midst of the campaign he claimed at a New York dinner that he had "asked Cardinal Spellman what I should say when people ask me whether I believe the Pope is infallible, and the Cardinal replied, 'I don't know, Senator—all I know is he keeps calling me Spillman.'"

BUILDING AN ORGANIZATION

While attacking the religious issue directly, he was also attacking it indirectly by demonstrating his appeal to all voters. We had no vast campaign organization in those early years, despite the rumors resulting from his progress. In advance of each trip, I worked on the speeches, schedules, transportation, accommodations, arrangements and publicity. Wires or letters would ask his supporters in each area to meet with him upon his arrival. On the plane, prior to each stop, I tried to brief him on whatever I had been able to learn about the state, its problems, leaders, candidates, factions and method of choosing delegates. In each city I arranged with a friendly state or county chairman or contact to collect all names and addresses for our growing political files. The Senator, neglecting neither the importance of an impressive speech nor the indispensability of personal contact—for he was one of the few politicians who excelled at both—talked in each state with key Democratic leaders, telephoned those not present, met with the press and visited with old friends. When there was an honorarium for his speech, he donated it to a local or national charity.

Back in Washington, we kept in touch with new and old political contacts through letters, Christmas cards, invitations and occasional telephone calls—sent out autographed copies of *Profiles in Courage* and later *The Strategy of Peace*—and built up a comprehensive state-by-state file of information on some seventy thousand party leaders, officeholders, labor leaders, fund-raisers, delegates, "key Kennedy contacts" and "grass-roots supporters."

The hectic schedule of appearances, and the other demands on our time, often diminished the quality of his speeches and often increased the number of generalities. With most college and many after-dinner audiences, he would call for questions from the floor and overcome the impression of a heavy speech with a sparkling command of all topics raised. In his speeches, moreover, he did not pull his punches or talk down to his audiences, but continued to spell out his high-minded views on controversial subjects. He chastised the United States Chamber of Commerce for its opposition to foreign aid, criticized several audiences of lawyers for the profession's indifference to racketeering members, and engaged in verbal battles with many local unions who were unaware of their stake in labor reform legislation. He spoke in factual and scholarly fashion, without "corn" or oversimplification, about the swift revolutions of our age—in weapons, nationalism, automation and life expectancy.

He would not, however, engage in any direct attacks on President Eisenhower. Upon his return to the Senate after his 1955 convalescence, he had replied to a question on Eisenhower's popularity: "He seems to be standing up pretty well in Palm Beach." In these pre-1960 years he felt Eisenhower was standing up pretty well everywhere, and inasmuch as Ike would not be the candidate in 1960, Kennedy saw no reason to take him on except by indirection. Whatever his differences with the President, moreover, he retained a basic respect for the office. When his mention of Eisenhower was hissed at a Dartmouth speech, he quickly interjected, "You mustn't hiss the President of the United States." And when a Democratic meeting in Tucson asked him about Mrs. Eisenhower's trip to a "beauty ranch," allegedly at the taxpayers' expense, he replied softly, "I wouldn't criticize anything she does—she is a very fine woman."

Whether his speeches were controversial or commonplace, it was clear that we were shorthanded in the speech-writing department. Final drafts with all his changes were often completed and retyped only hours before delivery. In Los Angeles in 1956 his reading copy was handed to him as he sat calmly but without manuscript listening to the toastmaster introduce him. In Oak Ridge, Tennessee, in 1959, my briefcase, containing his only speech copy, was delayed with me en route to a Rotary luncheon. It was with horror that I heard him introduced on the car radio, and with relief that I heard him give the essence of his text extemporaneously.

We made political mistakes as well. Some state party leaders on whose support we were counting deserted us when the showdown approached. Some gubernatorial candidates we were advised to support in their primary fights were defeated, and their victors not surprisingly had little regard for John Kennedy. One friendly Governor, Oklahoma's Howard Edmondson, lost control of his state's delegation. Local Kennedy leaders in some states proved unable to make good on their predictions. At least two of the experienced "professionals" we recruited for their political contacts produced a net loss. One antagonized more delegates than he won, and the other turned up as a chief organizer for Stevenson. One National Committeeman asked Kennedy to be the star attraction at a barbecue he was giving at his home for that state's leading Democratic donors—and then billed Kennedy for the cost. Letters and telegrams of invitation sent to unknown names in our massive files sometimes garnered eccentrics, children and Republicans.

On trips with several stops, the Senator, after an intensive visit of one state, would sometimes sigh at the prospect of "starting all over again" in another, meeting new faces and seeking new friends. Yet at the close of each visit he often expressed amazement at the number of men and women willing to devote time away from their jobs and families to help his candidacy, often with no thought and certainly with no assurance of any reward or recognition. He despaired in private at his inability to remember faces and names, but in time excelled all other candidates in this attribute. He also deprecated in private his knowledge of areas other than his own, but his zeal for learning and his ability to absorb information served him well.

In short, the primary purpose of these speech-making trips was not to talk but to listen and learn. He learned to tell the difference between volunteer workers who could talk and those who could also work, between a friendly comment ("We'll do all we can for you") and a firm commitment. (One governor, I noted in a 1959 memorandum to Abe Ribicoff before the National Governors' Conference, "has succeeded, at various times, in convincing the Kennedy, Stevenson and Johnson camps that he is really for their man.")

He learned also to tell the difference between those who were party leaders in name and those who actually spoke for delegates. In New York, for example, Congressman Charles Buckley had considerably less national fame but considerably more delegation influence than former National Chairman James Farley. In Illinois at that time, National Committeeman Jake Arvey had the national publicity, but Chicago's Mayor Dick Daley had the votes. In Puerto Rico Governor Muñoz Marín had more wisdom and stature, but State Chairman José Benítez had more Democratic delegates. Buckley, Daley and Benítez were for Kennedy.

Most of his fellow Senators, Kennedy found, had comparatively little political power in state and national conventions. Neither the veteran Carl Hayden of Arizona nor the freshman Tom Dodd of Connecticut, for example, could translate their endorsements of Johnson into a single vote in their pro-Kennedy unit-rule convention delegations.

He found factionalism and rivalries, based more on competing personalities than on ideologies, dividing the Democrats in nearly every state, and he learned to pick his way carefully through these contending forces. He did not confine his search for help to the possessors of high office. John Reynolds (later Governor of Wisconsin), Joseph Tydings (later Senator from Maryland), Robert McDonough (later State Chairman in West Virginia) and Teno Roncalio (later Congressman at Large from Wyoming), to name but four examples, were enlisted in the Kennedy cause long before their talents were equally recognized throughout their home states.

Just as John Kennedy represented a new era in Massachusetts

Democratic politics, he gradually built up a corps of new Kennedy Democrats throughout the fifty states. Some were old friends from college or Navy days (it must have been a very large PT boat to have contained all the shipmates we met). Some were delegates who had supported him at the 1956 Convention and enjoyed the special bond that created. Some were friends from the Congress or candidates he had helped. Some were Catholics who felt a strong affinity for his hopes for a political breakthrough—although we took pains not to have Catholics as the most prominent Kennedy leaders in any state. But most of these recruits were simply Democratic workers and voters whose response to our various mailings and meetings indicated their attraction to the unique Kennedy brand of energetic idealism and common sense. Few promises of future patronage were asked and none was given, although it was made clear that, if Kennedy were elected, he would be looking for talented people whom he knew, trusted and could work with.

In many of the smaller states the Kennedy nucleus was started by a series of meetings I held in 1959 and 1960. I also represented the Senator at conferences of the Western and Midwestern Democratic organizations (telling one protesting Michiganer that I still voted in Nebraska and resided in a state—Virginia—which extended further west than Detroit). While attending the Midwest Conference in Milwaukee, I asked—at the suggestion of Pat Lucey and John Reynolds—Mayor Ivan Nestingen of Madison, liberal, Lutheran and Scandinavian, to be our leader in Wisconsin. While attending the Western States Conference in Denver, I asked—at the suggestion of our key contact, Joe Dolan—an old Kennedy friend, Byron "Whizzer" White, to be our leader in Colorado. Both White and Nestingen were superb, as were others similarly recruited. In one state our Protestant-Scandinavian chairman not only had great ability and loyalty but so looked, talked and acted the part of the rustic, raw-boned corn-husker from what Eastern city dwellers called "the sticks" that the Senator accused me of finding him through some Hollywood type-casting studio.

But I knew full well that a national campaign required many more hands and far more experienced hands than my own. In a memorandum discussed with the Senator in December, 1958, in New York, I attempted to put his prior efforts into perspective and proposed the addition of several campaign aides. The most urgent need was for an administrative assistant to take over our lists of key Democrats, scheduling arrangements and political mail, and we agreed that his brother-in-law Steve Smith, who had smoothly overseen the administrative side of his 1958 Senatorial campaign, was the logical choice.

Steve did an outstanding job, quietly opening a political headquarters in the Esso Building located at the foot of Capitol Hill, and taking with him my card files, memoranda and assistant Jean Lewis. In time he was joined by two long-time Kennedy friends and hardheaded political aides from his Massachusetts Senate races, Larry O'Brien and Kenny O'Donnell; by Bob Wallace, formerly with Senator Douglas; by Pierre Salinger, a former newsman who left his post as investigator for the Senate Rackets Committee to become a superb campaign press secretary; and, finally, by Robert Kennedy, whose organizational and administrative skills, as well as his political judgment and ferocious dedication, made him the Senator's first and only choice for campaign manager, though neither he nor anyone else had a formal title and there was no organization chart. Bob's work with the Rackets Committee had made him controversial as well as famous, but the Senator shrewdly observed, "I'll take all his enemies if I can have all his friends, too."

In addition to these full-time campaigners, John Bailey of Connecticut and Hy Raskin of Chicago lent a part-time professional touch; Massachusetts Congressmen Macdonald and Boland helped out increasingly, as did Governors Ribicoff and Roberts; the Senator's brother Teddy and brother-in-law Sargent Shriver focused on the West and Midwest; his father talked to friends in New York, New Jersey, Illinois, Nevada and elsewhere; and Dave Powers of Boston, with his invaluable and indefatigable smile, began serving as the Senator's personal aide on most of the major trips. He also used Jacques Lowe of New York as a semi-official campaign photographer (although Jacques's single-minded pursuit of his art at times annoyed the Senator, and it was with genuine delight one day in a remote corner of Oregon that he ordered the *Caroline* not to wait for him).

While expanding his political organization, the Senator also acted to beef up the intellectual side of his staff. We tried out nearly a dozen potential speech-writers, making commitments to none, giving an opportunity to all. To one experienced author I wrote: "In fairness, I must repeat my warning that our past experience would indicate that the chances of satisfying the Senator's standards are slim." One full-time writer, Richard Goodwin, was finally hired, with occasional assistance from many other sources.

At the same time, with the help of Professor Earl Latham of Amherst College and a graduate student in Cambridge, I initiated at the Senator's request and in his name an informal committee to tap the ideas and information of scholars and thinkers in Massachusetts and elsewhere. Drawn primarily from the Harvard and Massachusetts Institute of Technology faculties, with a smattering of names from other schools and professions, the members of our "Academic Advisory Committee" held their first organizational meeting with me at the Hotel Commander in Cambridge on December 3, 1958. Thereafter they met infrequently with the

Senator or myself, answered written or telephoned inquiries, and produced a great number of well-documented position papers and recommendations on current problems and programs. Among the members of this group who would later occupy posts in the Kennedy administration or task forces were Professors Cox, Wiesner, Schlesinger, Galbraith, Rostow, Millikan, Keppel, Chayes, Nitze, Harris, Kaysen, Samuelson, Cohen, Hilsman and Tobin, as well as General James Gavin and numerous others.

Not all of their material was usable and even less was actually used. But it provided a fresh and reassuring reservoir of expert intellect at a time when the Senator's speech schedule was exhausting both our intellectual and physical resources. Those able to talk personally with him were deeply impressed. Some of them who had similarly briefed Stevenson in 1956 were amazed at Kennedy's familiarity with an even greater range of current issues.

No announcement was made at the time about the committee's formation, but its very existence, when known, helped recruit Kennedy supporters in the liberal intellectual "community" who had leaned to Stevenson or Humphrey. This was in part its purpose, for the liberal intellectuals, with few delegates but many prestigious and articulate voices, could be a formidable foe, as Barkley and Kefauver had learned. Suspicious of Kennedy's father, religion and supposed McCarthy history, they were in these pre-1960 days held in the Stevenson camp by Eleanor Roosevelt and others. Kennedy's "academic advisers" formed an important beachhead on this front.

An effort was also made, with limited success, to set up similar groups in some of the difficult Presidential primary states. In addition, many of the original committee members joined in written appeals to fellow professors and intellectuals in these states. Our largest single effort to woo the intellectuals was the mass mailing in the spring of 1960 of Kennedy's *The Strategy of Peace,* a collection of his speeches, with particular emphasis on foreign policy, which we had prepared for campaign purposes. Editors, scientists, columnists, educators, reporters, authors, publishers, labor leaders, clergymen, public opinion leaders and liberal politicians in great number received copies of the book "personally" from the Senator. One previously pro-Humphrey professor responded:

> *The Strategy of Peace* is incontestably the best campaign document I can imagine, for it communicates what various other books and most news reports inadequately convey. . . . You emerge from the book as the kind of reflective and purposeful candidate that many of us seek.

Despite all this activity, the formal preconvention organization remained small. Contrary to reports, no public relations agency or expert
was employed, no nationally known political professionals were placed
on the full-time payroll, and none of his father's associates or employees
was involved in campaigning. We did not have a paid political worker
in every state, and although the Senator did privately contribute to the
Congressional or Senatorial campaigns of numerous friends, many of
them were not delegates and many who were delegates voted for other
hopefuls. Irritated by Mrs. Eleanor Roosevelt's statement on television
that his father was spending lavish sums on his candidacy, he repeatedly
asked her for a retraction, which she refused on the grounds that her
"information came largely from remarks made by people in many
places." (He took in better humor a 1958 Gridiron skit which portrayed
him, to the tune of "My Heart Belongs to Daddy," as singing "Just send
the bill to Daddy." In his own speech that followed, he claimed to have
just received a wire from his "generous Daddy" reading: "Dear Jack:
Don't buy a single vote more than is necessary—I'll be damned if I'm
going to pay for a landslide.")

Our first organizational meeting took place in the Kennedy home in
Palm Beach on April 1, 1959. Most of us flew in the night before. In
attendance were John F. Kennedy, Joseph P. Kennedy, Robert F. Kennedy, Stephen Smith, Lou Harris, Larry O'Brien, Kenny O'Donnell, Bob
Wallace and myself. Since only the Senator, Steve Smith and I were at
that point engaged in the campaign, the meeting was a bit disorganized.
But each state was reviewed, assignments were improvised, strategy was
discussed and key names were checked. Polls were ordered for certain
states and delayed for certain others. Bob Kennedy's role as a labor
rackets-buster having secured him both popularity and speaking invitations throughout the South, it was decided that he could, even before
devoting full-time to the campaign, make contacts in states less likely
to invite the Senator.

Among the notes taken of that meeting, in addition to the state-by-
state notations, are the following:

> . . . Publicize poll results to key people. . . . Have Protestant
> staff member go out to certain states. . . . Get list of labor dele-
> gates. . . . Definite commitments. . . . System of checks on workers
> within states. . . . Keep the field crowded. . . . Foreign policy,
> peace emphasis. . . . Run against the other candidates—not God.

The atmosphere throughout the meeting, as at all subsequent meetings, was one of quiet confidence: there was a job to be done which
could be done; we had the best man; no state was impossible, no effort
was too great, no detail was too small. Indeed, this air of confidence

permanently characterized the entire Kennedy campaign. It was not smug or strident, but it reassured his followers and impressed the skeptics. It also impressed his wife, who loyally wanted whatever he wanted but had been worried about the strains of the Presidency on his health and family life. "I see, every succeeding day I am married to him," she wrote in a personal note in 1959, "that he has what may be the single most important quality for a leader—an imperturbable self-confidence and sureness of his powers."

At Palm Beach, and in all subsequent meetings, the Senator was in full command. He was still his own chief campaign manager and strategy adviser. He knew each state, the problems it presented, the names of those to contact—not only governors and Senators but their administrative assistants as well, not only politicians but publishers and private citizens. He coordinated the talks and travels of his campaign staff. He squeezed in with his Senate duties a series of private man-to-man conferences and phone calls with local political leaders and an increased schedule of travel. He invited friendly members of Congress to lunch in his office and sought their advice and assistance. He kept in touch with the Kennedy men in every state, acquired field workers for the primary states, made all the crucial decisions and was the final depository of all reports and rumors concerning the attitudes of key figures.

Rumors spread fast in politics—few secrets hold fast. Reports on who said what about whom poured steadily into our offices. Whenever word reached him of a politician who was being privately and persistently antagonistic, the Senator would often ask a third party to see the offender—not because he hoped for the latter's support but because "I want him to know that I know what he's saying." His own political agents were under instructions never to attack his competitors or argue with their supporters. Our approach instead was: "Once your man is out of the race, why not come with us?"

On October 28, 1959, a second organizational meeting was held in the Robert Kennedy house in Hyannis Port. Present were the participants in the Palm Beach conference and these additions: Ted Kennedy, John Bailey, Dennis Roberts, Pierre Salinger, Hy Raskin (a veteran of two Stevenson campaigns), Dave Hackett (friend and aide to Bob Kennedy), Marjorie Lawson (able Washington attorney working with Negro voters) and John Salter (an aide to Senator Henry Jackson). Again the Senator conducted the meeting, displaying his mastery of the political situation in each state. He knew without notes who was friendly and who was hostile, which states had primaries and which primaries were binding, which delegations might be governed by the unit rule, which could be instructed by state conventions and which contained wholly free agents.

No one at the meeting could match his knowledge of detail. The lines of responsibility were still unclear or overlapping in many areas. But to a far greater degree than had been true at Palm Beach in April, he was talking with a going political team which had a better grasp of its task. His travels that fall in twenty-two states had been better planned and executed, with efficient advance men and mailings to set up his public audiences and private conferences. Most of those present had already traveled extensively on his behalf, probing strengths and weaknesses, presenting arguments, building an organization. No one there had ever participated in the direction of a successful Presidential election campaign. All had different backgrounds, abilities and opinions of each other. But all were dedicated to the election of John Kennedy.

State by state the outlook was reviewed and assignments handed out. Larry O'Brien, under Bob Kennedy's general supervision, was given responsibility for the states with Presidential primaries:

> The Manchester delegate situation [an internal feud] should be straightened out. . . . A speaking date should be set up for the Negro district in Baltimore. . . . See DiSalle and make sure he is going to meet his commitment. . . . After local election is over, get invitation to Lake County [Indiana]. . . . Call Boyle [Nebraska] every so often to keep in touch. . . . Organization well set up in Wisconsin. . . . Make sure Mrs. Green [Oregon] selects an executive secretary. . . . No decision on West Virginia until poll has been taken. . . . Find out source of story stating that friends say Kennedy will run in California.

Those are but a few of the Senator's directions on the Presidential primary states as noted by a secretary. Omitting Minnesota, Missouri, Texas and the South (as strongholds of Humphrey, Symington and Johnson respectively), all states were similarly reviewed and assigned—including Puerto Rico, the Virgin Islands and the Panama Canal Zone, each of which is entitled to convention delegates. Reporting procedures were established. Trips were planned. Campaign films were planned. Polls were requested for Ohio and Wisconsin, delayed for Nebraska, West Virginia and California. A contemplated trip to Africa in December as chairman of the Senate African Affairs Subcommittee was ruled out for lack of time. A picture Christmas card was discussed which would be sent to every name in the political file. And near the close of the meeting the Senator disclosed his intention to announce—in a letter to some seventy thousand names in our files on January 1, 1960, and in a Washington press conference on January 2—his candidacy for the Presidency of the United States.

CHAPTER V

THE PRIMARIES

PROMPTLY AT 12:30 P.M., ON SATURDAY, JANUARY 2, Senator John Fitzgerald Kennedy strode into a crowded press conference and read a one-page declaration of his candidacy for the Presidency.

He was forty-two years old—and so youthful a candidate had never been elected President, nor in this century even been nominated by a Democratic Convention. He was a Roman Catholic—and no member of that faith had ever been elected President nor, after 1928, even seriously considered. He was a United States Senator—and only one Republican and no Democrats had ever been elected President from the Senate, nor had the Democrats even nominated a Senator for a hundred years. They had not nominated a New Englander for even longer.

Yet Kennedy hardly acted like a loser. Tanned and rested from a Jamaican holiday, he was not only crisp but confident:

> I am announcing today my candidacy for the Presidency of the United States. . . . In the past forty months, I have toured every state in the Union and I have talked to Democrats in all walks of life. My candidacy is therefore based on the conviction that I can win both the nomination and the election.

He knew he could not be coy or halfhearted in this statement. His supporters around the country needed to know he would go "all the way" and not leave them out on a limb. Political leaders who would soon make commitments needed to know he would make a real effort. He decided not to mention his religion directly but answered all questions on the subject without concern or hostility. He emphasized, as an answer to doubts about his age, his twenty years of travel "in nearly every continent and country" and his eighteen years "in the service of the United States, first as a Naval officer in the Pacific . . . and for the past fourteen years as a member of the Congress." He made no direct or downgrading references to other potential candidates—of whom only Humphrey had already announced—but challenged them to meet him in the primaries.

He flatly refused to consider accepting the Vice Presidential nomination "under any condition." Appearing on *Meet the Press* the next day, he said the situation was "somewhat different" than in 1956, and if he were not to be the Presidential nominee, "then I think I can best serve the party and the country in the Senate. . . . I don't want to spend the next eight years . . . presiding over the Senate . . . voting in the case of ties [which] . . . rarely occur, and waiting for the President to die." He might have added, as he did privately, that he could not accept his party's rejection for first spot on the ticket because of his religion and then its insistence that he take second spot because of his religion. He also believed, but did not say, that second spot on any other Democratic candidate's ticket in 1960 was likely to be second spot on a losing ticket.

The pundits of the press persisted throughout that first weekend, however, in believing that Kennedy was actually a candidate for the Vice Presidency or, in any event, had no reason to be as confident as he sounded about the Presidency. In the judgment of those political reporters who rarely left Washington, practically nobody who was anybody was for him. Almost all the nationally known Democrats thought he had the wrong religion, the wrong age, the wrong job and the wrong home state to be nominated and elected President. They all favored him for Vice President, partly to avoid charges of anti-Catholicism. He was everybody's No. 1 choice for the No. 2 place. But hardly anyone of whom anyone had ever heard favored him for the only place he would take.

Every Democratic leader of the House and Senate—except, it was assumed, for the inactive John McCormack—favored Johnson. The "titular leader" of the party, Adlai Stevenson, was publicly uncommitted and privately for himself. The past Democratic President, Harry Truman, was for Symington. The influential widow of Franklin Roosevelt was for Stevenson or Humphrey.

A poll of House Democrats favored Symington. A poll of Senate Democrats favored Johnson. A poll of editors predicted Stevenson. A poll of state chairmen predicted Symington. A poll of "influential intellectuals" favored Stevenson. The liberal ADA preferred either Humphrey or Stevenson. Most Negro leaders talked first of Humphrey. Most labor leaders, particularly those angered by the antirackets investigation and legislation, talked first of Humphrey or Symington. Most Southern leaders talked first of Johnson.

Among the best-known professional politicians, such as McKinney of Indiana, Lawrence of Pennsylvania and DeSapio of New York, most favored Johnson or Symington as more their type of candidate. Some, including the Catholics, were convinced that no Catholic could win, and nearly all preferred to take uncommitted delegations to the convention to "deal" with a compromise candidate. With such important exceptions as Daley of Chicago, Green of Philadelphia and Buckley of the Bronx, most of the leading Democratic politicians who were Catholics were against Kennedy—because they had conflicting ambitions of their own, because they wanted to avoid any anti-Catholic controversy in their own states, because they feared a charge of favoritism, or because they simply sincerely preferred one of his several opponents. Catholic Democrats running for state and local office thought their own faith would be less of a handicap if a Protestant headed the ticket. Those with Vice Presidential ambitions knew they had no chance if Kennedy headed the ticket. (A few with whom he had served in the Congress, Kennedy thought, were simply jealous.) National Chairman Paul Butler, to be sure, was by 1960 very friendly to Kennedy, but unfortunately he had more enemies than delegates.

Most governors of large Democratic states leaned to Stevenson, enough to keep Kennedy away from a convention majority. The spectacular number of potential favorite-son candidates—Governors Brown of California, Williams of Michigan, Meyner of New Jersey, Lawrence of Pennsylvania, Collins (or Senator Smathers) of Florida, Tawes of Maryland, Hodges of North Carolina, DiSalle (or Senator Lausche) of Ohio, McNichols of Colorado, Docking of Kansas, and Loveless of Iowa, plus Senators Hartke in Indiana and Morse in Oregon—seemed certain to deny to Kennedy the early-ballot victory he would need as front-runner.

But the Senator, while not ignoring those at the top, had been building his strength from the bottom up. Relying on new methods and new faces to match this formidable array of obstacles, he had acquired some formidable assets of his own. His power base was not Washington, where the big names were, but out in the states, where the delegates were. There were more voters, more rank-and-file Democrats, for Kennedy than for any other candidate.

Local party leaders—who usually possessed more delegate strength than those more nationally known—were influenced by Kennedy's popularity with their neighbors and friends and by his repeated visits to their states. He had spoken at their dinners and rallies, raised and given money for their campaigns, sought their advice and assistance, and maintained a genuine interest in them all. He never refused a phone call, ignored a letter or turned away a visitor. Political leaders, labor leaders, Negro leaders, intellectuals, had all been deluged with mail from Kennedy, from Kennedy's office and from their counterparts in Massachusetts; and all had been deluged as well with articles by and about Kennedy, phone calls from Kennedy, books by and about Kennedy and polls showing Kennedy ahead.

At the root of all other motivations, local political leaders and candidates want a winner, to help the local ticket and to replenish party patronage. To strengthen their future claims for help, they want to be with that winner early. Likely losers may be admired, advised and even quietly assisted, but they are rarely endorsed.

Kennedy did not look much like a politician, but increasingly he looked like a winner. He had a history of political victories which carried lesser candidates in with him. Perhaps more important, he gave the impression that he was playing for keeps. His organization, though inexperienced, was both competent and confident; and his "new pros," like O'Brien and O'Donnell, worked harder and knew more than the nation's best-known old "pros." He had a solid political base, comparable in size to any big state, in a united New England delegation.

Moreover, word was gradually spreading (with the encouragement of Kennedy supporters) that the North and East would block Johnson's nomination, that the South and East would block Humphrey, that Stevenson would not run and that Symington could not win. The latter two were the most acceptable compromise candidates, but uncommitted party leaders grew nervous waiting for Stevenson to declare and for Symington to get his campaign off the ground. Kennedy had taken pains to be "personally obnoxious" to no one. Many liberals preferred Kennedy to Johnson. Many conservatives preferred Kennedy to Stevenson. Symington was the second or third choice of almost everyone but the first choice of almost no one.

Within this perspective, each Democratic governor had to weigh his own ambitions for a role in the convention or future administration. If Kennedy's candidacy survived the primaries, he would be consulted about the convention's keynote speaker and he would need someone to place his own name in nomination. If nominated, he would need a Protestant Vice Presidential running mate from the Midwest or South. If elected, he would need a Cabinet.

The Senator and his staff quietly beamed on all such speculation. No commitments were made, no deals worked out, no falsehoods told. But both hints and frank talk flowed from the Kennedy camp to several governors about the kind of running mate and other talents needed, and all suggestions and applications were gratefully received from their spokesmen, their aides and, in a few cases, their wives. Notations on other Democratic governors in the aforementioned 1959 memorandum to Ribicoff illustrate these considerations (without divulging names):

. . . strong for Kennedy, partly because he considers himself a Vice Presidential possibility . . .

. . . for Stevenson first and Humphrey second . . . probably cannot be enthusiastic about Kennedy but may face tough fight for re-election and need help in areas where Kennedy is strong . . .

. . . irritated by tremendous Kennedy strength in his state . . . might be interested in Cabinet post if does not run for Senate . . . . . . enjoys being wooed and is looking for support to be keynoter or nominator . . .

. . . reportedly has been reached by the Johnson people though still far from committed . . .

. . . probably favors Johnson . . . also presumed to have Vice Presidential ambitions . . .

. . . presumably will have no voice in delegation . . .

. . . reportedly made a deal with Symington . . . can be wooed . . .

. . . favors either Kennedy or Johnson . . .

. . . a Catholic with Vice Presidential ambitions, he knows they will never be realized with Kennedy . . .

. . . committed to Humphrey . . . would be interested in Vice Presidency if Humphrey did not want it . . .

THE RELIGIOUS HANDICAP

But casting a shadow over all these bright spots was still the issue of Kennedy's religion. Democrats wanted a President, not a principle. If a Catholic could not be nominated, or, if nominated, could not be elected, no matter how outrageous the reason, that was sufficient grounds for any Democratic politician to oppose Kennedy's nomination without being guilty of bigotry. Many did. Nor did Kennedy regard every Democrat who doubted the electability of a Catholic as a bigot. He was not enlisting crusaders in a drive to remove the ban on Catholics from the White House. He had no deep desire to avenge the discrimination his grandparents had encountered in Boston. And he was not, contrary to some reports, interested in whatever glory attached to being the first Catholic President. He simply wanted to be President and happened to be a Catholic. Although his formal position was an expression of confidence in voter tolerance, he replied to one question with a wry smile: "I'll get my reward in the life hereafter—although I may not get it here."

He knew that his religion gave him certain political assets, as in the 1956 Vice Presidential speculation, although the thesis advanced by one friend that his religion was his greatest asset he regarded as "exaggerated." It gave him a link with potential political workers in many of the states he visited. And, if nominated, it gave him at least some hope of recapturing a portion of those Catholic voters who had stopped voting Democratic nationally. But he was never under the illusion that all Catholics, much less the Church hierarchy, would support him. On the contrary, all talk of a Catholic voting bloc—to which the 1956 Bailey Memorandum had contributed—would only encourage Protestant voting blocs. He was not surprised when Republican periodicals resurrected and reprinted the Bailey document, but he instructed his own aides never to talk in terms of Catholic voting strength—1960 was not 1956. Vice Presidential prospects were often judged in terms of their appeal to some particular sector of the electorate—farmers, Southerners or liberals, for example. But Kennedy was no longer a Vice Presidential prospect, answering arguments about the liabilities of his religion with offsetting statistics. In 1960, as he wrote me in a discussion of our approach:

> The question is how many people will vote for Kennedy, who, among other things, seems to be a Catholic. . . . Once we get into the argument . . . about there being a Catholic vote, we are on very treacherous grounds, indeed.

Thus he repeatedly said that he did not want anyone to vote either for him or against him on grounds of religion, that he did not expect to win because of or in spite of this irrelevant standard. He did not threaten his party, as some charged, with retribution from Catholic voters if the party failed to name him. He had neither the desire nor the power to use the feelings of Catholic voters as a bludgeon—and "I cannot believe," he said, "our convention will act on such a premise." But he was aware of the fact that, if he swept the primaries and led the polls and had the most delegates, he could be denied the nomination only by a few party leaders saying, "We won't take him because he's a Catholic"—and this, he knew, they would find politically difficult to do.

SELECTING THE PRIMARIES

If he swept the primaries . . . Only in this way could he demonstrate his electability, prove that a Catholic could win, scatter the favorite-son candidates, pick up a bloc of committed delegates and knock one or more competitors completely out of the race. Only then could he translate his voter strength in such states as New York, Illinois and Pennsylvania into solid delegate strength. Only by thus getting Humphrey and Morse out of the race could he secure his own majority by picking up some of whatever votes they acquired. And only by winning in an early convention ballot could he secure the nomination. "If it ever goes into a back room," he said, "my name will never emerge."

Actually he never took Morse's candidacy seriously and never thought Humphrey, in the absence of a Kennedy withdrawal, could claim more than 200 delegate votes. Nor, in his view, could Humphrey be nominated even if he knocked Kennedy out in the primaries. Campaigning had its supposed joys, he knew, but it also took its physical, emotional, financial and political toll. For Humphrey or anyone else to campaign without hope of success, no matter how loudly the crowds applauded or how hopefully one's managers talked, seemed to him—as he remarked to one reporter—"just a waste of time. . . . Why does Hubert do it?"

His real opposition, he knew, would be Symington, Johnson and Stevenson. The latter's participation in the 1956 primaries entitled him to vow he was not a candidate in 1960, but Kennedy argued that Johnson and particularly Symington should not be seeking nationwide delegate support without proving their voter appeal. At times he exempted Johnson from this charge because of his duties as Majority Leader. But often he referred generally to all his inactive opponents. "If the voters don't love them in March, April or May," he told a New Hampshire audience, "they won't love them in November."

Privately he thought that Symington, had he organized earlier, might have been able to defeat him among the more conservative Democrats of Indiana or Nebraska; and one defeat would have been enough to deny Kennedy the nomination. But Symington, he felt, preferred the strategy of compromise. Johnson, he was certain, would not enter and could not win any of the 1960 primaries in which Kennedy was running —although he would later speculate that LBJ might have carried West Virginia "if he'd made a fight out of it." But the Majority Leader's decision to stick to his Senate duties and enter no primaries at all was a fatal flaw in the Johnson campaign, Kennedy believed, the flaw that prevented Johnson's nomination.

Johnson had to prove that a Southerner could win in the North, just as I had to prove a Catholic could win in heavily Protestant states. Could you imagine me, having entered no primaries, trying to tell the leaders that being a Catholic was no handicap? . . . When Lyndon said he could win in the North, but could offer no concrete evidence, his claims couldn't be taken seriously.

Thus, while privately he had some qualms about the true desirability from his point of view of the inactive candidates getting into the primaries, he was so certain they would not, and so convinced of the unfairness of their staying out, that he continued publicly to challenge and chastise them. History, Kennedy knew from study, was on his side. "Even though my chief competitors in the convention remain safely on the sidelines, hoping to gain the nomination through manipulation," he said, in language that would grow even stronger as those on the sidelines tried to help the other team,

> for fifty years no Republican or Democrat has reached the White House without entering and winning at least one contested primary. . . . Primaries are the ordinary voter's chance to speak his own mind, to cast his own vote—regardless of what he may be told to do by some other self-appointed spokesman for his party, city, church, union or other organization.

In short, he was saying, if the bosses, bigots and Hoffas want to beat me with any other candidate, it should be at the polls and not in some back room.

In his opening declaration on January 2, therefore, he stressed that "any Democratic aspirant . . . should be willing to submit to the voters his views, record and competence in a series of primary contests." In that statement, and later the same day on New Hampshire television, he announced his entry into the nation's earliest primary in that state; and, for maximum local impact, a separate announcement was made— usually combined with a flying trip into the state to file his papers in person—for each primary he entered.

Humphrey responded to Kennedy's challenge by challenging Kennedy to enter Wisconsin and West Virginia.[1] Johnson responded by tending to his duties as Majority Leader. Stevenson responded with another declaration that he was not a candidate. Symington, whose strategy required the avoidance of possible defeat before the convention, responded by saying that he was not a candidate although he "certainly would like to be President," and he announced a nationwide speaking schedule to take his noncandidacy "into the homes, to the street corners . . . to the farms," but not to the voters.

Equally threatening to Kennedy as the contenders who did not wish to enter primaries were the local "favorite sons" who did not wish him to enter their primaries. If the Senator, out of deference to their wishes and in the name of party harmony, decided to step aside too often, he

[1] Humphrey was also entered in an unofficial balloting sponsored by his friends in the District of Columbia and as a favorite son in his native state of South Dakota, and Kennedy had no intention of entering either.

would shatter his whole strategy of sweeping the primaries and seeking an early convention majority.

The list of primary states had been carefully reviewed. Those in which the results did not bind the delegates were historically less important. Those with genuine Presidential or Vice Presidential hopefuls as "favorite sons"—such as Humphrey in South Dakota (where Kennedy was skeptical anyway of a newspaper poll showing him leading Humphrey), Smathers in Florida and Meyner in New Jersey (where the primary was not binding anyway)—were sufficiently few to be ignored. On the other hand, quietly yielding the field to DiSalle in Ohio, Tawes in Maryland, Brown in California, Morse in Oregon and Hartke in Indiana would have meant yielding 240 essential first-ballot votes, without a struggle, to five less genuine favorite sons, all of whom reportedly looked more favorably on some other candidate than Kennedy.

Though his loyal supporters in each of these states uniformly urged him to run, the Senator approached each one differently. In Indiana, as the Kennedy campaign mounted, Senator Hartke, though friendly to Johnson, made clear he had no intention of running. In Maryland Governor Tawes, after a stern Kennedy confrontation, reluctantly forgot his friendship for Maryland-raised Stuart Symington and welcomed Kennedy as the state party's candidate in the primary. In Oregon, inasmuch as a state law required Kennedy's name to be placed on the ballot, he was obliged to enter the primary.

In California and Ohio, however, Kennedy chose not to run, despite the size of their delegations. Governor Pat Brown, in the name of party unity (of which there had long been little in California), and in hopes of his own ambitions (with which fellow Catholic Kennedy's conflicted), asked all outsiders to stay out of his primary. At our Hyannis Port conference Kennedy had remarked that it was "not worthwhile to go into that primary without Brown's consent." For the Senator to oppose the Governor—who was not necessarily opposed to him—would involve an exhausting, expensive, party-splitting fight, after all other primaries were over, between two moderate Democrats, both Catholics; and inasmuch as the deadline for filing in California preceded most of the other primaries, Humphrey or some other contender might well enter the state and win, particularly since Brown might cut into Kennedy's vote more deeply than into anyone else's. Even a Kennedy victory, since it would be over the party regulars, might damage his chances of carrying the state in November. Worst of all, he said, "Pat might suddenly announce that he was running against me out there as a stand-in for Stevenson and beat me."

A judicious compromise was quietly worked out. If Brown would agree to back Kennedy after the latter won all the primaries (except Oregon, where Morse was the favorite son)—and if a proper proportion of Kennedy supporters could be placed on a delegation too liberal to hold out for Symington or Johnson—Kennedy would agree not to enter. Though later he would wonder whether he had erred, he dispatched Larry O'Brien to a California motel near the spot where the delegates were being selected. O'Brien was secretly shown the delegate list at a time when few Californians knew it, and he was able to secure a fair Kennedy representation (predicted: at least 25 percent; actual strength at the convention: 40 percent) in exchange for no primary contest.

In Ohio, on the other hand, Kennedy was willing and ready to run. He had too much support in the state, had heard too many reports of DiSalle's flirting with Symington and had too vivid a memory of DiSalle's opposition in 1956 merely to hope for the best in Ohio. At a 1957 Kennedy dinner in Boston, DiSalle, referring to Kennedy's 1956 Vice Presidential defeat, had declared the Senator to have been "spared for a greater political future," but the Governor's continued intransigence made the Senator wonder how long DiSalle would want to spare him.

The two men had a series of meetings and telephone calls. DiSalle pleaded the cause of Ohio party unity and the need to rebuild the organization. He warned that Senator Lausche might enter and defeat them both. He sought, between visits, to pressure his own county chairmen to take his side.

Kennedy was patient but adamant. He wanted Ohio's 64 convention votes committed to him, and, if necessary, he was prepared to run a wholly amateur slate of Kennedy delegates to humiliate a slate of party leaders pledged to DiSalle or anyone else. He had already campaigned throughout the state. He possessed—and showed DiSalle—a series of Lou Harris polls that backed up his prediction of victory. He felt he could obtain the support of the Cleveland *Press,* having fulfilled three speaking engagements for its editor, Louis Seltzer. He had backing from the Cleveland, Cincinnati and other Democratic organizations. He, too, emphasized a united Ohio delegation, and said the surest way to obtain that unusual goal was to unite the delegation behind Kennedy.

DiSalle, a realistic politician, finally agreed late in 1959. The week after Kennedy announced, the Governor irrevocably and unequivocally (inasmuch as our office had prepared a draft of his statement) pledged the Ohio delegation to the Kennedy candidacy. Combined with the Maine and Maryland endorsements that same week, Kennedy's capture of Ohio startled the Washington experts who thought he was really a Vice Presidential contender. (The following week Kennedy, in a National Press Club speech on the role of the Presidency which opened his campaign with a flourish, remarked that he felt as Abraham Lincoln must have felt when he wired after the 1863 elections: "Glory to God in the highest—Ohio has saved the nation!")

The list of primaries was now clear: New Hampshire (no real

opposition), Wisconsin (against Humphrey), Indiana (no real opposition), West Virginia (against Humphrey), Nebraska (no opposition), Massachusetts by write-in (no opposition), Maryland (against both Morse and, by state law, an uncommitted delegation) and Oregon (against Morse by his choice and against every potential candidate by state law). In short, with the exception of Ohio and California, he was entering every binding Presidential primary where no legitimate favorite son was running and most of the nonbinding primaries as well.

The map and calendar had advised him against it. The last five primaries, widely scattered from Maryland to Oregon, all fell within a three-week period. But he felt required to test the acceptability of his candidacy and competence in every part of the country. Few other candidates in history had done as much, and no other candidate in 1960 was willing to do it. But as he said in Maryland, "I would rather go into the convention with the endorsement of the people from this primary than with the backing of any major political figure in the United States."

In each of these states, as he announced his entry into the primary, he stated—with some variations in emphasis on the basis of his knowledge of the state's problems and a Harris Poll—the same basic issues confronting the nation:

> Whether we can achieve a world of peace and freedom in place of the fantastically dangerous and expensive arms race . . .
>
> Whether we can spur the nation's economic growth to provide a more secure life for all Americans, regardless of race, creed or national origin . . .
>
> Whether our food surplus can help us build a more stable peace abroad and feed our hungry here at home instead of wasting in warehouses . . .
>
> Whether the children of this state and nation can obtain safe, decent, adequate public school facilities.

No primary state was either written off or taken for granted. He wanted a big vote in every one. Even when battling from behind in West Virginia, he took time out to campaign in Indiana and Nebraska where he had no opposition. The fact that he had no opposition in conservative, agricultural Nebraska, despite Humphrey's identification with the farmer and Symington's location next door, was remarkable— but they had both found out too late that he had long been patiently touring every part of the state enlisting supporters and workers. The same was true in Indiana and Maryland.

The Senator and his wife opened the campaign in New Hampshire, where only a political unknown opposed him, as though he were in the fight of his life. Early in March he received a Democratic vote more than

twice the previous record, and more than two thousand write-in votes
on the Republican ballot at well. Richard Nixon, who ran unopposed
on that ballot, also piled up a record vote, and there was in that
primary a hint of trouble to come. Shortly before primary day, Nixon's
campaign manager, right-wing Republican Governor Wesley Powell,
denounced Kennedy as "soft" on Communism; and, although Nixon asserted he did not approve of the attack either before or after its issuance,
his congratulations to his campaign manager on the Republican turnout gave Kennedy a foretaste of the future.

WISCONSIN

The "stop-Kennedy" talkers (and they did little but talk) now turned
their attention to Wisconsin. Unlike those primary states where favorite
sons were a bane, this was one state where Kennedy would have preferred a neutral favorite son to avoid combating Humphrey in his own
"back yard." Minnesota and Wisconsin were distinguishable only by the
invisible boundary between them. Both states had a surplus of farm
products, a predominance of Protestant German and Scandinavian
descendants, and aggressively liberal Democratic parties with strong
farmer-labor backing. Minnesota newspapers and television stations
reached many parts of Wisconsin. Wisconsin's Democrats, in their long
years as a minority, had looked for inspiration and assistance to Minnesota's Humphrey. "He is better known here," said the Milwaukee
Journal, "than anywhere else outside of Minnesota."

But all attempts to reserve Wisconsin for a favorite-son Senator,
William Proxmire, foundered on the suspicions and ambitions of both
Humphrey and Proxmire's Wisconsin rival, Governor Gaylord Nelson.
Nor would Proxmire or Kennedy accept the Stevenson-Humphrey-leaning
Nelson as a favorite son. Humphrey, moreover, needed a victory to spark
his campaign even more than he needed delegates. Ignoring Kennedy's
comparison of Wisconsin and Minnesota to New Hampshire and Mas-
sachusetts, he challenged Kennedy to contest with him in the one state
Humphrey was confident of winning.

Kennedy knew the pitfalls. At our first organizational meeting in
Palm Beach he had spoken of a Proxmire favorite-son candidacy, hopefully pro-Kennedy but at the worst neutral, in order to "avoid a Catholic
vs. Protestant, urban vs. rural" split of the state which would be of no
help to his cause. Favorable Harris Polls had softened his view, but the
peculiar state primary law which awarded delegates according to the
results in each Congressional district guaranteed an uncertain and unhappy conclusion. Humphrey's clear-cut advantage in the areas border-
ing Minnesota might not be enough to stop a Kennedy victory but would

be enough to show Kennedy as nationally weak with Protestants and farmers. (To make matters worse, the pro-Humphrey State Democratic Committee—overriding its pro-Kennedy chairman, Pat Lucey, our most effective ally, who had hoped to abolish the district-by-district pattern for a single winner-take-all primary—would vote 14-12, *after* Kennedy's entry, to increase the proportion of district delegates, thus making it possible for a candidate in Humphrey's position to win a majority of the delegates with a minority of the state-wide popular vote.)

Kennedy's advisers were concerned. The polls were uncertain. The perils were plain. He resented having to enter a grueling fight against a likable candidate who had no chance for the nomination while the "inactive" candidates remained comfortably aloof. Symington, he told a New York audience, "is hoping Wisconsin will be a good clean fight— with no survivors."

He would have preferred a showdown with Humphrey almost anywhere else in the nation. He was tempted to rest his chances on other primaries and states. But Kennedy knew that, with his handicaps, he had to risk all to gain all. Contrary to press reports at the time—which we encouraged, to emphasize the state's difficulties—all his advisers knew it also. A final Lou Harris Poll was the clincher. To an almost apologetic Pat Lucey at the Madison airport, he said, with a reassuring half-grin, "You didn't force me. My chances for the nomination right now are less than 50 percent. If I can win here, they will be better than 50 percent."

He could not give all of his time to Wisconsin. He had to campaign simultaneously in other primaries, woo delegates in nonprimary states and stay on top of a full-scale national campaign. But Wisconsin, until the April 5 balloting, was the battleground; and there more than anywhere else John Kennedy learned to do battle.

"Whatever other qualifications I may have had when I became President," he would say after it was all over,

> one of them at least was that I knew Wisconsin better than any other President. My foot-tracks are in every house in this state. . . . I know the difference between the kind of farms they have in the Seventh District and the First District. . . . I suppose there is no training ground for the Presidency but I don't think it's a bad idea for a President to have stood outside of Maier's meat factory . . . at 5:30 in the morning with the temperature ten above.

More than one day started at 5:30 in the morning and ended at 1:30 that night. No one envied Dave Power's assignment of waking the candidate up after a few hours of sleep to shake two thousand hands at a dark factory gate until his own would be swollen and blue. But he always dressed quickly if not uncomplainingly, and Jacqueline, too, fought back fatigue and cold to keep pace with a demanding schedule.

Kennedy friends and family poured into the state, each assigned to a specific district. Writer-artist Bill Walton, asked by the Senator for a month of his life, gave the first of several months to political organization. So did Billings, Spalding and others not on the payroll. Brother Bob and his field organization moved fast and far in the bleak Wisconsin winter, mapping schedules, distributing pamphlets, securing endorsements, answering attacks. The Kennedy family—Jack, Bob, Teddy and often their mother and sisters—could be found all over the state making speeches, shaking hands and winning votes. To demonstrate the Kennedy spirit at a sports carnival, Teddy made the first ski jump of his career. "I feel," said Humphrey, "like an independent merchant competing against a chain store."

But Humphrey had some important allies of his own. Most of Wisconsin's local labor leaders, farm spokesmen and political liberals endorsed him. His own attractive family seemed more at home in Wisconsin than the sophisticated Kennedy girls. Symington and Stevenson supporters moved behind him. With paid television advertising, Wayne Morse came in to attack Kennedy. All the officialdom of Minnesota poured across the boundary to campaign for Humphrey. So did Teamster boss James Hoffa, the most powerful and dangerous figure of the labor movement to be exposed by the Rackets Committee. Humphrey emphatically repudiated Hoffa's endorsement, but he stepped up the vehemence of his own attacks on Kennedy's "Johnny-come-lately" farm record and on his wealth and campaign expenditures. (It should be emphasized that this chapter necessarily confines its discussion of Humphrey and other candidates to their opposition to Kennedy. Needless to say, their greater effort was not in opposing him but in advancing their own virtues, which were numerous.)

There were advantages of wealth, of which the airplane *Caroline* was the most ostentatious example. "But any candidate who attempts to finance his own campaign," Senator Kennedy pointed out, "will end up in jail because it is against the law." Kennedy himself had been raising money in Boston, Washington, New York and elsewhere for over a year, and his actual spending within Wisconsin roughly equaled Humphrey's.

More disturbing to Kennedy were the attacks circulated by many Wisconsin liberals. The President was saddened to see intelligent men, who had reviled Joe McCarthy's methods, themselves using methods which created an impression of anti-Catholicism. During the course of the primary fight, vicious falsehoods were whispered about Kennedy's father, Kennedy's religion and Kennedy's personal life. Anti-Kennedy letters-to-the-editor were printed in the Madison *Capital Times* over obscure signatures, such as "Confused Catholic." ("I see," said Kennedy, referring to political editor Miles McMillan of the *Capital Times*, "a face full of energy and full of hate.") Although Humphrey's friend Governor Nelson professed a pro-Stevenson neutralism, in order to offend no one who might make him convention keynoter, it was with his apparent approval that members of his staff—including those who would later ask the Kennedy administration for top jobs—were openly and bitterly anti-Kennedy. All the old stories of Kennedy's contributing to Nixon, of Kennedy's deriding foreigners in a Harvard background lecture, of Kennedy's admiring McCarthy, were resurrected without regard to well-documented past denials.

Humphrey, his speeches and his literature stepped up the attack on the still unruffled Kennedy: "If you can't cry a little in politics, probably the only thing you can do is hate. . . . Beware of these orderly campaigns. They are ordered, bought and paid for. . . . [Kennedy] voted for the Benson farm program . . . record is like Nixon's."

Still Kennedy remained, in the words of James Reston, "remarkably self-possessed. He has shown not the slightest trace of anger. He has made no claims of victory. He has made no charges against Humphrey." He continued his dawn-to-exhaustion schedule, talking about the pollution of Wisconsin's rivers, the future of the St. Lawrence Seaway, the development of Wisconsin's timber, the taxation of farm cooperatives and other topics selected from our file of over a hundred Wisconsin "speech sections."

His crowds, particularly in the farming areas, were not so openly responsive as the audiences of Irish and Eastern and Southern European ancestry with whom he had learned to gauge his own effectiveness. But they continued to grow; they included young voters, suburbanites and housewives who had not previously shown any interest in politics. "I don't care why they come out," said Kennedy to one reporter, "as long as they do. My problem here is to get myself known."

By April 5 the intensity of both men's campaigns had ended that problem. Kennedy was known. His views were known. His charm was known. And his religion was known.

Kennedy had tried to minimize the religious issue in Wisconsin. He made no direct appeals to tolerance or for Catholic support. (One plain-spoken Kennedy advance man, Paul Corbin, inviting all the Reverend Fathers at a Catholic Seminary to attend a rally in their town that evening, added, "But, fellows, please wear your sport shirts.")

The press, however, would not avoid the issue. The people of the nation, and to a lesser extent of Wisconsin, were largely unaware of Kennedy's talks on other subjects. Pictures of Kennedy greeting groups of nuns were quickly snapped, while other greeters went unnoticed. Frequent questions from student audiences about his religion were reported far more extensively than questions on labor or agriculture. On a TV panel interview one reporter asked the Senator if he would attend a summit meeting even if ordered not to do so by his Bishop. "Of course I would," bristled the Senator.

Several sermons were preached in Lutheran and other churches questioning the allegiance of a Catholic President. POAU pamphlets and far more unreasoning statements by anonymous hate sheets were distributed throughout the state. An advertisement in several Wisconsin newspapers said Catholics in both parties were "ganging up" on Kennedy's opponent and urged Protestants to give a "square deal for Humphrey." Humphrey promptly repudiated the ad and all other acts of bigotry, though one of his aides suggested it may have been inspired by those seeking to stir up Catholics for Kennedy.

Voters at Kennedy rallies were accosted by reporters outside the hall and asked their religion—"not their occupation or education or philosophy or income," remarked the Senator, "only their religion." One newspaper's political analysis of the primary, he noted, mentioned the word Catholic twenty times in fifteen paragraphs. And on the Sunday before the primary, the Milwaukee *Journal* listed the voting strength in each county of three types of voters: Democrats, Republicans and Catholics.

The primary results confirmed both his hopes and his fears. Kennedy won the state with more votes than any candidate in the history of Wisconsin's primary. He carried six of the ten districts and thus two-thirds of the convention delegates. He ran well in many farm areas, carried one farm district and carried labor's vote despite its leaders. His margin of 56 percent was greater than the press and pollsters had originally, though not finally, predicted, and a shift of less than three-tenths of one percent in the vote could have given him two of the four districts Humphrey carried.

But the loss of those four districts, after the press had talked of a landslide, encouraged many commentators—particularly pollster Elmo Roper on CBS, hard pressed to explain how Kennedy received more than the 53 percent his poll had predicted—to attribute Kennedy's win to Catholic Republicans and his losses to farmers and Protestants.[2] (Wisconsin Republicans, taking advantage of their state's open primary

2 Roper, who we had long heard was unfavorable to Kennedy's candidacy, had earlier downgraded the importance of a "Catholic vote." Kennedy was so angry at Roper's telecast that he wrote a letter of protest to the network.

laws, had actually crossed over in roughly equal numbers for both men, ignoring Nixon's unopposed listing on their ballot.)

Humphrey ran best, it was correctly reported, in the least Catholic areas. But few pointed out that all these areas were near the Minnesota border—that Humphrey also ran well in the *Catholic* areas near Minnesota—and that Kennedy ran well in the cities and in the eastern part of the state among non-Catholics as well as Catholics. Humphrey did well in the cities near Minnesota; Kennedy did well on the farms further away. Geography was more decisive than religion.

Obviously Kennedy's religion did help him—and hurt him—in Wisconsin. Undoubtedly most Catholics did support him. Unquestionably some were motivated by pride in their coreligionist. But it is equally clear that there were many other reasons for union members, Negroes, moderates, women, young people, retired workers, city dwellers, suburbanites and others to prefer Kennedy to Humphrey. Nevertheless, if they lived in a "Catholic community," their support was attributed solely to religion. "To submit the candidates to a religious test is unfair enough," said Kennedy. "To apply it to the voters themselves is divisive, degrading and wholly unwarranted." Attempts to correlate his showing with the location of Wisconsin Catholics were no more valid, he said, than one showing him running well "in the beech tree and basswood counties and not so well among the hemlock and pine."

WEST VIRGINIA

But Wisconsin threatened to make religion *the* issue, and Humphrey treated this "psychological blow" to Kennedy as a psychological boost for himself. Abandoning his earlier announced intention to withdraw from the race if he could not carry his neighboring state, the Minnesota Senator carried the fight to a new field of battle: West Virginia. "I know we can win here," he told his aides. Perhaps he recalled that in 1956 the Vice Presidential survey of his friend Louis Bean had flatly listed West Virginia as one of the states where "urban, Boston, Irish Catholic" Kennedy had "no appeal."

Kennedy had no choice but to accept Humphrey's challenge in West Virginia, as he had in Wisconsin, but he had even less reason to run there. He was running the same day—May 10—in Nebraska. He was running in the same area that very month in Maryland. The West Virginia primary had been of no historical importance. Its voters were not typical of the country. Its outcome was not binding on its delegates. The delegation itself was not large. And Senators Johnson and Symington, with no campaign at all, were certain to have many of that delegation's votes.

Unlike Wisconsin, not a single leading politician in the entire state was for Kennedy. He had entered West Virginia largely on the strength of a Lou Harris Poll which showed him 70-30 over Humphrey. Now a new Harris Poll, taken after the full impact of Wisconsin, showed a sharply new awareness of the religious issue in this 95 percent Protestant state—and a 60-40 landslide for Humphrey.

Kennedy was quietly disgusted with his own folly in setting such store by the earlier polls but equally embittered by Humphrey's refusal to withdraw. If a Minnesotan could not win in Wisconsin, he could not win the nomination, Kennedy reasoned. Humphrey, he was certain, was being urged on, exploited and financed by the backers of the other "stop-Kennedy" candidates. He approached friends they had in common in the liberal and labor movement on the possibility of obtaining a Humphrey withdrawal. He tried to persuade Stevenson backers to stop financing Humphrey to stop Kennedy. But it was all to no avail. ("Thank God," he would later remark in private, "that Humphrey did win the Second District in Wisconsin and didn't pull out of West Virginia, and that we did believe that poll of Lou Harris' and did enter it.")

While preparing his public position for a defeat, Kennedy set out doggedly in search of a victory. To neutralize the suspicion attached to his faith, he emphasized his other attributes, especially his family's war record and patriotism in a state justly proud of its war heroes. To offset the religious issue, he emphasized other issues, especially his efforts for the unemployed, in this most depressed of all states. He also stepped up his year-long cultivation of local county leaders as mapped by his first and shrewdest friend in the state, Bob McDonough ("our man in Havana," Kennedy had called him, when he was our only agent in a hostile territory).

Once again the smooth-running Kennedy team, under brother Bob, O'Brien and O'Donnell, assisted by local Kennedy leaders, organized each day and each county. (However, the Senator felt that his sisters were too glamorous to be used as extensively in this poverty-ridden state). A new speaker for Kennedy proved a special attraction, an old friend whose help he had earlier enlisted in his 1952 Senate campaign: Franklin D. Roosevelt, Jr., flashing the famous Roosevelt smile which had helped FDR, Sr. to carry West Virginia. Humphrey was campaigning through West Virginia in the Roosevelt image, making what his aides called his "FDR speech," with a New Deal ring more powerful and practiced than Kennedy's—but Kennedy had the Roosevelt image in the flesh. Cartons of letters to all West Virginia voters from Franklin, then a Washington automobile dealer, were shipped up to Hyde Park to be postmarked.

In deserted coal mining camps showing the effects of automation and the rise of competing fuels, to straggling groups of unemployed at the side of the road, to families eking out an existence on welfare checks and surplus food back in the hills and hollows, Jack Kennedy promised help—and asked for theirs. At first the sight of this wealthy Harvard graduate asking for help in their impoverished state astonished the West Virginians, but gradually his warmth and sincerity began to make an impression.

At the same time West Virginia was making a deep and lasting impression on Jack Kennedy. He was appalled by the pitiful conditions he saw, by the children of poverty, by the families living on surplus lard and corn meal, by the waste of human resources. He more deeply understood, as the distressed areas of Massachusetts had never made him understand, the unemployed worker, the pensioner, the relief recipient and the ghost town, and he more fervently endorsed their plea for more help. He talked of developing West Virginia's resources, with new highways, clean water and better parks and tourist attractions. He spoke of assisting the coal industry with new research, new by-products and the encouragement of "coal by wire"—shipping coal out of the state as electric energy, instead of by rail, through steam plants at the mouth of the mines (an idea quietly passed on to me by Kennedy's old Republican friend, Senator John Sherman Cooper of Kentucky). He called for better housing and better schools and better food distribution. And in his most effective use of the Humphrey-can't-win argument, he reminded his listeners that a Humphrey victory in the primary would only mean that neither of the two candidates familiar with West Virginia's problems would be the nominee.

He spoke in every town and hamlet, Jacqueline tirelessly at his side. "I am the only Presidential candidate since 1924, when a West Virginian ran for the Presidency," he would say later, "who knows where Slab Fork is and has been there." He shook every hand in sight. He campaigned day and night, and lost his voice in the process. For a few days his brother Teddy and I substituted for him, as he stood by on the platform smiling gamely. (Once, when Teddy made a particularly impassioned speech about the qualities needed in the White House, the Senator stepped close to the microphone to croak that Teddy was not old enough to meet the constitutional age minimum for the Presidency.)

Then came the television debate. Kennedy had agreed to debate Humphrey in West Virginia—which he never would in Wisconsin, believing Democrats should debate only Republicans—because he knew he was behind and hoped for a breakthrough. As he had predicted, there was no real clash, except for one acrimonious exchange about the "stop-Kennedy gang-up." Humphrey seemed less tense and more spirited than Kennedy. But Kennedy, speaking in softer tones and shorter answers, without notes, scored with local illustrations and specifics aimed chiefly at West Virginia. He held up a skimpy surplus food package and cited real-life cases of distress. He spoke in simple, straightforward terms. Local newspapers the following few days showed votes switching to Kennedy on the strength of this debate.

Making the most of his underdog position, Kennedy continued to deride the stop-Kennedy coalition, now aided by West Virginia mine workers and Teamsters angered by the labor reform movement. On the Saturday before primary day, Lyndon Johnson spoke in Clarksburg. The Symington backers were busy circulating their own slogan: "Symington for President, Kennedy for Vice President, Stevenson for Secretary of State and Nixon for Sports Writer" (the latter a reference to one of the many careers Nixon had asserted he once wanted to enter). One of Humphrey's West Virginia managers admitted he was actually for Stevenson or Symington. West Virginia's Senator Robert Byrd, an avowed Johnson supporter, openly endorsed Humphrey for the May 10 primary with the warning: "If you are for Adlai Stevenson, Senator Stuart Symington, Senator Johnson or John Doe, this primary may be your last chance to stop Kennedy." Other Johnson and Symington backers agreed. The people of West Virginia, Kennedy calmly replied, should be more interested in stopping Nixon.

Humphrey, meanwhile, asserting desperation for funds despite his continued confidence of victory, pushed the poor boy vs. rich boy theme to new heights. He went beyond stressing his own humble origins and Kennedy's wealthy background and began charging the Kennedys with illegal acts:

> I don't think elections should be bought. Let that sink in deeply. . . . I can't afford to run through this state with a little black bag and a checkbook. . . . I can't buy an election. . . . American politics are far too important to belong to the moneyman. . . . Bobby said if they had to spend a half a million to win here they would do it. . . . Kennedy is the spoiled candidate and he and that young, emotional, juvenile Bobby are spending with wild abandon. . . . Anyone who gets in the way of . . . papa's pet is going to be destroyed. . . . I don't seem to recall anybody giving the Kennedy family—father, mother, sons or daughters—the privilege of deciding . . . our party's nominee.

Weary, discouraged and angered by Humphrey's attacks, Kennedy said in an unaccustomed public complaint, "I have never been subject to so much personal abuse." Kennedy discussed with his campaign team whether to capitalize on his war record. Upon more sober reflection, he decided in the negative. An equally weary Frank Roosevelt, while driving through the state, was not at his thoughtful best when he told an interviewer that Humphrey was "a good Democrat, but I don't know where he was in World War II." It was an unfair comment, promptly headlined by the press and immediately regretted by Kennedy. Both he and Roosevelt later apologized to Humphrey; and though his own wounds in West Virginia were deep, he told a questioner even then that he was certain that he and Humphrey could be good friends again—"but it may take a day or two."

One issue still plagued him—Catholicism. Repeated newspaper surveys showed well over half of Humphrey's support was based solely on Kennedy's religion. It lay heavily on the minds of all Kennedy's listeners. It cropped up in every poll and press interview. It gave rise to anti-Kennedy sermons in all kinds of pulpits. Even the Humphrey campaign song was sung to the tune of "Give Me That Old Time Religion." "Protestants have nothing against Kennedy," said the Democratic leader of Madison, West Virginia. "They think he is intelligent. . . . But they are going to vote against him. That's the way they have been reared. It's like they like women, but won't vote for them for public office." "People here aren't anti-Kennedy," said the publisher of the *Coal Valley News*. "They are simply concerned about the domination of the Catholic Church."

In a complete switch in tactics, Kennedy decided that it was time to meet the issue head on. If he was to be downed by religious bigotry, he intended to go down fighting. In a series of telephone calls to me in Washington, he outlined three basic approaches: (1) He switched the subject of his address that month to the nation's editors in Washington from foreign aid to religion. (2) He wanted nationally prominent Protestant clergymen, in an open letter to their colleagues, to call for an end to religious divisions and prejudice. (3) He would make a direct and positive appeal in West Virginia for fair play and a fair chance.

His address to the American Society of Newspaper Editors was a success. It was his first full exposition of his views on church and state. He reviewed his position on education, birth control and relations to the Vatican and emphasized:

> There is only one legitimate question. . . . Would you, as President, be responsive in any way to ecclesiastical pressures or obligations of any kind that might in any fashion influence or interfere with your conduct of that office in the national interest? . . . My answer was—and is—no. I am not the Catholic candidate for President. I do not speak for the Catholic Church on issues of public policy, and no one in that Church speaks for me. . . . Are we to say that a Jew can be elected Mayor of Dublin, a

Protestant can be named Foreign Minister of France, a Moslem can sit in the Israeli Parliament but a Catholic cannot be President of the United States?

He would not, he made clear, accept the advice of those who wished him to withdraw to avoid the issue:

> If there is bigotry in this country, then so be it, there is bigotry. If that bigotry is too great to permit the fair consideration of a Catholic who has made clear his complete independence . . . then we ought to know it.

When he concluded, he called for questions, but there were no questions. The Senator was disappointed. Many of the editors in attendance, he told me, had printed stories—and would continue to print stories—about Vatican claims on all Catholics, about Catholic voting blocs and about their use by Kennedy as a candidate. He had answered all those questions and more. He wanted to answer them directly to the editors.

Meanwhile I was working on the public appeal to and from Protestant clergymen. I made it clear to those ministers whom I approached that the statement would not be released by the Kennedy office and that my role would not be made known to the press. It was to be no more than a nonpartisan appeal for tolerance and for an end to the religious issue.

Nevertheless I encountered difficulty from the outset. The Senator, encouraged by a conversation he had held with the Chaplain of the Senate, the Rev. Frederick Brown Harris, in which the latter expressed his confidence in Kennedy's ability to put his country first, suggested I start with him. Rev. Harris told me how much he admired Kennedy, how much he deplored bigotry and how unwilling he was to take part. Evangelist Billy Graham, encountered by chance by Pierre Salinger, gave it prayerful consideration and decided that his signing would help make religion an issue. (Later in the year he coupled negative comments on the Catholic Church with the declaration that religion would definitely be a legitimate, major issue, "whether we like it or not," and he proceeded that fall to lead a Nixon rally in prayer.) Other prominent pastors approached through friends in Protestant or political circles refused to sign. One said it might impair his efforts to raise funds for a Baptist hospital in Alabama.

But two courageous clergymen helped get the project under way. One was the Very Reverend Francis B. Sayre, Jr., Dean of the Washington Episcopal Cathedral, and grandson of President Woodrow Wilson, who instantly saw that the ugly repercussions of continued religious divisions could irreparably harm the nation. He agreed to serve as co-ordinator for the letter and drafted the basic document.

The other was Methodist Bishop Oxnam, whose long years of op-posing the Catholic hierarchy as a leader of the POAU gave him im-peccable credentials as a signer of this letter. Two years earlier, the Senator had joshed at the Gridiron Dinner, "Should I be elected, I do hope that Bishop Bromley Oxnam of the POAU will be my personal envoy to the Vatican—and he is instructed to open negotiations for that trans-atlantic tunnel immediately." But since then the Senator had appeared with Oxnam before the Methodist Council of Bishops and a seminar for Illinois Methodist ministers, corresponded with him about the Cushing article and answered all questions on church and state. The Bishop agreed to meet me in New York and after some improvement in the wording, Bishop Oxnam agreed to sign the letter and to help seek other signers.

Other Protestant leaders began to respond favorably. Finally, on May 3, one week before the West Virginia primary, an "open letter" to their "Fellow Pastors in Christ" was issued from Dean Sayre's office over the signature of thirteen nationally known Protestant leaders. "Quite apart from what our attitude toward the Roman Church may be," the letter read, religious lines should not be drawn. Protestant ministers should preach "charitable moderation and reasoned balance of judgment. . . . We are convinced that each of the candidates has presented himself before the American people with honesty and independence, and we would think it unjust to discount any one of them because of his chosen faith."

Copies of the letter went to every Protestant minister in West Vir-ginia. Like the ASNE speech earlier, it had a beneficial effect in West Virginia, where plans for a mass of anti-Catholic sermons on the Sunday before the primary had previously reached our ears.

The Senator, meanwhile, was presenting himself with the honesty and independence of which the letter spoke. Shortly after the Episcopal Bishop of West Virginia announced his opposition to a Catholic Presi-dent, Kennedy pleaded for fairness. "If religion is a valid issue in the Presidential campaign," he hoarsely told his audience, "I shouldn't have served in the House, I shouldn't now be serving in the Senate, and I shouldn't have been accepted by the United States Navy." For the oath of office was practically identical in each case, he pointed out—an oath sworn on the Bible to defend the Constitution.

While a Baptist minister in Chelyan, West Virginia, was distributing copies of a bogus Knights of Columbus oath, which showed Catholics seeking a war on Protestants, Senator Kennedy was at Bethany College telling questioning students that he did not approve of clerical political power in Spain, that he had no desire to impose his personal views on birth control or any other subject, and that, if he received a political directive from his Archbishop, "I simply would not obey it." He recalled that no one questioned his oath of allegiance "before I spent long months in a Veterans Hospital, or before my brother died on a mission to Germany." No priest or Pope would influence his decisions, he said, and no pastor or anti-Catholic pamphlet should influence their vote. He thought West Virginia deserved a fair shake, and he hoped West Virginia would give him one.

This was not a constant theme of his speeches—economics was still his chief issue—but it was stressed in his preliminary remarks and in his answers to questions. The Kennedy charm worked, too, even on his religious antagonists. One Kenneth Klinkert from Wisconsin, who had peddled anti-Catholic literature at Kennedy rallies in that state and then followed him around in West Virginia, suddenly returned to Wisconsin. The Senator had spoken kindly to him, he said, and showed no anger: "It takes a big man to . . . come up smiling and genuinely friendly after his religion is being constantly attacked." Klinkert was for Kennedy.

Finally, in a moving televised question-and-answer session with Franklin Roosevelt that closed the primary campaign, he made his position clear as West Virginia crystal. He answered fully and fervently the toughest religious questions I could devise for Frank to ask. He was opposed to the persecution of Protestants abroad, he could attend as President any Protestant funeral service, and he could, above all, swear unswerving allegiance to the Constitution. As President he

> would not take orders from any Pope, Cardinal, Bishop or priest, nor would they try to give me orders. . . . If any Pope attempted to influence me as President, I would have to tell him it was completely improper. . . . If you took orders from the Pope, you would be breaking your oath of office . . . and commit a sin against God. . . . You would be subject to impeachment and should be impeached.

Catholic Boston, he said, had in 1948 overwhelmingly supported Baptist Harry Truman "because of the man he is. I would like the same fairness Harry Truman was shown."

Some said his answers were only "fanning the controversy." Others said he was "running on the religious issue in West Virginia." And still others said he could hardly complain inasmuch as his candidacy had created the issue. The Senator made no complaint, but he steeled himself for defeat, arguing that he would still be in the race by virtue of his other victories. "After all," he said, "Franklin Roosevelt didn't win all the primaries in 1932." Putting aside the gloomy press and expert fore-casts (the *Wall Street Journal* predicted a 60-40 Humphrey victory), he remained in Washington on Primary Day and tried to relax at a movie.

Whatever his secret hopes, the returns late that night must have amazed him. The people of West Virginia, anxious to disprove the charge of bigotry, and convinced that this was the man who could relieve their plight, gave Jack Kennedy a thunderous endorsement by a 61-39 margin. He carried all but seven of its fifty-five counties. He carried towns domi-nated by the Mine Workers Union. He carried Negro wards (which linked Robert Byrd with the Ku Klux Klan), and he carried Robert Byrd's home town. He carried farm areas and urban areas. But, above all, he heavily carried the white Anglo-Saxon Protestant vote. He flew that night back to West Virginia, and there he accepted Hubert Hum-phrey's gracious statement of withdrawal from the Presidential race. The religious issue, he said with jubilation, had been "buried here in the state of West Virginia."

The attempt to disparage this victory, so successful in Wisconsin, was unsuccessful in West Virginia. Liberal analyst Louis Bean, the same man who in 1956 attacked the Bailey Memorandum on the grounds that there was no Catholic vote, issued a purported analysis of the results which said there was indeed a Catholic vote in 95 percent Protestant West Virginia and it was responsible for Kennedy's landslide victory. The *Christian Science Monitor* thought it significant that Ken-nedy had carried by a large margin a county which was only 70 percent Protestant. But little attention was paid to this kind of obvious bias. Instead, Kennedy was charged with winning with purchased votes. Several newspapers, the supporters of other Democratic candidates and the Republican Department of Justice all combed West Virginia for proof of irregularities. They found, as was customary in West Virginia, some vote-buying for local candidates and slates; and Kennedy campaign money may well have been diverted to this use. But no evidence could be found of Kennedy's "buying" popular votes, for none had ever existed. "We sent two of our best men out," wrote the editor of the Charleston *Gazette*. "They spent three to four weeks checking. Kennedy did not buy that election. He sold himself to the voters."

To be sure, the number of would-be adversaries who were publicly accusing Kennedy of illegal expenditures and other improprieties that spring (the wealthy supporter of one of his lesser competitors put a private detective on his trail) was nearly matched by the number of would-be friends who were privately asking for them. One self-appointed go-between was certain he could deliver the votes of a Southern dele-gation but wanted to talk to the Senator's father about their "trans-portation difficulties." A promoter suggested that $150,000 worth of

subscriptions would ensure the support of a certain publisher. Another
suggested we win the farm vote by purchasing a struggling farm newspaper. A veterans' convention was also offered "for sale" by a promoter
who neither owned it nor influenced it. Needless to say, the Senator was
not interested in any of these offers. He had heard similar offers in
Massachusetts politics and had rejected them all.

THE WRAP-UP

The Senator's victory in West Virginia was the signal for both pro-
Kennedy and anti-Kennedy delegates to come out of hiding. Those who
had counted on his losing either Wisconsin or West Virginia promptly
dismissed all primaries as, meaningless. Those who had hesitated to
endorse him for fear of a Humphrey victory eagerly rallied to his banner.
In New York, for example, DeSapio disclosed that more than a majority
of that 114-vote delegation was for Kennedy.

The Senator continued his nonstop campaigning in the primaries,
but the results were no longer uncertain. "There isn't any doubt in my
mind," Kennedy told West Virginians that fall, "that West Virginia really
nominated the Democratic Presidential candidate." In Nebraska, on the
same day as the West Virginia primary, he secured the largest Democratic vote since Roosevelt's 1940 record and most of the delegates as
well (though, as in West Virginia, they were not bound by the primary).
A week earlier in Indiana, and in impressive spontaneous write-in showings in Illinois and particularly in Pennsylvania (he did not campaign
in either primary), he continued to startle the "bosses" with his popular
appeal. In Maryland, one week after West Virginia, he overwhelmed
Wayne Morse with a nearly 4-1 margin.

Oregon, the final primary, was important. That state's model primary
law not only automatically entered all Presidential candidates but bound
its delegation to the winner until either he released them or his total
convention vote dropped below a specified level.[3] This unusual state
statute meant that Kennedy faced not only popular favorite son Morse,
whom many had picked to win, and familiar foe Humphrey, whose
name remained on the ballot. He also, at last, faced both Symington and
Johnson, who had refused to campaign though their names had been
entered. Stevenson's name was not entered only because he filed an
affidavit swearing "I am not now and do not intend to become a candi-

[3] The Oregon legislature in 1959 had changed the law to bind them for one
ballot only. But on a Western swing at that time I had talked with the counsel to
Oregon's ambitious Republican Governor, Mark Hatfield, pointing out that in some
future year Hatfield could carry the primary for Rockefeller only to have Nixonites
switch the delegation after one ballot. The bill, which ultimately proved irrelevant
to Kennedy anyway, was vetoed.

date for President . . ."—an affidavit which had a prominent place in our file on "other candidates" (along with such other choice items as Humphrey's record on McCarthy, Nixon's Senate votes against civil rights and a 1959 Lyndon Johnson letter which boasted of his support of the Taft-Hartley Bill).

One week before the Oregon vote, former President Truman, who had campaigned in the primaries in 1948, publicly blasted all primaries and endorsed Symington. All he had against Kennedy, he said, was the latter's residence in Massachusetts—to which Kennedy replied, "I have news for Mr. Truman. Mr. Symington was born in Massachusetts."

The religious issue was also raised briefly when the Vatican news-paper *L'Osservatore Romano* told Catholics that the church "has the duty and the right" to tell them how to vote. Vatican "sources" were reported as stating that the editorial applied to Americans as well as others, al-though it was believed to be aimed at Communist candidates, particu-larly in Italy. The Senator issued a statement that his support of church-state separation "is not subject to change under any conditions." Privately he remarked, "Now I understand why Henry VIII set up his own church," and once again he wondered whether the statement had been deliberately timed to harm his prospects.

In other respects the campaign was smooth. Kennedy's Oregon organ-ization drew from all the state's many Democratic factions. And in the end he polled more votes than all the other candidates combined.

The primaries were over, but not Kennedy's preconvention campaign. He still hoped to reduce the number of other candidates monopolizing first-ballot votes. He had an inconclusive meeting with Stevenson, who still talked of a dark-horse liberal, still dreamed of his own election and, according to our intelligence agents, had said of Kennedy to one Demo-crat, "If only he had ten more years." Kennedy had both private and public meetings with Hubert Humphrey, for whom he had never lost his respect and affection despite two bitter and heated campaigns. He tried in vain—as I had in an earlier meeting—to convince New Jersey's Governor Meyner that springtime was the time for Meyner to join the Kennedy team, which would surely be looking for talented friends to join its Washington team when Meyner's governorship ended. Kennedy aides also talked with Governors Pat Brown in California, Herschel Loveless in Iowa and George Docking in Kansas.

The most successful effort was with Michigan's Governor Mennen Williams. In the midst of the West Virginia contest, I had attended the Michigan State Democratic Convention. With the sympathetic help of Senator Philip Hart, UAW leader Leonard Woodcock and National Com-mitteewoman Mildred Jeffrey, I obtained a postmidnight conference with the state's Democratic leadership and a morning audience with Governor and Mrs. Williams. I answered a rough series of questions on Kennedy's liberalism, executive ability, financial interests, campaign expenditures, civil rights stand, foreign policy and devotion to new ideas. I denied rumors about vote-buying and wiretapping in West Virginia, gave assurances that Michigan would be represented in the highest councils of the campaign and committed the Senator to answering in writing a forty-one-part questionnaire covering his views on all national issues from automation to youth.

Michigan newspaper polls already showed Kennedy with more voter support than all other Democratic candidates combined, and the state Democratic ticket needed this kind of help, they knew, in 1960. Once Humphrey (and Williams himself) were no longer contenders, and the issue was posed as Kennedy vs. Symington or Johnson, Michigan Democrats were sufficiently realistic to know that the latter two (for whom they were not enthusiastic) would be aided by either a Stevenson endorsement or a delay; and that an appreciative and victorious Kennedy was more likely to make use of Williams' talent for public service than an unappreciative Kennedy or a nonvictorious Stevenson. On June 2, following a Kennedy visit to the Governor's summer home on Mackinac Island, Williams ringingly endorsed Kennedy—and 42 more votes out of Michigan's 51 were added to the Kennedy total.

In the midst of his travels, the Senator also found time for a major foreign policy address on the Senate floor. The downing of an American U-2 "spy plane" over the Soviet Union and the consequent break-up of the Paris Summit Conference had raised new fears about world peace, and about Kennedy's age and experience. Before a shopping-center crowd in Eugene, Oregon, he told a questioner that instead of the series of false, contradictory and then overly frank statements the administration had issued before suspending the flights, he would have been willing to cool the crisis by expressing "regret that the flight did take place . . . regret at the timing and give assurances that it would not happen again. . . . A week before the summit . . . was obviously the wrong time. . . . Every time we go up in a plane . . . it may come down sooner than we thought. The maintenance of peace . . . should not hang on the constant possibility of engine failure." His words were promptly distorted into a "suspicion of appeasement" by Republican Senator Scott of Pennsylvania, backed by Senator Dirksen of Illinois. He was attacked as "naïve" by Vice President Nixon. And Lyndon Johnson, now campaigning more openly, shouted to each audience as a part of his speech: "I am not prepared to apologize to Mr. Khrushchev—are you?"

Kennedy's Senate floor speech on June 14 ignored these critics and dealt comprehensively with America's foreign policy agenda. One of those assisting with the first draft was Congressman Chester Bowles of

Connecticut, who earlier in the year had been publicly entitled Kennedy's "foreign policy adviser." As a Connecticut Democrat, Bowles's endorsement meant comparatively little. But as a symbol to liberals in Wisconsin, Michigan, Minnesota, California and New York, his prominent role in the preconvention campaign was important. It had required, as a preliminary to his final meeting and exchange of letters with the Senator, a long winter afternoon's conversation with me at the Yale Club in New York. He told me of his own potential following for the Presidency, his chances for the Cabinet under other candidates, his unwillingness to campaign against Humphrey, and his hope that Kennedy, if unable to win a convention majority, might throw all his support behind him.

Finally, after flying trips to the Dakotas, Montana, Colorado and Iowa, and several to New York, the Senator could rest. He had decided not to give an image-building lecture in England. He still had his share of detractors—both Southerners and Negroes were criticizing him on civil rights, and both Hoffa and leading industrialists were attacking his labor reform bill. And he still had strong and active competitors—particularly Symington and Johnson, whose efforts have been necessarily unreported in these pages but were still powerful that June. For they, too, had likable families, extensive financial resources, appealing personalities, considerable ability and shrewd public relations. They won no popularity polls, but they were favored at the outset by most of the best-known "pols." They did not risk a single primary and had no fears of overexposure with the voters. Without declaring their candidacies, they had made their views known and their names available. Without formally collaborating to stop Kennedy (which would have required one to defer to the other), their supporters nevertheless could and often did approach state bosses and conventions in harmony. Their strategy seemingly had every desirable characteristic—save success.

This was primarily because Kennedy never faltered. He wooed those few leaders who could deliver other delegates. But where they couldn't or wouldn't, he wooed individual, independent delegates, recognizing that most delegates are no longer deliverable. He set new patterns for Presidential campaigning, and those accustomed to the old ways had to admire him. "He outsmarted all the pros," said Carmine DeSapio. "If he had ever stumbled just once, the wolves would have closed in on him." But the pros had underestimated Kennedy while overestimating themselves.

He had during 1960 alone traveled some 65,000 air miles in more than two dozen states—many of them in the midst of crucial primary fights, most of them with his wife—and he had made some 350 speeches on every conceivable subject. He had voted, introduced bills or spoken

on every current issue, without retractions or apologies. He had talked in
person to state conventions, party leaders, delegates and tens of thousands
of voters. He had used every spare moment on the telephone. He had
made no promises he could not keep and promised no jobs to anyone. He
had commissioned dozens of private polls. He had appealed to the
Humphrey delegates and made his peace with Humphrey. He had authorized a letter from his most liberal supporters urging all Stevenson
backers to join them. He had answered all questions about his religion,
demonstrated his executive skill in organization and shown forthright
courage on controversial legislative issues. Said Stuart Symington after
the convention, "He had just a little more courage . . . stamina, wisdom
and character than any of the rest of us." He also had, more than most
men, the will to win.

If no one else had run in the primaries, or if Stevenson had run in
Oregon, or if Symington had run in Indiana, or if Johnson had run in
West Virginia, or if Humphrey had lost Wisconsin's Second District
and not run in West Virginia, or if DiSalle had not yielded in Ohio,
or if Pat Brown had forced him to run in California, or if Dilworth had
been Governor of Pennsylvania, or if Johnson had gone all out for
Symington, Kennedy might already have been counted out. Instead, it
was with "High Hopes" (the title of a Frank Sinatra-sung campaign song
used in the primaries) that he sought ten days of rest at Cape Cod
before flying to the Los Angeles Convention. He was tired, almost hag-
gard, but as his father remarked, "He would be a lot more tired if he'd
lost."

TRUMAN AND THE YOUTH ISSUE

His rest was disturbed, however, by a blast on July 2 from Harry Truman.
In a nationally televised press conference, Truman, who had similarly
denounced Stevenson at the 1956 convention, repeated his endorsement
of Symington, added one for Johnson and, for good measure, tossed in
the names of Bowles, Meyner and six others he hoped to stir up. (Stevenson's name was omitted.) In bitter terms he attacked the convention
as a "prearranged . . . mockery . . . controlled . . . by one candidate,"
and he attacked Kennedy's "overzealous backers" for pressuring and
stampeding delegates. Privately, Truman had been reported by more
than one Democrat as opposing a Catholic nominee. Now he publicly,
though by implication only, raised the issue of Kennedy's religion as
well as his experience, forgetting that he had entered the White House
with far less Washington experience:

> Senator, are you certain that you are quite ready for the
> country, or that the country is ready for you in the role of Presi-

dent . . . ? [We need] a man with the greatest possible maturity and experience. . . . May I urge you to be patient?

I watched Truman's telecast from our Los Angeles Convention headquarters where advance preparations were already under way. A few hours later I was flying back across the country to Hyannis Port, where the Senator had asked and received television time to reply on July 4. I took with me a file on "youth and age" containing rebuttal material for just such an occasion, and the Senator, looking relaxed and confident, interrupted his vacation to work on the text. He knew his age affected his candidacy, both favorably and unfavorably, but he was unwilling to admit that it also affected his competence. "Sam Rayburn may think I'm young," he had said earlier, "but then most of the population looks young to a man who's seventy-eight. . . . I do not recall that I have demonstrated any lack of judgment under the heat of the past four years. The test is not in the age but in the man himself."

We flew on July 4 to New York for his own televised press conference. After dismissing Truman's other contentions,[4] he demolished the age argument with such force that his supporters were grateful to Truman for providing such a highly publicized occasion. He mentioned his eighteen years of service and expressed his willingness "to let our party and nation be the judge of my experience and ability." But, if "fourteen years in major elective office is insufficient experience," he said, "that rules out all but three of the ten names put forward by Truman, all but a handful of American Presidents, and every President of the twentieth century—including Wilson, Roosevelt and Truman." And if age, not experience, is the standard, he went on, then a maturity test excluding "from positions of trust and command all those below the age of forty-four would have kept Jefferson from writing the Declaration of Independence, Washington from commanding the Continental Army, Madison from fathering the Constitution . . . and Christopher Columbus from even discovering America." (He wisely struck out the one other name I had on this list, that of Jesus of Nazareth.)

In a young country such as ours, he continued, with young men in the Congress and state capitals, the voters are entitled to equal strength and vigor in the White House. He and Nixon were both in their forties and had entered the Congress together, and six previous Presidents (and many nominees) had served in their forties. While it was true that most major world leaders in 1960 had been born in the previous century and educated in a different era, "who is to say how successful they have been in improving the fate of the world?" The newer countries of Asia and

4 "Mr. Truman regards an open convention as one which studies all the candidates, reviews their records and then takes his advice."

Africa were selecting younger men "who can cast off the old slogans and delusions and suspicions." Then he closed with this summation of his pursuit of the Presidency:

> For there is a new world to be won—a world of peace and goodwill, a world of hope and abundance. And I want America to lead the way to that new world.
>
> Mr. Truman asks me if I think I am ready. And I am reminded that one hundred years ago Abraham Lincoln, not yet President and under fire from the veteran politicians, wrote these words: "I see the storm coming and I know His hand is in it. If He has a place and work for me, I believe that I am ready." Today I say to you that if the people of this nation select me to be their President, I believe that I am ready.

CHAPTER VI

❦❦❦❦

THE CONVENTION

JOHN KENNEDY WAS READY. He had helped turn his youth from a liability to an asset. And out in Los Angeles his convention organization was ready. As the Senator headed back to the Cape, and I crossed the continent for the third time in five days, Bob Kennedy and team were buttoning down the last details in our headquarters at the Biltmore Hotel. Arrangements for housing, transportation, communications, demonstrations, delegate hospitality, public relations and a host of other details had been under way for months, with deft on-the-spot supervision by Kennedy friends Robert Troutman and David Hackett, who had temporarily moved to Los Angeles.

There would be no repeat of the 1956 failure of communications. From the Kennedy command post on the eighth floor of the Biltmore a vast telephone network linked all offices with all residences, a cottage behind the Sports Arena Convention Hall and the seats of Kennedy leaders on the convention floor. Kennedy floor workers had their own walkie-talkies.

Salinger's press operation was in high gear with its own daily news sheet. Each day new support was announced to the press: North Carolina's Governor-elect Sanford, Minnesota's Freeman, New Jersey delegates. A wide assortment of volunteers—Massachusetts delegates, unoccupied spectators, old Kennedy friends—was assigned to eat, drink and live with each of the fifty-four delegations, to report regularly on their moods, questions and trends, and, above all, to keep track of their votes. The Kennedy "control room" had a file card on every delegate, and the Kennedy "delegate hospitality" room had the biggest crowds and the prettiest girls, dispensing free coffee with campaign pins and showing a movie about the candidate.

"I think we are going to win the nomination," said Kennedy on *Meet the Press*, after his arrival on Saturday, July 9, had been greeted by two thousand well-wishers. "But I don't think it is wrapped up. . . . No convention is." He knew that both Champ Clark in the Democratic Convention of 1912 and William McAdoo in 1924 arrived with a majority of delegates and lost the nomination. In those days, however, the rules required a nominee to obtain two-thirds of the delegate vote, and had Roosevelt and Farley not permanently liberalized the Democratic Party by repealing this rule in 1936, Kennedy could never have been nominated.

His own majority—which he was careful never to claim with finality, even when he received apparently clinching endorsements from the big Illinois and Pennsylvania delegations on Sunday and Monday respectively—was still too small and too shaky to inspire overconfidence. Pat Brown endorsed him but had lost control of the California delegation. Governors Herschel Loveless of Iowa and George Docking of Kansas said they would withdraw as favorite sons in favor of Kennedy, but it was not clear what they could do on the first ballot. Despite pressures from his own delegation, New Jersey's Meyner refused to withdraw. He was quoted as saying, "I want my twenty-five minutes on television—I'm entitled to it." Other Kennedy backers were restless. "Neither one of them is really for me," the Senator told me in his Los Angeles hotel room, referring to two powerful political supporters, "but each thinks I'm going to win because the other is for me. We'd better get out of here before no one is for me." He would win by the second ballot, he said, or "never."

As the convention opened on Monday, July 11, a growing Stevenson drive presented a new problem. Mrs. Roosevelt, echoing an earlier column by the respected Walter Lippmann, expressed the hope that Kennedy's "unselfishness and courage" would lead him to take the Vice Presidency, where he would have "the opportunity to grow and learn." Negroes, she said, would not vote for Kennedy. Hubert Humphrey, friendly since West Virginia, but never formally committed, announced he was "switching" from Kennedy to Stevenson out of "concern for my country." Pat Brown found he had lost to Stevenson many of the California delegates he had hoped to bring with him to Kennedy. A former Humphrey delegate from the District of Columbia told me she had been subjected to bitter and continuous pressures from the same Stevenson backers who complained most about Kennedy's high-pressure tactics. The convention galleries, both packed and picketed by Stevenson's Southern California supporters, noisily greeted their hero's arrival in Convention Hall as a delegate.

"I never said he couldn't be elected Mayor of Los Angeles," observed Kenny O'Donnell wryly.

Stevenson himself, who had been asked to place Kennedy's name in nomination, was repeatedly requested by those friendly to both men to halt these efforts, which could only help Symington or Johnson, to gain Kennedy's esteem by ending his own vacillation, and to return Kennedy's courtesy in 1956 of placing his name in nomination. It was with some disdain that Kennedy told me Stevenson had replied that he wanted to disengage but "just didn't know how."

Meanwhile Johnson supporters were increasingly active. After recessing the Senate until August, the Majority Leader, agreeing to the pleas but not with the views of anti-Kennedy, anti-Catholic Speaker Sam Rayburn, had formally announced as a candidate. His statement warned that "the forces of evil . . . will have no mercy for innocence, no gallantry for inexperience." Rayburn assailed Kennedy's "untested" leadership. John Connally and India Edwards cast doubt on his physical fitness. Other Johnson supporters said Joe Kennedy had been anti-Semitic and soft on Hitlerism. They contrasted Kennedy and Johnson on McCarthy. They sneered at the Kennedy wealth. Harlem leader Adam Clayton Powell endorsed Johnson. A $50,000 full-page advertisement campaign blossomed forth for Johnson. Old-line politicians talked knowingly of a deadlock—with Stevenson taking Kennedy votes, all favorite sons remaining in the race, Kennedy fading after two ballots, and then Johnson or possibly Stevenson emerging as the compromise choice. An attempt was made to amend the convention rules to prevent favorite sons from switching on the first ballot—an obvious stop-Kennedy move that was defeated.

At Los Angeles Johnson saw the opportunity for a break. Responding to a Kennedy form letter which sought meetings with all delegations but which was sent to the Texas delegation inadvertently, he challenged "young Jack" to a "debate" before the Texas group. Kennedy rejected the advice of those urging him to forget it, switched the forum to a joint Texas-Massachusetts delegation meeting, listened politely while Johnson somewhat provocatively contrasted his Senate leadership with the absenteeism of "some people," and then replied with his customary grace. Johnson, he said, had not identified whose shortcomings he was discussing so

> I assume he was talking about some other candidate, not me. . . .
> I want to commend him for . . . a wonderful record answering
> those quorum calls. . . . I was not present on all those occa-
> sions. . . . I was not Majority Leader. . . . So I come here today
> full of admiration for Senator Johnson, full of affection for him,
> strongly in support of him—for Majority Leader.

Most of the convention, watching on television, felt that Johnson's challenge had been neatly deflated by Kennedy. The Massachusetts Senator, despite all the Johnson and Stevenson efforts, remained unperturbed. Only winning candidates, he knew, were accused of driving "steamrollers," "bandwagons" and "well-oiled machines." Rumors, chaos and mob emotion are as much a part of convention business as brass bands, balloons, placards and oratory. But the truly important business was securing 761 delegate votes, a majority of the 1,520 total.

The headlines for Stevenson and Johnson were much larger than the number of actual delegate defections. Neither the Stevenson spectators inside, nor the Stevenson pickets outside, nor the organized Stevenson telegrams pouring in represented a cross-section of the American people or more than a handful of delegates. The Johnson and Symington forces could talk of a deadlock, but no Democratic convention had been deadlocked since the two-thirds rule had been repealed. The others had hopes, but Kennedy had delegates—and that was the difference.

They could all talk of making Kennedy their running mate, but he had made unmistakably clear his final rejection of that position. Once again on television he flatly ruled it out—and meant it. To one reporter speculating on a Stevenson-Kennedy ticket, he said, "Look, I'll make you an offer. If I take the Vice Presidential nomination with anyone, I'll let you have my next year's Senate salary." His father expressed the view we all held: "Not for chalk, money or marbles will we take second place." At a Los Angeles rally walking in amidst tumultuous applause, the Senator spotted a supporter whom he had not seen since a conversation two years earlier in which the latter urged him to be satisfied with the Vice Presidency. The supporter had long since forgotten the advice, but not Kennedy. "Do you still think I shouldn't go for it?" he said smiling.

Kennedy concentrated his public remarks, at an NAACP civil rights rally and a preconvention dinner for all candidates, not on personalities but on the issues. The only "health" issue, he said, "is the anemic health of the American economy today." The only "age" issue is the neglect of our older citizens. He devoted his time to making the rounds of those delegations and leaders who were still uncommitted, a cool, purposeful figure striding swiftly through the jumble.

Other problems kept the Senator and his organization busy. The platform, drafted largely under the direction of Platform Committee Chairman Bowles, promised, in Kennedy's private view, too many antagonistic specifics that could not be fulfilled, raising too many unwarranted hopes and unnecessary fears. Less divisive issues were raised in the Credentials and Rules Committee. Many of the convention's administrative and personnel problems had been worked out in advance by an informal, secret committee of labor and liberal representatives on which Kennedy and Humphrey were represented.

Still the main problem was 761 votes, preferably through switches at the end of the first ballot, otherwise on the second. If even a second ballot was necessary, some of those committed by law for only one ballot might move away from Kennedy, we feared, offsetting gains from favorite sons; and if a third or fourth ballot was necessary, a sense of deadlock could produce a back-room compromise.

On Wednesday afternoon, as the nominations and demonstrations for each candidate were in progress, I talked to the Senator by telephone from Convention Hall. His final effort had been to ask Governor Orville Freeman to make his principal nominating speech. Telegenic, a forceful speaker, Midwesterner, friend of the farmer, liberal, Protestant and Governor of a state from which we hoped to take delegates from Stevenson and Humphrey, Freeman possessed all the qualities needed, but the decision had been long postponed in the hopes of persuading Stevenson to do the job. Now the speeches and pageantry were drawing to a close, and the moment to which so much had been directed was drawing near.

If the Senator had any anxiety, it did not show in his voice. He scoffed at that day's headlines predicting vast gains for others. He liked Freeman's speech. He liked our line-up of seconding speakers. They included a woman and a Negro, a farm state Governor and a Southern Governor-elect, an older liberal and a younger moderate. They represented power in all sections, including several states not strongly for Kennedy, and they were all Protestants. He also admired the cynically brilliant speech nominating Stevenson, which had been delivered by Humphrey's friend and colleague, Senator Eugene McCarthy, who was actually for Johnson. But Kennedy sounded wholly unconcerned about the ensuing applause and demonstration for Stevenson. The hard work on the delegates was over for him. There was nothing he could do then but watch.

At 10:07 P.M. the roll was called.

Alabama, 29 votes: A year earlier, youthful Governor Patterson, admiring Bob's racket-busting and Jack's vigor, had publicly endorsed the Senator against the latter's wishes and to their mutual embarrassment; but only 3½ votes now remained with Kennedy as Johnson gained the bulk of the rest.

Alaska, 9 votes: A narrow majority of delegates decided during convention week to give all 9 to Kennedy under the "unit rule."

Arizona, 17 votes: Led by the hard-working and articulate Congressman Stewart Udall, Kennedy backers at the April state convention had fought off an astonished, previously confident Symington-Johnson coalition to capture for Kennedy, again under the unit rule, the full 17 votes.

Arkansas, 27 votes: Earlier in the week the state chairman had assured me that the controversial Governor Orville Faubus would lead his state to Johnson but would not walk out on a Kennedy nomination. All 27 for Johnson.

California, 81 votes: Stevenson received here his only large bloc of votes, as Kennedy wondered again whether he should have entered the primary; but the Stevenson delegates were far less numerous than his vocal supporters and Kennedy received 3 more votes than the 30½ he had anticipated.

Colorado, 21 votes: Byron "Whizzer" White and Joe Dolan, with the help of repeated Kennedy trips, had secured 13½ for JFK.

Connecticut, 21 votes: Ribicoff, Bailey, New England—all Kennedy.

Delaware, 11 votes: Majority cast all 11 under the unit rule for Johnson, a disappointment to Kennedy, who had counted on several.

Florida, 29 votes: Favorite-son Smathers.

Georgia, 33 votes: Johnson. Kennedy's increasing outspokenness on civil rights and Johnson's almost regional candidacy would give the latter a total of 307 Southern votes and the Massachusetts Senator 13.

Hawaii, 9 votes; and *Idaho*, 13 votes: Divided evenly between Johnson and Kennedy, who were now neck-and-neck in the totals. More important was our own tabulation which showed Kennedy more than half a dozen votes ahead of the number we had privately claimed for this quarter-way mark in the balloting.

Illinois, 69 votes: 2 votes for Stevenson in his home state, 5½ votes from southern Illinois for their Missouri neighbor Symington, and 61½ votes for Kennedy, due in large measure to Chicago's resolute Mayor and political leader, Dick Daley.[1] From this point on Kennedy was never behind.

Indiana, 34 votes: All Kennedy on the first ballot by virtue of the primary.

Iowa, 26 votes: In a major gain for Kennedy, favorite-son Governor Herschel Loveless—with the help of the convention Parliamentarian and Chairman, and over the protests of Kennedy opponents, who insisted Iowa was bound—withdrew before the balloting to give 21½ first-ballot votes to Kennedy, who had only been counting on 19 second-ballot votes from Iowa. This meant that if Kennedy strength in the rest of the states held as predicted on our private tally sheets, a majority would be obtained on the first ballot.

Kansas, 8 votes: The delegation was reported out caucusing. Some said the Kennedy and Symington forces in the state were evenly split, making another caucus at this time necessary. Others said their leaders

---

[1] It should be noted that powerful Kennedy supporters are referred to in this book as "political leaders," those in the opposition camp are called "bosses." By convention time, recognizing their inability to defeat him, most of the "bosses" had become "political leaders."

sought to gain more credit and glory by leading a trend to Kennedy at the close of the first ballot. Whatever the reason, Kansas passed. But Kennedy had not expected their votes on the first ballot anyway.

Kentucky, 31 votes; and *Louisiana*, 26 votes: 51½ for Johnson, 3½ for Kennedy.

Maine, 15 votes: All for Kennedy, the hope of a solid New England bloc of 114 votes finally having been realized.

Maryland, 24 votes: Kennedy's on the first ballot by virtue of the primary.

Massachusetts, 41 votes: Kennedy.

Michigan, 51 votes: 42½ Kennedy, as Mennen Williams had pledged.

Minnesota, 31 votes; *Mississippi*, 23 votes; *Missouri*, 39 votes: All had their own favorite sons, giving none to either Kennedy or Johnson. We had counted on none.

This was roughly the halfway mark, and Kennedy was not only well ahead of Johnson but within reach of a majority on this ballot. Outside of California, Stevenson thus far had 18 votes. Outside of Missouri, Symington thus far had 29 votes. Outside of the South, Johnson thus far had 26½ votes. Kennedy had only 7 Southern votes but was drawing strongly from all other sections.

Montana, 17 votes: 10 for Kennedy, ½ more than we had counted on.

Nebraska, 16 votes: 11 for Kennedy, winner of the state's advisory primary.

Nevada, 15 votes: 5½ for Kennedy, slightly fewer than hoped for.

New Hampshire, 11 votes: Kennedy—that long-ago first primary.

New Jersey, 41 votes: All for favorite-son Meyner, who still clung to the illusion that he would emerge as a compromise choice; Kennedy, counting on 35 to 40 second-ballot votes here to bring him victory, had done his best to keep eager Kennedy supporters in the New Jersey delegation from alienating their Governor.

New Mexico, 17 votes: After a bitter state convention fight in the spring with supporters of neighbor Lyndon Johnson, who claimed all 17, Kennedy forces had settled for 4 votes.

New York, 114 votes: Deluged with Stevenson telegrams, led by professionals more accustomed to candidates like Symington and Johnson, New York cast 104½ votes for Kennedy, ½ more than we had counted on.

North Carolina, 37 votes: Only 6 for Kennedy, but these included a courageous Governor-elect, Terry Sanford, whose announcement earlier in the week was Kennedy's first break in the Solid South, and who had seconded Kennedy's nomination when all other Southern governors were for Johnson.

North Dakota, 11 votes: Demonstrating that continued contact and effort with the smallest of states is worthwhile, North Dakota gave Kennedy all 11. Our supporters had started out the week with 5, raised it to 5½, then to 6, then voted 6-5 to impose the unit rule.

Ohio, 64 votes: Mike DiSalle's word was good—all for Kennedy.

Oklahoma, 29 votes: Governor Edmondson, a Kennedy friend, had lost control of his party and delegation—all for Johnson.

Oregon, 17 votes: All for Kennedy by virtue of the primary, except for one National Committee member who had half a vote.

Pennsylvania, 81 votes: Kennedy enthusiasm in Philadelphia and other counties had finally won over Governor Lawrence and 68 votes. Now we were looking ahead on our tally sheets to see if a majority was possible on this ballot.

Rhode Island, 17 votes; and *Vermont,* 9 votes: New England and Kennedy.

South Carolina, 21 votes; *Tennessee,* 33 votes; *Texas,* 61 votes; and *Virginia,* 33 votes: Southern and Johnson.

South Dakota, 11 votes: With Humphrey out, 4 to Kennedy.

Utah, 13 votes; and *Washington,* 27 votes: Neither the Mormons in Utah nor the Catholic Governor of Washington had been enthusiastic at first about Kennedy's leading their ticket, but our tally sheet predicted 19½ of their 40 combined votes would go for Kennedy and he received 22½.

West Virginia, 25 votes; and *Wisconsin,* 31 votes: Two hard-fought primaries (only the latter was binding) netted Kennedy 38 votes, most of the Humphrey delegates in Wisconsin refusing to switch.

Kennedy now had 750 votes of the 761 needed.

Wyoming, with 15 votes, was the last state, and 8½ of her votes were believed to be Kennedy's. The remaining 2½ votes, we were certain, could be obtained from the *Virgin Islands* (4 votes, all counted on by Kennedy) and *Puerto Rico* (7 votes, split between two conflicting groups but both for Kennedy), thus requiring no help from the *Canal Zone* (4 votes for Johnson) or the *District of Columbia* (9 former Humphrey votes supposedly divided between Kennedy, Symington and Stevenson).

But no more were needed. Wyoming, alerted by Teddy Kennedy to the important role it could play, triumphantly cast all 15 votes for Kennedy to put him over the top. To the dismay of all the experts predicting a deadlock, all the politicians awaiting the next ballot, all the would-be king-makers in New Jersey and Kansas, Kennedy had won on the first ballot.

The pattern of victory was not very different from that he had planned over a year earlier: "New England, plus the primaries, plus the big Northern states, plus half of the West and scattered other votes to make up for a near shutout in the South." If Iowa had been required by the convention Parliamentarian to vote for its favorite son on the first ballot, if Wyoming had consequently cast only the 8½ votes for Kennedy, if he had consequently missed a first-ballot majority by 4 or more votes, if second-ballot defections in Indiana, Maryland, California, Ohio or other states had started a trend elsewhere . . . but Kennedy's whole campaign had been keyed to making the "ifs" break his way.

The successful candidate had watched it all from a private home. Earlier in the day, to escape the press, which had located his "hideaway" apartment, he had scrambled down a fire escape and over a back fence with Dave Powers to go in private to see his parents. But when the roll call started, said Dave, "You never saw a man so calm in all your life. . . . He knew he had done the work." As the balloting started, a blown fuse knocked out his television reception. But it was back on long before he gleefully spied brother Teddy standing, equally gleefully, next to the Wyoming delegation chairman. Teddy's broad smile was the tip-off. "This could be it," said the Senator—and it was.

His first act as nominee was to use one of his four special telephone lines to call Jacqueline, who, expecting John, Jr., had remained in Hyannis Port. His next was to speed to the Convention Hall, where, surrounded by his family and key political supporters, he made a brief statement of appreciation. His next was to go back to his apartment for some eggs and some sleep. And his next was to select a running mate.

THE VICE PRESIDENCY

"I think he should be competent to fulfill the office of President," the Senator had said in outlining to an interviewer the qualities he would require of a running mate. "I think he should be a man experienced in problems of the United States, farm particularly . . . somebody from the Middle West or Far West." And earlier he had denied that his own rejection of the job meant he downgraded its importance:

I will select the best man I could get. If my life expectancy was not what I hope it will be . . . but that really is not . . . an enviable prospect for the second man . . . to exert influence in the course of events [only] if I should die.

In keeping with his usual practice of concentrating on one step at a time, the Senator would not decide on a running mate until his own nomination was a fact. But he had thought about it. Harris Polls showed Johnson and Humphrey helping in some areas and hurting in others, while most other prospects made little difference.

I had submitted to the Senator and brother Bob several weeks earlier, as had many others, a list of potential Vice Presidential nominees. On my list twenty-two names were reduced to fifteen and then to six. The Vice President-picking process invariably begins with a search for someone who will strengthen the ticket and invariably ends with a search for someone who won't weaken it. Those ruled out on my list were too liberal, too conservative, too inarticulate, too offensive to some groups in the party, too much like Kennedy in strengths and weaknesses or too young ("We don't want the ticket referred to as 'the whiz kids,'" I wrote). I placed at the top of my list, as did many others, the name of one man who had none of these disqualifications and many qualifications: Lyndon B. Johnson.

Many stories have circulated about Kennedy's choice of Johnson: that his father dictated it—that Johnson, or Rayburn on Johnson's behalf, took the initiative on it with an ultimatum to Kennedy—that Johnson and Kennedy secretly agreed on it before the convention opened—that Johnson told Kennedy he would fight for the nomination if Kennedy, having suggested it, later retracted. None of these stories is true.

Despite the regional nature of his support for the Presidency, Johnson was more of a national figure than a Southerner. The youngest Majority Leader in history, a Senator's Senator who had accomplished more in the Congress during the previous eight years than Eisenhower, he certainly was no stranger to agriculture and the West. He had strong voter appeal in areas where Kennedy had little or none. He was a Protestant with a capital P. His work on behalf of foreign aid, social legislation and particularly civil rights had modified liberal opposition. His assistance with a Kennedy Congress would be indispensable.

Above all, Kennedy respected him and knew he could work with him. Lyndon Johnson was, in his opinion, the next best qualified man to be President. He admired from firsthand observation Johnson's tireless ability to campaign, cajole and persuade. He admired his leadership of the party during its dark days and his sure-footed finesse in the Senate. Referring to Johnson's powerful position when introducing him to a Boston audience in 1959, he had observed, "Some people say our speaker might be President in 1960, but, frankly, I don't see why he should take a demotion." In his notes for that night, he had scrawled out many genuine compliments: ". . . the most skillful parliamentary leader since Henry Clay . . . speaks not just for Texas but for the country . . . the man whose personal friendship I value . . . a great American."

Johnson, in turn, had been grateful to Kennedy for defending him when liberal Democrats sought a post-1956 scapegoat. "I have always had great faith in your integrity and your independence of thought,"

Johnson wrote him, "and you have never let me down." And Johnson's selection of Kennedy over Kefauver for the Senate Foreign Relations Committee in 1957 had helped cement relations.

The campaign had not altered their friendly regard for each other. Johnson had started late, preferring his Senate position to the primaries and wary of losing face by losing a race with a younger Senator. Sam Rayburn did not think a Catholic could win or should win, but no hint of religious bias ever appeared in Johnson's speeches. He made no mention of Kennedy in announcing his own availability, and he repudiated the Connally-Edwards charge that Kennedy was too sick to be President. It was generally agreed that, if nominated, he would want Jack Kennedy as his running mate. ("I can see it now," one magazine had claimed a Johnson aide said. "He'll be standing there in the hotel room after the nomination and he'll say, 'We want that boy for Vice President. Go get him for me!' ")

Although the Massachusetts Senator had not been as close to the Majority Leader as many of his colleagues and competitors, he had refused to seek the favor of liberal Democrats—even in Wisconsin, where he needed their votes—by joining in their criticism of the Texan's leadership. He had tossed a few gibes Johnson's way. Referring to the latter's statement that the party needed a man "with a little gray in his hair," Kennedy told a crowd of enthusiastic supporters at Los Angeles that "we put that gray in his hair and we will continue to do so." In private he would sometimes speak far more sharply. But his basic attitude remained one of admiration and affection. A rumor that, if elected, he intended dislodging Johnson as Majority Leader was wholly false. Asked on television whether, as President, he could continue to work with Johnson as Majority Leader after "he said some rather harsh things about your youth and inexperience," Kennedy replied emphatically that he could.

As runner-up in the Presidential balloting (409 votes compared to Kennedy's 806), as leader of the party in the Senate, as candidate of the area most opposed to Kennedy, as spokesman for a large state that would be difficult for Kennedy to carry, Johnson was the strongest potential running mate and the logical man to be given "first refusal" on the job. Al Smith, the only previous Catholic nominee, had picked a Protestant Southern Senator, Joseph Robinson; and Franklin Roosevelt had picked a Texas Congressional leader, John Garner. Johnson, Kennedy felt, would strengthen the ticket in the South. And he was less certain that the Midwest and West, his other areas of weakness, could be carried by the Democrats in 1960 no matter whom he selected.

Yet neither Kennedy nor anyone else could have expected that

Johnson would accept, just as Johnson had not expected to be asked. Kennedy had publicly stated in January that he did not think Johnson, Humphrey or Symington would accept second place. A Johnson aide had reportedly said, "Can you imagine Lyndon sitting there watching some-one else trying to run his Senate?" Senate Majority Secretary Robert Baker, a Johnson confidant, cautioned me in June not to be so certain that his boss would reject a Kennedy-Johnson ticket. But Johnson himself commented emphatically only one day before the convention opened: "I wouldn't want to trade a vote for a gavel, and I certainly wouldn't want to trade the active position of leadership of the greatest deliberative body in the world for the part-time job of presiding." Earlier he had said, "The Vice Presidency is a good place for a young man who needs experience . . . a young man who needs training."

But friends of both men—particularly Philip Graham, publisher of the Washington *Post,* and columnist Joe Alsop—had urged Kennedy to try Johnson's availability; and a warm congratulatory telegram from Johnson after the balloting helped persuade the nominee to make a serious effort in that direction.

With only a few hours of sleep, he returned to his Biltmore head-quarters and called Johnson around 8 A.M. He asked to talk with the Majority Leader in Johnson's suite in that same hotel in two hours (Johnson had been awakened by his wife to take the call). At the meeting, laying stress on national and party unity, Kennedy asked about the Vice Presidency. Johnson said he was interested, and both men agreed to discuss it with other leaders.

Johnson encountered some opposition and considerable reluctance from those in his own camp who disliked Kennedy, the platform and the idea of second place. "Some changed their minds and some didn't," he said later. Some of his friends angrily refused to speak to him for weeks. But Speaker Rayburn, after talking with both Johnson and Kennedy, expressed a willingness to back LBJ's own decision to accept this new challenge and experience. So, ultimately, did Johnson's wife. "I felt," he said later, "that it offered opportunities that I had really never had before in either . . . the House or the Senate. . . . I had no right to say that I would refuse to serve in any capacity."

Kennedy, meanwhile, was encountering disappointment among the backers of Symington, Freeman and Henry "Scoop" Jackson—who were the most likely alternatives considered for the post—but found general support in the party, with one major exception. Several labor and liberal delegates were outraged at what seemed to be a concession to the defeated "bosses" and Southerners. They threatened a convention floor fight. Leaders of New York's Liberal Party threatened to nominate a ticket of their own. Bob Kennedy had the unpleasant task (not, as some have speculated, on his own initiative but at his brother's request) of conveying their views to Johnson, and mentioned the National Committee chairmanship as an alternative. Johnson's supporters—many of whom were not enthusiastic about second spot anyway—were angry at what they thought was a change in signals by Bob; but the Majority Leader said he would risk a floor fight if Senator Kennedy would.

By this time both principals had made up their minds, and both stuck by their initial view. The announcement was made, the emotional outbursts of many delegates were weathered or moderated, all possibilities of a floor revolt were quelled, and no alternative candidate was available. By a voice vote the rules were suspended, a roll call was avoided and Johnson's nomination was voted by acclamation.

Another precedent had been broken: it was the first ticket in history composed of two incumbent Senators.

There remained only the matter of the acceptance address. The nominee and I had received many suggested drafts but had hammered out the final text in the course of the convention week. Our final session was held at the private residence borrowed by his father, on the evening of the Vice Presidential race. Some elements of the speech were clearly needed:

• Acceptance of the nomination and platform.

• An olive branch of praise to Johnson, Symington, Stevenson and Truman in order to rebuild party unity ("I feel a lot safer now that they are on my side again").

• An effort to allay anti-Catholic suspicions ("The Democratic Party has . . . placed its confidence in the American people and in their ability to render a free, fair judgment—and in my ability to render a free, fair judgment").

• An attack on Nixon, which some advised against, and which later proved to be the one part of the speech most vulnerable to criticism, but which Kennedy felt, considering the size of his television audience, should be included ("His speeches are generalities from *Poor Richard's Almanac*").[2]

• A nonpartisan appeal to independents ("We are not here to curse the darkness but to light a candle. . . . My call is to the young in heart, regardless of age, to the stout in spirit, regardless of party").

• An account of the mounting problems this nation faced at home and abroad ("Seven lean years of drought and famine have withered the field of ideas. . . . More energy is released by the awakening of these new nations than by the fission of the atom itself").

---

[2] Unfortunately my lack of English history showed in a reference, while listing unfit heirs to power, to Richard Cromwell as the nephew of Oliver. Some Massachusetts elders, moreover, were astonished that Kennedy would mention Cromwell at all.

But the highlight of the speech was a summation of the Kennedy philosophy: the New Frontier. Many of the ideas and much of the language in this speech came from the drafts of other writers as well as earlier Kennedy speeches, including the televised reply to Truman. But the basic concept of the New Frontier—and the term itself—were new to this speech. I know of no outsider who suggested that expression, although the theme of the Frontier was contained in more than one draft. Kennedy generally shrank from slogans, and would use this one sparingly, but he liked the idea of a successor to the New Deal and Fair Deal. The New Frontier, he said,

> sums up not what I intend to offer the American people but what I intend to ask of them. It appeals to their pride, not to their pocketbook; it holds out the promise of more sacrifice instead of more security.
>
> But I tell you the New Frontier is here whether we seek it or not . . . uncharted areas of science and space, unsolved problems of peace and war, unconquered pockets of ignorance and prejudice, unanswered questions of poverty and surplus. . . .

The American people stood, he said, "at a turning point in history," facing a choice

> not merely between two men or two parties, but between the public interest and private comfort, between national greatness and national decline, between the fresh air of progress and the stale, dank atmosphere of "normalcy."

Speaking outdoors in a coliseum too vast for the occasion, speaking as the sun went down on what was once the last frontier, the Democratic nominee for President delivered his address with an air of conviction and determination:

> All mankind waits upon our decision. A whole world looks to see what we will do. We cannot fail their trust. We cannot fail to try. . . . Give me your help and your hand and your voice and your vote.

Earlier, as he had finished dressing for the occasion, his long-time aide Ted Reardon had asked him to autograph for Reardon's son a press release copy of the speech, and the Senator had written: "To Timmy, with best personal regards from your old friend, John Kennedy." Beneath his signature, he scratched initials which Ted thought were "N.D." for Notre Dame as a potential future school for Timmy. Was that it? he asked. "Hell, no," said John Kennedy. "That's N.P.—Next President. Let's go."

CHAPTER VII

THE CAMPAIGN

THE 1960 PRESIDENTIAL ELECTION CAMPAIGN OPENED on a low
note for John Kennedy. The Democrats were divided and fatigued.
His nomination had angered the party's already shaky Southern wing.
His selection of Johnson had angered the already suspicious liberals.
Skepticism marked the attitude of farmers toward Kennedy, labor
toward Johnson and Negroes toward both candidates. Stevenson die-
hards complained about Kennedy's ambition, wealth, father, brother
and refusal to commit himself on Stevenson for Secretary of State.
Republican nominee Nixon, on the other hand, supported by Rockefeller and Goldwater and certain he had a helpful running mate in
Lodge, had effectively rallied his followers with a brilliant acceptance
address.

The polls showed Nixon was far better known than Kennedy
on the basis of his national office and four nationwide campaigns; that
Nixon was considered the more experienced; and that Kennedy was
known primarily as a wealthy, inexperienced, youthful Catholic. Immediately after the two conventions the polls showed Nixon ahead by a comfortable margin, 50-44, with 6 percent undecided. The supposed "normal"
Democratic majority comprised a large majority in the South—now uncertain over religion and civil rights—and a seesaw split in the rest of
the country where the election would be decided. Eisenhower had given
the Democratic strongholds of the North the habit of voting Republican
at the Presidential level. Many of the key states, such as New York, New
Jersey, Michigan and Pennsylvania, had not been carried by the Democrats in a national election since Roosevelt in 1944. Democrats, moreover,
were more inclined to be ticket-splitters, party defectors and nonvoters

than were Republicans. Their party covered a far wider spectrum of divergent viewpoints that enabled individual Congressmen to win in individual districts but posed serious problems for a national ticket.

The Republicans, by way of contrast, were sitting pretty. They controlled the Executive Branch, with all its powers of patronage, publicity and public fund allocations. They had the larger share of the big financial contributors. Eisenhower's popularity and moderation had blurred the traditional Democratic issues, his prestige was a formidable Nixon asset, and his eight years had been marked by apparent peace and prosperity. In fact, observers could recall no instance of the electorate's switching parties in power under such generally contented conditions. By any historical test, even apart from his unprecedented religion and youth, Kennedy seemed likely to be defeated. His stern warnings about the superficial nature of this peace and prosperity seemed to some only to guarantee his rejection by a complacent electorate, much as Kennedy had seen Churchill rejected in the thirties.

Nixon, on the other hand, was more popular than his party and more able and likable than his enemies portrayed him. He had a quick and cool mind, a fluent tongue, vast campaign experience and intimate knowledge of television. To lead his united and well-financed party, he had an efficient organization and personal staff and could draw on the entire Executive Branch for research and ideas. His running mate, Lodge, was far better known nationally than Johnson and may well have been better known at that stage than Kennedy.

Although Kennedy in time won more editorial support than any Democratic Presidential nominee since Franklin Roosevelt, the nation's newspaper editors and publishers (in sharp contrast with the reporters covering the campaign) were overwhelmingly pro-Republican and pro-Nixon. Of the less than one out of six who supported Kennedy editorially, many had originally preferred Stevenson or some other Democrat and gave only lukewarm or belated endorsement to the ticket. The most noted example was the *New York Times*. But Kennedy, mindful of the fact that the influential *Times* had not endorsed a Democrat for President since 1944, was pleased that its editors had on balance favored him. ("I'm one of those," he later said, referring to a well-known *Times* advertisement, "who can truthfully say, 'I got my job through the *New York Times*.'")

The late summer and early fall of 1960 were also marked by Soviet Chairman Khrushchev's visit to the United Nations, highlighting Nixon's claim of superior experience in "standing up to Khrushchev," reminding voters of the Vice President's much-publicized argument with the Soviet Chairman at an American kitchen exhibition in Moscow, and occupying the front pages at a time when the lesser-known Kennedy needed the nation's attention. Demonstrating its toughness, the Republican administration announced that Khrushchev—and Castro, too, when he also arrived at the UN—would be confined to Manhattan ("But they have not confined them," said Kennedy on the campaign circuit, "in Latin America or around the world").

A mixed liability and asset was the determined and well-financed effort of Teamster boss Jimmy Hoffa to rally his large and powerful union against the Kennedys. He was joined in that effort by Longshoreman boss Harry Bridges and a few other leaders. (Brooklyn gangster Joey Gallo, asking Bob Kennedy if his influence could be helpful, was told, "Just tell everybody you're voting for Nixon.")

But the most frustrating handicap to the Democrats that summer had been self-imposed. Johnson and Rayburn had decided, prior to the Democratic Convention, to recess the Congress and reconvene it after the convention.

Whatever their motive, the reconvened session only embittered Kennedy. It embarrassed both him and Johnson because of their inability to push legislation past the Republican–Southern Democratic coalition, particularly in the House Rules Committee. The results offered fresh evidence of Democratic disarray in the South, where Nixon's initial forays were well received, and where he sent Senator Barry Goldwater to campaign extensively. The opposition of powerful Southern Democratic Senators and Congressmen to their party's legislative program, aided by the threat of Eisenhower's veto, rendered the Democratic majorities in both houses uncomfortably impotent, and encouraged the Republicans to disrupt Democratic plans still further through political and parliamentary maneuvers on civil rights. The increasingly vituperative and unproductive session also tied Kennedy and Johnson, far more than Nixon, down in Washington—where there were no votes to be won—until the Labor Day weekend.

ORGANIZING THE CAMPAIGN

Kennedy was not, however, wholly idle in the interval between the convention and Labor Day. After two days of rest with his wife and daughter at Hyannis Port (he had promised her a week), he plunged into a series of planning meetings with his brother and staff, strategy meetings with Johnson, unity meetings with disappointed Democrats, policy meetings with Stevenson and Bowles and quick trips about the country. He visited Eleanor Roosevelt in Hyde Park and Harry Truman in Independence, soliciting and securing their support. Feuding factions were coordinated, if not united, from New York to Florida to California. Despite the summer lull, a large, comprehensive nationwide registration drive was launched, emphasizing personal contact with millions of un-registered voters and securing in many states more new Democratic voters than Kennedy's ultimate margin. "Each of you go out and register one person between now and November," said the Senator, "and you are in effect voting twice."

From his summer cottage, now shielded from a stream of sight-seers by a new fence as well as police, came a series of manifestoes identifying Nixon with Benson, Eisenhower's unpopular Secretary of Agriculture. Nationality spokesmen, minority spokesmen, farm spokes-men, labor leaders and liberal leaders all paraded to Hyannis Port as the old Democratic coalition was rebuilt, the new convention wounds were patched up and the Kennedy campaign organization was made ready.

After three Congressional, two Senatorial and seven Presidential primary campaigns, all successful, John Kennedy knew how to cam-paign. He knew how best to use all the modern tools—air travel, tele-vision, advance men, a brain trust and polls (but not, as reported, computers). He knew how to create crowds and crowd appeal in a highly personal campaign that nevertheless focused on issues. The basic approach employed in Massachusetts had been applied and improved in the primaries, and it was further broadened for the election cam-paign.

One of the candidate's first, wisest and boldest moves was to refuse to be his own campaign manager. He recognized that all his own time and energy should be devoted to public and television appearances, mostly away from Washington, and that the administrative work of scheduling, fund-raising and organizing the fifty states (which he had supervised prior to the convention) should be directed by others. "All I have to do is show up," he said in admiring the handiwork of his team.

He insisted that the two-headed monstrosity of 1956, when Stevenson and the National Chairman had directed separate operations, be avoided by integrating his team with the Democratic National Committee. The entire operation was headed by the tireless Bob Kennedy as campaign manager, assisted by O'Brien as chief organizer, O'Donnell as chief schedule coordinator, John Bailey as chief contact with the professionals, Stephen Smith as chief administrator and moneyman, Pierre Salinger as chief press aide (with the help of Donald Wilson and Andrew Hatcher) and other preconvention regulars. Old campaign aides from Massachu-setts were recruited, including Richard Maguire, who handled schedul-ing when O'Donnell left with the candidate, and Richard Donahue, who assisted O'Brien on organization.

Byron "Whizzer" White headed Citizens for Kennedy, a network of local volunteer organizations whose efforts were combined with the regular party organization in some communities, "coordinated" by an out-of-state Kennedy man in others, and resisted or ignored by local party leaders in still others. New Jersey Congressman Frank Thompson led the successful registration drive. Senator Henry "Scoop" Jackson of Washington was interim chairman of the Democratic National Committee. Luther Hodges served as chairman of the business and professional men's group. Teddy Kennedy was in charge of operations in the Western states. Sargent Shriver and Harris Wofford worked with Negro leaders—including, after some high-level negotiations, the flamboyant but effective Adam Clayton Powell—attempting to improve a normally Democratic vote among Negroes that was clearly in doubt in 1960 owing to their cynicism on civil rights in general, Kennedy's voting record and running mate in particular, and the influence of prejudiced Protestant Negro preachers. A host of lawyers, legislative aides, Kennedy family friends and old National Committee hands volunteered or were drafted to serve as "advance men" for every Kennedy appearance and as "coordinators" for every state.

Advance men were the unsung heroes of the campaign. Arriving several days before the candidate, they worked with local party leaders to plan the schedule, determine the motorcade route, decide on platform sites and seating, turn out the crowds, work with the police and local press, and distribute flags, press kits and buttons. They arranged for most of the "spontaneous" hand-lettered signs, usually hoisted by the children of local party workers and volunteers, which impressed the press with such messages as "Baptists for Kennedy" and "Kennedy *Sí*, Nixon *No!*" (Some, of course—such as "Let's put a new John in the White House"—actually were spontaneous.)

Upon the *Caroline*'s arrival in each major city, the advance man came on board first to brief the Senator on names, faces and local color, and to distribute copies of a detailed schedule which included all room assignments, telephone numbers, press accommodations and baggage arrangements. If our hotel rooms were inadequate or our baggage late, we could blame the advance men. If there were enough cars and buses at the airport for the group of fifty aides and reporters with the candidate, and a band at the rally and a table for the press, we could thank the advance men. Some, such as Vince Gaughan of New York and Jerry Bruno of Wisconsin, often mastered a million details with remarkable precision. Others constantly encountered and contributed obstacles and delays. "I wonder," said the candidate to Mike DiSalle, as they waited patiently for an advance man outside of Youngstown, Ohio, to straighten out and start the order of procession, "how Napoleon ever got his army to Austerlitz." "It was easy," replied the Governor. "He didn't have any advance men."

Other specialists and campaigners were recruited. Harry Truman had a schedule which took him in particular to his fellow Baptists. Adlai Stevenson was especially helpful in California. Hubert Humphrey helped hold Minnesota and woo liberals elsewhere, as all primary feuds were forgotten:

HUMPHREY: I want to say . . . one thing about Senator Kennedy. If he gives you his word and says he is going to do it, he does it. He told me last year that he was going to lick me, and he did it.

KENNEDY: He made it so tough last winter that this fall is very pleasant. . . . It is much easier to play Harvard after you have played against Ohio State. . . . The great advantage I had [in the debates] was that Mr. Nixon had only debated with Khrushchev and I had debated with Hubert Humphrey. . . . That is much tougher.

The Kennedy girls—sisters, in-laws and mother—were given extensive speaking assignments, especially in suburban areas. Eunice, Pat and Jean all appeared with the Senator in their husbands' home states of Illinois, California and New York. "In preparation for this campaign," said the Senator to those audiences, "I had sisters living in all the key states."

A speakers' bureau was created. Liaison was established with organized labor, whose leaders worked more effectively than they had in any previous campaign. Transportation and television experts were brought in. An advertising agency was retained, not to provide campaign advice or slogans, but to purchase time and space in the commercial media and to help formulate and publish such materials as brochures, bumper stickers, banners and buttons.

The most successful "button" was a tie clasp in the form of Kennedy's old PT boat. It became a popular badge for Kennedy supporters and a fast-selling item in the "Dollars for Democrats" drive. It was part of an unprecedented Democratic effort to broaden their financial base and appeal to small donors—an effort based not only on the assumption that such donors are more likely to vote and work for the Democratic ticket following their donation, but also on the knowledge that the Republicans had nearly twice as many contributors giving $10,000 or more.

Fund-raising was a special problem. Those with large sums to give were primarily for Nixon. Those with small sums to give assumed Kennedy's wealth made their contributions insignificant. Both parties knew that a defeat is the most expensive campaign of all and that victors will not remain paupers. The Republicans were prepared to incur—and did incur—a level of expenditures exceeding both their 1952 and 1956 out-

lays for Eisenhower. Kennedy, lacking their sources of revenue but requiring the same resources for campaigning, was prepared to incur—
and did incur—the largest campaign deficit in American political history.
Both parties spent over ten million dollars at the national level. "They
spent it," Kennedy said of his campaign team later, "like they were
sure we were going to win." By the time the convention was over, the
cost of his campaigning had already exceeded contributions by more than
$200,000. In taking over the Democratic National Committee after the
convention, he inherited an additional debt of some $70,000. By the time
he was inaugurated in January, 1961, the party debt had climbed to
nearly four million dollars.

His fall campaign schedule had to make room for frequent fund-
raising stops: breakfasts, luncheons, dinners and receptions, at $10,
$100 or $1,000 a head, at least one in every state possible. "I am grateful
to all of you," he told one luncheon in Denver. "I could say I am deeply
touched, but not as deeply touched as you have been in coming to this
luncheon."

Both before and after his Presidential contest, Kennedy worried
over the rising cost of campaigns, including jet travel and television,
and the consequent dependence on powerful interest groups. As both
Senator and President, he expressed an interest in either Federal subsidies or tax credits for the small contributor. His only major policy
reference to the fund-raising problem during the campaign, outside of
fund-raising functions, came in his Wittenberg College speech on ethics
in government. "Campaign contributions," he pledged, "will not be regarded as a substitute for training and experience for diplomatic positions." ("Ever since I made that statement," the Senator joked a little
later, "I have not received one single cent from my father." Whether it
actually deterred any contributions will never be known, but the pledge
was carried out: of twenty-seven noncareer chiefs of mission appointed,
twenty had made no known contributions, one had contributed to Nixon,
one had served under Eisenhower, and others like Galbraith, Harriman
and Akers had all been talented members of the Kennedy campaign
organization.)

The organization was based on the Kennedy-O'Brien maxim that
"There is no such thing as too much campaign activity, properly directed."
The object was to involve as many people as possible. On a national,
state and local basis, Kennedy supporters created special groups for
Kennedy. A nationwide telephone campaign of women "Calling for Kennedy" was kicked off by Jacqueline's placing a conference call to eleven
ladies in eleven states. Each state had its own publicity chairman, announcing each new group's formation to small as well as large newspapers.

The Kennedy-O'Brien approach also called for detailed party organization—not merely in the key states but in every state—not merely in the big cities but in every county possible—not merely of the party regulars but of every volunteer. No one who volunteered in or out of Washington was ignored; some assignment was found for all. Volunteers, as pointed out by the "O'Brien Manual," and particularly women volunteers, are the backbone of any successful Democratic campaign organization.

At the same time, we were organizing to meet the religious issue. Prior to the convention, this had been primarily my assignment. Having been raised in a Unitarian and civil libertarian atmosphere that looked with some suspicion on Catholic political pressure, I could help the Senator understand the more reasonable fears he encountered. I had some credentials to talk without hostility or embarrassment to the Oxnams, Blanshards and others about the Senator's stand on these matters. But the Senator also delegated me to talk with his friend Bishop John Wright of Pittsburgh on the position of the Catholic Church (the Senator was pleased to be reminded that, contrary to popular belief, no public act of a President acting under the Constitution could conceivably lead to his excommunication by the Pope; that Confession is for the avowal of personal sins, not the discussion of public policies; and that he, as a Catholic, had not sworn any kind of allegiance to the Pope, least of all in political matters). He asked me to meet with Protestant clergy in Charleston, West Virginia, and elsewhere and seek their help. (In Houston in September, he asked me whether all my associations with Catholic clerics and defenses of Catholic doctrine had "rubbed off" on me a little Catholicism, and I replied that it had not, but that I still had hopes of my Unitarianism rubbing off on him.)

But once Kennedy was nominated in July, it was clear that his intensive speaking schedule would occupy all my time. The religious issue, we knew, was not dead. "It's a matter of continuing interest," said the Senator. "What we prevented in West Virginia was its becoming the *only* issue . . . but . . . it will come on the stage again."

Immediately after the convention I suggested to campaign manager Robert Kennedy that our headquarters include a "Community Relations" division to work on neutralizing the religious opposition. He agreed, and to head this operation I secured James Wine, an able, industrious staff member of the National Council of Churches with whom I had worked on the "open letter" at the time of the West Virginia primary. During the remainder of the campaign, with two assistants and two stenographers, Wine answered six hundred to a thousand letters every week on religion, ranging from the most thoughtful to the most scurrilous; helped clarify Kennedy's position on all church-state matters;

encouraged Protestant publications, clergymen and conventions to decry the religious issue; distributed leaflets and films of the Senator's remarks on this subject; counseled local Democratic leaders on how to handle the religious opposition in their locales; and helped establish a series of denominational, national and state committees designed to attack the problem. In addition, panel discussions were sponsored and high-level interfaith appeals were encouraged.

Wine's job was not to exploit the religious issue. He was under strict orders not to raise it or encourage others to do so. His memorandum to his contacts in each state emphasized the Senator's policy "to meet the issue only when raised by others . . . to combat an attack . . . to answer questions." No office in the Kennedy-Democratic National Committee headquarters worked harder or made a more important contribution to the campaign.

Finally, we were organizing in those early weeks on the "intellectual" level. Stevenson and Bowles were both named as foreign policy advisers, although Eisenhower denied Kennedy's request that they be included in the CIA and Pentagon intelligence briefings arranged for both candidates. (The briefings, Kennedy told me, were largely superficial anyway and contained little he had not read in the *New York Times.*) Although Nixon in the South scornfully referred to "the party of Schlesinger, Galbraith, and Bowles," Galbraith perhaps spoke for the others when he wrote me from his Vermont vacation retreat about the delights of being credited with so much power in return for so little work.

At the actual working level, Archibald Cox, who had headed our academic advisers since January, left Harvard to devote full time to coordinating our new writers and the preparation of position papers. These papers—which, unlike Nixon's, were mostly for internal use—were often invaluable in the writing of major speeches or statements on defense, Latin America, economics and agriculture. Myer Feldman, whom I would call day and night for needed facts, headed a superb staff of researchers whose resources included the "Nixopedia"—a somewhat unwieldy collection of everything Nixon had said and how he had voted on every subject, supplemented daily during the campaign by notations on glaring inconsistencies between his past and present, or North and South, speeches. Feldman and the research staff were important also in providing statements, answers to questionnaires and position papers for both internal and external use.

Although a group of new speech-drafters was assembled in Washington from various parts of the writing profession, Goodwin and I, traveling with the candidate, found ourselves drafting almost every text. Two of the new writers, however, Joseph Kraft and John Bartlow Martin, worked tirelessly and usefully as speech "advance" men, preparing notes and outlines of local lore and issues for use in brief talks at airports, train stations and shopping centers.

THE CANDIDATE'S SPEECHES

I do not mean to imply that all the speeches written and delivered on the campaign trail were models of oratorical grace and intellectual depth. "A man's campaign speeches," Henry Stimson once said, "are no proper subject for the study of a friendly biographer." John Kennedy would not want to be measured solely by the speeches we ground out day and night across the country—and neither would I. Nor did he even follow his prepared text on the vast majority of occasions, deviating sometimes slightly with his own interjections and interpretations, more often substantially and sometimes completely. When a line proved successful at one stop, whether planned or improvised, he used it at the next and many times thereafter.

He was more at ease with speeches that emphasized the positive above the partisan. His spontaneous remarks were consistently more effective than his prepared texts because they were delivered with more conviction and vitality—although both he and the press were sometimes surprised, upon reading the transcript of a particularly successful extemporaneous talk, to find that the passages that sounded so memorable in his impassioned delivery were less impressive in cold print. Some of his speeches reflected disorganization, haste (his and mine) and fatigue (his and mine). In one talk, speaking hurriedly with few notes and little sleep, he repeated the same phrase three times in a single sentence. The crowd laughed, and so did Kennedy. "We are going to put this speech to music," he told them, "and make a fortune out of it."

Many of his off-the-cuff speeches were largely repetitious. Some, particularly near the close, were overly caustic and captious in their criticism of Nixon. Many left his audiences unmoved by his elevated language, flat tone and often strident voice. But not one lacked sincerity. Excepting occasional ones marked by fatigue, not one lacked dignity. Not one offered patronizingly simple solutions to agonizingly difficult problems. Not one varied his views for various audiences or had to be disavowed later.

They were generally factual, direct and specific.[1] They were always brief—usually five minutes at daytime stops, twenty minutes for the day's major gatherings, and completed long before his audience had had its fill. They were quickly delivered, with few frills and few pauses for applause. They conveyed a sense of concern and conviction,

[1] After a Senate committee published all the campaign speeches, more than one writer for subsequent candidates told me he borrowed generously from them.

a vast command of information, a disdain for demagoguery and a mood of cool, decisive leadership. They were confident but never arrogant. "I would run a campaign," he had said to an interviewer in July, "which attempted to show . . . the responsibilities of the United States in the 1960's . . . [and] why I think that the Democratic Party and I . . . could do a better job than Mr. Nixon . . . [he is] a formidable candidate . . . [but] I have no doubt that I can beat Mr. Nixon."

Unlike Mr. Nixon, the Senator attempted to tackle a new subject or combination of subjects in almost every speech—ranging from undeveloped nations to America's unemployed, from our lag in outer space to our lack of urban space, from arms to disarmament, from the problems of youth to the problems of the aged. But these announced subjects, whether mentioned briefly and then discarded, or stressed throughout the speech, often served only as a springboard to the single theme he pressed throughout the fall: the challenges of the sixties to America's security, America's prestige, America's progress. "It is time to get this country moving again," he proclaimed over and over again, inserting the phrase or a variation of it in his opening speeches until we included it in all his texts.

He disliked political exploitation of "motherhood," but, told early in the campaign that housewives would disapprove of Jacqueline's absence, he reluctantly and self-consciously explained during his two-day train trip through California, "She's home having a boy." He never mentioned the subject again.[2]

He never referred to himself in the third person or spoke humbly of the receptions he received. He never reminisced about his childhood or told anecdotes about his daughter. Though he often joked with his audiences, his speeches were generally meaty, serious calls to action. "The New Frontier," he told his Labor Day audience in Cadillac Square, Detroit, in words anticipating his Inaugural, "is not what I promise I am going to do for you; the New Frontier is what I ask you to do for our country."

At times his fervent idealism spellbound his listeners, both spectators, who neglected to applaud, and reporters, who neglected to take notes. "It is our obligation and our privilege," he said over and over, "to be the defenders of the gate in a time of maximum danger. If we fail, freedom fails. Has any people since Athens had a comparable responsibility and opportunity?"

"I don't run for the office of the Presidency to tell you what you want to hear," he said in his Portland, Maine, opener and repeatedly thereafter. "I run for the office of the Presidency because in a dangerous

2 When newsmen later asked him the secret of finding out the sex, he said, "She told me—you would have to ask her."

time we need to be told what we must do if we are going to maintain our freedom and the freedom of those who depend upon us. . . . You cannot be successful abroad unless you are successful at home."

By avoiding the tired phrases and promises of the traditional Democratic campaign, he avoided tiring himself. So long as he could be himself—candid, informal, confident, without false pretensions of either humility or grandeur—he could endure and even enjoy the exhausting schedule, the lack of sleep, the endless travel and the raw ugly blisters on his swollen right hand.

For the campaign, involving as it did the most intensive speaking schedule of all time, was a physical ordeal for everyone, and especially the Senator. In addition to almost daily statements and letters issued by Feldman, Cox or Bob Kennedy in the candidate's name from Washington, he spoke eight or ten times every day, sometimes in four or five states. In one week of eighteen-to-twenty-hour days he visited twenty-seven states. His first full *weekend* took him to Massachusetts, New Hampshire, Maine, California, Alaska and Michigan.

He often spoke at a midnight airport arrival and at an early breakfast the next morning. "Every time I get in in the middle of the day," he good-naturedly told one audience, "I look down at the schedule and there's five minutes allotted for the candidate to eat and rest." At one stop he stressed the urgency of providing medical care for the aged "especially as we are all aging very fast these days." "I am going to last about five more days," he said on November 3, "but that is time enough."

Actually, he seemed to gain strength and steam with each new audience. Among the staff and press who accompanied him, the unprecedented pace took a heavy toll. I know that the search for a few moments of sleep—on the plane, on the bus, even during the speeches—began to dominate my own thoughts. But not Kennedy. "He doesn't eat, he doesn't sleep, he doesn't do anything to keep fit," observed his wife, "but he thrives on it."

At times, to be sure, he was hoarse and weary and dark circles formed under his eyes. "You are not as gay as you used to be," observed a Mormon leader in Salt Lake. But he never lost his voice as he had in the West Virginia and Oregon primaries; indeed it seemed to grow stronger. His weight fluctuated wildly, as he missed meals and sleep on some days and snacked constantly on milk and soup between airports on others. He found it increasingly hard to rise at dawn, even when Dave Powers would rouse him with a cheery "What do you suppose Nixon's doing while you're lying there?" But each day the spirit and enthusiasm of his growing crowds renewed and refreshed his own.

Never, however, did he lose his dignity, his self-restraint or himself in the exuberance of the crowd. Never was he to be seen waving both arms above his head, hugging local politicians or shouting banalities for the sake of applause. He spoke crisply, earnestly, with his chin thrust upward and forward. The chopping right hand with which he emphasized his points was his only gesture. "If I have to hold both hands above my head to be President," he told one friend, "I'm not going to be President." His magnetic appeal to youth—the phenomenon of female "jumpers," "leapers," "touchers" and "screamers" in the crowds along his route—the recurrent risks they took darting between his moving motorcycle escorts to grasp his hand (including one woman who nearly dislocated his shoulder holding on as though frozen)—the sound of thousands upon thousands of milling, yelling fans—the sea of outstretched hands along airport fences and barricades—all this surprised and amused him without instilling a speck of overconfidence or conceit. It did not detract him from either the issues or the realities of the campaign. Much of the yelling and jumping, he knew, came from children. "If we can lower the voting age to nine, we are going to sweep this state," he said at one stop.

He could still look and laugh at himself with detachment. "I will never know," he remarked one day as he watched the sidewalk throngs at suppertime, "why anyone would leave his home just to watch a politician go by." "Do you realize," he teased one of his liberal supporters, "the responsibility I carry? I'm the only person between Nixon and the White House."

When a turbulent crowd nearly deafened him with acclaim in the closing weeks of the campaign, he said in feigned solemnity to one reporter, "Do you figure this was how it was for Dewey in. . . . 1948?" When the crowd in Cincinnati laughed at his pronunciation of the city's name, he smilingly said that was what the city was called in Boston "and I am from Boston. We will explain to you how to pronounce it." When the microphone at the St. Paul airport failed to work, he was undisturbed. "I understand that Daniel Webster used to address 100,000 people . . . without a mike," he told the crowd. "We are a little softer than they used to be, however."

No situation ruffled his composure, every situation had its humor. When he was presented with a symbolic key to the city by the Republican Mayor of Niagara Falls, New York, he expressed the hope that the Mayor "will not take my key away if I make a few unkind remarks about his party. . . . I won't include him in them at all." When he had to be told by a Pocatello, Idaho, press conference that the local Burns Creek reclamation project had already come before the Senate, the Senator was embarrassed but not shaken. "It is early in the morning," he said. "I am sure . . . Frank Church . . . will tell me about it for the rest of the morning." (Kennedy also told his advance men and research men about it for the rest of the morning, in terms designed to make certain he was never caught napping again.)

When interrupted by an enthusiast in a Brooklyn arena, he calmly replied, "Let me speak first and then you—OK?" When his automobile loudspeaker was insufficient for one crowd, he stopped his speech, climbed to the top of a building and resumed: "As I was saying . . ." When a fire engine roared up, he said, "Tell the fire department it is just Democrats on fire." When Republicans at the American Legion Convention circulated copies of his famous 1949 attack, he said smilingly in his introduction, "I have learned a good deal about the Legion— especially since 1949." He had to cut short an airport stop in North Dakota to enable his plane to leave the unlit field before dark. But it was all right, he said—"The lights are going out for the Republican Party all over the United States."

Nixon supporters, signs and hecklers frequently appeared at his rallies in Republican areas, but they never fazed him. When a drunken, belligerent woman ran up to his motorcade in Milwaukee and flung a glass of whiskey in his face, he quickly wiped off the whiskey, handed back the tumbler and said in even tones, "Here's your glass." When, in the midst of another fatiguing motorcade through a working-class district, he saw among all his fervent well-wishers two well-dressed men in silk suits giving him a contemptuous gesture, he confided to me that he would enjoy nothing more than leaping out and punching them both in the nose—but he only smiled and waved.

"Just listen," he told a group of Young Republican hecklers at New York University. "You won't learn anything if you are talking." Later the same group interrupted his speech with chants of "We want Nixon." "I don't think you're going to get him, though," said the Senator good-naturedly as the crowd cheered. And he addressed the conclusion of his remarks to "all you young Nixonites—all eight of you."

In Owosso, Michigan, describing the pitiful surplus food packages he had seen in West Virginia, he heard boos in the crowd. "You can boo," he said with some emphasis, "but you can't eat it . . . you can't possibly dispose of [these] problems . . . by booing. You have to do something about it. That is what this election is all about." And to a Nixon picket perched on a telephone pole he had called, "If you just stay up there until November 9 we can settle this whole matter."

The campaign raised no clear-cut, decisive issue, and, except for the Peace Corps, no new proposals. Issues such as Cuba, agriculture, education, minimum wages, the missile gap and Quemoy-Matsu rose and faded throughout the fall. Kennedy did not attempt to create any single specific issue. Instead, he jammed his speeches with a whole series of facts and figures to express his dissatisfaction with standing still, his contention that America could do better. Fewer than a hundred people scattered throughout government are working on disarmament, he said, one-fifth as many as work for the U.S. Battle Monuments Commission.[3] Drawing on the administration's own figures on malnutrition, he overdramatized them by saying seventeen million Americans go to bed hungry every night ("Most of them on Metrecal," cracked one Republican).

Often in one speech—and sometimes in one paragraph or even one sentence—he would cite the average wage of female laundry workers in our five largest cities, the average Social Security check, the number of families with less than $1,000 income, the number receiving surplus food packages, the number of workers not protected by minimum wages, the number of families in substandard housing, the proportion of unemployed and their average jobless benefit, the proportion of steel capacity unused, the proportion of high school graduates unable to attend college, the rise in surplus food storage and the decline in home building. He gave precise figures on UN voting, Latin-American broadcasts, loans to Africa and Latin America and the number of Negro judges and Foreign Service officers. He compared our economic growth and our graduation of scientists and engineers with more impressive Soviet gains. He knew how many classrooms and how many jobs this nation would need over the next ten years. He quoted per capita income figures for Libya and India, and the number of college graduates in the Congo. Each torrent of statistics began with "I am not satisfied when . . ." or "Do you realize that . . ." or "Our party will be needed so long as . . ." And each one ended with "I think we can do better—we have to do better. . . . I do not accept the view that our high noon is past. Our brightest days can be ahead."

He used apt, sharp illustrations. In a farm speech, for example, he referred to the farmer who said he "hoped to break even this year because he really needed the money"—to the judgment that Khrushchev, if given his choice between fifty American scientists and fifty American farmers, would surely choose the latter—and to the children he saw in the hollows of West Virginia taking their free school lunch home to share with their impoverished parents while surpluses rotted nearby.

"The first living creatures to orbit the earth in space and return," he pointed out, "were dogs named Strelka and Belka, not Rover or Fido —or Checkers." Mr. Nixon, he was fond of recalling aloud, shook his finger in Khrushchev's face in their famous "kitchen debate" and proclaimed, "You may be ahead of us in rocket thrust but we are ahead of you in color television." "I will take my television in black and white,"

[3] Nixon replied that they had quality, not quantity. "I don't know who these geniuses are," said Kennedy, "but it is a terrible burden for a hundred men."

said the Senator. "I want to be ahead in rocket thrust. . . . Mr. Nixon may be very experienced in kitchen debates, but so are a great many other married men I know."

He repeatedly pointed to the inadequacies of the number of scholarships we had offered Black Africa, the number of Foreign Service personnel there (less than we had in West Germany alone) and the number of Voice of America broadcasts. The nationalist movements around the world, he said, had traditionally used American slogans and quoted American statesmen, not Russian. But now the United States was neglecting them. "There are children in Africa named Thomas Jefferson, George Washington and Abraham Lincoln," he said more than once. "There are none called Lenin or Trotsky or Stalin—or Nixon." (In Harlem, where Congressman Powell had given him a rousing introduction, he added: "There may be a couple of them called Adam Clayton Powell"—causing the Rev. Powell to lean forward and say, "Careful, Jack.")

He had local information at his fingertips as well. He decried the price of corn in Sanborn, Minnesota, the number of layoffs in International Harvester plants in Illinois, the amount of coal mined and food distributed in McDowell County, West Virginia, and the declining number of oil safety shoes sold by Sam Gray in Wichita Falls, Texas.

In Sharon, Pennsylvania, he could deplore Eisenhower's veto of the Sharpville Dam. In Schenectady he could compare our defenses to the failure of the early settlers of that city to prepare for an Indian massacre. In Rochester he quoted an earlier Republican candidate as having referred to it as Syracuse—proof, he said, that Republicans never did know where they were or where they were going. Repeatedly he said, "I want a world which looks to the United States for leadership, which does not always read what Mr. Khrushchev is doing or what Mr. Castro is doing. I want them to read what the President of the United States is doing."

He identified Nixon, who understandably preferred to forget party labels, with Republican "stand-pat" slogans and candidates of the last half-century or more—McKinley, Harding, Coolidge, Hoover, Landon and Dewey. "Where do they get those candidates?" he asked his audiences. But even as he criticized all the deeds and misdeeds of the last eight years, he avoided direct attacks on the popular Eisenhower. The latter, he said, was "a help to Mr. Nixon. I would be glad to have his cooperation, but I think he is already committed."

He knew that there was probably a greater gap between the views of Eisenhower and Kennedy—on space, defense, social welfare and all the rest—than between those of Nixon and Kennedy. But he also knew, and freely admitted in private, that had the Constitution permitted Eisenhower to seek a third term, no Democratic candidate including Kennedy could have defeated him. Had the Republicans, he felt, nominated Nelson Rockefeller, who would not need to defend the administration and who often sounded like Kennedy on defense and economic growth, the New York Governor might have been able to outflank the Kennedy position and win the race. (His only comment on Rockefeller's early 1960 withdrawal, however, had been an expression of sympathy for the fact that Nixon had now lost the chance to present his views in contested, and thus more interesting, primaries.)

Nixon, forced on the defensive, brought in references to Eisenhower, but not his party, whenever possible. The Vice President's speeches were rosy and reassuring about America's leadership, strength and economy, —and this, said Kennedy, "is the basic issue that separates us." It is a contest, he said, "between the comfortable and the concerned."

I have read since the close of the campaign that Kennedy's speeches were tailored to each audience through the advice of an official campaign psychologist, a professor of speech, a series of Harris Polls, a professional gag writer, and a "people machine" computer. Having drafted, revised or reviewed every text, I can categorically deny such assertions. Neither speeches nor debate preparations were based on any "people machine." Considerable self-advertising by a group called the Simulmatics Corporation has given the impression that their computer analyses of public opinion research were read and adapted by Kennedy and all his top advisers. In truth, their reports, when read at all, were no more valuable than the "issues polls" that were fed into their computers. They contained all the same faults: they restated the obvious, reflected the bias of the original pollsters and were incapable of precise application. Nor were any gag writers hired—or needed. To be sure, Harris Polls were taken and read. A voice teacher did try to warn the candidate against laryngitis. But most speech topics I discussed with the Senator only, and they were decided by him, in his plane or hotel and without reference to other materials, a day or two before the speech was given.

Ideas for speeches came from a variety of sources, including newsmen, advance men and the Washington research and speech staff. Some thoughts had been brewing for months. The Peace Corps proposal, for example, was based on the Mormon and other voluntary religious service efforts, on an editorial Kennedy had read years earlier, on a speech by General Gavin, on a luncheon I had with a Philadelphia businessman, on the suggestions of his academic advisers, on legislation previously introduced and on the written response to a spontaneous late-night challenge he issued to Michigan students.

In many cases the topic was suggested by the interests or economic conditions of the local community. But he made no effort to appease or comfort each audience. Addressing the Steelworkers Convention after their president had proposed a thirty-two-hour work week, he said the Communist challenge required this nation to meet its unemployment problems by creating abundance rather than rationing scarcity.

The "new" Nixon continually engaged in personalities. (Nixon favorites: "It's not Jack's money he's spending, it's yours. . . . He may have more dollars but you have more sense. . . . I'm sick and tired of his whining.") When Nixon called him too "naïve and inexperienced" to stand up to Khrushchev," and GOP National Chairman Morton accused him of "giving aid and comfort to the Communists" by deploring America's pace, Kennedy struck back hard: "It is not naïve to call for increased strength. It is naïve to think that freedom can prevail without it. . . . Personal attacks and insults will not halt the spread of Communism. Nor will they win the November election."

Kennedy, while constantly deriding Nixon's record and speeches, refused to touch rumors of a Nixon mortgage scandal, acquitted Nixon of any role in religious bigotry, and stepped over the borders of fair comment only twice that I remember: once when he called Nixon's original position on risking war for Quemoy and Matsu "trigger-happy" and once when, in answering a question, he referred to Nixon's support by the Ku Klux Klan (although he quickly went on to emphasize that he knew Nixon had no sympathy with the Klan viewpoint). Some time after Nixon had been hospitalized with a knee infection, Kennedy pointed out to a news conference that he had pledged not to "mention him, unless I could praise him, until he got out of the hospital—and I have not mentioned him."

But as soon as Nixon was out campaigning again, Kennedy was briefed daily on his opponent's speeches and tore into them almost daily. The Vice President, he reported on one occasion, had said unemployment "cannot become a significant issue in the minds of a great many people" unless it goes over 4.5 million. "I would think it would become a significant issue to the 4,499,000 . . . unemployed." And throughout Truman territory he said, "Last Thursday night Mr. Nixon dismissed me as 'another Truman.' I regard that as a great compliment, and I have no hesitation in returning the compliment. I consider him another Dewey."

He could be equally sharp with other attackers. Told at a press conference of the latest in a series of harsh statements by Senator Hugh Scott of Pennsylvania, with whom he had tangled in the Senate, he referred to Scott's membership on the Republican "Truth Squad" and added, "He may well have lost his membership today."

While campaigning was built around speeches, equally important were the motorcades, handshaking, personal appearances and repeated question-and-answer sessions. In the latter, Kennedy was at his best—

fluent, factual and deft, with a natural eloquence. When written questions were used, those selected were usually screened by Goodwin or me—not to avoid controversial issues, such as religion and agriculture, but to make certain they were included in the allotted time. Occasionally we planted a question, usually humorous or homey questions that had spontaneously appeared in earlier audiences. But even these were not told to the candidate in advance, for he preferred not to be forewarned.

Questions on his religion did not need to be planted in his first question-and-answer session. Asked whether a Catholic *could* be elected President, he replied, "With all due respect, it seems to me that question is worded wrongly. Can an American who happens to be a Catholic be elected President?" When he spoke from the rear platform of his train at Modesto, California, a question was shouted from the crowd: "Do you believe all Protestants are heretics?" "No," the Senator shot back. "And I hope you don't believe all Catholics are." At another train stop in Jackson, Michigan, a young student called up: "What shall I tell my parents who don't want to vote for you because of your religion?" "Ask them to study my statements and record," said the Senator, "and then . . . tell them to read the U.S. Constitution, which says there shall be no religious test for office."

"If 99 percent of the population were Catholic," he told a nationwide TV panel, referring to a POAU prediction that if the United States ever became 51 percent Catholic, Protestants would be treated as second-class citizens and damned souls, "I would still be opposed to . . . an official state church. I do not want civil power combined with religious power. . . . If some other Catholic in another country holds a different view, that's their right, but I want to make it clear that I am committed, as a matter of deep personal conviction, to this separation. Now what is there left to say?"

Campaigning also meant talking with the press, at first formally in press conferences and then informally on plane and train. Reporters covering Nixon soon memorized the banal sentimentalities he repeated in each speech and found them difficult to report. Their difficulty in reporting Kennedy's speeches was his tendency to be what they nicknamed a "text deviate," his rapid-fire interjection of more statistics and statements than they could note. But his unusual accessibility to reporters, his frank and friendly talks with them, his growing confidence, and the excitement generated by his crowds after the first television debate, all contributed to their growing respect for Kennedy and their glowing dispatches back home. There was, moreover, an atmosphere of conviviality in the Kennedy press entourage, encouraged by Salinger's efficient arrangements for their baggage, transportation, accommodations, instant speech transcripts and inflated crowd estimates from friendly local officials, and heightened by the attitude of enthusiasm and gaiety which spread from the candidate to his staff to the press. (The long weeks of travel together also encouraged the flowering of a certain amount of romance between secretaries, reporters and photographers, thereby adding to the atmosphere of camaraderie.)

For one long October day in Hyannis Port, and briefly in New York, on the plane and elsewhere, campaigning also meant strategy sessions with all the top team from Washington. But these sessions were largely confined to confirming the wisdom of what the candidate was already doing: identifying Nixon with Republicanism, not with Eisenhower.

Finally, campaigning meant seemingly endless travel, on and off planes, trains, buses, cars.

Although forty-five of the fifty states were visited, and no state could be taken for granted, those states with slender electoral totals or slim Democratic chances were visited only once in order to concentrate on more critical areas. Roughly three-quarters of the candidate's time was spent in the twenty-four most doubtful states and nearly three-fifths of his time in the seven largest. These seven, plus most of New England and the South, were the basis of his campaign strategy. The schedule was adjusted from time to time in accordance with the results of polls and political reports. Time did not permit him to carry out his original plan to open in Hawaii. Nevada, like Hawaii, had too few electoral votes to be squeezed in; and Nebraska was included only for a late-summer briefing at Strategic Air Command Headquarters. Arkansas was included only to the degree that the town of Texarkana is in Arkansas as well as Texas, and Alabama, Mississippi and Louisiana were thought better left to local loyalists and Lyndon Johnson.

In fact, the entire South depended considerably on Johnson, and Kennedy was delighted with the reports on his running mate's progress in that area. Campaigning as the grandson of a Confederate soldier and as a more hard-hitting partisan than previously, the Majority Leader whistle-stopped through Dixie decrying the religious issue, deriding Nixon's experience, detailing Republican shortcomings, warning of the dangers of divided government, praising Kennedy, mixing in a few homely Texas stories, reminiscing about his kinship with each state and refusing to back down on civil rights. Unlike his opposite number, Ambassador Lodge, Johnson at no time made any statement which caused Kennedy embarrassment or regret. He was aided, as had been the Kennedy girls on an earlier swing, by the remarkable campaign talents of his wife Lady Bird.

Equally as important as Johnson's platform "pitch" was the persuasive pressure he brought to bear on Southern Senators, governors and local leaders who had theretofore refused to work for a politically unpopular ticket. Many had merely announced their support, denounced the platform and done nothing further. Others had remained wholly mute. But Johnson impressed them with the practical political fact that, win or lose, he and Kennedy would have considerable influence over the passage of legislation and the pipeline to public funds—"and we're going to win." In Virginia Harry Byrd would not come to listen. In South Carolina Strom Thurmond was as opposed as always. But elsewhere Johnson's powerful listeners got the point and climbed aboard not only the campaign train but the campaign team.

While Lyndon Johnson stemmed the tide of Southern white revolt, John Kennedy's very human call to Negro leader Martin Luther King's pregnant wife on the occasion of his arrest by a Georgia traffic officer—combined with Bob Kennedy's indignant protest to the judge who jailed him—may have impressed both Negroes and whites because of the political risk. More on that and other underlying factors later.

THE PERSISTENT RELIGIOUS ISSUE

The roughest issue in the South, as elsewhere, was religion. The issue was quickly brought to a head on September 7 with the founding of a new organization of very prominent Protestant clergymen, the National Conference of Citizens for Religious Freedom. At the close of their day-long meeting behind closed doors, a public statement laid down a barrage of challenges to Senator Kennedy which made clear that, whatever his answers would be, his religion made him unacceptable for the Presidency. Kennedy, they said, had not repudiated all the teachings of his church and could not be free of its hierarchy's "determined efforts . . . to breach the wall of separation of church and state." Like Khrushchev, said the Rev. Harold Ockenga of Boston, Kennedy is "a captive of a system."[4]

Presiding over the Conference and serving as its spokesman to the press was a prominent Republican clergyman, author and lecturer, the Rev. Norman Vincent Peale of New York. (Peale was also a friend of Nixon's, and when asked why the group had raised no questions on Nixon's religion, Peale replied, "I didn't know that he ever let it bother him.") No Catholics, Jews or liberal Protestants had been invited, he said, and no details would be given out on who organized the Conference, who financed it or who drafted its declaration. During the Conference Peale had been overheard saying, "Our American culture is at stake. I don't say it won't survive [Kennedy's election], but it won't be what it was." (Upon hearing this Kennedy remarked, "I would like to think he was complimenting me, but I'm not sure he was.")

---

4 Hung on the Conference wall was the slogan: "Take Care to be Fair," and their statement opened with a declaration against "hate-mongering, bigotry [and] unfounded charges."

The "Peale group," as it was thereafter called, stirred a wave of anger and dismay from coast to coast. Many who had previously assumed that intolerance was confined to "backwoods Bible-thumpers" were shocked by the transparent unfairness of three aspects of the meeting:

1. Men well known to be Republicans had pretended their opposition to Kennedy was for religious reasons.
2. Protestant clergymen opposed to the Catholic Church's intervention in politics showed no compunction about openly intervening themselves.
3. The political position of the Catholic Church had not only been inaccurately described but also inaccurately ascribed to Senator Kennedy, whose own views and legislative votes the group largely discounted.

There was nothing new about any of these three phenomena. Similar attacks had been made in all parts of the country, in intellectual as well as scurrilous tones, and by prominent preachers as well as hate groups. But the "Peale group" was the best publicized. One result was the withdrawal by several newspapers of Peale's spiritual advice column and the withdrawal by Dr. Peale from the "Peale group." He had no disagreement with what was said and done but wanted everyone to know that he had nothing to do with it. "I do not now or never have had any relationship with the group, except attendance upon this one meeting," he wrote in a form letter which regretted his "distorted publicity" but not his participation in the meeting. "The press has continued to emphasize me personally, without reference to any of the [other] 150 persons present, which I must say seems unfair . . . perhaps I will be a wiser person in the future—at least, let us hope so." No more was heard during the campaign from the author of *Confident Living*.

The Peale publicity helped set the stage for Kennedy's major response to his attackers. He agreed, with considerable reluctance, to accept an invitation to appear before the Houston, Texas, Ministerial Association to discuss the religious issue on the evening of Monday, September 12. Nixon had declined a similar invitation from the same group.

We worked on the speech throughout a weekend "rest" in Los Angeles and overnight in El Paso. My chief source of material was Kennedy's own previous statements on religion to the ASNE, to the convention, to press conferences and to *Look Magazine*. One of the additional facts desired by the Senator, inasmuch as he was speaking at the Alamo in San Antonio on the way to Houston, was how many Catholics had died at that shrine of Texas independence. I telephoned Mike Feldman in Washington at 4 A.M. Texas time. A few hours later he had a list of possible Irish-American names but added that no religious affiliations were known. Thus was born a line in the speech: ". . . side by side with Bowie and Crockett died McCafferty and Bailey and Carey, but no one knows whether they were Catholics or not. For there was no religious test at the Alamo."

The Senator's desire was to state his position so clearly and comprehensively that no reasonable man could doubt his adherence to the Constitution. All year his critics had pointed to the Catholic attacks on his *Look* interview as proof that his church would resist his position. In the hopes of avoiding any loose wording this time that would unnecessarily stir up the Catholic press, I read the speech over the telephone to the Rev. John Courtney Murray, S.J., a leading and liberal exponent of the Catholic position on church and state. On the plane to Houston, the speech, along with all possible questions that might follow from the floor, was also reviewed with both James Wine and his temporary aide, John Cogley, a Catholic scholar formerly with *Commonweal* magazine. The Senator, resting his strained vocal chords, wrote out his questions and comments on a scratch pad, laughing at his lack of theological training and showing no apprehension over the trial he was about to face.

That night, in the ballroom of Houston's Rice Hotel, I sat in the audience with Cogley as we waited for the program to begin. Inasmuch as the meeting was to be televised throughout the state of Texas, all were silently in their places waiting for the hour to strike. The Senator, in black suit and black tie (but wearing brown shoes, his black shoes having been accidentally left on the plane to the chagrin of Dave Powers), flanked by the two ministers who presided, sat somewhat nervously behind the lectern. Glaring at him from the other side were the Protestant ministers of Houston. "They're tired of being called bigots for opposing a Catholic," Pierre Salinger had earlier reported to the Senator as he dressed. Also on hand was a large number of national press pundits who had flown in for the great confrontation. A sense of tension and hostility hung in the air. The few minutes of waiting seemed endless. John Cogley whispered to me, "This is one time we need those types that pray for Notre Dame before each football game!"

At last the Senator was introduced, and the atmosphere eased almost at once. It was the best speech of his campaign and one of the most important in his life. Only his Inaugural Address could be said to surpass it in power and eloquence. Both Protestants and Catholics acclaimed his succinct summation of belief: "not what kind of church I believe in, for that should be important only to me, but what kind of America I believe in."

I believe in an America where the separation of church and state is absolute—where no Catholic prelate would tell the President (should he be Catholic) how to act, and no Protestant minister would tell his parishioners for whom to vote—where no church or church school is granted any public funds or political preference . . . an America that is officially neither Catholic, Protestant nor Jewish—where no public official either requests or accepts instructions on public policy from . . . any . . . ecclesiastical source . . . where there is no Catholic vote, no anti-Catholic vote, no bloc voting of any kind . . . and where religious liberty is so indivisible that an act against one church is treated as an act against all.

He reminded his listeners that other faiths—including the Baptist—had been harassed in earlier days. "Today," he said, in a passage he had inserted in the final draft, "I may be the victim, but tomorrow it may be you."

The religious views of the American President, he said, must be "his own private affair, neither imposed by him upon the nation nor imposed by the nation upon him as a condition to holding that office." Citing his record on church-state issues, he asked to be judged on that basis and not on the

pamphlets and publications . . . that carefully select quotations out of context from the statements of Catholic Church leaders, usually in other countries, frequently in other centuries. . . .

I am not the Catholic candidate for President, I am the Democratic Party's candidate for President who happens also to be a Catholic. I do not speak for my church on public matters, and the church does not speak for me.

In the most controversial paragraph of the speech, Kennedy said he would resign his office rather than violate the national interest in order to avoid violating his conscience. That passage, which the Senator had long deliberated and which he rightly predicted would be criticized, was based on my talk months earlier with Bishop Wright. Although Kennedy did "not concede any conflict to be even remotely possible," this single sentence was designed to still those Protestant critics who were certain he would succumb to pressure and those Catholics critics who were certain he would stifle his faith. "I hope," he added, that "any conscientious public servant would do the same."

After the speech came a barrage of questions, none of them wholly friendly. More than one question related to the story circulated by a well-known preacher, publicist and onetime Republican candidate for Mayor of Philadelphia, the Rev. Daniel Poling. Congressman Kennedy had been invited by Dr. Poling to a fund-raising dinner in honor of a chapel, located in a Baptist church, which paid tribute to the heroic four chaplains (including Dr. Poling's son) who went down with the *S.S. Dorchester* in the Second World War. As stated in the Reverend's *Autobiography,* released in late 1959, Kennedy was to be the "spokesman for his Roman Catholic faith" at the dinner. A prominent Protestant and Jewish leader were also scheduled to speak. When the Congressman belatedly learned that the Archdiocese of Philadelphia did not support the project or dinner, he told Rev. Poling with some embarrassment that he could not accept the invitation after all because he had no credentials "to attend in the capacity in which I had been asked." He could and would have attended, he said repeatedly in 1960, in the role of Congressman, ex-serviceman or private citizen. Nevertheless, the incident was cited by Poling, and subsequently by thousands of others, as proof of Kennedy's subservience to the hierarchy.

"I had been in politics probably two months and was relatively inexperienced," said the Senator. "I should have inquired before. . . . [But] is this the best that . . . can be charged after fourteen years?" He had concluded a series of letters to Dr. Poling in July, 1960, by emphasizing that he would have no "reluctance in accepting an invitation to any public occasion in my capacity as a Massachusetts legislator or public official, without regard to any requests not to keep that engagement emanating from any source, ecclesiastical, political or otherwise." But the original story was still circulated in anti-Catholic literature, and Dr. Poling ignored Kennedy's reply when he was in touch with the Houston ministers.

The Senator fielded all questions with ease and without evasion. Asked if he would intercede with Cardinal Cushing to obtain the Pope's approval of his position, he said no ecclesiastical official should interfere in public policy and no public official in ecclesiastical policy. Asked if he had the approval of the Vatican for his statement, he said he did not need such approval. Asked what his response would be if his church attempted to influence his public duties, he said he would "reply to them that this was an improper action on their part . . . one to which I could not subscribe, that I was opposed to it . . . [as] an interference with the American political system."

He made clear that he had not read and was not bound by all the documents and doctrines quoted to him—that he believed not all but the "overwhelming majority of American Catholics" shared his views— that he could attend in his capacity as President any Protestant funeral or other service—and that he did not look upon those who sincerely asked his views as bigots. He concluded with the hope that the discussion would assist them "to make a careful judgment," although "I am sure I have made no converts to my church."

The Houston speech did make some converts to his candidacy. It impressed all who watched it then and later. "As we say in my part of Texas," said Sam Rayburn, "he ate 'em blood raw."

The Houston confrontation did not end the religious controversy or silence the Senator's critics, but it was widely and enthusiastically applauded, not only in the Rice Hotel Ballroom but all across Texas and the nation. It made unnecessary any further full-scale answer from the candidate, and Kennedy, while continuing to answer questions, never raised the subject again. It offered in one document all the answers to all the questions any reasonable man could ask. It helped divide the citizens legitimately concerned about Kennedy's views from the fanatics who had condemned him from birth.

But the issue did not die. Many who approved of the Houston speech demanded a statement by the Pope as well. Others said Kennedy was lying. Some said Kennedy was fine, but his election would pave the way for future Catholic Presidents who might not share his views. Some said they would still vote against Kennedy as a protest against his church. Others invented quotations of what he had said or cited Catholic criticisms of his earlier statements. "It's frustrating," said the Senator. "I've made my views clear month after month and year after year. I've answered every question. My public record is spread out over fourteen years . . . but it seems difficult to ever give some people the assurance they need that I'm as interested in religious liberty as they are."

But he maintained his good humor on the subject. When Harry Truman was chastised by Nixon for telling Southerners who vote Republican to go to hell, Kennedy said he would wire the former President "that our side [must] try to refrain from raising the religious issue."

To avoid charges that his side was raising the issue—a charge which always angered him, as he undertook only to defend himself—the Senator repudiated two labor-backed pamphlets which by implication connected Nixon and the Republicans with anti-Catholic propaganda. At all times he acquitted Nixon and Nixon's party of any responsibility for the growing tide of intolerance.

The Republicans were, in fact, handling the religious issue very shrewdly. To be sure, they continually mentioned the issue by deploring it.[6] Nixon repeatedly declared that both candidates should refrain from discussing the subject.[7]

6 The Gallup Poll, which showed only 47 percent of the electorate aware of Kennedy's religion in May, 1959, showed 87 percent aware of it in August, 1960, with the number rising steadily.

7 Refusing to answer questionnaires from the Baptists and others on all the church-state issues he knew Kennedy would have to answer, he did send one telegram saying each state should decide whether to use Federal funds for parochial schools. Had Kennedy so equivocated, he would have been denounced from a thousand pulpits.

Kennedy did refrain from raising it, but not his attackers. The President of the Southern Baptist Convention, Dr. Ramsey Pollard, insisted as he campaigned vigorously for Nixon:

> No matter what Kennedy might say, he cannot separate himself from his church if he is a true Catholic. . . . All we ask is that Roman Catholicism lift its bloody hand from the throats of those that want to worship in the church of their choice. . . . I am not a bigot.

In another "unbigoted" talk, the same Dr. Pollard warned: "My church has enough members to beat Kennedy in this area if they all vote like I tell them to."

There were, to be sure, scattered "declarations of conscience" by Protestant and Jewish groups denouncing the issue, commending Kennedy's stand or pointing out that the separation of church and state should not apply to Catholics only. But these were lonely voices, particularly among Southern Baptists, the Church of Christ and other Fundamentalist and evangelical sects. Opposition on religious grounds was not confined to any one group. While it was more open in the South, it was felt in all sections. While it was led by clergymen, it was aided by laymen. While it was worse in rural areas, it was bad in the cities. While the professional hatemongers were all active, they were outnumbered by supposedly respectable Protestant leaders.

Well over three hundred different anti-Catholic tracts, distributed to more than twenty million homes, and countless mailings, chain letters, radio broadcasts, television attacks and even anonymous telephone calls inflamed and assaulted the voters' senses, at a cost to someone of at least several hundred thousands of dollars. One rightist publication could not decide whether Kennedy's election was a Popish plot or Communist conspiracy, but thought the two worked together anyway. Another said Kennedy stirred up the religious issue to conceal the fact that he was a Communist. One theme persisted: that the Pope would soon be governing America. (Bishop Wright had told me that in 1959 Pope John, who had been trying to learn English, asked him about Kennedy's chances. "Very good," Bishop Wright replied—and the Pope, fully aware of the 1928 stories, jokingly added, "Do not expect me to run a country with a language as difficult as yours.")

Not all the peddlers of venom denied the label of bigotry. The Rev. Harvey Springer, self-named "the cowboy evangelist of the Rockies," seemed proud to be called a bigot. "Let the Romanists move out of America," he cried. "Did you see the coronation of Big John [Pope John]? Let's hope we never see the coronation of Little John. . . . How many Catholics came over on the *Mayflower*? Not one . . . The Constitution is a Protestant Constitution."

But others who rationalized the religious attack spoke in more subtle terms. David Lawrence, in his national news magazine, justified all religious votes for Nixon on the grounds that it was traditional that "citizens do vote their prejudices." Dr. George L. Ford of the National Association of Evangelicals declared that "religion definitely should not be an issue in politics—and wouldn't be if the Catholic Church hadn't made it so." His Association led, although with limited success, an attempt to convert Reformation Sunday on October 30, nine days before the election, into an excuse for anti-Catholic, anti-Kennedy sermons and rallies.

TELEVISION AND THE DEBATES

Kennedy realized that his most urgent campaign task was to become better known for something other than his religion. Over five hundred speeches, press conferences and statements in forty-five states would help, but even the most enormous crowds could total only a tiny fraction of the entire electorate. The answer was television.

Kennedy's style was ideally suited to this medium. His unadorned manner of delivery, his lack of gestures and dramatic inflections, his slightly shy but earnest charm, may all have been handicaps on the hustings, but they were exactly right for the living room. He had seen in West Virginia tiny ramshackle shacks with no plumbing, and no newspapers or magazines, but with large television aerials. He had seen surveys showing twice as many Americans citing television as their primary source of campaign information as those citing press and periodicals. Appearing on the Jack Paar network variety show was inappropriate for a dignified nominee, he concluded, after Nixon had appeared (and a Kennedy appearance had been promised). But otherwise the Kennedy campaign organization sought every possible use of the medium—obtaining state-wide television for his major address in each state, taping a series of presentations by the candidate on individual issues, showing as commercials selected excerpts from his campaigning in different areas, and making a few nationwide TV addresses, always before enthusiastic audiences instead of a studio camera. The timing of his half-hour shows was carefully selected with an eye to what programs would be displaced, thus displeasing their fans, and what programs would compete for an audience. Five-minute "spot" presentations were also strategically placed at the end of popular shows.

But the high cost of radio and television strained party finances— over one million dollars for network time alone. Steve Smith approached Nixon's campaign manager, Leonard Hall, about an agreement limiting the amount of broadcast time each candidate would purchase, but to no avail. We also tried to utilize every possible offer of free television time.

Invitations to appear on news panel shows, at-home-with-the-candidate shows, campaign documentaries and candidate profiles were all promptly accepted. But these, and all other uses of television save possibly the replays of the Houston ministers speech, pale in significance beside the Great Debates of 1960.

The national radio-television networks, at a cost of millions of dollars (and unknown numbers of disgruntled situation-comedy and Western fans), had earlier offered the two major parties free time for joint appearances, if Congress would suspend the rule requiring equal time for all fringe party candidates. The Congress, in what turned out to be the most important action of its postconvention session, passed the law and President Eisenhower signed it on August 24.

Like all leading Republicans, Eisenhower advised Nixon not to debate Kennedy, and he stressed in signing the bill that its use did not require "a debating atmosphere." Nixon was far better known nationally than his opponent. He was regarded as more mature and experienced. He had no reason to help build an audience for Kennedy, who had scored well debating Lodge in 1952, Humphrey in West Virginia and Johnson at the Los Angeles Convention.

But Nixon also had reason for self-confidence. He had launched his political career in 1946 by outdebating an able Congressman. His "Checkers" speech in 1952, defending his private political fund, was generally regarded as the most skillful use of television in the campaign that sent him to the Vice Presidency. His impromptu "kitchen debate" with Chairman Khrushchev in Moscow had measurably improved his ratings in the polls.

With this reputation to defend, with confidence in his ability to best Kennedy, with a desire to reach through the debates the millions of Democrats and independents whose votes he would need, reportedly with an eye to the financial advantages of free television, and mindful that the two National Chairmen had implicitly committed both candidates to accept in the public interest, Nixon felt unable to back away gracefully. In August, immediately after his nomination at the Republican Convention, the networks made a concrete offer. Kennedy immediately accepted with a blunt challenge to Nixon. Four days later, to the Senator's surprise and joy, the Vice President also accepted.

There followed a series of negotiations between representatives of the candidates and the networks. Kennedy TV chief Leonard Reinsch and I, representing the Senator, found the Nixon representatives as wary as we. The original network proposal was for four evenings of straight debate, one hour each, and four evenings of joint panel interviews, one hour each. Nixon, confident only that he was a better debater, preferred only three confrontations or less and emphasized no prepared texts.

Kennedy, confident only that increased TV exposure was to his benefit, preferred five or more joint appearances. Both men, anxious to avoid the role of prosecutor but anxious to see a sharp division, welcomed the presence of a panel. Both men were also anxious to settle the matter in order to arrange their schedules. Kennedy was opposed to including the Vice Presidential candidates. Nixon wanted the debates out of the way before he began the final three-week drive he thought would decide the election.

Agreement was finally reached on a series of four one-hour appearances to be carried simultaneously by all television and radio networks:

1. September 26: "Debate" on domestic policy, 8-minute opening statements by each candidate, questions from a panel of correspondents, 3-5 minute closing statements. Originating in Chicago.

2 and 3. October 7 and 13: Question periods only, with each candidate questioned in turn and given an opportunity to "comment" on the other's answers. Answers were limited to $2\frac{1}{2}$ minutes, "comments" to $1\frac{1}{2}$ minutes. No. 2 was held in Washington. For No. 3, Kennedy was in New York and Nixon in Hollywood.

4. October 21. "Debate" on foreign policy, same format as No. 1. Originating in New York.

The four debates, and the first in particular, played a decisive role in the election results. Nixon knew it. Kennedy knew it. Their advisers and party leaders knew it. Their crowds reflected it. Their polls showed it. The on-the-spot surveys, the postelection surveys and the surveys of surveys all showed it. Some seventy million adults, nearly two-thirds of the nation's adult population, watched or listened to the first debate, clearly the largest campaign audience in history. More than four out of five voters saw or heard at least one of the four debates, the average adult saw three, and more than half of all adults watched all four. Those who did not see or hear them soon read or heard about them. They were a primary molder in the public mind of campaign issues and candidate images. They were a primary reason for the increasing interest in the campaign and the record turnout at the polls. And they were a primary factor in Kennedy's ultimate electoral victory.

One survey showed 25 percent of those who in August had not expected to vote deciding to vote in November, with most of them voting for Kennedy. Most surveys showed the debates enabling Kennedy to solidify his own party, impress Republicans far more favorably than

Nixon did Democrats, and win over independents by more than two to one. Whatever may be said about who had the better line or logic, only one conclusion is possible: Kennedy won the debates.

He won in part because he recognized the unprecedented impact certain to be made by the most historic debates since Lincoln and Douglas, and viewed by more than a thousand times as many people. He directed that his schedule be arranged so as to allow him the maximum time for briefing, preparation and rest before each encounter. Reports that he listened to tapes of Nixon's speeches "to help put him in a properly aggressive mood," or that he rehearsed at the studio for more than seven hours before two of the debates, are wholly false. His only desire was to be properly prepared and informed. To this end, prior to the first debate, we reduced to cards and reviewed for hours the facts and figures on every domestic issue, every Kennedy charge and every Nixon countercharge. We threw at the Senator all the tough and touchy questions we could devise. One session was held on the sunlit roof of his Chicago hotel, another in his sitting room, the last in his bedroom after he had confidently napped for nearly three hours in the midst of a bed full of file cards. He had, in a sense, been preparing for this moment for years, in hundreds of rapid-fire question-and-answer sessions with newsmen, college audiences, TV panels and others.

As he dressed, he compared his anxiety to that of a prizefighter about to enter the ring in Madison Square Garden. To this Dave Powers replied, "No, Senator, it's more like the opening-day pitcher in the World Series— because you have to win four of these." In the car to the studio he was silent and a little tense. Bromidic advice from one aide on how to talk on television was curtly cut off. Traffic lights were regarded with irritation. In the studio he sent Dave Powers back to the hotel for a blue shirt, reviewed and then discarded his notes, and received (though the contrary impression was never corrected) a slight trace of makeup. Because of his continuing tan, reinforced that day on the hotel roof, little makeup was required. He and Nixon exchanged nervous smiles and amenities and waited stiffly for 8:30 P.M.

Kennedy spoke first, quietly and simply, perhaps too rapidly and undramatically, but with strength. His sentences were short and sharp. He drew upon the themes and phrases with which he had become familiar in the first few weeks of campaigning:

> I think the question before the American people is: Are we doing as much as we can do . . . ? If we fail, then freedom fails. . . . I am not satisfied as an American with the progress that we are making. . . . This is a great country but I think it could be a greater country.

"I'm not satisfied," he went on to say, with 50 percent of our steel capacity unused, with the lowest rate of economic growth among the industrialized nations, with nine billion dollars' worth of food rotting in storage while millions are hungry, with the Soviet Union producing twice our number of scientists and engineers, with overcrowded schools and underpaid teachers, with natural resources undeveloped and with racial discrimination wasting the talents of too many Americans. The utter conviction with which he closed his opening remarks could be felt on screens throughout the land:

> The reason Franklin Roosevelt was a good neighbor in Latin America was because he was a good neighbor in the United States. . . . I want people in Latin America and Africa and Asia to start to look to America . . . what the President of the United States is doing, not . . . Khrushchev or the Chinese Communists. . . . Can freedom be maintained under the most severe attack it has ever known? I think it can be and I think in the final analysis it depends upon what we do here. I think it's time America started moving again.

Then it was Nixon's turn, and those who expected his aggressive debating experience to destroy Kennedy were disappointed. He was as clever and articulate as ever. But hoping to submerge among Democrats and independents his old image as a "gut-fighter" in exchange for the new image of a statesman, he began by agreeing with Kennedy's goals:

> The things that Senator Kennedy has said, many of us can agree with. . . . I subscribe completely to the spirit that Senator Kennedy has expressed tonight. . . . I know Senator Kennedy feels as deeply about these problems as I do, but our disagreement is not about the goals for America but only about the means to reach those goals.

It sounded weak. What was worse, Nixon looked weak. Between the bleak gray walls and the bright floodlights of the television studio, his gray suit and heavily powdered jowls looked flabby and pallid beside Kennedy's dark suit and healthy tan. The Vice President's delivery was at times hesitant and uneasy. Both men were tense and unsmiling in their opening remarks, but Nixon looked drawn and tired. The preachy platitudes and dramatic gestures which had scored for him on the public platform seemed too pat and political in the living room next to Kennedy's fresh and forthright precision.

The contrast continued throughout the question-and-answer period. In all four joint appearances, the press panelists—with some notable

exceptions—were to be the least effective performers. Their unimaginative questions were increasingly but ineptly aimed at tripping a candidate
or creating a headline instead of eliciting specific issues and information.
They rarely had continuity in a single debate but became repetitious in
the course of all four. Nor did two-and-a-half-minute answers permit
any real debating.

But they did produce different impressions of the candidates. In the
question period for the first debate, Kennedy, by then more relaxed,
gave informed, incisive, forceful answers. His rapid-style delivery
crowded more facts and arguments into each severely limited time period
than Nixon could answer. The Vice President appeared equally well
prepared and quick-witted but less specific in his facts, less certain of his
memory and more defensive and evasive on hard questions. As in his
opening statement, he seemed strained and less assured. His eyes
shifted and darted. He used none of the aggressive lines or folksy
examples he was using for local audiences—except for the one plaintive
plea, "I know what it is to be poor." At one point, intending to say
"farm surplus," he said we "must get rid of the farmer," then quickly
corrected himself. He was irritated by a question referring to Eisenhower's statement to the press (meant to be facetious, said Nixon) that,
if they would give him a week, he might think of an example of a Nixon
idea that had been adopted.

On one of Kennedy's answers, Nixon weakly said "No comment,"
while Kennedy carried the fight at all times, correcting a questioner's
assertion, taking time when answering subsequent questions to refute
earlier Nixon statements. When Kennedy deplored the Republican
frustration of a $1.25 minimum wage, medical care for the aged and aid
to education, Nixon said, among other things, that it was because "they
were too extreme"—a remark which Kennedy immediately picked up
and demolished. Perspiration and lip-licking multiplied the Vice President's problems with makeup. He projected no warmth and little depth.

In their closing remarks, Senator Kennedy, after first answering
briefly a few remaining charges, largely ignored Nixon. He spoke directly
to his listeners with more fervor than either participant had shown up to
then: ". . . only you can decide . . . what you want this country to be,
what you want to do with the future. I think we're ready to move." Nixon,
whose summation had sounded thin and defensive, glowered as Kennedy
confidently closed still keeping the initiative.

The television producer in charge of the show later concluded, after
rerunning a tape of the first debate a dozen times, that the only thing
wrong with Nixon's appearance was an oversized shirt collar. Others
charged sabotage by Nixon's makeup man. Some said Nixon's schedule
had left him fatigued. Others blamed the television studio for its bright

lights and intense heat. Some said it was just Nixon. "Kennedy did not necessarily win the debates," one survey concluded, "but Nixon lost them."

The first debate, James Reston wrote the next day, "did not make or break either candidate." Most of the headlines called it a draw. Very few voters said they had switched their allegiance from one candidate to the other. Many said Kennedy had talked too fast. Teachers of debate said both had scored equally. Many who listened on radio were amazed to hear TV viewers' reaction to Nixon. (But not all radio listeners had this reaction. When I hailed a cab to return to my hotel, the driver said the debate had stifled his business. Everyone was staying home or in bars to watch. He, like many others, had pulled over to the curb to listen. He didn't know who I was and he didn't care whom I supported. "Kennedy," he said, "clobbered him.")

Even a draw, if it was a draw, was a Kennedy victory. Millions more voters now knew Kennedy and knew him favorably. Doubting, dissident Democrats now rallied to his cause. Shocked Republicans could no longer talk about his immaturity and inexperience. Protestants no longer thought of Kennedy only as a Catholic. Nixon talked less of who could best stand up to Khrushchev. Seventy million or more people, most of whom knew little of Kennedy before, many of whom had not made up their minds, had scrutinized both candidates in a unique situation of stress and judgment, and while both candidates were impressive, it was Kennedy who impressed the great majority as being more decisive, more informed and more vigorous.

The fact that large proportions of both parties had expected a Nixon victory made Kennedy's showing all the more effective. They may not all have understood the issues he presented. They may have marveled at Nixon's highly informed presentation also. But they liked Kennedy's informal style, his alert and forceful manner, his cool strength. He looked both more poised and more determined. In the surveys, more Republicans than Democrats agreed that the opposing party's candidate had "won," whatever that meant. More Democrats than Republicans became more negative to the opposing candidate. And more independent and undecided voters moved in Kennedy's direction.

"I switched from being an anti-Nixon Democrat to a pro-Kennedy Democrat," said one Stevenson die-hard. An Alabama Protestant who switched from Nixon to Kennedy said Nixon "seemed more easily ruffled. . . . It appeared they wanted things covered up that they didn't want us to know about." A Nebraska independent decided to vote for Kennedy because he liked the sound of the New Frontier. A Massachusetts lady felt the debates showed Nixon "wasn't as smart as I originally thought he was. . . . Also, when it was divulged that his party was against the majority of the people, I felt more against him." Nixon may well have scored more debating points, but Kennedy scored with the voters.

Neither Kennedy nor Nixon needed these later surveys to know what had happened. Both had quick polls taken minutes after the debate was concluded. As the *Caroline* flew late that night to Ohio, the Senator, relaxing with a beer and a bowl of soup, reviewed his role and replies with almost total recall. He was physically and emotionally exhausted. But he was confident and happy. He had no regrets. He did not worry over what he wished he had said on any point. "You can always improve afterward," he remarked later, "but I would settle for the way it went. I thought it was all right."

He soon discovered that millions more thought it was all right. The size and enthusiasm of his crowds increased immensely and immediately. Nixon's press secretary had to issue a release to the effect that his candidate was "in excellent health and looks good in person." Kennedy was warmly congratulated in a wire from the previously dubious Southern Democratic governors, who watched the debate nine strong from their conference in Hot Springs. Nixon was besieged with Republican politicians telling him to look healthier and talk tougher. Ohio's conservative Senator Frank Lausche decided to join the Kennedy caravan. Democrats who had been cool since long before the convention— Stevenson supporters, big-city bosses and, above all, Protestants—started working for Kennedy.

The second, third and fourth "debates" were almost an anticlimax. Not only were they viewed by fewer voters (though still a phenomenal number)—particularly by fewer uncommitted and uninformed voters— they also had less impact. All three were judged to be very close. Nixon changed to an aggressive style, but it was too little and too late. He put on weight and changed to a new kind of makeup to conceal his stubborn beard stubble, but he still looked less appealing than the handsome Kennedy. Some say he "won" the third round—when he and the Senator were screened from separate cities, which apparently made Nixon feel more at ease—but it was to no avail. The debates as a whole, said the surveys, were won by Kennedy.

The remaining three joint appearances served Kennedy's interest primarily by preserving and reinforcing the gains he had achieved in the first one. Nixon's own pollster reportedly summed up the debates to his client by concluding that Kennedy, who had started out lesser known and with doubts in his own ranks, "has increased his standing on every issue test . . . [and] has succeeded in creating a victory psychology."

Kennedy's quick mind was equal to even the new, aggressive Nixon (some said it was the old Nixon). While Kennedy continued to pour out facts and arguments in answer to each question, Nixon hedged some on the grounds that he would later have a speech or "white paper" on the subject. While Nixon was berating one Kennedy answer and demanding a retraction, the camera caught Kennedy broadly grinning. When Nixon accused Kennedy of weakening the country with his criticism, Kennedy fired back:

> I really don't need Mr. Nixon to tell me about what my responsibilities are as a citizen. I've served this country for fourteen years in the Congress and before that in the service. . . . What I downgrade, Mr. Nixon, is the leadership the country's getting, not the country.

When Kennedy was questioned on Harry Truman's profane language in the campaign, his answer sharply contrasted with Nixon's:

KENNEDY: I really don't think there's anything that I can say to President Truman that's going to cause him to change his particular manner. Perhaps Mrs. Truman can, but I don't think I can.

NIXON: One thing I have noted as I have traveled around the country are the tremendous number of children who come out to see the Presidential candidates . . . mothers holding their babies up. . . . It makes you realize that whoever is President is going to be a man that all the children of America will either look up to or will look down to. . . . And I only hope that, should I win this election . . . whenever any mother or father talks to his child, he can look at the man in the White House and say . . .

One major issue in the debates, which related to Kennedy's entire campaign and which worked to his advantage, was that of American prestige abroad. The decline in that prestige, as evidenced by a variety of riots and adverse reactions in foreign capitals, fit well into Kennedy's major themes. Nixon retorted that our prestige was at an all-time high. Upon learning that the administration had refused to release to the Congress certain USIA overseas surveys on this subject, Kennedy called upon Nixon to show his influence and answer Kennedy's charges by obtaining their release. Nixon said the polls supported his contentions—but the polls remained secret.

In October Mike Feldman in Washington was told he could obtain copies of the polls from a source outside the USIA. He telephoned me about his acquisition, and I asked him to forward them to me at our next overnight stop. The polls strongly backed the Senator's position and made Nixon's claims about them look like deliberate misinformation. To avoid charges that he had improperly obtained classified material, Kennedy turned the polls over to the *New York Times*, who immediately printed them without mention of how they had been acquired, and the Senator was then free to quote them as official proof of our plummeting prestige. An Eisenhower aide promptly asked USIA Director George Allen to issue a statement saying his polls showed American prestige at a record high, but Allen refused, and the issue continued to help Kennedy.

Two other foreign policy issues arose in the last three debates, and neither of them worked to Kennedy's advantage or, fortunately, persisted in the public mind. The question of the two Nationalist Chinese islands off the coast of Communist China, Quemoy and Matsu, was raised, not by either candidate, but in questions directed to Kennedy by newsmen— both one week before the second debate and near the close of that debate. Kennedy's reply, citing considerable military authority, opposed "withdrawal at the point of a Communist gun" but felt the chances of being dragged into an unnecessary war would be lessened if the Nationalists could be persuaded to draw the line of defense specifically and exclusively around Formosa and the Pescadores. Nixon went beyond the Eisenhower policy of leaving their status in doubt:

> The question is not these two little pieces of real estate; they are unimportant. It isn't the few people who live on them; they are not too important. It's the principle involved. These two islands are in the area of freedom. . . . [Kennedy's answer] is the same kind of woolly thinking that led to disaster for America in Korea.

For the next several days Nixon and the Republicans charged Kennedy with policies of appeasement, defeat, retreat and surrender. "I oppose handing over to the Communists one inch of free territory," said the Vice President, misquoting Kennedy's stand and implying it meant abandoning Berlin also. (On Formosa, Generalissimo Chiang Kai-shek joined in denouncing Kennedy.) The Senator responded in New York City with a full-scale speech pointing out that the Eisenhower administration had long advocated evacuation of these islands for the same reasons it evacuated the neighboring Ta-chen Island, and for the same reasons it had opposed the Nationalist build-up on Quemoy and Matsu— namely, on grounds that they were "indefensible." He favored resistance, he said, to any direct or indirect attack on Formosa, but not enlarging our treaty obligations to fight for these islands alone. His closing quotation, which he often cited thereafter, had by luck been telephoned to me by an unknown researcher for the New York Democratic Committee: " 'These islands,' said Admiral Yarnell, former commander of our Asiatic Fleet, 'are not worth the bones of a single American.' "

Nixon, replying in the third debate, said no Republican President had led this nation into war in the last fifty years and "there were three

Democratic Presidents who led us into war. I do not mean by that that one party is a war party." He then reviewed the history of the two islands as he saw it. "I don't think it's possible," retorted Kennedy, "for Mr. Nixon to state the record in distortion of the facts with more precision than he just did."

But Kennedy also recognized that his position, while correct, was too sophisticated for the average viewer who understood Nixon's refusal to surrender one square inch of free soil. Consequently both Kennedy and Nixon began to emphasize the official administration position: defending these islands only from a Chinese Communist attack that was actually aimed at Formosa. Kennedy said they should not be defended *unless* the attack was aimed at Formosa. Nixon said they should be defended *because* any such attack was clearly aimed at Formosa. Each insisted that the other had originally been at odds with the official policy and backed down. But the issue died. Nixon later was to claim that he patriotically dropped the matter as the result of a request conveyed by Chester Bowles to Secretary of State Herter, but Bowles's own notes of that conversation reflect no such request and certainly Kennedy never authorized one.

The other foreign policy issue involved in the debates was also dropped by mutual assent and adjustment of positions, and because both candidates thought it was harming them. The Communist-Castro takeover of Cuba had been steadily cited by Kennedy as an example of Republican ineptitude. The only Republican comeback was citation of a pre-1960 essay in *The Strategy of Peace*—unlike the bulk of the book, it had never been delivered in a Kennedy speech—which appeared to link Castro with the Latin-American revolutionary tradition of Simón Bolívar. Kennedy, even though he regretted the implication, was angry he had not caught it and was embarrassed by Republican attacks on this passage; nevertheless he refused to disown either the words or the junior staff member who had written them from a wholly different perspective. But he did maintain his own attack on Republican failures in Cuba. When Nixon, aided by a belated administration embargo, outlined his program to solve this problem, Kennedy called it "too little and too late," and he then outlined in a statement a four-point program of his own which included an "attempt to strengthen the non-Batista democratic anti-Castro forces in exile, and in Cuba itself, who offer eventual hope of overthrowing Castro."

Kennedy—who had not, contrary to Nixon's subsequent assertions, been informed by the CIA that it was covertly training an exile invasion force—had no specifics in mind. Nor did his advisers, who were equally unaware of the invasion plan. It was, in all candor, a vague generalization thrown in to pad out an anti-Castro "program." In the fourth debate,

Nixon, who was aware of the CIA operation but could not disclose it, assailed Kennedy—as did many liberals—for proposing illegal intervention in internal Cuban affairs. A better solution was our procedure in Guatemala, said the Vice President, where our quarantine produced a "spontaneous" anti-Communist revolt. In fact, as both Kennedy and Nixon knew, the American CIA had engineered the Guatemala revolt, but Kennedy thought it inappropriate to say so publicly just as Nixon felt he could not disclose the Cuban invasion plans publicly.

That issue also faded, as Kennedy explained he was referring not to direct intervention but to stepped-up propaganda and political positions. Other issues rose and fell throughout the debates. The strain was at times relieved by some trivia. Kennedy complained in Round 2 that the studio, cooled at Nixon's request to end the perspiration on his makeup, might require him to debate in a sweater. Nixon's research staff discovered an old Kennedy text which included compulsory arbitration in a list of tools the White House should have available in case of national emergency strikes, but didn't discover that Kennedy had deleted the phrase from his delivery and issued a corrected release. "I always have difficulty recognizing my positions when they are stated by the Vice President," Kennedy commented. As Kennedy kept pressing that America must move again, Nixon twice said that "America cannot stand pat."

The Senator enjoyed telling his staff and an occasional audience how Nixon, as the photographers gathered after one of the debates, raised his finger in Kennedy's face as he had in the "kitchen" with Khrushchev. "I thought, here it comes, he is going to tell me how wrong I am about the plight of America—and do you know what he said? 'Senator, I hear you have been getting better crowds than I have in Cleveland.'"

As the fourth and final round approached, only the networks were eager for a fifth to be added. But correctly sensing that Nixon was even less eager for a fifth debate than he, the Senator publicly called for such a debate, pressed for negotiations between the staffs (which we carried out to no avail) and, in a barrage of telegrams and public statements, continually chided Nixon's refusal to meet him once again.

THE WIND-UP

All this was consistent with the continuing atmosphere of Kennedy confidence. The campaign had entered its final phase. The debates were over, the World Series was over, Khrushchev had left the UN and a crucial 11 percent of the voters had still to make a final choice. The crush of Kennedy's crowds continued to grow, people often waiting several hours, on occasion until 1, 2 and 3 A.M. His motor tour of economically hard-hit Pennsylvania cities from Bethlehem to Wilkes-Barre was, Governor

Lawrence said, "like the coming of a Messiah," as 500,000 shouting, crowding people hurled confetti at the candidate, gifts into his car, and flags and Kennedy banners into the air. Crowds choked his car engines with paper streamers in Los Angeles, trapped him in a phone booth at Roanoke and paraded one million strong for him in Chicago. "I hope they won't all be too tired to get to the polls Tuesday," said the candidate to Mayor Daley. "They'll be there," said the Mayor (and they were).

His audience in New York's garment district covered twelve blocks, and he touched all the hands he could. Jacqueline, who always joined him in New York, despite her doctor's warning ("If he lost," she said, "I'd never forgive myself for not being there to help"), felt the sides of the car almost bending. A motorcycle policeman with his sleeve torn off said it was worse than the Battle of Omaha Beach.

Kennedy was, if anything, calmer as the campaign closed around him. He radiated confidence as he preached concern. His speeches were more aggressive, more poised, more humorous and less tense. He was still informal, relaxed and unafraid. He was still himself. He fought off the effects of fatigue and pushed his vocal chords into one final drive. His anger exploded only once, when a series of motorcade errors marred his last visit to New York.

His hand was wrenched, scratched, swollen and infected. His face was creased with lines that had not been there a year before. "This campaign," he told crowds in New York, "fortunately for us all, is coming physically and financially to an end. . . . If somebody told me the election is November 16 instead of November 8, I might just fade right out." "Four more days," he told a Phoenix airport crowd at 3 A.M., November 3. "We can hang on that long. The election is Tuesday. . . . We have timed it very well."

Nixon, although his speeches had an increasing ring of desperation, felt *his* timing was right and that Kennedy had "peaked" too soon. Predicting an electoral landslide "if the tide continues," he stepped up his attack, increased his television and unlimbered his biggest weapon: Ike. Kennedy, while still refraining from attacking the President, needled Nixon for needing Eisenhower, as well as Lodge and Rockefeller, to escort him through New York and to serve as his future peace council. Why not add Goldwater, Dewey, Hoover and Landon? he asked.

But Eisenhower's intervention was hurting. Nixon, effectively taking to the rails, used more savage adjectives than he ever had in the debates. He stepped up his charges that Kennedy was the captive of left-wing labor bosses, would spend this nation into inflation and depression, would raise food prices 25 percent and the domestic budget by $25 billion. "In the last seven days," remarked Kennedy in the Bronx, "he has called me an ignoramus, a liar, a Pied Piper and all the rest. I just confine myself to calling him a Republican . . . and he says that is really getting low." Nixon accused him of telling "a bare-faced lie," said the Senator in Albuquerque. "Having seen him four times close up . . . and made up, I would not accuse Mr. Nixon of being bare-faced, but the American people can determine who is telling the truth."

Nixon also began to unveil a new spectacular proposal each day, mostly a series of conferences and committees on "peace." He began to go far beyond the Eisenhower position on housing, health, education and natural resources. He founded his housing proposals on the Democrats' Federal Housing Act of 1949 (Congressman Nixon, pointed out Kennedy, had voted against that Act). Moving to foreign affairs, he proposed sending Lodge to Geneva and Eisenhower, Hoover and Truman to Russia, while he and his wife, Pat, would travel through Eastern Europe. ("If I am elected," said Kennedy, "I am going to Washington, D.C., and get this country to work.") The Nixon staff, building the "tide" psychology, released polls showing their candidate carrying Pennsylvania, Ohio, Illinois, California and Texas. A newspaper poll of editors on the results in their respective states predicted an overwhelming Nixon victory.

The administration announced it was releasing an additional $155 million for B-70 development it had previously declined to use in the unemployed aircraft centers of California. By coincidence it chose November 3 to launch, with considerable ballyhoo about our space effort, a new Explorer satellite. (A Mercury capsule launching timed for Election Day, November 8, was a failure.)

Other problems persisted. Democratic politicians and volunteers were still quarreling in California. Not all the hate literature related to religion. The chairman of Texans for Nixon said Kennedy was not a Communist, only a Khrushchev-lover. Anonymous pink cards made their appearance in Miami: "One Mr. K. is enough—vote Republican."

Ironically, the cruelest blow came from within the Catholic Church. Except for Cardinal Spellman's public appearances with Eisenhower and Nixon, appearances which convinced Kennedy of the Cardinal's opposition, the hierarchy kept silent during the fall; the Catholic press reflected growing resentment of unfair attacks; and the Catholic clergy— in contrast with Kennedy's Protestant critics and contrary to the latter's belief—abided by their customary rule of neither endorsing nor opposing any candidate from the pulpit, enduring vitriolic and violent harassment of every kind in admirable silence. Catholic voters leaned increasingly though not uniformly to Kennedy, with many still opposed to his "defensive" attitude on religion, his "boast" of attending public schools and the "leftist" advisers around him.[8]

8 When a Lou Harris Poll showed Catholic support and particularly Irish Catholic support lagging behind that of the Jews, Ambassador Kennedy, who had been

Then, in the closing weeks of the campaign, the Catholic hierarchy in the American Commonwealth of Puerto Rico directed all Catholics on that island how to vote: against Governor Luis Muñoz Marín and his Popular Democratic Party for permitting birth control instruction, tolerating common law marriage and opposing religious education.

Their action aroused a bigger storm in our election than in Puerto Rico's, where it was only the latest blow in an age-old battle.[9] American Protestant leaders saw in the Puerto Rican pastoral letter a confirmation of their worst fears. On this basis, said Denver's Methodist Bishop, "I shall not mark my ballot for a Roman Catholic candidate for the Presidency." Another called it an "alarming illustration of the pressure the Roman Catholic hierarchy can exert." Instantly the incident was featured in publications ranging from hate sheets to denominational newspapers, often under the heading, "They said it couldn't happen in America." Senator Kennedy knew he had been hurt. "If enough voters realize that Puerto Rico is American soil," he remarked to me, "this election is lost."

Many of his advisers, fearful that it was lost, urged him to make a nationally televised appeal for fairness on the Sunday night before election. They pointed to the increase in hate literature, to evidence that too few Americans still knew his Houston views. The pollsters said more people talked hostilely of Kennedy's religion than mentioned any other issue or factor in the campaign.

The plan was to announce the subject of religion in advance and ask for written questions. But Kennedy, sensitive to the charge that he was keeping the issue alive even by answering questions, decided against it. Instead, though he was almost superhumanly fighting off fatigue and irritability, he canceled all rest periods for the final two weeks and vowed to campaign right up to Election Eve.

A lack of funds—which long before had curtailed distribution of Kennedy signs and stickers, long-distance phone calls and expense accounts —made it impossible for Democrats to match a last-minute Republican television saturation. Even some of the time which we had earlier reserved was released. Nixon topped off a TV "blitz" with a four-hour, half-million-dollar telethon the day before the election. It seemed insipid to us, but we could not know how many voters would like it.

The Gallup Poll had shown the two candidates seesawing within a few percentage points of each other since the campaign began, and now it concluded that the race was too close for prediction.

---

assailed in a barrage of New York newspaper advertisements as an anti-Semite, fumed: "I think I'd better become a Jew. They and the Negroes are the only reliable friends we have."

9 Ninety percent Catholic Puerto Rico voted overwhelmingly for Muñoz Marín.

Except for a brief Western swing—far too brief in California, he later concluded—Senator Kennedy concentrated those last two weeks on Illinois, Michigan, Pennsylvania, Ohio, New Jersey, New York and New England. The weather was freezing, particularly in Waterbury, Connecticut, at 3 A.M., on November 6, where one of his largest crowds for a city of that size would simply not let him go to bed.

Finally and suddenly, it was November 7. After six speeches that day in five states, Election Eve began in Manchester, New Hampshire, with his three sisters. They had been to forty states, he said proudly, but "when somebody last week asked my sister Patricia if I was her kid brother, she knew it was time this campaign came to an end." His own fatigue was evidenced by a rare show of public irritability and incaution in blasting one local publisher for saying once again that Kennedy was a Communist sympathizer:

> I would like to have the *Union Leader* print a headline that we carried New Hampshire. [Applause] I believe there is probably a more irresponsible newspaper in the United States but I can't think of it. [Applause] I believe that there is a publisher who has less regard for the truth than William Loeb but I can't think of his name. [Deafening applause]

Still in Manchester, he moved to a TV studio for a nationwide question-and-answer session, with his sisters asking questions we had selected. They covered all the most difficult issues—Communism, Castro, Catholicism, agriculture, education, the budget, small business and peace.

The evening continued with a noisy inspirational rally with his original boosters, back home in the Boston Garden. There he concluded:

> I thank you for your past support. I ask you to join us tomorrow. And, most of all, I ask you to join us in all the tomorrows yet to come, in building America, moving America, picking this country of ours up and sending it into the sixties.

Finally, at 11 P.M., he closed out the 1960 Presidential campaign with a televised presentation from Boston's old Faneuil Hall. It included brief talks by his wife from Hyannis Port and Lyndon Johnson from Austin, taped interviews with various voters and filmed excerpts from his campaign travels. The Senator spoke quietly but movingly. "I come back to this old city," he said, "with the strongest possible confidence in the future of the United States, in the ability of its people to meet its responsibilities . . . [and] to strengthen our cause."

CHAPTER VIII

THE MARGIN

IT WAS OVER. "We have done everything that could be done," he said. He and Jacqueline voted in Boston and rested at the Cape. The remaining job was one of organization, for which Bob Kennedy had relentlessly prepared with no allowance for overconfidence. Symbolic of the nationwide network of poll workers and watchers he had built was the network of thirty telephones and four teletypes in his house adjoining the candidate's. Reports on "indicator" precincts were received, trends were projected and leaders were called throughout the long day and night that followed.

The first news of the day was word of a record turnout—nearly 69 million voters: good news. Then came word of an especially high turnout in the South—among white, Protestant Southerners: bad news. Except for Philadelphia, Chicago, New York and Los Angeles, the turnout in the big cities was off: bad news. Finally the Senator, relaxed with a cigar, in sport shirt, sweater and slacks, settled back to watch the returns, sometimes in Bobby's house, where aides manned the phones, sometimes in his own house, where Jacqueline watched quietly with him.

He made a few calls on his own. Soon after the returns began trickling in, he called John Bailey in Connecticut, one of the first states to report. "Who's this?" asked Bailey as the questions were fired at him. "Who do you think it is?" said Kennedy. "The candidate." He joked after a call to his running mate that "Lyndon says, 'I hear *you're* losing Ohio but *we're* doing fine in Pennsylvania.'" He did not conclude the race was over on the basis of his early landslide win among his Connecticut neighbors, any more than he did on the basis of Thurston Morton's premature claim of a Nixon victory. He was equally skeptical of those television computers which early in the evening predicted Nixon winning and those later predicting a Kennedy sweep. When Nixon, trailing in the early returns, refused to concede, Kennedy alone was unnettled: "Why should he? I wouldn't under these circumstances." He felt that Nixon had only embarrassed himself and Mrs. Nixon by a half-concession statement to a group of unruly supporters.

The Senator refused to make any statement, despite pleas from the press, until the outcome was clear—and it was far from clear. Even before 8 P.M. Huntley-Brinkley were using the phrase "cliff-hanger." After 10 P.M. Kennedy's early lead shrank steadily through the night. The experts hedged their predictions. The statistics were uncertain. The TV network computers, said one commentator, were producing at best "a definite maybe." The Senator watched television impassively, for the most part silently. Generally calm, he was briefly upset about not spending more time in California. He could not understand Ohio. For a time it looked like the 1956 Vice Presidential nominating contest all over again, with Kennedy racing to a near majority only to find himself unable to win enough Western and Midwestern votes to clinch it. But he was cool, often jovial, switching his TV set to a new channel each time local returns displaced the national. Shortly before 4 A.M. John Kennedy went to bed, reasonably but not completely confident that he had won, reasonably but not completely content with his effort and, as always, unwilling to worry once there was nothing more he could do.

The minute he awoke around nine the next morning, I mounted the stairs and congratulated him on his election as President. "What happened in California?" were his first words. I told him—mistakenly as it turned out—that he had carried California and that, in any event, he had carried Minnesota, Michigan and Illinois as well as Pennsylvania and Missouri, to guarantee an electoral majority. I also informed him that the Secret Service had surrounded the house. Almost instantly his bedside phone rang, and he picked it up hoping it was the final verdict. It was his mother-in-law—a lifelong Republican who had publicly supported him—and they chatted as though nothing else was on his mind. He dressed once again in sports clothes, uncertain of how long it would be until Nixon bowed out. He knew politics well enough to know that nothing was certain until then.

His popular vote margin continued to dwindle, dropping finally to less than 120,000 out of nearly 69 million votes cast (in contrast with his electoral vote margin of 303–219). When the gracious wires of concession and congratulation finally came shortly after noon from Nixon and Eisenhower (after the Minnesota verdict was final), he was all business, deliberating his replies and his statement of victory. His elation over achieving the long-sought prize of the Presidency was tempered by the fatigue that had finally caught up with him, by the responsibilities that lay ahead of him and by the narrowness of his hard-won victory.

What accounted for Kennedy's victory after his initial lag in the polls? The margin was so narrow that almost any important aspect of the campaign could probably be said to have provided the final margin. In my view, any list of decisive factors in Kennedy's favor, excluding his defensive actions on religion, would have to include the following seven, without attempting to ascribe relative weight to any one of them:

1. *The Television Debates*

Kennedy's sincerity and vitality, in the most televised campaign in history, and in the televised debates in particular, appealed to millions of voters who would otherwise have dismissed him as too young or known nothing about him but his religion. One survey showed four million voters making up their minds on the basis of the debates, with a three-to-one margin for Kennedy.

Nixon, confident of his superior debating experience, did not avail himself of the many excuses he could have employed to refuse Kennedy's challenge to debate, and thereby gave the far lesser-known Senator his most highly publicized forum and most highly prized opportunity of the entire election campaign. Handicapped in the vital first debate by a poor television appearance, and hoping to win Democratic votes by erasing the image of the "old" more militant Nixon, he enabled Kennedy to appear more vigorous by seemingly agreeing with many of the Senator's most pointed thrusts.

2. *Campaign Tactics*

Kennedy's campaign style, tested and sharpened in seven spring primaries, was more attractive, more vigorous and more consistently on the offensive. Driving hard from the outset, he appealed to an inner feeling that the soft and easy life was not enough, that our national potential was unful-

Nixon's campaign effort, handicapped at the outset by two weeks in the hospital with an infected knee, and further diluted by the fulfillment of his convention pledge to speak in all fifty states, had less substance and style than Kennedy's. In contrast to the Kennedy theory on timing, Nixon's strategy

filled. He had been well behind at the close of the conventions. He had been behind midway through the campaign both in the big states and in the South. The opinion polls concealed the unusually large number of undecided and wavering voters. Subsequent analysis by the University of Michigan showed that, contrary to our fears of a late Nixon "tide," Kennedy won two to one among those making up their minds in the last two weeks before election. Indeed, had more time permitted, he might have carried such additional states as Virginia, Florida and California. His incredibly intensive campaign had convinced the unconvinced, projected his own convictions, demonstrated his quick intelligence, converted his youth into an asset and showed Democratic anti-Catholics that he was not only a Catholic.

called for a careful pacing of campaign efforts, going all out the last two weeks to reach his peak on Election Eve, but his pacing was too slow and his peak fell short.

3. Party Identification

Kennedy's party, despite Eisenhower's personal appeal and successive victories, was the majority party in this country in terms of both registration and voting below the Presidential level. The majority of Senators, Congressmen, governors and big-city mayors were Democrats, capable of helping with organization and registration; and Kennedy appealed strongly and frequently to party unity, history and loyalty. To make the most of this majority, a highly skilled well-organized registration drive helped

Nixon wished to be identified in the campaign with Eisenhower, but not with his party, not with all his policies and not at the expense of his own independence. At the outset, neither Nixon nor Eisenhower seemed certain of their relation or the extent to which the President's participation in the campaign might overshadow the Vice President. Kennedy meanwhile was placing Nixon on the defensive for all the failings of the preceding years. The full-scale entry of Eisenhower, whose immense popularity bring out nearly seven million more people than voted four years earlier, over four million of whom it was assumed were Democrats.

more than made up for his lack of political enthusiasm, was thus delayed until it was too late to switch enough states.

4. *Running Mate*

Kennedy's running mate, Lyndon Johnson, helped salvage several Southern states the Republicans had counted on capturing, with an intensive campaign mixture of carrots and sticks, and campaigned effectively in some forty states. The maltreatment to which he and his wife were subjected by a shoving, booing crowd of disorderly Republican fanatics in Dallas undoubtedly helped switch more than the 23,000 voters who provided the Democratic margin in Texas; and had it not been for the return of Texas and Louisiana to the Democratic column from their 1956 Republican sojourn, and for the Carolinas' staying Democratic against a predicted Republican victory, Nixon would have won the election.

Nixon's running mate, Henry Cabot Lodge—whom the press and pollsters (but never Senator Kennedy) all said would strengthen the Republican ticket more than Johnson would help the Democrats —proved to be the least industrious campaigner on either ticket; and both his blatant pledge of a Negro in the Nixon Cabinet and his subsequent vacillation on the matter offended voters of all areas and races. Lodge was nationally known as "the man from the UN"; and had more political appeal than either Secretary of Labor James Mitchell, whom Nixon might have selected in pursuit of Catholic votes had Kennedy not been nominated, or Senator Thruston Morton of Kentucky, whom Nixon might have selected in pursuit of Southern votes had Johnson not been nominated. Kennedy regarded Lodge as an attractive, able addition to Nixon's team, but he also predicted in August, on the basis of his own race against Lodge in 1952, that sooner or later a Lodge blunder would cause Nixon regret—and he was right.

5. *Negro-Southern Choices*

Kennedy's phone call of concern and interest to the bereaved and pregnant wife of Negro leader

Nixon's hope of an unprecedented Republican Southern sweep kept him quiet on the Rev. King's

Martin Luther King, imprisoned in Georgia on a traffic technicality—a call which almost all his advisers initially opposed as a futile "grand-stand" gesture which would cost more votes among Southerners than it would gain among Negroes—was hailed throughout the Negro community, which then voted overwhelmingly for Kennedy in numbers exceeding his margin of victory in several Northern and Southern states. Many of those who advised against the call to Mrs. King still argue that, even without it and Bob Kennedy's subsequent call to the Georgia judge, Kennedy's popularity among Negroes would have reached this level anyway as the result of economic issues. Although two million copies of a Democratic Committee pamphlet on the episode were distributed outside Negro churches on the Sunday before election, Kennedy was sufficiently uncertain of its impact to make no speech or press release on his call, revealing it with one simple but powerful sentence: "She is a friend of mine and I was concerned about the situation."

fate, and also caused him during the final week to neglect close states in the North for a flying and futile trip to South Carolina and Texas.

6. *Foreign Policy*

By chance, an American U-2 "spy" plane had been downed in Russia in the spring of 1960. The subsequent break-up of the Paris Summit Conference, cancellation of Eisenhower's trips to the Soviet Union and Japan, public fear of a space and missile lag and the increasing realization that the Communists controlled Cuba "only ninety miles from our shore," all clouded the atmosphere of "peace" which a year earlier had seemed certain to silence any Democratic critic. Nixon, dependent on Eisenhower's goodwill, and defensive of the Republican record, was required to make rosy assertions about American leadership and prestige abroad which Kennedy continually exploded.

7. *Recession*

In the last month of the campaign, the nation could clearly feel the effects of a recession which had actually started in April, three months after Eisenhower predicted "the most prosperous year in our history." It was the third recession in seven years, giving urban voters in the large industrial states good reason to be dissatisfied. Kennedy, on the offensive, was able to emphasize the downturn; Nixon publicly denied its existence and privately failed to persuade his administration to take sufficient action to counteract it. The Federal Reserve Board, as he urged, loosened credit in June but this was not enough. The votes of newly unemployed workers alone in Illinois, New Jersey, Michigan, Minnesota, Missouri and South Carolina were greater than Kennedy's margin in those states, and their electoral votes were greater than his margin in the Electoral College. Nixon ran worst not, as many believe, in the cities with the highest proportion of Catholics but in the cities with the highest proportion of unemployed.

Each of these seven factors worked in Kennedy's favor. This was fortunate, for the eighth and by far the largest factor in the campaign worked against him: religion. Obviously there were other reasons for Protestants and others to vote against him—or for him. I cannot agree with Ambassador Kennedy, who, when asked how many states his son would have carried had he been an Episcopalian, snapped without hesitation: "Fifty!" Most of the more superficial analyses completed immediately after the election concluded that Kennedy's religion had on balance helped him. But subsequent studies in depth concluded that it was, other than Republican Party loyalty, the strongest factor against him.

Catholic voters were not uniformly Kennedy's strongest supporters. Conservative, well-to-do and suburban Catholics continued to vote Republican, particularly in the West, Midwest and upper New England. Among the states listed in the Bailey Memorandum, Catholic votes for Nixon helped the Republican ticket carry Ohio, Wisconsin, New Hampshire, Montana and California.

Nevertheless Kennedy's religion was undoubtedly a help in bringing back to the national Democratic ticket most of the Catholic Democrats who had twice preferred Eisenhower to Stevenson while still considering themselves Democrats and voting Democratic locally. More than three out of five Catholics who voted for Eisenhower in 1956 switched to Kennedy in 1960.[1] Hardly any of them, however, were regular Republicans. Most analysts agree that their return to the Democratic column in 1960 was likely anyway for any candidate, Protestant or Catholic, with the probable exception of Stevenson. But to what extent these Catholic Democrats were *also* moved by pride in Kennedy's religion, by resentment of the attacks upon it, or foreign policy, economics or a dozen other reasons, cannot ever be measured. We cannot be certain that all of them would have voted for Kennedy had he been a Protestant, although it is revealing to note that: (1) Kennedy carried Boston and other heavily Catholic areas by little more than a Protestant Democrat had carried them in 1948; (2) he received roughly the same proportion of Catholic support nationally (over three to one) that all Democratic Congressional candidates had received in 1958; and (3) the Protestant Democrat who succeeded Kennedy would also obtain this same proportion in 1964.

What is certain is that had Kennedy not scored large majorities among other types of voters, including Negroes, Jews and union members—had he not convinced almost as many Protestants as Catholics who had voted for Eisenhower to switch to him—he would not have won the election. His increased support from Catholics alone would not have been sufficient to secure him a plurality in Connecticut, Delaware, Illinois, Maryland, New Jersey, New York, Nevada or any of the Southern and border states he recaptured. In Massachusetts, Rhode Island, Michigan, Pennsylvania and possibly Minnesota, the return of Catholic voters to the Democratic ticket may well have been one of the keys to the electoral votes of those five states returning to the Democratic column, but these electoral gains alone clearly would not have been enough to beat Nixon.

Thus it cannot be said that Kennedy's religion elected him. Many assumed that Nixon's inability to draw a higher proportion of the Protestant vote than Eisenhower (nearly two out of three) showed religion was not a factor. But the more detailed surveys showed that this was evidence of the opposite conclusion. Protestants, like every other group in the electorate, switched strongly from Eisenhower in 1956 to Kennedy in 1960, but these Protestant switches were almost exactly offset by Protestant Democrats switching from Stevenson to Nixon.

Analysis of all the switches on both sides provides the answer. Comparatively few long-time Republican Catholics deserted Nixon, but lifelong Democrats who were Protestants deserted Kennedy in droves. Both

---

[1] In the 171 counties across the nation with the largest Catholic populations, only 3 voted more strongly for Nixon than they had for Eisenhower and only 20 were below the national average in Democratic gains, although the existence of those 23 helps disprove the fear of a solid bloc vote.

Protestants and Catholics who had voted for Eisenhower switched in great numbers to Kennedy. Inasmuch as the Protestants did so for reasons other than religion, it cannot be said that religion was the sole motivation of the Catholics. But inasmuch as Protestants comprised nine-tenths of those switching from Stevenson to Nixon, the Republican pull on loyal Democrats for any reason *other* than religion must have been fairly weak.

Kennedy's over-all loss nationally from Protestant Democrats, reported the University of Michigan survey, was at least 4.5 million votes, far more than any Catholic vote gains could offset. In terms of electoral votes, the five states in which the return of Catholic votes helped supply his winning margin outweighed those states which can be clearly identified as lost because of religion. But the Michigan survey analysts, convinced that most of the Catholics voting for Kennedy would have returned to the Democratic fold anyway, concluded that Kennedy's religion prevented him from winning by a comfortable popular majority. And Professor V. O. Key, Jr. summed up the results of the later surveys with the judgment "that Kennedy won in spite of rather than because of the fact that he was a Catholic."

The fact remains that he won, and on the day after election, and every day thereafter, he rejected the argument that the country had given him no mandate. Every election has a winner and a loser, he said in effect.[2] "The margin is narrow, but the responsibility is clear. There may be difficulties with the Congress, but a margin of only one vote would still be a mandate."

If the Electoral College members from Louisiana, Georgia, South Carolina and the rest of Alabama had decided to join their six Alabama and eight Mississippi colleagues in voting for Harry Byrd (and this had been a real threat in each of those states, defeated in Louisiana, for example, by only one vote on the hundred-member state committee)— or if fewer than 7,000 people in Illinois, Nevada, Mexico and Hawaii had voted for Nixon instead of Kennedy—neither one of them would have received a majority of the electoral vote, the election would have been thrown into the House of Representatives, and its outcome would have been in doubt. If fewer than 12,000 people strategically located in the above four states plus Missouri had voted for Nixon instead of Kennedy, Nixon would have received an electoral vote majority and become the next President.

But continued reference to these statistics did not faze the President-elect. No one pointed out that a shift from Nixon to Kennedy of less than one-tenth of one percent of the popular vote could have given him six

[2] His electoral vote total of 303 was the same as Truman's 1948 total and larger than Wilson's 1916 victory.

more states—California, Alaska, Virginia, Washington, New Hampshire and Montana—for 64 more electoral votes and an overwhelming victory. Nor did anyone point out that every state in the nation, save six Southern and border states, had given Kennedy an increase in his party's proportion of the two-party vote, even though some states showing the largest increase had too large a deficit of Democratic voters to overcome. Among the latter, for example, were Maine, Vermont and New Hampshire, but the other three New England states gave their favorite son whopping majorities.

As he watched the election returns on the night of November 8, and reviewed them in the weeks that followed, he had reason for both satisfaction and disappointment. He had never counted on any support from the rural, Protestant, conservative states of the Midwest and West. Farm labor supported him more strongly than farm owners, but he knew that the much predicted Farm Belt "revolt" would fall far short, that most of its anti-Benson force had been spent in 1956, and that its remaining benefits for Democrats would be felt at the Congressional level but not by an Eastern urban Catholic. He had been hopeful but had not counted on winning Nevada and New Mexico (nor had he counted on Delaware in the East. He won all three). He knew Utah and Idaho were no contest once the head of the Mormon Church (long wooed by Kennedy) endorsed Nixon, even though Kennedy ran well ahead of the 1956 Democratic vote in every county in both states. But he was as surprised at his loss of Alaska as he was by his win in Hawaii (where it was not clear that he had won until a December 28 recount).

He had held some hopes for Montana, and possibly even Colorado, where the Denver *Post* had given him its first Democratic Presidential endorsement since 1916. He lost both. He was disappointed that National Chairman Jackson had not been able to deliver Washington. He was chagrined at not having spent more time in California, where migrants from the Bible Belt to the central valley had switched to Nixon in sufficient numbers to defeat him in a contest so close it was decided by the Republican absentee voters. That is why, conceding the strongly anti-Catholic Oklahoma, he had sent its Governor to campaign for him in the rural centers of California—but to no avail. Democratic factionalism had undermined him there as well.

The other state where a lack of time and unity defeated him was Virginia. "We could take this state away from Harry Byrd if we only had more time," he had said to me leaving Roanoke less than a week earlier, but we did not have time and fell short by 42,000 votes out of more than three-quarter million cast.

He had counted on most of the larger, more urbanized and industrial states of the Midwest, but expected to lose (and did lose) Indiana, where his reception seemed the coolest of the entire campaign. He won in Minnesota, with the help of Hubert Humphrey, where his victory was due more to the depressed Mesabi Iron Range than to the big cities. ("I used to think the Democrats were pretty strong in South Boston," he had said in Hibbing, "but we are going to send them out here for indoctrination.") He won in Illinois, where he was helped by strong candidates for Governor and Senator, Otto Kerner and his old friend Senator Douglas. He barely won in Missouri and in Michigan. He lost Wisconsin, where he had hoped his spring primary efforts would overcome a built-in Republican edge.

But his biggest disappointment by far was Ohio, where his Harris Poll had showed him ahead. In few states had he spent so much time or had larger or more enthusiastic crowds. Although he increased the Democratic vote in Ohio over 1956 by the same proportion as he did elsewhere, and increased it in 96 percent of its counties, that was not enough. He carried Cleveland by strong proportions, but the total turnout was too low. He carried Akron, Toledo, Youngstown, Warren and other labor centers, but did not do well enough in Cincinnati (which he barely carried), in Dayton or in Columbus to offset the Nixon sweep of Protestant small-town and rural voters, few of whom the Senator had ever seen on his travels. "There is no city in the United States," Kennedy would later tell a Columbus audience, "in which I get a warmer welcome and less votes."

With these exceptions—and the exceptions of Ohio, California, Wisconsin and Virginia made all the difference between a massive victory and a narrow squeak—the electoral results were about as he had hoped and expected. (My own expectations, as recorded in an office pool, had been too optimistic. I had predicted 408 electoral votes, lower than some of my colleagues but far above his final total of 303, to which Pierre Salinger came closest in our group. All of us predicted his proportion of the two-party popular vote would be in the 53-57 percent range, not in the 50.1-50.2 percent range it ultimately was.)

Candidate Kennedy had known that he had a tough fight, taking on a powerfully entrenched administration that had brought on no war or depression. He had known, reviewing Eisenhower's margins in 1956, that it would be no easy task to change enough voters to regain enough states. Both his own polls and the published ones told him it would be close nationally and close in the key states, but he could not have known it would be the closest in seventy-six years. He won twelve states with less than 2 percent of the two-party vote and lost six in the same range.

He had known also that no significant number of Republicans—Catholics or any other kind—would shift to him (and they didn't), and that to offset the loss of Democratic Protestants he had to pick up even more members of all faiths who had voted for Eisenhower (and he did). He had known that he would have to convert the sizable Republican majorities of 1956 in the major industrial states—an Eisenhower plurality of more than a million and a half in New York alone, for example—into new Democratic majorities (and he did).

He had known he would have to win a tremendous vote from labor, Catholics, Negroes, Jews, young voters and other city dwellers, and break even in the suburbs if he was to offset the rural and small-town Republican vote. He did. He broke even in the total vote cast in thirty-seven major suburban areas, carried twelve of the nineteen most important and increased the Democratic vote in all but one. He carried twenty-six of the forty largest cities, compared to Stevenson's four years earlier carrying only eleven. Of the fourteen Nixon carried all were in the Midwest, West or South (the one big city most opposed to Kennedy was Dallas, Texas).

Finally, he had gambled that Lyndon Johnson would not hurt him in the North and would help him in the South. That gamble paid off. Nixon, who emphasized states' rights in the South, had consistently criticized Johnson's nomination in the North—but with no effect. The Liberal Party in New York, which had threatened at Los Angeles to nominate its own ticket because of Johnson, cast more votes for Kennedy and Johnson than the margin by which they carried the state. In the South, where Johnson had wisely spent nearly half the campaign, the Democratic ticket, despite a growing tide of Republicanism, racism and religious bigotry, regained from the Republican column not only Texas—with the help of a large Negro and Latin-American vote, and resentment of the Johnsons' mistreatment in Dallas—but also Louisiana, where an independent elector movement split the opposition.

Tennessee, said its Governor, would have been two to one for Kennedy had it not been for his religion. While his ratio may be exaggerated, the Michigan survey estimated that the religious issue alone cost Kennedy an estimated net loss of one out of every six Southern voters, more than enough to account for Nixon's margin in Florida, Kentucky, and Virginia, as well as Tennessee, Oklahoma and possibly other Southern, border and Western states.

Protestant Democrats in the small towns of Ohio and the central valley of California, many of them originally from Oklahoma, Arkansas and the South, overcame Kennedy's lead in the cities of both states. French Catholics in Louisiana and Mexican Catholics in Texas may have helped overcome the anti-Catholic votes in those states. South Carolina was held despite the opposition of Senator Strom Thurmond and a final Nixon appearance with the Rev. Billy Graham. Mississippi, however, was carried by a slate of unpledged electors who voted for Harry Byrd, as did six of the eleven Democratic electors from Alabama. Nor could the border states of Kentucky and Oklahoma be saved from the anti-Catholic tide which very nearly carried Missouri, Illinois and Texas along with them. But West Virginia, his old friend, had stuck with Kennedy.

The statistics and surveys could be read in such a way as to produce the most sobering effect. Including votes for minor party candidates and unpledged electors, he had been denied a majority of the total popular vote—as had Lincoln one hundred years earlier, and as had every Democratic President, with the exception of Franklin Roosevelt, in the intervening hundred years. Even including only the two-party vote, a majority of the voters outside of Massachusetts had voted against him. A majority of the states (twenty-seven out of fifty) had voted against him. A majority of his own race had voted against him. So had a majority of his fellow college graduates and his fellow high-income earners. Contrary to crowd impressions, so had a majority of women voters. So had a majority of Protestants, farmers, old people, small-town inhabitants and business and professional men (although he made spectacular gains in the latter group, receiving more than twice the proportion of their vote that Truman had received in 1948).

But the very narrowness of his victory had, in another sense, broadened its base. John Kennedy could not have been elected President without the votes he received from Protestants as well as Catholics and Jews—indeed, more Protestants voted for him than all his Catholic and Jewish supporters combined. He could not have been elected without both Negro and Southern support. He could not have won without the votes he received from farmers and businessmen, young and old, rich and poor, cities and suburbs. His victory actually related to regions, religions and races only in the minds of the analysts. Millions of Americans who fitted into no category other than "citizens," and who acted on the basis of no pressure other than their own convictions, elected John Kennedy President of the United States.

One week earlier he had assailed an anonymous Republican poster distributed to San Diego defense plant workers which bore the caption: "Jack Kennedy is after your job." "That shows," he said, "how desperate and despicable this campaign has become. . . . I am after Mr. Eisenhower's job."

Now—after an uphill fight, against all odds, breaking all precedents and by the narrowest of margins—the job was his. That he had won at all, he admitted upon reflection, was "a miracle."

PART THREE

The Kennedy Presidency

CHAPTER IX

THE BEGINNING

O N THE NINTH DAY of November, 1960, shortly after noon, John
Fitzgerald Kennedy became President-elect of the United States.
It was an unwieldy mouthful by which to address him, the press
said, and he suggested that they continue to call him "Senator—a good
title." After a walk near the beach with Caroline on his back, he
watched Nixon's noontime concession on television, received and
acknowledged the congratulatory wires of Nixon and Eisenhower, and
changed his sweater and slacks for a suit and tie to make a brief statement of appreciation to the national television and press assembled at
the Hyannis Port Armory. He was jubilant about his victory. At the same
time he was deeply touched by it. Above all, he was tired, terribly tired.
He wanted and needed long hours of sleep, seclusion, relaxation in the
sun, and a peaceful life with his daughter and wife and with the new
baby expected soon. But as his car returned from the Armory to his Cape
cottage he counted up seventy-two days.

There were seventy-two days to inauguration.

. . . Seventy-two days in which to form an administration, staff the
White House, fill some seventy-five key Cabinet and policy posts, name
six hundred other major nominees, decide which incumbents to carry
over, distribute patronage to the faithful and fix personnel policies for
the future . . .

. . . Seventy-two days in which to work with Eisenhower on an orderly
transfer of power, with Nixon on a restoration of national unity, with
Democratic leaders on reshaping the National Committee, and with his
own aides on handling all the administrative problems of the transition

period, including finances, transportation, accommodations, press relations and attention to the enormous number of letters pouring in from
heads of state, well-wishers, job-seekers, old friends and myriad others . . .

. . . Seventy-two days in which to make plans for the inaugural
festivities, making certain nothing and no one was overlooked, arranging
for the right successor to be appointed to his seat in the Senate, selling
or transferring his financial holdings to avoid a conflict of interest, and
writing an Inaugural Address . . .

. . . Seventy-two days in which to make plans for the organization of
Congress (which would convene before his inauguration), to prepare
a legislative program that could be promptly incorporated into messages
and bills, and to formulate concrete policies and plans for all the problems
of the nation, foreign and domestic, for which he would soon be
responsible as President.

The number and nature of those problems might well have benumbed
the brain of another man. The postwar world was ablaze with change.
Yet the nation's seeming indifference and opposition to needed changes
had hampered progress. An endless, constantly frustrating "cold war"
had only increased the appeal of extremists with short and simple answers. "I think the President [Eisenhower] is going to escape," Senator
Kennedy had said earlier in the year, "and that all the pigeons are coming home on the next President."

In October, 1957, the Soviet Union had launched simultaneously the
first space capsule to orbit the earth and a new cold war offensive to
master the earth—an offensive relying on Western disunity in the face
of nuclear blackmail and on anti-Western nationalism in the under-
developed areas. In the three years that followed, the freedom of West
Berlin had been threatened by a Soviet ultimatum, backed by boasts of
medium-range ballistic missiles targeted on Western Europe. The existence of South Vietnam had been menaced by a campaign of guerrilla tactics and terror planned and supplied by the Communist regime in Hanoï.
The independence of Laos had been endangered by pro-Communist
insurgent forces. The Soviets had invested several billions of dollars in
military and economic aid in the developing nations, including arms for
Indonesia, the Aswan Dam for Egypt, steel mills for India and more arms
for the Algerian rebels. The Russian and Chinese Communists had competed for a Central African base in Ghana, in Guinea, in Mali and particularly in the chaotic Congo. The Russians had obtained a base in
the Western Hemisphere through Fidel Castro's takeover in Cuba and
his campaign to subvert Latin America. Red China was busy building
its own Afro-Asian collection of client states and its own atomic bomb.

In response, American military might was too thinly stretched and
too weakly financed to meet our global commitments. Our missile and
space efforts had started late. Our foreign aid was underfinanced,

as was the flexibility of our military potential, and populations and poverty grew faster in the developing countries than all their resources and our assistance combined. The United Nations was in disarray. The Paris Summit collapse, along with anti-American riots in Japan and Venezuela, had made democracy seem on the defensive. Our policies were not aligned in Latin America with the new forces of economic development and social justice, or abreast in Western Europe of the new forces for economic unity and growth. Other nations were uncertain *what* we meant when we talked—or *whether* we meant it when we talked—about the equality of man or about our desire for disarmament or about our commitment to defend freedom.

Within our own borders still more pigeons were coming home to roost. The third recession in seven years had caused the highest unemployment in over twenty years. The highest deficit in the nation's international balance of payments during peacetime had depleted our gold reserves to their lowest level in over twenty years. The growing frustrations of our oppressed Negro population, the growing cost of subsidizing large farms, the growing number of overcrowded college classrooms and uncared-for elder citizens—all these and more, Kennedy knew, were not merely matters for Democratic campaign talk, but concrete problems about to confront him. And he knew that they were not as susceptible to ready political solution as the partisans of either party had argued in the campaign.

THE PROBLEMS OF TRANSITION

Seventy-two days gave him very little time. But he did not start wholly from scratch. The Brookings Institution—which deserves a large share of the credit for history's smoothest transfer of power between opposing parties—had urged both nominees after the conventions to prepare for the problems of transition; and Senator Kennedy had named, as both his liaison with Brookings and his adviser on the interregnum, his friend from the Drew Pearson incident, Washington attorney Clark Clifford, formerly Special Counsel to President Truman and Stuart Symington's preconvention manager. Clifford's counsel was constantly sought during the transition—although, Kennedy quipped to one audience, Clark had asked him for nothing whatsoever in return except the right to advertise the Clifford law firm on the back of the one-dollar bill. In typical Kennedy fashion, he also asked Columbia Professor Richard Neustadt, a leading student of the Presidency, to outline, preferably without consultation with Clifford, his own views on the personnel problems with which the winner of the election would be faced.

Both men produced helpful reports, and both continued to advise throughout the transition period. With no attempt at collaboration or coordination, their recommendations in no way conflicted and largely coincided. Neustadt's memorandum contained more cautions and more details on the problems of transition, with particular emphasis on the White House staff. Clifford's memorandum was more basic. ("I am never certain," one Kennedy staff member observed, "whether Clark Clifford is a genius in making the complex sound simple or in making the obvious sound profound, but either way he's a genius.")

With these two reports, and a more detailed analysis from Brookings, before him on the living room coffee table, the President-elect on the morning of November 10 met in his brother's house with his closest advisers. We had instinctively risen when he came in, sensing the automatic change in our relations. He wanted the next few hours behind him so he could fly to Florida and rest. The crisp, compartmentalized approach of the campaign seemed somewhat dulled by fatigue. But he knew, as the memoranda in his hand confirmed, that certain decisions had to be immediately and carefully made.

He would need during the transition and throughout his term in the White House an aide for administration and appointments, an aide for press relations and an aide for program and policy. To these positions he named the three men who had in effect occupied them during the campaign: O'Donnell, Salinger and me. I had the honor of being named first—the title, which Clifford was anxious to see restored to its former status, was that of Special Counsel to the President—and it was the one post I wanted most. O'Brien and Shriver were placed in charge of the talent hunt for Cabinet and other officers. No specific role was spelled out for Bob Kennedy, the other man present, but clearly it would continue to be a key one.

Neustadt had recommended that, in the interest of national unity, smooth continuity and political balance, five incumbents in sensitive positions be considered nonpartisan and continued by Kennedy in those same jobs, with prompt announcement to prevent contrary pressures and speculation: the Directors of the FBI and CIA, the President's Science Adviser, the Civil Service Commission Chairman, and the Executive Secretary of the National Security Council. Kennedy kept only the first two, whom his dinner guests the previous evening had reportedly suggested be the first to be ousted. He placed calls to Messrs. Hoover and Dulles from our meeting, and included their names in his first press announcement as President-elect.

Other business delayed his departure. Of all the messages of congratulations he received, he was most concerned about his answers to two: a cable from French President De Gaulle which rang with elegant eloquence and one from Soviet Chairman Khrushchev with a ring of "peace" propaganda. For his answer to De Gaulle's "Welcome, Dear

Partner" message, he turned to his own tutor in French language and literature, Jacqueline Bouvier Kennedy, and with her drafted a warm and perceptive reply.

Khrushchev, after his outburst at Paris, had made plain his intention to have no more dealings with Eisenhower and to await the election of his successor. His message to Kennedy hinted at a summit and somewhat hypocritically called for a return to the Soviet-American relations "developing in Franklin Roosevelt's time." For an answer, the President-elect asked me to call one of the foremost Russian experts in the Foreign Service, his old friend "Chip" Bohlen. The latter's one-sentence suggestion seemed more curt than courteous, and the President-elect, convinced that "civility is not a sign of weakness," drafted a less brusque reply which was equally cautious in substance but more friendly and hopeful in tone.

Even as the President-elect departed for the peace of Palm Beach, the orderly transfer of executive responsibility was going forward. It was enormously aided by the cooperation of President Eisenhower. His initial wire of congratulations from Washington on November 9 (not counting the premature congratulations accidentally sent the night before) was promptly followed a few hours later by another from Augusta, Georgia, where he had flown for a brief vacation. This second message dealt wholly with the transition, offering to meet with Kennedy "at any mutually convenient time," assigning chief aide Wilton Persons as his liaison with the Kennedy operation, and making clear that his Budget Director, his Secretary of State and all other officials stood ready to help. Kennedy asked Clifford to meet with Persons, asked me to meet with White House and Budget Bureau officials, asked each appointee when named to meet with his counterpart, and on December 6 and January 19 personally met with Eisenhower at the White House.

In both meetings Eisenhower was joined after an interval by his Secretaries of State, Defense and Treasury, and in both meetings the President-elect probed hard on the problems he was about to face. Eisenhower, who had regarded Kennedy with disdain in the campaign, and who had apparently delayed their first meeting until it was clear no recount could change the voters' verdict, reportedly told a friend that the young Senator had "tremendously impressed" him. Kennedy in turn found Eisenhower "better than I had thought," and he was grateful for his cooperative attitude, remarking after the second meeting, "I don't think we have asked for anything that they haven't done."

He also met briefly and cordially on November 14 with Nixon, to whose gracious wire of concession he had responded with congratulations "on a fine race" and his conviction "that you and I can maintain our long-standing cordial relations in the years ahead." For the unprecedented meeting he requested with Nixon, which both men described as amicable, and for which ex-President Herbert Hoover served as intermediary, Kennedy flew from Palm Beach to Nixon's vacation retreat in Key Biscayne, Florida.

Eisenhower and Nixon, merely by meeting with Kennedy, were patriotically recognizing the certainty of his election, and thus helping to put an end to the bitter charges of fraud, the demands for recounts and the threats of Southern independent electors. In few other nations could so narrow a result have been so smoothly accepted. A framework of good feeling was established; and in sharp contrast to the rancor, the cool relations, the absence of communication and the casual indifference which had marked almost all previous Presidential transitions, the Eisenhower-Kennedy transfer was characterized by an atmosphere of cordiality and continuity. It demonstrated to the nation and the world a spirit of unity which John Kennedy was anxious to preserve.

There were some disagreements, to be sure. As I reviewed with Eisenhower's Budget officers the document with which he would take his leave of the Congress in January, it was clear that its precarious balance relied upon legislative actions, expenditure reductions and revenue expectations which they knew full well would never be realized. But it was equally clear that they had no intention of revising their estimates in the light of changed conditions, preferring to let Kennedy take the blame for the deficit. At the same time, the President-elect thought it inappropriate and unwise, until he had full responsibility and information, to participate in, commit himself to, or even comment or be consulted upon those actions taken by the outgoing administration between election and inauguration—including a mission to Western Europe to improve the payments balance and the ending of all diplomatic relations with Cuba.

Below the Presidential level, the results varied from department to department. One appointee told us that his predecessor had spent most of their conference on transition problems urging him to retain that departing official's personal private secretary. From my interview with the genial General Wilton Persons, who had succeeded Sherman Adams as the Assistant to the President, I learned enough to confirm Kennedy's wisdom in abolishing the duties of that post, which included: permitting no memorandum, letter or document to go before the President without Persons' initialed approval; seeing Cabinet members, Congressmen and White House aides who would otherwise "overwhelm" the President; granting interviews to few, if any, reporters except when the Press Secretary said it was necessary; and similar functions more appropriate to the chief of staff in a military chain of command. Although I was disappointed at the time that a promised list of pending problems was never forthcoming from Persons, I now realize that the personal and political nature of White House posts would have made such a list wholly speculative.

For the most part, the collaboration was smooth and useful. Kennedy men emulated their leader in showing respect for their predecessors and gratitude for their assistance. The whole process was further facilitated by the Eisenhower administration's generous agreement to put two incoming personnel on the payroll of each department as of January 3, 1961, with ten in both State and Defense.

Despite this move, one of the unsolved problems of that transition period, on which Kennedy would later successfully urge Congressional action for the sake of future Presidents-elect, was its cost. His personal fortune, homes, plane, telephone and Senate office payroll could absorb much of it. Many new appointees and advisers took care of their own expenses, although not without considerable hardship on their part. Many were granted office space in their prospective departments. But more funds had to be found for the many people required to handle mail, screen appointments, meet the press and assist the President-elect, for their wages, hotel rooms, office space, supplies, telephones and travel. It was unfair to saddle either the Kennedy family or the National Committee with the total bill, which was estimated in excess of $350,000 from election to inauguration.

Except for brief visits to Nixon, Boston and the LBJ ranch in Texas, Kennedy divided his time between Palm Beach, Washington and the Carlyle Hotel in New York. His air travels totaled an insignificant (compared to the campaign) fifteen thousand miles. For the first two weeks, and from time to time thereafter, he basked in the sun at Palm Beach— where he quickly gained fifteen pounds—but felt it was too fancy and faraway for serious announcements. He enjoyed his own home in Washington, but found himself more subject there to interruptions and requests than in New York. Moreover, his Georgetown house was not large, and the ever-present crowd of newsmen, policemen, Secret Service agents and onlookers was forced to freeze outside while the Senator met inside with aides and possible appointees.

One prolonged stay in Washington commenced earlier than planned. He had flown from Palm Beach to Washington to share Thanksgiving dinner with his wife, whose pregnancy kept her at home. When he left that evening to return to Florida, all was well. But upon landing in Palm Beach, he was told that John F. Kennedy, Jr. had been suddenly and prematurely born, and he immediately flew back to Washington.

FAREWELL TO MASSACHUSETTS

The trip to Boston served three purposes: (1) to attend a meeting of the Harvard Board of Overseers, whose obligations of membership he took very seriously (when nearly mobbed by cheering students in the Harvard Yard, he responded, "I'm here to go over your grades with President Pusey, and I'll protect your interests"); (2) to confer with prospective appointees from the Boston and New England area, in a brief session at the Arthur Schlesinger, Jr. home; and (3) to bid farewell to Massachusetts in an address to the state legislature on historic Beacon Hill.

The last was approached with some concern. Kennedy the historian was not unmindful of Lincoln's farewell to the people of Springfield. Kennedy the politician was not unmindful of the debt he owed the state of his birth for making possible his public career. And Kennedy the President-elect was not unmindful of his inability to be as proud of all the politicians in Massachusetts as Massachusetts was of him. Few state governments in the United States have a record free from corruption, but in January, 1961, few had a record that could surpass the repeated disclosures of official wrongdoing that had rocked his home state. The President-elect felt he could neither avoid that issue nor deliver a self-righteous lecture about it.

There had been little time to prepare the speech, and I had reluctantly dipped into our file of phrases collected for the Inaugural Address in order to meet his specifications. It was not a lengthy speech—less than three dozen sentences. But it was one of his best, and it proved to be a moving occasion. It was his first formal address since the election, and to all those watching on television he looked and sounded like a President as he spoke of government as "a city upon a hill."

> For of those to whom much is given, much is required. And when at some future date the high court of history sits in judgment on each of us, recording whether in our brief span of service we fulfilled our responsibilities . . . our success . . . will be measured by the answers to four questions:
> First, were we truly men of courage . . . ?
> Second, were we truly men of judgment . . . ?
> Third, were we truly men of integrity . . . ?
> Finally, were we truly men of dedication . . . ?
> These are the qualities which, with God's help, this son of Massachusetts hopes will characterize our government's conduct.

FORMULATION OF A PROGRAM

By the time he flew to Boston, the pace of the President-elect very nearly matched the furious rate of the fall campaign, though it was far less physically punishing. Two months earlier he had concluded his brief statement of victory at the Hyannis Port Armory by saying, "Now my wife and I prepare for a new administration—and a new baby." In the weeks that followed, he had welcomed the new baby and largely formed the new administration. He had slept long hours, fished, golfed regularly, visited the LBJ ranch, attended the theater in New York and enjoyed the company of his family. Shunning a host of applicants, he had recommended his old roommate, the former Mayor of Gloucester, Benjamin Smith, to fill his Senate seat. He had sold all his corporate stocks and bonds and converted them into Government Bonds. He had read both pertinent and pleasurable books by the score, reviewed dozens of reports and conferred repeatedly with his expanding number of associates. Building wider public acceptance, he had seen not only Eisenhower and Nixon but Herbert Hoover, Billy Graham, labor leaders, farm leaders, Negro leaders and many more. He had held nineteen press conferences of one kind or another. He had conferred with Lyndon Johnson and with the leading Democrats in both houses of Congress. He had received regular intelligence briefings, and conferred with the British Ambassador and German Vice Chancellor, and he would later confer before inauguration with the Chairman of the Joint Chiefs of Staff.

His "office" was the living room or library of whichever home he inhabited at the time—Palm Beach, Georgetown or the Carlyle Hotel penthouse—and his "office" continually throbbed with activity. While the Senator interviewed one prospective appointee, another waited in the bedroom, sometimes along with a Kennedy aide waiting to brief the President-elect and a delegation invited to see him. Press and Secret Service clustered outside, telephones rang constantly inside.

My notes on the instructions which he gave me one afternoon (largely because I happened to be there on other business) indicate the range of his activities:

> Get Wiesner on the phone. . . . Ask Lovett if Fisk would take it and let us know before this afternoon's meeting. . . . Find an office in Agriculture or somewhere for Ken Galbraith. . . . Ask Roosa when the Sproul group should report to the White House. . . . Ask Rusk about McCone staying on compared to McKinney. . . . Check with the Speaker on Hays. . . . F.D.R., Jr. for the Philippines? . . . Get Mills's voting record. . . . Consult Marcy. . . . Which spot at Treasury for Surrey? . . . Magnuson wants educational TV and oceanography mentioned in Inaugural or State of the Union. . . . Ask Morse about minimum wage report.

By chance this last call to Senator Morse, then with the UN delegation in New York, was returned when I was again in conference with the President-elect and he answered the phone: "Yes . . . He's here, operator, but I'll take it. . . . This is Senator Kennedy and I'm answering Mr. Sorensen's calls for him today."

But far from this often frenzied atmosphere the formulation of a new Presidential program was quietly under way. It was a remarkable job. A Democratic President had not succeeded a Republican since 1933, and that occasion offered little by way of precedent. Another President might have awaited his inauguration and then appointed study groups, after the pattern in 1953, to give him time and ideas. But Kennedy had a different conception of his duty. When asked, prior to the convention, what his first effort would be as President, he had replied: ". . . to determine what the unfinished business was, what our agenda was, and set it before the American people in the early months of 1961." To do that required unusual efforts in the late months of 1960.

The previous summer, following his nomination, the Senator had commissioned with appropriate publicity a series of advisory committee reports to be delivered in the transition period: a report on Defense Department reorganization under the chairmanship of Stuart Symington, a report on foreign policy problems under Adlai Stevenson, a "nonpartisan, bipartisan" report on national security measures under Paul Nitze, and a report on natural resource needs under Congressman Frank Smith. In addition, Averell Harriman was to tour Africa, and Senator Joe Clark and Congressman Emanuel Celler were to prepare new civil rights recommendations. The political and public relations value of announcing each of these studies at the start of the campaign was obvious.

But after noon on November 9, it was no longer a matter of politics and public relations. Many more reports were needed as foundations for new programs and policies. Public reports were useful, also, as trial balloons to test the political atmosphere, and as public evidence of continuing Kennedy momentum.

Several of the topics generally touched upon in the Stevenson report —including foreign economic policy, food surpluses, Africa, USIA, overseas personnel and disarmament—were assigned to a series of new task forces directed by Stevenson associates George Ball and John Sharon. James Landis was asked to report on regulatory agencies and Richard Neustadt on government reorganization. My first two assignments as Special Counsel to the President-elect were (1) to recruit a task force on ways to combat the recession and (2) to work out with him other studies needed. The latter list rapidly expanded to include depressed areas and West Virginia, housing and cities, health and Social Security, education, taxation, minimum wages, outer space, Latin America, India, cultural exchanges, USIA and the Peace Corps.

The obvious overlapping in these lists caused confusion at times but represented a deliberate Kennedy pattern. Rejecting one suggestion for coordination, he said, "I simply cannot afford to have just one set of advisers." One major subject omitted was agriculture, and an effort to establish a task force on this subject failed. We found many men with open minds on agriculture, and we found many experts, but we could find no open-minded experts.

Except for the depressed areas—West Virginia committee—which kept an old Kennedy commitment by immediately organizing for hearings in West Virginia under Senator Paul Douglas—the formation of these task forces was not announced. The close to one hundred men serving on them were drawn largely from the professions, foundations and university faculties, including two college presidents, in an unusually swift mobilization of the nation's intellectual talent. The names of those of the thirteen for which I was responsible were drawn from the personal files, friendships and memories of various members of the Kennedy team and from recommendations by the chairman of each group.[1]

Partly because it was a time of intellectual hope and cooperation with the new administration, and partly because it was a time when talent was being recognized in prestigious appointments, no one, to my recollection, refused a request to serve on a task force. In some cases their acceptance did sound a little less eager than their initial response to the operator's statement that "Mr. Sorensen is calling from Palm Beach."

The members of these task forces received no compensation and usually no expense money. In many cases only the chairman received public credit and a personal visit with the President-elect. Many of these specialists were sooner or later offered positions in the administration— men such as Jerome Wiesner, Walter Heller, Wilbur Cohen, Mortimer Caplin, Henry Fowler, James Tobin, Stanley Surrey, Adolf Berle, Joe McMurray, Tom Finletter, Robert Schaetzel, Donald Hornig, Frank Keppel, Lincoln Gordon, Jerry Spingarn, Champion Ward, Arturo Morales Carrión and many others, including those previously mentioned in our list of "academic advisers." But some were not asked and some were unable to accept. Moreover, fiscal limitations, legislative opposition or other practical inhibitions often reduced the implementation of their work so sharply as to cause them disappointment if not dismay.

The President-elect's private judgment on the task force reports, as they were delivered in early January, ranged from "helpful" to "terrific."[2]

1 Testimony to the high regard in which his fellow academicians held Walter Heller was the fact that his name was suggested for three separate task forces.
2 The reports, or summaries thereof, were usually released after delivery to the President-elect, although certain recommendations—for example, those on Cuba in the Latin America report and those on reform in the taxation report—were

Some, such as the Symington report calling for a wholesale reorganization of the military services along functional lines, were too controversial to be more than a stimulant to future planning. Others, such as the nine-billion-dollar program urged by Purdue's President Frederick Hovde and his blue-ribbon task force on education, set a standard which could not immediately be reached. But all provided useful facts, arguments and ideas, and nearly all were directly reflected in legislation. Paul Samuelson's antirecession task force, for example, had a major role in shaping the new administration's early economic proposals (and also redoubled Kennedy's futile efforts to induce Samuelson to leave the academic calm that he relished and join the "New Frontier").

But composition of the new President's program neither awaited nor depended upon completion of the task force reports. In November and December, with the help of the Budget Bureau staff and my associates, a master check list of all possible legislative, budgetary and administrative issues for Presidential action was prepared.[3] This list was then refined and reduced to manageable proportions in a conference with our new Budget Director and his hold-over Deputy Director; and on December 21 a list of over 250 items, ranging from area redevelopment to Nike-Zeus, was reviewed in a rugged all-day and late-night session with the President-elect in Palm Beach. "Now I know," he said, looking over the length and complexity of the list, "why Ike had Sherman Adams."

He was well rested by then. His mind was far more keen and clear than it had seemed when I had last visited Palm Beach two weeks after the election. He had still seemed tired then and reluctant to face up to the details of personnel and program selection. Now he was deeply tanned, and as he changed from his swimming trunks in his bedroom, he joked about how fat he looked. His comments were precise and decisive, and it was a tonic to me to see that he could hardly wait until the full responsibility was really his.

When we interrupted our session for lunch, he told us with a touch of humor about the assassination attempt uncovered the week before. A deranged New Hampshire resident had driven his car to Florida, filled it with dynamite and planned to crash it into Kennedy's. When finally picked up on December 15 by the Secret Service tracing a tip from his

deemed better left confidential. They were also made available to the appropriate Cabinet and sub-Cabinet members as appointed, and the latter in some instances met with the task forces working within their jurisdiction of subject matter.

[3] It was based on Kennedy campaign pledges and written statements, as indexed by both our staff and the Budget Bureau; the 1960 Democratic platform and our various campaign conferences and committees; Democratic and nonpartisan legislation left unenacted by the Eighty-sixth Congress; expiring laws in need of renewal and possibly revision; and other Budget Bureau briefing materials on an agency-by-agency and issue-by-issue basis, including Eisenhower recommendations which were unrelated to party philosophy.

home town, he said that he had foregone a perfect opportunity the previous Sunday only because Jacqueline and the children were also present. The President-elect seemed more intrigued than appalled by the man's ingenuity in planning a motiveless murder, and then he dismissed it from his mind and returned to work.

On some items he asked questions of his new Budget experts who were present; on some he requested memoranda of additional detail or arguments from his Cabinet appointees who were not. Some matters he postponed as of lower priority or doubtful desirability. Some he referred to his task forces for recommendation. A few he preferred to delete altogether. He also added a few items on his own: a commission on campaign costs, a memo to all appointees to hold down Federal employment and another to divest themselves of all conflicts of interest.

It has since been widely reported that Kennedy, alarmed by the narrowness of his winning margin, had decided to retreat from his original plans for his first year. Certainly no alarm or retreat was sounded in this meeting. The President-elect was aware of the legislative realities. He exercised caution consistent with his new responsibilities. And he did not feel free, with the dollar appearing slightly shaky, to reverse in one month the fiscal philosophy that he felt had weakened the economy for years. But reviewing my notes on that December 21 check list, I see no signs of a slowdown. Not a single one of his major campaign pledges was ignored or interred.

On the basis of that December 21 conference, a detailed letter of questions and requests was sent to each prospective member of the Cabinet, assignments were meted out for the drafting of detailed proposals and documents, new budget estimates were prepared, the task force reports were fitted in—and a Kennedy Presidential program took definite shape well before Kennedy became President. The amount of preparation was unprecedented. Clearly it made it possible for the new President to take the legislative initiative immediately. In almost every critical area of public policy—including recovery from the recession, economic growth, the budget, balance of payments, health care, housing, highways, education, taxation, conservation, agriculture, regulatory agencies, foreign aid, Latin America, defense and conflicts of interest— comprehensive Presidential messages and some 277 separate requests would be sent to the Congress in Kennedy's first hundred days.

Kennedy was irritated, however, by widespread press speculation that he intended to emulate the first hundred days of Franklin Roosevelt, who had taken office with a landslide vote, in the midst of a depression and with heavy Congressional majorities, and consequently rushed through far-reaching legislation almost immediately. Kennedy had emphasized the necessity of "setting forth the *agenda*" in the first hundred days, but had no illusions that the Congress and country of 1961 bore any resemblance to 1933.

INAUGURATION

Early in January, with work on his program well under way and his principal nominees named, the President-elect's thoughts turned more and more to his inauguration. He took a lively interest in plans for the Inaugural Concert and five simultaneous Inaugural Balls (all of which he would attend), in plans for the four-hour-long Inaugural Parade (all of which he would watch in twenty-degree temperature), the million-dollar Democratic fund-raising Inaugural Gala (which he greatly enjoyed, despite a two-hour delay due to blizzards) and in all the other festivities. He asked Robert Frost to deliver a poem at the inauguration ceremony. He wanted Marian Anderson to sing "The Star-Spangled Banner." He sought a family Bible on which he could take the oath of office without arousing the POAU. He indicated that top hats instead of Homburgs would be in order for the official party. And, finally and most importantly, he began to work on his Inaugural Address.

He had first mentioned it to me in November. He wanted suggestions from everyone. He wanted it short. He wanted it focused on foreign policy. He did not want it to sound partisan, pessimistic or critical of his predecessor. He wanted neither the customary cold war rhetoric about the Communist menace nor any weasel words that Khrushchev might misinterpret. And he wanted it to set a tone for the era about to begin.

He asked me to read all the past Inaugural Addresses (which I discovered to be a largely undistinguished lot, with some of the best eloquence emanating from some of our worst Presidents). He asked me to study the secret of Lincoln's Gettysburg Address (my conclusion, which his Inaugural applied, was that Lincoln never used a two- or three-syllable word where a one-syllable word would do, and never used two or three words where one word would do).

Actual drafting did not get under way until the week before it was due. As had been true of his acceptance speech at Los Angeles, pages, paragraphs and complete drafts had poured in, solicited from Kraft, Galbraith, Stevenson, Bowles and others, unsolicited from newsmen, friends and total strangers. From Billy Graham he obtained a list of possible Biblical quotations, and I secured a similar list from the director of Washington's Jewish Community Council, Isaac Franck.

The final text included several phrases, sentences and themes suggested by these sources, as did his address to the Massachusetts legislature. He was, in fact, concerned that the Massachusetts speech had pre-empted some of his best material and had set a mark that would be hard to top. Credit should also go to other Kennedy advisers who reviewed the early drafts and offered suggestions or encouragement.

But however numerous the assistant artisans, the principal architect of the Inaugural Address was John Fitzgerald Kennedy. Many of its most memorable passages can be traced to earlier Kennedy speeches and writings. For example:

Inaugural Address	*Other Addresses*
For man holds in his mortal hands the power to abolish all forms of human poverty and all forms of human life.	. . . man . . . has taken into his mortal hands the power to exterminate the entire species some seven times over. —*Acceptance speech at Los Angeles*
. . . the torch has been passed to a new generation of Americans. . . .	It is time, in short, for a new generation of Americans. —*Acceptance speech and several campaign speeches*
And so, my fellow Americans, ask not what your country can do for you; ask what you can do for your country.	We do not campaign stressing what our country is going to do for us as a people. We stress what we can do for the country, all of us. —*Televised campaign address from Washington, September 20, 1960*

No Kennedy speech ever underwent so many drafts. Each paragraph was reworded, reworked and reduced. The following table illustrates the attention paid to detailed changes:

First Draft	*Next-to-Last Draft*	*Final Text*
We celebrate today not a victory of party but the sacrament of democracy.	We celebrate today not a victory of party but a convention of freedom.	We observe today not a victory of party but a celebration of freedom.
Each of us, whether we hold office or not, shares the responsibility for guiding this most difficult of all societies along the path of self-	In your hands, my fellow citizens, more than in mine, will be determined the success or failure of our course.	In your hands, my fellow citizens, more than mine, will rest the final success or failure of our course.

First Draft	*Next-to-Last Draft*	*Final Text*
discipline and self-government.		
Nor can two great and powerful nations forever continue on this reckless course, both overburdened by the staggering cost of modern weapons . . .	. . . neither can two great and powerful nations long endure their present reckless course, both overburdened by the staggering cost of modern weapons . . .	. . . neither can two great and powerful groups of nations take comfort from our present course—both sides overburdened by the cost of modern weapons . . .
And if the fruits of cooperation prove sweeter than the dregs of suspicion, let both sides join ultimately in creating a true world order—neither a Pax Americana, nor a Pax Russiana, nor even a balance of power—but a community of power.	And if a beachhead of cooperation can be made in the jungles of suspicion, let both sides join some day in creating, not a new balance of power but a new world of law . . .	And if a beachhead of cooperation can push back the jungle of suspicion, let both sides join in creating a new endeavor, not a new balance of power, but a new world of law . . .

Initially, while he worked on his thoughts at Palm Beach, I worked at my home in a Washington suburb with telephoned instructions from the President-elect and the material collected from other sources. Then I flew down, was driven to his father's oceanside home, and gave him my notes for the actual drafting and assembling. We worked through the morning seated on the patio overlooking the Atlantic.

He was dissatisfied with each attempt to outline domestic goals. It sounded partisan, he said, divisive, too much like the campaign. Finally he said, "Let's drop out the domestic stuff altogether. It's too long anyway." He wanted it to be the shortest in the twentieth century, he said. "It's more effective that way and I don't want people to think I'm a windbag." He couldn't beat FDR's abbreviated wartime remarks in 1944, I said—and he settled for the shortest (less than nineteen hundred words) since 1905.

"I'm sick of reading how we're planning another 'hundred days' of miracles," he said, "and I'd like to know who on the staff is talking that up. Let's put in that this won't all be finished in a hundred days or a thousand."

That afternoon, as he was busy with other meetings at the house, I put his notes, changes and additions into a clean draft, working beside the Palm Beach Towers Hotel swimming pool.

The next morning, on the patio in sport clothes, he reworked it further. "Let's eliminate all the 'I's,' " he said. "Just say what 'we' will do. You'll have to leave it in about the oath and the responsibility, but let's cut it everywhere else." The ending, he said, "sounds an awful lot like the ending of the Massachusetts legislature speech, but I guess it's OK." He worked and reworked the "ask not" sentence, with the three campaign speeches containing a similar phrase (Anchorage, Detroit, Washington) spread out on a low glass coffee table beside him.

Later that day—January 17—as we flew back to Washington from Palm Beach, working in his cabin on the *Caroline,* the final phrasing was emerging. A Biblical quotation that was later used in his American University speech was deleted. The opening paragraphs were redictated by the President-elect to Evelyn Lincoln en route, and he smilingly placed in the plane's desk drawer his handwritten notes from which he had dictated, saying, "An early draft of Roosevelt's Inaugural was discovered the other day—and brought $200,000 at an auction."

Arriving back in Washington, the work went on at his house and in our Senate offices. Kenneth Galbraith suggested "cooperative ventures" with our allies in places of "joint ventures," which sounded like a mining partnership. Dean Rusk suggested that the other peoples of the world be challenged to ask "what together we can do for freedom" instead of "what you can do for freedom." Walter Lippmann suggested that references to the Communist bloc be changed from "enemy" to "adversary." The President-elect inserted a phrase he had used in a campaign speech on Latin America—"a new alliance for progress." At the last moment, concerned that his emphasis on foreign affairs would be interpreted as an evasion on civil rights, he added to his commitment on human rights the words "at home and around the world."

On January 19, one day before inauguration, it was finished. The Arrangements Committee was asked to check on the height of the reading lectern. A large-type reading copy was encased in a loose-leaf notebook. A copy sat beside the Kennedy chair at home, and by his seat on a quick trip to New York, so that any spare moment could be used to familiarize himself with it. (He never memorized a speech.) It was beside him when he took time out, amidst the last day's hectic schedule of conferences and arrangements, to meet seven of my little nieces and nephews as well as their parents.

Inauguration morning dawned cold but clear. Three thousand servicemen stationed in the Washington area had done an amazing job of working through the night with seven hundred plows and trucks to remove the eight inches of snow which, on the previous day, had nearly strangled the city. (On hearing the order go out for snow shovelers, one new Kennedy economic adviser, already burdened with a dozen assignments, had wearily remarked to his chairman, "Don't be surprised if they call us.") Visitors from every state, jubilant Kennedy workers we had hardly seen since the primaries, foreign diplomats and dignitaries, outgoing and incoming officials, a specially invited group of 155 writers, artists and scholars, and thousands of ordinary citizens of every age and background, all crowded the capital city and Capitol Hill. On the temporary wooden grandstands raised on the east front of the newly painted Capitol, under a glittering sun but in bitter cold, the Cabinet and White House officers of the New Frontier assembled. We bore some resemblance to "frontiersmen," wearing sweaters beneath our formal togs and woolen gloves along with top hats. As we greeted each other gaily, the chill in the air merely added a certain warmth to the spirit of youth and vigor.

Few will forget the memorable moments of that solemn ceremony at twelve noon:

Robert Frost, with the glare of the sun and the snow making it impossible for his aging eyes to read a new dedication (". . . a Golden Age of poetry and power, of which this noonday's the beginning hour . . ."), resolutely reciting his older poem from memory . . .

Richard Cardinal Cushing, delivering a proud (and prolonged) prayer for his famous parishioner while firemen and Secret Servicemen contended with smoldering short-circuited wires in the lectern . . .

John Fitzgerald Kennedy, thirty-fifth President of the United States, in that marvelously clear voice, repeating after Chief Justice Earl Warren the oath of office he had told the Houston ministers he could take without condition or reservation, "so help me God."

Few will forget the striking contrast presented by the outgoing and incoming Presidents. One was the likable, dedicated product of the rural Midwest and the Military Academy. The other was the urbane product of the urban East. Both had spent their entire adult careers in the service of their country, yet they were vastly different, not only in age, religion and political philosophy, but in their views of politics as a profession and the Presidency as power. Every eye watched them take their places, the oldest man ever to serve in the office of the Presidency and the youngest man ever elected to it. Dwight Eisenhower, aged seventy—still looking remarkably ruddy, his successor observed—sat next to John Kennedy, aged forty-three, bareheaded as always in the twenty-two-degree air, carrying the top hat he had decreed all should wear. Their contrast lent added meaning to the phrase: "Let the word go forth from this time and place, to friend and foe alike, that the torch has been passed to a new generation of Americans."

Grouped behind Kennedy as he removed his overcoat to speak were the young men of his new administration—men with strikingly successful backgrounds in business, law, politics, government and academic affairs—men who were, with few exceptions, unschooled in the old pre-World War I dogmas and pre-depression doctrines—men who had witnessed the folly of unpreparedness and appeasement, the tragedy of war, the dawn of the nuclear age, and the harmful rejection of intellectuals by McCarthyism and the new materialism. These were men who had been concerned about the lack of ideas and idealism in the sterile clash between repressive Communism and narrowly negative anti-Communism, but who were also determined, as their leader put it that day, to "pay any price, bear any burden, meet any hardship, support any friend [or] oppose any foe in order to assure the survival and the success of liberty."

I know of no way to summarize, condense or excerpt the Kennedy Inaugural Address. It was itself a compact summary of the new President's hopes and resolves—his pledges to our friends and allies, old and new—his request to the Communists for a new quest for peace—and his summons to his fellow citizens to bear with him the burdens of freedom. Each of these imperatives was contained in phrases too brief to be summarized and too important to be omitted. They were addressed to the American people of our time but have meaning for all people for all time. For they embody the best of our heritage from the past and the best of our hopes for the future. This one speech, of all John Kennedy's speeches, must be set forth here in full:

We observe today not a victory of party but a celebration of freedom, symbolizing an end as well as a beginning, signifying renewal as well as change. For I have sworn before you and Almighty God the same solemn oath our forebears prescribed nearly a century and three-quarters ago.

The world is very different now. For man holds in his mortal hands the power to abolish all forms of human poverty and all forms of human life. And yet the same revolutionary belief for which our forebears fought is still at issue around the globe, the belief that the rights of man come not from the generosity of the state but from the hand of God.

We dare not forget today that we are the heirs of that first revolution. Let the word go forth from this time and place, to friend and foe alike, that the torch has been passed to a new generation of Americans, born in this century, tempered by war, disciplined by a hard and bitter peace, proud of our ancient heritage, and unwilling to witness or permit the slow undoing of those human rights to which this nation has always been committed, and to which we are committed today at home and around the world.

Let every nation know, whether it wishes us well or ill, that we shall pay any price, bear any burden, meet any hardship, support any friend, oppose any foe to assure the survival and the success of liberty.

This much we pledge—and more.

To those old allies whose cultural and spiritual origins we share, we pledge the loyalty of faithful friends. United, there is little we cannot do in a host of cooperative ventures. Divided, there is little we can do, for we dare not meet a powerful challenge at odds and split asunder.

To those new states whom we welcome to the ranks of the free, we pledge our word that one form of colonial control shall not have passed away merely to be replaced by a far more iron tyranny. We shall not always expect to find them supporting our view. But we shall always hope to find them strongly supporting their own freedom, and to remember that, in the past, those who foolishly sought power by riding the back of the tiger ended up inside.

To those peoples in the huts and villages of half the globe struggling to break the bonds of mass misery, we pledge our best efforts to help them help themselves, for whatever period is required, not because the Communists may be doing it, not because we seek their votes, but because it is right. If a free society cannot help the many who are poor, it cannot save the few who are rich.

To our sister republics south of our border, we offer a special pledge: to convert our good words into good deeds, in a new alliance for progress, to assist free men and free governments in casting off the chains of poverty. But this peaceful revolution of hope cannot become the prey of hostile powers. Let all our neighbors know that we shall join with them to oppose aggression or subversion anywhere in the Americas. And let every other power know that this hemisphere intends to remain the master of its own house.

To that world assembly of sovereign states, the United Nations, our last best hope in an age where the instruments of war have far outpaced the instruments of peace, we renew our pledge of support: to prevent it from becoming merely a forum for invective, to strengthen its shield of the new and the weak, and to enlarge the area in which its writ may run.

Finally, to those nations who would make themselves our adversary, we offer not a pledge but a request: that both sides begin anew the quest for peace, before the dark powers of destruction unleashed by science engulf all humanity in planned or accidental self-destruction.

We dare not tempt them with weakness. For only when our arms are sufficient beyond doubt can we be certain beyond doubt that they will never be employed.

But neither can two great and powerful groups of nations take comfort from our present course—both sides overburdened by the cost of modern weapons, both rightly alarmed by the steady spread of the deadly atom, yet both racing to alter that uncertain balance of terror that stays the hand of mankind's final war.

So let us begin anew, remembering on both sides that civility is not a sign of weakness, and sincerity is always subject to proof. Let us never negotiate out of fear, but let us never fear to negotiate.

Let both sides explore what problems unite us instead of belaboring those problems which divide us.

Let both sides, for the first time, formulate serious and precise proposals for the inspection and control of arms, and bring the absolute power to destroy other nations under the absolute control of all nations.

Let both sides seek to invoke the wonders of science instead of its terrors. Together let us explore the stars, conquer the deserts, eradicate disease, tap the ocean depths and encourage the arts and commerce.

Let both sides unite to heed in all corners of the earth the command of Isaiah to "undo the heavy burdens . . . [and] let the oppressed go free."

And if a beachhead of cooperation may push back the jungle of suspicion, let both sides join in creating a new endeavor, not a new balance of power, but a new world of law, where the strong are just and the weak secure and the peace preserved.

All this will not be finished in the first one hundred days. Nor will it be finished in the first one thousand days, nor in the life of this Administration, nor even perhaps in our lifetime on this planet. But let us begin.

In your hands, my fellow citizens, more than mine, will rest the final success or failure of our course. Since this country was founded, each generation of Americans has been summoned to give testimony to its national loyalty. The graves of young Americans who answered the call to service surround the globe.

Now the trumpet summons us again—not as a call to bear arms, though arms we need; not as a call to battle, though embattled we are; but a call to bear the burden of a long twilight struggle, year in and year out, "rejoicing in hope, patient in tribulation," a struggle against the common enemies of man: tyranny, poverty, disease and war itself.

Can we forge against these enemies a grand and global alliance, North and South, East and West, that can assure a more fruitful life for all mankind? Will you join in that historic effort?

In the long history of the world, only a few generations have been granted the role of defending freedom in its hour of maximum danger. I do not shrink from this responsibility; I welcome it. I do not believe that any of us would exchange places with any other people or any other generation. The energy, the faith, the devotion which we bring to this endeavor will light our country and all who serve it, and the glow from that fire can truly light the world.

And so, my fellow Americans, ask not what your country can do for you; ask what you can do for your country.

My fellow citizens of the world, ask not what America will do for you, but what together we can do for the freedom of man.

Finally, whether you are citizens of America or citizens of the world, ask of us here the same high standards of strength and sacrifice which we ask of you. With a good conscience our only sure reward, with history the final judge of our deeds, let us go forth to lead the land we love, asking His blessing and His help, but knowing that here on earth God's work must truly be our own.

It seemed to me, as I watched the faces of the crowd, that they had forgotten the cold, forgotten party lines and forgotten all the old divisions of race, religion and nation. It was time to begin.

SETTLING IN

January 21 started early. Orders had gone out for all White House staff to be on duty by 9 A.M., and the President was there before anyone. (It did not start that early for me. My alarm clock failed to function and I barely made the staff swearing-in ceremony.) The President called me in with Mike Feldman, who brought, as earlier requested, Executive Order No. 1: increasing the variety and doubling the quantity of surplus foods for four million needy Americans. Mike and I felt a bit stiff and awkward in the Presidential office for the first time, bare though it was, and I suspect the President did too. It was also the first time I called him "Mr. President," but that seemed natural to the tongue. The Order was signed at 10:30 A.M. and issued at 11.

Between meetings and swearing-in ceremonies he acquainted himself with his office and its various buttons and buzzers. He strolled into other offices, talked with his staff, visited with stenographers, opened mail, used the phone and generated work for himself. The unaccustomed long uninterrupted hours of solid working time came as both a shock and a blessing. "It's awfully quiet over there sometimes," he remarked to me at lunch the first week on the second floor of the Mansion, thinking of his noisy quarters in the Senate, on the *Caroline* and during the interim.

It was not all quiet. The exhilaration of securing the prize he had sought so long had not yet worn off. The adjustment from the days of constant compaigning was not complete. Politicians and reporters were constantly in and out of his office. The new President's first visitor had been former President Harry Truman, welcomed for the first time to his former home. Organizations, celebrities and award winners of every kind, from Baptists to beauty queens, were greeted daily in the oval office. Thirty thousand letters poured in every week. Twelve speeches were made in the first two months. Old friends were visited in their homes. Departmental meetings were visited in person. Press conferences and background briefings were held regularly. Legislative requests were contained in separate messages spaced for maximum publicity.

His activist, enthusiastic approach was contagious throughout the Executive Branch. The lights burned late in his office and in every department in Washington. It was an exciting and inspiring time in our lives, and nothing could dampen our delight in being in that place at that time. "Those were the days," Bob Kennedy would recall somewhat wistfully some hundred days later, "when we thought we were succeeding because of all the stories on how hard everybody was working."

The new President never got over the small boy's sense of pride and excitement about living in the White House. On his second full day in office, returning from Mass with Paul Fay and his brother Teddy, he invited them in for an inspection; and sitting in the only chair in the still bare and nearly empty oval office, he spun around and asked with a pleased look, "Paul, do you think it's adequate?" And Fay spoke for all of them in replying, "I feel any minute somebody's going to walk in and say, 'All right, you three guys, out of here.' " On at least two other occasions that week, he and Jacqueline took guests on a top-to-bottom tour of what he called "the property," asking Franklin Roosevelt, Jr. the history of a particular room or furnishing, pointing out to Ken Galbraith the holes in the floor caused by his predecessor's golf shoes. The whole tour, said Galbraith, "was sheer delight. He turned over furniture, looked at the labels, complained that there were too many reproductions, dismissed something here as 'Grand Rapids,' tried the

Lincoln bed, and kept up a running conversation about political problems."

In New Ross, Ireland, nearly three years later, he told the story of the old-time Irish immigrant who had his family's picture taken in front of the White House and proudly told his friends back in Ireland it was their summer home and his friends should pay a visit. "Well," concluded the President proudly, "it is our home also in the winter, and I hope you will come and see us."

CHAPTER X

❧❧❧❧❧

THE KENNEDY TEAM

NOTHING GAVE THE NEW PRESIDENT a greater sense of satisfaction and security on the day of his inauguration than the men he had selected to work with him.

THE TALENT HUNT

Only seventy-two days before his inauguration, Kennedy had started with a wholly clean slate. American politics provides for no "shadow Cabinet" in the party out of power, and Kennedy's staff and advisers were not an equivalent. He had secured the nomination without obligating himself to any leader of his party. After the convention he had mobilized a campaign team and raised a campaign fund without promising any posts in return. He had not even made any tentative designations in his own mind. During the campaign he had steadfastly resisted the efforts of reporters and Stevenson supporters to persuade him to reveal a preference for Secretary of State. To do so, he said, would be inappropriate, presumptuous and, recalling Dewey's decision to the contrary in 1948, needlessly defiant of fate. The premature announcement of any names, he felt (and Nixon took a similar position), would only confuse the issue between the two candidates. His full time and attention were devoted instead to winning the election. The press could and did speculate on a possible Kennedy Cabinet but with no help or hints from the candidate.

Consequently, as the great talent hunt of 1960-1961 began on November 10, his choice was not limited by any definite political debts or campaign commitments. The ten department heads comprising the official Kennedy Cabinet, selected in the five weeks that followed, reflected this lack of political restriction in at least five ways.

1. The Cabinet contained no figures with a nationwide following of their own. Wilson in 1913 had felt bound to take Bryan, and Roosevelt in 1933 took a former National Chairman and prominent Southern Congressman, Cordell Hull. But Kennedy felt free to by-pass Stevenson, Bowles and other nationally known names for the little-known Dean Rusk as Secretary of State. An even lesser known figure, Robert Mc-Namara, was named to the other top post, Secretary of Defense, instead of Presidential rival Stuart Symington or retiring National Committee Chairman Henry Jackson. Kennedy had met both Rusk and McNamara for the first time a full month after his election—coincidentally but separately on the same day, December 8. Other top posts were similarly filled, and Stevenson was named to a post for which he was ideally suited, United Nations Ambassador, and given Cabinet rank.

2. The Cabinet contained only one member who had contributed $1,000 or more to the 1960 campaign: Douglas Dillon, who, together with his wife, had contributed over $26,000. But the Dillons had contributed to Nixon and the Republicans, not to Kennedy.

3. The Cabinet contained no dissenting spokesman for some opposition group he needed to appease—such as labor leader Durkin in the Eisenhower Cabinet and all the factional leaders in Lincoln's Cabinet—nor did it contain any free-wheeling individualists of the Henry Wallace–Harold Ickes variety. His Cabinet members had a variety of backgrounds and gave him independent judgments, but they were uniformly dedicated to him and to the broad public interest, and all, including the two Republicans among them, approached their assignments with a philosophy consistent with their chief's. His Secretary of Agriculture was sponsored by no farm organization and had sponsored no farm legislation. His Secretary of Labor, despite long association with the labor movement as a lawyer, was not regarded as one of their own by organized labor's leaders, and his name was not on the list of acceptable names they put forward.

While Kennedy recognized his vote losses among segregationists, anti-Catholics and farmers, he made no appointments from their ranks, just as he would not name a woman or a Negro to the Cabinet merely for the sake of show.[1] An example of his unwillingness to appease occurred when he asked me what I knew of Henry Fowler's background for Under Secretary of the Treasury, and I said I believed Fowler had fought

[1] One unsubtle gesture was made in this direction, however, by arranging with Negro Congressman William Dawson the announcement that he had "declined" Kennedy's offer of the postmaster-generalship.

in Virginia against the powerful political machine of Finance Committee Chairman Harry Byrd. "That," said the President-elect, "is a
strong point for him, not against him."

While he obviously would have been concerned had his entire
Cabinet turned out to be Catholics, he paid no regard to religion in their
selection. When I felt it necessary to bring to his attention the fact that
all three of my proposed White House associates—Mike Feldman, Lee
White and Dick Goodwin—were of Jewish ancestry, he replied matter-
of-factly, "So what? They tell me this is the first Cabinet with two Jews,
too. All I care about is whether they can handle it."

4. The Cabinet contained only one official from the Roosevelt-Truman
era, Dean Rusk, who had been a Deputy Under Secretary of State, and
not one man who had held elective office as long as Kennedy had. At
the Cabinet and particularly the sub-Cabinet level there was a wealth
of experience in public affairs, but in place of the old, familiar faces were
new men. It was the youngest Cabinet in the twentieth century. Luther
Hodges was the only member born before 1900. Kennedy made no effort
to balance youth with age. On the contrary, at an early stage when I
mentioned that Paul Samuelson had suggested Robert Roosa as Secretary
of the Treasury, with the warning that he was only forty-three years old,
Kennedy's reply was: "A forty-three-year-old Secretary of the Treasury
. . . hmm—might be a good combination with Mac Bundy as a forty-one-
year-old Secretary of State."

5. The Cabinet was nonpolitical and bipartisan to an extent unusual
for Democratic Presidents in particular. It contained only four men who
had ever sought public office (Ribicoff, Udall, Freeman and Hodges),
none of them national figures, and only four members of the FKBW
(For Kennedy Before Wisconsin) Club (Bob Kennedy, Ribicoff, Udall
and Goldberg). These four were joined in the campaign by Freeman and
Hodges, but Kennedy had no political or even personal tie with either
Rusk (who had supported Stevenson for the nomination) or Republican
McNamara and knew Dillon had supported Nixon. An Eisenhower hold-
over in the Pentagon, Research Director Herbert York, pointed out to me
the curious fact that he was the earliest Kennedy supporter in the top
ranks of the new Defense Department, for he had favored JFK at a
time when all the others were for Rockefeller, Symington, Johnson or
Stevenson. The postmaster-generalship, in another break with tradition,
was turned over, not to a patronage politician or National Committee
Chairman, but to a skilled administrator, J. Edward Day, a Stevenson
supporter whom JFK had met only in passing.

Contrary to a report that the appointment of Dillon, Eisenhower's
Under Secretary of State, contradicted a Kennedy pledge to "make a
clean sweep" of all Ike men, "superior ability" had been practically the

only positive test enunciated in the campaign. The candidate had also
touched briefly on what he did *not* want. He did not want his Cabinet
drawn entirely from a single segment of society, such as business. He
did not want men unwilling "to commit themselves to stay on the job
long enough to learn what they must learn."

The financial sacrifice required was considerable. Even by the standards of state and local government, Federal executives were paid shock-
ingly low salaries. The Superintendent of Schools in La Due, Missouri,
received a higher salary than the Secretary of Defense (and McNamara's
earnings at the Ford Motor Company had been $410,000 the previous
year). The Chief Probate Judge of Cook County, Illinois, was paid more
than the Secretary of State. The city of Los Angeles alone offered twenty-
eight positions more highly paid than any Cabinet post.

Kennedy wanted a ministry of talent. Several limitations and pressures beset him in his hunt for the best. Most of his previous contacts
and friendships were in two fields—politics and journalism. Most of
them were in the East. Many of the best members of Congress preferred
the security and seniority of their seats to the Executive Branch, and
in many cases could help us more by staying where they were. Each
private pressure group in a particular field, such as labor or agriculture,
put forward names unacceptable to other groups in the same field. It
was difficult, the President-elect found, to check quietly on a man's
ability and philosophy without arousing his expectations, his Democratic
Senator's irritation and some party faction's opposition. Names of those
supposedly under consideration—some of which he had never even
heard or considered—continually leaked out to the press, which promptly
concluded they were deliberate "trial balloons" on the part of Kennedy.
Even personality problems cropped up. He was, for example, irritated
by Stevenson's delay in deciding on the UN Ambassadorship and publicly
announced that it had been offered in order to make rejection all the
more difficult.

There were also pressures of time. Clifford and Neustadt both urged
him to appoint a Budget Director almost immediately. Eisenhower, the
press emphasized, had announced his final Cabinet choice by December 1, which was the day Kennedy announced his first (Ribicoff). Even
after he had completed his full Cabinet on December 17 (with Day),
some sixty additional key policy posts and several hundred more key
positions remained to be filled, and he was determined not to delegate
to the Cabinet full discretion in the selection of the "sub-Cabinet."

The process was arduous as well as long and deliberate. "This is
the one part of the job I had hoped would be fun," the President-elect
had remarked somewhat sardonically as we wearily reviewed names one
night in Palm Beach. "But these are the decisions that could make or
break us all." He lacked neither advice nor assistance. In the first large-

scale organized effort of its kind ever undertaken by a newly elected political party, Larry O'Brien and Sarge Shriver did a skillful job of meticulously screening the qualifications of tens of hundreds of applications and recommendations, for positions high and low. Aided by Dungan, Wofford, Donahue and Adam Yarmolinsky, they not only received names but searched for new ones. Their vast card file of candidate evaluations was both less systematic and more sensible than some news stories reported.

In this operation Bob Kennedy played a major role, and each Cabinet member, when appointed, had an important voice in the selection of his subordinates. Kennedy advisers with backgrounds in special areas— particularly Paul Samuelson on economics and finance, Jerome Wiesner on science and defense and Chester Bowles on foreign affairs—submitted influential lists. Those of us who had no direct responsibility for personnel were nevertheless deluged by calls and communications from campaign workers, contributors, friends and old college classmates (including a great many never previously heard of). Advice poured in from most members of the Senate and from several members of his family.[2] Clifford and Neustadt on occasion gave names to fit the jobs their memoranda described. Other sages were consulted, including the Vice President-elect, Dag Hammarskjöld, Dean Acheson, Walter Lippmann, John McCloy and particularly Robert Lovett (with Kennedy trying in vain to draft the latter two for Cabinet positions—McCloy did accept a temporary assignment in the disarmament effort and filled it admirably).

But for the top thirty to fifty jobs, the bulk of the work and all the final decisions rested with Kennedy. He personally interviewed dozens, studied the writings and qualifications of others and placed calls all over the country to check references. "What do you know about this man?" he would ask. "How well do you know him—is he just a lot of talk?" He was endowed with unusually good instincts for sizing up good men. He was also fortunate in possessing both the personal magnetism and the powers of persuasion that enabled him to attract good men, to win them to his banner and to induce them to serve their country. He stayed in close touch with the Shriver office (calling Shriver's office late one night from Palm Beach and finding only a secretary present, he good-naturedly "demanded" that she confess "who is leaking all the names"), but he kept his list of Cabinet possibilities in his head rather than in a card file.

He preferred to avoid any names that would not receive Senate confirmation or a security clearance. But he had no hesitation about

[2] He heard from his sister-in-law how the wife of one man highly recommended to be Secretary of State had wept bitter tears over Kennedy's nomination at Los Angeles, but there is no truth to the allegation that his father was responsible for the selection of Rusk and McNamara and the formal draft of brother Bob.

naming all the favorite targets of the extreme right, many of whom violently disagreed with each other: Bowles, Stevenson, Acheson, Galbraith, Mrs. Roosevelt, Schlesinger, Kennan, Bohlen, Nitze, the Bundys, Robert Weaver, Murrow and Mennen Williams. He was neither impressed by great fortune nor afraid of great intellects. When his brilliant economic adviser James Tobin at first demurred on the grounds that he was something of an "ivory tower economist," the President-elect replied, "That's all right—I'm something of an ivory tower President." He did, in fact, appoint to important posts a higher proportion of academicians, including fifteen Rhodes scholars, than any other President in history including Roosevelt—more even than those European governments in which intellectuals abound only in the lesser civil service positions. His appointees, it was observed, had among them written more books than the President could read in a four-year term, even at twelve hundred words per minute.

But most of Kennedy's academicians had previous government experience, just as many of his politicians and businessmen had previously been writers or teachers. He wanted men who could both think and act, "men of ability who can do things . . . people with good judgment." The qualities he sought largely mirrored his own: an outlook more practical than theoretical and more logical than ideological; an ability to be precise and concise; a willingness to learn, to do, to dare, to change; and an ability to work hard and long, creatively, imaginatively, successfully.

His search succeeded. The men he picked were for the most part men who thought his thoughts, spoke his language and put their country and Kennedy ahead of any other concern. They were scrupulously honest; not even a suspicion of scandal ever tainted the Kennedy Cabinet. They were, like him, dedicated but unemotional, young but experienced, articulate but soft-spoken. There were no crusaders, fanatics or extremists from any camp; all were nearer the center than either left or right. All spoke with the same low-keyed restraint that marked their chief, yet all shared his deep conviction that they could change America's drift. They liked government, they liked politics, they liked Kennedy and they believed implicitly in him. Their own feelings of pride—*our* feelings, for I was proud to be one of them—could be summed up in a favorite Kennedy passage from Shakespeare's *King Henry V* in his speech on the St. Crispin's Day battle:

> . . . we . . . shall be remembered—
> We few, we happy few, we band of brothers . . .
> And gentlemen . . . now abed
> Shall think themselves accurs'd they were not here.

Those finally appointed were not always his first tentative selections. A farm leader—whom he had practically chosen to be his Secretary of Agriculture on the basis of a review of all the names—talked, when summoned to his first meeting with the President-elect in Georgetown, only in terms of generalities and stereotypes. "It was so boring," the President-elect told us afterward, "and the living room was so warm, that I actually fell asleep." Orville Freeman, who had resisted the job, but was far more in the Kennedy image, was induced the next day to accept it.

Although he named far fewer businessmen than his predecessor, Kennedy scoured the business community seeking able administrators, particularly for the foreign aid program. And while he insisted on men loyal to his philosophy, he retained a far larger proportion of the previous administration's officials and appointed far more opposition party members to sensitive posts than his immediate predecessor had done eight years earlier. I doubt, in fact, whether any new President bringing a change of party displayed so much bipartisanship in his initial appointments.

He worried longest over his selection of a Secretary of State, admitting to me that those aspirants whom he did not know had an advantage over those whose deficiencies as well as abilities he knew well. He worried the least over the postmaster-generalship, deciding almost as an afterthought that it would be well to have a Westerner. He privately predicted that the nomination of his brother as Attorney General ("Let's announce it at midnight," he said) would prove to be his most controversial choice then and one of his wisest choices later, and he was right on both counts.

There were other controversies. A New Deal economist said Kennedy had surrounded himself with too many "businessmen and bankers," and a top businessman said the team contained too many academic "theorists." Republicans stressed that four of the ten Cabinet members were Harvard graduates (overlooking the fact that Eisenhower's Cabinet also had four and Theodore Roosevelt's five, although not all at the same time). Actually his appointees came from every background. But John Kennedy, in selecting his associates, did not pretend or attempt to achieve an average cross-section of the country—he wanted the best.

The entire list of several hundred appointees would not prove to be wholly free of mistakes, from the Cabinet level on down. Some exceeded the President's expectations and some failed to fulfill them. Noted men rarely equal their reputations—some are better, some are worse. In some instances the right kind of man was given the wrong kind of job. But as a group the remarkably high quality of Kennedy's appointees reflected his own remarkable search for a true "ministry of talent."

THE WHITE HOUSE STAFF

My participation as a member of the Kennedy White House staff is still too recent to permit me to give an objective account of its personnel and their part in the government, but that part was too important to omit from any account of the Kennedy Presidency.

Our roles should not be exaggerated. We wielded no secret influence. We did not replace the role of Cabinet officers, compete with them for power or publicity, or block their access to the President. We could not impose our own views, nor assert the President's views, nor speak in the President's voice, without his prior or subsequent approval. "I will continue to have some residual functions," the President said drily when told of the tremendous powers being ascribed to one aide.

President Kennedy tremendously increased and improved his own impact on the Executive Branch by the use of his personal staff. He knew that it was humanly impossible for him to know all that he would like to know, see everyone who deserved to be seen, read all that he ought to read, write every message that carried his name and take part in all meetings affecting his plans. He also knew that, in his administration, Cabinet members could make recommendations on major matters, but only the President could make decisions; and that he could not afford to accept, without seeking an independent judgment, the products and proposals of departmental advisers whose responsibilities did not require them to look, as he and his staff looked, at the government and its programs as a whole. He required a personal staff, therefore—one that represented *his* personal ways, means and purposes—to summarize and analyze those products and proposals for him, to refine the conflicting views of various agencies, to define the issues which he had to decide, to help place his personal imprint upon them, to make certain that practical political facts were never overlooked, and to enable him to make his decisions on the full range of *his* considerations and constituencies, which no Cabinet member shared.

Contrary to reports that President Kennedy, in Rooseveltian fashion, encouraged conflict and competition among and between his staff and Cabinet, our role was one of building governmental unity rather than splintering responsibility. Two dozen or more Kennedy assistants gave him two dozen or more sets of hands, eyes and ears, two dozen or more minds attuned to his own. They could talk with legislators, bureaucrats, newsmen, experts, Cabinet members and politicians—serve on inter-departmental task forces—review papers and draft speeches, letters and other documents—spot problems before they were crises and possibilities before they were proposals—screen requests for legislation, Executive Orders, jobs, appointments with the President, patronage and

Presidential speeches—and bear his messages, look out for his interests, carry out his orders and make certain his decisions were executed.

In those areas where his interest and knowledge were limited, the scope of our discretion was often large. But even in those instances we did not make major decisions for him. Our role was to enable him to have more time, facts and judgments with which to make them himself —to increase *his* influence, not ours; to preserve his options, not his ego; to make certain that questions were not foreclosed or answers required before he had an opportunity to place his imprint upon them. In the words of Neustadt's postelection memorandum, our task was to get "information in his mind and key decisions in his hands reliably enough and soon enough to give him room for maneuver." That imposed upon him heavy burdens of overseeing everything we were doing, but he much preferred those burdens to the handicaps of being merely a clerk in his own office, caught up in the routines and recommendations of others.

We advised him when he sought our advice; more often we enabled him to assess the advice of others. At the risk of displeasing Congressmen and Cabinet members—and the President—our task was to be skeptical and critical, not sycophantic. There was no value in our being merely another level of clearances and concurrences, or being too deferential to the experts—as the Bay of Pigs acutely showed.

No doubt at times our roles were resented. Secretary Hodges, apparently disgruntled by his inability to see the President more often, arranged to have placed on the Cabinet agenda for June 15, 1961, an item entitled "A candid discussion with the President on relationships with the White House staff." Upon discovering this in the meeting, I passed the President a note asking "Shall I leave?"—but the President ignored both the note and the agenda.

Some overlapping was inevitable. The President frequently assigned the same problem to more than one aide, or kept one in the dark about another's role or involved whoever happened to be standing nearby at a critical moment.

He often expressed impatience with lengthy memoranda from certain aides which boiled down to recommendations that he "firm up our posture" or "make a new effort" on some particular problem. Such generalities, he observed, were sufficient for a candidate's speeches but not for Presidential action. When he returned one assistant's six-page, single-spaced memorandum with the request that the author set down its action consequences, he received back another long memorandum recommending: two Presidential speeches, a policy paper and a "systematic review of the situation"—and shortly thereafter that aide was moved to one of the departments.

Those of us in the White House staff with policy responsibilities often differed from each other and from the President in the deliberations preceding a decision. But none of us ever questioned his decision once it was final.

The selection of the White House staff—which began, as noted, on the day after his election was confirmed—was a personal Presidential process. He chose men to meet his personal needs and mode of operation. No Senate confirmation was required and no particular public impression was desired. One powerful politician brought heavy pressure to have his long-time personal aide made a member of our staff, but the President-elect did not respect that aide and would not be bound by anyone else's preferences.

No staff member was appointed in order to please, or to plead for, the advocates of disarmament or defense, Negroes or Jews, the State Department or the Commerce Department, farmers or labor, or any other goal, group or government agency. Nor was any staff member appointed with an eye to any particular pattern—balancing liberals and conservatives, regions or religions. We were appointed for our ability to fulfill the President's needs and talk the President's language. We represented no one but John Kennedy. And no one but John Kennedy could have drawn and held together the diverse and disparate talents of such strong-minded individuals, with all their differences in manner and milieu.

His staff, to be sure, was neither as efficient as we pretended nor as harmonious as he thought. Failure of communication appeared more than once. A degree of envy and occasionally resentment cropped up now and then. A group of able and aggressive individualists, all dependent on one man, could not be wholly free from competitive feelings or from scornful references to each other's political or intellectual backgrounds. Below the level of senior adviser, a few personnel changes did occur in due course. But Kennedy's personal interest in his aides, refusal to prefer one over another, and mixture of pressure and praise achieved a total command of our loyalties. We worked for him ten to twelve hours every day, and loved every minute of it.

The President showed his appreciation to us not by constant expressions of gratitude—which were in fact rather rare—but by returning in full the loyalty of his staff and other appointees.[3] "Congressmen are always advising Presidents to get rid of Presidential advisers," he told a news conference. "That is one of the most constant threads that runs through American history." The statement was occasioned by the suggestion of conservative Democratic Congressman Baring that Kennedy get rid of Bowles, Ball, Bell, Bunche and Sylvester. "He has a fondness

[3] He took particular delight in striking back in a press conference at Republican Congressman Broyhill, who had assailed Pierre Salinger for holding a reception for Broyhill's opponent. "I can see why he would be quite critical of that," said the President. "But I will say that I've never read as much about a Congressman . . . and seen less legislative results."

for alliteration in B's," observed the President smilingly, "but I would not add Congressman Baring to that list, as I have a high regard for him *and* for the gentlemen that he named. . . . Presidents ordinarily do not pay attention [to Congressmen urging dismissal of their advisers], nor do they in this case."

When Arthur Schlesinger was under fire for calling a columnist an "idiot"—when Dick Goodwin was accused of meddling in diplomacy—when Pierre Salinger's trip to the Soviet Union was under attack—when the hard-working Bundy, Rostow and Galbraith were maligned as "the dancing professors"—and when Walter Heller, Stuart Udall, Willard Wirtz, Arthur Sylvester and many others were assailed for some supposed mistake or misstatement—the President took pains to reassure each of us in private and, if asked, to defend us in public. Jerome Wiesner, after the newspapers had distorted a sailing accident which temporarily laid him low, told how the President cheered him up with an offer "to give me lessons in sailing and press relations." When another aide apologized for a personal incident which had appeared in the press, the President replied, "That's all right, I've been looking over the FBI files and there isn't one of us here that hasn't done something."

Outside observers often attempted to divide the staff into two camps: the intellectuals or "eggheads" and the politicians or "Irish Mafia" (a newspaper designation bitterly resented by its designees when first published). No such division, in fact, existed. Those with primarily political roles were men of high intelligence. Those who came from primarily academic backgrounds often had political experience. Many could not be simply classified as either "intellectuals" or "politicians" (and I insisted I had a foot in each camp). All the President's principal staff members shared his high hopes for a better world and his practical acceptance of the present one. All recognized that Presidential policies and politics were inseparable, respected each other's individual talents and functions, and accepted the possibility of error in their own conclusions as well as those of their colleagues.

While few of us had a "passion for anonymity," most of us had a preference in that direction. In December, 1960, I reviewed with the President-elect a series of speaking invitations I had received, as well as requests for magazine profiles. "Turn them all down," he said, and I did. "Not only will you not have time. Every man that's ever held a job like yours—Sherman Adams, Harry Hopkins, House, all the rest—has ended up in the ————. Congress was down on them or the President was hurt by them or somebody was mad at them. The best way to stay out of trouble is to stay out of sight."[4]

---

[4] He had a different motivation for telling me not to accept the invitation to be the Gridiron Club speaker one year. "It will take too much time to work up a funny speech," he said, "besides, we don't have enough jokes for our own speeches."

The wisdom of his words was brought home several months later when I represented the President at his request at a George Norris Centennial Dinner in my home state. My speech deplored the number of young people leaving Nebraska to seek better schools for their children, and it was bitterly attacked out of context. The Republican National Committeewoman, for example, said if I came back to Nebraska to die "it would be too soon." Word of the uproar reached the Washington newspapers, and the President greeted me with the comment: "That's what happens when you permit a speech-writer to write his own speech!" When I apologized, not for what I had said but for any embarrassment I had caused him, he laughed. "I don't mind," he said. "They can criticize *you* all they like!"

Kennedy wanted his staff to be small, in order to keep it more personal than institutional. Although in time a number of "special assistants" accumulated for special reasons, he kept the number of senior generalists to a minimum. Both my office, which dealt mostly with domestic policy, and that of McGeorge Bundy, which dealt exclusively with foreign policy, combined in relatively small staffs the functions of several times as many Eisenhower aides. Instead of adding specialists in my own office, I relied on the excellent staff work of the Bureau of the Budget and Council of Economic Advisers.

The President wanted a fluid staff. Our jurisdictions were distinguishable but not exclusive, and each man could and did assist every other. Our assignments and relations evolved with time, as did the President's use of us. There was no chief of staff in the Sherman Adams–Wilton Persons role supervising and screening the work of all others. Instead, Kennedy was his own chief of staff, and his principal White House advisers had equal stature, equal salaries and equal access to his office. He compared it to "a wheel and a series of spokes."

There were no distinctions in rank connoted by staff titles and very few differences in title. Nearly everyone was officially a "Special Assistant." A few were "Administrative Assistants." No one was "The Assistant to the President." The President, in fact, remarked in January of 1961 that he wished everyone had been called Special Assistant. As the heir to a very honorable title, I could hardly share his sentiments, but only one title was ever used within the walls of the White House, and that was "Mr. President."

Not one staff meeting was ever held, with or without the President. Nor was one ever desirable. Each of us was busy with our separate responsibilities, and each of us met when necessary with whatever staff members had jurisdictions touching our own. For example, in my role of assisting the President on his program and policy, with particular emphasis on legislation, I might meet in one day but at separate times with National Security Assistant Bundy on the foreign aid message, Budget Director Bell on its cost, Press Secretary Salinger on its publication, Legislative Liaison O'Brien on its reception by the Congress, and Appointments Secretary O'Donnell on the President's final meeting on its contents, as well as the Secretaries of State, Defense and Treasury and the Foreign Aid Director. I also kept abreast of the President's thinking by attending all the more formal Presidential meetings around which policy was built: the Cabinet, the National Security Council, the legislative leaders breakfasts, the pre-press conference breakfasts and the formulation of the Budget and legislative program. He and I continued to be close in a peculiarly impersonal way. Of course, no man is truly an "alter ego" to the President of the United States.

The President retained at all times the highest regard for each of his principal aides. McGeorge Bundy's sagacious and systematic coordination of the President's myriad foreign affairs headaches made him a logical candidate for Secretary of State in the event of a second-term opening. His brisk, sometimes brusque manner, which occasionally annoyed his intellectual inferiors (who were legion), suited Kennedy perfectly—as did the cry of outrage emanating from Foster Furcolo over the appointment of this Republican Harvard dean, surprisingly never used by Eisenhower, who had worked for Dewey in 1948, attacked Furcolo in 1958 and supported Kennedy in 1960.

"Dave Bell," said Clark Clifford to the President-elect in November, 1960, "is your kind of man." That was precisely correct, as the Budget Director proved to be a source of few words but unflagging work, unfrenzied advice and unfailing calm. Tough beneath a bland exterior, he loyally agreed later to take on the thankless task of the foreign aid directorship only after the President had overridden my protest that this was cutting off my right arm. Bell's replacement as Budget Director, Kermit Gordon, fortunately proved equally able.[5]

Ken O'Donnell, handling appointments, trip arrangements and White House administrative duties, customarily exhibited such a cool countenance, and such a grim resistance to those undeserving of the President's time, that many were unaware of his shrewd sense of judgment and delightful sense of humor which helped the President through his day. The only chink in O'Donnell's defense of the Presidential front door was the existence of a back door less strictly guarded by the President's softhearted personal secretary, Evelyn Lincoln, still as unruffled and devoted as in her days in our Senate office.

Larry O'Brien, who shared political chores with O'Donnell when not

5 Kermit had already served brilliantly as a member of the Council of Economic Advisers, and there was no truth to the story that I had opposed his selection in 1961 on the ground that two years earlier he had refused to serve as an academic adviser.

wrestling with the Congress, possessed the extraordinary patience, resilience and affable political instincts which enabled him not only to survive but to succeed in the struggle for Kennedy's program.

Press Secretary Pierre Salinger's work was more closely followed by the President on a daily basis than that of any other staff member, with the exception of O'Donnell and Mrs. Lincoln. While maintaining good relations with his counterparts in both the Soviet Union and Allied nations, Pierre did not intrude on Presidential policy-making. Transcripts of his twice-daily briefings of the press were quickly read by the President and staff for both illumination and entertainment—the latter covering such subjects as portly Pierre's fitness for a Presidentially prescribed fifty-mile hike and his distinction as the only known golfer ever to hit the clubhouse at Hyannis Port.

Many others in the White House served Kennedy well and deserve to be mentioned: including Ralph Dungan, who continued the talent hunt in the White House and worked with Bundy as well; Ted Reardon, ever loyal to his old chief as Cabinet assistant; and Arthur Schlesinger, Jr., who served as a constant contact with liberals and intellectuals both in this country and abroad, as an adviser on Latin-American, United Nations and cultural affairs, as a source of innovation, ideas and occasional speeches on all topics, and incidentally as a lightning rod to attract Republican attacks away from the rest of us.

As Bundy was aided by the astute Carl Kaysen and others, as O'Brien and Salinger were backed by their able staffs, so I depended in the Special Counsel's office on Mike Feldman and Lee White to handle many agency problems and pressure groups under the direct supervision of the President. Feldman, for example, served among other things as the channel for most business requests—on tariffs, airline routes and subsidies, to name but a few. "If Mike ever turned dishonest," said the President one day, "we could all go to jail."

Indispensable to the President was the ever-smiling presence of his old friend Dave Powers, who kept everyone else smiling with his unending supply of Charlestown, Massachusetts color, baseball lore and statistics, and unprecedented greetings of the great and near-great (examples: "He's our type Shah" and "Is this the real Mikoyan?").

Housed in the Executive Office Building across a small avenue from the White House West Wing were the President's economic and science advisers. Walter Heller, Chairman of the Council of Economic Advisers, was learned without being doctrinaire and liberal without being rigid. Once he learned to adjust to Kennedy's methods, views and emphasis on the possible, Heller and his associates became the most highly influential and frequently consulted Council of Economic Advisers in history. In fact, both Heller and Science Adviser Jerome Wiesner, by learning to adapt their pedagogy to the President's preference for brevity and to accept philosophically his decisions contrary to their advice, greatly raised the stature of their offices.

The economic, science, Budget and other advisers in the Executive Office Building worked closely with the President's office and those adjoining it in the West Wing of the White House. More distant in many ways were the offices in the East Wing, containing military aides, social secretaries, administrative officers, correspondence clerks, Mrs. Kennedy's staff and assorted others. With certain notable exceptions such as Schlesinger, the occupants of those sedate and serene offices were regarded almost as inhabitants of another world. "Sometimes," sighed the President one day on the telephone to an aide of Mrs. Kennedy, "I don't think you people in the East Wing have any understanding of our problems over here in the West Wing."

THE DEPARTMENT HEADS

Ranking the Cabinet has long been a favorite game among the Washington columnists and cocktail circuit-riders. Who is "in," "out," "up," "down"? Who is slated to go and who will replace him? The game is based more on fun than fact, for there are very few facts available to the public which are relevant to such rankings. A Cabinet member who sees the President often may be considered by the latter to be an intimate or a bore. One who sees the President rarely may have been given broad discretion or the "deep freeze." It is much easier for a Secretary of Labor to be judged a "success" by the press than it is for a Secretary of Agriculture. The value of a Postmaster General cannot be compared with that of an Attorney General; nor will a President preoccupied with world crises turn to his Secretary of Commerce as often as to his Secretary of State.

The nature of their responsibilities and the competence with which they did their jobs brought six senior national executives particularly close to the President: Vice President Johnson, Attorney General Kennedy, Secretary of Defense McNamara, Secretary of the Treasury Dillon, Secretary of State Rusk and Secretary of Labor Goldberg. The other Cabinet officers—Secretary of Agriculture Freeman, Secretary of Labor (II) Wirtz, Secretary of Health, Education, and Welfare Ribicoff, Secretary of the Interior Udall, Secretary of Commerce Hodges, Secretary of Health, Education, and Welfare (II) Celebrezze and Postmasters General Day and Gronouski—all enjoyed, for the most part, the President's fullest confidence and respect, though he necessarily spent less time with them.

The President and Vice President, to the astonishment of many and somewhat to the surprise of them both, got along famously. Their initial wariness gave way to genuine warmth. Johnson's vast energies were enlisted in a wide range of undertakings: Chairman of the antidiscrimination in employment committee, Chairman of the coordinating Space Council, Chairman of the Peace Corps Advisory Board, member of the Cabinet and National Security Council, participant in the legislative and pre-press conference breakfasts, emissary and fact-finder on foreign missions of major importance, Democratic campaigner and fund-raiser, and a channel to both houses of Congress, particularly Texans and Southerners who were not otherwise easily reached. His advice was particularly sought by the President on legislative and political problems. Presiding over the Senate and substituting at ceremonies were the least of his duties.

The President did not delegate decisions to the Vice President, and Johnson did not expect to make them. In foreign affairs he sometimes advocated within the White House a slightly more militant policy but strongly supported whatever course the President adopted. In domestic affairs he often made suggestions accepted by the President—including a less sweeping reform of oil and other depletion allowances in the tax bill, and the inclusion of both a large scale job-training and illiteracy elimination effort and a voluntary conciliation service in the civil rights program. He was not voluble at meetings and did not volunteer advice on matters on which he felt insufficiently informed. On a few of these occasions Kennedy felt Johnson could have been more forthright or forthcoming, and on occasion Johnson felt Kennedy could have kept him better informed. But expressions of irritation on both sides were, to the best of my knowledge, comparatively few. The President never doubted his Vice President's loyalty, as so many Presidents have, took pains to have him present at all the major meetings earlier mentioned, and publicly praised him as "invaluable."

He was angered by false reports that he was having Johnson spied upon or that he was considering dropping him from the ticket (this last rumor he traced to rival Texas politicians). He made clear at two separate news conferences his intentions to have the same ticket in 1964. "The merger of Boston and Austin was one of the last that the Attorney General allowed," he told a political banquet, "but it has been one of the most successful." The former Majority Leader in turn never complained about his new position's comparative lack of publicity and power and never crossed or upstaged his leader. "Frankly," he was quoted by one reporter as saying, "I believe he [the President] is more considerate of me than I would be if the roles were reversed."

The possibility of succession through death was ever-present but rarely seriously mentioned. The President often joked about it in casual banter with both the Vice President and his own staff. "If that plane goes down," he said to me with a laugh one day in his bedroom, dressing with the help of valet George Thomas for a storm-threatened flight to Ohio, "Lyndon will have this place cleared out from stem to stern in twenty-four hours—and you and George will be the first to go." But the President knew that in fact his staff and Cabinet, with occasional exceptions, had excellent relations with the Vice President, and that Johnson was sufficiently informed to take over smoothly, if necessary.

Kennedy asked Congress in 1961 for legislation to provide Secret Service protection for Vice Presidents without their request and for those next in line when the Vice President assumed the Presidency. Also in 1961 he and Johnson agreed without difficulty on the procedures by which the Vice President would serve as Acting President if so required by Presidential disability. These procedures were identical to those adopted by their predecessors, with one addition. "Appropriate consultation" by the Vice President, in case the President was unable to communicate his disability, was spelled out in the Kennedy-Johnson agreement to include the support of the Cabinet and a legal justification from the Attorney General. The fact that the latter was a member of the Kennedy family gave additional assurance to both President and Vice President.

The Attorney General remained his brother's closest confidant. As an invited member of the National Security Council and its various offshoots, as a bearer of the President's flag, name and purpose in foreign lands, and as a participant in every major crisis meeting, he gave advice and assistance in foreign affairs to an extent unprecedented for his position. By chance several of the major crises in domestic affairs, including civil rights and steel prices, fell normally within the purview of his department. With the exception of juvenile delinquency and poverty, he was not consulted on or directly concerned with most other domestic measures or on day-to-day foreign operations, although he often lent a hand in legislative relations and high-level personnel selection.

With the help of an unusually talented group of associates, he achieved without detracting from these other duties a remarkable record at the Justice Department: not only in advancing civil rights but in attacking juvenile delinquency, organized crime, monopolistic mergers and price-fixing; intervening in the landmark reapportionment cases; securing counsel for impoverished defendants; broadening the use of pardons; humanizing the Immigration Service; improving (with some exceptions) the quality of the Federal Judiciary; turning the FBI to more effective work against organized criminal syndicates and civil rights violators; and ending abuses of bail and excessive or improper punishment. For twenty-five years the Federal Prisons Director had tried unsuccessfully to overcome opposition to the closing of archaic Alcatraz;

the Kennedys closed it. The department also obtained more legislation from Congress than it had in thirty years. The large number of Democrats indicted for Federal offenses, and the small number of Republicans appointed to the Federal bench, caused some grumbling among the respective officials of both parties, but the Attorney General, on these as on all other matters, willingly took the heat for decisions the President had approved.

There were disadvantages to having a brother in the Cabinet. Bob's errors on the side of candor could not so easily be repudiated. His enemies could attack "the Kennedys" instead of merely attacking the Cabinet. His intervention in the problems of other departments was more intimidating to colleagues, who might have more stoutly resisted anyone other than a Kennedy. But these liabilities were more than offset by his assets: a mature judgment that belied his youth, and unusual drive, dedication and loyalty. His various errors and enemies thus occasioned light banter between the two brothers more often than expressions of regret.

Bob Kennedy in 1961 had far more warmth and depth than when I had first met him in 1953, and this was not merely because he and I were by then getting along well. His work in the Cabinet added to his human as well as his professional stature. Working with the victims of racial prejudice and with the causes of juvenile delinquency made him more compassionate. Working with the problems of peace and war made him less militant. Working with his brother made him more patient and willing to listen, less demanding and certain of his solutions.

Between them was built a bond of confidence and affection that is rare even among brothers. They communicated instantly, almost telepathically. Even the President observed that their communication was "rather cryptic." Both joked about Bob's reputation as second only to the President in the government. When a phone call from the Attorney General interrupted one conference in the oval office, the President said with a smile, "Will you excuse me a moment, this is the second most powerful man calling."

Like all Cabinet members and the President, they did not always agree. The President authorized a start on the Volta River Dam project in Ghana, even though, as he told the National Security Council, "I can feel the hot breath of the Attorney General breathing down my neck" from his customary seat in the back row. The President did not like it when a press interview with his brother revived the Bay of Pigs controversy. Bob did not like it when the President joked at a post-inaugural dinner that he saw no harm in naming his brother Attorney General to give "him a little experience before he goes out to practice law." Actually, Bob (who preferred not being called Bobby, but could never persuade the President to change) had been sensitive to the nepotism charge, and had long resisted his brother's desire to name him Attorney General, despite his rackets-busting background. But the alternatives of his serving as a private Presidential adviser without responsibility, or as a White House adviser without command, or as a subordinate to the Secretaries of State or Defense, presented obvious practical difficulties.

The Secretary of Defense, Robert McNamara, was clearly the star and the strong man among the newcomers to the Kennedy team. His own staff and subordinates ranked with Bob Kennedy's and Douglas Dillon's as the best in Washington and possibly in history; and it was largely through the President's confidence in McNamara's competence that the Department of Defense began to play a far greater role in areas in which other agencies were concerned: civil defense, space, intelligence, paramilitary operations, foreign aid and foreign policy in general. Unlike some Secretaries of Defense, McNamara even delved deeply into military matters. In addition, his business experience was drawn upon in the steel price dispute, while his previous status as the independent Republican President of the Ford Motor Company was a useful deterrent to Republican attacks.

McNamara, whose name had been produced by the Shriver talent scouts and recommended by several sages, had at first refused to leave this business background. Shriver, in Detroit, refused to take "no" for an answer. McNamara then repeated to the President-elect in Washington his doubts about his own qualifications. "I wasn't aware," Kennedy replied, "that there was a school for Cabinet officers." McNamara reconsidered, obtained the President-elect's assurance that he would not be bound by either the Symington task force on Pentagon reorganization or by any political commitments on the choice of his subordinates, and decided that one could not say "no" to a President.

Neither ever regretted that decision. The two men forged a close personal as well as official relationship. They reinforced each other in reasserting civilian control of the military. Both put in long, hard hours. Both preferred precise decisions to prolonged attempts to please everyone. In eleven years with Kennedy I never saw him develop admiration and personal regard for another man as quickly as he did with Robert McNamara, enabling the McNamaras to be excepted from the general Kennedy rule of keeping official and social friendships separate.

Repeatedly, publicly and privately, the President praised his Defense Secretary in glowing terms. But he did not refrain from overruling him. He was impressed but never overwhelmed by McNamara's confident, authoritative presentations of concise conclusions. Presidents of the United States, he also felt, knew more about press and Congressional relations than presidents of large automobile companies. And aware that McNamara's energetic involvement in foreign affairs was often resented in the Department of State, Kennedy had a shrewd sense of when to rely on him, when to restrain him and when to hear from the Secretary of State.

Dean Rusk possessed many qualities ideally suiting him to be Kennedy's Secretary of State. Many had predicted that Kennedy would be "his own Secretary of State"—a phrase incapable of practical application to the administration of a huge department and Foreign Service, the daily relations with more than one hundred nations, and the simultaneous negotiations with allies and adversaries on several different fronts. Kennedy looked to Rusk for the bulk of this work, and he made clear that the latter—not McNamara, Bundy or any of the many he consulted on foreign affairs—was his principal adviser and agent in foreign relations.

But Kennedy was one of the few Presidents who, in someone else's administration, would have made a first-rate Secretary of State himself, and his interest, energy, experience and enterprise in this area exceeded those in all other departments combined. Like MacMillan, De Gaulle, Khrushchev and most modern chief executives, he regarded peace as too important to be left to the diplomats and took the reins of foreign policy into his own hands. An Acheson, Dulles or Charles Evans Hughes, accustomed to asserting strong-minded leadership from the Secretary's chair, would not have worked so comfortably with Kennedy. The gentle, gracious Rusk, on the other hand, deferred almost too amiably to White House initiatives and interference. He was quiet, courtly and cautious, noncommittal in his press conferences and unaggressive in his excellent relations with the Congress. Intelligent and well informed but never patronizing, he chose his words coolly and carefully, avoiding unnecessary controversies with bland and lucid logic. Recognizing in Rusk a hard worker, a knowledgeable negotiator and an experienced diplomat, Kennedy liked his terse, low-key Secretary of State—though he could never come to call him "Dean." Rusk in turn was wholly loyal to the President and wholly committed to his objectives.

(His loyalty was early demonstrated when I solemnly handed him, during the transition period, a clipping from a Costa Rican newspaper which contained, on that nation's equivalent of April Fool's Day, a faked photograph and news story to the effect that President-elect Kennedy, "on his way" to Palm Beach, had stopped off in San José to promise an outsized foreign aid grant. Rusk looked at the bogus clipping and nodded gravely that any commitment made would have to be kept. Although he later proved to possess a wry sense of humor, he looked more reassured than amused when I confessed it was a hoax.)

Rusk's strong points were also his weaknesses. At times the President wished that his Secretary—whose judgment he found thoughtful when expressed—would assert himself more boldly, recommend solutions more explicitly, offer imaginative alternatives to Pentagon plans more frequently and govern the Department of State (where his subordinates included four former governors not of Rusk's own choosing) more vigorously. Rusk at times seemed almost too eager to disprove charges of State Department softness by accepting Defense Department toughness. Too often, Kennedy felt, neither the President nor the department knew the Secretary's views, and neither in the public mind nor in Congressional wars did Rusk share with the President, as most of his colleagues did, in the criticism for controversial decisions. The Secretary did bear with almost too much composure another kind of criticism, —that aimed at the frequent sterility of the State Department bureaucracy.

Rusk had been highly recommended by Lovett and Acheson. Kennedy, who had never met him, summoned the former diplomat from a meeting of the Rockefeller Foundation of which he was President (and where he had just met Trustee Dillon), talked briefly and somewhat vaguely with him about an article Rusk wrote on *The Presidency,* and called him the next day to say the job was his.

At no time, press reports to the contrary, did the President regret having selected him. He in fact admired the Secretary's patience in the face of repeated press speculation on his demotion. Kennedy neither demoted him nor wished that he had started his administration with any of others originally considered and gradually eliminated. He could not take Dillon, he was advised, because he was a Republican, Bundy because he was still young, Bruce because he was already an elder statesman, and Fulbright because he had taken the Southern position on race. (Among other names mentioned, Stevenson, Bowles and Bunche had never been seriously considered, and Lovett had refused to accept this or any other post.) Kennedy recognized that Rusk's unobtrusive modesty had more advantages than disadvantages in his kind of Cabinet, and concealed qualities and accomplishments not always known to the public.

Douglas Dillon, Eisenhower's Under Secretary of State and Nixon's probable preference for Secretary of State or Treasury, became Kennedy's Secretary of the Treasury. His acceptance annoyed many leaders of both parties. It reassured many leaders of finance. Democratic Senator Albert Gore protested that Dillon was merely an "affable easygoer" at a time when bold economic policies were needed. (Two years later Dillon was leading the fight for the boldest economic measure in at least fifteen years—the tax cut—and Gore was in the opposition.)

While he was more likely to resist or delay Presidential pressures than any of his Cabinet colleagues, particularly on international monetary matters, Dillon was also skilled at sensing which way the President leaned. He remained a liberal Republican, but never acted out of partisan motives, never differed publicly with the President and loyally supported the entire Presidential program. He became more and more of an expansionist at home, an activist abroad and a personal friend of the Kennedy family, although, except for a brief encounter at the 1956 Harvard Commencement, he had not known the President previously. In contrast with his party's traditional policies, Dillon supported deficits to ease a recession, tax cuts at a time of deficit, the closing of tax loopholes, an expansion of foreign aid and greater economic growth to finance greater budgets.

During our first week in office, Dillon, Heller and Bell (known by some of us as the Troika) worked late one night with me on Kennedy's first Budget design, which required an increase in the deficit. When the President reluctantly accepted it the next morning, I observed, "The press will say, Mr. President, that a spendthrift Democratic President insisted on this deficit over the protests of his Republican Secretary of the Treasury, but the truth is exactly the opposite!"

Kennedy, in securing Dillon's acceptance, had made no commitment on fiscal policy. "A President," he said, "cannot enter into treaties with Cabinet members." But he did make clear at his first Cabinet meeting that the office of the Secretary of Treasury was being removed from its customary partisan role. Dillon, Rusk and McNamara were all exempted from attending any political function. Dillon, whom Kennedy had appointed only after ascertaining that he was not a candidate for Governor of New Jersey, often made speeches on behalf of Kennedy's policies but never for either party. "If Goldwater is nominated in 1964," he told me, "that would make the choice for all of us [liberal Republicans on the Kennedy team] much easier."

Although on our first meeting in Palm Beach he said Joe Alsop had warned him that I was suspicious of Eastern bankers, we worked closely and harmoniously, often at night and on weekends. Like the Kennedys, millionaire Dillon could have been taking his ease on the beach instead of serving as a target for Congress. Like Bob Kennedy's and Robert McNamara's, his enlarged role in Presidential decision-making was aided by a reputation for thoughtful judgment, a topnotch staff and an invitation to sit with the National Security Council. And like the entire Kennedy Cabinet he was cool under pressure, more pragmatic than dogmatic and possessed of considerable intellectual capacity.

No Secretary of Labor ever possessed more intellectual capacity or boundless energy than Arthur Goldberg. An articulate adviser even beyond the field of labor, he might have been Attorney General had Bob Kennedy's initial "no" been accepted. A tireless activist, and a skillful mediator respected by both sides, he was touring unemployment centers and settling labor disputes within days of his assumption of office. His legislative work for the labor movement in earlier years, which first brought him together with Kennedy, also endowed him with both contacts and judgment that were helpful in getting bills passed.

Early in 1962 the President was faced with the first of what he regarded as among his most important tests—the opportunity to fill a Supreme Court vacancy. He was not unaware of Arthur's judicial interest and ability or unappreciative of his labors in the Cabinet. The fact that his appointment would place two Jews on the Court did not disturb John Kennedy in the slightest. Neither did the lack of precedent for moving a labor lawyer to the highest court in the land. But the administration's economic recovery and expansion program—and, more particularly, its anti-inflation drive and hopes to contain steel wages and prices—had not yet reached the point where he felt he could risk losing Goldberg. He was reluctant to lose any key Cabinet member and close adviser, in fact, even though Goldberg was to be replaced by his Under Secretary, the able Willard Wirtz—equally thoughtful, equally articulate and frequently with far fewer words. After weighing several names for several days—including those of Harvard Professor Paul Freund, Negro Federal Judge William Hastie and several state judges and lawyers— the President selected the scholarly Deputy Attorney General, Byron White. But when another opening occurred on the Court later in the year, he nominated Arthur Goldberg without a moment's delay.

Two other members of the original Kennedy Cabinet resigned their posts voluntarily. The President was genuinely sorry to lose Abraham Ribicoff as his Secretary of Health, Education, and Welfare, though he could appreciate Abe's preference for the Senate. Ribicoff, who had practically his pick of jobs, had been a long-time Kennedy friend, adviser and supporter since their days in the House together. Contrary to press speculation, Abe had preferred the HEW post to the more controversial (especially for a Jew, he said) attorney generalship; and for the HEW post Kennedy had preferred Ribicoff to the more controversial (and thus less productive of legislation) Mennen Williams. As a Cabinet member, like McNamara, Bob Kennedy and Orville Freeman, Ribicoff loyally accepted abuse and attacks for being out in front on administration positions.

The President's original intention had been to name as Ribicoff's successor the outstanding Housing and Home Finance Administrator, Robert Weaver, already the highest-ranking Negro in Federal Government history. Weaver's race had blocked Congressional approval of the plan to elevate his agency into a Cabinet-level Department of Housing and Urban Affairs, but it had not, contrary to earlier predictions, blocked comprehensive housing legislation or widespread admiration for Weaver's work. Regrettably, by the time Ribicoff had been nominated for the Senate from Connecticut and resigned from the Cabinet, a shaky stock market and increased business hostility had so darkened the atmosphere in Congress that any further revolt by Southern legislators would have endangered the entire Presidential program. There were rumblings from Northerners also that Weaver was needed in the Housing Administration post, for which he had long prepared, and that shifting him to HEW would look like politically inspired racism-in-reverse.

The President decided then on Anthony Celebrezze, who had been seeking, and even preferred, a Federal judgeship. While ethnic considerations for the first time were not irrelevant (Italian-Americans had been complaining of insufficient appointments from their ranks, and the President asked me to check with Census on their relative weight in the electorate), Kennedy had long known and admired Celebrezze for his exceptionally efficient administration as Mayor of Cleveland. After a year of Cabinet meetings, however, in which Celebrezze at some length analyzed every world and national problem in terms of his experiences in Cleveland, the President was more amused than admiring. Celebrezze performed yeoman political service, however, and during his tenure the success of HEW legislation in the Congress continued, aided not only by the Kennedy-O'Brien effort from the White House but also by such able HEW sub-Cabinet officials as the indefatigable Wilbur Cohen, Frank Keppel and Boisfeuillet Jones.

Ethnic politics also played a minor role, but no more than a minor role, in the selection of Wisconsin Tax Commissioner John Gronouski to succeed Day as Postmaster General. Gronouski had been an able administrator as well as an early Kennedy supporter and friend of Pat Lucey. "I don't know why," the President told his press conference,

> it causes so much excitement when the name is Gronouski as
> opposed to . . . Smith or Brown or Day . . . or even Celebrezze. . . .
> [They say if an appointment] is of Polish extraction . . . therefore
> it must be political but if it is not of Polish extraction it is not
> political. I am not sure that I accept that test.

These were almost the exact words he had used at breakfast that morning in saying he hoped he was asked about Gronouski. But at the press conference he added to his praise of Gronouski's qualifications a candid conclusion: "I think we just happen to be fortunate that his grandparents came from Poland."

The President regretted losing Ribicoff but fully understood his reasons. On the other hand, he felt less regret over the resignation of J. Edward Day as Postmaster General and never fully understood Day's reasons. He liked Day's peppery personality, his comments at Cabinet meetings and, above all, his businesslike administration of the huge Post Office bureaucracy. In naming Day in December, 1960, Kennedy had observed, "Having just mailed a letter from Washington to Boston and having it take eight days to get there, I am hopeful we can improve the postal service." Later in his administration he addressed a testimonial luncheon for Day by wire instead of letter "to be certain that [it] reaches you in the right place and at the right time." In fact, Day did improve the service, cut costs, reduce frills and obtain an unpopular but necessary rate increase. Unfortunately he was more capable of making uncleared and uncalled-for public statements than of dealing with the practical political problems channeled through his deputy, William Brawley; and after a bitter falling-out with Brawley, who moved to the National Committee, his own decision to leave government was only a matter of time.

The other member of the Cabinet with a tendency to state publicly individual views at variance with administration policy was Secretary of Commerce Luther Hodges. Just as Goldberg was suspected by some labor leaders of leaning backwards too far to prove he was not prolabor, so Hodges was accused of going too far to prove he was not probusiness. His ouster of the prestigious Business Advisory Council from its privileged place within the administration, and his hard-hitting speeches on business ethics, damaged his rapport with many of his most influential "clientele." The oldest man in the Cabinet, and a successful Southern businessman and politician, Hodges presented an image that was helpful with the Congress and some elements of the business community. He was energetic in his efforts to revive a department that had long lacked effective leadership, imaginative in his new drive for export expansion and helpful in the steel price crisis. But his subordinates, with few exceptions, did not compare with the aides assembled by McNamara, Dillon and Bob Kennedy, and the President tended to turn to Dillon, Heller and private consultants to learn about both the business forecast and the business viewpoint. While Hodges was not held responsible for the frayed relations between the administration and the business community in 1962, President Kennedy briefly deliberated at that time whether a Secretary of Commerce who enjoyed greater business confidence might not be better able to repair those relations. But it was not easy to think of an alternative who would have been (1) wholly loyal to Kennedy, his party and program, (2) enthusiastically greeted by business leaders and (3) willing to leave his present position and income to take on the unwieldy conglomeration of bureaus and administrations known as the Department of Commerce. Hodges, Governor of North Carolina when Kennedy first met him at the 1956 Convention, was willing; he was loyal; and he was making some headway with business. No change was made.

Secretary of Agriculture Orville Freeman and Secretary of the Interior Stewart Udall were more vigorous and progressive than Hodges, equally successful with the Congress and far more influential with the President. But they were handicapped, as Hodges was, by the President's inability to give their departments and problems the same time and attention he gave to national security affairs. Freeman, the former Minnesota Governor, was highly regarded by the President, particularly once Orville realized that his role in Kennedy's eyes was not representing the interests of agriculture in the administration but carrying out the administration's objectives in agriculture, including the reduction of storage subsidies.

When the administration indicted Billie Sol Estes for his manipulations under the previous administration's cotton and grain program, Freeman unhesitatingly fired three employees (out of 100,000 in his department) who had accepted gratuities from Estes, and satisfied himself that no Federal funds had been lost. He acted without waiting for a Congressional investigation. When it came, it was seeking his scalp, and when it departed, it was praising his tighter administration.

Freeman had originally not wanted the thankless task of running this swollen department, where the number of employees had so increased under Benson as the number of farmers declined that the Congress considered only half-jokingly requiring no more employees than farmers. Nor had Kennedy originally wanted Freeman for this job, in accordance with a self-adopted rule against defeated politicians in his Cabinet. But the Agriculture prospects soon boiled down to two defeated politicians, both of whom had lost votes through identification with Kennedy and his religion: Freeman and ex-Congressman George McGovern. He named Freeman Secretary of Agriculture and placed the equally dedicated McGovern in the newly expanded and independent Food-for-Peace post in the White House. Neither ever showed any symptoms of defeatism.

Representative Stewart Udall of Arizona had never been defeated. His experience in Congress encouraged him into independent ventures and statements in the interest of his department and party that were not always consistent with White House policy, but it also enabled him to serve as an additional channel to the Congress and as an effective campaigner and campaign adviser (including planning of the President's "conservation" tours to dedicate dams in key states).

Coincidentally I had first met both Freeman and Udall at odd hours, although the President had met them both casually in 1955. Udall, after adjournment of the 1959 Congress, had come to our office at 3 A.M. to declare his support for Kennedy's candidacy. Seeking Minnesota delegates following Humphrey's withdrawal in the spring of 1960, I had sipped Jane Freeman's homemade hot chocolate with Orville at 4 A.M. in his St. Paul living room after adjournment of Minnesota's State Democratic Convention, at which Udall delivered a plea for Kennedy.

All in all, the Kennedy Cabinet was a group of gifted men. I felt tremendously pleased and impressed on the Sunday before inauguration, as the President worked in Palm Beach, when the Cabinet, with several absentees, gathered for its first informal get-together at the home of Arthur Goldberg, brunching on lox and bagels. For several it was their first look at some of their colleagues. Some may not have been sure upon arrival who all of the others were—or even what lox and bagels were. But it was a harmonious group from that first meeting onward, and a loyal one. Not one sought to advance his own political interests at the expense of his colleagues or leader, and all willingly subordinated their own interests and identities to those of John Kennedy.

Equally remarkable was the number of men of Cabinet stature and ability serving in sub-Cabinet posts, including, in addition to those mentioned earlier, and a wide range of talent in the Department of State to be mentioned later, such indispensable Deputy or Under Secretaries as Gilpatric in Defense, Gudeman and Roosevelt in Commerce, Roosa and Fowler in Treasury, Katzenbach in Justice and Murphy in Agriculture. Edward R. Murrow immensely improved the United States Information Agency, its stature in the eyes of Congress and the world and its voice in the NSC. Space Administrator Webb and Atomic Energy Chairman Seaborg both brought unusual ability to their positions. Kennedy admired such Assistant Secretaries and Bureau Chiefs as Esther Peterson and Jim Reynolds at Labor, Surrey and Caplin at Treasury, Marshall at Justice, Scammon at Census, and Vance and Nitze at Defense. He felt confident leaving Civil Service matters to Macy, District affairs to Tobriner and Horsky, Federal procurement to Boutin, airlines to Halaby and Boyd, and Export-Import Bank matters to Linder. He frequently consulted Archie Cox on legal matters beyond the Solicitor General's jurisdiction. He was proud of the caliber of such regulatory agency appointees as Cary at the SEC, Minow at the FCC, Swidler at the FPC and McCulloch at the NLRB.

OTHER PERSONNEL

Kennedy and his co-workers regarded the Civil Service and Foreign Service as honorable professions. Custom and Congressional criticism, the President knew, had driven many members of these services into an excess of caution, committees and clearances. The President sought to inspire confidence. He spoke directly on the phone to career specialists who had rarely been called by their own Secretaries. He attended and addressed staff meetings of the leading agencies. He gave new recognition to employee unions. He adhered to the merit system in new appointments. He protected career servants from security "witch-hunts" and Congressional harassment.

He obtained from the Congress increases in both civilian and military pay and, more importantly, a new and rational standard of comparability with private enterprise salaries. He told the Congress in his First State of the Union Message that he had found the Executive Branch

> full of honest and useful public servants. . . . Let every public servant know, whether his post is high or low, that a man's rank and reputation in this Administration will be determined by the size of the job he does, and not by the size of his staff, his office or his budget. . . . Let the public service be a proud and lively career.

He also acted promptly in four ways to improve both the quality and effectiveness of our ambassadors abroad:

1. In too many countries our ambassadors and many of their officers were required to reach deep into their own pockets or go in debt to finance the normal entertainment expenses accompanying their posts—including hospitality for visiting Congressmen—as the result of legislative penny-pinching on what some Congressmen called "booze allowances." Kennedy, even before the inauguration, worked (though with only limited success) to make possible the appointment of more career and other nonwealthy ambassadors by applying Palm Beach pressure to the key subcommittee chairman, Congressman John Rooney of New York.

2. In too many countries our ambassadors were unable to coordinate the activities of all the various American operatives in their country—intelligence agents, foreign aid technicians, agricultural attachés, information specialists and many others. Kennedy, early in 1961, issued a directive clarifying each ambassador's authority as America's principal spokesman and the President's personal representative. He backed up his words by frequent personal messages and probing White House talks which at times disconcerted envoys more accustomed to being left undisturbed.

3. In too many countries the President and Department of State were in dangerous lack of rapid, reliable and secure communication channels with many of our own ambassadors. This became known to the President in the midst of the Cuban missile crisis. An order that a duty officer stand by the embassy telephone night and day throughout that crisis, for example, produced the embarrassed response from one ambassador that the only telephone operating at night in his somewhat isolated embassy was next to his wife's bed in their bedroom. Cuban planning was briefly interrupted to initiate sweeping, long-range technical improvements.

4. In too many countries America's representation had long been characterized by unprepared political appointees and unimaginative career appointees. Kennedy, despite some major exceptions and mistakes,[6] appointed a record high proportion of men trained in the language, culture and problems of their posts. Two out of three had risen through the ranks of the career service. His noncareer ambassadors, including a higher proportion of Negro and Spanish-speaking Americans, were usually nonpolitical in background, recruited from universities, foundations and the professions. Among the best were Professors Reischauer in Japan, Gordon in Brazil, Badeau in Egypt and the irresistible Galbraith in India; writers Attwood and Loeb in Geneva, and Martin in the Dominican Republic; lawyers Finletter at NATO, Blair in Denmark and Wine in the Ivory Coast; university presidents Cole in Chile and Stevenson in the Philippines; and many others. General James Gavin may not have moved General De Gaulle, but no other Ambassador to France could have done more (and De Gaulle might have been more friendly had he known of Gavin's increased tendency to accept De Gaulle's version of Franco-American relations). Even a frankly political appointee like Matt McCloskey was regarded in Ireland as the best American Ambassador in memory.

In addition to these noncareer appointees, able young career men were promoted to ambassador, such as Gullion in the Congo, Meyer in Lebanon, Stephansky in Bolivia and Berger in Korea; and the best of the old State Department hands—Bruce, Bunker, Bohlen, Thompson, Labouisse, Merchant and others—were all used to good advantage.

OBTAINING TEAMWORK

From the diversity of talent which he had assembled, John Kennedy drew the divisions of opinion which he encouraged. He also knew that so many strong-minded men would inevitably be engaged from time to time in clashes of jurisdiction, which he did not encourage.

6 Including one ambassador whose constant presence on the golf course, even when due at official functions, earned him the deep disrespect of his host country and another termed unacceptable by the host country before he could be nominated.

He hardly needed to encourage them. The Food-for-Peace office, for example, wanted more independence from Agriculture, which wanted certain functions from State, which wanted less authority over balance of payments for Treasury. Treasury was angry about Justice's blocking bank mergers. Justice detected softness on civil rights within Commerce. Commerce tangled with Labor over maritime strikes. Labor differed with Agriculture over migrant farm workers. Agriculture fought Interior on National Parks and Forests. Interior accused the Federal Power Commission of blocking orderly power development. And the Kennedy appointees on the Federal Power Commission were split amongst themselves.

These and similar disputes—between the CAB and the FAA, between NASA and the Air Force, between the Army Engineers and Reclamation, between State and Commerce, between Defense and the CIA—were not all settled by the President, though many were. Some were settled by the White House[7] or Budget Bureau, some by the parties themselves. Some smoldered on indefinitely, although the traditional rivalries between Labor and Commerce, State and Defense, and Agriculture and Interior were significantly lessened. Kennedy knew how to sooth and smooth over ruffled feelings and when to check and balance the views of competing departments. Better informed, he had a broader perspective. Keeping his top team intact to an unusual degree, he took pains to win over to each policy those who would be chiefly responsible for implementing it—and thus did not feel, for example, that he could push the Joint Chiefs too far on their budget or Secretary Dillon too far on international monetary reform.

One incident stands out in my mind, more as an exception than an example. At the close of a meeting on balance of payments problems, the President cautioned all those present to keep it confidential. Treasury Secretary Dillon murmured that it was too late, that Jean Monnet in Paris was already discussing such proposals and that State must have let it out. At that Under Secretary of State George Ball, already resentful of Treasury's domination of diplomacy in this area, sharply retorted that the Dillon statement was wholly false and Monnet's proposals were spontaneous. The President calmed everyone down before he left, but remarked to me later in his office, "I hope that doesn't mean there is bad blood between Doug and George. If there is, it's the only case of it anywhere in this administration."

While that may have been overly optimistic, the dedication of his

7 When one Commission head protested as improper my informal invitation to lunch at the White House to settle his feud with a Cabinet member, his Budget request remained at the bottom of my "in" box until he decided such a lunch would be delightful.

associates to his success did in fact produce an unusual degree of unity—
and Kennedy was proud of it. There were no cliques, much less cabals,
in the Cabinet. To be sure, the six department heads not on the NSC felt
somewhat neglected during the Cuban crisis. Those whose budgets were
cut back to help make room for the tax cut were not enthusiastic about
its proposal. Those less often invited to share the Kennedys' social life
after hours may have felt some envy of the McNamaras and Dillons—
or if they didn't, their wives no doubt did. But there were no clear or
continuing splits along political or philosophical lines.

More than good feeling and good fellowship, however, was required
to mold nearly three million civilian and military men and women on the
Federal payroll into a smooth-running governmental machine. Three
special Kennedy approaches deserve mention: (1) reorganization of
the executive decision-making forces; (2) the clearance and coordination
of public statements; and (3) personnel changes.

THE DECISION-MAKING PROCESS

Kennedy brought to the White House unusual firsthand knowledge of
the foreign, domestic, legislative and political arenas but no experience
in the Executive Branch. He was always more interested in policy than
in administration, and would later admit that "it is a tremendous change
to go from being a Senator to being President. In the first months it is
very difficult." He continued to reshape executive procedures throughout
his term, but from the outset he abandoned the notion of a collective,
institutionalized Presidency. He ignored Eisenhower's farewell recommendation to create a First Secretary of the Government to oversee all
foreign affairs agencies. He abandoned the practice of the Cabinet's and
the National Security Council's making group decisions like corporate
boards of directors. He abolished the practice of White House staff meetings and weekly Cabinet meetings. He abolished the pyramid structure
of the White House staff, the Assistant President–Sherman Adams-type
job, the Staff Secretary, the Cabinet Secretariat, the NSC Planning Board
and the Operations Coordinating Board, all of which imposed, in his
view, needless paperwork and machinery between the President and his
responsible officers. He abolished several dozen interdepartmental committees which specialized in group recommendations on outmoded problems. He paid little attention to organization charts and chains of
command which diluted and distributed his authority. He was not interested in unanimous committee recommendations which stifled alternatives to find the lowest common denominator of compromise.

He relied instead on informal meetings and direct contacts—on a
personal White House staff, the Budget Bureau and *ad hoc* task forces to

probe and define issues for his decision—on special Presidential emissaries and constant Presidential phone calls and memoranda—on placing Kennedy men in each strategic spot. Particularly in 1961 and particularly on National Security matters, he talked at the White House or by telephone to lower-level officers and experts with firsthand knowledge or responsibility. (At least one State Department subordinate was embarrassed by the profanely skeptical reply he gave when the voice on the other end of the line announced itself as the President's.) "The President can't administer a department," Kennedy said when asked about this practice,

> but at least he can be a stimulant. . . . There is a great tendency in government to have papers stay on desks too long. . . . One of the functions of the President is to try to have it move with more speed. Otherwise you can wait while the world collapses.

Abolishing the Operations Coordinating Board, he made clear his intention to strengthen departmental responsibility "without extensive formal machinery" and to maintain

> direct communication with the responsible agencies, so that everyone will know what I have decided, while I in turn keep fully informed of the actions taken to carry out decisions. We of course expect that the policy of the White House will be the policy of the Executive Branch as a whole, and we shall take such steps as are needed to ensure this result.

A reporter compared the Eisenhower-Kennedy methods of obtaining teamwork with the differences between football and basketball. The Eisenhower football method relied on regular huddles and rigid assignments. In the Kennedy administration all team members were constantly on the move.

Kennedy called huddles, but only when necessary and only with those necessary, those whose official views he required or whose unofficial judgment he desired, regardless of protocol or precedent. Attendance varied with each subject, but it was not haphazard. McGeorge Bundy made certain that no responsible officer or point of view was omitted from meetings on foreign policy, and I tried to do the same on domestic. For example, if Walter Heller and George Ball wanted to meet with the President on the balance of payments, I made certain Dillon was also invited. The President's own accessibility, and his insistence on dealing with subordinates as well as chiefs, made certain that he was not denied any relevant counsel or criticism, and both he and his staff improved our ability to use channels and coordinate decisions during those first crucial months. But he never altered his view that any meeting larger than necessary was less flexible, less secret and less hard-hitting.

As a result, with few exceptions, he held Cabinet meetings only be-cause "I suppose we should—it's been several weeks since the last one," and with few exceptions these meetings bored him. He rarely made any attempt at such sessions, as President Roosevelt had, to engage Cabinet members in light banter, to seek their political advice, to suggest that they volunteer problems or to call on them one by one for discussion.

No decisions of importance were made at Kennedy's Cabinet meet-ings and few subjects of importance, particularly in foreign affairs, were ever seriously discussed. The Cabinet as a body was convened largely as a symbol, to be informed, not consulted, to help keep the channels of communication open, to help maintain the *esprit de corps* of the mem-bers and to prevent the charge that Kennedy had abolished the Cabinet. There were no high-level debates, or elaborate presentations, or materials circulated in advance.[8]

Kennedy relied considerably on his Cabinet officers, but not on the Cabinet as a body. On the contrary, he thought

> general Cabinet meetings . . . to be unnecessary and involve a
> waste of time. . . . All these problems Cabinet officers deal with
> are very specialized. I see all the Cabinet officers every week, but
> we don't have a general meeting. There really isn't much use
> spending a morning talking about the Post Office budget and tying
> up Secretary Freeman, who has agriculture responsibilites. . . . If
> we have a problem involving labor-management . . . it is much
> better for me to meet with Secretary Hodges from Commerce and
> Secretary Goldberg from Labor. . . . I think we will find the
> Cabinet perhaps more important than it has ever been but Cabinet
> meetings not as important.

He also felt, but could not add, that he usually had little interest in the views of Cabinet members on matters outside their jurisdiction. He summoned former Under Secretary of State Dillon to most major meet-ings on foreign policy and former Ford President McNamara to advise on the steel price dispute. But he did not want McNamara's advice on debt management or Dillon's advice on Nike-Zeus. In his opinion, that only wasted his time and theirs.

Problems involving all Cabinet members, and thus appropriate to Cabinet discussion, were few and far between: Civil Service and patron-age, the Budget outlook, legislative relations and somewhat superficial briefings, not consultations, on administration policy and current events. Occasionally more important matters appeared on the agenda—the

[8] In the first few months of 1961, Fred Dutton tried valiantly but in vain to make meaningful his role of "Cabinet Assistant" by promoting an impressive agenda, detailed planning, an outline for the President and some of the other characteristics of the Eisenhower Cabinet. But Dutton, and Ted Reardon who succeeded him to these duties, soon gave up.

responsibility of Cabinet officers for advancing civil rights or accelerating Federal projects during the recession, for example—but more typical by far was this Cabinet agenda for December 10, 1962, set forth here in its entirety:

1. Review of Foreign Situation—The Secretary of State
2. Review of Economic Situation and Outlook—Honorable Walter Heller
3. Status Report on 1963 Legislative Program—Honorable T. C. Sorensen

While Heller and I were often asked to make presentations of this kind—as were O'Brien, the Budget Director and the Civil Service Chairman—only the ten department heads (and Ambassador Stevenson, when in town) sat at the long Cabinet table. None of them brought any staff or subordinates with them and most of them said comparatively little. The Cabinet Assistant, the Budget Director, the Science Adviser, the Economic Adviser and I sat behind the President, who kept the meetings as brief as decorum permitted. Often he would cut discussion short. Occasionally he would ask the Vice President to "chair" the meeting during his temporary absence—and then disappear permanently into his office.

Much the same was true of the large formal meetings of the National Security Council, which dealt exclusively with foreign affairs. It had a more significant agenda prepared by McGeorge Bundy, papers were circulated in advance and the meetings were more interesting to the President. He ran them in every sense of the word, first asking the CIA Director for the intelligence summaries on the situation under study, then asking the Secretary of State to give his recommendations, and then throwing it open to Defense and others. (Usually the senior official was addressed by the President as "Mr. Secretary" or "Mr. Dulles," but his own aides by their first names.)

At times he made minor decisions in full NSC meetings or *pretended* to make major ones actually settled earlier. Attendance was generally kept well below the level of previous administrations, but still well above the statutory requirements. He strongly preferred to make all major decisions with far fewer people present, often only the officer to whom he was communicating the decision. "We have averaged three or four meetings a week with the Secretaries of Defense and State, McGeorge Bundy, the head of the CIA and the Vice President," he said in 1961. "But formal meetings of the Security Council which include a much wider group are not as effective. It is more difficult to decide matters involving high national security if there is a wider group present."

For brief periods of time, during or after a crisis, the President would hold NSC meetings somewhat more regularly, partly as a means of getting on record the views of every responsible officer (who might otherwise complain that he wasn't consulted and wouldn't have approved), but mostly to silence outside critics who equated machinery with efficiency. "The National Security Council," he said, when asked about various positions reportedly taken by its members in the Cuban missile crisis, "is an advisory body to the President. In the final analysis, the President of the United States must make the decision. And it is his decision. It's not the decision of the National Security Council or any collective decision." This he meant quite literally, for he often overruled the principal NSC members and on at least one occasion overruled all of them.

There were some complaints about the Kennedy approach to organizational machinery. Secretary Hodges grumbled publicly that there should be more Cabinet meetings. State Department aides grumbled privately that their prestige suffered if they were not present for key decisions. Secretary Rusk complained that he did not like to offer his views in meetings at which "people like Sorensen and Kaysen with no responsibility were making academic comments." He preferred to save his arguments for the President's ear only. But in general the department heads concurred with Willard Wirtz's conclusion that, without many formal meetings, there had been an "extraordinary degree" of close communication, both ways, "between the President and his Cabinet . . . and among the Cabinet members."

SPEECH AND STATEMENT CLEARANCES

The President's standing rule requiring White House clearance for all major speeches and Congressional testimony was rarely enforced except in critical periods. Salinger and his staff and Ted Reardon checked routine speech drafts, and my staff and Bundy's checked major statements on domestic and foreign policy respectively. The President reviewed some speeches on his own. Occasionally he would ask us to coordinate in advance and monitor in progress all Congressional testimony by administration witnesses with differing points of view on a sensitive issue under hearing—the Cuban missile crisis or the 1962 economic and tax outlook, for example.

Some important gains resulted. Several Defense Department speeches were rendered less "missile-rattling." A State Department aide was informed that he could not assert his own visionary proposals for civil rights. But it was an imperfect system. Several controversial high-level statements were given without clearance, and there was no way to clear answers to press or Congressional questions.

The speeches most difficult to check—and most dangerous to leave unchecked—were those by high-ranking military officers, whose remarks had not always reflected the President's point of view about peace. When it became known in Kennedy's first week that a strong anti-Soviet speech by Chief of Naval Operations Arleigh Burke had been toned down in the White House lest it disrupt the release of the RB-47 fliers, a great hue and cry arose about "muzzling" the military. Actually, Admiral Burke had voluntarily submitted the speech and the procedure was not unusual. But it was clearer than ever that military officers on active duty were not to undermine the final decisions of their Commander in Chief in their speeches or legislative testimony, not to confuse the world about the nature of America's foreign policy, and not to undertake as an official responsibility the political indoctrination of either their troops or public opinion.

The most flagrant example of the last was Major General Edwin Walker's use of right-wing extremist material with his troops in Germany. The President read about Walker's wild charges in the newspaper and asked McNamara to investigate. In November, 1961, having been admonished and ordered to the Pacific, the General resigned from the Army.

There was nothing radical or even new, said Kennedy, about protecting the military from direct political involvement, requiring their educational talks to be nonpartisan and accurate, and requesting that their official speeches reflect official policies. Nor was any new curb placed on the military's freedom of speech and opinion, or on their frank answers to Congressional questions. But

> if a well-known, high-ranking military figure makes a speech which affects foreign policy or possibly military policy, I think that the people—and the countries abroad—have a right to expect that that speech represents the opinion of the national government. . . . The purpose of the review . . . is to make sure that . . . the government speaks with one voice.

And he pointed out that his own speeches were reviewed in State and Defense with this objective.

In time, however, a Senate investigation, sparked by Strom Thurmond, sought to link this "censorship" with "softness" toward Communism. The situation was complicated by former President Eisenhower's statement, "after thoughtful reconsideration," that his own administration's policy of requiring speech clearances should be dropped. But several high-ranking officers testified to the wisdom of the practice, and General Walker's ranting testimony served to confirm it. The most prominent military supporters of his policy on clearances were all distinguished officers, said the President with some pleasure,

who understand the importance of the proper relationship between
the military and the civilian . . . which has existed for so many
years, which provides for civilian control and responsibility. . . .
In fact, the military seems to understand the problem better than
some civilians.

Not all the military understood. Not all agreed to speak with one
voice, that of their civilian Commander in Chief. Some still grumbled to
the press and Congress about decisions on which they felt inadequately
consulted or unwisely overruled. But, on the whole, official Washington
spoke publicly with one strong voice more clearly than ever before.

PERSONNEL CHANGES

Very few important officials inherited or appointed by Kennedy were
overtly dismissed from the Federal service. One Kennedy critic in a
major holdover post was the object of such intentions, but upon reading
Bundy's memorandum explaining that by statute the only hope for
removing this gentleman would be to "get him on bad behavior," the
President scrawled at the bottom: "No—he might do the same to us. JK."

Nevertheless those who could not keep up, those whose contributions
did not match their reputations and those who did not share his energy
and idealism were reassigned, if not asked to retire. The most prominent
case of reshuffling—known in some quarters as "the Thanksgiving Massacre of 1961"—occurred in the Department of State.

The President was discouraged with the State Department almost as
soon as he took office. He felt that it too often seemed to have a built-in
inertia which deadened initiative and that its tendency toward excessive
delay obscured determination. It spoke with too many voices and too
little vigor. It was never clear to the President (and this continued to
be true, even after the personnel changes) who was in charge, who was
clearly delegated to do what, and why his own policy line seemed consistently to be altered or evaded. The top State Department team—
including Secretary Rusk, Under Secretaries Bowles and Ball, UN Ambassador Stevenson, Roving Ambassador Harriman, Assistant Secretary
Williams, Latin America coordinator Berle, all men of Cabinet stature,
and many others—reflected an abundance of talent ironically unmatched
by production. Kennedy felt the men recommended by Bowles had done
better than Rusk's; Rusk felt confined by subordinates appointed personally by Kennedy, some of them even before Rusk had been named,
and by all the White House aides and other outsiders brought in on
foreign policy; Bowles felt unable to get Rusk's backing on the administrative rebuilding which the Secretary was too busy to perform; and
Stevenson, enveloped in the United Nations–New York atmosphere where

world opinion weighed heavier than domestic, felt out of touch with decisions in Washington. In addition, reorganization of the foreign AID program was hampered not only by ineffective direction but by the refusal of Congress, the No. 1 critic of AID overstaffing and inefficiency, to authorize the elimination of "deadwood" personnel, many of them placed there through Congressional influence.

State's relations with the Congress, the press and the White House were in some disarray. Holdovers in the department talked longingly of Acheson—or Nixon. The Foreign Service, many of its brightest lights having been darkened or dimmed during the McCarthy-McCleod days and by Dulles' one-man diplomacy, still suffered from low morale and from a tradition of grumbling about interference by aggressive amateurs and by other agencies, and from a system of looking so long at every side of every decision that often only indecision emerged. (A veteran diplomat told the President, however, that the Foreign Service had become much like a badly trained horse whom punishment could only make worse.)

The President had no desire to change the Secretary of State. But Rusk left administration to his Under Secretary, Chester Bowles, who preferred exploring long-range ideas to expediting short-gap expedients, and to the Deputy Under Secretary for Administration, Roger Jones, a former Civil Service commissioner. As one observer summed it up to the President, "Rusk finds it hard to use a deputy and Bowles finds it even harder to be a No. 2." The President liked Bowles, liked most of his ideas and liked most of his personnel recommendations. But the State Department team needed a manager.

Many names were considered. Bundy had already rejected the job in January. Sargent Shriver and David Bell were needed where they were. Bob Kennedy would not have fitted there. Arthur Dean and John McCloy, both highly regarded for their work on disarmament and the UN, preferred not to accept permanent full-time responsibilities. Harvard's Robert Bowie had been more of a thinker than an administrator. Finally the solution was clear, as perhaps it should have been earlier: promoting Under Secretary for Economic Affairs George Ball, No. 3 man in the department, into the No. 2 position.

But premature word of Bowles's impending reassignment in the summer of 1961 brought glee to his enemies, who mistakenly assumed that the President had "leaked" it to his columnist friends, and this postponed Bowles's fate. The Foreign Service cliques, the CIA professionals, the Pentagon generals and the right-wing editorials were all opposed to Bowles for the wrong reasons. Kennedy was not motivated by any criticisms that Bowles was too "soft," or too naïve, or had attempted to clear himself of responsibility for the Bay of Pigs failure. At the same time, some of Bowles's supporters in the press, party and government (nicknamed by some "the Chet Set") began to pressure the President to retain Bowles for equally irrelevant reasons. Bowles himself ignored all hints and opportunities to request reassignment as a matter of service and loyalty to the President.

Kennedy let the controversy die down, but he began relying more on Ball than on Bowles. While Ball also had little time or inclination to take on the management of the department, he was able to give the President more expeditious service on major projects. In a press conference, while praising Bowles, Kennedy made clear his intention to "make more effective the structure and the personnel of the State Department. . . . If I come to the conclusion that Mr. Bowles could be more effective in another responsible position, I would not hesitate to ask him."

By late November he was ready to move with a whole series of closely held, swiftly executed changes "better matching men and jobs." Dick Goodwin's ambitious efforts on Latin America and Walt Rostow's generalized planning on foreign policy belonged in State, which was weak in these areas, rather than in the White House. Fred Dutton, whose abilities had not found a firm foothold in the White House, would take over State's sorry Congressional relations (where he did a good job despite the continuing practice of the more timid bureaucracy to appease those legislators who controlled the purse strings). Averell Harriman, whom the President noted had already held more important posts than anyone since John Quincy Adams, and whose performance as Ambassador at Large (once he swallowed pride and wore a hearing aid) had far surpassed Kennedy's expectations, agreed to serve as Assistant Secretary for the Far East, where the problems of Laos, Vietnam, Red China and Formosa had not been adequately handled. Rostow was to take the place of Rusk man George McGhee, McGhee was to take Ball's place (where he was later succeeded by Harriman), Ball was to take Bowles's place, and Bowles was to be offered a specific or roving ambassadorship.

Obviously the whole chain of moves depended on Bowles. Fearful that Bowles might resign in an uproar, the President asked me to "hold his hand a little, as one 'liberal' to another, after Rusk breaks the news to him." I liked Chet Bowles and his ideas about the Foreign Service and the kind of men it needed. I had stayed in contact with him since 1959. It was the Sunday afternoon after Thanksgiving when the news was broken to each of the men moved, and Rusk, concerned by Bowles's reaction, called me at home where I had been standing by and urged me to see the Under Secretary immediately.

In the all-but-empty new State Department Building I found Bowles sitting disconsolate and alone in his office. He was hurt and angry at

Kennedy, at Rusk and at the world. He had no intention of taking any post. He had his pride and his convictions, he said. He had been loyal and received no loyalty in return. He would resign and speak his mind.

We talked. On behalf of the President, I sympathized with Chet's feelings. I rejected his threats. I shared his grief. I admired his efforts. It grew darker and darker, but neither of us moved to turn on the lights. Salinger's prescheduled Hyannis Port press conference, ·at which the changes had to be announced before they "leaked," was about to begin. We talked on and on.

Finally a solution began to emerge. Bowles would be a part of the prestigious White House team, the President's "Special Representative and Adviser for Asian, African and Latin-American Affairs" with the rank of ambassador. He would have a raise in pay, reflecting a raise in responsibility. He would have his own office and staff, use of the White House cars, and access to the White House dining room. He would report directly to the President.

It was not a real post, as became clear to all later. Bowles was far more suited to return to India as Ambassador, which he did promptly on Galbraith's retirement in mid-1963, and where he served with loyalty and distinction. But it was a post which saved faces and prevented fights in November, 1961. Bowles accepted it. The President, who would nail it down the following day in a personal conversation, liked it. Salinger announced it. All those who a few months earlier had denounced the prospect of Bowles's removal could not effectively object to it. And the President, who looked with some amusement on my assignments as a missionary to liberals, commented, "Good job, Ted—that was your best work since the Michigan delegation."

CHAPTER XI

❦

THE EARLY CRISES—
THE BAY OF PIGS

JOHN KENNEDY ONCE RECALLED with humor the day at Cape Cod when he sat handicapped by his bad back in the eye of a New England hurricane. The only two other people in the house had been a servant who was drunk and a chauffeur enraged at the servant. While they chased each other threatening murder, the then Senator sat alone with his crutches in the deadly still air, watching nature's fury swirl about him and wondering whether he would survive.

In 1961 he found himself once again in the eye of a hurricane. Sitting alone in the unnatural quiet that becalms the summit of power, beset by economic and military handicaps and quarrels within the free world, he saw the international horizon explode about him in one storm after another. "Every President," wrote John Fischer in *Harper's Magazine*, "needs about twelve months to get his executive team organized, to feel his way into the vast and dangerous machinery of the bureaucracy. . . . While [Kennedy] was still trying to move in the furniture, in effect, he found the roof falling in and the doors blowing off."

Kennedy had been forewarned. The CIA briefings he received from Allen Dulles and his deputy in Palm Beach were far more revealing than those he had received as a candidate, and the still fuller familiarity with world trends that came with his assumption of power "staggered" him, as he willingly confessed. But he had never entertained any illusions about avoiding or postponing these crises. "That's stupid," he had said to me in Palm Beach upon hearing that sources within his administration

were supposedly reporting that he had asked Soviet Chairman Khrushchev for a six-month moratorium on world tensions to give the new
administration time to look for new answers. The national interests of
the Soviet Union, he said, like those of the United States, could not be
waived or suspended for any person or period, and where those two sets
of interests conflicted, there was trouble ahead.

During his first week in office we worked intermittently on his first
State of the Union address. As each successive draft was reviewed, he
sought to make more somber his warning to the country of the perils
that lay ahead. His original foreign affairs passage struck me as already
rather ominous, preoccupied as I was with his legislative program:

> Our problems are critical. The tide is unfavorable. The news
> will be worse before it is better. And while hoping and working
> for the best, we should prepare ourselves now for the worst.

But on Saturday, January 28, two days before the message was to be
delivered, he decided, in reviewing a near-final draft completed in an
all-night session, that these words of warning were still insufficient. He
inserted another paragraph:

> Each day the crises multiply. Each day their solution grows
> more difficult. Each day we draw nearer the hour of maximum
> danger. . . . I feel I must inform the Congress that . . . in each of
> the principal areas of crisis, the tide of events has been running
> out and time has not been our friend.

And then on Sunday, going over the finished draft in the Mansion
after church, he added one final prediction: *There will be further setbacks before the tide is turned.*

On Monday the message was delivered, and immediately much of
the press called these passages unnecessarily grim and gloomy. No one
could have foreseen that the rate of world crises in the following eight
months would so rapidly outpace that message that a unique second
State of the Union address would be required in the spring and that
even grimmer dangers would appear in the summer.

Two weeks after his speech, on February 13, the Soviets threatened
new intervention in the Congo following the assassination of former
Premier Lumumba.

On March 9 Communist-led forces were so close to taking over all of
Laos that detailed plans for the introduction of American forces were
presented to the President.

On March 18 NATO ally Portugal was required to rush troops to
Angola to repress a nationalist uprising supported by America's African
friends.

On March 21 the Soviet delegation at the Geneva test-ban talks announced its new demand for a Troika veto over all inspection, making doubtful any nuclear disarmament.

On April 12 the Soviets dramatically demonstrated their superior rocket boosters by orbiting the first man in space.

On April 19 Fidel Castro completely crushed an invasion at the Bay of Pigs by a band of U.S.-supported Cuban exiles hoping to free their homeland.

On May 1 the Communist-sponsored National Liberation Front of South Vietnam and the Communist Party newspaper in North Vietnam announced that the rate of progress in the guerrilla war would enable them to take over the country by the end of the year.

On May 15 an internal military coup overthrew the government of U.S.-defended South Korea.

On May 30 the assassination of dictator Trujillo introduced an atmosphere of revolt and unrest into the Dominican Republic that is still continuing as of this writing.

On June 4 Khrushchev at Vienna warned Kennedy that a peace treaty with East Germany, ending Western access rights in West Berlin, would be signed before the end of the year.

On July 19 fighting broke out between two nations friendly to the U.S., France and Tunisia, over a French base on Tunisian soil at Bizerte.

On August 13 the Communists closed off East Berlin through barricades, barbed wire and a stone wall.

On August 25 Brazil, our largest Latin-American neighbor, was thrown into a constitutional crisis by the resignation of President Quadros.

On August 30 the Soviet Union announced that it was breaking the three-year moratorium on nuclear testing with a series of high-megaton explosions.

On September 18, touring the Congo where fighting had broken out once again, UN Secretary General Dag Hammarskjöld was killed in a plane crash, subjecting the UN to insistent Soviet demands for a Troika.

There were other foreign crises during these first eight months. There were others in the months that followed, one of them—in October, 1962 —the most critical in our nation's history. But these eight months were the darkest period for the President personally and for freedom—eight months in which he labored to fit our strength to our commitments and to reshape our ends and our means. Often his plans were altered by fast-moving events even before they were executed. "It is easier," he commented somewhat sourly, "to sit with a map and talk about what ought to be done than to see it done."

During these eight months he could at times be privately bitter about the mistakes he had made, the advice he had accepted and the "mess" he had inherited. But, while learning his lessons, he never lost his sense of confidence. Red Fay has said that PT boat skipper Kennedy was cheerful in the South Pacific before the tide was turned against the Japanese simply because he was happy to be in the midst of it and certain of success in due time. In the crisis councils of various names and sizes that met daily or oftener in his office or in the Cabinet Room during this difficult eight-month period, President Kennedy generally displayed the same qualities. "Last year, in its way, was a pretty tough year too," he said to me one noon en route from his office to the Mansion— referring to West Virginia, Truman's attack, the Houston ministers and the TV debates. "I think we can handle whatever hits us."

Nor did he lose his sense of humor. He opened one troubled NSC meeting with the remark: "Did we inherit these problems, or are these our own?" To a reporter he quipped, "The only thing that surprised us when we got into office was that things were just as bad as we had been saying they were." When McGeorge Bundy or another aide would bring an urgent message to his desk, the President would ask, in a voice resigned to bad news and not wholly able to make light of it, "What's happened now?" He liked quoting General MacArthur's reminder to him in late April: "The chickens are coming home to roost, and you happen to have just moved into the chicken house." And to another NSC meeting he remarked, "Oh, well, just think of what we'll pass on to the poor fellow who comes after me."

THE BAY OF PIGS

The worst disaster of that disaster-filled period, the incident that showed John Kennedy that his luck and his judgment had human limitations, and the experience that taught him invaluable lessons for the future, occurred on April 17 in the Zapata Swamp at the Cuban Bay of Pigs. A landing force of some fourteen hundred anti-Castro Cuban exiles, organized, trained, armed, transported and directed by the United States Central Intelligence Agency (CIA), was crushed in less than three days by the vastly more numerous forces of Cuban dictator Fidel Castro. America's powerful military might was useless, but America's involvement was impossible to deny. Both publicly and privately the President asserted sole responsibility. Many wondered, nevertheless, how he could have approved such a plan. Indeed, the hardest question in his own mind after it was all over, he told one reporter, was "How could everybody involved have thought such a plan would succeed?" When I relayed to the President late in 1962 the request of a distinguished author that he be given access to the files on the Bay of Pigs, the President replied in the negative. "This isn't the time," he said. "Besides—we want to tell that story ourselves."

This is the time to tell that story—at least those parts about which I can speak with confidence. I am limited by the fact that I knew nothing of the operation until after it was over. When I asked the President a few days earlier about the bare hint I had received from another meeting, he replied with an earthy expression that too many advisers seemed frightened by the prospects of a fight, and stressed somewhat uncomfortably that he had no alternative. But in the days that followed the fiasco the President talked to me about it at length—in the Mansion, in his office and as we walked on the White House lawn. He was aghast at his own stupidity, angry at having been badly advised by some and let down by others, and anxious, he said, that I start giving some time to foreign affairs. "That's what's really important these days," he added.

What was really important in the Bay of Pigs affair was the very "gap between decision and execution, between planning and reality" which he had deplored in his first State of the Union. John Kennedy was capable of choosing a wrong course but never a stupid one; and to understand how he came to make this decision requires a review not merely of the facts but of *the facts and assumptions that were presented to him.*

The Eisenhower administration authorized early in 1960 the training and arming of a Cuban exile army of liberation under the direction of the CIA. Shortly before the Presidential election of 1960, it was decided (although Eisenhower was apparently not informed of the decision) that this should be a conventional war force, not a guerrilla band, and its numbers were sharply increased.

On January 20, 1961, John Kennedy inherited the plan, the planners and, most troubling of all, the Cuban exile brigade—an armed force, flying another flag, highly trained in secret Guatemalan bases, eager for one mission only. Unlike an inherited policy statement or Executive Order, this inheritance could not be simply disposed of by Presidential rescission or withdrawal. When briefed on the operation by the CIA as President-elect in Palm Beach, he had been astonished at its magnitude and daring. He told me later that he had grave doubts from that moment on.

But the CIA authors of the landing plan not only presented it to the new President but, as was perhaps natural, advocated it. He was in effect asked whether he was as willing as the Republicans to permit and assist these exiles to free their own island from dictatorship, or whether he was willing to liquidate well-laid preparations, leave Cuba free to subvert the hemisphere, disband an impatient army in training for nearly a year under miserable conditions, and have them spread the word that Kennedy had betrayed their attempt to depose Castro. Are you going to tell this "group of fine young men," as Allen Dulles posed the question later in public, "who asked nothing other than the opportunity to try to restore a free government in their country . . . ready to risk their lives . . . that they would get no sympathy, no support, no aid from the United States?" Would he let them choose for themselves between a safe haven in this country and a fighting return to their own, or would he force them to disband against their wishes, never to be rallied again?

Moreover, the President had been told, this plan was now or never, for three reasons: first, because the brigade was fully trained, restive to fight and difficult to hold off; second, because Guatemala was under pressure to close the increasingly publicized and politically controversial training camps, and his only choice was to send them back to Cuba, where they wished to go, or bring them back to this country, where they would broadcast their resentment; and third, because Russian arms would soon build up Castro's army, Cuban airmen trained behind the Iron Curtain as MIG pilots would soon return to Cuba, large numbers of crated MIGs had already arrived on the island, and the spring of 1961—before Castro had a large jet air force and before the exile army scattered in discontent—was the last time Cubans alone could liberate Cuba. (With an excess of candor during the week prior to the landing, the President revealed the importance of this factor in his thinking when he stated in a TV interview, "If we don't move now, Mr. Castro may become a much greater danger than he is to us today.")

Finally, the President was told, the use of the exile brigade would make possible the toppling of Castro without actual aggression by the United States, without seeming to outsiders to violate our principles of nonintervention, with no risk of involvement and with little risk of failure. "I stood right here at Ike's desk," Dulles said to Kennedy (as Kennedy told me later), "and told him I was certain our Guatemalan operation would succeed,[1] and, Mr. President, the prospects for this plan are even better than they were for that one."

With heavy misgiving, little more than a week before the plan was to go into effect, President Kennedy, having obtained the written endorsement of General Lemnitzer and Admiral Burke representing the Joint Chiefs and the verbal assent of Secretaries Rusk and McNamara, gave the final go-ahead signal. He did not regard Castro as a direct threat to the United States, but neither did he see why he should "protect" Castro from Cubans embittered by the fact that their revolution had been sold out to the Communists. Cancellation of the plan at that stage, he feared,

[1] The operation of June, 1954, that restored a non-Communist government to Guatemala. Apparently this should not be confused with a later conversation with Eisenhower, reported in *Mandate for Change*, in which Dulles estimated the prospects of the Guatemalan operation, by then already under way, as "about 20 percent" if aircraft could be supplied.

would be interpreted as an admission that Castro ruled with popular support and would be around to harass Latin America for many years to come. His campaign pledges to aid anti-Castro rebels had not forced his hand, as some suspected, but he did feel that his disapproval of the plan would be a show of weakness inconsistent with his general stance. "I really thought they had a good chance," he told me afterward, explaining it this way: If a group of Castro's own countrymen, without overt U.S. participation, could have succeeded in establishing themselves on the island, proclaimed a new government, rallied the people to their cause and ousted Castro, all Latin America would feel safer, and if instead they were forced to flee to the mountains, there to carry on guerrilla warfare, there would still have been net gain.

The principal condition on which he insisted before approving the plan was to rule out any direct, overt participation of American armed forces in Cuba. Although it is not clear whether this represented any change in policy, this decision—while in one sense permitting the disaster which occurred—in another helped to prevent a far greater one. For had the U.S. Navy and Air Force been openly committed, no defeat would have been permitted, a full-scale U.S. attack would ultimately have been required, and—assuming a general war with the Soviets could have been avoided—there was no point in beginning with a Cuban brigade in the first place. Once having openly intervened in the air and on the sea, John Kennedy would not have permitted the Cuban exiles to be defeated on the ground. "Obviously," he said later, "if you are going to have United States air cover, you might as well have a complete United States commitment, which would have meant a full-fledged invasion by the United States."

The results of such an overt unilateral intervention, "contrary to our traditions and to our international obligations," as the President said, would have been far more costly to the cause of freedom throughout the hemisphere than even Castro's continued presence. American conventional forces, moreover, were still below strength, and while an estimated half of our available Army combat divisions were tied down resisting guerrillas in the Cuban mountains, the Communists could have been on the move in Berlin or elsewhere in the world. Had such intervention appeared at all likely to be needed, Kennedy would never have approved the operation.

This decision not to commit U.S. forces emphasized the assumption underlying the pleas for the plan by its authors that it would succeed on its own. It also led to other restrictions designed to make the operation more covert and our involvement more concealed, restrictions which in fact impaired the plan's military prospects.

Yet no one in the CIA, Pentagon or Cuban exile movement raised any objection to the President's basic condition. On the contrary, they were so intent on action that they were either blind to danger or willing to assume that the President could be pressured into reversing his decision once the necessity arose. Their planning, it turned out, proceeded almost as if open U.S. intervention were assumed, but their answers to the President's specific questions did not. Could the exile brigade achieve its goals without our military participation? he asked. He was assured in writing that it could—a wild misjudgment, a statement of hope at best. Were the members of the exile brigade willing to risk this effort without our military participation, the President asked, and to go ahead with the realization that we would not intervene if they failed? He was assured that they were—a serious misstatement, due at least to bad communications on the part of the CIA liaison officers. But as the result of these assurances, the President publicly pledged at an April 12 press conference:

> . . . there will not be, under any conditions, any intervention in Cuba by United States armed forces, and this government will do everything it possibly can—and I think it can meet its responsibilities—to make sure that there are no Americans involved in any actions inside Cuba . . . the basic issue in Cuba is not one between the United States and Cuba; it is between the Cubans themselves. And I intend to see that we adhere to that principle . . . this administration's attitude is so understood and shared by the anti-Castro exiles from Cuba in this country.

That pledge helped avoid any direct American attack the following week, thus limited our violation of international law and—despite pressures from the CIA and military—was never reversed or regretted by the President. But he was shortly to realize that he should have instead canceled the whole operation.

Early in the morning of Monday, April 17, 1961, the members of Cuban exile Brigade 2506—some fourteen to fifteen hundred Cubans of every race, occupation, class and party, well trained, well led and well armed—achieved tactical surprise in their place of landing, fought ably and bravely while their ammunition lasted, and inflicted heavy losses on a Castro force which soon numbered up to twenty thousand men. The proximate cause of their defeat, according to the full-scale investigation later conducted under the chairmanship of General Maxwell Taylor, was a shortage of ammunition, and the reasons for that shortage illustrate all the shortcomings of the operation.

The men had ample supplies with them, but, like most troops in their first combat, said General Taylor, they wasted ammunition in excessive firing, particularly upon encountering more immediate opposition than expected. A ten-day supply of ammunition, along with all the communications equipment and vital food and medical supplies, was on the freighter *Rio Escondido*; but that freighter was sunk offshore by Castro's tiny air force effectively led by two or three rocket-equipped jet trainers (T-33's) on the morning of the landing, along with another supply-laden freighter, the *Houston*.

Additional supplies and ammunition were carried by two other freighters, the *Atlántico* and the *Caribe*. But, although the President's rule against Americans in the combat area was violated in other instances, no Americans were on board these freighters or in a position to control their movements. When their sister ships were sunk, these two, ignoring the order to regroup fifty miles from shore, fled south so far so fast that, by the time the U.S. Navy intercepted them, the *Caribe* was too far away to get back in time to be of help. By the time the *Atlántico* returned Tuesday night and transferred her ammunition supplies into the five small boats prepared to run them fifty miles in to the beach, it was too late to complete the run under cover of darkness. Certain that they could not survive another Castro air attack when dawn broke, the Cuban crews threatened to mutiny unless provided with a U.S. Navy destroyer escort and jet cover. With the hard-pressed exiles on the beach pleading for supplies, the convoy commander requested the CIA in Washington to seek the Navy's help; but CIA headquarters, unable to keep fully abreast of the situation on the beach and apparently unaware of the desperate need for ammunition in particular, instead called off the convoy without consulting the President.

That was the only request for air cover formally made from the area, and it never reached the President. Yet that very night, in a somber postmidnight meeting in the Cabinet Room, the CIA and Joint Chiefs were asking him to reverse his public pledge and openly introduce American air and naval power to back the brigade on the beach. The President, still unwilling to precipitate a full-scale attack by this country on Cuba, and mindful of his public pledge of nonintervention and his global responsibilities, agreed finally that unmarked Navy jets could protect the anti-Castro force of B-26's when they provided air cover the next morning. As noted below, these B-26's were capable of providing air cover for no more than an hour. But receiving their directions from the CIA, they arrived on the scene an hour before the jets, who received their directions from the Navy; and whether this tragic error was due to a difference in time zones or instructions, the B-26's were soon downed or gone, the jet mission was invalidated before it started, and without ammunition the exiles were quickly rounded up.

Thus, while the lack of ammunition led directly to disaster, Castro's control of the air had led directly to the lack of ammunition. The landing plan had not neglected to provide for air control. There had been, on the contrary, unanimous agreement that the Castro Air Force had to be removed. But confusion persists to this day about the President "canceling the air cover" that U.S. jets were to have provided. Actually no U.S. Air Force jet participation had ever been planned, much less canceled. Nor was there any cancellation of any other combat air cover over the battle front. Instead, the plan was to destroy Castro's air force on the ground before the battle began, and then to provide air support, with an anti-Castro "Air Force" consisting of some two dozen surplus planes flown by Cuban exiles. That plan failed.

The exile air arm, other than transports, was composed solely of lumbering B-26's as part of the covert nature of the plan. These World War II vintage planes were possessed by so many nations, including Cuba, that American sponsorship would be difficult to prove, and the prelanding attack on Cuban airfields could thus be attributed to defecting Castro pilots. No Florida, Puerto Rico or other bases nearer than Nicaragua were to be used for similar reasons. But the B-26's were slow, unwieldy, unsuited to air cover and constantly developing engine trouble. The fuel used flying between Nicaragua and Cuba restricted them to forty-five to sixty minutes over the island. The limited number of exile crews, exhausted by the long, dangerous flights, and overcome on the final day by fear and futility, had to be replaced in part on that day by volunteers from their American instructors, four of whom gave their lives. Although one reason for selecting the Bay of Pigs site was its airstrip, Castro's superior ground forces and ground fire made it almost completely useless. Supplies dropped from the air blew into the jungle or water, and half of the usable B-26 force was shot down over the beach on the first day by Castro's T-33's.

The failure to destroy Castro's planes on the ground in two strikes before the fight started thus affected control of both the air and the beach. The first strike went off as planned early Saturday morning, April 15. But its effectiveness was limited by the attempt to pretend it was conducted by pilots deciding to defect that day from Castro. Only B-26's were used, no American napalm was used, and the planes had to fly in from Nicaragua and return, except for one flown to Florida to act out the cover story.

The cover story was even less successful than the air strike. It was quickly torn apart—which the President realized he should have known was inevitable in an open society—not only by Castro's representatives but by a penetrating press. Adlai Stevenson's denials that Saturday afternoon at the United Nations were disproven within twenty-four hours by photographs and internal inconsistencies in the story, contrary to all the assurances given the President that the strike could be accomplished without anyone knowing for some time where the attackers came from, and with nothing to prove that they weren't new defectors from Castro. The whole action was much bigger news than anticipated. The world was aroused by this country's deliberate deception. No one would have believed that the second strike, scheduled for dawn Monday after the landing party was ashore, was anything other than an overt, unprovoked attack by the United States on a tiny neighbor. The Soviet Union said American intervention would not go unmet, and our Latin-American friends were outraged.

As a result, the President was urged on Sunday by his foreign policy advisers—but without a formal meeting at which the military and CIA could be heard—to call off the Monday morning strike in accordance with the previous agreed-upon principle of avoiding overt American involvement. The President concurred in that conclusion. The second strike was canceled. The CIA objected strongly but, although given an opportunity, chose not to take the matter directly to the President. All hoped that the first strike had done enough damage to Castro's air power, as had at first been reported. After the events on Monday made clear that these hopes were in vain, the second strike was reinstated for that night, but a cloud cover made this postponement fatal. The last opportunity to neutralize the air over the beach by destroying the T-33's and other planes was gone. In retrospect General Taylor concluded that both in the planning stages and on Sunday the military importance of the air strike and the consequences of its cancellation should have been made more clear to the President by the responsible officers. But in fact the first strike, designed to be the key, turned out later to have been remarkably ineffective; and there is no reason to believe that Castro's air force, having survived the first and been dispersed into hiding, would have been knocked out by the second.

The President's postponement of the Monday morning air strike thus played only a minor role in the venture which came to so inglorious an end on Wednesday afternoon. It was already doomed long before Monday morning, and he would have been far wiser, he told me later, if, when the basic premises of the plan were already being shattered, he had canceled the entire operation and not merely the second air strike. For it was clear to him by then that he had in fact approved a plan bearing little resemblance to what he thought he had approved. Therein lies the key to the Bay of Pigs decision.

With hindsight it is clear that what in fact he had approved was diplomatically unwise and militarily doomed from the outset. What he thought he was approving appeared at the time to have diplomatic acceptability and little chance of outright failure. That so great a gap between concept and actuality should exist at so high a level on so dangerous a matter reflected a shocking number of errors in the whole decision-making process—errors which permitted bureaucratic momentum to govern instead of policy leadership.

1. The President thought he was approving a quiet, even though large-scale, reinfiltration of fourteen hundred Cuban exiles back into their homeland. He had been assured that the plan as revised to meet his criteria was an unspectacular and quiet landing of patriots plausibly Cuban in its essentials, of which the air strike was the only really noisy enterprise that remained. Their landing was, in fact, highly publicized in advance and deliberately trumpeted as an "invasion," and their numbers deliberately and grossly overstated—in part by exile groups and officials hoping to arouse the Cuban people to join them, in part by Castro to inflate first his danger and then his victory, and in part by headline writers to whom "invasion" sounded more exciting than a landing of fourteen hundred men. The CIA even dictated battle communiqués to a Madison Avenue public relations firm representing the exiles' political front. After all the military limitations accepted in order to keep this nation's role covert, that role was not only obvious but exaggerated.

2. The President thought he was approving a plan whereby the exiles, should they fail to hold and expand a beachhead, could take up guerrilla warfare with other rebels in the mountains. They were, in fact, given contrary instructions to fall back on the beaches in case of failure; the immediate area was not suitable for guerrilla warfare, as the President had been assured; the vast majority of brigade members had not been given guerrilla training, as he had been assured; and the eighty-mile route to the Escambray Mountains, to which he had been assured they could escape, was so long, so swampy and so covered by Castro's troops that this was never a realistic alternative. It was never even planned by the CIA officers in charge of the operation, and they neither told the President they thought this option was out nor told the exiles that this was the President's plan.

3. The President thought he was permitting the Cuban exiles, as represented by their Revolutionary Council and brigade leaders, to decide whether they wished to risk their own lives and liberty for the liberty of their country without any overt American support. Most members of the brigade were in fact under the mistaken impression, apparently from their CIA contacts, that American armed forces would openly and directly assist them, if necessary, to neutralize the air (presumably with jets), make certain of their ammunition and prevent their defeat. They also mistakenly assumed that a larger exile force would land with them, that the Cuban underground or guerrillas would join them and that another landing elsewhere on the island would divert

Castro's forces. (A small diversionary landing was, in fact, scheduled but called off after two tries.) Their assumptions were not made known to the President, just as his were not made known to them; and the Revolutionary Council was similarly kept largely uninformed on the landing and largely out of touch with the brigade. Its President, Dr. José Miró Cardona, who believed that only American armed might could overturn Castro, did not pass on the message he received from Kennedy's emissaries that no American military help would be forthcoming.

4. President Kennedy thought he was approving a plan calculated to succeed with the help of the Cuban underground, military desertions and in time an uprising of a rebellious population. In fact, both Castro's popularity and his police state measures, aided by the mass arrests which promptly followed the bombing and landing, proved far stronger than the operation's planners had claimed. The planners, moreover, had no way to alert the underground without alerting Castro's forces. Cooperation was further impaired by the fact that some of the exiles' left-wing leaders were mistrusted by the CIA, just as some of their right-wing leaders and brigade members[2] were mistrusted by the Cuban underground. As a result, although the brigade was aided after its landing by some defectors and villagers, no coordinated uprising or underground effort was really planned or possible, particularly in the brief time the brigade was carrying the fight. In short, the President had given his approval with the understanding that there were only two possible outcomes—a national revolt or a flight to the hills—and in fact neither was remotely possible.

5. The President thought he was approving a plan rushed into execution on the grounds that Castro would later acquire the military capability to defeat it. Castro, in fact, already possessed that capability. Kennedy was told that Castro had only an obsolete, ineffective air force not in combat condition, no communications in the Bay of Pigs–Zapata Swamp area and no forces nearby. All these reports were wrong: expected mass defections did not materialize; Castro's T-33 jet trainers were much more effective than predicted; and Castro's forces moved to the beachhead and crushed the exile force with far greater strength, equipment and speed than all the estimates had anticipated. Indeed, the jet trainers—which were largely responsible for the ammunition losses and other failures—had been largely overlooked by the planners.

The President, having approved the plan with assurances that it would be both clandestine and successful, thus found in fact that it was too large to be clandestine and too small to be successful. Ten thousand exiles might have done it—or twenty thousand—but not

[2] Whose very presence was contrary to the President's instructions that all pro-Batista suspects be purged from the operation.

fourteen hundred, as bravely and brilliantly as they fought. General Taylor's subsequent review found the whole plan to have been militarily marginal: there were too few men in the brigade, too few pilots in the air arm, too few seconds-in-command to relieve fatigued leaders, too few reserves to replace battle losses and too many unforeseen obstacles. The brigade relied, for example, on a nighttime landing through uncharted reefs in boats with outboard motors. Even with ample ammunition and control of the air, even with two more air strikes twice as large, the brigade could not have broken out of its beachhead or survived much longer without substantial help from either American forces or the Cuban people. Neither was in the cards, and thus a brigade victory at the Bay of Pigs was never in the cards either.

These five fundamental gaps between what the President actually approved and what he thought he was approving arose from at least three sources:

1. In part they arose because of the newness of the President and his administration. He did not fully know the strengths and weaknesses of his various advisers. He did not yet feel he could trust his own instincts against the judgments of recognized experts. He had not yet geared the decision-making process to fulfill his own needs, to isolate the points of no return, to make certain he was fully informed before they passed, and to prevent preshaped alternatives from being presented to him too late to start anew. Nor were his advisers as frank with him, or as free to criticize each other's work, as they would later become.

2. In part these gaps arose because supposed pressures of time and secrecy permitted too little consideration of the plan and its merits by anyone other than its authors and advocates. Only the CIA and the Joint Chiefs had an opportunity to study and ponder the details of the plan. Only a small number of officials and advisers even knew of its existence; and in meetings with the President and this limited number, memoranda of operation were distributed at the beginning of each session and collected at the end, making virtually impossible any systematic criticism or alternatives. The whole project seemed to move mysteriously and inexorably toward execution without the President being able either to obtain a firm grip on it or reverse it. Under both Eisenhower and Kennedy it grew, changed and forced decisions without any clear statement of policy or procedure. No strong voice of opposition was raised in any of the key meetings, and no realistic alternatives were presented (consideration was given to putting the action off until a true government-in-exile could be formed to give it a more genuine "civil war" flavor). No realistic appraisal was made of the chances for success or the consequences of failure. The problems of turning back a preconceived project ready to go, supposedly without overt American involvement,

seemed much more difficult than permitting it to go ahead.

3. Finally, these gaps arose in part because the new administration had not yet fully organized itself for crisis planning, enabling the pre-committed authors and advocates of the project in the CIA and Joint Chiefs to exercise a dominant influence. While not all his associates agreed, Kennedy's own feeling was that—inasmuch as he had personally polled each individual present at the "decisive" meeting—no amount of formal NSC, Operations Coordinating Board or Cabinet meetings would have made any difference. (In fact, this type of operation would never have been considered in a large, formal meeting.) "The advice of every member of the Executive Branch brought in to advise," he commented wryly a year and a half later, "was unanimous—and the advice was wrong." In fact, the advice was not so unanimous or so well considered as it seemed. The Chiefs of Staff, whose endorsement of the military feasibility of the plan particularly embittered him, gave it only limited, piecemeal study as a body, and individually differed in their understanding of its features. Inasmuch as it was the responsibility of another agency and did not directly depend on their forces, they were not as close or critical in their examination as they might otherwise have been, and depended on the CIA's estimates of Castro's military and political strength. Moreover, they had originally approved the plan when it called for a landing at the city of Trinidad at the foot of the Escambray Mountains, and when Trinidad was ruled out as too conspicuous, they selected the Bay of Pigs as the best of the alternative sites offered without informing either Kennedy or McNamara that they still thought Trinidad preferable.

The CIA, on the other hand, although served by many able military officers, did not have the kind of full military staff required for this kind of operation. It was not created or equipped to manage operations too large to remain covert; and both the CIA and the President discovered too late the impossibility of directing such an operation step by step from Washington, over a thousand miles from the scene, without more adequate, direct and secure communications. The CIA's close control of the operation, however, kept the President and the Cuban exile force largely uninformed of each other's thinking; and its enthusiasm caused it to reject the clear evidence of Castro's political and military strength which was available from British and State Department intelligence and even from newspaper stories.

Both the CIA and the Joint Chiefs were moved more by the necessity of acting swiftly against Castro than by the necessity for caution and success. Answers to all the President's doubts about the military and intelligence estimates came from those experts most committed to supporting the plan, and he had no military intelligence expert of his own in the

White House. Instead of the President telling the bureaucracy that action was necessary and that they should devise certain means, the bureaucracy was telling the President that action was necessary and that the means were already fashioned—and making his approval, moreover, appear to be a test of his mettle.

Yet it is wrong now—and was wrong then—to expect the CIA and military to have provided the necessary objectivity and skepticism about their own plan. Unfortunately, among those privy to the plan in both the State Department and the White House, doubts were entertained but never pressed, partly out of a fear of being labeled "soft" or undaring in the eyes of their colleagues, partly out of lack of familiarity with the new President and their roles, and partly out of a sense of satisfaction with the curbs placed on U.S. participation. The CIA and Joint Chiefs, on the other hand, had doubts about whether the plan had been fatally weakened by those very curbs, but did not press them.

Yet nothing that I have set forth above should be read as altering John Kennedy's verdict that the blame was his. He did not purchase, load or fire the gun, but he gave his consent to its being fired, and under his own deeply held principles of executive responsibility only a plea of "guilty" was possible.

Moreover, his own mistakes were many and serious. He should never have believed that it would be arrogant and presumptuous of him, newly arrived on the scene, to call off the plans of the renowned experts and the brave exiles. He should never have permitted the project to proceed so early in his first year, before he knew the men he was listening to and while he was still full of deep-rooted doubts. He should never have permitted his own deep feeling against Castro (unusual for him) and considerations of public opinion—specifically, his concern that he would be assailed for calling off a plan to get rid of Castro—to overcome his innate suspicions. He should have tried to keep the brigade in some other camp in view of the impossibility of keeping it in Guatemala, while considering its future more carefully; and even had he disbanded it, the consequences clearly would have been mild compared to those of the course he chose.

Inasmuch as he was unwilling to conduct an overt operation through the Department of Defense, he should have abandoned it altogether as beyond the CIA's capability. He should have insisted on more skepticism from his staff, and made clear that their courage was not to be questioned by the advocates.

He should have realized that, without wartime conditions of censorship, his hope of keeping quiet a paramilitary operation of this magnitude was impossible in an open society. He should have re-examined the whole plan once all the publicity about a big invasion began appearing. In fact, the Cuban refugee community in Miami, the American press and the Castro government were all talking about the "secret" training camps and invasion plans long before those plans were definite.

Finally, he should have paid more attention to his own politically sound instincts and to the politically knowledgeable men who did voice objections directly—such as Fulbright and Schlesinger—on matters of Cuban and Latin-American politics and the composition of a future Cuban government, instead of following only the advice of Latin-American experts Adolf Berle, Jr. and Thomas Mann.[3] While weighing with Dean Rusk the international consequences of the plan's being quietly and successfully carried out, which they decided were acceptable, he should also have weighed the consequences of the plan being neither quiet nor successful—for those consequences were unacceptable. But for once John Kennedy permitted his hopes to overcome his doubts, and the possibilities of failure were never properly considered.

When failure struck, it struck hard. Tuesday's postmidnight meeting in the Cabinet Room was a scene of somber stocktaking. The President, still in his white tie and tails after the annual Congressional reception, was stunned by each new revelation of how wrong he had been in his expectations and assumptions. He would not agree to the military-CIA request for the kind of open commitment of American military power that would necessitate, in his view, a full-scale attack by U.S. forces—that, he said, would only weaken our hand in the global fight against Communism over the long run. He dispatched Schlesinger and Berle as personal emissaries to the angry exile political leaders who had been held incommunicado by the CIA in Florida. Finally, around 4 A.M., after ordering the ill-fated "air cover for the air cover," and talking half-heartedly with those aides who remained after all officials departed, he walked out onto the South Lawn and meditated briefly alone.

On Wednesday, in a solid day of agonizing meetings and reports as the brigade was being rounded up at Zapata, he gave orders for American Navy and Air Force to rescue as many as possible; and he talked, at Schlesinger's suggestion, with the exile political leaders flown in from Florida. He found them remarkably understanding of his resolve to keep the fight between Cubans, and they found him, they remarked later, deeply concerned and understanding, particularly for those with sons in the brigade. "I lost a brother and a brother-in-law in the war," the President told them. "I know something of how you feel." In truth, words alone could not express how he felt, for I observed in the days and months that followed that he felt personally responsible for those who had lost their lives—miraculously few compared with Castro's heavy

[3] Schlesinger did draft an excellent White Paper on Castro's betrayal of the revolution, but there was too wide a gap between the understanding implicit in that paper and the premises implicit in the landing plan.

losses—and that he was determined above all else to prevent the execution and to seek the liberation of the 1,113 men his government had
helped send to their imprisonment.[4]

In public and with most of his new associates, the President remained hopeful and calm, rallying morale, looking ahead and avoiding
the temptation to lash out in reproach or recrimination. He asked
General Maxwell Taylor to chair an investigation of the truth, to
determine not *who* was wrong and deserved to be punished but *what*
was wrong and had to be righted. As both mobs and diplomats the
world round decried American imperialism, deception and aggression,
he remarked privately that many of those leaders most anxious to see
Castro removed had been among the first to assail the U.S. in speeches
for regarding tiny Cuba as a threat. Nevertheless, he held his tongue in
public.

Despite this outward composure, however, so necessary to the
country at that hour, he was beneath it all angry and sick at heart. In
later months he would be grateful that he had learned so many major
lessons—resulting in basic changes in personnel, policy and procedures
—at so relatively small and temporary a cost. But as we walked on the
South Lawn Thursday morning, he seemed to me a depressed and lonely
man. To guard national unity and spirit, he was planning a determined
speech to the nation's editors that afternoon and a series of talks with
every Republican leader. The Bay of Pigs had been—and would be—the
worst defeat of his career, the kind of outright failure to which he was
not accustomed. He knew that he had handed his critics a stick with
which they would forever beat him; that his quick strides toward gaining
the confidence of other nations had been set back; that Castro's shouting
boasts would dangerously increase the cold war frustrations of the
American people; and that he had unnecessarily worsened East-West
relations just as the test-ban talks were being resumed.

"There's an old saying," he later told his press conference, "that
victory has a hundred fathers and defeat is an orphan. . . . I am the
responsible officer of the government and that is quite obvious." But

[4] Some twenty months later, on Christmas Eve, 1962, the prisoners, kept alive
by Kennedy's stern warnings to Castro, were freed in exchange for $53 million in
drugs, baby food, medical equipment and similar non-embargoed supplies donated
without any use of Treasury or CIA funds under an impressive operation directed
by the Attorney General and negotiated with Castro by lawyer James Donovan
representing the Cuban Families Committee. Since mid-1961 various negotiation
attempts had waxed and waned; and while the basic responsibility and financing
were kept private, the President was proud of the assistance his administration
provided by way of tax exemptions, coordination, surplus food and encouragement.
Receiving the brigade leaders at his Palm Beach home after their release, the
President and First Lady were deeply impressed by their bearing and spirit, and the
President predicted, in an Orange Bowl address two days later to the brigade members and friends, that its flag would someday fly "in a free Havana."

as we walked that Thursday morning, he told me, at times in caustic tones, of some of the other fathers of this defeat who had let him down. By taking full blame upon himself, he was winning the admiration of both career servants and the public, avoiding partisan investigations and attacks, and discouraging further attempts by those involved to leak their versions and accusations. But his assumption of responsibility was not merely a political device or a constitutional obligation. He felt it strongly, sincerely, and repeated it as we walked. "How could I have been so far off base?" he asked himself out loud. "All my life I've known better than to depend on the experts. How could I have been so stupid, to let them go ahead?"

His anguish was doubly deepened by the knowledge that the rest of the world was asking the same question.

CHAPTER XII

THE PRESS

THE GAP BETWEEN public opinion and the public interest, which had been the theme of *Why England Slept* and *Profiles in Courage*, became a theme of John Kennedy's campaign, Inaugural and first State of the Union Message in what he regarded as an age of dangerous complacency. He recognized his obligation to "lead, inform, correct and sometimes even ignore constituent opinion, if we are to exercise fully that judgment for which we were elected." And no problem of the Presidency concerned him more than that of public communication—educating, persuading and mobilizing that opinion through continued use of the political machinery, continued traveling and speaking and, above all, continued attention to the mass media: radio, television and the press.

PRESS RELATIONS

John Kennedy knew the newspaper profession as few politicians knew it. He had served two brief stints as a working reporter.[1] He often considered purchasing a newspaper once he left public life. He discussed with a reporter how the low quality of most typography could be improved. He numbered several Washington newsmen among his closest friends. He mingled with them informally and formally, socially and professionally, and enjoyed both joking with them and talking seriously with them, just

---

1 When, as President, he became a member of the National Press Club, its bulletin board solemnly pronounced: "John F. Kennedy, a former newspaperman now in politics, was approved for membership." The President at a news conference summed it up more casually: "A lot of journalists have bad luck."

as he did with fellow politicians. His wife was a former newspaperwoman for the old Washington *Times Herald,* and his father had passed on to him a flair for public relations and some painful lessons of experience. Many of John Kennedy's good friends in the journalism fraternity, in fact, had been his father's harshest critics, and many of his father's newspaper friends became the President's harshest critics.

During his long quest for the Presidency, Kennedy had been helped by his unusual accessibility to reporters. He knowingly timed his major campaign releases to meet their A.M. and P.M. deadlines, sometimes evaluated a speech draft as if he were writing the headlines, and subjected himself to more interviews, press conferences, "backgrounders" and assorted other news gatherings than his opponents in both parties combined. Political reporters were impressed by his candid and never exaggerated review of the potential delegate and electoral count. In the White House Pierre Salinger was superb, but Kennedy was his own best Presidential press secretary. His activities, aims, announcements and family dominated the news, and exclusive interviews with the President, once a rare event in journalism, took place almost daily.

Yet there remained a curious dichotomy in his attitude toward the press. He regarded newsmen as his natural friends and newspapers as his natural enemies. He was more concerned about a news column read by thousands than a newscast viewed by millions. He both assisted and resented the press corps as they dogged his every footstep. He had an inexhaustible capacity to take displeasure from what he read, particularly in the first half of his term, and an equally inexhaustible capacity to keep on reading more than anyone else in Washington. He always expected certain writers and publications to be inconsistent and inaccurate, but was always indignant when they were. While he fortunately grew insensitive to old critics, he remained unfortunately too sensitive to new ones. He could find and fret over one paragraph of criticism deep in ten paragraphs of praise. He dispensed few favors to his journalistic friends, but ardently wooed his journalistic foes. He had an abhorrence of public relations gimmicks, but was always acutely aware of what impression he was making.

Few, if any, Presidents could have been more objective about their own faults or objected more to seeing them in print. Few, if any, Presidents could have been so utterly frank and realistic in their private conversations with reporters and so uncommonly candid in public—but few, on the other hand, could have been so skillful in evading or even misleading the press whenever secrecy was required. Finally, few, if any, Presidents could have been more accessible and less guarded with individual reporters and editors—or more outraged when anyone else "leaked" a story.

If there is a logical inconsistency in these attitudes, it stems from similar inconsistencies in political life. The President knew that the fairness, if not the favoritism, of the reporters covering his campaign had helped to elect him—but he also knew that the overwhelming proportion of editors and publishers had been out to defeat him. He valued the role of the press in calling his shortcomings to his attention—but that did not make him enjoy it any more than any proud man.

This was not simply a matter of "image." The public and posterity would judge him and his program on the basis of the "news," and, he felt, more on the basis of the written than the spoken word. He needed to know, therefore, what was being written and how he could make it, if not more favorable, at least more objective and accurate.

At the heart of it all was an attitude he had expressed to me as Senator when complimenting me on my friendships with Massachusetts reporters. "Always remember," he had added, "that their interests and ours ultimately conflict." From 1957 through 1960 through 1963, John Kennedy's tide of favorable publicity, only some of which he stimulated, helped build his popularity. Certainly it irritated his opponents. But gradually the conflict to which he referred, which had nothing to do with partisan loyalties or charges of a "one-party press," grew clearer to both of us, particularly in the White House:

• As President, in order to promote his program and his re-election, he was required to use the newspapers and other media, and the newsmen resisted and resented the feeling of being used. "He wants us as a cheering squad," complained one reporter. Indeed he did.

• As President he sought to control the timing of his announcements with a view to obtaining maximum effectiveness. His best interests, even on many nonsecurity matters, often required at least temporary secrecy, either to protect proposals that were still in the discussion stage, and too weak to face public fire, or to give a helpful element of surprise and initiative to his actions. But the best interests of the news media, even on many security matters, required penetration of that secrecy. They had to publish something every day or week, regardless of whether it was speculative, premature or wholly invented.

• As President he preferred to correct his errors before they were exposed—the press preferred to expose them before they could be corrected. "We're looking for flaws," was the way one White House reporter summed up his role, "and we'll find them. There are flaws in anybody." When the newspapers erred, however, as they sometimes did, Presidential corrections or even press retractions rarely had the impact of the original story.

• As President he wanted as much privacy as possible for his personal family life, but these were subjects on which the press wanted as much publicity as possible, and his attractive, photogenic family and his own good looks had led to much of his favorable publicity in the pre-Presidential days.

• As President his progress in many areas was often characterized by small, dull or complex steps, but newspaper headlines in the same areas more often dwelt on the simple, the sensational and the controversial. Good news, when printed, would reflect more favorably on a President—but "bad news is news," he said ruefully, "and good news is not news, so [the American people] get an impression always that the United States is not doing its part." The press was far more interested in finding out, for example, who in the government or among our allies had disagreed with the President than who had agreed. Criticism and dissent invariably made bigger and better headlines and columns than praise; and two and one-half million honest civil servants were not nearly so newsworthy as one sinner.

• As President, finally, he preferred to decide for himself which were the major issues requiring decision and when, but newspaper stories could blow up minor, premature, past or even nonexistent subjects into issues in the national mind. Kennedy never doubted the accuracy of Oscar Wilde's observation: "In America the President reigns for four years, but Journalism governs forever."

All these differences of perspective posed a conflict of interest, and, with a greater degree of tolerance each year, the President philosophically made up his mind to accept it. "I think that they are doing their task, as a critical branch," he smilingly said of the press one day, "and I am attempting to do mine; and we are going to live together—for a period— and then go our separate ways."

The President shrugged off many but by no means all critical stories with a favorite phrase: "They have to write something." Those who wrote in 1961 that he was enamored with power, he noted, were writing in 1962 that he was preoccupied with its limitations. Those who wrote in 1962 that he was not spending his popularity were writing in 1963 that he had taken on too many fights. The reporter who purported to discover "Kennedy's Grand Strategy" for an article in 1962 wrote another article, in the same magazine one year later, entitled "The Collapse of Kennedy's Grand Design."

Moreover, he never lost sight of the invaluable assistance to him of a free and critical press. While Mr. Khrushchev's "totalitarian system has many advantages as far as being able to move in secret," he said,

> . . . there is a terrific disadvantage in not having the abrasive quality of the press applied to you daily. . . . Even though we never like it, and even though we wish they didn't write it, and even

though we disapprove, there isn't any doubt that we could not do the job at all in a free society without a very, very active press.

Nor would Kennedy take up Eisenhower's earlier advice that it is better not to read the newspapers. "I am reading more and enjoying it less," he told one press conference, parodying a popular slogan. "I talk to myself about it," he said (and at times he would also talk back to his TV set), "but I don't plan to issue any general [indictment] of the press." It is not surprising that Kennedy was more disappointed by unjust errors or abuse in the columns of those newsmen or newspapers he considered fair or friendly than of those he had long since dismissed as hopelessly unfriendly. He rarely saw the latter—although he never gave up trying with some, such as *Time*—and he rarely made comments to them on their stories. With the many newsmen he knew well, however, he felt free to praise stories he liked and to criticize those he disliked. Particularly in his first eighteen months in the White House, his chastisements of newsmen for stories he felt were unfair or inaccurate (chastisements which he often conducted secondhand through directions to his staff, in one of our less pleasant assignments) unfortunately led to charges that he was not only oversensitive to unfavorable stories, which he was, but also attempting to intimidate their authors' thinking, which he was not. Contrary to reports, there were no threats to secure an offending reporter's dismissal or deny him access to the White House (though no doubt we talked more freely and frequently to our friends).

The President in time also became more philosophical about a reporter's role in securing unauthorized information. It takes two to "leak" a secret, and he blamed the premature or unauthorized publication of official information on the source, not the reporter, sometimes even requesting an FBI or informal investigation to find out who in government had violated security regulations.[2] When one high official with close friends in the press was resigning, the President told me he was tempted to tell this man, as he took his farewell, the name of his still undisclosed successor, but the wrong name, simply to see if it turned up in certain columns or newscasts.

He was a good source himself with his candid, private interviews, and he paid little attention to the complaint from opposition papers, who had been more favored in the White House under Eisenhower, that Kennedy was discriminating in favor of his friends. But his general rule was to say comparatively little to a newsman in confidence, even "off the record," that he could not afford to have published. Occasionally, in fact, he would confide "secrets" to a newsman, in the gravest of tones, with the full knowledge that this was the best way to get them published. Mid-

---

[2] His general experience, particularly with the State Department and Pentagon, was that those who knew didn't tell and those who told didn't know.

week before his announcement of the Cuban quarantine, when complete secrecy was essential to our security, he, Bob and I marveled aloud one night that not a word had gone to the press from any of the participants in our conferences—"Except," I added with a straight face, "for your talk with Joe Alsop." He started to launch into a vehement denial before realizing we were joking, and laughed as heartily as we did.

Occasionally one of his journalistic friends—not Joe Alsop—would take what the President thought was improper advantage of his familiarity with life at the Kennedys'. His refusal to end his long-standing personal ties with these newsmen also caused some resentment among their competitors. But when mistakenly charged with authorizing, encouraging or providing the erroneous information in a Bartlett–Stewart Alsop article on the Cuban missile crisis, the President, unwilling either to repudiate his friends or to cause more damage by specifying where they erred, was equally unwilling to take responsibility for what his friends wrote. "I am responsible for many things under the Constitution," he said, "but not for what they write. That's their responsibility and that is the way we will continue it." He meant that very seriously, he said to me later. "I've never told Bartlett what to write, so I can't start telling him what not to write."

He could never stay angry at either friends or strangers in the newspaper profession, because both their virtues and their vices were so familiar to him. Like most of his aides, they tried—but not always successfully —to separate fact from fiction and to discount personal prejudices in meeting their professional responsibilities.

Time and again he remarked on how sensitive his journalistic critics were to criticism. One of his favorite examples in the pre-Presidential days involved one of his favorite friends, Charlie Bartlett. "I got another Bartlettism today," the Senator would remark, referring to the fact that his pal invariably brought him bad news. I had learned during that period to combine bad news with good, or with a word on how to make it good, but Charlie seemed always to have just heard only something gloomy. Finally the Senator told Charlie one day that, in conversation with a group of reporters (wholly fictitious), he had heard them say that Bartlett was regarded in the press gallery as a high-hat ever since he won the Pulitzer Prize. "He absolutely collapsed," the Senator laughed later. "They all think we should take it, but they're angry if anyone says a bad word about them." In 1962, the target of editorial attacks about "too many Kennedys," he wondered what some of these same newspapers would say if he pointed out publicly the nepotism with which they were run.

His White House and other aides were also directly accessible to the press. In addition we found it necessary, in order to answer the President's inquiries intelligently, to read a number of newspapers and read them early. JFK—as he persuaded the headline writers to call him, not to imitate FDR but to avoid the youthful "Jack"—read (actually, in about half of these, skimmed) all the Washington newspapers (*Post, Star, News*), most of the New York newspapers (*Times, News, Wall Street Journal*, at one time the *Herald Tribune* and frequently most of the others), the Baltimore *Sun*, the Boston *Globe* and *Herald*, the Miami *Herald*, the Chicago *Sun-Times*, the Chicago *Tribune*, the Philadelphia *Inquirer* and the St. Louis *Post-Dispatch*. When he had time, he read the sports page as well as the front page, social news as well as financial news, and gossip columnists as well as political columnists. He liked the political cartoonists—Herblock, he remarked, was "very gentle" with him —and he enjoyed the humor and "inside dope" columns, at times using privately but never maliciously nicknames he had read in those columns such as "Nose McCone" and "By George McBundy."

His magazine reading was equally omnivorous, covering at least sixteen periodicals ranging from the *New Republic* to *Sports Illustrated,* from *The New Yorker* to *Look*. He read several British newspapers and journals as well, and regarded *Le Monde* in Paris as one of the world's finest. But he did not read everything. He almost never read *U.S. News & World Report,* for example, on the grounds that it had little news and less to report. Yet he read *Time* and *Newsweek* faithfully, and felt their condensed hindsight often influenced their readers more than daily newspaper stories. He had his disagreements with *Newsweek,* particularly on the inaccuracies in its political gossip column in the front, but *Time* was a source of special despair. For, unlike *U.S. News & World Report,* it was well written. Unlike the Chicago *Tribune,* it gave an impression of objectivity. And unlike its White House correspondent, Hugh Sidey, unlike its sister publication *Life,* and unlike what he regarded to be its general pre-1961 attitude toward his efforts, it was in John Kennedy's opinion consistently slanted, unfair and inaccurate in its treatment of his Presidency, highly readable but highly misleading.

Nothing pleased him more than *Time*'s embarrassed confession that its story about a Michigan tennis coach being secretly flown to Cape Cod for the Kennedys was wholly wrong; or the magazine's confirmation of his suspicion that, of two Annigoni portraits, it was *Time* and not the artist who selected the cover showing an unrecognizable Kennedy with his tie and one eye askew; or the opportunity a press conference question gave him to call a *Time* article (or the *Fortune* article from which it was condensed) "the most inaccurate of all the articles that have appeared on Cuba."[3]

[3] He regarded the author of that particular article as particularly biased and hostile, and upon learning that he had secured a sensitive Pentagon post for his temporary active duty in the Air Force, the President wasted no time in changing his orders—"preferably out in some desert," he told the White House Air Force aide.

As a perpetual optimist, however, he continued to believe that fair and friendly stories filed by Sidey—whom the President continually befriended, chastised and sought to enlighten—were being rewritten in a hostile and one-sided fashion without the knowledge of *Time* chief Henry Luce, an old friend of the Kennedy family. On several occasions he saw Luce to call misleading omissions or conclusions to his attention, and he asked me to have prepared for two of these sessions two documents which he thought were greatly interesting. One, after continuous *Time* harping on the size of the Budget, was an estimate by the Postmaster General that the various Luce publications paid in postage less than 40 percent of the cost of their mail handling, resulting in a subsidy to Luce publications from the taxpayers of some $20 million a year. The other was a study of *Time*'s treatment of Eisenhower's first year as compared with Kennedy's. The study, several weeks in preparation by an admittedly sympathetic researcher, amassed considerable evidence to show that, by the use of loaded adjectives, clever picture captions and a careful selection of quotations out of context

> the two Administrations are put in very different lights. . . . The Eisenhower Administration was given every benefit of the doubt . . . in general it was dealt with in only glowing terms and heroic prose—but the Kennedy Administration, in contrast, was nary given a chance and criticism was never spared. . . . Sympathy is offered to one side, ridicule to the other.

The increasing tendency of the once-respected New York *Herald Tribune* to adopt a similarly oversimplified and smart-alecky style in place of straight factual reporting led to the President's public cancellation of the White House subscriptions to that newspaper. When the *Herald Tribune,* after a series of speculative front-page stories implying Democratic complicity with Billie Sol Estes, then seemed uninterested in covering the costly and possibly corrupt errors exposed in the administration of the National Stockpiles under Eisenhower, the President decided to call attention to this contrast by his dramatic cancellation.

But the *Herald Tribune* cancellation was a mistake. He liked many of its feature writers (and his wife wanted to smuggle in its fashion column). More importantly, the greater-than-foreseen publicity accorded this act led to the assumption that he wanted to read only friendly words when he actually read hostile writers and newspapers every day. He once told me, for example, that we should all quit reading columnist Arthur Krock on the grounds that his old friend's attacks were a waste of time to read. But at breakfast the very next morning he asked me about Krock's latest jab.

The openly Republican editorials of the *Herald Tribune,* in fact, were regarded by the President as more balanced on most subjects than those of the *New York Times,* which had endorsed him and most of his policies. He thought the *Times* one of the most influential newspapers in the nation, less guilty of bias and sensationalism in its news stories than any other publication. He had read it regularly since his days in Choate, which may be one reason why he worried more over its editorials than those of a dozen more widely distributed newspapers combined. But he could not understand how its editors could agree with 90 percent of his program and still write what at times seemed to him 90 percent unfavorable editorials. "I'm convinced," he said after calling me early one morning about a particularly snide piece, "that they keep in stock a canned editorial on our 'lack of leadership' and run it every few weeks with little change."

The purpose of these calls to me and other associates, which were frequent and stimulated by more than editorials in the *Times,* was varied. Occasionally he wanted action in response to a criticism or information about its validity. Sometimes he simply wanted me to list the factual errors in a specific piece or have someone write a letter to the editor. Usually he wanted to share his indignation with a staff member or friend and listen to us join in it. (Once he called Pierre Salinger on a *Time* issue which Pierre agreed was particularly atrocious, which pleased the President greatly until he learned Pierre was complaining most about *Time's* article on Salinger, not Kennedy.) In short, these calls—like the calls to the reporters, which gradually became rarer—were simply his way of giving vent to the frustrations of "living on the bull's-eye," as he described it, and by doing so, he could more easily forget the barbs and get back to work.

MANAGED NEWS

He never tried to use his position to intimidate a reporter's thinking, to secure his dismissal, to withhold news privileges from opposition papers, to require the publication or suppression of timely stories, to falsify facts deliberately as a means of covering up errors, to blanket as "secret" or "private" any matters that deserved to be known or to shift the blame for his errors to others. He was careful not to change the date or method of economic data releases, such as the monthly unemployment figures, preferring to let both good news and bad news come from the departments at the regularly scheduled times. While he would, on the rarest of occasions, arrange for "planted" questions at a press conference, he preferred that his television and other interviews not be staged in advance.

If these practices, in which he did *not* engage, are the elements of news management, as I had assumed, then the Kennedy administration stands not guilty of that offense. If, on the other hand, those who are concerned about this label wish to apply it to the following eight practices, as apparently some do, then it is true that at least we tried.

1. It is true that Kennedy believed that the government, as distinguished from the nation, should speak with one voice; and that he not only insisted on clearing speeches but on particularly sensitive matters—after the steel and Cuban missile crises, for example—requested (in vain) that all participants refer reporters' inquiries to the White House.

2. It is true that he sought out not only the company but the counsel of newsmen, as individuals and in groups, both reporters and their bosses, dispensing as many informal views in private—both for the record and off the record—as he gave formal statements in public. He did not see how his accessibility to so many reporters could be classified by Arthur Krock as being more "cynical" than Roosevelt's or Truman's, who gave exclusive interviews only to Arthur Krock. He took pains to address all the Washington press banquets—where he was often at his funniest off the record—and he broke all precedents in his attentions to editors and reporters in the White House. But he was seldom indignant if one day's guest was the next day's critic. Some of his newspaper guests at luncheons or in his office did in fact change their views because they found him more moderate than they had assumed and both articulate and reasonable in explaining his burdens.

3. It is true that he informed his friends in the press corps of stories they had written which he liked and stories which he disliked, through phone calls, notes and staff relays. As a Senator he had gone even further, writing a letter of thanks in response to every friendly editorial and answering many of the critical ones. A Portland, Maine, editor told me his publisher had suggested to him when he was hired, "Any time you think no one in Washington is reading you, put in a good word about Senator Kennedy, and you'll get a letter the next week."

4. It is true that he believed the press had responsibilities as well as rights—including the responsibility to get the facts straight, to consider the national interest and to save their bias for the editorial columns —and he did not hesitate to remind those who he thought had failed to meet their responsibilities.

5. It is true that he sought to get his story across to the public, to emphasize his accomplishments instead of his setbacks, to clarify and justify his actions, to stress good news to offset the bad and to time his announcements for maximum effect.

6. It is true that he permitted photographers and cameramen to in-

trude into his office and home, with an eye on both current publicity and future history—but never at the cost of his essential dignity and privacy. ("My predecessor did not object, as I do," he told a dinner of publishers, "to pictures of one's golfing skill in action. But neither, on the other hand, did he ever bean a Secret Service man.") He gave up trying to keep reporters away from his church, although he never specified in advance which Mass he would attend. As a Senator he had been far more sensitive, and as a result more secretive, on stories about his money and health, until he decided secrecy was causing stories far worse than the truth. He had also been far more sensitive about stories on his sister Rosemary, until the whole family decided that a more matter-of-fact attitude better served the fight against mental retardation.

7. It is true that he permitted full press coverage of all U.S. space shots, despite the accompanying chaos and the notoriety given to failures. "In a free society," he said,

> if a newspaperman asks . . . to come, then he can come. . . . We are not going to do what the Russians did of being secret and just hailing our successes. . . . For people to suggest that it's a publicity circus, when at the same time they are very insistent that their reporters go down there, does seem to me to be unfair.

8. Finally, it is true that he sought to prevent the publication of information harmful to the security of the United States and, in a few instances, requested newspapers to hold off printing stories their reporters had uncovered lest premature disclosure upset careful planning.

But it was by no means an administration zealous to suppress information. Both Kennedy and Salinger expended considerable effort in persuading the departments to use their "Top Secret" and "Executive Privilege" stamps less frequently. It was thus unfair and unfortunate that much of the so-called "news management" controversy stemmed from two incidents incorrectly interpreted as proof of the administration's devotion to secrecy.

After the Bay of Pigs, the President, in an address to the nation's publishers, asked them to "recognize the nature of our country's peril . . . which knows no precedent in history," to consider whether "the interest of the national security" should be weighed as well as news value, and to recognize that

> this nation's foes have openly boasted of acquiring through our newspapers information they would otherwise hire agents to acquire through theft, bribery or espionage; details of this nation's covert preparations to counter the enemy's covert operations have been available to every newspaper reader, friend and foe alike; the size, the strength, the location and the nature of our forces

and weapons, and our plans and strategy for their use, have all been pinpointed in the press and other news media to a degree sufficient to satisfy any foreign power; and, in at least one case, the publication of details concerning a secret mechanism whereby satellites were followed required its alteration at the expense of considerable time and money.

The furor that followed this speech overlooked the fact that it had explicitly opposed either compulsory or voluntary censorship machinery, had recommended no legislation (as an earlier Eisenhower commission had done) and had, in fact, called for far greater public information through an independent and critical press. A committee of editors and publishers was designated to meet with the President, and for this meeting he had his staff prepare examples of harmful disclosures and alternative ways of cooperating to prevent them. But the committee members, to his suppressed surprise and indignation, said in effect that they recognized no special peril. The "constructive dialogue" for which the President had hoped was impossible, and the whole matter was dropped.

The second incident followed the Cuban missile crisis. Assistant Secretary of Defense for Public Affairs Arthur Sylvester, using terms the President felt were both unclear and unwise, spoke candidly and informally about news as a "part of the weaponry" available to the government in the cold war and Cuban crisis, including "the right, if necessary, to lie to save itself" from nuclear war—meaning the right to lie to our enemies in statements also heard by our citizens. We felt that General Eisenhower had said much the same thing on television some weeks earlier, but Sylvester's words were attacked out of all context and proportion by a torrent of newspaper and Congressional critics. The President immediately asked me to draft a letter for Sylvester which explained his choice of language, admitted that it "should have been more carefully phrased and considered," and emphasized his own and his department's abhorrence of censorship. But Sylvester, with a show of spunk the President had to admire, refused to sign any letter that appeared to appease his accusers, and so the sound and fury continued.

At the time of the Cuban missile crisis the President also approved restrictions on Pentagon and State Department news contacts, stressing his willingness to drop them once they appeared to curb the free flow of essential news. At the same time he tried briefly to require all White House aides to clear in advance with Salinger all conversations with newsmen, and to report in writing on the subject matter of those conversations, but the rule was so rarely and so humorously observed that it soon fell into disuse.

Former Florida Governor LeRoy Collins, then head of the National

Association of Broadcasters, accused the administration of "news suppression" in the Cuban crisis, but the President had no apologies:

> It would have been a great mistake and possibly a disaster if
> this news had been dribbled out when we were unsure of the
> extent of the Soviet build-up in Cuba, and when we were unsure of
> our response, and when we had not consulted with any of our
> allies. . . . During the [following] week . . . we attempted to have
> the government speak with one voice . . . newspapermen were
> not permitted to go to Guantanamo because obviously that . . .
> area might be under attack.

The crisis having eased, he added, the curbs did not seem to be too
tight, inasmuch as Adlai Stevenson's highly secret report on U Thant's
visit to Cuba, distributed in the State Department one morning at
8 A.M., was appearing in wire service copy by 10 A.M. before Dean Rusk
had seen the original report. U Thant's understandable reaction "caused
Governor Stevenson some pain," said the President. "So I think that
information has been flowing out, but if it isn't, we will get it out."

Having joined in the criticism of Eisenhower's refusal to give
Congress access to USIA "prestige" polls, he initially changed the nature
of these polls and later authorized both their immediate availability to
appropriate Congressional leaders and their public release at dates sufficiently later to prevent Allied embarrassment. When this led to an
outcry that he was suppressing unfavorable findings, we arranged with
a friendly legislator who rightfully had access to them to "leak" their
very favorable findings to the press. The outcry soon stopped.

So long as the news was free, the citizenry informed and the channels of information open, the President regarded the whole "managed
news" charge as a manufactured controversy of little interest. "We aren't
losing any votes on that one," he said privately. "Does anyone think we'd
be getting 'belted' every day if we could control it ourselves?" He was
amused by a poll of newsmen declaring (1) that his administration
worked harder than all others at "managing the news" and (2) offered
more accessibility than all others to news sources.

PRESS CONFERENCES

The Presidential press conferences were one of Kennedy's most effective
means of communicating with the American people. Indeed, once he
decided that they would all be directly transmitted, in full and without
editing, by radio and television to all parts of the country, their primary
purpose was to inform and impress the public more than the press. No
previous President had tried it, and columnist James Reston, certain it

would produce some slip of catastrophic proportions, called it "the goofiest idea since the hula hoop." But the President wanted the American people to see and hear his answers and opening statements as he gave them, without having to rely on newspaper accounts and headlines.

It was a bold but highly effective innovation. Some reporters, who could have filed stories quicker merely by watching television, wondered whose purpose they were serving, and some publishers may have objected to their reporters acting as performers for the benefit of the television industry. But "it is highly beneficial," the President reassured them with a touch of sarcasm, "to have some twenty million Americans regularly . . . observe the incisive, the intelligent and the courteous qualities displayed by your Washington correspondents."

Prior to almost every press conference, he protested privately and only half-seriously that he did not feel like facing the press—that he envied General De Gaulle's practice of meeting correspondents only twice a year and accepting only questions carefully planted in advance to which the answers had been carefully memorized—that Salinger and the rest of us were launching him unprepared and unprotected into a hostile sea. He always returned pleased with his own performance, however, occasionally resentful of a nasty question, but eager to tune in to watch its rebroadcast, chuckling appreciatively at some of his own answers.

He was not unprotected and unprepared. For protection, he had his own skill in parrying and answering questions. And he was always thoroughly prepared. The day before the conference, which was usually fixed publicly two or more days in advance, Salinger met with the information officers of major departments to gather their materials on current issues. The State Department prepared a large briefing book, listing all possible questions and answers on foreign policy. The Council of Economic Advisers prepared a list of major questions and answers on major economic developments. All the weekly reports from the departments and agencies since the last conference were gathered. The President pored over this material, much of which was not too useful, and then breakfasted at 8:45 A.M. on the morning of the conference with Salinger or his deputy from the Press Office; myself and Feldman from the Special Counsel's Office; Rusk, public affairs Assistant Secretary Robert Manning and usually Under Secretary Ball from the State Department; Bundy from the White House foreign affairs shop; Walter Heller from the Economic Advisers; and the Vice President. On the basis of our own reading, Salinger and I prepared lengthy lists of possible difficult questions—usually far more difficult than most of those asked—and the breakfast was customarily spent reviewing those questions and their answers.

His own extensive reading, and his participation in every level of government, was his best preparation. On most of the questions which Salinger or I read off, he simply nodded for the next one, a signal that he felt confident he could handle that subject. On others, he asked questions of those present or directed that more information be obtained. His answers were never written out or practiced—he simply wanted to feel comfortable with each possible subject. Our discussions frequently produced humorous answers, which were usually too barbed for his serious consideration but which at times I could detect him deliberating as he listened to an actual question at the conference. "It is dangerous to have them in the back of my head," he once told me, and he predicted from the tone of our discussion one morning that the press conference that evening would become "The 6 O'clock Comedy Hour."

In actuality his own humorous responses, nearly all of them spontaneous, were both funnier and more appropriate than any we suggested. He poked fun at many subjects, but particularly his Republican detractors. Refusing to comment on various charges by Nixon and Goldwater, he expressed "sympathy" for the "problems" they were encountering. Told about a Republican resolution that he was a failure, he observed drily, "I am sure it was passed unanimously." Asked if he had any judgment on a series of Republican leadership seminars, he wondered aloud who could be supplying them with leadership—"But I'm sure they'll have a varied program." Equally often he laughed at himself. Told that the appearance of a Band-Aid on his finger would surely cause inquiries from viewing editors, he explained, "I cut my finger when I was cutting bread—unbelievable as it may sound."

At times, on more serious matters, he would threaten during the breakfast to speak some harsh truth or opinion that caused shudders in the Department of State. "If I followed your advice on every topic which you want me to avoid answering," he said one morning, "I would stand up there with nothing to say." Later, when it was suggested that he might be asked about a recent stream of astonishing remarks former President Truman had volunteered on such subjects as taxes and racial intermarriage, President Kennedy observed, "Compared with Truman's advisers, you fellows don't have any problems."

Often Bundy, Salinger and I spent most of the hours between the breakfast and the conference, usually held at 4 P.M., securing additional information or working on his opening statements, which also had been reviewed at breakfast. The President preferred to have from one to three opening statements or announcements of importance for each news conference, not to take time away from the questions but to provide some focus for them, and to make use of this rare opportunity and sizable audience. Pending bills in particular were pushed in this form rather than in a long speech. During a sensitive world crisis an opening statement of policy might also be used to ward off further questions on that subject.

From 3:00 to 3:40 P.M. we usually met with him once more as he dressed in his bedroom, reviewing last-minute changes and developments. Then he would hurry out with Salinger, muttering once again that he felt doubtful and defenseless about the whole thing.

Regular press conferences—and, equally important, the preparation for them—had many values. "It's like preparing for a final exam twice a month," the President commented. These sessions kept him, and his staff, on top of everything going on in the government, in the press and in the public mind, instead of concentrating on a few crises. They enabled him to fix a deadline for the announcement of various projects. They gave him an opportunity to articulate the administration's policy for everyone in the administration, and I always detected a greater sense of direction and pride throughout the Executive Branch following a particularly good press conference. They provided him with a low-key excuse to speak directly to Congress and to foreign governments. They enabled him to dominate the front pages, for which Congress and the Republicans were competing.[4]

Above all, the televised press conferences provided a direct communication with the voters which no newspaper could alter by interpretation or omission. "We couldn't survive without TV," remarked the President one evening, as he watched a rebroadcast of that day's conference.

For these reasons, after abandoning the idea of weekly news conferences in the crisis-filled year of 1961, he finally decided, partly as a matter of self-discipline, to subject himself to regularly scheduled news conferences at intervals of one to three weeks even when he felt there was insufficient news to supply them. Even then he took some delight when a trip, a holiday or the substitution of other press activities led to a longer interval, and during the Cuban, Berlin and race relations crises he did not hesitate to avoid news conferences for seven- or nine-week stretches. Nevertheless, in thirty-four months in the White House, he held sixty-three formal televised news conferences in Washington as well as numerous other special Presidential question-and-answer sessions. No one of these was either called, or canceled once called, because of any sudden emergency.

On very few occasions Kennedy received advance word, usually

4 A comparative survey by Professor Elmer Cornwell has shown that the Kennedy press conferences generated far more newspaper stories, not only in the number of articles but in total space, than those of any of his predecessors. In a single year, Kennedy in his conferences produced more news than Roosevelt had meeting the press three or four times as often.

through Salinger, that a particular question would be asked, and on even fewer occasions, no more than a dozen in three years, he arranged to plant a pertinent question in advance. While his own preparations were designed to anticipate as many questions as possible, the twenty to twenty-five questions raised in each conference invariably included at least one not remotely foreseen in the several dozen topics we had reviewed. Nor did he attempt to select only friendly reporters in singling out one of the many on their feet after each answer. He often seemed to point more to his right than to his left, but this had no hidden ideological significance.

Many of those with whom he was most friendly asked unfriendly questions, to which he never objected. He preferred hard, controversial questions to soft, generalized queries. The sharper the question, the more sharply he felt he could answer. He listened patiently to long statements concealed as questions and engaged in no direct debate with reporters. Often he was champing to give his answer before the question was completed.

At no time did he lose his dignity, his temper or his control of the situation. He made a few misstatements of fact but no major blunders. His answers were almost always brief. Some of the best were no more than a sentence or even a word. Would he comment on the possibilities of a neutron bomb? "No." Was he certain the Soviets really put two men in orbit? "Yes."

Questions asked by female correspondents invariably provided an element of entertainment, if not information. He knew that May Craig's questions were more likely to be puzzling than weighty, but he always shared the television viewers' curiosity about what her question would be, and he always called on her. One lady reporter provoked a rare show of anger by using a question to brand two State Department employees as "well-known security risks." The President responded immediately that he was familiar with both men, their records and their assignments, which he believed they could carry out "without detriment to the interests of the United States, and I hope without detriment to their characters by your question." But he continued to call on this reporter at every conference. "I'd like to pass her by," he once confided, "but something always draws me to recognize her."

CHAPTER XIII

THE PUBLIC

BUT THE PRESIDENT would not rely on the press conferences alone to inform the American people. Every working day Kennedy filled the news with statements, releases, proclamations, memoranda, public letters, messages and reports to the Congress and remarks to small groups in the White House. Every time he signed a bill, presented a medal, toasted a prime minister, swore in an official, lamented a death or approved a commemorative stamp, he spoke with a larger audience in mind. The press received twice as many White House news releases each year as had ever been true before.

Salinger held two press briefings every day. Comprehensive background briefings were inaugurated to explain every Presidential message to the Congress. A few special news sessions were held by the President at Cape Cod and Palm Beach. He was the author of several magazine articles, on subjects ranging from the arts to physical fitness, and the subject of cover stories in every kind of magazine.

Kennedy also initiated a series of White House luncheons with editors and publishers, mostly on a state-by-state basis (although one friendly get-together was limited to prominent newspapers which had opposed him in 1960). Well briefed in advance on their names, views and state's problems, he talked informally, confidentially and extremely frankly about their interests and his. Wary news executives suspicious of being taken in by his charm went away impressed by his competence. "You ought to talk to the people this way," said one publisher. To which the President replied, "What do you think I'm doing right now?"

During his Christmas holiday in Palm Beach, both in 1961 and 1962, he invited the two dozen or so regular White House correspondents accompanying him to a free-wheeling three-to-four-hour "backgrounder" in his home on the year behind and the year ahead, dividing each session into domestic and foreign affairs discussions. Year-end "think pieces" (which would have been written anyway, he reasoned) were in this way better informed of views attributable to "the highest authority" or "sources close to the administration." Although these phrases deceived no one in the know, it made for a freer and fuller exchange than would have been true of a regular press conference or a larger background group in Washington. The State Department also sponsored regular background briefings for editors at which the President spoke off the record. He also made frequent public addresses, usually followed by question-and-answer sessions, to various organizations of editors, publishers, business publications, inter-American press executives and cartoonists.

TELEVISION

But his greatest weapon, he said more than once, was television. In addition to his televised press conferences and major speeches, the President frequently issued short statements on television from the White House and frequently granted special television interviews. The most successful of these was the unprecedented interview conducted by the three White House correspondents for the major networks, carried by all three to a vast audience in December, 1962. The President did not influence the choice of either questioners or questions. Relaxed in his White House rocker, with no crowd of reporters and with the cameras concealed, he spoke with astonishing candor—almost as if he thought it was a private interview—about his views of the office, his problems and prospects. Receiving a tremendously favorable response, he planned to make such an appearance an annual affair, and scheduled a repeat performance for December 17, 1963, the anniversary of the first.

The President, along with his office, his family and the White House, also became the focal point of numerous television (and illustrated magazine and newspaper) presentations which took the public behind the scenes. Reporters and cameramen stayed with the President in the course of his duties to record "a typical day at the White House," "the actual conduct of Presidential business" or "how a decision is made." These were not simulated conferences of the types staged in the previous administration. The reporters or cameramen were simply there when one of us walked into the President's office for a wholly unrehearsed meeting.

At times some of his associates were less comfortable than he with a camera crew observing their deliberations, and at times we found it necessary to make somewhat oblique references to sensitive subjects.

Some critics worried that the presence of cameramen or reporters might interfere with the natural flow of business. But the President never permitted their presence when it might do so.

Kennedy wearied of hearing how much more often Roosevelt had used the "fireside chat," and he discovered with much satisfaction that the faulty memory of its advocates had greatly exaggerated its frequency. The largest number of "fireside chats" FDR ever made in one year was a total of four in his first year, at the depth of the depression and the height of his influence. He made only four more during the rest of his entire first term, and throughout his whole tenure averaged fewer speeches from his office than Kennedy.

The danger which limited both men was not too much "exposure," as commonly assumed, but too little selectivity. "The public psychology," wrote Roosevelt, expressing sentiments which Kennedy shared, "cannot . . . be attuned for long periods of time to a constant repetition of the highest note in the scale."

I do not believe it is possible to "overexpose" a President like Kennedy. Nevertheless he could not, with any effectiveness, go on the air to denounce Big Steel, or announce a Cuban quarantine, or deliver some momentous message, every month of the year. Selectivity was the key— selecting the right time and the right issues. As a commander saves his biggest guns for the biggest battles, so Kennedy limited his direct national appeals to situations of sufficient importance to demand it and sufficiently fluid to be helped by it. "I made a speech," he reminded a press conference pressing him for a "fireside chat" on the Birmingham race conflict, "the night of [the] Mississippi [crisis] at Oxford, to the citizens of Mississippi and others, that did not seem to do much good. But this doesn't mean we should not keep on trying. . . . If I thought it would [be helpful], I would give one."

At a time when the international scene and the narrow Congressional margins required all the national unity possible, John Kennedy saw no sense in dividing the country, or alienating the Congress, or squandering his limited political capital, or feeding the fires of extremism, or wearing out his welcome and credibility, by making major appeals for public support on too many hopeless or meaningless causes. "I will," he said early in his term, "at such time as I think it most useful and most effective . . . use the moral authority or position of influence of the Presidency. . . . [But] I want to make sure that whatever I do or say does have some beneficial effect."

The most frequent complaint concerned Kennedy's refusal to employ more "fireside chats" on behalf of legislation.[1] He employed them where he thought they would help vital measures, such as the Test Ban Treaty,

[1] Actually Roosevelt had rarely used his "fireside chats" to put pressure on the Congress, and often delivered them when Congress was out of session.

tax cut and civil rights bill and in his constant televised plugs for foreign aid, and he was also willing to fight for his program in press conference statements and speeches around the country. But he had to consider the legislative and political consequences of opening a "cold war" with a Congress that was in fact passing, even though it was very slowly passing, most of the important Kennedy items and that was nominally a Democratic Congress. If the public response, in the form of letters to the Congress, turned out to be light—as it usually is—he would have laid his full prestige on the line for little gain and possibly a loss.

The fact is that a large proportion of the public will not listen to a Presidential speech on legislation. Many of those who do listen will resent being deprived of their regular TV entertainment. Very few of the rest feel sufficiently affected to write their Congressmen, and very few Congressmen feel sufficiently flexible to change their votes on the basis of such letters. Most members of Kennedy's bipartisan opposition in Congress were either irrevocably committed by the time a speech was in order or permitted by their seniority and safe districts to disregard both the President and any petitions he might stir up. No speech could have sprung the Department of Urban Affairs free from the House Rules Committee, for example. No speech could have obtained passage of an education bill which lacked a hundred or more votes, or made the Senate Finance Committee move faster, or forced Louisiana's Otto Passman to like foreign aid.

Whether on TV or the public platform, John Kennedy's major speeches were an important tool of his Presidency. He often used them to define administration decisions in specific terms and to convey those decisions throughout the government as well as the rest of the world. We had more experts from whom to seek ideas, facts and first drafts than we had in pre-Presidential years. Next-to-final drafts were usually submitted to the agencies concerned for their views, and this process was so slow on foreign policy speeches that McGeorge Bundy would gather all concerned around a table in his office to go over the draft in one sitting. We also had more pressures for completing authorized texts well ahead of time for advance distribution and foreign-language translation.

But in other respects the texts of most major speeches, messages and other documents, including many of his letters to Khrushchev, were still produced basically in accordance with the rules described in Chapter II. The basic pattern of our collaboration remained the same. Major speeches and other policy statements reflected decisions taken in meetings in which I participated, enabling me to spell out the reasons and sometimes the very words he had used in those meetings. Groups of advisers could suggest outlines and alterations, and they could review drafts, but group authorship could not produce the continuity and precision of style he desired, or the unity of thought and argument he needed. "The big difference," he said to me one day, "is all the different audiences that hear every word. In the Senate and campaign we didn't have to worry so much about how Khrushchev and Adenauer and Nehru and Dirksen would react."

He took pains to have a hand in every major Presidential paper—not only speeches but letters, messages and proclamations—and he still chose his words and their arrangement with great care. His Inaugural, State of the Union, American University, United Nations, Berlin, Irish Parliament and other addresses, including those televised from the White House on Cuba and civil rights, earned him the title of one of the most articulate and eloquent Presidents since Lincoln.

Eloquence depends not only on the words but on the man, the subject and the situation. Kennedy was still no orator. Others could be more forceful in voice, gestures, emphases and pauses. But as Lord Rosebery said of the impassioned oratory of Pitt, it was "the character which breathes through the sentences" that was impressive. Kennedy's character could be felt in every word, and the dramatics his style may have lacked were supplied by the subject and situation.

While we were more acutely aware of weighing each word in a speech, we still joked over what he insisted was my outrage at his changes and my determination to find some future use for every paragraph he cut. Some texts, such as the speech on peace at American University, represented primarily Presidential initiative with very little departmental contribution. Some, on necessary topics of little interest to him, such as reclamation, were basically unchanged from the products he received from collaboration between the departments and my office. And some, as in the past, were virtually ignored when he rose to speak. He became, however, so skillful at moving back and forth between his text and his interpolations that the press, unable to follow him on their copies, often assumed that an entire speech was extemporaneous when it was not.

On speeches televised from the White House he stayed close to his carefully cleared texts. On political stump speeches, particularly outdoors, he often ignored them. One near mishap occurred during his noted outdoor speech before the West Berlin City Hall, which had all the air of a political rally. Departing from his text, fired by the enthusiasm of his audience, he delivered an inspiring series of challenges to all naïve advocates of the Communist system, each one closing with the words: "Let them come to Berlin!" He included in this series: "And there are some who say in Europe and elsewhere we can work with the Communists. Let them come to Berlin!" Inasmuch as he had said only two weeks earlier at American University that we should try to find

ways of working with the Communists, and inasmuch as he was looking
forward to nuclear test-ban negotiations the following month in Moscow,
this ad lib caused some consternation. Between City Hall and the Free
University of Berlin it was discussed, and at the university he inserted
this passage of Kennedy interpreting Kennedy:

> As I said this morning, I am not impressed by the opportun-
> ities open to popular fronts throughout the world. I do not believe
> any democrat can successfully ride that tiger. But I do believe in
> the necessity of the great powers working together to preserve the
> human race.

POLITICS

His unwillingess to make still more public TV appeals for legislation
was hardly a matter of "hoarding" his personal and political popularity,
as often charged. "No President in the past eighty years incurred greater
political regional liabilities," as the *Saturday Review* observed, and only
Roosevelt in the past eighty years was the subject of so much hostile
comment in parts of the business community. He was a President willing,
if necessary, to risk defeat for his principles, but he preferred preserving
both his principles and his power to effect them.

Consequently politics was an ever-present influence in the Kennedy
White House, not as the sole subject of many meetings in his office, but
as a criterion for trips, visitors, appointees and speeches, as an unspoken
force counterbalancing the unrealistic, checking the unreasonable, occasionally deterring the desirable and always testing the acceptable. It
was automatically assumed by the staff that part of our role was to weigh
the effect of every move and statement, large and small, on various voter
groups, on Congress, on national unity and on the 1962 and 1964
elections. Kennedy retained in the White House his unusually acute
political antennae, with which he sensed the public mood both quickly
and accurately. He understood what moved people, what touched their
hearts and what touched only their pocketbooks. He was good at distinguishing their momentary whims from their enduring convictions.

There was no single source of this sensitivity. He read every
fiftieth letter of the thirty thousand coming weekly to the White House,
as well as a statistical summary of the entire batch, but he knew that
these were often as organized and unrepresentative as the pickets on
Pennsylvania Avenue. (Pickets and their placards never interested him—
although he made friends one stormy day by arranging for a group of
youthful peace marchers to be served coffee.) "Mail, unfortunately," he
told a 1962 press conference, "is not true as an indicator of the feelings

of the people. . . . I got last week 28 letters on Laos . . . [and] 440 letters on the cancellation of a tax exemption for a 'mercy' foundation."

He also remained an avid consumer of public opinion polls. He did not commission any polls directly, as rumored, but Lou Harris and others reported findings of many polls taken for their political clients, and the published polls of Gallup and his colleagues were studied with care. Nevertheless the President remained a skeptic. He told Orville Freeman that a survey of farmers showing Kennedy's job performance rating higher than his Secretary of Agriculture's merely proved that the latter was doing a good job—but that the whole poll was dubious, since it also claimed that Bostonian Kennedy ranked higher than Kansan Eisenhower. He told a press conference that a Gallup Poll showing 72 percent against a tax cut which produced deeper debts might have had a different result had it asked opinions on a tax cut necessary to prevent a recession, unemployment and consequently greater debts. At the peak of the 1963 civil rights furor, he privately speculated to a visitor that his poll ratings could drop below 50 percent for the first time—and then was amused by the rash of rumors which promptly spread throughout Washington and even appeared in the press citing an about-to-be-published poll revealing such a slide. (The next Gallup Poll showed him still above 60 percent.)

He relied on more than mail, public petitions and polls. He talked with hundreds of people every week in the White House. He read news-papers and magazines from all over the country. He judged the reactions of his crowds when he traveled (although not necessarily their size, which was partisan and planned). He observed the pressures reflected in Congress and heard reports from his Cabinet on their trips. But some-how his political intuition was an amalgamation of all these that was greater than the sum of its parts.

His political instincts had always been good. As a young reporter in London after the war, he had sensed that Churchill and the Tories would lose the 1945 elections. His editors, noting that no senior cor-respondent agreed, severely took him to task. As a result, by election time he had gradually crawled off that limb to report a Churchill rally and certain victory. Churchill lost.

Since that day he had been engaged in his own campaigns and calling them correctly. John Kennedy liked politics. He liked talking about it, participating in it, speculating on it. He looked upon it as the noblest profession. He never tired of encouraging young men and women to enter politics and public service, and by his own example, I believe, he worked a profound change in this nation's respect for that calling.

HIS CRITICS

The most oft reported charge made by President Kennedy's liberal and intellectual critics was that he made no crusading commitments of the heart, that he neither possessed nor inspired any warmth. They wanted him to go in more for lost causes, bigger deficits, grand designs and "fireside chats." They wanted him to pay more attention to Bowles and less to Acheson, to denounce the Republicans and do everything at once. They thought it proof of their complaints that his popularity exceeded Eisenhower's.

At the sophisticated Georgetown cocktail parties, in the scholarly and leftist journals, in the political columns and in letters-to-the-editor, they imitated, with little consistency, each other's charges: that Kennedy relied too much or not enough on his advisers, that he sent too much or too little to the Congress, that he engaged in too much "arm-twisting" or too little "leadership." They resented his wealth, his "style," his youth. Some liberals talked nostalgically about the good old days of Harry Truman, just as in Truman's day they had yearned for Roosevelt. "Every generation," said the President understandingly, "remembers its youth."

At times he would muse aloud over the academic isolation of many of his intellectual critics and their previous record of misjudgments. Though they assumed to speak for the voters, most of them talked mostly to each other—in Washington, on a campus or on an editorial staff. Their criticisms, he noted, generally lacked accurate information or feasible alternatives. They would, he hoped, judge him on the basis of his entire term in office, not merely individual episodes. "It is," he said, reflecting on his own candidacy as well as his critics, "much easier to make speeches than it is finally to make the judgment." He also frequently quoted Melbourne, under fire from the historian Macaulay, saying he "would like to be as sure of anything as Macaulay seemed to be of everything." Many of the noted analysts of public opinion and foreign policy, he commented, rarely left Washington. However, said Kennedy of his liberal critics in typical understatement, "I guess criticism is their special business."

While the left called Kennedy too timid, the right assailed him as power-hungry. Because he was uniquely a man for his time, because he recognized the revolutionary changes sweeping our globe and nation, and wanted our attitudes and institutions changed accordingly, he was assailed for being ahead of his time by those opposed to change.

John Kennedy never hated, and he worked hard to cast out hate in human and national affairs. But he was hated. The White supremacists hated "the Kennedys" more than they hated Truman or Eleanor Roosevelt. Bitter-end businessmen, ignoring all he had done for their prosperity, condemned him as a traitor to his class as they had once condemned Franklin Roosevelt. The far-right fringe of professional cold warriors and anti-Communists denounced him with poisonous passion, just as in the heyday of Joseph McCarthy they had denounced the fourteen Kennedy appointees mentioned in Chapter X, and Harry Truman, Henry Wallace, Robert Oppenheimer, Philip Jessup, James Conant, Francis Sayre, Arthur Miller and Walter Reuther, all of whom Kennedy honored by one means or another.

The publisher of the Dallas *News* embarrassed his fellow Texans at a White House luncheon by demanding "a man on horseback to lead this nation—many people in Texas and the Southwest think you are riding Caroline's bicycle." But the President was not embarrassed. He knew that he "didn't get elected President by arriving at soft judgments," and that he and only he had to weigh the multiple burdens, balance the conflicting responsibilities and produce the concrete solutions which would assure the survival and the success of 180 million Americans.

He deplored "the discordant voices of extremism" which peddled their frighteningly simple solutions to citizens frustrated and baffled by our nation's burdens. We had never heard of the John Birch Society until campaigning in Wichita in 1960, but in the years that followed, this and similar fringe groups increasingly recovered the noisy voices that had been stilled since McCarthy's demise. In his speech prepared for Dallas on November 22, 1963, the President lashed out at those who "confuse rhetoric with reality" and assume "that vituperation is as good as victory." And earlier he had said of these fanatics:

> They look suspiciously at their neighbors and their leaders. They call for a "man on horseback" because they do not trust the people. They find treason in our churches, in our highest court, in our treatment of water. . . . Unwilling to face up to the danger from without [they] are convinced that the real danger is from within.

But hate groups are not softened by reason or charm. Indeed, John Kennedy's obvious charms and cool reasoning only seemed to make them angrier. A man who loves, as Kennedy loved his fellow man, regrets hate, but Kennedy nevertheless expected it. When a pre-Presidential profile complained because no one hated him, the then Senator had written me:

> It is only after you wield the powers of the Presidency that you get hated. Morse, Hoffa, Al Hayes, etc., all hate me now merely because of one bill. Presidents are bound to be hated unless they are as bland as Ike.

John Kennedy was not going to be bland. He was bound to arouse either enthusiasm or anger with everything he did, and he was not a man to do nothing. "Public sentiment" on most controversial matters, he said to a fellow politician, "says don't act. But that's not enough. Somebody ought to see over the hill, even if he risks defeat. If that isn't the President's function, we should never have quarreled with Eisenhower."

He was always defying the most powerful interests in Washington— the AMA, the Truckers, the billboard users, the private-power, drug-manufacturer and junk-mail lobbies, even the leaders of his own church. He fully shared Theodore Roosevelt's concept of the White House as a "bully pulpit," calling for new standards of excellence in every endeavor, large and small, from staying in school to staying physically fit, from historical publications to cultural appreciation. "The American people are rather evenly divided on a great many issues," he coolly said. "As I make my views clearer on these issues, of course some people increasingly are not going to approve of me."

His prediction was correct. One morning we had talked about criticism at his pre-press conference breakfast—about the wide range of attacks that week, from Alabama's Governor Wallace to Vietnam's Madame Nhu, from right-wing author Victor Lasky to Communist Chinese boss Mao Tse-tung. No one, it turned out, had read the Lasky diatribe except its target. And the target was bearing up very well. He was not insensitive yet—or ever—but as each day passed he became more committed to his own self-examination and his own sense of responsibility. He took great delight in reciting a poem by bullfighter Domingo Ortega, as translated by Robert Graves:

> Bullfight critics ranked in rows
> Crowd the enormous Plaza full;
> But only one is there who knows—
> And he's the man who fights the bull.

PART FOUR

President Kennedy
and the Nation

CHAPTER XIV

❦

THE CONGRESS

For a man with no interest in mathematics, John Kennedy spent a large proportion of the years I knew him counting. Prior to July, 1960, he was counting convention delegates; and he came up with a bare majority. From July to November, 1960, he was counting electoral votes; and he again gained a slender majority. After November, 1960, he was counting Congressional votes; and this time he could not make the sums come out right.

His experience with the Eighty-sixth Congress, particularly that miserable postconvention session in August, 1960, made it clear that larger Democratic majorities were needed in both houses to pass the bills blocked (often in the House Rules Committee and sometimes with the use or threat of a veto) in 1960—including bills on housing, education, minimum wages, depressed areas, civil rights and medical care. But in the 1960 election those larger majorities were not forthcoming. For the first time in this century a party taking over the Presidency failed to gain in the Congress. The Democrats lost only one seat in the Senate. But in the House the Republicans lost seven incumbents while displacing twenty-nine Democrats, every one of them a Kennedy progressive. Twenty of those twenty-nine districts had gone Democratic in the 1958 mid-term landslide by less than 2.5 percent of the vote, and most of them were predominantly Protestant areas carried by Nixon in the closest Presidential race of the century.

The Democratic Party still had large paper majorities in both houses —262-174 in the House and 65-35 in the Senate—and Northern and Western Democrats in agreement with Kennedy's program still held a majority of their party's seats. In both houses they had a minority of the total vote, however, particularly in the House of Representatives. In the balky Eighty-sixth Congress they had substantially outnumbered House Republicans. But in the Eighty-seventh, the most conservative Congress since Eisenhower's Republican Eighty-third, the opposite was true. The balance of power appeared to have swung decisively in the direction of the conservative coalition of Republicans and Southern Democrats who had since 1937 effectively blocked much of the progressive legislation of four Presidents.

Reviewing these dismal figures with Lyndon Johnson and the Democratic Congressional leaders in Palm Beach, the President-elect decided nevertheless to confront the conservative coalition with an immediate showdown of strength—over control of the House Rules Committee. That committee, dominated since 1937 by the conservative coalition and in more recent years by its wily chairman, Howard Smith of Virginia, had been the chief bottleneck on the Kennedy-Johnson bills the previous August. No bill reported by a House committee could be considered in the regular manner on the House floor, and no bill passed by both houses in differing forms could proceed to a Senate-House conference committee, unless Smith's committee granted a "rule." Many "rules" were not granted at all, and others were granted only after long delays and the attachment of conditions or amendments. Although the committee was 8-4 Democratic, neither Smith nor ranking Democrat William Colmer from Mississippi had ever supported Kennedy's campaign, much less his program, and their two votes, joined by the four conservative Republican members against six loyal Democrats, produced a 6-6 tie on most major issues, guaranteeing, in the President's words, that "nothing controversial would come to the floor of the Congress. Our whole program would be emasculated."

The showdown had been building up for years, as Speaker Sam Rayburn found it increasingly difficult to deal with Smith, Colmer and the Republican members. Asking the new President to stay out of the fight, the Speaker took over its command from the House liberals. By threatening to "purge" Colmer from the committee for his support of anti-Kennedy electors in Mississippi, Rayburn impressed upon the Southerners—to whom the seniority system was a sacrosanct source of strength—that he was serious enough to act. Moderate Southern leaders asked Rayburn to compromise. He had not purged Negro Adam Clayton Powell for endorsing Eisenhower. He had not purged other members convicted of crimes. By singling out Colmer, he would so anger the South that no Kennedy bill could be passed. Rayburn, aware all along of these facts, offered a compromise: the temporary addition to the Rules Committee of two Democrats and one Republican, making possible an 8-7 majority on most bills. The moderates were agreeable, but a floor vote was required, and Republican Leader Charles Halleck announced that his party was officially opposed.

The fight was on. Rayburn employed every asset at his command. Kennedy could hardly remain aloof. Rayburn obtained an endorsement of his move in the House Democratic caucus. Kennedy declared at his first press conference that, although the Constitution made it a matter for the House,

> it is no secret that I would strongly believe that the members of the House should have an opportunity to vote . . . on the programs which we will present—not merely the members of the Rules Committee. . . . But the responsibility rests with the members. . . . I merely give my view as an interested citizen.

The Vice President, the Attorney General, the Secretaries of Commerce and the Interior as well as other Cabinet members, and particularly White House aide Larry O'Brien, used all the influence a new administration could muster—patronage, sentiment, campaign commitments and Federal actions of all kinds. Rayburn and his lieutenants canvassed every vote, staking the deeply respected Speaker's personal prestige on the outcome. Lobbyists for the Chamber of Commerce, National Association of Manufacturers, American Medical Association and American Farm Bureau launched a mail assault against the change, and labor, liberal and civil rights lobbyists were pressed into action on its behalf.

The infighting became vicious. The vote was put off until the day after the President's First State of the Union Message, in hopes that his eloquence and restraint would win fence-sitters. Moderate Southerners and Republicans were begged not to undermine the President before he was barely under way, not to humiliate the Speaker in one of his last great fights and not to handicap the country at a critical time. The President made several last-minute phone calls. The Vice President urged Texans to stand by their colleague. The Speaker made one of his rare impassioned speeches before the vote. The proposal carried 217-212.

"With all of that going for us," the President repeated many times in the months that followed, "with Rayburn's own reputation at stake, with all of the pressures and appeals a new President could make, we won by five votes. That shows you what we're up against." Sixty-four Democrats had voted against their President. Only 22 Republicans had voted with him, 17 from states he had carried. Without the votes of more than one-third of the Southern Democrats and one-eighth of the Republicans he would not have won at all.

The meaning was clear. No bill could pass the House of Representatives without somehow picking up the votes of 40 to 60 Southerners or Republicans, or a combination of the two, out of the 70 or so Southerners and Republicans who were not intransigent on every issue.

The situation was better in the Senate, although progressive Democrats there, too, had substantially less than 50 percent of the votes. The President and his Senate leadership decided against intervening in a fight to curb filibusters. The filibuster's chief damage was limited to civil rights bills, which appeared unlikely of passage anyway; and incoming Majority Leader Mike Mansfield opposed making the fight at that time, certain that it could not be won and that Westerners as well as Southerners would be antagonized by the President's intervention.

In his continuing confrontation with the conservative coalition in both houses, the President could not afford any additional antagonists. He could not bring the same pressures to bear on every fight that he had brought on the Rules Committee roll call. Just as the experts were predicting that only his housing bill stood a chance, the House approved his emergency farm bill by seven last-minute votes and turned down his minimum wage bill by one vote (a defeat he later reversed).

The Republicans taunted Kennedy for his inability to cash in on his Democratic majorities, but the President made no bones about the fact that Southern Democratic defections made every vote a cliff-hanger. "You can water bills down and get them by," he said, "or you can have bills which have no particular controversy to them. . . . But . . . we have a very difficult time, on a controversial piece of legislation, securing a working majority." Yet, as Theodore White has pointed out, "More . . . new legislation was actually approved and passed into law . . . than at any other time since the 1930's."[1]

For three years, a handful of votes were often decisive. Accelerated public works carried the Senate by one vote. The 1962 farm bill, designed to reverse the absurd, if not scandalous, increases in farm subsidies and surpluses at a time when the number of farms and farmers was declining, lost in the House lacking only five votes, supported by only one Republican (a lame duck later appointed to a job in the Department of Agriculture).

Of all his narrow losses, the most discouraging to Kennedy was the defeat of his "Medicare" bill—the long-sought plan enabling American working men and women to contribute to their own old-age health insurance program under Social Security instead of forcing them, once their jobs and savings were gone, to fall back on public or private charity. The President had pushed this bill hard in the campaign. He had drawn up a new version on the basis of a transition task force report. The cost of his own father's hospitalization, he told the legislative leaders at break-

1 Appendix A lists the major Kennedy enactments.

fast, made him all the more aware of how impossible it was for those less wealthy to bear such a burden. For three years he kept looking for one or two more votes to sway the House Ways and Means Committee on this bill. For three years he kept after the chairman of that committee.

But Chairman Wilbur Mills had his hands full with other administration bills. Although tentatively opposed to the bill, he told House Majority Leader John McCormack at the outset of the Kennedy administration (and McCormack so reported to the President at breakfast) that "something can be worked out if he is given time" and that the bill might better be added in the Senate to a House-passed measure and then taken up in conference. Kennedy also hoped that Senate passage would make House approval more likely.

With Senate passage as the target, pressure on the "Medicare" fight gradually built up on both sides. With the crowding of the 1961 Congressional calendar with antirecession legislation, it was made a priority item for 1962. The President wanted a vote before the fall Congressional elections. In many a press conference and speech he strongly endorsed the bill. He ridiculed the attacks of the American Medical Association as "incomprehensible" and met with a group of leading physicians supporting his position. On May 20, 1962, nationwide television carried his address to a mammoth rally of senior citizens in Madison Square Garden. It was a fighting stump speech, loudly delivered and applauded. But the President had forgotten the lesson of his campaign that arousing a partisan crowd in a vast arena and convincing the skeptical TV viewer at home require wholly different kinds of presentation. He already had support from the senior citizens; he needed more support from the home viewers, and that speech did not induce it.

The AMA replied with a bitter attack the following night ("I read their statement," said the President at his news conference, "and I gathered they were opposed to it"), and a further barbed exchange followed in public letters. At the same time new pressures were applied to the House Ways and Means Committee in the hopes of reversing its attitude. But the real arena was the Senate. Early in July the House-passed Public Welfare Bill presented itself as an appropriate vehicle for the "Medicare" amendment. A desultory Senate debate opened on July 2. On three successive Tuesday mornings—July 3, 10 and 17—tactics and tallies on this measure were the first subject of discussion at the legislative leaders breakfast with the President. Senate passage in the previous Congress had failed 51-44. Now there was one more Republican in the Senate, one less Democrat, and few votes capable of being switched. Alabama moderate Lister Hill, for example, a leading sponsor of health legislation, was under too much doctor pressure, and kept his moderate colleague John Sparkman with him. The President's personal friend George Smathers, an usher at his wedding in 1953, was aware of AMA influence in Florida. ("Smathers," commented one of my White House colleagues, "hasn't stood up for Jack Kennedy since the wedding!") Moderate Oklahoman Mike Monroney felt bound to stick with his colleague Bob Kerr, the immensely powerful Senator who was floor manager of the anti-Medicare forces.

Nevertheless, on July 10 O'Brien reported a head count of 51-49 in favor. At least four liberal Republicans and one Southern Democrat were switching from their 1960 opposition. On July 17, the day of the vote, he reported a new count: "50-50 at best, and Senator Randolph has a problem."

West Virginia's Democratic Senator Randolph's problems included a concern that controversy over Medicare would defeat the Public Welfare Bill—which contained important provisions for his state—and a commitment to Medicare's opponents that he would switch from his 1960 position of support in exchange for more welfare aid for West Virginia. Forty-eight votes were solid for Medicare. If Randolph supported it, Carl Hayden would support it out of party loyalty; and fifty votes, with Vice President Johnson breaking any tie, would pass the bill.

The President talked to Randolph. He arranged for West Virginia and national party leaders, labor leaders and welfare group leaders to talk to him. The pressure was unprecedented—and unsuccessful. Randolph voted with those tabling the Medicare amendment; waiting to the end, so did Senator Hayden; and, except for the amendment's five Republican cosponsors, so did every Republican. The measure was lost, 52-48, and the President went immediately on television to declare that this "most serious defeat for every American family" would be a key issue in the fall campaign. (He also instructed his Budget Director to notify Randolph that a costly and controversial project sponsored by the Senator was being dropped from the Budget, although I have no doubt that Senator Kerr could channel more funds into West Virginia than we could reroute.) The Eighty-seventh and Eighty-eighth Congresses would in time pass more health legislation than any two Congresses in history—including landmarks in mental health and mental retardation, medical schools, drug safety, hospital construction and air and water pollution—but the President never got over the disappointment of this defeat.

KENNEDY VS. THE CONGRESS

Even before the Rules Committee fight, and well before his subsequent setbacks on Medicare and other bills, the President and the Congress regarded each other with misgiving. More than arithmetic or ideology was at the root of this mutual mistrust. It represented as well a struggle for power between two different branches of the government and two different generations of politicians.

Had John Kennedy remained throughout his public life in the House, or had he remained after 1960 in the Senate, he would by 1963 have been among the exclusive 20-25 percent of Democrats whose seniority usually entitled them to positions of influence in those bodies. But he had not, and the seniority system had elevated into the most powerful committee chairmanships of both houses many men who were not only unfriendly to much of his program but as old as or older than his father. The average member of the House was a decade older than the President, and the average Senator even older. Most of them had known Jack Kennedy as a comparatively brief and youthful member of their legislative bodies. They were less suspicious of him than of the brisk young men around him, and they had no qualms about ignoring his programs while wrangling endlessly with each other. The worst of an increasing number of petty feuds between the House and Senate, which delayed bills and frazzled nerves, was a dispute between Senate Appropriations Committee Chairman Hayden, eighty-four, and House Appropriations Committee Chairman Cannon, eighty-three, which held up action on the Kennedy Budget in 1962 for three months while they fought over who should call conference meetings when and where.

Kennedy, particularly in his first year—despite the advantages of being the first President in a hundred years to have served in both houses—felt somewhat uncomfortable and perhaps too deferential with these men who the previous year had outranked him. Although his opening State of the Union remarks had called the assembled legislators his "oldest friends in Washington," he knew that he had always been too junior, too liberal, too outspoken and too much in a hurry to be accepted in their inner ruling circles; and they knew that he spoke a different language and seemed more at home with a different breed of friends. Many of his efforts to bridge this gap seemed futile. In one unusual tribute, for example, the President dropped in by helicopter on Senate Finance Committee Chairman Harry Byrd's annual birthday picnic. But that did not discourage Byrd from decrying at the following year's picnic the number of airplanes and other means of costly transportation wastefully made available to the President.

"What would the world be like," the President meditated aloud to me one day, "if all public officials had to retire at age seventy?" And he rattled off a list of international as well as Congressional leaders who had not been making life easy for him. But when asked at a press conference about an Eisenhower suggestion for reform, floated from the safety of Gettysburg, that Congressmen as well as Presidents should have a limited number of terms, he replied, "It is the sort of proposal which I may advance in a post-Presidential period, but not right now."

He knew he lacked the votes to put through any of the sweeping reforms required to enable a majority to work its will in each house, and the spotty success of past reforms made him skeptical of most new proposals. His Department of Justice did intervene strongly in the Supreme Court reapportionment cases, in hopes of ultimately weakening the domination of the House by rural conservatives. But, as he said late one evening in the summer of 1962 as we talked in his office, no reform could end the basic hostility which then existed between the Congress and the White House, and he ticked off the reasons:

1. Most of the Democrats on Capitol Hill had never served in the Congress with their own party in the White House. By custom and Constitution, they thought principally of their own districts and states, not the national interest. They had no experience in the Executive Branch, "yet they look at you fellows as incompetents because you've never run for office. What's more, some of them figure they can make more news by opposing me than by going along."

2. "Party loyalty or responsibility means damn little. They've got to take care of themselves first. They [House members] all have to run this year—I don't and I couldn't hurt most of them if I wanted to. Most of them ran ahead of me last time, and most of them had been for Stu or Lyndon for the nomination. They figure I've put them in the middle on trade or civil rights or parochial schools, and there's little the National Committee can do to help them."

3. "Some of them aren't as important as they were under Eisenhower, especially in the Senate. A lot of the spotlight has shifted down here now and they get damn little credit for their part. Every time I ask them for more power—over aid or trade or taxes—they think I'm invading their prerogatives." ("And they may be right!" I interjected.)

"The Congress," he said publicly a short time later,

> looks more powerful sitting here [in the White House] than it did when I was . . . one of a hundred in the Senate. . . . From here I look . . . at the collective power of the Congress . . . there are different views, different interests [and] perspectives . . . from one end of Pennsylvania Avenue to the other. . . . There is bound to be conflict.

That conflict was made all the more inevitable by Kennedy's refusal to leave the legislating solely to the legislative branch. He spelled out his own legislative program in detail and stirred public and private pressure on its behalf. No major legislative measure was ever presented to the Congress by his Cabinet or passed by the Congress for his signature without his prior approval. He vetoed minor bills that he did not like, impounded appropriated funds that he did not need, ignored restrictive amendments that he found unconstitutional and improvised executive action for bills that would not pass.

Example: The Congress specifically exempted the Federal government from the 1961 minimum wage increase, and also omitted private laundry workers from its coverage, but the President directed his agency heads to make certain that all Federal employees, including laundry workers, were paid the new statutory minimum.

Example: When Congress buried a bill for a Federal Advisory Council on the Arts, he created one by Executive Order.

Example: Drawing upon a variety of funds and authority, he created the Peace Corps by Executive Order before even requesting enabling legislation from the Congress, with the result that the Corps was in full operation by the time the legislation passed some six months later.

He did not feel obligated to risk unnecessary delay and possible defeat by sending every important international agreement to the Senate for approval as a formal, long-term treaty. Nor did he follow Eisenhower's precedent of seeking Congressional resolutions of approval for major foreign policy initiatives. He dispatched personal and official advisers on important missions abroad, stationed Lucius Clay in Berlin for seven months with the rank of ambassador, and inserted Maxwell Taylor between himself and the Joint Chiefs of Staff without recourse to Senate confirmation. He told one career servant called to testify on a matter not yet settled by the administration "to tell them you're sick and you'll be up there next week." He invoked the claim of executive privilege to prevent Congressional investigators from harassing State and Defense Department civil servants over the individual deletions or alterations they made when clearing speeches. He resisted the attempts of powerful Congressional committee chairmen to force unwanted increases in his Budget—for veterans' pensions, research and defense.

The issue of increased funds for defense—specifically for the B-70 aircraft—brought the two branches close to a head-on collision in March, 1962. The powerful House Armed Services Committee, agreeing with Air Force and industry pressures on behalf of a new "RS-70" version of the same dubious project, sought to prevent the President from once again impounding the sums appropriated above his request. Reflecting anger at both the de-emphasis of manned aircraft and the disregard of Congressional will, the military authorization bill was deliberately worded by Committee Chairman Carl Vinson to "direct" the Pentagon to spend nearly half a billion dollars on the RS-70—roughly three times the President's request. The report not only directed but "ordered, mandated and required" that the full amount be spent, adding: "If the language constitutes a test as to whether Congress has the power to so mandate, let the test be made . . . [for] the role of the Congress in determining national policy, defense or otherwise, has deteriorated over the years."

McNamara urged the President to do battle against the wording. Democratic leaders urged him not to tangle with Vinson. His lawyers advised him that he could ignore the language if it passed, relying on the Constitutional separation of powers. O'Brien advised him that any floor fight against Vinson would be lost, and costly in future fights.

Kennedy attained the one course his advisers assumed was impossible: he persuaded Vinson to withdraw the language. He did it by inviting "the Swamp Fox" to the White House for a private chat and a walk in the garden on the afternoon before the debate. "Uncle Carl," he said in effect, "this kind of language and my ignoring it will only hurt us and the country. Let me write you a letter that will get us both off this limb."

McNamara and I drafted the letter that afternoon, and O'Brien and I immediately took it in draft form to Vinson's office. We could not know what his reaction would be. The letter strongly restated the President's constitutional authority, urged deletion of "directed" and promised nothing more than a restudy of the RS-70[2] in the interests of comity. But Vinson liked it; the formal letter was sent that night, and Congressmen gathering for a bloody antiadministration battle on the floor the next day were disappointed to hear Vinson and his committee meekly withdraw the "test" language. The President, refusing to crow, said only that it would be "chaotic" if each branch pushed its powers to the limit.

WOOING THE CONGRESS

Vinson, moreover, was one of the key Southern leaders upon whom the President depended. The Rules Committee fight had made clear that he could not win hotly contested bills without substantial Southern Democratic or Republican support. Kennedy set out to seek both, in effect building a different coalition of his own on each bill.

The labor and civil rights lobbies, the National Committee, even his own promises of campaign help meant little to Southern Democrats more concerned about their conservative-dominated primaries. Prior to 1961, the ninety-nine Democratic Congressmen from eleven Southern states had consistently voted at least three to one, and often five to one, against their party. But working through Vinson and other old friends in the House, through Kerr and Smathers in the Senate, and through O'Brien and Henry Wilson on his own staff, Kennedy obtained a majority of the Southerners on four out of five major issues.

[2] The project was restudied but no extra funds for the B-70 or RS-70 were ever spent.

Every gain has its cost. During 1961-62 Kennedy concentrated his civil rights efforts on executive actions. He increased price supports on cotton, rice, peanuts and tobacco. He added overly enlarged rural aid provisions to the Depressed Areas and Accelerated Public Works bills.

Neil MacNeil, author of *Forge of Democracy* and one of Washington's shrewdest observers of the House, has written me:

> For me the most astonishing thing about President Kennedy's dealings with Congress was his ability to pull those Southerners into his camp after their quarter-century of wandering in the conservative camp. This was well underway by the end of 1961, reached its fulfillment in the 1962 session and didn't erode until the civil rights disturbances in 1963 began to spook those Southern Congressmen. I mention this only because some of our "profoundest" observers here now are saying that Kennedy didn't know how to deal with Congress. . . . That, as I'm sure you know, is patent nonsense.

Kennedy's attentions to Democrats could not be confined to Southerners. He gave preferential recognition—in his speeches, trips, invitations to White House dinners and ceremonies, patronage and seats in the Presidential box—to all those whose votes he appreciated or sought. He wrote letters of "appreciation" to helpful Congressmen facing primary fights in which he could not officially take sides. He conferred in his office with each Democratic committee chairman, occasionally with all the Democrats on a committee. A series of White House receptions covered all Democrats in both houses in groups of fifty, and at the beginning or end of each session, the full Democratic membership of each house was brought in for a Presidential pep talk, complete with graphs and charts. In his individual conferences he was not good at the small talk which most Congressmen relished, but several told me how amazed they were at his knowledge of a bill's detail.

Patronage, the President said candidly, "does give us some influence . . . [but] there are not many jobs." There are, he might have added, more headaches. Patronage squabbles in several states gave him more enemies than friends. Three-quarters of a century earlier, seven thousand out of every eight thousand Federal jobs were non-merit-system appointments. By 1961 the ratio was more nearly twenty out of eight thousand, and only four of those twenty were Presidential appointments. A large proportion of the twenty, moreover, required trained experts at low pay. But occasionally, with Republicans as well as Democrats, a specific personnel opening at the time of a crucial vote enabled both the President and a key legislator to please each other.

Kennedy was generally unsuccessful, however, in his efforts to woo Republican votes, particularly on domestic policy. After 1961 only his gains with Southern Democrats enabled him to continue winning four out of five roll calls on the House and Senate floors. But on foreign policy, civil rights and a few other issues, his good relations with conservative GOP leaders Dirksen and Halleck were rewarding. He liked both men, respected them as fellow professionals and enjoyed bantering with them over their successes and defeats. In fact, by 1962 his relations were so good with Dirksen—whom he had always found entertaining and at times movable by invocations of patriotism (or patronage)— that both men had to reassure their respective party members that each had not embraced the other too much. The President went campaigning in Illinois for Dirksen's opponent and the Senate Minority Leader protested good-naturedly that he had not "gone soft on Kennedyism."

No fight better illustrated both the necessity and the difficulty of winning Republican votes than the annual battle over foreign aid. Kennedy's hope in 1961 was to obtain long-term borrowing authority for his reorganized AID program, thus permitting a new nation's development to be planned on a more orderly basis than one year at a time. It also would have facilitated a more precise determination of how much other nations should contribute and how much self-help was expected from the recipient country. But Congress not only denied the long-term financing, relenting only to the extent of permitting long-range commitments without money to back them up; it also forced the President to fight a major battle each year to prevent heavy slashes in the program.

Seeking Republican help, Kennedy included legislative leaders from both parties on foreign policy briefings, relied heavily on his Republican appointees in top posts, obtained statements on the AID bills from Eisenhower and other G.O.P. leaders, and publicly recalled the support he and his party had given Ike in earlier years.

Seeking Democratic support, he talked to key members by telephone or in his office, rounding up votes in much the same manner as he once rounded up delegates: "I know your district, Sam, and this won't hurt you there. . . . This is a tough one for you, Mike, I realize, but we'll go all the way with you this fall. . . . Vote with us on recommittal, where it's close, Al, and then you can vote 'no' on final passage." He agreed to help with their pet projects or to speak in their districts. On one California trip he pointedly excluded the local Democratic Congressman from the platform for consistently deserting him on the foreign aid bill in committee, and another recalcitrant found the new Federal Office Building scheduled for his district suddenly missing from the Budget. More than one visiting prime minister from a new nation, the President remarked to me one evening, had confessed his inability to understand why a Democratic President could not tell what a Democratic Congress would do on foreign aid,

Seeking public support, he repeatedly promoted the program in his televised speeches and press conferences and in his talks around the country. The opponents of foreign aid, he said,

> should recognize that they are severely limiting my ability to protect the interests of this country. They are not saving money. . . . Our assistance makes possible the stationing of 3.5 million Allied troops along the Communist frontier at one-tenth the cost of maintaining a comparable number of American soldiers. A successful Communist breakthrough in these areas, necessitating direct United States intervention, would cost us several times as much as our entire foreign aid program.

In proportion to our effort in the early days of the Marshall Plan, he added, his program was one-fourth as burdensome, yet the need was greater. "I don't understand why we are suddenly so fatigued," he told his last news conference. "The Congress has its responsibility, but . . . I cannot fulfill my responsibility in the field of foreign policy without this program."

But Appropriations Subcommittee Chairman Otto Passman of Louisiana felt *his* annual responsibility was to cut back foreign aid as sharply as possible. Immune to the President's personal pleas, and aided by members of both parties, North and South, liberal as well as conservative, Passman had no difficulty in finding examples of waste and error in a program rendered incapable of consistently maintaining efficiency and attracting quality by constant Congressional carping, constant executive reorganization, constant appropriation delays and constant shifts in emphasis among its most fervent advocates. No powerful constituencies or interest groups backed foreign aid. The Marshall Plan at least had appealed to Americans who traced their roots to the Western European nations aided. But there were few voters who identified with India, Colombia or Tanganyika.

Each year Kennedy lost more ground to Passman, and each year the President blasted a little more sharply "those who make speeches against the spread of Communism . . . and then vote down the funds needed . . . to stave off chaos and Communism in the most vital areas of the world." With what he privately acknowledged to be a "calculated risk," he named a panel of conservative private enterprise skeptics to review his 1963 AID request. That panel, under General Lucius Clay, recommended cuts while strongly defending the program. Passman and Company ignored the defense, accepted the cuts and made still more cuts—and Kennedy's gamble backfired.

Kennedy was not embittered by his legislative defeats. He had no difficulty working with Kerr or Mills or Dirksen the day after they had successfully worked against him, just as his administration had room for those who had opposed his nomination. He often reminded his wife and brothers not to be bitter against those who fought or failed him, voicing two political maxims: "In politics you have no friends, only allies" and "Forgive but never forget."[3]

His margin, however, was too narrow to grant him the luxury of attacking all Republicans or all Southerners. "I have to have the Congress behind me," he told one interviewer, pointing to the list of mounting world crises. "I can't afford to alienate them." Legislative defeats, and the drop in his Gallup Poll rating which usually accompanied them, were accepted as part of the job. "There is a rhythm to a personal—and national and international—life," he said, "and it flows and ebbs. . . . If I were still 79 percent [in the Gallup Poll] after a very intense Congressional session, I would feel that I had not met my responsibilities." When I congratulated him on an October, 1961, Gallup Poll showing he would defeat Nixon 62-38, he replied that the margin would rise and fall many times before his re-election. He knew it was no coincidence that both his personal morale and his Gallup Poll ratings rose each time Congress adjourned for the winter. But the sheer volume of bitterly contested administration bills required each session to be longer than the one before. "It is much easier in many ways for me," said the President frankly to a news conference, "when Congress is not in town. But . . . we cannot all leave town."

His legislative leaders warned him that he was sending to the Congress more than it could digest—a record of 1,054 requests in three years—but he wanted to lead, to set forth the agenda, to begin. "They are only going to pass part of what I send up anyway," he said to me as we readied his 1963 program in Palm Beach. "If I had sent up half as many major bills in '61-'62, they would have passed only half as many as they did." Unless it was "completely emasculated . . . a shadow of success and not the substance," he preferred a compromise to no bill at all—"compromises of our political positions but not ourselves . . . of issues, not of principles."

Example: He deeply disliked dropping laundry workers—whose plight he had often cited in the campaign—from the extended coverage provisions of the minimum wage bill. But the alternative was no bill at all and thus no protection for millions of others.

Example: By personally persuading Senator Eastland to report out a drug reform bill broader in its consumer protection provisions than the Kefauver drug bill, he gave both Kefauver and consumers a notable victory. Kefauver had been consulted all the way, but the Tennessean's

---

[3] He still remembered, for example, which stores in Boston had accepted window signs for his first congressional campaign and which had refused.

aides denounced the administration for not including their patent proposals, which would clearly have blocked the whole bill.

1962 CONGRESSIONAL ELECTIONS

No compromise or setback, moreover, was regarded as permanent. Each one, Kennedy promised, would be an item for a future, more favorable Congress and an issue in a future campaign. In the 1962 Congressional campaign, however, his task was to keep the Congress at least as favorable as it was.

Within his own party he attempted no purge of those voting against his program but made clear his intention to campaign only for its supporters. Inasmuch as most of the Democrats who opposed him neither wanted nor needed his help in their one-party districts, this was hardly, as some claimed, a "purge" in reverse. He also gave indirect help in primary fights to those who had helped him, even when it meant helping an "old guard" Democratic incumbent against a "reform" challenger. Reformers moaned, for example, when a testimonial dinner for Bronx Boss Charles Buckley received a laudatory wire signed "Joe, Jack, Bobby and Teddy Kennedy." Although he had earlier snubbed New York's "old guard" leaders, he generally paid little attention to such labels. The "old guard" bosses who once ordered his defeat now gladly took orders from him, he noted, and the reformers tended to become the old guard once they were in.

His real problem in 1962 was with the Republicans, in stemming the historical trend of mid-term elections, which, with the exception of 1934, had invariably cost the party in the White House some three dozen seats in the House and a comparable number in the Senate. His own margin had been so thin in 1960 that few observers gave him much chance of keeping GOP gains down even to the fifteen to twenty additional House seats he publicly conceded. Aide Arthur Schlesinger, Jr. argued in a thoughtful memorandum that Roosevelt had made no campaign at all for the Congress in 1934, the one exception to the mid-term rule, and that Roosevelt had lost Democratic seats in both houses when he did campaign in 1938 and 1942. Kennedy's intervention in the campaign, it was argued, would only invite blame for a historical trend beyond his control, and to avoid this loss of prestige he should remain above the battle.

A prominent Republican also suggested that a President should limit himself to nonpartisan appearances representing all the people. No, said Kennedy,

> . . . it is a responsibility of the President of the United States . . .
> to have a program and to fight for it. . . . I do not believe that

in this most critical and dangerous period that Presidents . . .
should confine themselves to ceremonial occasions, ornamenting
an office at a time when this country and this world need all of
the energy and the action and the commitment to progress that
[we] can possibly have.

In 1962 the opinion polls showed less than 30 percent of the Democrats,
compared with 43 percent of the Republicans, planning to turn out to
vote. To offset this apathy, the President planned a mid-term campaign
more vigorous than that of any President in history. "I have never overstated what a President could do in these matters," he told his news
conference, and he was not campaigning, as most people assumed,
simply because he enjoyed it. "I don't enjoy it very much," he told a
surprised interviewer.

> One of the great myths in American life is that those who
> are in politics love to campaign. Well, maybe some do; but it's
> hard work making a lot of speeches, and I have a good many other
> things to do. But . . . [this] is going to decide what kind of
> Congress we're going to have for the next two years. So . . .
> there's no place that I ought to be in these weekends that is more
> important.

A Western "conservation tour" in the summer, a Southern space
missile tour in September, and then quick trips to a dozen states by
mid-October were indeed hard work. Then the Cuban missile crisis intervened to cancel the rest of his schedule. But the hard work paid off,
aided to an undeterminable extent by his handling of the crisis. It was
the largest turnout, except for 1938, of eligible voters in any mid-term
election recorded, and it was the best showing, except for 1934, by any
party in power in modern political history. The Republicans gained only
two seats in the House and lost four seats in the Senate. "We are about
where we were the last two years," said the President; but he knew it
was better than he had hoped.

LEGISLATIVE LEADERS AND LIAISON

One of those Senate races had given him extra joy—and extra anxiety.
His youngest brother Ted, long touted as the most natural campaigner
in the family, defeated Henry Cabot Lodge's son George to keep the
President's old Senate seat in the Democratic column. Because the loss
of his own state would have been a heavy blow, because the polls showed
that only Teddy could carry the state for the Democrats, and because
he would not stand in his younger brother's way, the President was
willing to endure far more complaints than he had foreseen about

"nepotism" and "dynasty." But the greatest strain growing out of Teddy's candidacy was that placed on the President's relations with the new Speaker of the House, John McCormack, whose nephew Eddie sought the same Senate seat.

In Washington all the old stories about bad blood between the two families were revived. In Massachusetts the lines were tightly drawn for a bruising battle. But neither the President nor the Speaker took any public part or, at our weekly legislative breakfasts, any private notice. Both felt strongly about the outcome, but neither blamed the other for the contest and both were determined not to let it interfere with their collaboration, despite statements to the contrary by their Boston backers. Comparing the primary by implication to Vietnam, where American troops were officially present only as advisers and trainers, the President quipped to the Gridiron Club off the record:

> I have announced that no Presidential aide or appointee would be permitted to take part in that political war in Massachusetts. Of course, we may send up a few training missions. . . . All I can say is: I'd rather be Ted than Ed.

I made a few "training missions," as did others, and both the President and Attorney General helped coach their younger brother—who in fact was less nervous when performing out of their presence. The President was nervous, too, over his own reputation rising or falling with each controversial question Teddy might be asked—on aid to parochial schools or civil rights, for example—and for this reason turned off one TV panel interviewing his brother.

But without requiring any overt help or improper pressure from either brother, Ted Kennedy won the nomination in September, 1962. The Speaker, while deeply disappointed, merely chewed his cigar more vigorously at the next legislative breakfast.

These weekly Tuesday morning breakfasts, like meetings of the Cabinet, usually served little more than as a means of maintaining rapport, *esprit de corps* and open channels of communication. The President, leading the discussion on the basis of memos prepared by O'Brien and me, valued the meetings as a regular check for him on all pending bills, but the information he received and delivered was usually available without a full meeting.

O'Brien, O'Donnell, Salinger and I attended from the staff. Majority leader Mike Mansfield, Majority Whip Humphrey and Democratic Conference Secretary Smathers attended from the Senate. In 1961 Sam Rayburn was Speaker of the House, John McCormack was Majority Leader and Carl Albert Assistant Leader or Whip. Rayburn died at the close of that session, McCormack and Albert each moved up and Hale Boggs succeeded Albert as Whip.

Each of these men became devoted to Kennedy, including Rayburn who had bitterly opposed his nomination, Humphrey who had fought him in the primaries, Smathers who voted frequently against him and McCormack with whom he had differed over Bay State politics. After Rayburn's death, each of them was as new to his post as Kennedy and Johnson were to theirs, and together they made mistakes as they learned.

Sam Rayburn had been increasingly grumpy and uncommunicative in his last months, but no man, including Henry Clay, ever served as Speaker for more years or with more distinction. He knew how, when and from whom to wheedle votes, dispense favors, intimidate new-comers and appease old-timers. In his absence, more power inevitably seeped to the conservative committee and subcommittee chairmen, and John McCormack, accustomed to the more aggressively partisan role of Majority Leader, found himself unfairly assailed from both wings of his party for failing to fill "Mr. Sam's" shoes.

Kennedy had, in fact, been strenuously urged to oppose McCormack's elevation to Majority Leader. But the President noted that those so urging had no clearly electable candidate of their own, and no candidate with any better claim than McCormack to either the President's help or the post itself. Unable to risk gaining many more enemies in high places, he stayed out of a fight he felt certain he would lose. Party organization in the House, moreover, had been steadily improving ever since that day early in 1961 when the minimum wage bill had been defeated by one vote with sixty-four Democrats absent.

In the Senate, Majority Leader Mike Mansfield was also being un-fairly and unfavorably compared with his predecessor, the Vice President. The kind and careful Mansfield, faced with the very different task of enacting the program of his own party's President, was endowed with very different personal assets. A gentle, usually soft-spoken Mon-tanan, he was even more low-key and low-pressure than Kennedy. At times the President, who had been fully consulted on the makeup of the Senate leadership team, was frustrated by what he felt were Mansfield's excessive pessimism, caution and delays. But in view of his consistent string of successes in the Senate, he was deeply appreciative of Mans-field's loyalty and labors, held him in close personal affection, and felt that no Senate leader in those years could have done better in the long run.

Working closely with the House and Senate leaders was the most organized White House legislative liaison effort in history under Larry O'Brien. His aides, unlike the rest of the White House staff, were selected with a careful eye to geography: Wilson of North Carolina, Manatos of Wyoming, Donahue of Massachusetts, Daley of California and DeSautels of Maryland. Although charged with employing high-pressure tactics and threats, the O'Brien team pumped far more arms than they twisted and brandished far fewer sticks than carrots: advance notification of Federal contracts, special privileges for White House tours, detailed data on a bill's effect, material for speeches and releases, birthday notes from the President, campaign help from the National Committee, autographed pictures from the President, and whatever flexibility was possible on patronage, public works and other budget items.

O'Brien, genial, tactful and tireless, added names and dates to the President's lists of dinner guests, baseball companions, speaking engagements, appointment calendar and phone calls. Aware that the President's interest in domestic legislation and the time he had available for any legislation were both limited, he increased the value of personal Presidential appointments for Congressmen by keeping their number low, but he never denied access to anyone insisting on seeing the President. A thoroughgoing political professional, he spent his evenings as well as his days with Congressmen, lobbying them, listening to them, laughing with them, always offering more blandishments than bargains. He mobilized pressure from Democratic state and party leaders back home, from labor and other lobbyists, and from each of the departments and agencies. He maintained a card file on every Senator and Representative, complete with personal and political data and information on their districts. As crucial votes approached, he and his aides stationed themselves outside the doors of the appropriate chamber or set up temporary headquarters in the Speaker's or Majority Leader's office. On votes where there was no roll call, an O'Brien aide sometimes sat in the gallery watching how each member voted, although Larry himself felt it improper for him ever to appear there.

EDUCATION AND RELIGION

O'Brien's original hope was to be named National Chairman—especially when he learned that the President, presumably on the assumption that the religious issue was now dormant if not dead, was paying no attention to those who insisted that the tradition of a Catholic chairman should be broken with a Catholic in the White House. But within a few months of inauguration, Kennedy, O'Brien and the rest of us were once again embroiled in the religious issue—only this time, remarked the President wryly, "with new teams."

Kennedy had in fact never agreed with those who wrote that the 1960 election had banished religion for all time as an issue. An un-American tradition had been broken. Clearly a Catholic could be elected.

The campaign had illuminated many a dark corner of intolerance and ignorance. But the real test, he remarked soon after his victory, was not his election but his administration. The hard-core religious opposition which nearly defeated him would remain and flourish, to be cited by future conventions against the practicality of nominating a Catholic, *if* he lowered the bars between church and state, yielded to the pressures of the hierarchy or otherwise confirmed the religious opposition's suspicions. But if his conduct of the office was in keeping with his campaign pledge and constitutional oath, then, while unreasoning bigotry would always remain and legitimate church-state questions would always be raised, the unwritten law against a Catholic President would be not only temporarily broken but permanently repealed.

The issue was presented swiftly and forcefully on the one domestic subject that mattered most to John Kennedy: education. Throughout his campaign and throughout his Presidency, he devoted more time and talks to this single topic than to any other domestic issue. Without notes he would cite all the discouraging statistics: only six out of every ten students in the fifth grade would finish high school; only nine out of sixteen high school graduates would go on to college; one million young Americans were already out of school and out of work; dropouts had a far higher rate of unemployment and far lower rate of income; 71 percent of the people, according to Gallup, expected their children to go to college but only 51 percent had saved for it. As he climbed back onto his plane after a speech in Ohio, he said to me, "That's the fifth governor I've talked to who doesn't see how he can squeeze any more from property taxes to build enough schools."

Both as a Senator and President he addressed countless college audiences, imploring them

> to give to the world in which you were reared and educated the broadest possible benefits of that education. . . . I would not adopt from the Belgian Constitution of 1893 the provision giving three votes instead of one to college graduates—at least not until more Democrats go to college. . . . But I do strongly urge the application of your talents to the great problems of our time.

Each year he was in the White House he sent to the Congress a message on education more forceful than the previous year's. He linked education to our military, scientific and economic strength. "Our progress as a nation," he said, "can be no swifter than our progress in education. The human mind is our fundamental resource."

No number of setbacks discouraged him. When an omnibus bill failed, he tried for each of its parts, and vice versa. When elementary and secondary school aid was blocked, he worked on higher education.

Racial and religious[4] overtones, sniping from public school lobbyists and quarrels between the House, the Senate and individual members all combined to block passage of his higher education bill in 1962, even after both houses had passed it in different forms. But patience on the part of the President, perseverance by a new and talented Commissioner of Education, Francis Keppel, and a more constructive leadership in the National Education Association produced the Higher Education Act of 1963, authorizing several times more college aid in a five-year period than had been appropriated under the Land Grant College Act in a century, and providing classrooms for several hundred thousand students, twenty-five to thirty new community colleges a year, ten to twenty new graduate centers, several new technical institutes and better college libraries. A separate bill enacted the same year provided similar assistance to medical and dental schools.

When Congress dropped scholarships out of these bills, the President broadened student loans and scholarships under existing laws. When general Federal aid was defeated, he invented or expanded new means of specialized aid: quadrupling vocational education, allocating Presidential funds to stop dropouts, authorizing literacy training under Manpower Development, providing funds to teach the deaf and the handicapped and the retarded and the exceptional child, increasing funds for school lunches and libraries, working with schools on delinquency—in all these ways not only attacking serious educational problems but freeing local funds for use on general construction and salaries. Other enactments aided community libraries, college dormitories and educational television. An estimated one-third of all principal Kennedy programs made some form of education a central element, and the Office of Education called it the most significant legislative period in its hundred-year history.

Nevertheless his bill for general aid to elementary and secondary education failed, unable to survive a harsh combination of controversies of which religion was only the most conspicuous. For nearly fifty years similar bills had been the victim of arguments over civil rights, states' rights, academic freedom, balanced budgets and financial equalization. Its supporters in the Congress could not agree among themselves, and most of its organizational backers were inept, uncooperative and inconsistent. "He's simply against all Catholics, regardless of whether his position endangers an education bill," Abe Ribicoff told us in summing up the views of one long-time school lobbyist.

[4] The President—and a HEW–Justice Department brief—concluded that the Constitution and tradition made possible the equal treatment of both private and public institutions at the college level, where no state was required to furnish a free education to all, no student was compelled to attend, and no standards of curriculum or admission were required by law.

On the other hand, said a Catholic cleric, some of his colleagues were simply against all Federal aid to education bills, regardless of whether they included constitutional aid to children attending parochial schools. Kennedy expressed no surprise at this. But he noted that a bill limited to public schools had nearly passed in 1960 with no major protest from the hierarchy, and he hoped that his church would be equally understanding of his campaign pledge to obtain such a bill.

His hopes were soon dashed. Even before inauguration, Cardinal Spellman denounced the Kennedy task force report on education as "unthinkable" for not including parochial schools equally. "He never said a word about any of Eisenhower's bills for public schools only," muttered the President, "and he didn't go that far in 1949 either." But he refused to duck the issue or alter his view, and he presented early in the year a massive Federal aid to education bill limited, as he emphasized, to public schools "in accordance with the clear prohibition of the Constitution." The National Catholic Welfare Conference, representing the full hierarchy in America, immediately called for the Kennedy bill's defeat unless loans to nonpublic schools were added. Pastoral letters in many churches urged parishioners to write their Congressmen.

The President, wondering once again why he had been singled out, pointedly referred in a press conference to the fact that there had been no similar agitation during the Republican administration. "The Catholic, Protestant and Jewish clergy are entitled to their views," he added, but "they should not change their views merely because of the religion of the occupant of the White House."

His campaign commitment and the Constitution were both clear on this matter, in his opinion, and a comprehensive brief by the Departments of Justice and Health, Education, and Welfare reinforced his view. He saw nothing discriminatory about helping local taxpayers of all faiths finance schools that were open to all faiths—and which, in fact, roughly half of all Catholic children attended, as he had. His continued reliance on the Constitution in messages and press conferences seemed to make some Catholics angrier; but no matter how many different versions of the question the President received, his answer always reflected his determination (1) to promote public school education *and* (2) to preserve church-state separation. The problem was to find some means of removing Catholic objections to the former without violating the latter.

Secretary Ribicoff and I met quietly and informally with a local Catholic cleric who in turn was in touch with officials of the National Catholic Welfare Conference. These discussions ultimately focused on possible amendments—to be proposed in the Congress, and not by the President—to the National Defense Education Act (NDEA).

The NDEA, enacted in 1958, already included loans for private school education in categories essential to defense. It thus provided the most convenient and constitutional vehicle for demonstrating that it was "across-the-board" aid to Catholic schools, not "categorical aid" to Catholic schoolchildren, which the Constitution forbade. While the President remained formally committed only to his original program, advocated no other and did not want it amended to cover parochial schools, he had no constitutional or policy objection to the Congress, by separate bill, removing Catholic opposition to his bill by broadening the NDEA's categories and increasing its loan funds. As a young Congressman he had made a similar effort more than a decade earlier to bridge the gap between public and parochial aid adherents by introducing an auxiliary services "aid to the child" amendment in committee in keeping with the *Everson* school bus case.

But the public school advocates had been suspicious of his amendment then, and they were suspicious of widening NDEA in 1961. The Kennedy Federal Aid to Education Bill, having passed the Senate early in 1961, and having been reported out of committee in the House, ran afoul of his one-vote margin in the House Rules Committee. Democrat Jim Delaney sincerely believed, along with a majority of his constituents, that distinguishing between Catholic and other schoolchildren was unconstitutional and unfair. Having sensed the gathering Protestant storm over the NDEA amendments, he concluded—and no doubt rightly—that once he agreed to the public school bill, the NDEA bill would be mutilated or killed. As he waited until both bills reached the Rules Committee, religious feelings boiled up on both sides; and with no prospect of joining the two bills together or passing the NDEA bill first, Delaney joined Smith, Colmer and all five Republicans in voting the Kennedy bill down by 8-7. No amount of pleading or pressure by the President or Ribicoff could budge him. More adamant than many leaders of his church, he had no interest in bargains or trades on other subjects. "He didn't want a thing," said O'Brien. "I wish he had." The more Delaney was attacked by editorials and Protestant spokesmen, the more he was applauded by his Catholic constituents and colleagues.

The battle lines were now drawn in Congress and the country. A new organization, Citizens for Educational Freedom, threatened to defeat any Congressmen opposed to aiding parochial schools. Legislators received an avalanche of letters on both sides, some accidentally including instructions on how to write your Congressman on parochial school aid. One bloc of House members vowed to oppose any bill that included parochial aid, another bloc vowed to oppose any bill that excluded parochial aid, and the rest, with divided constituencies, devoutly hoped no bill would ever be reported that would force them to take a stand. John McCormack came out for across-the-board loans to parochial schools. Sam Rayburn said opposition would be less without inclusion in the bill of teachers' salaries. The education lobbies denounced any deletion of teachers' salaries. House leaders agreed that no bill on this subject could pass without first obtaining Rules Committee approval, and that—in the atmosphere then prevailing—no bill could win the support of both Delaney and the Southerners to provide that Rules Committee approval.

Nevertheless the President fought on, urging those "members of Congress who support this [bill] . . . probably the most important piece of domestic legislation . . . [to] use those procedures which are available to them under the rules of the House to bring this to a vote." There were only three doubtful routes of resurrecting on the House floor a bill the Rules Committee had killed: (1) discharge petitions signed by a majority of House members—which had produced legislation only twice in fifty years; (2) suspension of the rules to bring up a blocked bill—requiring a two-thirds vote, which this bill clearly lacked; and (3) bills called up by committee chairmen on "Calendar Wednesday"—these could be delayed and debated to death. Nevertheless this last route was pursued on a compromise bill sponsored by the House leadership.

It was a sorry ending to a sad story. Solid Republican opposition, joined not only by conservative Democrats but by those unwilling to face voting the bill up or down on its merits, overwhelmingly defeated a motion even to bring the bill up for consideration. Federal aid to education was dead.

Most Catholic members, including Delaney, voted to consider it. But only 6 out of 166 Republicans voted for it, compared to 44 the previous year, and nearly every Southern segregationist voted against it. The repeated headlines and editorials stating that it was the Catholics who had caused the bill's defeat, said the President, were unfair. The bill's House sponsor, he pointed out, was a Catholic. Of the three Catholics on the Rules Committee two had voted for it; of the ten Democrats seven had voted for it; but of the five Republicans not one had voted for it, when only one was needed to report it. In short, seven of the eight opponents—five Republicans and two Dixiecrats—had not supported Kennedy's election and were not influenced by Kennedy's wishes. "That's who really killed the bill," he said, "just as they've killed it for fifty years, not the Catholics."

The death of his aid to education bill, however, was accompanied by one of the most far-reaching changes in American politics effected during the Kennedy years. To a much greater extent than had been true the previous November, the ban on Catholics in the White House was dead also. John Kennedy had demonstrated that a Catholic could withstand the full pressures of the hierarchy on a bill of real significance to both sides, and he was toasted from Protestant pulpits throughout the land. One of his most violent opponents in the campaign a few months earlier, for example, Dr. W. A. Criswell of Dallas, called upon his flock "to stand behind President Kennedy and the Constitution." Even the POAU reported it was "extremely well pleased with President Kennedy" whose "strong stand . . . will reassure and inspire all who believe in the separation of Church and State. . . . We hope that the American people will support President Kennedy against the Bishops of his church."

Many Catholic laymen, and a few Catholic publications such as *Commonweal,* supported the President's position, and his friend Cardinal Cushing called upon Catholics to recognize the majority's opposition to tax-supported parochial schools and "neither force such legislation through at the expense of national disunity or use their political influence in Congress to block other legislation of benefit to education because they do not get their own way." But the President felt once again that most members of the hierarchy were opposed to both him and his program. At the 1961 Gridiron Dinner he referred to the old anti-Catholic legend that Al Smith, when his defeat in 1928 prevented the Pope from "taking over" America, had sent the Pontiff a one-word wire: "Unpack!" "Well," Kennedy said, "after my stand on the school bill, I received a one-word wire from the Pope myself. It said 'Pack!' "

At the 1963 Dinner, with no change in the situation in sight, it having been somewhat exacerbated by the Supreme Court's decision outlawing compulsory prayers in the public schools, he summed up the measure's chances with a realistic quip. "The Chief Justice," he said, "has assured me that our school bill is clearly constitutional—because it hasn't got a prayer."

The Court's decision on school prayers, and another on Bible-reading in the schools, threatened to raise new religious issues for the 1964 Presidential campaign. Many of the same conservative Protestants who in 1960 had denounced all Catholics—for supposedly seeking to break down the barrier between church and state, to upset the delicate constitutional balance on religious liberty and to threaten the secular nature of the public schools—were in 1963, with no sense of inconsistency, denouncing the Supreme Court for banning the recitation of formal prayers and Bible-reading in the public schools, and demanding a constitutional amendment to permit them. Most Catholic leaders, and many liberal Protestants, also attacked these decisions, as did the United States Governors' Conference and many powerful members of Congress.

A new ugly battle loomed, with all the controversies over the Court, the school bill, the Catholic President and his re-election being twisted together. The President, however, took much of the sting out of these decisions and much of the force out of any drive to amend the Constitution. He did it by his thoughtful response to a news conference question on the prayer case:

> I think that it is important . . . that we support the Supreme Court decisions even when we may not agree with them. In addition, we have in this case a very easy remedy and that is to pray ourselves. . . . We can pray a good deal more at home, we can attend our churches with a good deal more fidelity, and we can make the true meaning of prayer much more important in the lives of all of our children. That power is very much open to us.

That answer to me symbolized Kennedy's mastery of the religious issue throughout his stay in the White House. He disappointed all critics who had warned that he would weaken the Constitution and any Catholics who had hoped that he would. His administration made clear that this country is not officially Catholic, Protestant or even Christian, but a democratic republic in which neither religion in general nor any church in particular can be either established or curbed by public act.

True to his word, he showed no religious favoritism in the selection of his appointees, no fear of ecclesiastical pressures and no divided loyalty of any kind. No ambassador was sent to the Vatican. With his support, the Federal Government quietly but extensively increased its activities in the area of birth and population control—increasing its research grants, supporting an expansion of UN efforts and offering to help make more information available to other countries requesting it. A 1962 bill providing for the censorship of obscene publications in the District of Columbia—the kind of bill his critics had assumed heavy clerical pressures would force him to sign regardless of merit—was vetoed, not because he favored such publications but because the bill had grave constitutional defects. Having told the Texas preachers that he would have no hesitancy in attending a Protestant service in his capacity as President, he flew in his first year to Texas for the funeral of Sam Rayburn.

He attended Protestant prayer breakfasts with a now very friendly Billy Graham, received various Protestant clergymen at the White House and met privately—in my office, so that even visitors in the White House could not know—with anti-Catholic pamphleteer Paul Blanshard, seeking his agreement to the inclusion of private colleges in the higher education bill, and he kept me in touch with Blanshard generally. He felt as free as any other President to visit the Pope (but did not, in keeping with his own precedents as well as the protocol applicable to heads of state, kneel or kiss Pope Paul's ring but simply shook hands).

Partly as a result of John Kennedy's example—and the example of another John whose brief tenure as Pope overlapped Kennedy's brief tenure as President, but who by tragic chance died before they could meet—the Catholic Church in this country became less subject to recriminations from without and more subject to reform from within.

But the President at no time changed or downgraded his Catholic faith; he did not reduce or conceal his church attendance; and he possessed with pride a set of military identification "dog tags" inscribed with the unprecedented combination: "Kennedy, John F.—Commander-in-Chief—O [for blood type]—Roman Catholic."

One other note might be added. To me, the least explicable religious objection encountered during the entire campaign was the fear that a Roman Catholic Mass might be held in the White House. To those who expressed this worry, I can give assurance that it happened only once—on November 23, 1963.

CHAPTER XV

❧

THE MAN IN THE WHITE HOUSE

JOHN F. KENNEDY WAS A HAPPY PRESIDENT. Happiness, he often said, paraphrasing Aristotle, is the full use of one's faculties along lines of excellence, and to him the Presidency offered the ideal opportunity to pursue excellence.

He liked the job, he thrived on its pressures. Disappointments only made him more determined. Only once do I recall his speaking with any bitterness about his post. It was a few minutes before he was to go on the air with his Cuban missile speech, and the Congressional leaders whom he called in for a briefing had presented a thousand objections and no new suggestions. More weary from their wrangling than his own week of deliberations, he remarked to me in disgust as he changed clothes for TV, "If they want this —— job, they can have it."

But moments later he was once again full of determination and drive; and at all other times he made clear his pride of office. When I handed him a letter from my eight-year-old son Eric, who volunteered the information that he liked the White House and would like to live there someday, the President wrote on it in reply: "So do I . . . sorry, Eric, you'll have to wait your turn." When asked at a press conference, in reference to his brother Teddy's comment on the unattractive burdens of the office, "whether, if you had to do it over again, you would work for the Presidency and whether you can recommend the job to others," he replied, "Well, the answer . . . [to] the first is Yes, and [to] the second is No, I don't recommend it to others—at least for a while."

Without minimizing the difficulties of the office, he made clear in a variety of other press conferences and interviews that he was very happy in his work:

> This job is interesting. . . . It represents a chance to exercise your judgment on matters of importance. . . . I find the work rewarding . . . the Presidency provides some happiness (under Aristotle's definition). . . . There are a lot of satisfactions to the Presidency. . . . You have an opportunity to do something about all the problems . . . and if what you do is useful and successful . . . that is a great satisfaction. . . . This is a damned good job.

Life was not all satisfaction and happiness, even in a damned good job, but it was personal adversity that affected him more deeply than any political attack or policy setback. He wept over the death of his infant son Patrick, the first child born to the wife of a President in office in this century. The President, more at home and involved with his children in the White House than he had ever been before, had looked forward with special pleasure to the arrival of this child; and he seemed even more broken than Jacqueline when a lung ailment took Patrick less than two days after his premature birth in August, 1963. "He wouldn't take his hands off that little coffin," said Cardinal Cushing, who presided at the Mass. "I was afraid he'd carry it right out with him."

For the grieving father, rushing in vain to reach his wife's side before the baby was born, then flying back and forth between her hospital bed on Cape Cod and the Boston hospital to which Patrick had been taken for special treatment, those few days were like a grisly nightmare. But he was due to send to the Senate that week his special message on the Nuclear Test Ban Treaty—a message of hope—and nearly every day during his ordeal it was necessary for him to discuss the message with me by telephone in a downcast but factual manner. Presidents have little time for formal mourning, and President Kennedy was soon back in the swirl of office. But he also took time out the following October for an unpublicized visit to Patrick's grave.

Earlier in his term another family tragedy had struck, and this, too, temporarily broke his spirits but not his stride. On Thanksgiving, 1961, he expressed concern to me about his father's health, and the following month he received word in the White House that the Ambassador had suffered a stroke in Palm Beach. Moving swiftly to the Presidential plane, "Air Force One," he asked me to continue en route the review of the 1962 legislative planning we had barely begun.

It was with difficulty and incredible self-discipline that he engrossed himself in our work on that sorrowful flight. The mutual bonds of affection and admiration between father and son had not diminished in the White House, and Joseph P. Kennedy's subsequent inability to communicate freely to his son removed a welcomed source of encouragement and cheer for the President. Saddened to see the old man suffering both physical and mental agony in his permanently crippled and virtually speechless condition, the President later wondered out loud about the decision facing doctors who work desperately to keep alive any man hovering between a peaceful death and a fraction of life. In the months that followed his father's stroke, he continued to return in full all the love and loyalty his father had for so long lavished upon him, frequently talking to (not really with) the Ambassador by telephone, visiting him at Palm Beach and Cape Cod, and inviting him for long stays at the White House.

His own physical pain was the other chief source of personal stress. More fit than ever in every other way, a picture of health and vitality, he was still plagued by his aching back. The rocking chair was moved over from his Senate office and more rockers were acquired, becoming a nationally recognized symbol of the traditional values, reflective patience and practical informality prevailing in the White House. A cloth brace, three hot baths a day, rest on a heating pad after lunch, prescribed calisthenics before supper and daily swims in the heated White House pool all helped, but the pain was almost always with him. "He never complained," said Dave Powers. "You . . . might have an idea by some of his silences that maybe his back was bothering him, but he never ever complained."

His injury was aggravated when he planted a tree in the capital city of Canada on his May, 1961, visit. It was not until later that month, as I watched him ease himself slowly and carefully into an ornate bathtub upon his arrival in Paris, that I realized the pain he was in. Back in Washington, he was forced to use crutches around the White House, although, still opposed to evidencing any physical weakness, he stoically put them away when talking to outsiders or departing the grounds. But he had to deliver one speech seated in 1961, and had to cancel a few others.

At times the pain was worse, at times better. "It depends," he said, "on the weather—political and otherwise." But at all times he approached climbing stairs, stooping and lifting somewhat gingerly. He was cautious about his annual ceremonial duty of throwing out the first baseball of the professional season, but never satisfied with less than the best in any endeavor, he secretly practiced on the White House lawn. He golfed more rarely than he desired and lifted his children less frequently than both he and they would have liked. The Presidency was by no means the same physical endurance contest as the campaign. But the Kennedy Presidency required of both the man and his aides long hours, relentless activity and steady concentration, and John Kennedy rarely slowed his pace to ease his pain.[1]

The rigorous series of calisthenics he practiced daily under the direction of Dr. Hans Kraus of New York after the 1961 injury helped immensely. They not only strengthened his back but made him more muscular and trim. At times his vanity was still hurt by pictures showing him puffy in the face, but his weight finally stabilized at 175 pounds. He dieted frequently, once asking the chef to cut out his favorite chocolate soufflé until a forthcoming television appearance was over. He also acquired a few more lines on his face and a little more gray in his hair, and, as Dave Powers put it, "he looked more like a President every day." To save time both his barber and his tailor worked on him in his office.

He still favored dark-colored, lightweight, two-button suits, with a monogrammed shirt and a PT-boat tie clasp. Not surprisingly, most of his aides did also. Even at Palm Beach and Hyannis Port he felt that the dignity of his office required him to don a coat and usually a tie whenever he was to be photographed at work, and on more than one occasion he handed out coats and ties to his aides before our pictures were taken with him. (He also smilingly chided us at Paris that our button-down collars were out of place in that capital of fashion.) Averell Harriman, reporting at Hyannis Port on his return from Moscow and the Test Ban Treaty negotiations, was touched when the President insisted on his taking a swim, and a Kennedy shirt and tie, before meeting the press.

Neither back pain nor bad luck could ever dim his sense of humor. The public saw part of it at his press conferences. The press saw more of it at their various annual dinners, where he invariably stole the show. Around the White House we saw it every day, on every subject. It was never forced or feigned, and far funnier than it was in public. It flowed naturally, good-naturedly, casually. It was dry, wry, ironic and irreverent. His humor was largely an integral part of his own thinking rather than a deliberate attempt to amuse others. He did not pause before his witticisms for effect or afterward for appreciation, but simply dropped them as part of his comments. Sometimes one could see the eyes twinkling and the smile breaking as he deliberated whether a particularly biting barb should be cast.

At no time did he show disrespect for his office or country, but no other subject was spared. The Attorney General and others thought it

[1] On the plane back from his exhausting barnstorming tour of Europe in 1963, he told me his back was better than ever and speculated that giving vent to all his energies and feelings in some forty speeches in ten days had relieved the tension.

almost sacrilegious for him to parody his own solemn Inaugural at a Democratic anniversary dinner, but he went ahead:

> We observe tonight not a celebration of freedom but a victory of party. For we have sworn to pay off the same party debt our forebears ran up nearly a year and three months ago. . . . If the Democratic Party cannot be helped by the many who are poor, it cannot be saved by the few who are rich.

He kidded his staff, his wife, his brothers, his critics, his opponents, foreign leaders, Congressional leaders, columnists ("I'd rather be Fleesonized than Krocked"), everyone without regard to race, rank or relationship. His delicate relations with Prime Minister Diefenbaker of Canada could not restrain him from saying, upon his arrival in Ottawa, that he was less reluctant to try a few words in French after listening to the Prime Minister try it. He good-naturedly razzed Pierre Salinger about his weight, Evelyn Lincoln about her Methodism and me about an obviously borrowed dinner jacket. When Ken Galbraith complained that the otherwise favorable *New York Times* profile of him as the new Ambassador to India had called him arrogant, the President responded, "Why not? Everybody else does."

Above all, he could still laugh at himself—at the solemnities he pronounced, at the praise he received, at the setbacks he suffered. He still took his problems seriously but never himself.

"I used to wonder, when I was a member of the House," he told one dinner in the presence of the previous Democratic President, "how President Truman got in so much trouble. Now I am beginning to get the idea. It is not difficult."

Addressing the 1961 graduating class of the Naval Academy at Annapolis, he might well have dwelt nostalgically on his days in the Navy, or lectured them sternly on the fight then raging over the military in politics. Instead, he was himself. "In the past," he told the Midshipmen,

> I have had some slight contact with this service, though I never did reach the state of professional and physical perfection where I could hope that anyone would ever mistake me for an Annapolis graduate. . . . I know you are constantly warned . . . not to mix . . . in politics. I should point out, however . . . that my rapid rise from a reserve lieutenant of uncertain standing to Commander in Chief has been because I did not follow that very good advice.

He assumed that we all would have to live indefinitely with national and international tensions and imperfect humans and solutions, and he was blessed with qualities which helped him to prepare to make the best of it. The discipline of his mind and emotions was of a piece with his self-knowledge and his knowledge of his time and trials. He never self-consciously thought of himself as "courageous," but he lived by the Hemingway definition with which he had opened *Profiles*: "grace under pressure." (He could even rib that definition, saying it also described a girl he knew by that name.)

The sobering education and searing experiences of the Presidency obviously contributed to his growth but did not otherwise change him. Looking back, I am even more amazed that the White House did not alter his personal qualities. Upon his election, everyone about him automatically became more deferential, his life became more privileged and powerful, his every word became history. Yet he remained natural, candid, measuring his own deeds and words with doubt and amusement as well as pride. He entertained no delusions about himself or others, neither affecting nor accepting any pretensions of grandeur.

As usual, some mistook his humor, gaiety and gentle urbanity for a lack of depth, and some mistook his cool calculation of the reasonable for a lack of commitment. But his wit was merely an ornament to the earnest expressions that followed, and his reason reinforced his deep conviction and ideals.

HABITS OF WORK

President Kennedy's day at the White House did not begin at any heroic predawn hour. Awakening around 7:30 A.M., he quickly read the morning papers and often placed calls on their contents. Throughout the day and night, as more newspapers and reports came in, more Presidential phone calls or terse memoranda would follow, inquiring, requesting, suggesting. Action was always expected as soon as possible. He was on the telephone, according to one estimate, more than fifty times in an average day, with a large portion of the calls taking place in the Mansion before and after his hours in the office.

After a bath, shaving as always in the tub to save time, breakfast was around 8:45—sometimes with his family if they were available, sometimes in bed with the newspapers, and once or twice a week on official business, with legislative leaders, staff members or others.

Between 9:00 and 9:30 A.M. he arrived in his office, checked his mail, read a three-thousand-word CIA briefing and plunged into the day's round of conferences. In addition to the official calendar of appointments released to the press, he had a far larger number of off-the-record meetings and a still larger number of informal talks with staff aides. Daily events often required new meetings to be squeezed into the schedule. During the first few weeks, before the crush of crises began, he had received far more outsiders—politicians, newsmen, friends— just as he had found more time to visit friends around the city. In later months his work increasingly confined him to his office, but he still managed to avoid reliance on official channels of information only. "I sit in the White House," he said, "and what I read . . . and . . . see is the sum total of what I hear and learn. So the more people I can see, or the wider I can expose [my mind] to different ideas, the more effective [I] can be as President."

He refused to take the chance that his subordinates were screening out criticisms, alternatives or information on his or their errors. His compulsive curiosity was a valuable Presidential instinct. He made certain that he had the final decision on whom he would see and what he would read. He made certain that Bundy's office received copies of every important cable moving in and out of State, Defense and CIA (and he arranged to receive some cables directly from individuals such as Galbraith). Each department made a weekly report on its activities in addition to the usual mountain of memoranda and messages. "I never heard of a President who wanted to know so much," said one long-time career servant.

Ambassadors paying formal calls of farewell were interrogated as well as instructed. News interviewers found themselves being interviewed. Officials and journalists returning from overseas tours were invited to inform him fully on their findings. His wife was encouraged to report in writing on her observations of American officialdom in India and Pakistan (and those reports held back nothing by way of either praise or criticism). In preparation for Budget decisions, he toured firsthand several military, space and atomic energy installations. (His helicopter pilot had difficulty persuading the President that they should not attempt to land on a fourteen-hundred-foot crater at the Nevada atomic test site.)

He kept meetings as brief as the subject permitted, many no more than fifteen minutes, very few running over an hour, but when necessary sitting for several hours. For long afternoon meetings, he often ordered coffee served to all hands. He kept his own comments to a minimum and often cut short others, no matter how important or friendly, who were dealing with generalities or repeating the obvious. Frequently he saw their point long before they had finished. Focusing full attention upon each speaker, even while doodling on a pad before him, he had a remarkable ability to absorb detail while keeping in view the larger picture. When he considered a subject exhausted or a decision final, he would gather up all his papers as a sign that the meeting was over and, if this hint was not taken by persistent conferees, suddenly rise to his feet to say good-bye.

Despite these efforts, despite a new-found desire to be punctual, and despite Ken O'Donnell's deliberate interruption of less crucial visits that were running overtime, the President was often an hour behind schedule by the end of his day. It was always an exhaustingly full and long day, as he remained in the office until 7:30, 8:00 or even 8:30 P.M., sometimes returning after his customarily late dinner, and usually reading reports and memoranda in the Mansion until midnight. Even when he had guests for dinner and a movie, he would often slip away after fifteen minutes of the film to work, and then rejoin them when it was over. More than once we worked in his West Wing oval office or in his bedroom or oval study in the Mansion until well past midnight. More than once after a late dinner I would invite guests to view the Presidential office only to find him there going over mail or other documents. Saturdays, when he was in Washington, were usually a shorter working day, and on Sundays no regular office hours were kept. But it all added up to an average of forty-five to fifty-five hours of work weekly in his office and still more over in the Mansion. "He lived at such a pace," his wife has said, "because he wished to know it all."

He helped himself maintain such a pace by wisely breaking his day for two hours or so at lunch. Around 1:30, and, if possible, a second time in the evening, he would take a fifteen-minute swim in the heated (90-degree) White House pool, usually with Dave Powers. Even at the height of the Cuban crisis he made time for his dip in the pool. Listening to recorded show music in the background, exchanging sports stories or anecdotes with Powers, he regenerated his energies and ideas, often giving Dave a list of messages he wanted delivered during the lunch hour. The swim, a rubdown and his calisthenics were followed by lunch—occasionally official affairs with foreign dignitaries, editors, or business or labor leaders, but more often private. He continued to read while lunching if he were alone—and then he would read or nap in bed while easing his back on a hotpad. Between three and four o'clock he was back in his office or on his way to a press conference, refreshed and ready to act.

Nor was every office hour spent on matters of state. His conversations with visitors sometimes turned to a kind of nineteenth-century court gossip about public figures and private lives, astonishing strangers from all fields with his curiosity about the personalities and politics of their professions, his knowledge of high and low goings-on, and his willingness to spend time in lighthearted conversation. He found time in 1963 to plan a surprise birthday party for Dave Powers and to attend one the staff had planned for him.

Those parties typified the rapport between the President and his staff. He was informal without being chummy, hard-driving but easy-mannered, interested in us as people without being patronizing. While neither he nor we ever forgot that he bore the responsibilities of leadership, he treated us more as colleagues or associates than employees. He made clear that we were there to give advice as well as to take orders. All of us, no matter how long or how well we had known him, addressed him only as "Mr. President," and all of us referred to him in private as well as public only as "the President." (I found this a bit awkward when talking with his wife, but not with the Attorney General, who largely followed the same practice.)

Above all, the President was remarkably accessible. He could not afford to be bothered by insignificant details and did not like listening to whiners, but no staff member, Cabinet member or Congressman with important business to lay before him had any difficulty seeing him alone. "You might have to wait until late in the night," as Maxwell Taylor said, "but if you sent word you needed to see the President you got to see him."

O'Donnell and Salinger—and usually Bundy, O'Brien and myself—were in and out of the oval office several times a day. No appointment was necessary for most of these quick informal visits, but we did not interrupt other conferences, and O'Donnell often suggested when we might catch him between appointments. Many times I would walk in to find the President totally absorbed in reading a report or writing a letter, and he would completely concentrate on that effort, unbothered by my presence, until he had completed it. Other times I would obtain answers to a series of questions or report on new developments as I walked with him over to his quarters before lunch or dinner, or talked with him as he changed clothes or lay in bed. On rare occasions he would come to my office down the hall from his.

There was no pattern to the number of times I would see him in a given day. Most days one or more of his formally scheduled meetings involved my participation. Often I would be summoned to his office by telephone. Frequently I would catch him between meetings or before lunch to review quickly a number of smaller problems. Only a few words from him on each topic would usually suffice.

Around 7:30 in the evening, after the last of his official conferences, was often the best time for me to drop in and raise miscellaneous matters not covered during the day. He was usually in a relaxed mood then, sometimes in his shirt sleeves, sometimes watching the news on TV or signing mail while we talked, sometimes striding out to Mrs. Lincoln's office to read whatever was on the top of her desk. He was at his reflective best in those hours, relating some crisis or anecdote of the day, asking me to check into some new problem or suggestion, or raising some question on which he sought my opinion. One evening, for example, he was absorbed in the task of selecting names for new

Polaris submarines. He was amused that the Quakers had objected to William Penn, a pacifist hero, and that the Pentagon had objected to those Indian chiefs who had fought against the U.S. The Navy felt that the name of Chief Red Cloud had particularly unfortunate international connotations. Those talks were among my most treasured, and I often dropped in at that hour with only the flimsiest excuse of official business.

The same time period was utilized by other aides unable to see him during the day, and it was not uncommon for two or three of us to be standing simultaneously at his desk presenting problems. His daughter Caroline and son John, Jr. would also frequently drop in at this hour for a prebedtime romp with their father and a piece of candy from Mrs. Lincoln's desk, just as they sometimes would during the day. Their father, depending upon his work, would either encourage their questions and antics or continue his work oblivious of them until finished. At times he would introduce them to his guests, Caroline curtsying and John giving a little bow, and then ask them to wait in the outer office, where his daughter might draw pictures while his son played with the toys kept for him by Mrs. Lincoln.

John Kennedy, Jr. (contrary to popular impression, his parents did not call him "John-John" and in fact disliked the nickname) liked to crawl through the "secret door" in the side of his father's desk or play somewhat dangerously with the works of scrimshaw (finely engraved whale tooth) which ornamented the office. The entire room, in fact, had been redecorated by the President and his wife with a nautical motif. Ship models graced the shelves, and pictures of ships and naval battles dominated the walls. A whaling harpoon and the sword and flag of Commodore John Barry stood on one side of his desk, facing the American and purple-and-gold Presidential flags on the other. Even his desk, discovered by Jacqueline in a White House storage room, had been made in the nineteenth century of battleship timbers; and on it was the coconut shell on which Kennedy had carved the message that rescued his crew and himself. Family photographs, a picture painted by his wife and bird models of two Cape Cod sandpipers varied the decor.

The desk was usually disordered during the day, as was the table crowded with newspapers and magazines behind it. Its other fixed items included a metal prop for his daily schedule, a black alligator desk set presented by General De Gaulle, the usual paraphernalia for writing and, between two bookends, specially leather-bound copies of his five books: the private volume he edited about his brother, *As We Remember Joe; Why England Slept; Profiles in Courage;* and his two books of speeches, *The Strategy of Peace* and *To Turn the Tide* (publication of *The Burden and the Glory* was not completed while he was President).

The whole White House crackled with excitement under John Kennedy, but the soundproof oval office, the very center and stimulant of all the action, symbolized his own peace of mind. The tall French windows opened onto the completely renovated flower garden of which he was inordinately proud. Even on gloomy days the light pouring in through those windows on the blue rug and freshly painted cream-colored walls bathed his ash splint rocking chair and two beige couches, brought in for more friendly talks, in a quiet glow. He tried the fireplace only once and, to his embarrassment, promptly filled the entire West Wing with smoke. (I rushed in offering to save George Washington's portrait.)

RELAXATION

In a larger sense, the President's office is wherever the President may be. For unlike the Congress and Supreme Court, the Presidency never recesses or adjourns. Unlike the arrangement in most departments and states, his absence from the country does not make his running mate Acting President. Wherever he went, Kennedy was linked by telephone to the White House switchboard, guarded by the Secret Service, and discreetly followed by one of an alternating team of Army warrant officers carrying in a slender black case the secret codes by which the Presidential order for nuclear retaliation would be given. Wherever he went, he received the same daily CIA briefing from a military or other aide and read most of the same daily newspapers, which were flown in to him if necessary. Wherever he went, he took with him the bulky black alligator briefcase he had carried since his first days in the House—the same bag he often took over to the Mansion in the evening—bulging with whatever he and his staff felt he needed to read by way of mail, magazines, books, briefing memos and assorted dispatches and documents. During absences of forty-eight hours or more, additional materials were flown to him regularly. Wherever he went, he kept in constant touch with Washington, signed bills and Executive Orders, and conferred on or contemplated current crises.

Despite these continuing burdens, a break in the routines helped prevent them from breaking him. The President thought it best for his family life and personal outlook to get away from the White House, when possible, for at least twenty-four hours on a weekend, for the whole weekend in the summer and for a longer holiday on occasion. In the summer, and occasionally in the fall, he traveled to his home at Hyannis Port on Cape Cod, with additional visits to the summer home of his wife's family in Newport, Rhode Island. (The persistent recurrence of weekend rain and fog at the Cape in 1961 brought on a debate, only partly humorous, between the First Lady and her father-in-law about whether the climates of the two communities differed.) In the winter and spring Palm Beach was the site for the longer stays; and for a brief weekend respite the Kennedys would sometimes use Camp David, the official Presidential retreat in the Maryland Hills, or the rented estate Glenora in the Virginia countryside. A home of their own in the same area was built in 1963.

During these family weekends the President, when it was time for play, could, whatever the strains of the moment, devote every inch of mind and body to leisure as intensively as he had to work, completely shaking off and shutting out the worries of the world beyond.

When at the seaside, he took long walks and swims, played with his children in the sand, devoured light as well as heavy reading and went boating with his father and family. He held to no official schedule, alternating work and play, reading and resting, talking to his children and talking to one of us on the telephone or in person. Occasionally I accompanied him to Cape Cod or Palm Beach for working weekends, and Salinger and a military aide always traveled with him on such trips. But, except for his daily briefings, he tried to keep Glenora and Camp David free from official visitors.

If we were working at Cape Cod he usually asked me to meet him at his house after church. Having changed into sport clothes, he would work over my latest draft or memorandum in his living room or on the back porch, usually smoking a cigar and sometimes, just before supper, drinking a daiquiri. On a very few occasions we worked during his daily boat ride, lunching on fish chowder and other preparations of the White House assistant chef, watching his wife water-ski, and lounging on the fantail talking in a lighthearted manner about people more than problems.

He relaxed best of all on the water. Although he sailed less frequently than he had in his younger days, and had perhaps forgotten the channels, judging from his embarrassment one day upon running aground on a sandbar, he loved the sea, as he had since childhood. (When he first sailed with his brother Joe, his father recalled, they were still "so small you couldn't see their heads and it looked from the shore as if the boat were empty.") On board either the family or Presidential cruiser, the President read history or biography or fiction, chatted with family and friends, waved at passing boats, watched local sailing races and enjoyed the distance between himself and the Secret Service. Birthday outings or weekends—his father's, his wife's, his children's, his own—were very special, for the President could be quite sentimental about presents and reunions. At night he would watch a movie, though he was increasingly inclined to walk out on bad ones, and in Hyannis Port he would each weekend drive his children, and whichever of their twenty or so cousins were around, to the local candy shop.

Sundays included not only attending church but watching the political panel shows on television, as though he did not get his fill of that during the week. When I appeared at his request on *Meet the Press* at a delicate time—between the Cuban crisis and the 1962 election—the program had no sooner ended than the telephone rang in the studio. "They didn't lay a glove on you," said the President from Glenora.

When his back permitted, he played golf, often immediately upon arrival at whichever weekend home was near a course. Although neither his back nor his duties permitted much practice, he was a natural golfer and a good one, shooting in the low 80's. Red Fay told of the game in May of 1960 at Cypress Point, California, when the candidate pleaded with a drive headed straight for the hole not to drop in. The publicity from a hole-in-one, he said, would not help a Democratic candidate at a time when Presidential golfing was a subject of not always friendly comment. He never used the putting green Eisenhower installed behind the White House, and was amused by the children's forts dug in the sand trap and the toys planted near the cup. At least once, however, he was out in the back driving golf balls toward the Washington Monument.

His friends have related how he fancied himself to be Ben Hogan, Arnold Palmer or some other professional champion whenever he swung a golf club (or Y. A. Tittle, the famed New York Giants quarterback, whenever he picked up a football). "He never started a game [of golf]," said British Ambassador David Ormsby-Gore, a frequent partner, "without working out a very complicated system of bets" in a discussion that usually lasted through the first three holes, with all bets doubling on the ninth.

The Ormsby-Gores (later Lord and Lady Harlech) were often guests of the Kennedys at Cape Cod, Camp David and Palm Beach, but their discussions rarely centered on British-U.S. affairs. They had been personal friends for many years, and the President felt no obligation either to transform all his personal relationships to an official level or to transfer all his professional relationships to the social level. I saw them socially on comparatively rare occasions, without the slightest embarrassment about this on either side.

When he was not working, he and Jacqueline liked having people around who were cheerful, amusing, energetic, informed and informal. While the friends mentioned in Chapter I also served as sources and sounding boards for independent ideas and information, they sought, with rare exception, no influence or favors, and they were all as candid and casual with the Commander in Chief as they had been when he was a Congressman. He found, after the first few weeks, that it was difficult for him as President to take walks with an old friend around the Washington Monument or to drop in on one as casually as he had dropped in at Joe Alsop's his first night as President (where he hungrily devoured terrapin soup, the only food that could be located, while discussing the experiences of Inaugural Day). But he did continue his practice of calling his old friends by telephone at all hours of the day and night.

HIS FAMILY

No friend ever drew as close to John Kennedy, or contributed so much to his spirit and strength, as his wife, his daughter and his son. He would rather eat fettucine with them in the family dining room than preside over the most important formal banquet in the State Dining Room. Whatever cares or crises pressed upon him, he kept time free for his family and kept his family life free from the strains of office. He deeply loved his wife and children; he was deeply proud of them; and their love and pride in turn provided him with both essential relief from his burdens and additional reason to bear them.

His children often played on the equipment newly set up on the lawn behind the Mansion, and that was also the play area for a small White House school which the First Lady organized to make life more normal for Caroline and John. Whenever he saw either of them playing out on the lawn or walking with one of their several dogs, the President would interrupt all but the most formal conversations in his office, stand in the outside door and clap his hands until both children and dogs came rushing over. Awkwardly stooping down, he ignored pain and passers-by to pick them up, his face more relaxed in those moments than I had ever seen it with any adult.

Back in the days when he was traveling the long, hard road that had led him to the White House, John Kennedy had had too little time to spend with Caroline (whose first word was "plane"); and John, Jr. was not born until his father was President-elect. Consequently it was in the White House, and on their holidays together, that the President truly discovered his children. How best to rear children, a subject of no interest to him in earlier days when his friends and siblings raised it about their offspring, suddenly became one of his favorite topics of discussion.

Like their parents, both Caroline and John, Jr. were unusually bright, alert and constantly inquisitive, bursting with restless energy, reserved with newcomers but always friendly. While legend has already made them sound more like angels than normal children, they were as capable of mischief and misbehavior in the White House as any other children in any other house; and their mother, referring during the campaign to the books of Kennedy supporter Dr. Benjamin Spock, said she found it "a relief to know that other people's children are as bad . . . at the same age."

President Kennedy, that intellectual, sophisticated man, considered cold by his critics and complicated by his admirers, possessed a gift for communicating with children—with his children, with my children, with all children. He never talked down to them, and they always understood him. "He talked to me," confided one aide's thirteen-year-old son to his diary, "with an air of business-like equality." At the same time he was realistically aware of how limited an adult's influence is in the small child's world. Secretary McNamara liked to tell of the time he saw the President accost Caroline in the midst of the Cuban crisis just before her supper hour. "Caroline," he said, "have you been eating candy?" She ignored him. The question was repeated and it was again ignored. Finally, summoning up his full dignity as Commander in Chief, he asked his daughter, "Caroline, answer me. Have you been eating candy—yes, no or maybe?"

Similarly, when he was accompanied by John, Jr. one morning to our pre-press conference breakfast, he found his son's continued presence unbusinesslike but not easily ended. After shaking hands and bowing all around with a gusto worthy of Honey Fitz himself, John took over a proffered chair and very nearly took over the meeting. His father's suggestions to leave, accompanied by bribes to take him to the office later, were loudly resisted. Deciding to ignore him, the President opened his request for questions with the usual "What have we got today?" The first answer was John's: "*I've* got a glass of water." Accepting defeat, the President sent for the children's long-time nurse, an unflappable English "nanny" who soon persuaded John that he should join his sister. "Marvelous," said the President, "there would have been a storm of tears if I had tried that."

Caroline Kennedy quickly became a national figure—tottering somewhat unsteadily into her father's Palm Beach press briefing in her mother's shoes, offering a rose to India's Nehru, wandering into the press lobby to report that her father was "sitting upstairs with his shoes and socks off not doing anything," emerging from church with her large rag doll in her father's custody, wading into a friend's swimming pool over her head, and asking Speaker Rayburn why he didn't have any hair. She took to horses like her mother, to the sea like her father and to books like both. Together with John, Jr., she met more heads of state than most Cabinet members, often watched ceremonies on the White House lawn from upstairs (once with cries of "bang" to echo each volley in a twenty-one-gun salute) and one hot day took a dip in the South Lawn fountain.

Her father, who gave up calling her "Buttons" when she acted so grown-up at age four, was fascinated by her retentive memory, a trait both he and his wife had long possessed, and as she grew older, the bedtime stories at which he excelled were supplemented by the poetry which he delighted in hearing her repeat. Addressing on the South Lawn a group dedicated to preserving the White House and other historical buildings, he had occasion to quote spontaneously one of the couplets he had taught his daughter and which he had long promised her he would use in a speech:

> *Safe upon the solid rock the ugly houses stand:*
> *Come and see my shining palace built upon the sand!*

He correctly attributed these lines to Edna St. Vincent Millay. But later he told me with some embarrassment that he had almost said Emily Dickinson and that Caroline's memory was better than his.

Both parents, the wife more than the husband, worried about the effects of too much publicity on both children, the daughter more than the son. In the hectic preinaugural days, watching over his daughter between appointments and task forces while Jacqueline was in the hospital with infant John, the President-elect suggested to the reporters and photographers who followed Caroline's every move that it was "time we retired her." But this was not easily done in the White House, with the press and public wanting more and more pictures and feature items. Jacqueline came to the conclusion that neither her husband nor his Press Secretary was as concerned as she that publicity would alter the children's attitudes. When I remarked that one authorized article on Caroline of which she was complaining had been regarded as excellent by the President and Salinger, she replied a bit tartly, "Well, *they* are not very good judges, if you ask me."

Providing a normal life for her children and a peaceful home for her husband was only one of Jacqueline Kennedy's contributions to the Kennedy era, but she regarded it as her most important. "It doesn't matter what else you do," she said, "if you don't do that part well, you fail your husband and your children. That really is the role which means the most to me, the one that comes first." No one should have been surprised by her refusal to give more speeches, press interviews and women's receptions. In the campaign candidate Kennedy had avoided mawkish references to his wife, made no pretense of involving her in political and policy decisions, and, even had she not been expecting their son, would not have urged upon her a large campaign role apart from his own. And Jacqueline, when asked about her role in the White House, had replied:

I'll always do anything my husband asks me to do. . . . [But]
I think the major role of the First Lady is to take care of the
President . . . [and] if you bungle raising your children, I don't
think whatever else you do well matters very much.

In the White House husband and wife were very close. His election,
to her surprise, strengthened instead of strained their marriage. Those
were their happiest years. Jacqueline and the children, contrary to her
fears during the campaign, saw more of her husband than ever before,
and he found with her a happiness and love he had never known before.
He became more relaxed, less demanding and very proud of his wife.
Often, as I boarded a helicopter on the White House lawn to begin some
Presidential journey, I would see Jacqueline walking with her husband
to his plane, hand in hand, without regard to the police or politicians
all about them.

She never interfered with his work or volunteered advice on his
decisions, wisely content to let him be concerned with the country's life
while she concerned herself with their family life. She provided not only
a welcome change from his political and official chores but a fresh
perspective on the world as well. Equipped with a gentle satirical wit
of her own, she could deflate any pompous Presidential posture he did
not immediately deflate himself. Refusing to let either her tastes or
time be swept away by a sea of strong-minded Kennedys, she gave her
husband new interests and tastes to round out the old, even as she
studied history and golf to keep up with him. They learned from each
other.

Like her husband, Jacqueline remained essentially unchanged
by either adulation or adversity. She was herself at all times, even when
not everyone wanted her to be herself. During the campaign we had
received constant advice on how Jacqueline Kennedy should be more
of a politician like Eleanor Roosevelt or more homespun like Bess
Truman. Her clothes, it was said, were too expensive, her hair-do too
fancy, her interests too rarefied. Even in her first months in the White
House she was criticized for not addressing countless women's groups,
for not equaling Mrs. Khrushchev's response to a women's peace petition,
and for not devoting more time to a hundred worthy causes and cru-
sades.

But Jacqueline Kennedy, sensitive but strong-willed, so long as her
husband would not be harmed by her decision, had no desire to be
anyone else. By maintaining her own unique identity and provocative
personality, she never bored or wearied the President, and had full
time for him and her children. As the Attorney General once commented,
"Jack knows she'll never greet him with 'What's new in Laos?'" In
addition, by continuing with her "fancy ways" and fox hunting, her

water skiing and antique hunting, by refusing to appear more folksy at political rallies or less glamorous in poorer nations, by carrying her pursuit of quality and beauty into White House decorations and dinners, she brought great pleasure to millions in every land, rich and poor alike. She became a world-wide symbol of American culture and good taste, and offered proof in the modern age that the female sex can succeed by merely remaining feminine.

Her televised tour of the White House was a memorable gift to the American people. No longer bothered by crowds, she became John Kennedy's proudest asset when accompanying him on state visits abroad and on political trips in this country. She also won countless friends for her husband and country on an official trip of her own to India and Pakistan (where she had, as the President told an audience that week, "her first—and last—ride on an elephant") and on quieter vacation visits to the Mediterranean. On the night of November 21, 1963, she told her husband how happily she looked forward to being able to campaign with him in 1964. Earlier that evening, says Dave Powers, the President had asked him for a comparison of crowds between that visit to Houston and the President's previous trip there in 1962. "Just about as many came out to see you as they did on our last visit, Mr. President," replied Dave, "but there were about a hundred thousand more for Jackie." And the President, beaming at his wife, said, "You see, you do help."

The vicious rumors about the President and his wife which had circulated in the campaign recurred from time to time. None angered him more than the report that, as a young man, he had been previously married. "I wouldn't be the last to know *that!*" he said bitterly.

The fact is that Kennedy's own candor and humor, his refusal to take himself too seriously, his constant stimulation of excitement and controversy, his recognition of intellect and art, his assault on myths and complacency, and perhaps even his genuine attachment to his family in an age when some thought that "unsophisticated"—all made possible an unprecedented atmosphere in which the President of the United States and his family could be mimicked, mocked, criticized, insulted and made the subject of countless stories, songs and skits. It was a lively, new and healthy atmosphere, and President Kennedy was willing to take its bad points along with its good.

He was amused, and amusing, about success symbols of this new atmosphere. Asked at a news conference whether he was annoyed by a sometimes funny recording of skits about "The First Family" by a very skillful Kennedy impersonator named Vaughn Meader, the President said, "I listened to Mr. Meader's record, but I thought it sounded more like Teddy than it did me—so *he's* annoyed."

INTELLECTUAL AND CULTURAL REVIVAL

This atmosphere of gaiety and verve was by no means limited to critics and mimics. A wave of intellectual interest and excitement rippled out from the White House. Learning and culture were in style. "The quality of American life," said the President, "must keep pace with the quantity of American goods. This country cannot afford to be materially rich and spiritually poor."

He cared deeply and personally about education, human rights, better health, cleaner cities and greater dignity for the aged. Believing that "A nation reveals itself not only by the men it produces but also by the men it honors," he initiated the new Medal of Freedom Awards as an annual civilian honors list for those who have enriched our society, personally worked on the medal's design, and insisted that awards go to several controversial figures, including some critical of his administration. He kept in touch with Robert Frost, whose poetry had graced his inauguration, visited with him at the White House, corresponded with him through the years and paid a posthumous tribute to him at Amherst. He gave as much attention to French Cultural Affairs Minister André Malraux as he gave to the foreign affairs ministers of many other nations.

The White House became both a showplace and a dwelling place for the distinctive, the creative and the cultivated. It was also, cracked the President to one gathering of intellectuals, "becoming a sort of eating place for artists. But *they* never ask *us* out." At a dinner honoring American Nobel Prize winners, their first official recognition by our government, he announced: "This is the most extraordinary collection of talent . . . that has ever been gathered together at the White House— with the possible exception of when Thomas Jefferson dined alone." One of the Nobel scientists honored, pacifist Linus Pauling, sought to attract attention to his cause by picketing the White House that day. But the President merely congratulated him on expressing his opinions so strongly, and the First Lady chided him that Caroline had asked, "What has Daddy done now?"

State dinners at the White House, I can testify from my few first-hand experiences, had an atmosphere of warmth as well as elegance. Formal protocol was held to a minimum. Changing clothes in my office and walking over, I was given my seat assignment and introduced to my dinner partner by one of the military or social aides. As the guests talked in the East Room, martial music announced the arrival on the staircase of the President and Mrs. Kennedy and the guests of honor. A receiving line formed, the President usually laughing at being formally introduced to me by a military aide and adding some humorous twist to my job description as he introduced me to the visiting chief of state.

From my seat well below the salt at dinner, I could observe the President amusing the ladies on either side of him, then knitting his brow as he asked a guest a more serious question, then laughing once again at some bantering exchange. The guests on either side of me were among those personally selected by the President, who used dinner invitations as a means of honoring, influencing, thanking or meeting all kinds of people. Occasionally, the long horseshoe-shaped banquet table was replaced by a cluster of little tables. The food, the wine and the background music were delightful, the toasts short and frequently funny.

After the toasts, we went into the redecorated Red, Green and Blue Rooms of the White House.[2] Fires burned in the fireplaces, flowers filled every niche, and all the guests talked about Jacqueline's transformation of those rooms from a cold museum and hotel lobby into authentic restorations of the best in American history. The President and First Lady moved from group to group, talking informally about newly collected paintings or heirlooms, and joking with me on one occasion about the antique chair which had suddenly cracked and collapsed under the President at our legislative breakfast that morning.

A performance was then presented in the East Room which honored both guests and artists by selecting the best in the nation, including a Shakespeare company (the first in the White House since 1910), a ballet troupe, a musical comedy, opera stars, Frederic March reading from Hemingway, Isaac Stern, Igor Stravinsky and Pablo Casals in his first visit to the White House since playing for Theodore Roosevelt. At the end of the evening, all of us felt we were truly in the First House of the land.

Jacqueline Kennedy acted to preserve the Mansion's greatness for posterity. She obtained legislation from the Congress placing the White House under the National Park Service, permitting unneeded objects to be stored or exhibited in the Smithsonian Institution and preventing the loss or neglect of any heirloom. She appointed a Fine Arts Committee of experts (mostly Republicans) to advise her on historical re-creations and to receive contributions. She established the post of White House Curator. She created a White House Historical Association to publish a guidebook and other pamphlets about the Mansion, its history, its occupants and its contents, and the guidebook (which the President had been warned would be assailed for commercializing the White House) was a one-dollar best-seller which raised still more money for the work of restoration.

2 Jacqueline had been nervous about JFK's reaction to her redoing the Olive Room in white. "I like it," he said, "if you can get away with it."

Nor did she confine herself to the rooms toured by the public. She redid the private living quarters above the first floor to fit her own tastes and family needs with art and furniture of her own choosing. (She and her husband also insisted that the private quarters remain truly private, and a staff member who had taken friends on a tour of the upstairs, even though the Kennedys were absent, was severely reprimanded.) The White House library was restocked and restored with the best in American literature. She rearranged furniture and pictures in the West Wing's offices and Reception Room. She and the President were particularly proud of the once dilapidated Rose Garden which became a blazingly beautiful flower garden.

Kennedy had ambitious plans for beautifying the District of Columbia. With Jefferson's love of architecture, he initiated a master plan for the sweeping redesign of Pennsylvania Avenue between Capitol Hill and the White House. With advice from his wife and Bill Walton, he took action to prevent historic, graceful Lafayette Park, across the street from the White House, from being permanently ruined by modernistic Federal structures on either side.

John and Jacqueline Kennedy had more than an architectural effect on the capital city. They had both lived there throughout most of their adult lives, they were more widely acquainted with its residents than any previous First Family, and they cared deeply about its role and stature.

Some skeptics said that the President was trying to prove that he was for "culture" in the same way that he was for Medicare or Mass Transit. Many artists, on the other hand, looked upon Kennedy as one of their own. Neither, in my view, was wholly right.

Clearly he was an intellectual, if that term has any solid meaning, although many of his fellow intellectuals would have disputed that conclusion almost as vehemently as he. He meditated, but on action, not philosophy. His was a directed intelligence, never spent on the purely theoretical, always applied to the concrete. He sought truth in order to act on it. His mind was more critical and analytical than creative, but it was better balanced by humor, practicality and even profanity than that of the typical intellectual.

Typical intellectuals, in fact, were rarely among his closest friends. He preferred the Waltons and Bundys and Galbraiths of this world, whose interests were not confined to their artistic or intellectual specialties. But he enjoyed the exchange of specific facts and ideas with almost anyone from whom he could learn.

To be sure, his own artistic talents and interests were limited. He had dabbled briefly in oil painting after his 1955 back operation, and some of the results, hung in his home, were considered good,

But he felt he had "no gift" for it, soon tired of it and turned to more active pursuits. Nor could he sing, although at times, when the spirit (or, more likely, spirits) moved him, he was known to render a passable version of "Won't You Come Home, Bill Bailey." In Dorchester, Massachusetts, on the last night of his 1958 campaign, too tired to present another speech to an already solid audience, he instead presented the three Kennedy brothers singing "Heart of My Heart." They were awful.

His wife and his curiosity drew him to several cultural fields, but not in depth. He had a strong feeling for architecture, but pretended no expertness. He became interested in French period furniture, but deferred to Jacqueline's judgment. He bought some ancient pieces of sculpture but was more impressed by their antiquity than their form.

In general his respect for artistic excellence exceeded his appreciation. He had no interest in opera, dozed off at symphony concerts and was bored by ballet. His taste in records ran from Broadway show tunes such as *Camelot* to romantic ballads to "Irish Sing Along." In earlier days our Senate office, indeed the whole Senate Office Building, was enlivened once a year by a visiting Bostonian whom he induced to sing "Danny Boy." (His wife once teased him that the only music he apparently liked was "Hail to the Chief.") He liked stage shows, but preferred musicals and comedies to heavy drama. He liked movies such as *Casablanca* and *Spartacus* but nothing too arty or actionless. He liked the seascapes and ship scenes hung in his office, and the George Catlin paintings of Western scenes he placed in his living quarters, and, according to Walton, he liked Impressionists.

He was genuinely interested in sports and enjoyed meeting leading athletes in his office as much as artists. He had championship boxing matches, available to the public only on closed circuit television, piped into the White House, and he once delayed leaving for a more "cultural" event until a final knockout had been scored. Football, both college and professional, was his favorite sport. He enjoyed his annual ceremony opening the professional baseball season, but he remarked to me after one such outing that "Baseball is an awfully slow-moving game."

His reading is best summed up by an incident related by a White House visitor who noticed, amidst the official volumes and weighty histories on the President's shelves, a book by Abel Green, editor of the entertainment trade newspaper *Variety*. Assuming it was there by error, for comparatively few politicians or public officials had heard of either the magazine or its editor, he later asked the President what a book by Mr. Abel Green was doing in his bookcase; to which Kennedy punned in reply, "Don't you think a President is entitled to variety?"

Variety was the keynote of his reading habits. Despite the volume of newspapers, magazines and memoranda he devoured daily, he continued in the White House to read a surprising number of books. History, biography and current affairs dominated the list. He was willing to quote poetry in his speeches (but only occasionally, and never more than a few strong and simple lines) and he liked to teach it to Caroline and read it aloud to his wife. ("I always thought that was his Celtic side," said Jacqueline, pointing to the poetry anthologies in their sitting room.) Novels and mysteries were relatively rare in his reading, but for relief from the rigors of his office he sometimes turned to the fantastic escapades and escapes of Ian Fleming's delightfully exaggerated British Secret Agent, James Bond. ("Why," the President was heard to remark after the Bay of Pigs, "couldn't this have happened to James Bond?") *Talleyrand, Marlborough* and *Melbourne* remained favorites. He studied *The Guns of August,* an account of the origins of the First World War, as a warning to his own generation.

Variety was also the keynote of all his interests and tastes. He liked Schlesinger's books as well as Ian Fleming's. He liked meeting the Jerome Robbins dance group and heavyweight champion Floyd Patterson. He was interested in the worlds of Carl Sandburg and Frank Sinatra. He could enjoy communicating at the level of the Bundy brothers and the Cassini brothers. His offhand observations could be profound and profane. He could laugh at quips from Ken Galbraith and Dave Powers. He was amused to learn one summer that his press aide's son was going to music camp and his cultural aide's son to baseball camp. He felt equally at home with Italian-American sopranos and Irish-American politicians.

But whatever limits there may have been to John Kennedy's own artistic talents and interests, they in no way limited his respect for cultural achievement or his sincerity in promoting it nationally. Nor did he promote culture for the sake of appearances or for the sake of politics.

His effort, to be sure, had political advantages—which were not lost on this highly political President—just as his Academic Advisory Committee in 1959-1960 had political advantages. It was not the endorsements and entertainment which artistic celebrities could provide in future campaigns. That was never a reason. More important was the fact that liberal Democrats, reformers, wealthy contributors and independent Republicans were most often among the culturally minded. They warmed to an intellectual President who patronized the arts when his position on fiscal and other matters might well have cooled them. Nor was his view of art limited to its interest for the elite. The President frequently sought statistics on how many Americans (i.e., voters) played musical instruments, visited art galleries and museums or in some other way participated in our cultural life.

His desire to encourage the arts, to give recognition and support and leadership, was not hypocritical merely because he was not more artistic, just as his attack on poverty was no less sincere because he was wealthy. The artists and scholars whom he invited to the White House recognized that he was honoring their work, not merely using their names—that he recognized this nation's debt to its artists for their contribution to our national heritage. He was a President who pursued excellence, and excellence in creative activity, he believed, was essential to excellence in the nation both now and generations from now. "If we can make our country one of the great schools of civilization" like Athens, he said,

> then on that achievement will surely rest our claim to the ulti-
> mate gratitude of mankind. . . . I am certain that, after the dust
> of centuries has passed over our cities, we will be remembered
> not for victories or defeats in battle or in politics but for our
> contributions to the human spirit.

THE POWERS OF THE PRESIDENCY

One of John Kennedy's most important contributions to the human spirit was his concept of the office of the Presidency. His philosophy of government was keyed to power, not as a matter of personal ambition but of national obligation: the primacy of the White House within the Executive Branch and of the Executive Branch within the Federal Government, the leadership of the Federal Government within the United States and of the United States within the community of nations.

And yet he almost never spoke of "power." Power was not a goal he sought for its own sake. It was there, in the White House, to be used, without any sense of guilt or greed, as a means of getting things done. He felt neither uplifted nor weighed down by power. He enjoyed the Presidency, thinking not of its power but its opportunities, and he was sobered by the Presidency, thinking not of its power but its obligations. He was a strong President primarily because he was a strong person.

He was slightly annoyed by all the newspaper fuss during the transition over the fact that he enjoyed reading Dick Neustadt's *Presidential Power,* with its emphasis on "personal power and its politics; what it is, how to get it, how to keep it, how to use it." For Neustadt would be the first to agree that John Fitzgerald Kennedy, a third-generation practitioner of political power, already knew its nature without being obsessed by either its burdens or its glories.

As a Senator he had supported more power and discretion for the President in foreign aid, trade, item vetoes and national emergency disputes, and opposed curbs on the President's treaty-making power and electoral base. As an author and historian he had praised the independent Presidency and the men who stretched its limits and preserved its prerogatives. As a candidate he both launched and closed his campaign with addresses focused upon Presidential responsibility as the No. 1 issue. And as President he both expanded and exerted the full powers of that office, the informal as well as the formal, "all that are specified and some that are not." In my judgment, few features of the Kennedy Presidency were as distinctive as his concept and conduct of the office itself.

Any affront to his office—whether it came from Congress on the B-70, Khrushchev on Cuba, Big Steel on prices, or his own church on education—was resisted. What he could not accomplish through legislation—to fight recession, inflation, race discrimination and other problems—he sought to accomplish through Executive Orders, proclamations, contingency funds, inherent powers, unused statutes, transfers of appropriations, reorganization plans, patronage, procurement, pardons, Presidential memos, public speeches and private pressures.

Example: In the summer of 1963, unable to obtain passage of his education bill and concerned about growing youth unemployment, he used his Presidential "emergency fund" to distribute $250,000 for guidance counselors in a drive against school dropouts.

Example: His first Executive Order, improving surplus food distribution to the needy, had been previously held up by his predecessor for lack of clear statutory authority. Kennedy issued it immediately, drawing upon his constitutional powers and on revenues available from customs fees.

"The Constitution has served us extremely well," he explained to a group of students in the White House flower garden, "but . . . all its clauses had to be interpreted by men and had to be made to work by men, and it has to be made to work today in an entirely different world from the day in which it was written."

Within the Executive Branch he accepted responsibility for every major decision, delegating work but never responsibility to Cabinet, National Security Council, Joint Chiefs of Staff, White House aides or other advisers. He did not wait for unanimity among them or permit them to disregard his instructions. In reporting on executive actions to the Congress, he deliberately worded his messages to read "I have directed the Secretary . . ." rather than "I have requested . . ."

He had no intention of using his staff, he said, "to get a pre-arranged agreement which is only confirmed at the President's desk. That I don't agree with." He wanted no one shielding him from anticipating problems and seeking to initiate solutions. Told in one conference by a sub-Cabinet member that the issue at hand involved the biggest decision he would ever have to make, he replied drily: "We get one of those every week."

He was very clear about the distinct roles of advisers and Presidents. The Joint Chiefs of Staff, he said, "advise you the way a man advises another one about whether he should marry a girl. He doesn't have to live with her." And in the three-network television interview of December, 1962, which contained his remarkably candid views on the Presidency, he stated:

> There is such a difference between those who advise or speak or legislate and . . . the man who must . . . finally make the judgment. . . . Advisers are frequently divided. If you take the wrong course, and on occasion I have, the President bears the burden of the responsibility quite rightly. The advisers may move on— to new advice.[3]

He deliberately had many advisers of varying points of view. Some outsiders mistook their clash of ideas for confusion, and assumed that a multiplicity could only produce uncertainty. Because they could not tell whether Dillon or Heller was in charge of tax planning, or whether Acheson or Rusk was in charge of Berlin planning, they assumed the President was either equally confused or compromising two views. Actually, he was in charge and liked hearing alternatives and assumptions challenged before he made up his mind.

His decisions were not fixed by any "grand design" for the future. He started his term with basic convictions and broad goals just as a scientist begins with faith in his hypothesis, but each new discovery and experience would broaden his perspective and recast his strategy. Because he had a shrewd judgment of the possible, he did not exhaust his energies or hopes on the impossible. Asked what kind of world he hoped to leave his successor in 1969, he replied in mid-1961, "I haven't had time to think about that yet."

Yet ever since his youth he had possessed an unusual ability to take the long view. "I sometimes think," he said, "we are too much impressed by the clamor of daily events. Newspaper headlines and the television screens give us a short view. . . . Yet it is the . . . great movements of history, and not the passing excitements, that will shape our future." Despite his fascination with the past, he oriented his policies to the future. His speeches were increasingly addressed to the next generation as well as his own, and he wanted to make sure there would be one. "Each President," he wrote, "is the President not only of all who live, but, in a very real sense, of all those who have yet to live." To help the next generation, he was always fashioning, not grand designs, but single steps—toward disarmament and space discoveries and salt water conversion and an end to illiteracy and disease. He talked of laying

[3] In discussing this concept with me before the program, he mentioned a series of poor recommendations he had received from Senator Smathers on the Dominican Republic, adding, "And now he's telling me what to do about Cuba."

the groundwork now for foreign policy beyond the cold war—of preparing now for coming water shortages, doctor shortages, classroom shortages, power and timber and park and playground shortages—of an Alliance for Progress a decade from now and an Atlantic Partnership a generation from now and wilderness preserves a century from now. Maintaining our forest lands is a "challenge to our foresight," he said, because "trees planted today will not reach the minimum sizes needed for lumber until the year 2000."

In fact, one of his favorite stories, which he repeated again on the fifteenth of November, 1963, related how French Marshal Lyautey's gardener sought to put off the persistent Marshal by reminding him that the trees which he wanted planted would not flower for a hundred years. "In that case," the Marshal had said, "plant it this afternoon." John Kennedy believed in planting trees this afternoon.

As his months in office increased, however, he talked more and more about the limitations of power.

"Every President," he wrote in the Foreword to my book on *Decision Making in the White House,* "must endure a gap between what he would like and what is possible." And he quoted Roosevelt's statement that "Lincoln was a sad man because he couldn't get it all at once. And nobody can."

His strategy in the Presidency, as in politics, was to keep moving, looking for openings, hoping to make the breaks fall his way. He was wise enough to know that in a nation of consent, not command, Presidential words alone cannot always produce results.

Near the end of November, 1963, he wrote a letter to Professor Clinton Rossiter, whose work on *The American Presidency* he greatly admired. Rossiter had dedicated his book with a line from Shakespeare's *Macbeth:* "Methought I heard a voice cry, 'Sleep no more!'" Kennedy, who could sleep with his perils but not always waken others to them, suggested in his letter as "more appropriate" the exchange between Glendower and Hotspur in Part I of Shakespeare's *Henry IV:*

GLENDOWER: I can call spirits from the vasty deep.

HOTSPUR: Why, so can I, or so can any man;
             But will they come when you do call for them?

CHAPTER XVI

❦

THE FIGHT AGAINST RECESSION

URING THE FOUR YEARS following John Kennedy's inauguration the United States experienced the longest and strongest economic expansion in this nation's modern history, as the output of goods and services increased more in four years than it had in the previous eight. The rate of national economic growth in 1960 was less than 3 percent, and a major talking point in his campaign. The three-year average during 1961-1963 was nearly double that level.

Nixon in 1960 had derided Kennedy's complaints about the growth rate, and some of Kennedy's own advisers were doubtful that these figures meant much to most voters. But to Kennedy they meant jobs. By the end of 1963 a record $100 billion, 16 percent growth in the nation's total output had provided more than two and three-quarter million more jobs and a record rise in labor income. The amount of idle manufacturing capacity had been reduced by half, and for the first time the seventy-million-job barrier had been shattered. The postwar trend of recurring recessions had been broken; the recession which was "due" in 1963 had been skipped; and nearly every indicator of the state of the economy was at a record level.

The President was far from satisfied with these gains. Too many men were still without work. Too many families, in Appalachia and Harlem and other centers of poverty throughout the country, were still without hope. He had plans to do more in the years ahead. He had regrets that he had been unable to do more in the years that had passed. But those who throughout his tenure were demanding that he do more and do it all at once clearly misjudged both the man and the mood of the

Congress and country. Partly because he did move cautiously, deliberate carefully, talk conservatively and seek counsel from a Republican Secretary of the Treasury, he obtained from the Congress a host of far-reaching economic measures, all while under heavy Republican attack, and all while confronted with a delicate and dangerous imbalance of international payments, an "independent" Federal Reserve Board and a conservative coalition in Congress.

The President would not claim that Federal actions alone had been responsible for all the economy's gains. Nor do I claim that he devised all his own economic policies. Kennedy had little formal background in economics. Nixon accused him in the campaign of being an "economic ignoramus . . . who doesn't understand simple high school economics." Young Jack Kennedy probably didn't learn much economics in high school—few do—or, for that matter, anywhere else. At Harvard he had received a "C" in a beginning economics course from instructor Russ Nixon, whom Congressman Kennedy later enjoyed cross-examining when Nixon turned up as an official with a union kicked out of the CIO for its relations with Communist fronts. Republican fears to the contrary, illness had prevented him from obtaining much exposure to Harold Laski at the London School of Economics. His letters home from college indicated that he was operating on a "budget" and occasionally dabbling in stocks, and he sought as a Senator to keep at least his household operations within the confines of his Senate salary. But he had little interest in his father's business or most of his own economic environment, had no taste for economic theory and, even as a legislator, defied classification on the economic spectrum. As President he was generally more cautious on spending than the Republicans thought but more liberal than his tight-fisted handling of the Budget indicated. He did not regard government planning as socialism, but neither did he believe the Budget should never be balanced. He recognized limits on "big government's" attempts to do everything, but few limits in combating unemployment and poverty.

He never mastered the technical mysteries of debt management and money supply. He once confided in his pre-Presidential days that he could remember the difference between fiscal policy, dealing with budgets and taxes, and monetary policy, dealing with money and credit, only by reminding himself that the name of the man most in charge of monetary policy, Federal Reserve Board Chairman William McChesney Martin, Jr., began with an "M" as in "monetary."

But as President he more than compensated for his limited background in economics by his superb ability to absorb information and to ask the right questions. He was surrounded with probably the most knowledgeable group of articulate economists in U.S. history. He recognized the role of economics in all his decisions, and included Walter Heller in his pre-press conference breakfasts and pre-State of the Union meetings.

The members of the Council of Economic Advisers, led by Walter Heller and absolutely invaluable to the President (whom they kept buried in a tide of memoranda), emphasized more than the others the "gap" between our production and our potential. Treasury Secretary Dillon emphasized more than the others the international dangers of too large a Budget deficit. Part-time adviser Ken Galbraith—who helped work on our 1961 economic messages before taking up his duties as Ambassador to India (in what the President called Galbraith's "period of penance")—emphasized more than the others the benefits of more public spending. Labor Secretary Arthur Goldberg emphasized more than the others the uses of massive public works and other pinpointed solutions. The President's leading "outside" economic adviser, Professor Paul Samuelson, emphasized more than the others the value of a temporary tax cut. Banker Martin, Businessman Hodges, Trader Ball and other department and agency heads emphasized more than others the needs of their respective clienteles. Budget Directors Bell and Gordon usually sided with Heller. My role, untrained as I was in economics, was simply to analyze and synthesize, refining issues for the President's consideration and relating them to the larger legislative and political outlook.

All these advisers, it should be stressed, whatever their differences in emphasis, agreed on the same basic principles: that unemployment was too high, that Budget deficits at such times were both unavoidable and useful, and that consumer purchasing power should be more strongly supported by Federal actions than had been true under the previous administration. The President paid most attention to Heller and Dillon, but he also mixed in his own readings, observations and sense of the national and Congressional mood. He was slow to grasp many of the theoretical economic doctrines presented to him, but on practicable proposals and problems he learned fast. An old friend and part-time adviser, Professor of Economics Seymour Harris, invited with his wife to watch the 1962 America's Cup races at Newport with the Kennedys, spent most of the time discussing economics and later wrote:

> His major responsibility is our security. What astonishes me is how much time the President nevertheless devotes to economic problems, how interested he is in them and how much he has learned in the last two years. He is now by far the most knowledgeable President of all time in the general area of economics.

Harris, recalling that Keynes had called Roosevelt economically "illiterate," was no doubt biased, and the President thought Harris was hurting more than helping when, in reply to one of Kennedy's liberal critics, he called the President a good Keynesian economist. But there was no doubt that John Kennedy, long after graduating from Harvard, had learned far more economics than most men in either public or academic life.

RECOVERY IN 1961

The task force report on the economy which Kennedy commissioned as President-elect in 1961, prepared by Paul Samuelson, bluntly used the term "recession," which had been avoided throughout the campaign. Indeed, in every way it painted a dark picture of the economy. The recession, the report made clear, would not cure itself. "Not even the ostrich can avert the economic facts of life," said Samuelson in the report. "He misreads the role of confidence in economic life who thinks that denying the obvious will cure the ailments of a modern economy."

"That's well put," commented Kennedy to Samuelson as they reviewed the report in New York's Hotel Carlyle two weeks before inauguration. He made no attempt in his first State of the Union address to deny the obvious:

> The present state of our economy is disturbing. We take office in the wake of seven months of recession, three and one-half years of slack, seven years of diminished economic growth, and nine years of falling farm income. . . .
>
> Save for a brief period in 1958, insured unemployment is at the highest peak in our history. Of some five and one-half million Americans who are without jobs, more than one million have been searching for work for more than four months. . . .
>
> In short, the American economy is in trouble. The most resourceful industrialized country on earth ranks among the last in the rate of economic growth. Since last spring our economic growth rate has actually receded. Business investment is in a decline. Profits have fallen below predicted levels. Construction is off. A million unsold automobiles are in inventory. Fewer people are working, and the average work week has shrunk well below forty hours. . . .
>
> This Administration does not intend to stand helplessly by . . . to waste idle hours and empty plants while awaiting the end of the recession. . . .
>
> I will propose to the Congress within the next fourteen days measures . . . aimed at insuring a prompt recovery and paving the way for increased long-range growth.

"I painted the picture as I saw it," said the President. "Anyone who makes the judgment that it was laid on thick for political reasons . . . is making a serious mistake." Three days later, on February 2, 1961, he sent to the Congress the comprehensive Economic Message which had been in preparation for several weeks, proposing legislation (1) to add a temporary thirteen-week supplement to unemployment benefits; (2) to extend aid to the children of unemployed workers;[1] (3) to redevelop distressed areas: (4) to increase Social Security payments and encourage earlier retirement; (5) to raise the minimum wage and broaden its coverage; (6) to provide emergency relief to feed grain farmers; and (7) to finance a comprehensive home-building and slum clearance program. The first of these seven measures became law the following month, and all seven had been signed by the end of June. It had been 161 days of action.

These seven measures were not, as some suggested, too little and too late, for recovery, while beginning early, was a long, slow process. Nearly $800 million in extended jobless benefits for nearly three million unemployed, over $200 million in additional welfare payments to 750,000 children and their parents, more than $400 million in aid to over 1,000 distressed counties, $175 million in higher wages for those below the new minimum, and an estimated 420,000 construction jobs under the new Housing Act could not be termed "too little."

Nor did the President limit his moves to Congressional action or wait for it. The need was to get more money into the economy fast. On his own initiative, under existing authority, he directed all Federal agencies to accelerate their procurement and construction, particularly in labor surplus areas. He compressed a long-range program of post office construction into the first six months, released over a billion dollars in state highway aid funds ahead of schedule, raised farm price supports and advanced their payment, and speeded up the distribution of tax refunds and GI life insurance dividends. To expand credit and stimulate building, he ordered a reduction in the maximum permissible interest rate on FHA-insured loans, lowered the interest rate on Small Business Administration loans in distressed areas, expanded its available credit and liberalized lending by the Federal Home Loan Banks. To aid the unemployed, he broadened the distribution of surplus food, directed that preference be given distressed areas in defense contracts, created a "pilot" Food Stamp program for the needy and expanded the services of U.S. Employment Offices. Finally, he encouraged the Federal Reserve Board to help keep long-term interest rates low through the purchase of long-term government issues.

[1] Made permanent the following year, this is the bill by which Kennedy was best known in the darkest corners of despair in this country.

While most of these administrative moves of the first 161 days added to the deficit—some by tens of millions of dollars, some by billions—none of them had to wait for legislation or appropriations. The money, instead of being stretched out, was paid out when the economy needed it most. While passage of a public works acceleration bill, for example, would have helped even more, the President to the extent possible accelerated them on his own. At the same time he made clear—and this may have had the most important effect of all—that he would not cut back Federal spending when the recession reduced Federal revenues, or permit a tightening of credit when recovery began.

The combined impact of these legislative and administrative steps, which largely implemented the recommendations of the Samuelson task force, had an impressive effect. The natural strength of private spending may well have ended the recession sooner or later anyway, but prompt action provided not only an initial impetus for recovery but grounds for the basic consumer and business confidence needed to unloosen that spending.

The President, moreover, did not want a repeat of the anemic recovery staged by the economy after the 1958 recession. That time production, employment and plant use had never returned to their normal rates before another recession ensued. This time, he said in his February 2 message, he wanted "full recovery and sustained growth. . . . If these measures prove to be inadequate to the task, I shall submit further proposals to the Congress within the next seventy-five days."

The seventy-five-day reference reflected pressure from within the administration, from liberal Congressmen and from organized labor, for two other measures: a massive public works program and a temporary tax cut. The President promised that he would review the situation with his advisers in the spring to ascertain whether either step would then be recommended. By late spring he was convinced that the recovery would continue without either, and that the Congress would pass neither.

Make-work public works, in his view, were not likely to create many full-time jobs until too late to fight the recession, and they would, with considerable waste, add to the published Budget deficit during the very spring and summer he was requesting more defense funds. That extra defense spending, he ruled, would have to serve as a substitute stimulant. Arthur Goldberg, convinced that the President should wage a fight for the bill in 1961 even if he lost, reminded him that Robert Frost had advised him to be "more Irish than Harvard." But Kennedy only smiled. "As President," he said, "I have to be both Harvard and Irish." He promised Goldberg and organized labor that he would consider a more careful public works bill the following year.

Walter Heller and the tax cut advocates, on the other hand, were not only denied their request; they suddenly found themselves fighting to keep taxes from being *increased*.

A Federal income tax increase at that stage, even though it took no more money out of the economy than new defense spending was putting in, might well have aborted the shaky recovery that was then under way. Establishing a precedent of new tax increases to pay for every increase in defense spending would have plagued Kennedy the rest of his term. Such a mistake in his first summer in the White House could have equaled for domestic affairs the foreign affairs fiasco at the Bay of Pigs in his first spring. Interestingly enough, the proposed tax increase originated not with his economic advisers but among his foreign affairs advisers, but it was tentatively approved by the President and came dangerously close to being announced.

The occasion was the Berlin crisis of 1961. Those advocating a declaration of national emergency and massive mobilization originally recommended both stand-by price and wage controls and a tax increase in order to offset panic buying, prevent inflation and cover the cost of the mobilization. Later, when the military plans were scaled down to a lower key, the idea of a "special Berlin surtax"—either increasing all tax rates by a flat 2 percentage points or everyone's tax by a proportionate 7.5 percent—still had great appeal. Applying to both individuals and corporations, it was to be a one-year addition only.

The President liked it as a means of requiring all Americans to share the burden of the crisis as well as those called to active duty. The Attorney General liked it as an answer to those asking what they could do for their country. The foreign policy makers liked it as a clear demonstration of America's determination. Secretary Dillon, though with some reluctance, at first liked it as a step toward the principle of balanced budgets. Senate Leader Mansfield liked it—both "sound policy and sound politics," he told the President—and saw no reason to limit it to one year. Only the economic advisers were against it, arguing that taxes were already too high for solid growth. Inasmuch as they did not sit in on the Berlin crisis meetings, I undertook to represent their views.

Our first alternative was to argue that the threat of panic buying had been exaggerated—that there was ample slack in the economy and ample supplies of goods to absorb this small increase in spending—and that only discretionary authority to increase taxes, in case of an emergency, should be requested. That position was rejected as politically unfeasible.

The next tack was to point out that the proposed tax increase would not take effect until January 1, 1962—that well over half its revenues would be realized, not in fiscal 1962 when the new funds were being spent, but in fiscal 1963—and that the President should simply promise that he would propose a tax boost the following January if, but only if, he was unable to present a balanced fiscal 1963 Budget. While this committed us to a restricted Budget effort the following year, that was far better than a tax increase in the midst of recovery, for we were determined to find fair means or foul of making that Budget look balanced and dropping all thought of new taxes. We also pointed out that there was plenty of unenacted sacrifice already pending in the Congress to which the President could point, including proposals to increase postal rates, close tax loopholes and withhold taxes on dividends. Secretary Dillon now endorsed this view, and the President, still sensitive to the charge that no concrete calls for sacrifice had followed his ringing Inaugural, reluctantly agreed.

Then the opposite faction produced a new scheme. As a means of sacrifice, why not drop from the domestic budget new expenditures equal to the new amounts required for defense? This, too, at first appealed to the President. But we argued, backed up this time by some "domestic" Cabinet officers, that such a move would indicate that the Republicans had been right all along in saying we couldn't afford "both guns and butter"; it would confirm their suspicions that we didn't need all the funds we requested; it would undermine our argument that strength in our economy and health and education was the backbone of our strength overseas; it would set a precedent which the opponents of these domestic programs could always find some emergency to invoke; and it would in effect give Khrushchev the ability to determine the size of our domestic budget and the strength of our economic recovery. Moreover, had not the President rejected the massive public works program partly on the grounds that this extra spending for defense would take its place?

PERSISTING PROBLEMS

In the end the President sided with us. He realized that he faced a deep-rooted sluggishness in the economy which posed a more serious and longer-range problem than mere recovery from recession. In a sense, his problem was the companion of Roosevelt's a generation earlier. The thirties were confronted with an extraordinarily low supply of jobs for those looking for work. The sixties were confronted by an extraordinarily high number of potential workers far exceeding the supply of jobs. Unless the economy grew fast enough to create new jobs as rapidly as the manpower tide increased, there would be no end to recurring recessions, or even to high unemployment in the midst of prosperity. From 1947 to 1962 the civilian labor force grew by nearly twelve million men and women, but the number of jobs grew by only ten million. As a result, said the President, our loss of man-hours even in a year of prosperity, as measured by those willing but unable to find full-time work, "was a staggering one billion workdays, equivalent to shutting down the entire country with no production, no services and no pay for over three weeks."

As unemployment declined for skilled breadwinners who were white, it remained high for the unskilled, the Negro and the young. As jobs increased in new industries and service establishments, they decreased in old industries—coal, textiles, railroads and others. The economists called much of it "structural unemployment," the pessimists said it was unavoidable, and after each recession it grew worse.

John Kennedy's wealth had never made him immune to the suffering of others, and poverty in the midst of plenty disturbed him. His experiences in New England and West Virginia had made him more attuned to specific solutions for specific problems—depressed areas, untrained workers, substandard wages. But he recognized that both the general economy and the specific problems had to be treated. "Large-scale unemployment during a recession is bad enough," he told the Congress. "Large-scale unemployment during a period of prosperity would be intolerable."

Long-range growth required long-range efforts—particularly the education of our youth, the conservation of our resources, the expansion of our science and health—and it was no coincidence that the Eighty-seventh and Eighty-eighth Congresses set unequaled marks in those same areas. In addition, as a spur to industrial modernization and expansion, the Kennedy administration proposed in 1961 the payment of a 7 percent tax credit for business investment in new machinery and equipment. Passed in 1962, it was accompanied by an administrative liberalization of the timetables and guidelines applied by Internal Revenue to the depreciation of machinery and equipment, speeding up by nearly a third the rate at which firms could write off those assets for tax purposes and purchase more productive replacements. This depreciation reform—long the No. 1 item on business' list of requests, but abandoned by the previous administration as too difficult—provided, when combined with the investment tax credit, a 1962 reduction in business taxes of some $2.5 billion, an 11 percent tax cut for corporations.

Yet the tax credit bill was constantly in difficulty. Businessmen were suspicious of a Democratic administration doing them favors. Labor leaders had to be persuaded not to oppose it. Democrats complained that we were forcing, ironically over Republican opposition, American businessmen to accept a tax "handout" they didn't want and wouldn't use. Douglas Dillon told of explaining the bill's merits at length to a businessman on a plane who then said, "Wonderful, wonderful. Now would you tell me again why I'm against it?" But finally the bill was passed, its tax credit was widely used, outlays for plant and equipment in 1963 crossed the $40 billion mark for the first time in history, and the administration's two tax changes were estimated by an independent business survey to have been responsible for nearly half of this expansion.

The President recognized, however, that new equipment and machinery formed a threat as well as a promise: higher productivity was the promise; increasing automation was the threat.

There was nothing new about advancing technology costing jobs. But in the fifties and sixties there was something new in the economy not expanding rapidly enough to absorb the displaced workers. There was growing alarm about the pace at which the machines moved in, spreading from one branch of industry to another, from the farm to the factory, from the assembly line to the office, displacing workers at a rate of 35,000 jobs a week. When John Kennedy entered Congress, fewer than 15 percent of the locomotives on the railroads were electric diesel engines. During his government service the figure rose to 97 percent. In West Virginia he saw machines enabling forty-six men to dig as much coal as one hundred men dug when he first entered Congress, and he saw despair on the faces of miners who had been waiting several years for work. The Federal Government itself under his Presidency made more use than ever before of computers and automatic processors in place of office and clerical workers.

The steady prosperity of Western Europe, observed the President, offered proof that rapid automation need not cause heavy unemployment. He directed his economic advisers to keep him posted on the economic policies of European governments. "Automation," he said at a news conference,

> does not need to be, we hope, our enemy. . . . I think machines can make life easier for men, if men do not let the machines dominate them. . . . It can provide new jobs, but . . . it is going to take a good deal of wisdom by those of us in the government as well as labor and management.

Technological unemployment, which Kennedy understood, was a basic problem in our farm economy, which he never understood. New fertilizers, machinery, insecticides and research had made American agriculture one of the productive miracles of the world, a sharp contrast with Communism's collective farms. But while farm output increased by nearly a third, the number of man-hours worked was cut in half, with a decline of three million workers. That is comparable, said the President with his flair for vivid illustrations, to seeing each year for the last fifteen years enough people thrown out of work to populate Akron, Ohio.

Kennedy and Secretary of Agriculture Orville Freeman, while keeping food prices relatively stable, took steps to raise net farm income per farm to a record high, a billion dollars a year over its level in 1960 (when he had largely unsuccessfully sought farm votes). They also took more steps than had ever previously been taken to reduce farm surpluses in storage, which during the previous administration had soared from $2.5 billion to $9 billion—by expanding welfare food distribution at home, increasing farm exports by 70 percent, and reducing wheat and feed grain acreage at a savings in storage costs of several hundred thousand dollars a day. A new Rural Areas Development program helped low-income farmers not only find new jobs and improve their homes but also turn surplus cropland into recreation areas for fun and profit.

Nevertheless the major efforts of Kennedy and Freeman to fit food production to consumption encountered immovable opposition. It came from the larger and more prosperous farmers, who enjoyed being subsidized to produce crops for storage. It came from Congressmen opposed to the kind of controls needed to make this chaos manageable (although we called it "supply management" instead of "controls").

Nor could there be any reversal in the trek of former farm workers and youth to the cities searching for work. The President was disturbed by the estimate that only one out of every ten boys growing up on our farms would find a living in agriculture.

In their search for work in the city, farm youths were joined not only by older men replaced by machines but by other young people crowding the nation's labor market. This was the President's special concern. He warned that the crest of the postwar baby flood, which for nearly two decades had crowded our elementary and then our secondary schools, was about to engulf the labor force with 26 million new workers in the 1960's, of whom nearly a third would not have finished high school. The youthful, the untrained and the unskilled, he said, were the largest factors in our high unemployment rates—rates which were dropping far too slowly even after the recession had ended. He urged the nation's youth to stay in school, emphasizing the difficulties facing dropouts. He pressed for enactment of his education program, his vocational education bill, and a young people's Job Corps to take boys off the streets for training. He explored the use of existing Selective Service procedures to identify young men needing vocational as well as physical help.

The labor movement, impatient with the progress of Kennedy's proposals, called with increasing force for a thirty-five-hour week at the same wages a forty-hour week could command. But the President cited the adverse effects these increased costs would have on American business competing in world markets, and on his own efforts to prevent inflation from eating up their gains in purchasing power. He recognized that in time a shorter work week might be standard, but his goal was to create more jobs instead of dividing up the too few already available.

He emphasized in particular the training of unskilled workers and the retraining of skilled workers for the new skills which industrial change demanded. This concept could be found in a whole series of Kennedy programs: depressed areas, public welfare, vocational education, civil rights, trade expansion, youth employment, literacy training and the first full-scale Federal program of Manpower Development and Assistance. The related technique which could not be used as boldly as desired, however, was worker relocation. Kennedy, when campaigning in West Virginia, remarked to me in his car that the best thing for many of the men in those deserted mining towns would be to help get them out of there. But Congressmen willing to vote funds for the retraining of their constituents were not as willing to relocate them elsewhere, and most of the unemployed were equally reluctant to move.

In 1961 the Area Redevelopment Act sought to move industry and help into these hard-hit areas. In 1962, to supplement that Act, Kennedy obtained passage of the first Accelerated Public Works program since the days of the New Deal. In 1963, even before completing work on his bill to aid Appalachia—the mountainous belt of abandoned coal mines and poverty which stretched across the Middle Atlantic States— he developed with state and local officials a coordinated Federal effort.

In the fall of 1963, moved by a *New York Times* story on the desperate plight of families in eastern Kentucky, he directed a special Federal program for their relief, and planned to tour the area himself. That fall he also gave orders for the formulation of a new Federal antipoverty program. In a November strategy session on the 1964 campaign, he was warned by one election analyst that the balance of political power was held by affluent suburbanites who did not identify with antipoverty, minimum wage and depressed area programs. After I passed this caution on to Walter Heller, he asked the President whether work should continue on the antipoverty bill. The answer was in the affirmative, and the bill passed in 1964, thanks to the leadership of Kennedy's successor.

But it is true that, even when Kennedy took over at the low point of the recession, there was little public interest in his attack on unemployment. "The 94 percent employed," he remarked more matter-of-factly than bitterly, "couldn't care less about the 6 percent unemployed." And once the recession was over, Congress balked at some of the big planks in his economic platform, especially a permanent strengthening of unemployment insurance and Presidential stand-by authority to lower taxes and speed up public works in case of a recession. The legislators went along with his proposals to strengthen housing and small business credit, to broaden the depressed area program and to revamp public welfare. But in our affluent society, remarked the President, major expenditures and innovations were resisted "by people who like it the way it used to be. Change is always pleasant to some people and unpleasant to others." His own philosophy had been summed up in his Inaugural: "If a free society cannot help the many who are poor, it cannot save the few who are rich." He did not apply that philosophy only to foreign countries.

THE BALANCE OF PAYMENTS AND TRADE

The tools of deficit spending and easy credit were not so readily available to President Kennedy's fight on unemployment for economic as well as political reasons. The main economic reason was a problem of concern to few, comprehended by even fewer, and practically ignored by the party platforms and the popular press: the balance of payments. Yet few subjects occupied more of Kennedy's time in the White House or were the subject of more secret high-level meetings.

The problem, essentially, was a chronic and mounting deficit in our international accounts as a nation. More dollars went out of this country than came in. What Americans spent or invested in other countries —as importers, tourists, investors and soldiers—was far exceeding the amounts we received from our exports, from purchases made by foreigners in this country, from dividends on our overseas investments and other sources. As a result, for a period of ten years prior to Kennedy's inauguration, the quantity of American dollars held by foreigners mounted steadily; but until 1958 our reserves of gold, into which foreigners were permitted to convert those dollars, remained stable. The deficits in our balance of payments were moderate in size and helped provide war-torn economies suffering from a "dollar gap" with dollars for their own use.

But between 1957 and 1960 a combination of events raised this chronic problem to crisis proportions. In 1958-1959 the failure of high-priced American goods to penetrate increasingly competitive European markets sharply reduced our usual surplus of exports over imports, and it was this surplus which had helped offset our overseas military, foreign aid and other expenditures. Western Europe's growing economy had become an attractive place for investment. More time and money were spent abroad by tourists, while relatively few visitors came here. Foreign governments also restricted the amount their citizens could invest in our enterprises, while short-term commercial credits inevitably grew with our export trade. As a result of all these factors, our balance of payments deficit, normally about a billion dollars a year, suddenly rose to nearly four billion; and those holding dollars abroad, now that they were no longer in short supply, decided to cash in some three billion dollars' worth in those two years for American gold.

In 1960, although our export surplus improved, the other trends continued or worsened. Bonn and London raised their short-term interest rates, causing the transfer of foreign capital previously deposited in New York banks. European international bankers, concerned by charges that forthcoming Democratic deficits would cheapen if not endanger the dollar, decided not only to withdraw their American funds but heavily convert their dollars into gold. Aggravated by speculation on the London gold market and by unfavorable comparisons of our uncommitted gold reserves with foreign dollar holdings, gold left this country by amounts totaling almost two billion dollars in that year alone. Last-minute efforts by the outgoing administration failed to stem the tide, and there were widespread reports that America's gold reserves would be insufficient to meet the demands of foreign dollar-holders unless the new President raised the price of gold and thus "devalued" the dollar.

But the new President had no intention of doing so. The balance of payments problem had been of little interest to him during the early stages of the campaign. As the gold outflow and speculation dangerously mounted, both sides sought to use it as an issue against the other, Kennedy blaming our lagging economy, Nixon blaming Kennedy's attitude on spending.

"I must say," Kennedy told a partisan crowd in Moline, Illinois, "the Vice President does show some signs of tension. Now he blames me for the increase in the cost of gold on the London Market. . . . Mr. Nixon, if you are listening, I did not do it, I promise you." Kennedy requested his "Academic Advisory Committee" to work out a formal comprehensive public statement. He issued it in Philadelphia on October 31, after a long night's work hammering out the final draft with Ken Galbraith at the other end of the telephone.

In the transition between his election and inauguration, he became far more concerned. In January the outflow of gold rose to proportions which could not continue without disaster. The need for world confidence in the dollar, and the danger of a "run on the bank" by dollar-holders turning them in for gold, dominated several of his conversations as President-elect. They were the decisive influence in his choice of a Secretary of the Treasury. They started us working on the balance of payments program he presented in February. In his State of the Union Message he emphasized the priority he was giving the problem, his refusal to devalue the dollar by raising the price of gold and his determination to do whatever had to be done "to make certain that . . . the dollar is 'sound.' "

Some foreign apprehensions were heightened by the fact that two-thirds of our gold was officially untouchable because it was required as backing for our currency and Federal Reserve deposits. But no matter how strongly sophisticated bankers and economists assured him that this commitment should be repealed, that it represented merely an unnecessary inducement to foreign dollar-holders to scramble for the other third, the President was certain that any such proposal to the Congress from him in 1961 would be seized upon as "Democratic funny-money finagling." Inasmuch as the Federal Reserve Board could suspend the rule, and certain that Congress would repeal it in an emergency, he preferred simply to pledge, in his State of the Union address, that *all* our gold reserves, plus our International Monetary Fund drawing rights, were "available" for use if needed. That pledge—and his pledge a week later in the Special Message on the Balance of Payments that the dollar would continue to be "as good as gold"—went a long way toward restoring confidence in the dollar and slowing the gold outflow. The gold speculation in London ceased almost completely, and the President reversed Eisenhower's curb on military dependents overseas on the grounds that its small contribution to our balance of payments was more than offset by the loss of morale.

He had no intention of devaluing. Nor would he stop the outflow of dollars and gold by shutting off credit, imports or dollar convertibility. He refused to believe that he had to choose between a weaker economy at home or a weaker dollar abroad. But he did recognize that the crisis limited his full use of monetary policy—lower interest rates—in fighting the recession. His concern, in fact, was that the powerful and independent Chairman of the Federal Reserve Board, William McChesney Martin, might hamper recovery through higher rates. The traditional fear of the men at the "Fed" was inflation, not unemployment, and balance of payments pressures plus economic expansion called for higher interest rates in their book. Kennedy could not, by law, order Martin to do anything. But he talked privately and frequently with him, praised his work publicly and reappointed him to the chairmanship. He invited Martin to regular, confidential sessions in his office with the "Troika" (Heller, Dillon and Bell) in which the needs of the economy were stressed. For two and a half years long-term interest rates on bonds as well as mortgages were held down, in contrast with their record rise in the previous few years, while short-term rates were nudged high enough to discourage continued large outflows of short-term capital.

Kennedy's Budget freedom was also restricted by the balance of payments problem. Too large a Budget deficit resulting from new Kennedy programs, said Dillon, could cause foreign bankers to believe, correctly or not, that the value of the dollar was in doubt and to take more American gold. At the first meeting of the Cabinet on January

26, the Treasury Secretary set forth the problem for his colleagues and warned of its effects on their budgets. During the months and years that followed, that same room would contain countless meetings on that same subject.

Almost to a man, Kennedy's associates in the administration thought he was excessively concerned about the problem. Even the Treasury resisted his prodding for faster, more far-reaching solutions, opposing in particular any restrictions on American capital going abroad. (The Treasury, confided one nongovernmental adviser to the President, "is subject to the banker syndrome, which is to foresee disaster but prefer inaction." And the President himself once remarked to Dillon in one of our meetings that "the Treasury is very skillful at shooting down every balloon floated elsewhere in the administration" on this subject.) The economic advisers, more concerned with the domestic economy, pointed out that the totals owed this nation by others far exceeded the claims upon our reserves, and that the wealthiest nation in history, possessing two-fifths of the free world's gold stocks, was hardly in dire straits.

Privately some advisers told the President that even devaluation was not unthinkable—a drastic change in the system but preferable to wrecking it altogether. But the President emphasized that he did not want that weapon of last resort even mentioned outside his office—or used. By disrupting the international monetary system that we had done so much to create, devaluation would call into doubt the good faith and stability of this nation and the competence of its President.

"I know everyone else thinks I worry about this too much," he said to me one day as we pored over what seemed like the millionth report on the subject. "But if there's ever a run on the bank, and I have to devalue the dollar or bring home our troops, as the British did, I'm the one who will take the heat. Besides it's a club that De Gaulle and all the others hang over my head. Any time there's a crisis or a quarrel, they can cash in all their dollars and where are we?" He also had some evidence to back his suspicions that the gloomy rumors which triggered the gold withdrawals of 1960 had been deliberately spread by American bankers to embarrass him politically, and he did not want to be vulnerable to the same tactic in 1964.

Aided by Dillon and his talented Under Secretary, Robert Roosa, the President chipped away at the international deficit and gold flow. Despite the reluctance of European nations to keep a larger portion of their reserves in dollars instead of gold, the outflow of our own gold reserves, in Kennedy's first thirty-two months, was less than half as much as it had been in the previous thirty-two months. But the over-all payments deficit was more stubborn. The third quarter of 1963 showed the best balance of payments position of any quarter since the Suez crisis had given us a temporary surplus. But that particular quarter's showing was partly due to the beneficial effects of the President's proposing a special tax on foreign bond issues floated in our market. This bill, he said, was the kind of proposal he wished Treasury had put forward much earlier. The flow of American investments abroad was largely unrestricted, a policy he continued to doubt. "Sure they bring more in earnings in the long run," said the President, "but by then this problem will be over. It's a ridiculous situation for us to be squeezing down essential public activities in order not to touch private investment and tourist spending—but apparently that's life." Every time General De Gaulle and his aides talked menacingly about keeping American investments out of Europe, Kennedy secretly wished they would.

Nevertheless progress was slowly being made in other ways. American goods were kept competitive while foreign costs and prices rose. The Treasury constructed a complex network of arrangements with other countries and with the International Monetary Fund to protect the dollar with other currencies. The State, Defense and Treasury Departments persuaded other nations to buy more of their military equipment from us and to pay their old debts off in advance. Despite the Berlin build-up, a more modern military establishment led all other departments in cutting down on expenditures abroad. Federal civilian agencies, which had previously regarded it as a mark of prestige to open a branch office overseas, were discouraged from doing so.

The laws were tightened against Americans avoiding our income taxes abroad. Progress was made in getting other countries to pay their share of the foreign aid and military burden, and our own outlays in these efforts were tied almost wholly to purchases in America. In addition to higher short-term interest rates, new tax incentives helped keep more short-term foreign capital here. The President also pushed Treasury hard, although with limited success, to work with other nations in formulating a far stronger long-range international monetary system to finance future high levels of world trade.

These and other arrangements were generally approved by the Congress, whenever legislation was required, but they were generally unknown to most Americans. Two efforts did win wider attention. One was the effort to close the growing "tourist gap," by attracting more foreign tourists to this country with a new United States Travel Service and simplified visa procedures and by reducing the duty-free amount our own citizens could spend abroad from $500 to $100. "If we're restricting servicemen," said the President, "I don't see why these rich ——— can't do with a little less—including my sisters." Walter Heller suggested in the fall of 1963 that perhaps Jacqueline Kennedy, whose travels abroad

were well publicized and by some unfavorably criticized, might take a
"See America First" trip as part of our effort to get more Americans to
vacation in their own country. "Next year," the President laughed. "Next
year I'll ask her to do that." At the same time he thought it unfair to
restrict—or, as some proposed, tax—all overseas travel, with ill effects
on teachers, students and other less affluent tourists, when those proposing such measures would not place equivalent restrictions on the
movement of American capital.

The public's attention was called even more strongly to the administration's effort to increase our export trade. A variety of tools was employed, under the direction of Secretary of Commerce Hodges—including
trade missions, market surveys and export promotion and education
among American businessmen. A wholly new program of export credit
insurance was developed. But the major effort—and one of the major
legislative efforts of the Kennedy administration—was the Trade Expansion Act of 1962.

Like the antirecession program in 1961 and the tax cut in 1963 (and,
later in 1963, civil rights), the 1962 trade bill became the centerpiece
of all that year's efforts—the subject of extra emphasis in the State of the
Union Message, the subject of the year's first special legislative message,
the subject of a pep talk with charts to Democratic legislators, the subject
of several Presidential speeches, and the subject of an intense White
House lobbying effort with priority over almost all other bills. The new
proposal would help our balance of payments, said the President, hopefully by increasing our exports faster than imports, and by enabling our
businessmen to sell on more equal terms to the European Common
Market instead of building plants within the Market.

But balance of payments considerations contributed only one of
many long-range arguments for trade expansion. The Reciprocal Trade
Agreements Act of Franklin Roosevelt and Cordell Hull had become
outmoded and inadequate, as successive renewals narrowed the President's negotiating authority. The remarkable growth and bargaining
strength of the European Economic Community, known familiarly as
the Common Market, and the application of Great Britain and her
European trading partners for membership in 1961, produced new pressures for new legislation. If American business and agriculture could
not share on suitable terms in the growth of that market, the President's
hopes for both greater Atlantic unity and greater American prosperity
were clearly less likely to be realized.

The Reciprocal Trade Act expired in mid-1962. As we prepared in
the fall of 1961 for Kennedy's second legislative program, some advisers
counseled merely a twelfth extension of the existing Act, with the usual
minimum of amendments. That strategy would allow time to prepare

the Congress and country and to await the EEC's action on Britain's application. But the President felt that the evidence was clear, that events might pass us by, and that the fierce fight which even a simple extension would entail might better be fought, and fought only once, for a wholly new trade instrument. "The United States," he said, "did not rise to greatness by waiting for others to lead. . . . Economic isolation and political leadership are wholly incompatible."

He established a special operation in the executive offices, headed by Philadelphia banker Howard Peterson, to help promote the bill in the Congress and mass media. Because his courtly Secretary of Commerce was better received by skeptical Congressmen than international lawyer George Ball, who was our trade and EEC expert, he directed Hodges rather than the Under Secretary of State to take the lead in all Hill testimony and negotiations. But he kept matters closely coordinated by the White House.

The Congress, accustomed to grumbling about even superficial changes in the old Reciprocal Trade Act, had been ill prepared for an unprecedented bill giving the President a five-year authority to cut all tariffs by as much as 50 percent and to cut tariffs down to zero on those commodities traded predominantly by the U.S. and the Common Market. The President never avoided the fact that, in order to sell more, we would have to buy more; and he proposed as part of the trade bill a measure (which he had first introduced as a Senator years earlier) to provide Federal "adjustment assistance" to firms and workers injured by any increases in imports deemed desirable. He did not expect that revolutionary provision to pass. It contained a variety of social welfare and economic aids which could never be passed on their own. Including it, however, helped our labor friends support the bill among their skeptical, traditionally protectionist members. It also served as a lightning rod to draw fire away from other sections, and as bargaining material if a compromise had to be made. The best evidence of the bill's expert management and amazing success was the continued presence of those readjustment provisions when it came to the White House to be signed.

Democrats in every state, Kennedy had unsurprisingly discovered in his pre-1960 campaign travels, favored the traditional party policy of liberalized trade only if their own state's products were protected. The fragmentation of Congressional power along state and local lines made that body protectionist by nature, as he knew from the pressures on him as a Congressman. And in 1961 three Lou Harris Polls—in Florida, West Virginia and Illinois—had failed to find a majority supporting trade expansion.

The President in 1962 set out to get a majority. It is time we recognized, he said, that trade is "no longer a matter of local economic interest but of high national policy." He emphasized that the united Western economic might implicit in the bill would dwarf the Communists economically. "This bill," he said, "by enabling us to strike a bargain with the Common Market, will 'strike a blow' for freedom." Meeting frequently with those Senators and Congressmen concerned about particularly vulnerable commodities, he gradually built a majority in both houses without any compromise of principle or important loss of flexibility.

With the defeat of Republican attempts to strike out "adjustment assistance" and of all other crippling amendments, the bill passed virtually intact the same year it was offered. The following year, De Gaulle's veto of Britain's Common Market application slowed down progress toward Western unity and watered down the "down-to-zero" portion of the Act. Some insisted the administration should have fought for an amendment that took care of this contingency. But the President could not in 1962 have offered legislation assuming anything other than Great Britain's acceptance, nor would he throw the whole subject open again in 1963 for a new set of Congressional pressures.

His authority over trade was still several times broader than any predecessor had enjoyed, and even as the new bargaining with Europe began—the "Kennedy round," as the Europeans named it in 1963 somewhat to his discomfort—both our exports and our export surplus showed striking increases over their earlier levels. Nevertheless trade was only a long-range answer to the balance of payments problem. The Common Market was slow to lower its own tariff walls, particularly on agricultural products, where this country's competitive advantages were great. ("Is the Grand Alliance going to founder on chickens?" the President asked one day in mock despair.)

In short, despite all his efforts, the payments "club" still hung over his head, limiting the size of his domestic economic program. In November, 1963, he weighed still stronger deterrents to the flow of American capital abroad, and talked of calling those of us working on the problem to an all-day planning session at Camp David.

BUDGET AND DEBT

But even had there been no balance of payments pressures, the President would not have felt free to unbalance the Federal Budget by as much as his liberal critics would have liked. He recognized that the "Administrative Budget" presented to Congress was not an accurate account of the government's effort. He realized that a period of sizable Budget deficits would be required before the country regained its full potential of employment and growth, and he increasingly realized that the Budget was not merely a set of accounts but a powerful instrument of economic policy.

Although he looked upon his increased domestic spending in 1961 primarily in terms of the benefits offered by particular programs, instead of the benefits of Budget increases in general, by 1963 he was fitting his spending and tax policies to economic conditions, appreciating the effect of all spending on prosperity and employment. Nevertheless his political judgment told him that a period of gradual re-education would be required before the country and Congress, accustomed to nearly sixteen years of White House homilies on the wickedness of government deficits, would approve of an administration deliberately and severely unbalancing the Budget.

His success with the Congress and country depended, he felt, on weakening the traditional Republican charge that Democrats were spendthrifts and wastrels who would drown the nation in debt. Nixon in 1960 had accused him of being fiscally irresponsible, a radical whose programs would invite runaway inflation. Had the young moderates in the suburbs and other independents who switched to Kennedy believed Nixon, Kennedy would have been defeated. He felt that he had to shed the "big spender" image to get his programs through, and that restraint was also required to keep some accord with Eisenhower and other Republicans whose support he would need on foreign policy.

The widespread acceptance of the sanctity of balanced budgets, moreover, made it politically impossible to convert overnight either the voters or the Congress to the merits of Budget deficits. Even in 1963, when his combination of a tax cut with a large deficit and rising expenditures represented the boldest fiscal move in a generation, he felt inhibited by the limitations of Congressional and voter opinion. Far more money could well be spent in many domestic areas, he knew. "But it still is a large budget, a large deficit," he told his news conference, "and I think we have done about as much as we now can do. In other years we may have to do more." And in other years he hoped the public and Congress would better grasp the wisdom of doing more.

He approached this problem of the nation's fiscal re-education in three different ways:

1. First, while quietly accepting the necessity of unbalanced budgets, he made clear that he was no wastrel. To the despair of the liberals, he talked the lingo of the Budget-balancers even as he incurred sizable deficits. It was Kennedy's only means, as Paul Samuelson pointed out, of "quieting irrational opposition" to his Budget increases. He stressed his objective of balancing the Budget "over the cycle" of good years and bad combined. He said all the right phrases about getting "a dollar of service for the dollars we spend." He stressed in 1961 that his domestic program, of and by itself, would not unbalance the Budget his predecessor left behind, in 1962 that his Budget as presented was in balance, and even in

1963 that his Budget, although in deficit due to the proposed tax cut and military and space expenditures, nevertheless reduced "civilian" spending.

While none of these statements was false, they were no more "the whole truth and nothing but the truth" than any other Presidential Budget statement in modern history. They imposed ceilings on those of us helping to prepare his budgets and legislation, but within those ceilings there were a number of ways in which the figures could be fitted without drastically altering major programs. The Budget is only a set of estimates —of how much taxes will bring in, how many contracts will be let before the fiscal year ends, at what date new programs will be started, which payments can be speeded up or deferred, and many other unknowns. Those estimates depend on other estimates—of the economy that produces the revenue, of the weather that affects the crops, of the wars that change defense spending—and those estimates are based on still more estimates.

Low ceilings, in short, can still permit several rooms. The best example was the badly unbalanced "balanced" Budget President Eisenhower left behind for Kennedy's first full fiscal year. It assumed prosperity revenues at a time of recession. It recommended projects and programs for which no funds were included. It assumed, contrary to all experience, that a proposed postal rate increase would be approved by the Congress and in effect within ten weeks. It greatly underestimated expenditures for farm price supports. It proposed, with tongue in cheek, that Congress would terminate or sharply cut back several basic housing, airport, REA and other programs which everyone knew Congress would expand. And it omitted certain financial obligations to which the Federal Government was wholly committed. I can truthfully say that no Kennedy Budget ever resorted to this extreme to feign fiscal responsibility.

But to the surprise of many of his appointees, President Kennedy not only talked but acted the role of true economizer. His two chief tasks upon taking office were to revive the economy and shore up our defenses, and neither could be accomplished by slashing a wholly inadequate Budget. But he regarded deficits necessitated by excessive unemployment as wholly different from deficits produced by uncontrolled spending, and he had no intention of permitting the latter. "Washington is filled," he observed, "with dedicated men and women who feel that government funds should be spent for one purpose or another," and he intended to make certain they were his purposes. Leaving most program funds relatively untouched, he was suspicious of all personnel requests, and he was willing to start with the White House, cutting back on the grounds and service personnel and keeping expenses down. (Judging from his delight over a letter Thomas Jefferson had written requesting White House gardeners who could double as musicians after dinner, he may have had similar proposals in mind.)

He personally scrutinized every agency request with a cold eye and encouraged his Budget Director to say "no." From the amounts requested by the individual agency heads and service chiefs, the President and his Budget Director (aided, in the latter case, by his Defense Secretary) cut as much as $20-25 billion before each Budget was submitted to the Congress. He increased funds actually allocated for true social and economic benefits faster than his predecessor; but, by reducing the postal deficit through higher rates, by avoiding higher storage costs for surplus grain and cotton, by selling mortgages and other Federal financial assets to private creditors, by increasing automation in the Post Office and other agencies, by putting the Interstate Highway program back on a self-financing basis through increased truck and gas taxes, by requiring the agencies to absorb through other reductions nearly half the cost of their Federal pay raise, by clamping down on personnel increases, by abolishing unnecessary operations and offices, by not spending all the moneys appropriated by the Congress, and by holding the cost of new domestic programs to the lowest possible level, he was able to show in 1963 a cumulative increase in "domestic civilian expenditures" over his three years smaller than the increase over the preceding three Eisenhower years. To do that, while adding new programs and expanding old ones, was quite a feat. The reduction in domestic spending proposed in January, 1963, had, in fact, been accomplished only four times in the preceding fifteen years.

He learned anew, however, that most members of Congress favored economy only where it did not impinge upon their own interests. Many of those who forced him to ask constantly for increases in the artificial ceiling on the public debt were far more willing to vote unwanted funds for military or farm programs than to raise postal rates, close tax loopholes, charge barges for their use of Federally financed waterways or restrict farm surpluses. Fiscal years 1962 and 1963 produced deficits, instead of the balances predicted, largely because of lagging recession revenues and increased defense and space spending, but also because of Congressional opposition to Kennedy's farm and revenue measures.

President Kennedy's largest and most controversial savings were in the area of his largest expenditure increases—national defense. The Budget Bureau estimated that the first-year costs of our entire new legislative programs in 1963 were not so great as the annual savings already being achieved in the Pentagon. Those savings were achieved through more efficient logistics, organization and procurement, through the reduction of civilian personnel to their lowest levels since pre-Korean days, through the termination of obsolescent or unworkable weapons systems and bases, and primarily through the managerial genius of the Secretary of Defense and the political courage of the President who backed him.

Robert McNamara found a chaotic budget situation when he entered the Pentagon. In practice each service submitted and received individual budgets largely unrelated to each other, with no logical analyses of how much fire power was actually needed. He found no internal consistency— no matching of our available forces with all the elaborate NSC planning papers, war plans and contingency plans, no correlation between ground forces and air support, or between munitions and men. He began immediately to question, to study, to plan, and he began to build and to cut simultaneously.

On occasion Kennedy's budget, science and other White House advisers would press for even more reductions in weapons systems than the Secretary would support. McNamara, while acknowledging the possibility of surplus destructive capacity or "overkill" in his recommendations, frankly told the President that neither of them could count on the continued confidence of the service chiefs if much more was cut. As it was, the Air Force, its contractors and friends in the Congress resented the cutback in the B-70, the phase-out of the B-47 and Snark missile and the cancellation of further Titan missiles, of Skybolt and of the nuclear-powered plane; the Army and its friends resented the limitations on the Nike-Zeus antimissile missile; and the Navy and its friends resented his hostility to more carriers.

The "military-industrial" complex, of which Eisenhower's farewell message warned in one of his greatest services as President—a complex combining powerful economic and political pressures on behalf of these military projects—brought constant pressure on the President and Secretary through unions, community leaders, businessmen, scientists, politicians and magazine advertisements. "I see nothing wrong with that," said the President in his December, 1962, panel telecast.

> Every time you cancel a weapons system, it affects a good many thousands of people . . . it is a very difficult struggle with the Congress. Twice now Congress has appropriated the [extra] money [for the B-70], twice we have not spent that money. But I must say as of today I don't feel that the pressure on us is excessive.

A few months later he felt differently, as a Senate investigation tried unsuccessfully to force a change in McNamara's awarding of the contract for a new TFX aircraft. "What we are really dealing with in the TFX investigation," read an internal government memorandum, is the spectacle of a large corporation, backed by Air Force Generals, using the investigatory powers of Congress to intimidate civilian officials just because it lost out on a contract. If . . . successful, it will be impossible for any civilian official ever again to exercise judgment . . . [without] measuring the influence of large corporations with Congress or . . . to control the military men who are theoretically under his direction.

But the effort failed, and so did all the other complaints about such McNamara innovations as (1) five-year projections of cost effectiveness; (2) budgeting according to each major type of mission rather than each branch of the service; (3) the comparison of systems and support elements within each service to eliminate duplications; and (4) the use of computers and civilian intellectuals to analyze performance. More importantly, the Kennedy administration refused to commit itself to:

• Spending another several billion dollars on a nuclear-powered plane that, after fifteen years and one billion dollars, still couldn't fly.

• Spending another $13-15 billion on the B-70 bomber, its name temporarily changed to the RS-70 in the hopeless attempt to find a mission for it that was feasible, necessary and, in JFK's words, "worth the money we would have to put into it."

• Spending another several billion dollars on a Skybolt air-to-ground missile that still combined all the disadvantages of the B-52 bomber that fired it (comparatively vulnerable on the ground and slow to reach targets) with all the disadvantages of the poorest missiles (comparatively less accuracy and destructive power).

• Spending another $11-12 billion on a battery of twenty-six Nike-Zeus antimissile missiles, at best protecting less than a third of our citizenry, and still unable to discriminate between an incoming missile and the flock of decoys that accompanied it. To be sure, said the President, the first nation to perfect a missile defense would have an immense psychological as well as military advantage. "But it will cost billions. There is no sense going ahead until that system is perfected."

Moreover, these projected costs were only estimates. History showed that the final costs for acquiring advanced weapons systems in modern times have averaged three times the original estimates. John Kennedy did not believe that the economic health of either the country or any community had to depend on excessive or inefficient armaments. Money saved by McNamara's ax was used to strengthen our sword and shield. Defense spending rose some eight billion dollars under Kennedy, constituting most of his Budget increase, but it was spent on more solid and dependable deterrents from which the above systems might otherwise have taken money.

McNamara and Kennedy also made certain that defense dollars were not spent on "gold-plating" needlessly fancy and expensive specifications,[2] on surplus installations, or on an overreliance on cost-plus-fixed-fee contracts and noncompetitive bidding. They formed a single Defense Intelligence Agency, which produced one confidential daily report instead of the previous eleven. They formed a single Defense Supply Agency, which tightened up procurement practices on everything from different belt buckles to missiles, noted that Army helicopters could use the one million too many small rockets in Air Force stockpiles (savings: $41 million), abolished eighty-one different Pentagon shipping forms for one standard bill of lading and avoided dozens of other duplications. They undertook an initial reorganization of the National Guard and Reserves, which had been wholly inadequate for modern emergencies but the pet project of most Congressmen and governors, and they shut down, sold or cut back nearly three hundred inefficient installations. "The defense establishment," said Kennedy, "must be lean and fit."

2. Kennedy's second approach to the public's fiscal education was to bridge the gap between myth and reality by placing the goals of the former in the perspective of the latter. Those who wanted balanced budgets were informed that all three Kennedy cash budgets would have been balanced *if* we had full employment, or if there were no arms race, or if repayable loans and long-term capital outlays (which private business budgets would treat differently) were not included in full. Those who talked of swollen Federal payrolls were informed that the ratio of Federal employees to every hundred Americans was declining, and that nearly three-fourths of all Federal civilian employment was in three agencies: Defense, Post Office and the Veterans Administration. Those who were concerned about the national debt were informed that that debt, as a *proportion* of our economic output, was being reduced to a postwar low.

The Federal debt and spending figures had to be *compared,* said the President. Even the average businessman and homeowner had gone proportionately more deeply into debt than the Federal Government, despite all the talk about running the government like a housewife's or grocery store's budget.

He particularly liked to compare the Federal Government's record with that of state and local governments. Their payrolls, debts and civilian expenditures were climbing much higher and faster than their Federal counterparts. He was waiting for the day when an attack on his fiscal "irresponsibility" by Senator Harry Byrd would give him an opening to compare Virginia's fiscal record under the Byrd machine with the Federal Government's:

---

[2] By substituting molded plastic for stainless steel, for example, the cost of a small turbine wheel was reduced from $175 to $2.

PERCENT INCREASES BETWEEN 1948 AND 1961

	General Expenditures	Civil Service and Other Employees	Outstanding Debt
Federal Government	163	27	17
Virginia State Government	199	70	864

But his favorite comparison of all, not surprisingly, was with the fiscal record of his Republican predecessor. On occasion he would ask visitors: considering Truman's expenditures in Korea and at the end of the Second World War, how do you think Eisenhower's eight budgets compared with Truman's eight budgets? No one ever came close to the correct answer: Eisenhower outspent Truman by $182 billion. "You could win a bet on that in any bar in the country," the President told me when I first gave him the figure. He would also cite Eisenhower's record of five deficits in eight years, including an all-time peacetime high of $12 billion, the $23 billion Eisenhower added to the national debt and the 200,000 civilian employees he added to the Federal payroll. All Presidents, Kennedy would then continue, outspend their predecessors in a growing, progressive nation. Eisenhower's Budget Director had issued a study forecasting continued Budget increases regardless of the party in power. The Kennedy administration's "domestic" increases, which were less than a quarter of his new expenditures, didn't sound so outrageous when shown to be less than in the last three years of his predecessor.

However, despite criticisms from the left that he ought to be spending much more, the President recognized that comparatively few of the voters who were concerned about too much spending, and who read publications concerned about too much spending, would ever regard him as more thrifty than Eisenhower. He tried. He asked the Council of Economic Advisers and Budget Bureau to prepare detailed answers to inaccurate editorials on his fiscal policies in *Life* and the *Reader's Digest*, calling one of Walter Heller's assistants at home one Sunday afternoon to ask questions on each line in the latter's suggested reply. He commented in a news conference on the failure of the press to assist his fiscal re-education program, with almost all newspapers persisting in repeating the same clichés about rising outlays, debt and payrolls, instead of the declining ratio of those figures to the national population and output. "One of the reasons we have such difficulty getting an acceptance of our expenditures and our tax policies," he said, "is because people misread the statistics or are misled."

3. The third and final approach to obtaining a more sophisticated understanding of debt and budget problems was the most direct: to impress upon the public, without comparisons or contrivance, the necessity and desirability of not only the increases in his Budget but the

increases in the deficit. Each year his Economic Report grew a little bolder along these lines. In 1961 one had to look hard to find in his Message on Economic Recovery the conclusion that "deficits accompany —and indeed help overcome—low levels of economic activity." But by 1963, dropping any pretense of offering a balanced Budget, he was more boldly pointing out—even in a speech to the nation's editors, the watch- dogs of our fiscal integrity—that "carefully screened and selected Federal expenditure programs can play a useful role, both singly and in combina- tion; to cut $5-10 billion [from the Budget], unless the private economy is booming . . . would harm both the nation and the typical neighborhood in it."

He reminded several audiences of Eisenhower's experience in 1958— that trying to cut back expenditures to fit revenues meant contract cancellations, payment stretch-outs, grant-in-aid suspensions, employee layoffs, and thus less taxable income, more outlays for the jobless and still more Budget deficits. Over and over he stressed that point: it is un- employment and recession that cut revenues and produce deficits.

He tried to get people to think about what the Budget is, what their money goes for. "The Federal Government is the people . . . not a remote bureaucracy," he said, "and the Budget is a reflection of their needs. . . . To take the expenditures required to meet these needs out of the Federal Budget will only cast them on state and local governments"—and they are doing worse fiscally.

In a chart session with Congressional Democrats in January, 1963, he showed that four-fifths of his Budget increases had gone for defense, space and the cost of past or future wars—that the Budget represented not a bureaucratic grab but loans to farmers and small businessmen, aid to education and conservation, urban renewal and area redevelop- ment. Using similar charts in a talk to the editors, he used an imaginary cross-section community, "Random Village," to illustrate how all families are benefited by Federal programs. He spoke to bankers, students, labor groups, business groups, economists and others in his effort to put across the facts of economic life.

He also encouraged articles on the need for spending and encouraged his economic advisers, Treasury Secretary and Budget Director to talk plainly. Heller, by testifying in 1963 that popular opposition to tax cuts must be due partly to a "basic puritan ethic," invited the delightful riposte by one Republican that he'd "rather be a Puritan than a Heller." New Budget Director Gordon, in office only five weeks, testified that deep cut- backs in Federal spending would reduce prosperity, profits and employ- ment but not the deficit, and Harry Byrd promptly called for his dismissal. "I must have set some kind of record," Gordon wryly told the President, to have invited ouster demands so quickly. But even earlier the President's leading Republican adviser, Secretary Dillon, had, to the dismay of his former colleagues in the GOP and on Wall Street, stated the need for deficit financing to treat economic slack, a truth which even previous Democratic Secretaries of the Treasury had been consistently unwilling to acknowledge.

THE 1962 PAUSE

The economy, which had expanded vigorously in 1961, slowed its pace in mid-1962. The growth continued but the zip was gone, and some of the figures were disturbing. The rate of private inventory accumulation —which had been built up to an abnormally high level of seven billion dollars in the first quarter, partly because a steel strike was anticipated —fell off to one billion in the third quarter. Unemployment leveled off at an uncomfortable 5.5 percent. Consumers were saving more instead of spending. Business investment in new plant and equipment, for which the tax credit had not yet been enacted, was low.

The most dramatic cause for concern was a severe drop in the stock market. After reaching a peak on December 12, 1961, the average price of stocks bought and sold on the New York Stock Exchange declined by roughly one-quarter, and roughly one-quarter of this drop occurred on Monday, May 28. It was only the twenty-fourth largest proportionate drop in market history. But it was the sharpest one-day drop in the number of points on the Index since the crash of 1929, and immediately fears and rumors arose—and in some quarters were inspired—that it was 1929 all over again. *Time* magazine speculated on Kennedy becoming "the Democratic version of Herbert Hoover." Wild stories spread that the decline was due to a business plot to hurt Kennedy, to a European withdrawal of funds or to Kennedy's attack on Big Steel. Some said it was a once-in-a-generation break, others said that it was due to increased competition from Europe, others attributed it to excess capacity in our sluggish economy.

The simplest explanation to many businessmen was that Kennedy was against profits and free enterprise. His mail and press were filled with blame for "the Kennedy market." "I received," the President noted a year later when the market was setting record highs,

> several thousands of letters when the stock market went way down in May and June of 1962, blaming me and talking about the "Kennedy market." . . . Now that it has broken through the Dow-Jones average . . . I haven't gotten a single letter . . . about the "Kennedy market."

Harried stockbrokers who found their customers taking their money elsewhere were busy looking for a scapegoat. And, in what even the financial community's idol, William McChesney Martin, Jr., termed "childish behavior," many brokers and businessmen placed sole blame upon the President.

They had few facts to support them. Those who blamed it on his steel price fight of early April neglected to mention that the decline had begun back in December, that the ratio of advances to declines had been adverse since the previous August and that stock values in many of the basic industries had been going down for several years. Those who blamed it on Kennedy's policies neglected to mention that the decline had merely brought prices back to where they stood on the day of his election. Those who said it was a certain sign of recession neglected to mention that the thirteen such drops since the thirties had not even all preceded, much less produced, a recession and that, on the contrary, a sharper drop over a shorter period in May, 1946, had been followed by record-breaking prosperity. Those who compared it to 1929 neglected to mention the fact that the earlier crash had been twice as large and twice as fast in a much smaller economy, preceded by months of declining business and construction, and aggravated by uncontrolled speculation, questionable brokerage practices, a recession in Europe and a lack of Federal floors beneath the economy such as unemployment compensation and insured bank deposits.

Nevertheless the highly publicized break in the market, and the three days of gyrations and four weeks of sag that followed, seemed certain to disturb business and consumer spending. The President called an emergency meeting for May 29 in the Cabinet Room. It was not a cheerful way to spend his forty-fifth birthday. But somewhat to his surprise, he found Dillon, Heller, Federal Reserve Chairman Martin and the other economists present generally unperturbed. The critical loss of confidence, they said, was in the market, not in the economy or even in the administration. Most financial analysts had been predicting for some time that stock prices could not long continue to rise further and faster than potential profits, reaching paper values twenty or more times their earning power. But too many investors, large and small, had been bidding prices up and up, not out of an interest in dividends or corporate ownership, but out of a desire for tax-favored capital gains in an inflationary economy. Now inflation was over, a fact for which the steel price rescission may have served some as a reminder. Once investors started weighing the actual earning power of their shares instead of hoping for continued price rises, many of them realized that bonds and savings banks offered a better return on their money than overpriced and risky stocks. This long-expected downward re-evaluation, the President was told, while temporarily worsened by speculation and its own momentum, would in the long run put the market on a sounder basis.[3]

But the President expressed concern in our meeting about the market continuing to fall and dragging the economy down with it. Essentially, in addition to pressing for pending economic legislation, three new courses of action were considered:

1. First was a Presidential "fireside chat" to reassure the nation, to place the market drop in perspective, to review the basic strength of the economy, to contrast the situation with 1929 and to call for calm and confidence. But after work on a possible speech was well under way, this course was suspended, to be revived only if selling went completely out of hand. Stocks were gyrating up, down and up again. Less than 2 percent of the total volume of stock was actually being sold by panicky or margin-called owners, and a nationwide television speech might only spread their panic to others. By staying out of it, by keeping calm, the President hoped to help spread calm, and in time turn the paper losses of the 98 percent who held on into actual gains. He decided, as a "low-key" substitute, simply to open his press conference on June 7 with an over-all look at the economy, using a very mild and very brief analysis of the stock market as a springboard for a review of his program.

2. The second possible action considered that Tuesday was to lower the "margin requirement," the percentage of actual cash which a stock buyer must put up when he buys on credit. No legislation, only a change in Federal Reserve regulations, was required to reduce this cash requirement from 70 percent, where it then stood, to 50 percent, thus enabling and encouraging more investors to buy more stocks.

The Council of Economic Advisers favored an immediate reduction, partly as a demonstration of Presidential determination (although, due to the peculiar status of the Federal Reserve Board, the President could only request, not direct, the Board to do anything). But there was no evidence that a lack of credit was the market's immediate problem, and it was agreed by the others that any immediate move might

3 A year later, when the market was once again high and the belief that Kennedy's steel fight had caused the May drop was well accepted, an expert study sponsored by the SEC, whose careful investigation of shoddy stock practices had also been blamed by some, presented facts and figures which exploded all myths. It was not a plot of the professionals against Kennedy. Although many of them were buying bargains while the public was unloading, there was no evidence of manipulation. But neither had Kennedy caused the drop. Long before the steel fight the market was going down, the mutual funds were selling, the big-name stocks were declining to a more reasonable ratio of earnings, and investors were finding more attractive security in bonds and banks. Some of the market letters had been warning that prices were overvalued, but high-pressure merchandising techniques had continued to push up sales. The end of inflation had brought the inevitable shake-out, long overdue after a get-rich-quick public had speculated feverishly on glamour stocks "with scientific sounding names ending in -namics, -omics, or -mation."

be interpreted as an admission of serious trouble. Instead, margin requirements were quietly lowered to 50 percent some six weeks later, and by late October the market had started booming again, soaring a year after the May scare back up to its December, 1961, high, from which it continued to rise.

3. The third proposal considered in our May 29 meeting, which was considered throughout the balance of the summer, and which related more to the general economy than the stock market alone, was a "quickie" income tax cut of $5-10 billion. It was to apply to both individuals and corporations, and last one year or even less. The Council of Economic Advisers was for it, unless the economy improved. Secretary Dillon was against it, unless the economy worsened. The President reserved judgment until he saw which way the economy moved. Another meeting was scheduled for one week later, and similar meetings were held regularly throughout the summer.

Even during that first week the pressures increased. Senate Democratic Whip Humphrey called for a temporary tax cut. So did Secretary of Commerce Hodges. Secretary of the Treasury Dillon assured Senator Byrd in open hearings that none was planned. The President was irked by Cabinet members publicly committing him either way in advance of his decision, and irked as well by press speculation that he had secretly decided for a "quickie."

At the June 6 meeting Heller was more gloomy about the economy. He was backed by outside advisers Samuelson and Robert Solow, who used language that hit the President where it hurt. While not yet foreseeing a new recession in 1962, they felt that

> for the first time the prudent odds for a so-called "Kennedy recession" . . . have ceased to be negligible. . . . The first Kennedy expansion may be no larger than the 25 months of Eisenhower's last recovery. . . . Why can't America take the initiative needed to forestall unnecessary recessions? . . . Only an early tax cut appears to be capable of giving the economy the stimulus it needs in time.

By the end of June, Samuelson had raised the odds on a 1962 recession from 20 percent to even. By mid-July Samuelson and Solow spoke, they said, for "a majority of economists inside and outside the government"[4] in asserting that, without a temporary emergency tax cut, losses of profits, production, employment and total output in 1962 would characterize "the developing recession." Walter Heller feared a downturn "before the snows melt" (they melt late in his native Minnesota). Rockefeller and labor, the Chamber of Commerce and the ADA, the academic eco-

---

[4] Though not for Galbraith, who continued to advise the President from abroad on the virtues of more public spending.

nomic advisers to the Treasury, all joined in urging a tax cut in 1962, though they all differed sharply on what kind.

But in each of our meetings throughout the summer, Douglas Dillon and others offered persuasive arguments to the contrary. The economic indicators were, as the President described them, "a mixed bag," some down, some up, some steady. If the Congress would act promptly on the tax bills already before it—including the investment tax credit, a repeal of surface transportation taxes and, above all, a bill providing stand-by authority to adjust taxes in an emergency—that would be enough. If Congress was balking at these, then sending up a new bill would not help and might only endanger the tax credit bill then before the Senate. Moreover, argued Dillon, the President had already indicated early in 1961 that a comprehensive tax reform bill, to be submitted after passage of the "little" tax reform bill which contained the investment credit, would include some reduction in tax rates. That hope should be enough. It involved waiting only a few months; and any reduction taken in 1962 could not be used in 1963 as sugar coating for an otherwise unpalatable reform bill.

The legislative and economic arguments, in fact, overlapped. If the Congress passed a temporary tax cut and it proved premature, the President's overreaction, an attribute he sought always to avoid, might make action more difficult when it was really needed. Nor did political arguments aimed at the 1962 mid-term elections impress him. Not only was he loath to be charged with partisan motivations, the record did not support them: whatever party was in control of the Congress during the three tax cuts enacted since the war had on each occasion lost the next election. Nor did he want a big tax cut to push his deficit beyond that Eisenhower record he liked to cite.

But the greater likelihood, O'Brien, Dillon and others reported, was that a temporary tax cut could not be passed. Too many key figures were against it or unconvinced. For the President to assert that a "quickie" tax cut was essential to our economic health, and then have it rejected, might well worsen the climate of confidence, further depress the stock market and impair prospects for the 1963 tax bill. Even the supporters of a temporary tax cut in the Congress and business community could not agree on its size, scope, timing, nature or conditions. The number of amendments certain to be offered held out the prospects of at best delay, at worst a bill so bad it would have to be vetoed, and, most likely, no bill at all.

Senator Douglas, a long-time advocate of tax cuts to fight recessions and an eminent economist, opposed a cut in 1962 in a thoughtful memorandum to the President. Senator Byrd not unsurprisingly was strongly opposed, and, most importantly, Chairman Wilbur Mills of the House Ways and Means Committee—who, in an unusual Presidential move, had been invited to sit in on one of Kennedy's sessions with his economists—remained unconvinced that a cut was needed or could pass. Other solons were for such a bill only if its economic impact were canceled by cutting out of the Budget the same amount of funds as the tax cut would release into the economy, thus rendering it meaningless.

In short, it was clear to Kennedy that, in the absence of overwhelming evidence that a tax reduction bill was needed to prevent a recession, the Congress, which had already spent a year and a half on his first tax measure, would not pass such a bill in that session. The President had no choice but to wait for that overwhelming evidence, and it never came.

Did Kennedy really want a quickie tax cut in 1962 which the Congress prevented him from obtaining? Its advocates thought so. The press said so. But, having taken part in all the meetings, my own judgment is that he, too, was unconvinced that a temporary cut at that time was essential, as distinguished from merely being helpful, in the absence of that overwhelming evidence that was required to get the bill through. "We want to be convinced," he told a news conference questioner, "that the course of action we are advocating is essential before we advocate it." Cool as the pressures built up around him, accused of undue delay and indecision, he refused to be stampeded into an unnecessary and unsuccessful fight that could only impair his long-range economic goals and his relations with the Congress. "Wilbur Mills," he said one day, "knows that he was chairman of Ways and Means before I got here and that he'll still be chairman after I've gone—and he knows I know it. I don't have any hold on him."

While he waited for the evidence, he pursued an alternative program, quietly and administratively increasing expenditures in a number of areas, publicly pressing for Congressional action on the tax credit, on public works and on other economic measures, liberalizing tax rules on depreciation, and telling each press conference that "we will continue to watch the economy." Finally, after a review of the figures for July showed no signs of a recession sufficiently strong to convince him or the Congress, he delivered on August 13 an economic report to the nation by television from the White House. He concluded that report by promising a permanent tax cut bill in 1963 and by rejecting a temporary tax cut unless subsequent events made it necessary to recall the Congress for that purpose.

> Under the right circumstances that is . . . a sound and effective weapon . . . [to be] fired only at a period of maximum advantage. . . . Proposing an emergency tax cut tonight, *a cut which could not now be either justified or enacted*, would needlessly undermine confidence both at home and abroad.

The operative words, which are italicized, satisfied both sides within the ranks of his advisers. Those opposed to the temporary tax cut agreed with his judgment that it could not be justified, and those favoring it accepted his judgment that it could not be enacted.

The speech, however, was in every other respect less satisfying. We tried every possible way to make a dull economics speech interesting. The President used charts beside his desk. He cited real-life human interest examples of individuals helped by his programs. But despite these efforts and despite, or perhaps partly because of, the President's effort to extemporize informally as he moved from desk to chart, that speech was the worst speech he ever gave from the White House on television. It sought to educate the American people on the new fiscal philosophy. It urged action by the Congress on pending economic measures. It was, in short, the kind of "fireside chat" the critics said he needed. But it dealt not with a new crisis, only an explanation of why there was none —not with a new bill, only an explanation of why there would be none— and that kind of speech cannot be exciting. "I would call it," said the President to one professor, "a C-minus performance."

THE 1963 TAX BILL

Nevertheless that drab speech, and the aforementioned June 7 opening press statement on taxes, laid the groundwork for one of the boldest and most far-reaching domestic economic measures ever proposed—the $10 billion tax cut bill of 1963, offered without experiencing or even predicting for the immediate future any of the three traditional occasions for a tax cut: a Budget surplus, a reduction in spending or a recession. While it would be convenient to assert that this bill was conceived solely by President Kennedy as a defiant challenge to the fiscal troglodytes, or that massive tax reduction to keep the expansion going had long been his plan for 1963, the actual facts are more haphazard.

The origins of that bill can be traced to the preinaugural task force on taxation, commissioned by the President-elect and headed by Professor Stanley Surrey, who was later Assistant Secretary of the Treasury. That report, like the President's comprehensive Message on Taxation in April, 1961, recommended without details a sweeping, long-range, tax reform bill which would broaden the tax base by closing loopholes, end all inequities of benefit to the few, and thereby make possible lower rates for all. It was a tax reform bill, not a tax cut, and while it was agreed by Surrey and Dillon that the reforms would make possible the same amount of revenues at lower rates, and could only be passed with the help of such a "sweetener," there was no mention or intention at that time of reducing the government's net take. The President publicly emphasized, in fact, that with "budget problems as difficult as they are . . . we cannot carry out a tax reduction in these critical times." He planned to offer this bill in January, 1962, enabling the Congress to concentrate in 1961 on the "little" tax bill, a bill designed to help the economy and balance of payments with no net loss of revenue. In the unlikely event that he could achieve a Budget surplus, he planned a tax cut and a debt reduction as well.

But the "little" bill did not pass until late in 1962, making impossible the proposal of a larger, more controversial tax reform before January of the following year. Meanwhile the President was rejecting Walter Heller's advocacy of a quickie tax cut in the spring of 1961 and the summer of 1962. But even as he rejected them—and particularly as he listened to the arguments against a temporary tax hike in the 1961 Berlin crisis—the President gave thought to a favorite Heller theme: namely, that the Federal tax rates, established in wartime to prevent inflation, were taking in so much money as the economy recovered that they were draining off the private funds needed for full growth. Heller wanted a quickie tax cut as a down payment on a permanent reduction.

Between the two crucial meetings in the late spring of 1962—the first held just after the stock market tumble and the second just before the President's June 7 press conference—Douglas Dillon, aware of the strength in Heller's argument, and trying to fight off a temporary tax cut that might block the 1963 reform bill, accepted the view that the 1963 bill should provide a net tax reduction. In a speech on June 4 he said that reforms would offset reductions in the 1963 bill "in whole or in part." But in our June 6 meeting it became "in part"—not because he was as yet an advocate of massive tax reduction, but because he thought a small net reduction would help pass tax reforms.

On the following day the President, seeking to give the nation more cause for confidence after the drop in the market and the pause in the economy, and seeking to answer public pressures for a tax cut that summer, included in his press conference review of the economy an almost hidden pledge:

> *Three:* A comprehensive tax reform bill . . . will be offered for action by the next Congress, making effective as of January 1 of next year an across-the-board reduction in personal and corporate income tax rates which will not be wholly offset by other reforms —in other words, a net tax reduction.

The emphasis was still on tax reform but the commitment had been made. The August economic "fireside chat" gave slightly more prominence to a tax cut but no more details: "An across-the-board, top-to-bottom cut in both corporate and personal income taxes . . . a creative tax cut creating more jobs and income and eventually more revenue." It also cited the Heller doctrine that "our present tax system is a drag on economic recovery and economic growth, biting heavily into the purchasing power of every taxpayer and every consumer."

Nevertheless the President remained unenthusiastic, if not skeptical, about tax reduction. He still thought in terms of tax reform more than a tax cut for 1963. He was committed to no figure. He barely mentioned it in the mid-term campaign. Division, moreover, was deep within the administration and its advisers. Some economists wanted all reforms dropped as too controversial a drag on the tax cut. Some department heads wanted the cut small to prevent its reducing room in the Budget for their programs. Some wanted cuts and reforms in separate bills. The Vice President argued that oil depletion reforms would handicap the whole bill. There were arguments over whether to include corporations at all, whether to exclude all but corporations, whether to stretch the cut over two or three years or include it all immediately, whether to concentrate on lower-bracket or high-income relief.

But when the bill was finally hammered out, first in Washington and then in our annual planning sessions in Palm Beach over the holidays, the internal arguments had largely vanished. It was the classic example of everyone getting something and no one getting everything. All agreed that the economy needed a boost, that many tax reforms would help growth and that a wholesale reduction in tax rates was the best reform of all. Proposals for rate changes, reforms, the Budget and the statutory debt limit were all juggled, rearranged and revised in relation to each other, as the President insisted that Eisenhower's $12 billion deficit could not be exceeded, that "civilian domestic" spending had to decline, and that the Budget could not create headlines by going over $100 billion. He knew the Budget had to grow if the economy was to grow. But he felt that passage of the tax bill was far more important to our economic growth than the difference between his proposing spending estimates of $98 billion instead of $100 billion, and that the latter figure was sufficiently more dramatic that it should be avoided.

Throughout the fall, however, as these agreements were reached, the President, preoccupied with the Cuban missile crisis, was still almost indifferent to the tax bill. With the help of his newly enacted tax incentive for investment, continued liberal credit and increased public spending, the dark clouds of recession which had first caused all the tax talk had vanished. The stock market was climbing again. The growth of the economy was still too slow to create enough jobs, but that seemed a difficult premise on which to sell to the Congress a far-reaching bill of this kind.

The President did not become fully enthusiastic until December, and it was the convincing effect of one of his own speeches that helped convince him. The speech, designed to unveil the basic tax and Budget outlines, was delivered to a conservative gathering of mostly Republican businessmen, the Economic Club of New York. The President realized that the economy had resumed its growth and that any attempt to use an antirecession justification for his bill would seem strained. He planned to talk instead of "the burden on private income and the deterrents to private initiative imposed by our present tax system . . . that . . . reduce the financial incentives for personal investment, effort and risk-taking." It sounded like Hoover, but it was actually Heller.

Earlier in the week, the words of Wilbur Mills in a magazine interview had been interpreted as opposition to any tax cut unless it was accompanied, as it could not be, by a Budget cut. But Mills, with whom the President had been in close contact, had actually used the words "increased control of the rises in expenditures." And in his Economic Club speech the President revealed the planned reduction in nondefense spending as well as other increased Budget controls.

Ken Galbraith, stopping by the White House from India as the speech was being finished, called it "the most Republican speech since McKinley." He preferred releasing into the economy an additional $10 billion in Federal expenditures, on top of normal Budget increases, instead of a $10 billion tax cut. But the President felt that that alternative was unobtainable in the Eighty-eighth Congress (and told Galbraith he had usually found it helpful to have his lanky friend on the other side anyway). The key member of the Senate Finance Committee on whom the President was depending, Senator Robert Kerr of Oklahoma, also made suggestions for the speech, shortly before he entered the hospital from which he did not emerge. Mills read it without commitment. Dillon, Heller and others all added their views.

But the man most concerned about the speech was the President. He worried less about the policy than the Economic Club audience, wondering how they would swallow a large tax cut at a time of increasing deficits, increasing expenditures and increasing prosperity. "If I can convince them," he said as we reviewed the final draft in his New York hotel room, "I can convince anybody."

He did convince them. The speech—sounding, said *Time* magazine, like that of an officer of the National Association of Manufacturers—was well received (partly because it gave no details on either reforms or the size of the deficit). The President's own enthusiasm grew. He began to look to the tax cut as his most potent weapon against the persistent unemployment still plaguing him. He began to concentrate on it in his conferences, his speeches, his Budget, his legislative program and his State of the Union Message; and tax cuts, rather than tax reform, dominated his talks about the bill.

But the public was initially indifferent, and despite broad business and labor support the Congress was still far from enthusiastic. If Congress had been unwilling to pass a tax cut the previous summer when recession threatened and the Budget (as proposed) was in balance, why did Kennedy think he could suggest a cut in 1963, when no recession threatened and the Budget was both larger and out of balance? Almost every Democrat had some better scheme for reducing rates. Almost every Republican denounced the Budget. Almost every lobby group denounced one or more reforms. The difficulties encountered by the "little" reform bill of 1962, which limited expense account abuses and cracked down on overseas tax havens, were minuscule compared to the opposition to the new reforms. Every legislator's favorite reform closed some other legislator's favorite loophole. And even the tax cut created quarrels among its supporters as to whether business or low-income groups were getting too large a share. Congressmen perfectly willing to leave farm, military and other policies to the more specialized committee members had no hesitancy in feeling expert on tax changes.

The Republicans called the tax cut the "biggest gamble in history" and predicted that unemployment would not decline. But having long talked about removing the heavy hand of government, they were unable to quarrel with the President's reasons for a tax cut and quarreled instead with the Budget. We had strained painfully but successfully to reduce that Budget to meet the three Presidential limitations earlier mentioned. But Everett Dirksen called it "incredible," Clarence Cannon called it "monstrous" and Charles Halleck said it made "a mockery of the administration's brave talk." The President calmly emphasized that the choice was not between a Budget deficit and a Budget surplus but between two kinds of deficits—one from "waste and weakness" as the result of slack growth and lagging taxable income and one "incurred as we build our future strength" on the way to a full-employment economy. With full employment, he said, we would have no deficit, but delaying a tax cut until expenditures could be equally cut meant waiting until our population stopped growing and the Communists stopped threatening.

Then former President Eisenhower entered the fray with a letter to Halleck. He called the combination of "a massive deficit . . . lavish new spending and a huge tax cut . . . fiscal recklessness," leading in time not to "a free country with bright opportunities but a vast wasteland of debt and financial chaos." He endorsed a cut of some $13 to $15 billion from Kennedy's Budget. "May I stress," said the former Republican President in closing to the Republican House Leader, "there is not a trace of partisanship in the views here expressed."

The President made no direct reply. But a few weeks later, in answering a question from the nation's editors, he reviewed both the Budget economies he had made and the necessity of major Budget increases, and then added, without a trace of partisanship:

> I am strongly against the wholesale Budget cuts of the kind that have been talked about, $5-$10-$15 billion. I can think of nothing more ruinous to the security of this country and our economy. And I think that those who advocate it were in many cases the architects of the fiscal and monetary policies which brought us into a recession in '58, a $12.5 billion deficit in '58, the largest outflow . . . of gold and dollars . . . and a recession in 1960. We hope to do better.

From the other side liberal Democrats complained that the reforms were inadequate, that wealthy individuals and corporations would benefit too much, that the timing was too slow or the amounts too low. Labor spokesmen preferred job-creating public works, fearful that business would use its tax cuts merely to increase automation. New Dealers, preferring public spending, called the President's basic premise contrary to thirty years of Democratic philosophy.

Dillon and Hodges had analyses showing the benefits of the bill to business—cuts in the top brackets and in corporation taxes, combined with the tax gains given business the previous year—and Heller and Secretary of Labor Wirtz had tables to show labor and liberals that the lower-income groups had the largest proportionate cut. Both were right. But the President emphasized that the usual class warfare jargon was inappropriate, that his effort was not how to divide the economic pie but how to enlarge it for everyone. Helping business profits led to more jobs. Helping consumer income led to more sales.

The key to House approval was Ways and Means Chairman Mills. A long-time advocate of tax reform, he was doubtful about tax cuts when no recession threatened. Slowly the President brought him around. Initially Mills agreed to a major tax reform bill, with a little tax reduction to help pass it. When presented, it was a tax reform and tax reduction bill. In testimony, it became a tax reduction and tax reform bill. And when it was finally reported out by Mills, the President had his major tax cut bill with a little tax reform. More reforms, the President agreed, were overdue, but they could not even pass Mills's committee.

Wilbur Mills, as he had proved the previous year on the trade, "little" tax and other bills, was an invaluable ally, respected by his colleagues, well-informed on his work and a cautious head-counter. No committee chairman had a firmer grip on his committee. Having been embarrassed by a defeat on the first bill he ever reported out as Ways and Means chairman back in 1958, the Arkansas Congressman never thereafter took a bill to the House floor without knowing he had the votes. He worked slowly, carefully, deliberately. The lengthy hearings and delays were at times exasperating to the President. "Do you realize," he said to me one day, "that the British prepared, proposed, passed and put into effect a proportionately larger tax cut than ours, and are getting the benefits from it, while we are still holding hearings?"

Finally, as the House prepared to vote, the President went on television once again. This time the speech was worked and reworked, simplified and clarified. One draft was prepared by economics columnist Sylvia Porter, whose prose the President admired. Illustrations of how the bill would reduce the taxes of a typical family, and how their tax savings would be used to create more jobs, were inserted. So were the President's favorite statistics: ten thousand new jobs had to be created every day; recessions have occurred on the average every forty-four months since World War I; seven million more young people will come into the labor market in the sixties than in the fifties. Some of his own familiar phrases were included: "We need a tax cut to keep this present drive from running out of gas"; "this nation is the keystone of the arch."

This time the speech was a success, and so was the bill.

The Kennedy tax bill, as finally enacted with the help of his successor, and the unparalleled period of expansion both its anticipation and enactment helped bring to the American economy, stand as monuments to the economic wisdom and political tenacity of John Kennedy. They embody a repudiation of the most persistent fiscal myths and fears which have so long dominated this nation. Prevented by the balance of payments and a conservative Congress from relying too heavily on the familiar Democratic remedies of still lower interest rates and still higher budgets, he had nevertheless broken the trend of postwar recessions by blazing new trails and rejecting old dogma. While it cannot be claimed that either the country or the Congress fully accepted his philosophy along with his bill, his actions shed more light on the once "dismal science" of economics than a generation of speeches and lectures.

In the process, John Kennedy's own thinking had come a long way in a short time. In a message to Galbraith requesting information on a particular problem on the balance of payments, he asked for "as much technical detail as seems appropriate and without the limitations that you might feel in discussing the matter with one who is not a professional economist." To this he added in a scrawl: "—but who knows a hell of a lot about it after taking Ec-A under Russ Nixon at Harvard."

Whatever he had learned in Ec-A, he had received a good education in economics in the White House. For a man pressed with other problems, he had been a good student; and for the country as a whole, he had been a good teacher.

CHAPTER XVII

❧

THE FIGHT AGAINST INFLATION—
THE STEEL PRICE DISPUTE

"R EMEMBER," shouted Richard Nixon to a Cleveland, Ohio, crowd in 1960, "if you want to inflate your money, if you want to raise your prices, you have our opponents to vote for." In 1961 many an expert, who assumed that inflation was certain to accompany recovery, thought the Vice President's reasoning wrong but his prediction right. John Kennedy proved his prediction to be wrong as well.

The experts did not lack faith in Kennedy. They simply knew that price rises had usually occurred during rapid economic expansion —that Kennedy's increases in defense, space and antirecession spending would produce the kind of large Budget deficits assumed to produce inflation—that traditional Democratic sympathies for the worker and farmer usually led to higher wages and food prices—that traditional Democratic opposition to high interest rates and hard money also invited inflation—and that the President had no power to prevent powerful industries and unions from adopting inflationary price and wage increases. They calculated that prices had risen nearly 10 percent in the second term of a Republican administration dedicated to halting inflation, so how could Democrat Kennedy, dedicated to greater growth, ever hope to do better?

But John Kennedy was determined to do better. The precedents of party and history did not dissuade him, for he faced a world-wide threat to the dollar and a chronic slack in the economy that knew no modern precedent. The imbalance of payments posed a clear and present danger which could never be averted if American goods were too high-priced for world markets. His whole concept of growth would mean little if prices rose as rapidly as income. Increases in Social Security, minimum wages and welfare benefits would represent little progress if the recipients could buy no more with those larger checks than previously. His efforts to show a prudent Budget posture were doomed if Defense and other procurement agencies had to pay more to buy less. His efforts to persuade the Federal Reserve Board to keep long-term interest rates low were doomed if an inflationary spiral began. And his efforts to help those living on fixed incomes—pensioners, annuitants and others clearly in need—would suffer the most from this "cruel tax upon the weak," as his Economic Message termed it. In short, his whole economic program would be impaired unless this tradition of inflation could be broken.

He was not obsessed by this problem over all others. He paid no heed to those who said inflation was a greater danger to our economy than unemployment, or to those opposing every proposal for increased spending or decreased taxes on the grounds that runaway inflation was just around the corner. But neither would he listen to those alluring voices of the easy excuse, including even such citadels of conservatism as *Time* magazine, which asserted on June 1, 1962, that economic growth and price stability were incompatible, that "inflation has long been a companion to economic boom," that "the price of a prosperous and growing economy is a 'normal,' or controlled, inflation of 2% to 3% a year," and that "the alternative to 'normal' inflation . . . is economic stagnation or downright recession."

He would not countenance continued slack in the economy in order to postpone fighting inflation. He would not tighten long-term credit or avoid necessary spending in order to fight it. Yet neither did he favor peacetime controls or a tightly managed economy. The challenge was clear; the answer was not. But the challenge had to be met. Just as Woodrow Wilson had pioneered in the creation of a modern money and banking system, just as Franklin Roosevelt had pioneered in the adoption of more realistic Budget policies, so John Kennedy, convinced that the new balance of payments problem made continued inflation intolerable, decided that the time had come to confront the even more elusive problem of constantly rising prices in a free and expanding economy.

Once he had made that commitment, he did not back away from it. His battle with Big Steel was both the chief symbol and the chief crisis in this war on inflation, and, as he said of that battle, "There is no sense in raising hell and then not being successful. There is no sense in putting the office of the Presidency on the line and then being defeated."

He succeeded. Prices remained stable under the Kennedy administration to a degree unmatched in the tenure of his precedessor or, during the same period, by any other industrial country in the world. It was the first of the postwar recoveries from recession in which wholesale industrial prices actually fell while production and income were rising. Three years after Kennedy's inauguration, the Wholesale Price Index was lower than when he took office; and the Consumer Price Index was comparatively steady, well below the "normal inflation" of 2-3 percent a year. A record rise in national output, business profits and labor incomes was real, undiminished by any noticeable rise in prices.

While this was partly a continuation of the stability which had prevailed since 1958, and partly due to a persistent surplus in manpower and plant resources as well as increasing foreign competition, it was also due to some intense Presidential leadership. "For the first time since Grover Cleveland's day," wrote one observer, "a Democratic President had succeeded in stabilizing the internal value of the dollar."

This was not achieved by the imposition of any direct controls. It was not achieved by the substitution of government for business or labor in the setting of prices and wages. But neither was it achieved without bringing some chill to President Kennedy's political relations with both business and labor. And that is the real story of this chapter.

Just as most Congressmen are all for economy measures so long as they fall on someone else's state, so most business and labor leaders are against inflation for each other but not for themselves. It should not have been a surprise, therefore, that both sides, in varying frequency, expressed resentment with a President who brought the prestige of his office and the power of public opinion to bear on their decisions—who promulgated economic guidelines within which their price-making and collective bargaining should take place—and who believed it was his obligation, as Kennedy said in his 1960 National Press Club speech, to be "a vigorous proponent of the national interest, not a passive broker for conflicting private interests."

Walter Heller called it the "jawbone" method of keeping wages and prices down.[1] The Kennedy approach was not founded on any statute or backed up by any sanctions. He commented almost enviously one day on the variety of weapons and controls used by De Gaulle to fight price increases in France, an impressive array of powers which called into question the thesis that European inflation would eventually equalize our balance of payments. But he sought to make up for what he lacked in statutory authority by greater ingenuity and greater effort.

The effort was focused partly on a variety of legislative proposals and administrative steps, including the first Presidential message to

[1] Presumably a Biblical reference to Samson never used by the President, possibly suspecting that some opponent would note that Samson used "the jawbone of an ass."

Congress on consumers' interests and a Special Consumers' Council. Administration bills sought to lower the price of housing, transportation, education, medical care, drugs, credit and other items, and to increase competition through strengthening antitrust laws, lowering tariff barriers and stimulating small business. The Department of Justice Antitrust Division was particularly successful against price-fixers in a record number of prosecutions which not only ended those conspiracies but deterred others. Legislation favoring "Fair Trade" or resale price maintenance was strongly opposed, and tax incentives for the purchase of new machinery were aimed at the higher productivity which could raise profits and wages without raising prices.

But the bulk of the effort was not legislative. It lay in an unprecedented, ceaseless, tireless use of the "jawbone"—in general and specific warnings to labor and management, in Presidential messages, press conferences and speeches, in talks to their conventions, letters to their negotiators and private conferences with their leaders.

The bulk of the ingenuity lay in two new techniques:

First was the President's Advisory Committee on Labor-Management Policy, with members drawn from unions, business and the public. Tripartite bodies of this kind in peacetime had consistently failed in the past. This one succeeded, stayed together and served as a useful channel to and for the President on labor-management relations and wage-price stability.

Second was the enunciation of national wage-price guidelines, promulgated with Presidential approval in their first annual report by his Council of Economic Advisers. The guidelines represented the first attempt by the Federal Government to indicate a general standard by which the public could measure whether wage and price increases were in the national interest. Stressing that no hard and fast rules were possible, these guidelines were based on the recognition of the fact that labor and management obtain their greater gains out of greater productivity; that, as new skills and machines enabled each worker to turn out more of the employer's product in each hour worked, those savings would permit increased profits and wages without any price increases and possibly with price reductions; and that excessive wage settlements, paid for by price increases, on the other hand, would merely pass the bill on to the rest of the economy with inflationary results hurting everyone. When specifically applied to a single industry or company, the guidelines raised more controversies than they settled, but they were a courageous injection of the public interest into an area where it had long been overlooked.

The President refuted, in his talk to the editors in 1963, the notion that private wage-price decisions were none of his business. If they lead to a national emergency strike, then the law made that his business, he said. If they wreck the balance of payments, then the maintenance of our troops overseas was his business. "When things go badly . . . if we have another recession, the President of the United States is to blame," he said. "So I think it is our business."

LABOR RELATIONS

The jawbone method was directly applied most often to labor. An arbitrarily shortened work week was opposed by the President at every opportunity. He called upon the AFL-CIO Convention, in a 1961 address, to recognize labor's responsibility in keeping our goods competitive, urging "those of you who are in the areas of wage negotiations [to] recognize the desirability of . . . maintaining stable prices." He called upon the Steelworkers Union, by letter in the fall of that year, to "ensure that their collective bargaining proposals are fashioned so that . . . the public interest in price stability is protected." He called upon the leaders of the Communications Workers, gathered in the flower garden in February, 1962, to meet their responsibility to the country as they prepared their bargaining position. And he called upon the United Auto Workers Convention, in the spring of that year, to seek "a non-inflationary and peaceful settlement . . . in your forthcoming negotiations in the aircraft and missile industries." Meanwhile, his Secretary of Labor, economic advisers and other appointees were carrying the same message to union meetings even more frequently and specifically.

Throughout his term this process and prodding continued, and with success. Average wage rate increases during Kennedy's tenure were this nation's lowest for any comparable period since the Second World War. They were generally within the "guidelines" and less than the increases then occurring in the plants of our trading competitors in Europe. This does not mean labor was poorly off under Kennedy. Productivity gains made noninflationary wage increases possible, and, as the recession ended, work weeks returned to normal. Consequently factory workers raised their average wages for the first time to $100 a week, and, with two and three-quarter million more men and women working, total labor income rose to record levels.

Nevertheless the fact remains that most union leaders did listen to Kennedy, and their wage demands were more moderate. "Part of it is political and emotional," the President told me after his UAW speech. "I go to the Chamber of Commerce last week and talk about all we're doing for business and profits—and they sit on their hands. I go to the UAW and warn them about the necessity of restraint, following the guidelines, no unjustified wage demands—and they cheer every word."

Part of it was political and emotional. Labor leaders were unaccustomed to a Democratic President who thought there could be such a thing as excessive wage increases in peacetime. They recognized the truth of Labor Secretary Goldberg's statement that "labor and management will both be making a mistake if they believe that the Kennedy administration is going to be prolabor." They recognized that Kennedy had meant it when he stressed during the campaign that his would "not be a businessmen's administration nor a labor administration nor a farmers' administration, but an administration representing and seeking to serve all Americans." Nevertheless, with a few outstanding exceptions (led by indicted Teamster boss Jimmy Hoffa), most labor leaders regarded Kennedy as a friend—a friend who treated them not with favoritism but with dignity and equality.

They worked more closely with the President and his team on legislation than they ever had before. They were consulted on policy and politics. They were invited to the White House for conferences and ceremonies. Their names showed up on State Dinner lists and in nominations for appointive offices outside as well as within the Department of Labor. One union leader was made an ambassador. Another was named to the Communications Satellite Board of Incorporators, and another Deputy Housing Administrator. A former labor lawyer was named to the highest court in the land. A Chamber of Commerce publication, quoted by Barry Goldwater, expressed outrage that the Kennedy administration had filled "high government offices with the largest number of union officials and adherents in history," citing the Departments of Commerce, State and Interior as well as those previously listed (but making no mention of the number of businessmen also appointed to high posts).

Appearing for AFL-CIO President George Meany at a Berlin Trade Union Conference on his 1963 trip to Europe, the President took Meany with him on the remainder of his Berlin visit and then introduced him throughout Ireland, a gesture not forgotten by Meany back in Washington.

The President in turn felt more at home with a labor audience. Addressing the AFL-CIO Convention in sunny Miami in December, 1961, the day after he addressed the National Association of Manufacturers in wintry New York, he commented, not too cryptically, "It's warmer here today than it was yesterday." After receiving an overwhelming welcome from the UAW the following May, he observed: "Last week, after speaking to the Chamber of Commerce and the Presidents of the American Medical Association, I began to wonder how I got elected. And now I remember."

But labor and Kennedy had their differences. Labor disliked the wage-price guidelines, often resented the government asserting the "national interest" in labor disputes, felt he overstressed the balance of payments as a limitation and still wanted a thirty-five-hour work week.

A related problem was labor's long-standing request for changes in the Taft-Hartley Labor-Management Relations Act. The President wanted it changed also. He was particularly convinced that the Executive Branch should possess a wider arsenal of tools in national emergency strikes in addition to an injunction, although he did not hesitate to use the injunctive powers when necessary. But he was equally convinced, from his experiences in the Senate—and labor came around slowly to his view—that raising the issue in the Eighty-seventh or Eighty-eighth Congress would only produce a worse law. He preferred to use existing laws, his inherent powers, and the initiative and imagination of his own office and Secretary of Labor to keep down the number of harmful strikes and to stave off harmful legislation.

The publicity accorded Secretary Goldberg's activities in this area, making mediation proposals "on behalf of the President" in labor disputes ranging from toilets at General Motors to musicians at the Metropolitan Opera, led to still more charges of too much government intervention. Actually neither the Secretary nor the President wanted either labor or management to look to Washington for help in every dispute, and their formula was to act only when both sides in a major industry remained far apart after all other steps had been exhausted. They encouraged both sides to adopt new techniques for labor peace, more use of outside arbitrators and mediators, more machinery for constant contact and study (instead of at contract time only) and more voluntary recognition of the public interest (and the public's impatience).

But when all else failed, the President felt an active Federal role was justified in any dispute with nationwide impact. The Metropolitan Opera was a unique exception, and when the President, after receiving wires from top opera performers such as Risë Stevens and Leontyne Price, asked Goldberg to intervene, he replied to his Secretary's warning of criticism, "We'll have to take that risk. Bricks and mortar are not the only assets of America." "I was often termed in praise and criticism a very activist Secretary of Labor," Justice Goldberg later recalled. "But really I was a Secretary of Labor for a very activist President."

The activism worked, aided once again by some executive ingenuity and initiative, including the establishment by Executive Order of a Missile Sites Labor Commission to head off restrictive legislation, Presidential appeals by wire or in person to both labor and management representatives, mediation and arbitration by Secretaries Goldberg and Wirtz, and a variety of special boards, commissions and panels. Man-hours lost due to strikes during the Kennedy years were the lowest in any three peacetime years since the war, less than half of their previous rate. The public, to be sure, was aware of the trouble areas. But while a few strikes were making headlines, the number of peaceful settlements was making history.

This is not to say that labor relations were everywhere rosy. In the maritime trades they continued to be chaotic. In the building trades they were restless. Unreasonable demands by a New York Printers Union and by the Flight Engineers Union were publicly denounced by the President at press conferences. A Presidential commission in the latter case finally succeeded in abolishing certain inefficient work rules—sometimes called "featherbedding"—by finding that three men instead of four were adequate for the cockpit of commercial jet aircraft.

As the tide of automation replacing men with machines rolled across the country, disputes over work rules and cries of "featherbedding" threatened to drown out the usual economic issues of collective bargaining. They also threatened the Kennedy administration with its most serious disruption of labor peace and its most difficult challenge from the labor movement—the railway labor dispute.

Throughout most of Kennedy's term, the persistent threat of a nationwide rail shutdown obscured the labor peace which elsewhere prevailed. The problem was principally one of work rules and labor utilization in an industry where rigid jurisdictional lines and job guarantees had been carried over from the prediesel age.

Five unions representing the men who operate the nation's railroads, beset by declining employment and membership and rising internal strains, presented for nearly four years a solid front of resistance to changes in their work rules necessitated by automation, demanded by the railroads and approved in whole or in part by a series of Presidential commissions, panels and Labor Secretaries. Collective bargaining had completely failed, with each side accusing the other of intransigence. The nation's railroads were ready and eager to put their rules changes into effect, reducing the number of firemen in diesels, changing the roles of brakemen and similar moves. The unions, in turn, were ready to shut down all rail transportation if the rules were changed.

Some said, "Let them strike." The unions accused the administration of encouraging management resistance by making clear no strike would be allowed. Management warned that it would accept no further government postponement of its right to lay off men. Both sides moved steadily toward a final showdown and strike.

But President Kennedy would not stand idly by and let the strike occur. He doubted those who said a walkout would bring both parties to their senses in a hurry. "This is no dollar-and-cents issue they can split down the middle," he said. "This is do or die for both sides, and they'll stay out and stand it a lot longer than the country can stand it." A strike of 200,000 union members would immediately idle 500,000 other railroad employees, and by its thirtieth day, his economic advisers estimated, the shutdown of affected industries would have idled some six million nonrailroad workers in the worst unemployment since 1930.

Consequently, in June of 1963, with the final "final" rules change and strike deadline approaching, the President asked both sides to try again, with a further postponement of any action. Labor Secretary Wirtz, who devoted night and day to the problem for months along with Assistant Secretary James Reynolds, made his own recommendations for a solution. As was true of each previous impartial recommendation, the railroads accepted and the brotherhoods would not.

With only one day remaining before a new deadline, the President, after consultation with the then Supreme Court Justice Arthur Goldberg on the alternatives to legislation, recommended that the parties accept arbitration by the Justice. It was a drastic move, and Chief Justice Warren, whom I reached in Athens at the World Bar Association Conference, expressed his traditional reluctance to see Court members involved in other endeavors, a reluctance which the President shared but felt obligated to shed in this emergency. The railroads accepted the proposal; the unions foolishly did not. Not many weeks later, a union leader confided to me that they had made a mistake in rejecting Goldberg.

But that dramatic proposal at least served the purpose of awakening the nation and Congress to the crisis about to engulf them. A stormy session in the Cabinet Room with Democratic Congressional leaders convinced the President that they were wholly unwilling to face up to any legislation preventing a strike and obviously unable to pass it that day. That afternoon in a private meeting with the chief railroad negotiator, only hours before the deadline, the President obtained one more postponement to enable a special subcommittee of his Labor-Management Advisory Committee to report on the issues. His hopes for a new breakthrough in the interim were based on his appointment to that subcommittee of both a responsible rail union leader not involved in the strike and a progressive railroad president suspected of being "soft" by some of his colleagues. In the days that followed, agreement seemed several times within reach, and then faded each time.

Finally, all postponements, existing procedures and personal appeals having been exhausted, the only alternative to a catastrophic strike was legislation. All the legislative choices looked bad. Some would still permit a strike and some would merely freeze the status quo. Some wanted labor punished and some wanted it rewarded. Some proposed Presidential seizure of the railroads, a solution which neither solved the work rules problem nor recognized the railroad's cooperative attitude. One agent of the rail unions, who had channeled many a campaign contribution to members of the Senate Labor Committee, wanted that committee to arbitrate. Some management representatives wanted permanent amendments to the Railway Labor Act incorporating compulsory arbitration.

The President, hoping to avoid a precedent for undiluted compulsory arbitration in this or any other industry, decided in the end on a temporary resolution requiring the Interstate Commerce Commission to pass on employment security rules in dispute, weighing their effects on the parties and the public service. The Commission was already empowered to judge the employment security arrangements of railroad mergers. It was a logical and orderly solution which fulfilled the request of our legislative leaders that we send them no "pure" compulsory arbitration bill. But the rail unions, convinced of bias on the part of the ICC, lobbied vehemently against the proposal, and ultimately the ICC features were ripped out and a straight compulsory arbitration law passed and signed, the first in the nation's peacetime history. No one was happy, and the rail unions blamed the President—but there was no strike, and the economy continued to grow.

THE 1962 STEEL PRICE DISPUTE

The most direct and dangerous challenge by a powerful private interest group to the President's anti-inflation efforts—and to the President's office and trust—came from the steel industry in 1962.

While the dramatic confrontation between John Kennedy and United States Steel reached its climax in April of that year, the President's own concern went back more than a year earlier. In one of his first post-inaugural conversations with Secretary Goldberg, a former counsel to the Steelworkers Union, he expressed concern over the effects any steel price rise would have on his balance of payments and anti-inflation efforts.

The President's concern was well founded. Not only was steel one of our largest industries; its prices were also a direct or indirect cost in almost every other commodity. It played so large a part in the American economy, and its products were an essential part of so many other capital and consumer products, that its price actions had long been a bellwether for all industry. "As goes steel, so goes inflation" had long been the epigram which accurately summarized this nation's price movements.

Senator Robert Taft of Ohio, in Senate hearings of 1948, scolded the industry for raising its prices, predicting that such an increase would force up other prices and encourage further wage demands by labor. His scolding was in vain, but his forecast was unfortunately accurate. Between 1947 and 1958 steel prices more than doubled, increasing more than three times as fast as other industrial prices. Economists estimated that the largest single cause of the rise in the Wholesale Price Index prior to 1958 was inflation in steel.

Labor was partly to blame. Because of the dominant influence of a comparative handful of companies, both sides in steel labor negotiations privately assumed that management would be able to adjust its prices to pay for whatever wage bargain was reached. As a result, steel wages had been rising between 1947 and 1958 faster than productivity, and steel prices had been rising even faster than labor costs.

Since 1958 steel prices had been stable, and so had wholesale prices as a whole. But, as earlier noted, our balance of payments and gold supply were far from stable. American steel prices having risen in earlier years far more rapidly than those of our competitors overseas, this country's share of world steel export markets had steadily declined, while foreign imports into this country more than tripled, accounting for nearly one-fourth of the rise in our payments deficit between 1957 and 1961. American machinery, machine tools, equipment and vehicles, which comprised the bulk of our durable goods exports, also depended on steel products and prices—as did our exports of most other important commodities—and it was clear to President Kennedy in 1961 that another major price rise in steel could potentially spark not only a new inflationary spiral but a disastrous payments deficit and gold outflow.

His immediate concern that year was an automatic increase in steel wages scheduled to take place on October 1 and the growing talk in the steel industry, as reported in the press, of a price increase at that time. The October 1 wage rise was the third and final increase promised under a 1960 settlement which had ended the longest steel strike in history. That settlement, under the auspices of Vice President Nixon, was accompanied by solid rumors that the companies had agreed not to increase prices until after the election. Kennedy asked Goldberg, who had helped negotiate the contract, whether the Steelworkers Union should be asked to forego the October 1 wage increase in the national interest. But this would have been a dubious precedent for the stability of collective bargaining contracts, and analysis by the Council of Economic Advisers showed that the October 1 step was within the range of rising productivity and could be absorbed without a price increase. Labor costs per ton of steel, said the CEA, in figures the industry would later dispute, were no higher than they were in 1958. The real problem, warned Secretary Goldberg, would be the 1962 negotiations for a new contract.

On September 6 the President wrote an open letter to the presidents of the twelve largest steel companies, urging that prices not be increased on October 1 or thereafter, detailing the damage higher steel prices would do to the nation's balance of payments and price stability in general and to steel exports in particular, pointing out the excellent profit and income position of their stockholders, and reminding them that the restrictive monetary and fiscal measures required to halt any inflationary spiral they started would retard our nation's recovery from recession and steel's hopes for greater capacity utilization. He then made this key point:

> I do not wish to minimize the urgency of preventing inflationary movements in steel wages . . . the steel industry has demonstrated a will to halt the price-wage spiral in steel. If the industry were now to forego a price increase, it would enter collective bargaining negotiations next spring with a record of three and a half years of price stability. It would clearly then be the turn of the labor representatives to limit wage demands to a level consistent with continued price stability. The moral position of the steel industry next spring—and its claim to the support of public opinion—will be strengthened by the exercise of price restraint now.

Some of the replies were thoughtful, some were rude, none made any promises—but prices were not raised. A week later the President wrote an old friend, President David McDonald of the Steelworkers, emphasizing the need in 1962 for a steel-labor settlement "within the limits of advances in productivity and price stability . . . in the interests of all of the American people." Republicans protested that Presidents should concern themselves with "inflation," not with price rises in particular industries. But no one misunderstood the President's desire that the 1962 settlement neither necessitate nor lead to a price increase.

To lessen disruptive stockpiling of steel by customers who thought either a strike or a large price increase was inevitable, the President requested both parties, through Secretary Goldberg and in a press conference, to accelerate their negotiations. With his approval, the Secretary talked first with the industry's chief negotiator, R. Conrad Cooper, then with Steelworkers President McDonald, and subsequently with others on both sides, including a telephone conversation with U.S. Steel Chairman Roger Blough. On January 23, 1962, Kennedy met privately with Goldberg, Blough and McDonald at the White House, having also met with Blough the previous September.

In all these talks both the President and Goldberg emphasized their interest not only in an early settlement, which by itself was not of great importance, but in a settlement which would make a price rise unnecessary. More specifically, President Kennedy's considerable influence with the union and the good offices of the Secretary of Labor were offered as a means of helping achieve such a settlement if both sides were agreeable. No formal pledge from the industry to hold prices steady, if the President succeeded, was requested, and none was forthcoming. For the government to have asked for such a commitment, the President said, would have been "passing over the line of propriety." But, while Blough and other industry spokesmen grumbled on each occasion about rising costs and the profit squeeze in what was assumed to be the usual "poor-mouthing" that opens labor negotiations, the industry accepted the administration's help without any illusion as to the President's only purpose and without any indication that it intended to raise prices no matter what settlement was reached.

While Roger Blough would later claim that all kinds of public hints about a pending price rise had been made—hints which no one else in either industry or the press seemed to have grasped—he and other industry officials in direct contact with the administration made no use of those opportunities to inform the President of such an action. On the contrary, the industry voluntarily made itself party to what was in effect a tripartite transaction clearly based on the President's premise that steel price increases were undesirable and, unless necessitated by a wage increase exceeding productivity increases, not to be attempted.

Nor was it a passive acceptance of minimal help. Goldberg did not even talk to McDonald until Cooper had advised him, after talking with his colleagues in the industry, that they were agreeable. A series of wires, calls and visits from the Secretary on behalf of the President helped to get the negotiations started several months early in February, helped get them resumed when they had broken up in March and, most importantly, helped persuade McDonald to accept the industry's most modest settlement in postwar history. "They did it in part," concluded the President later, "because I said that we could not afford another inflationary spiral, that it would affect our competitive position abroad—so they signed up." The agreement provided for no general increase in wage rates at all, and fringe benefit improvements costing about 10 cents an hour, or 2.5 percent.

This over-all figure—well under the 17 cents originally sought by the union, well under the 1960 settlement, less than one-third the cost of the average steel settlement for twenty years, and based on an earlier Council of Economic Advisers analysis—had been presented by Goldberg to Blough in a private conversation on March 6 as a figure well within the capacity of the industry to absorb without a price increase, a conclusion which neither Blough nor other industry leaders disagreed with. Goldberg then urged the same figure upon McDonald in a private conversation on March 12 as appropriate to price stability. Negotiations were resumed on March 14 and concluded on March 31.

The 1962 steel settlement, the first without a strike since 1954 and the first clearly and completely within the bounds of productivity increases in memory, was hailed throughout the nation. The President, in identical telephoned statements to management representatives and union headquarters, praised the agreement as "responsible . . . high industrial statesmanship . . . obviously noninflationary . . . a solid base for continued price stability. I . . . extend to you the thanks of the American people." The union members, he remarked to me as he put down the phone after the second call, had cheered and applauded their own sacrifice, while the management representatives had been "ice-cold."

But neither side expressed any disagreement with his conclusions on price stability. Newspapers and magazines representing every shade of opinion breathed a sigh of relief that steel price increases were no longer a danger. The following week, as the individual companies executed their formal contracts with the union, the President telephoned Goldberg that Charlie Bartlett had a tip from steel sources that a price rise was imminent. The Secretary scoffed at the report. Nothing had happened to alter the cost picture of the industry in the preceding months. On the contrary, the competition from low-cost foreign producers, competing metals and other materials, and the higher profits which could be realized from greater sales and capacity utilization, would cause any normally competitive industry at such a time to be considering price decreases.

The price of scrap, iron ore and coal, the three major materials used by the steel industry, were below their 1958 levels. Under the new labor contract, which did not even go into effect until July 1, employment costs per ton of steel would continue to decline. In the years of general economic slack since 1958, the profit position of several companies had improved and others had worsened, making it impossible to justify a uniform price decision by all. "We should be trying to reduce the price of steel, if at all possible," President Edmund Martin of Bethlehem Steel was quoted as telling his annual meeting on April 10, "because we have more competition, particularly from foreign sources."[2]

On Tuesday, April 10, the last major contract having been signed, the President was surprised to note that his appointment calendar included a 5:45 P.M. appointment for Roger Blough. O'Donnell said Blough had requested it that afternoon. Goldberg said he had no idea what Blough might have in mind but agreed to stand by in his office.

What Blough had in mind was soon clear. Seated on the sofa next to the President's rocking chair, he handed him U.S. Steel's mimeographed

[2] To a stockholder urging the corporation not to give any grants to Harvard University, "where they study deficit spending," Martin said, "I agree with you. . . . I don't think we could get any Harvard men anyway—they're all in the government."

press release announcing a $6-a-ton price increase, four times the cost
of the new labor settlement. The President was stunned. He felt that his
whole fight against inflation, his whole effort to protect our gold, was
being reduced to tatters. If the industry in which he had made his
greatest effort for stability, an industry plagued by foreign competition
and underutilization, could make a mockery of his plea for self-restraint
in the national interest, then every industry and every union in the
country would thereafter feel free to defy him.

Above all, he felt duped. The man sitting across from him had
personally, knowingly accepted his help in securing from the workers a
contract that would not lead to an increase in prices. The prestige and
powers of the Presidency had been used to help persuade the Steelworkers
to accept less from the companies in the interest of price stability, and
now the contract had no sooner been signed than the industry was
announcing a large, across-the-board price increase for all products.
"The question of good faith was involved," as the President said later.
"The unions could have rightfully felt that they had been misled"—and
no other union would ever listen to his plea for self-discipline again.
"I think you're making a mistake," he coldly told Blough, who would
not learn until later the enormity of his mistake.

Angry but contained, the President sent for Arthur Goldberg, who
was less contained. The Secretary, learning that Blough's press statement
had already been distributed to the wire services and networks for 7 P.M.
release, harshly rejected the U.S. Steel Chairman's explanation that as an
act of "courtesy" the President of the United States had been handed a
mimeographed press release about an accomplished fact. Goldberg called
it a "double cross," an act of bad faith, contrary to what was obviously
understood by all concerned in the negotiations, contrary to the best
interests of both the nation and the industry, and contrary to the assurance Goldberg had given the President that both Blough and McDonald
could be relied on. Blough expressed his regrets, attempted to justify
his action as necessary for his stockholders and departed. "They were
not willing to accept my explanation," he said later with some degree
of understatement.

The President's next scheduled appointment was a review of
questions for the next day's press conference—an extra session, before
the usual breakfast, which Assistant Press Secretary Andrew Hatcher
had scheduled in Salinger's absence. Hatcher, Walter Heller, McGeorge
Bundy and I were waiting for this meeting in Ken O'Donnell's office outside the President's door. When Blough left, the President asked us to
come in and told us the news. His own anger was rising. His trust had
been abused, his office had been used. He had intervened only with the industry's consent, with the unmistakable intention of holding the price
line, and that intervention was now being made to appear at best weak

and at worst stupid to the workers and to the American people. "My father always told me," he said, recalling the Ambassador's brief service in the steel industry and his fight with its leaders while on the Maritime Board, "that steel men were sons-of-bitches, but I never realized till now how right he was."

Little time was spent on recriminations. A price rise at that time and in that context was not only an economic setback—it was an affront to the office of the Presidency and to the man who held it. "If I had failed to get a rescission," he said later, "that would have been an awful setback to the office of the Presidency." No President should have accepted it without a fight; no one could have thought that John Kennedy would. "U.S. Steel," one of those present would remark later, "picked the wrong President to double-cross."

The steel industry had successfully defied Presidents, however, for more than half a century. Its challenge to Kennedy was in an arena where he had few weapons and no precedents. Had it not been for the fact that the industry, in addition to its economic defiance, also accepted his good offices and then failed to honor his trust, history might well have been different. But the first question the President asked us after breaking the news was: "What can we do about it?"

Our primary *hope* was to create a climate that would discourage other companies from joining in the increase and encourage U.S. Steel to rescind. We recognized that market pressures would force the price leaders to back down if only one or two important companies refused to go along with the increase. Our primary *obligation* was to ascertain whether the ability of a powerful company to announce an unjustifiable price increase, with confidence that it could be sustained despite all the obvious economic pressures against it, reflected a violation of the laws against monopoly. With these two courses in mind, the President promptly telephoned for press statements from the Attorney General and the chairmen of the Senate and House Anti-Trust Subcommittees, similarly discussed what the government was doing for or with U.S. Steel with his Secretaries of Treasury and Defense, and directed Goldberg, Heller and me to prepare a statement for his Wednesday afternoon press conference. He could not meet with us later that night, he complained, because of the annual White House reception for all members of Congress. Recalling that the previous year's reception had been similarly marred by the Bay of Pigs fiasco, he said with a rueful smile, "I'll never have another Congressional reception."

Moving to my office, Goldberg, Heller and the latter's colleague from the Council of Economic Advisers, Kermit Gordon, discussed with me the information needed for the next day's statements. Through the long night that followed, the Council and the Bureau of Labor Statistics worked to produce the necessary data on why the industry needed no increase and how it would harm the whole nation. At the Congressional reception the President, in between smiles and handshakes, talked action with the Vice President, with Senator Gore and with Goldberg and me when we arrived. Earlier, by telephone, he had talked almost apologetically to David McDonald, who assured him that the Steel Union members would not feel the President had intentionally misled them.

The press conference breakfast the next morning, Wednesday, was devoted almost entirely to steel. Arthur Goldberg, who attended, told the President that he intended to submit his resignation, that he could no longer preach wage restraint to any union, and that he wished to acknowledge publicly his failure in exposing the Presidential office to such abuse. The President deferred this request, and he also agreed finally to defer his own suggestion for an immediate message to Congress seeking legislation, and to concentrate instead on mobilizing public opinion in his press conference opening statement.

Presidential anger, Arthur Krock has written, "must be reserved for those rare occasions when the office and the nation as well as the man are basically offended." This was one of those rare occasions. With the economic data before me, with continuous news announcements of other steel companies raising their prices by identical amounts, and with considerable alterations by both the President and the Attorney General, the opening statement for that press conference was written and rewritten. Each new version reflected more strongly the President's by then wholly unemotional determination to impress upon the industry and the public the seriousness of the situation. It was completed only as we rode over to the State Department Auditorium in his limousine.

His voice was ice-cold but calm as he read, sounding more like Roosevelt indicting the Japanese for Pearl Harbor than a man displaying "unbridled fury" as some of those not present would later claim:

> The simultaneous and identical actions of United States Steel and other leading steel corporations, increasing steel prices by some six dollars a ton, constitute a wholly unjustifiable and irresponsible defiance of the public interest.
>
> *In this serious hour in our nation's history, when we are confronted with grave crises in Berlin and Southeast Asia,* when we are devoting our energies to economic recovery and stability, when we are asking reservists to leave their homes and families for months on end, and servicemen to risk their lives—*and four were killed in the last two days in Vietnam*—and asking union members to hold down their wage requests, at a time when restraint and sacrifice are being asked of every citizen, the American people will find it hard, as I do, to accept a situation in

which *a tiny handful of steel executives whose pursuit of private power and profit exceeds their sense of public responsibility* can show such utter contempt for the interests of 185 million Americans.

Seated in the audience, I heard a gasp from the reporters around me as the President continued:

If this rise in the cost of steel is imitated by the rest of the industry, instead of rescinded, it would increase the cost of . . . most . . . items for every American family . . . businessman and farmer. It would seriously handicap our efforts to prevent an inflationary spiral . . . make it more difficult for American goods to compete in foreign markets, more difficult to withstand competition from foreign imports, and thus more difficult to improve our balance of payments position, and stem the flow of gold. . . .

Price and wage decisions in this country, except for very limited restrictions in the case of monopolies and national emergency strikes, are and ought to be freely and privately made, but the American people have a right to expect, in return for that freedom, a higher sense of business responsibility for the welfare of their country than has been shown in the last two days. *Some time ago I asked each American to consider what he would do for his country and I asked the steel companies. In the last twenty-four hours we had their answer.*

The words italicized above were among those added to the statement by the President just prior to the conference or inserted spontaneously as he delivered it. Less pointed remarks, he was convinced, would have been noted, answered and then forgotten.

The statement also cited convincing and detailed facts on the industry's strong economic position without an increase, on the widespread damage the increase would cause and on the various branches of the government already looking into the matter; and it was followed by equally harsh comments in answer to all questions. Example:

. . . the suddenness by which every company in the last few hours . . . came in with . . . almost identical price increases . . . isn't really the way we expect the competitive private enterprise system to always work.

Even answers to unrelated questions on service wives and Vietnam were related by the President to the actions of the steel companies. From the moment of that press conference on, he had the initiative in the fight.

But as we discussed the situation back in his office, the steady parade of companies rushing to imitate precisely U.S. Steel's increase cast gloom over his hopes for a rescission. Nevertheless he was determined to fight on, and he asked me to call a meeting for him in the Cabinet Room early the next morning to coordinate the various efforts needed or already under way, some of them initiated the previous evening.

Days later, when it was all over, several Republicans—who had remained discreetly silent during the fight, refusing to approve either the price hike or the President's opposition to it—would term these various administration efforts an example of "overreacting," "tyranny" and "executive usurpation." Roger Blough spoke of "retaliatory attacks," and said that "never before in the nation's history had so many forces of the Federal Government been marshaled against a single industry." Clearly there was at the time an atmosphere of mobilization and crisis, much of it more apparent than real, based on words rather than actions, and deliberately designed to encourage rescission. But once the smoke of battle had blown away, it should have been clear to all—as it had been clear to the group which met Thursday morning in the Cabinet Room— that the only concrete governmental actions available were two rather modest steps, neither representing "illicit coercion" or "intemperate retaliation":

First, the Defense Department sought to meet its obligation to the taxpayers to purchase steel at the lowest available price. Secretary McNamara reported to the President that the steel industry's action could increase the cost of national defense by one billion dollars, not, as widely reported, merely because of increased steel costs, which were but a fraction of that total, but because of increased costs in all other sectors of the economy which followed steel. "To minimize the effect of the price increase on Defense costs," McNamara directed, the use of alternative materials would be studied, and "where possible, procurement of steel for Defense production shall be shifted to those companies which have not increased prices."

Any prudent steel customer would have done the same. McNamara, whom the President had called regarding this approach after Blough's visit, underscored his intentions by announcing the award of a small Polaris armor-plate contract to the tiny Lukens Steel Company, which had not raised prices. He noted publicly that U.S. Steel and Lukens were the only producers of this kind of high-strength steel. Similar announcements were planned for the General Services Administration, the Agency for International Development and others. But this was not a massive weapon. It was insufficient by itself to persuade the few holdout companies not to join the price increase parade and wholly useless once they did. The Lukens award, in fact, was announced after the fight was almost over.

Second, the Justice Department sought to meet its obligation to law enforcement by initiating an inquiry as to whether a series of simultaneous and identical price increases, justified neither by cost nor by demand, and undertaken by companies in totally different financial positions, reflected normal free market behavior, coincidence, collusion or monopoly. Whatever the answer, I doubt that any self-respecting Antitrust Division under any administration could have sat back and idly watched this occur, given the long history of price conspiracies in steel. In no fully competitive industry could one company raise its prices in confidence that virtually all others would follow. The Federal Trade Commission, which had ordered the industry in 1951 to halt certain monopolistic practices, also announced a reopening of its inquiry. "Steel," said an eminent scholar commending the President's action, "is not really a competitive market. It's one big company." And a leading professor of antitrust law wrote us:

> Price leadership without overt collusion is inevitable in tightly organized oligopolies, schooled to habits of cooperation, afraid to discriminate, without possible new entrants. . . . Using the latent powers of the Sherman Act . . . the Courts have plenty of power . . . to reorganize industry leaders.

No such reorganization was attempted. Those who assailed the Kennedys for immediately summoning a Grand Jury investigation, however, had less to say when seven major antitrust indictments for secret price-fixing conspiracies were returned against the steel industry in the two years that followed. The largest indictment was returned in April, 1964, by a Grand Jury receiving information from its predecessor organized by the Kennedys.

One of the items that particularly interested the trust-busters in April, 1962, was the statement by Bethlehem President Martin, made shortly before the Blough announcement, that this was no time to raise prices. Bethlehem was the first to join U.S. Steel in the increase. Was this evidence of conspiracy, monopoly power, deliberate deceit or, as claimed, a misquotation? The Antitrust Division had an obligation to find out. Federal Bureau of Investigation agents, in their normal role as investigators and fact-finders for all divisions of the department, interviewed not only all company officials (U.S. Steel's General Counsel told them that he and his associates were "too busy" to talk to them then) but also the three reporters who had covered the Bethlehem meeting (all of whom stood by their stories).

Unfortunately, two overzealous agents, misunderstanding either their role or their instructions, called and visited one of the reporters in the middle of the night to check his story, and telephoned another who put them off. The latter, as well as the third reporter, were interviewed at their offices, although subsequent reports talked of "state security police" swooping down unannounced to grill all three in their beds. Some members of the newspaper fraternity—who never, as the President pointed out, showed the slightest hesitation in waking anyone else up at night—encouraged violent Republican talk about "Gestapo tactics," "press suppression" and accusations that the Kennedy brothers had personally ordered a 3 A.M. "third degree." As always, neither of the Kennedys would publicly blame the career men responsible, but the Attorney General's deputy had in fact specified to the FBI that all those to be interviewed should be telephoned at their place of business, not their homes, for an appointment in the usual hours. No orders were ever given to awaken anyone or to obtain the information by 7 A.M., and neither Kennedy knew about the calls until the next day.

The antitrust and Defense procurement actions were the only two tangible items on the list I drew up for Thursday's meeting in the Cabinet Room, and, although both contributed to the general atmosphere of concern, neither provided a means of rescission. Among those present at 8:50 that morning, in addition to the President and myself, were Messrs. Robert Kennedy, Goldberg, McNamara, Hodges, Under Secretary of the Treasury Fowler, FTC Chairman Dixon, Walter Heller, Larry O'Brien and several sub-Cabinet members and assistants. Roughly the same strategy group met the following day as well.

The only other concrete action available, it appeared, would be new legislation. The President regarded this as a difficult route, despite early Democratic support for his stand on the Hill. Remembering Truman's ill-fated move to draft railroad strikers, and having reconsidered his position of the previous morning, he did not want to act in haste. The Steelworkers having fulfilled their obligations, he did not want to take action against the industry—on its tariffs or tax proposals, for example—that would diminish its employment. Secretary Dillon, on vacation in Florida, argued against any change for the time being in the proposed investment tax credit and depreciation reform. But if rescission could not be obtained soon, said the President, he would go to Congress. His press conference statement had not been an act.

But the legislative alternatives, canvassed in a meeting in my office Friday morning, were not too promising. They ranged all the way from a simple resolution condemning the price rise to permanent legislation placing steel and similar price and wage decisions under various degrees of governmental supervision. A proposed ninety-day "Steel Price Emergency Act of 1962" would have temporarily rolled back prices to their April 9 level until a Presidential board of inquiry could report on what increase, if any, was proper and in the national interest; and the industry, though not bound to accept the Board's recommendations, would be on notice that further legislation was the alternative. A proposed amendment to the existing Defense Production Act would have revived Presidential authority to stabilize, with a March, 1962, base, prices and wages either in all industries or in those producing basic commodities. Other suggestions called for a variety of Executive Orders, Presidential panels, court reviews or temporary roll-backs and controls. Most suggestions were too little, too late or too much. They either failed to assure correction of the immediate problem or went so far as to be undesirable.

The President was left chiefly with his effort to obtain a voluntary rescission without legislation through both public and private appeals. At our Thursday morning meeting Secretary of Commerce Hodges was designated to hold a press conference in reply to one scheduled by Roger Blough that afternoon. Arrangements were made to supply Hodges with rebuttal material, and to supply a few friendly reporters at the Blough conference with pertinent questions. Other Cabinet members and agency heads were asked to hold press conferences on the impact of a steel price increase on their various concerns—defense, balance of payments, farmers, small businessmen.

All the economists in government were to pull together a "Fact Book" or "White Paper" on steel to be widely distributed. Democratic governors were asked through the National Committee to deplore the increase and request local steel men not to join in it. Administration spokesmen were to be supplied to the various TV interview shows.

On Capitol Hill Senator Kefauver had already welcomed the President's call to arms and scheduled an investigation by his Anti-Trust Subcommittee. The House Anti-Trust Subcommittee, the Small Business Committees in both houses and other committees and individual members threw their weight behind the President. The Republican candidates for Senator and Governor of Pennsylvania, Congressmen Van Zandt and Scranton, wired Roger Blough that the increase was "wrong for Pennsylvania, wrong for America and wrong for the free world." With a handful of expected exceptions, the nation's editorial writers and columnists refused to support the price rise and most supported the President.

Blough's press conference statements that afternoon were defensive but mild. Hodges in his reply struck back hard against a "handful of men who said in effect that United States Steel comes first, the United States of America second." He ridiculed Blough's contention that price *increases* were justified by foreign competition, and refuted the corporation's plea that increasing the cost of everyone else's machinery was the only way U.S. Steel could obtain enough funds to modernize its own.

But while the public barrage continued, the President was exploring private avenues of persuasion as well. He had early in the fight asked all those in his administration with business ties—including Hodges, Gudeman, Heller, McNamara, Gilpatric, Fowler, Dillon, Goldberg, Roosa and others—to place calls to any contacts they had among steel companies still holding the price line, among steel companies who might consider rescinding, among steel bankers and steel buyers and steel lawyers. No threats were made, no inducements were offered, but the nation's interest in price stability and a better balance of payments was made clear, and reliable channels of communication between the government and the steel companies were established.

There was little time, very little time. When steel prices had last been increased in 1958, all the major companies had been in line two days after the first company's announcement. The rush of other companies to join U.S. Steel on Wednesday, both before and after the Kennedy press conference, cast gloom over the possibility we had discussed the previous night of bringing U.S. Steel back by persuading the others to hold fast. "I am hopeful," the President said at his press conference, "that there will be those who will not participate in this parade. . . . But we have to wait and see on that, because they are coming in very fast."

Many of the hopes for this divide-and-conquer strategy focused on the Inland Steel Company of Chicago. Inland's President, Joseph Block, was regarded as an "industry statesmen" and served on the President's Labor-Management Advisory Committee. Block was in Japan, but a series of administration calls reached other Inland officials. Recognizing the national interest in preventing a worsening in balance of payments and inflation, and recognizing the administration's role in helping obtain a noninflationary labor settlement, Inland agreed that April, 1964, was no time to be raising prices, and announced Friday morning that it would not. Promptly the President called another friend, Edgar Kaiser of Kaiser Steel, and that much smaller company made a similar announcement. Still another company, Colorado Fuel and Iron, announced that it would consider at most only selective price increases on some items in the future.

A note of optimism entered our Friday meeting in the Cabinet Room. The companies announcing no price raise, along with an as yet uncertain holdout, Armco, probably had no more than 15 percent of the industry's capacity and could, by holding out, increase it to no more than 25 percent. "But," said Robert McNamara, on the basis of his days with Ford, "none of the others will be willing to give up any part of that additional 10 percent, and they'll all have to come down." We agreed that a primary effort should be made to reach Armco.

Absent from this Friday conference was Arthur Goldberg, on his way to New York for the last of three secret meetings with U.S. Steel officials.

The President, after the first blush of anger, had no animosity toward either the company or the industry which had challenged him. He sought not revenge but rescission. Those with a more oversimplified class warfare view of big business argued that the steel industry had deliberately abused him and should be the object of punishment, not negotiations. But my own belief is that the industry's misdeeds—which resulted in the President of the United States being misled as to its intentions, informed too late of its action and made to look bad by its timing—were the product of thoughtlessness rather than malicious intent; and, while most steel executives, having held the line in 1960 after a far more expensive settlement, might have been a little less thoughtless had the occupant of the White House been Richard Nixon,[3] I believe their motivations were based primarily on narrow and shortsighted economic grounds rather than political ones.

U.S. Steel, unlike most of those imitating its action, had in fact suffered a decline in profits, although it had maintained its usual dividends; and Roger Blough, the man whom it paid each year several times the amount the United States people paid their Chief Executive, impressed Kennedy as a sincere, if somewhat dull, individual. Some of Blough's colleagues in the industry may well have had a "let's show that man in the White House who's boss" attitude, but Blough and others seemed genuinely surprised and concerned by the President's response.

The President, therefore, upon learning late Wednesday night through the Charlie Bartlett channel that a meeting of the minds might be possible, directed his Secretary of Labor to meet with U.S. Steel Finance Chairman Robert Tyson; and later, when Goldberg's history as an adversary seemed to prevent the company from bending, Kennedy asked Clark Clifford, as a corporation lawyer with no job in the government, to represent him also. Earlier, two bankers friendly to Blough had been asked to point out to him the error of his ways. Wilbur Mills, whose Ways and Means chairmanship commanded respect in the industry, had wired Blough to revoke the increase. And Walter Heller had been removed by the President from a televised debate with Tyson when the latter suggested through intermediaries that it might only harden the lines.

Tyson met separately with Goldberg and Clifford on Thursday afternoon, meeting the latter on board U.S. Steel's private plane at the Washington airport. Neither meeting made any progress. But word reached the President that Blough wanted talks to continue, and a luncheon meeting of Goldberg, Clifford, Tyson, Blough and U.S. Steel President Worthington was scheduled for Friday.

[3] To whom they contributed twenty-five times as much money in the 1960 campaign as they gave to John Kennedy.

Goldberg—who had not, contrary to Blough's later report, initiated the negotiations—pressed hard on both days for a rescission of the increase and for the appointment of a high-level Presidential review committee. Both Goldberg and Clifford stressed that the timing of the increase, after Blough had failed to use many opportunities to warn the President of his intention, looked like a double cross, whether it was or not. Under instruction from the President, they warned of the darkening climate between steel and government, expressed doubt that Kennedy could restrain the more fiery members of Congress intent on harsh legislation, and insisted that there was one, and only one, action acceptable to the President: a complete rescission.

But by the time lunch was served on Friday, their arguments were largely unnecessary. The holdouts in the industry had prevailed. During the luncheon both Blough and Goldberg received telephone calls with the same message: Bethlehem Steel, the nation's second largest producer, a rival of Inland's in Midwest markets and of Kaiser's on the West Coast, and a major Defense Department contractor, had rescinded its increase.

Back in the White House the Bethlehem announcement caused jubilation. Already on his way to a review of the Atlantic Fleet off the Carolina coast, the President asked me, first, to prepare a brief statement thanking, on behalf of all consumers and businessmen, those companies who had held the line, and, second, to check with the others with whom we had worked as to whether any Presidential statement was desirable. Late that Friday afternoon, as I reported on this by telephone through Andy Hatcher at a Norfolk, Virginia, naval base, a secretary from the Press Office placed a scrap torn from the wire service ticker in front of me:

> Bulletin—New York, A.P.—United States Steel Corporation rescinded today the steel price increase it initiated Tuesday.

Roughly seventy-two hours had passed since Roger Blough's visit to the White House—seventy-two hours in which nearly every waking moment of the President, regardless of whether he was toasting the visiting Shah and Empress of Iran, preparing for his press conference and trip, hosting the Congressional reception or fulfilling a dozen other duties, had been spent in either meditation or action on how best to preserve his purpose and policies in this struggle. Even the Chicago *Tribune* could not avoid admiring such "decisiveness in the executive." Foreign newspapers were almost unanimous in their praise of his victory, although the Communist press was hard put to explain how a government controlled by capitalist monopolists had cracked down on one of its masters. "Oh," cried Robert Frost, "didn't he do a good one! Didn't he show the Irish all right?" But what he had shown primarily was not his Irish temper, not "naked power" as the *Wall Street Journal* called it, but the ability to mobilize and concentrate every talent and tool he possessed and could borrow to prevent a serious blow to his program, his prestige and his office. While steel 1962 was the key battle in John Kennedy's war on inflation, his victory was less a victory against Big Steel than a victory for the American Presidency.

BUSINESS RELATIONS

Magnanimous in victory, as always, the President promptly turned his attention to the problems of reconciliation. He permitted no gloating by any administration spokesman and no talk of retribution. The "White Paper" was buried. The scheduled "tough-talk" press conferences by Dillon and others were canceled. The Grand Jury, having been called for legitimate and necessary purposes of investigation, not intimidation, could not be called off, but in a brief meeting in which the Attorney General and I participated, the President decided against seeking in the courts a break-up of U.S. Steel, as strongly recommended to him in some quarters. Nor would he support Kefauver's attempt to cite for contempt steel industry witnesses unwilling to reveal cost data.

He considered somewhat longer the creation of a Presidential panel to make voluntary recommendations on if, whether and how much steel prices deserved to be increased, but in the end rejected it as more likely to hurt than help relations. He made a special effort to be gracious to Roger Blough, toward whom he had no trace of bitterness. He invited him to the White House a few days later, and frequently thereafter, to confer on business confidence, and he also asked Blough to head a Business Council Presidential advisory committee on balance of payments problems.

He utilized every opportunity to make clear that, while he had no regrets or apologies for his assertion of the public interest, he had no desire to intervene generally in either price or wage decisions—that free collective bargaining and competition, with consideration of the national interest, should fix wages and prices generally, as they ultimately had in this instance—that this industry and this situation were unique requiring a response that was unique, because the timing and context of Big Steel's action had challenged not only his economic policies but his office and good faith as well—and, finally, that he harbored "no ill will against any individual, industry, corporation or segment of the American economy. When a mistake had been retracted," he told his next press conference, "nothing is to be gained from further public recriminations."

Privately he made clear that he did not wish to be placed in that kind of situation very often, that he could not hope to repeat that kind of success very often, and that steel and every other industry had to be able to change its prices from time to time without creating a government crisis. (He also predicted privately that a violent press campaign and the traditional American sympathy for the underdog would soon swing the pendulum of public opinion away from his position in the steel dispute.) In his next press conference opening statement, and in an address shortly thereafter to the United States Chamber of Commerce, he stressed his concern for the steel industry's and all industries' need for higher profits, lower costs, faster modernization and greater markets in an expanding economy. "There can be no room on either side," he said, "for any feelings of hostility or vindictiveness."

But the olive branch held out by the President to the steel industry in particular and all business in general was met in many instances with poisoned arrows. Roger Blough, without altering his politics or philosophy, was cooperative and constructive at all times. Had administration-business relations depended on him—and on men like Tom Watson, Jr. of IBM, who was an effective liaison—all would have been well. Even most Republican leaders had little to say about steel. But right-wing columnists and commentators maintained a steady attack on the President's action. And after a week or so of mixed feelings and constant agitation, many businessmen—who had, in private conversations with administration officials, condemned Big Steel's increase as bad economics, bad public relations and bad judgment, and who had, inwardly, breathed a sigh of relief at the President's preservation of the prices they paid for steel products—began a torrent of abuse against the President's success. Any industry that raised prices, they said, was inviting the "steel treatment."

U.S. Steel's announcement of rescission had cited as reasons "competitive developments today, and all other current circumstances, including the removal of a serious obstacle to proper relations between government and business." But the very surprise and swiftness of Big Steel's retreat convinced those who had thought it impossible that the government must have used excessive power, and new obstacles to proper relations between government and business soon followed.

Amidst all the talk of "dictatorship," "blind fury" and "socialism" among these business critics, three specific complaints on the steel incident stood out, all of them more superficial than substantive. The first was the FBI's nighttime inquiry, already mentioned. The second was a doubt that the President would be equally stern with labor, forgetting that the whole crisis had been precipitated because the President *had* successfully insisted on the Steelworkers moderating their demands.[4]

The third was a widely repeated story from *Newsweek* and the *New York Times* that the President, in our first conference after the Blough visit, had quoted his father as saying "all businessmen" were sons-of-bitches. Having been one of those whom the President addressed, I could not be clearer in my recollection that he was talking only about the steel industry. But the erroneous story became a *cause célèbre* in the business community, and arose at a press conference:

QUESTION: Mr. President, at the time of your controversy with the steel industry, you were quoted as making a rather harsh statement about businessmen. I am sure you know which statement I have in mind.

THE PRESIDENT: Yes. [Laughter] You wouldn't want to identify it, would you? [More laughter]

QUESTION: Would you talk about it, Mr. President?

THE PRESIDENT: . . . the statement which I have seen repeated is inaccurate. It quotes my father as having expressed himself strongly to me, and . . . I quoted what he said, and indicated that he had not been, as he had not been on many other occasions, wholly wrong. [More laughter]

Now the only thing wrong with the statement was that, as it appeared in a daily paper, it indicated that he was critical of the business community, I think the phrase was "all businessmen." That's obviously in error, because he was a businessman himself. He was critical of the steel men. . . . He formed an opinion which he imparted to me, and which I found appropriate that evening. But he confined it, and I would confine it. . . . I felt at that time that we had not been treated altogether with frankness, and therefore I thought that his view had merit. But that's past, that's past. Now we are working together, I hope.

His correction was ignored and his hope was unfulfilled. Buttons for businessmen appeared bearing the caption "S.O.B. Club." Bumper stickers appeared reading "Help Kennedy Stamp Out Free Enterprise" or "I miss Ike—Hell, I even miss Harry." Another said: "Goldwater for President, Kennedy for King of Palm Beach." A *New Yorker* cartoon enjoyed by the President portrayed one tycoon saying to another in their lavishly upholstered clubroom: "My father warned me that all Presidents were S.O.B.'s."

[4] Coincidentally, he had also invoked his Taft-Hartley injunction powers against the West Coast maritime unions on the very day of his attack on Big Steel, and in time several other unions, as mentioned earlier, felt both his pressure and his wrath on their wage or job demands.

Most of the jokes circulated, particularly after the May stock market slide, were much more bitter. Typical was the crack: "When Eisenhower had a heart attack, the market went down. If Kennedy had a heart attack, the market would go up." But the President enjoyed the story of a businessman supposedly visiting at the White House, whom JFK sought to reassure with the words: "The economic outlook is good, no matter what the market says. If I weren't President, I'd be buying stock myself." To which the businessman replied, "If you weren't President, so would I." And he enjoyed another which had Joseph P. Kennedy staring disgustedly at the ticker tape muttering: "And to think I voted for that S.O.B.!"

Occasionally the President replied with a little humor of his own. At a New York Democratic rally on his forty-fifth birthday in May, he joked that he had received a wire from Roger Blough reading: "In honor of your birthday, I believe that you should get a raise in pay. . . . P.S. My birthday's next month." In June he revealed that the "nicest" letter he had received in a long time came from a Bethlehem Steel executive writing: "You are even worse than Harry Truman." And a year later, at another New York dinner, he referred to the fact that down the hall in the same hotel Eisenhower was receiving an award as the man who had done the most for the steel industry that year. "Last year," claimed Kennedy, "I won the award . . . they came to Washington to present it to me, but the Secret Service wouldn't let them in."

But there was little humor that summer of 1962 in the attitude of many outspoken executives. As mentioned in the previous chapter, careful analysis made clear that Kennedy's attitude toward business in general and steel in particular had no more to do with the stock market slide of 1962 than it did with its record climb in 1961 and 1963; but those searching for a scapegoat convinced not only themselves but the nation that the market decline, inasmuch as its worst day was less than two months after the steel fight, must have been caused by it.

Nor did they stop there. They accused Kennedy of favoring socialism and price controls, opposing free enterprise and profits, and retaining too many antibusiness advisers—mentioning Bob Kennedy, Heller, Goldberg, FTC Chairman Dixon and Arthur Schlesinger, Jr. (although the latter had nothing to do with the steel case or other economic decisions). They assailed Dillon for being a traitor to his class and Hodges for not representing them in the Cabinet.

To these critics, every conciliatory Kennedy speech was duplicity, every favorable Kennedy move was a menace. They wanted him to oppose inflation in general, but not specific price increases. They wanted him to improve the balance of payments, but not by curbing foreign tax havens. They wanted him to cut back subsidies, but had in mind aid to education and welfare, not the Federal subsidies paid to ship-owners, shipbuilders, publishers and sugar importers. They wanted him to reduce corporate taxes, but not with the investment tax credit.

If he remained calm during the stock market slide, they said he was indifferent to recession. If he sought new antirecession measures, he was power-hungry. If he met their demands to be equally tough on labor, he was intervening too much in private enterprise. If settlements recommended by a panel of impartial Federal mediators cut back union demands for railroad firemen or jet flight engineers, that was the result of simple justice, but if they provided for a union shop in the aerospace industry, that was the result of Kennedy bias. "No matter what he did," said the head of the Michigan Chamber of Commerce, "I'd be suspicious."

Much of this opposition was emotional, illogical, political and inevitable. It was led largely by men who were Republicans or right-wing Democrats by conviction, habit and association. Nothing any progressive President could conceivably do would have appeased them, and Kennedy was not only a progressive Democrat but a stranger to balance sheets and market reports, a friend of labor and—worst of all—an intellectual from Harvard. "He has never attacked Khrushchev or Tito or any other enemy half as hard as he attacked our own steel industry" was one comment more prevalent than relevant.

Most of these bitter businessmen could not agree in their own ranks on any specific complaints or proposals. They talked loosely of S.O.B. references, midnight raids and radical advisers, but, when asked for concrete suggestions on government policy, they tended to complain of Congressional actions that long antedated Kennedy: income tax rates, antitrust laws, big government and regulatory agencies. None of them agreed on what economic policies they wanted him to push. Some wanted a quickie tax cut in 1962 and some didn't. The President's bold new transportation program, calling for less regulation and more competition, and pushed by the President over strong opposition from Commerce and the ICC, was regarded as probusiness by the railroads and antibusiness by the truckers. The coal and textile industries liked the investment tax credit but opposed the trade bill. Others supported the trade bill but resented the tax credit.

One poll of businessmen cited at his press conference showed them two to one for both bills while simultaneously convinced that the administration was hostile to business. Asked "what this apparent inconsistency suggests," the President said it suggested "that most businessmen, number one, are Republicans, and, number two, that they realize what is in the best interests of business and the country." A Gallup Poll at the height of the supposed "crisis of confidence" showed fewer than one in five businessmen who thought Kennedy was antibusiness. Nevertheless, most Republican leaders and newspapers continued to say that business was anti-Kennedy (which was only partly true) and that Kennedy was antibusiness (which was not true).

"I don't think," said Douglas Dillon, "that there had been a President in a long time who had basically done as much for business . . . [but] it took the business community a long time to recognize this." John Kennedy was no more probusiness than he was prolabor. If appeasing business required suspension of the food and drug and wage-hour laws, or a toleration of inflation and tax loopholes, or a withdrawal of his reforms for stock exchange transactions and for the businessman's cherished "travel and entertainment" deductible expense accounts—or "if to stop them saying we are antibusiness, we are supposed to cease enforcing the antitrust laws," he told a press conference, "then I suppose the cause is lost."

But more than any previous Democratic leader in this century, he looked upon private enterprise with an objective, unjaundiced eye as an essential, constructive part of the American economy. He stressed repeatedly that his hopes for economic growth, plant modernization and government revenues depended on ample business profits. Corporate profits throughout his administration rose some 43 percent, higher and longer than ever before. Production rose, capacity utilization rose, and business confidence—as reflected not in speeches and newspapers but in actual plant expansion and investment—continued strong throughout his tenure.

To help keep business costs down and their markets growing, Kennedy pursued policies designed to achieve wage moderation, competitive transportation, low-cost credit, lower tariff barriers abroad, a supply of trained workers, expanding consumer purchasing power and lower taxes. After all their suspicions and criticisms, businessmen found that the investment tax credit increased the profitability on the purchase of new equipment more than an equivalent reduction in corporate income taxes. They found that Kennedy, unlike his predecessor, was willing to promulgate the modernization of tax depreciation rules they had long sought, to relegate the government from senior partner to junior partner in their enterprises through a reduction of corporate income taxes below the 50 percent level, and to reduce top-bracket personal income taxes and transportation excise taxes.

A variety of other programs extended credit and other aid to small business, to businessmen located in depressed communities or rundown neighborhoods, to bankers, builders, railroads, exporters, textile mills, coal mines, small lead and zinc producers, the lumber industry, the fishing industry and many others. Nor would a President dedicated to "big government" instead of private enterprise have directed that the national stockpiles be drastically reduced, that surplus government plants and installations be sold, that private industry be permitted patents on discoveries Federally financed and that a new communications satellite system be governed by a privately owned corporation. The latter bill, despite built-in protection of the government's interest and assurances of public participation without domination by any single company or stockholder, was filibustered by Senate liberals as a giveaway to big business at the very time many business spokesmen were assailing Kennedy as a socialist.

But those who assumed that business hostility to Kennedy began in the spring of 1962 made a mistake which the President never made. Except for an early clash between the Department of Commerce and its Business Advisory Council—resulting in the Council's divorcing itself from its special position within government—relations between business and the Democratic administration were normal; and normal, for Democratic administrations, meant more suspicion on the part of business than praise. The President recognized this inevitable political gulf. "It would be premature to seek your support in the next election," he told one business group his first month in office, "and inaccurate to express thanks for having had it in the last one." "I do not think it wholly inaccurate to say that I was the second choice of a majority of businessmen for the office of President," he told the U.S. Chamber of Commerce. ("Their first choice," he added a week later, "was anyone else.")

"I'm not sure you have all approached the New Frontier with the greatest possible enthusiasm," he said to the National Convention of Manufacturers, but he added that he felt reassured upon learning that the same group in earlier years had denounced the Marxist "swollen bureaucracy" and the new "paternalism and socialism" under Calvin Coolidge and Herbert Hoover.

The matter often arose at his press conferences:

QUESTION: Mr. President . . . The other day General Eisenhower described the Republican Party as the party of business. Now, do you consider this fair or accurate . . . ?
THE PRESIDENT: . . . I dislike disagreeing with President Eisenhower, and so I won't in this case.
QUESTION: Mr. President, there is a feeling in some quarters, sir, that big business is using the stock market slump as a means of forcing you to come to terms . . . their attitude is, "Now we have you where we want you." Have you seen any reflection of this attitude?
THE PRESIDENT: I can't believe I am where business, big business, wants me!

Many liberals advised the President to be more indifferent to business complaints. Asked at a special news conference with business editors and publishers whether his administration was "unduly sensitive to the alleged hostility of the business world," he replied, "We are—unduly and alleged, I would say." But he also recognized, as Keynes warned Roosevelt in 1938, that a climate of bitter hostility between Main Street and the White House—in which businessmen were convinced, however incorrectly, that their profits would be curbed and their efforts harassed—might well reduce their willingness to invest and expand, and adversely affect the economy, the stock market, the Congress and the elections.

In June of 1962, when the attacks reached almost the point of hysteria in some quarters, he asked me to prepare an analysis of his administration's business relations and all possible means of improving them. Inasmuch as the opposition was more psychological than substantive, the recommended means were also—for the President had no intention of changing either the personnel or the policies under attack. The memorandum led the following month to the President's request that I lead a discussion with the Cabinet on its role in improving relations, and I introduced a list of possible steps each Cabinet member could take with the following observations:

> We cannot do much about most of the emotional and political criticism, which focuses on personalities and clichés. Nor can we discharge every appointee that comes under attack, withdraw our legislative program, relax our enforcement of the law or join the Republican Party. . . .
>
> Nevertheless it is both possible and desirable for each member of the Cabinet . . . to take certain steps designed to show both business in particular and the public in general that this administration is not engaged in an unfair, unreasonable harassment of American businessmen.

The steps suggested, which were then listed in a memorandum sent to each Cabinet member, included informal luncheons and dinners with the business clientele of each department, formal business advisory groups (such as the Defense Industry Advisory Council), more speeches to business organizations, temporary avoidance of controversial remarks not cleared at the White House (such as Hodges' speeches on business ethics and an Archibald Cox speech on wage-price machinery), better liaison with the business press, and a reasonable, nonhostile attitude on the part of those employees engaged in law enforcement. Top aides were dispatched to all meetings of the Business Council, and other business organizations similarly received high-level speakers from the administration, all stressing the need for cooperation—as they had in fact since 1961.

Also planned were a series of off-the-record seminars in cities throughout the country, bringing together leading administration spokesmen and leading businessmen to exchange views and increase understanding. The first of these was a success in Denver. But the political campaign and the Cuban missile crisis postponed a followthrough, and by the start of 1963, with the market climbing, the economy expanding and a tax cut in the offing, much of the meanness in business attitudes had ebbed.

When smaller and more selective price increases were initiated by the Wheeling Steel Company in April of 1963, on the anniversary of the previous fight—a date the President doubted was coincidental—there was a brief revival of tension. New memoranda were prepared in the White House on the industry's economic position. New secret meetings were suggested by self-appointed intermediaries. New calls were placed to other companies by administration officials. And new crisis meetings were held in the Cabinet Room. The President, reported in the press only as watching the situation "with great interest," made a point of postponing by one day his departure for an Easter vacation while the steel companies waited and watched.

But unlike the previous year, no affront to his office and no abuse of his good faith were involved, and the President confined himself, after a long and heated debate within the administration, to releasing a low-key statement which strongly opposed a general across-the-board price increase of the kind attempted the previous year but recognized that

> selective price adjustments, up or down, as prompted by changes in supply and demand, as opposed to across-the-board increases, are not incompatible with a framework of general stability and steel price stability and are characteristic of any healthy economy.[5]

But both the reasonableness and the warning reflected in this statement helped U.S. Steel and Bethlehem announce smaller and more selective increases, and Wheeling and all other producers adjusted back to their level, resulting in an average increase of little more than 1 percent. Only a third of all steel products were involved, and selected price reductions several months earlier largely offset the over-all effect.

[5] I suggested, to the President's amusement, that the statement, with its strong arguments against an increase followed by the above, was based on a line from *Don Juan:*

"A little still she strove, and much repented,
And whispering 'I will ne'er consent'—consented."

Actions on both sides, in short, prevented another massive confrontation, and both reflected and continued the improvement in government-business relations which had taken place during the previous twelve months.

This whole "take a businessman to lunch" campaign, stressed particularly in the last six months of 1962, appears in retrospect an unusual effort to woo a single segment of the electorate, but it was comprised largely of better communication, not substantive concessions, and in a sense it only matched the attention already received by other segments of the electorate from a Democratic administration. Nor was it a hypocritical act to beguile business. For the major burden of this effort, as always, rested with the President, and he neither started nor stopped it in the summer and fall of 1962 when the hostility was at its peak. Both for political and economic reasons, he had preferred from the start of his administration to neutralize the hostility of those business executives he could not win over, rather than merely denounce them as other Democrats had done.

Over and over since his inauguration he had sounded the theme of harmony and cooperation: "Far from being natural enemies, government and business are necessary allies."

In addition to addressing the major business organizations and holding a special press conference with business writers, the President was effective in meetings, luncheons and receptions at the White House with smaller groups of business leaders, showing a genuine interest in their problems and giving them a better grasp of his. A public exchange of letters with banker David Rockefeller on balance of payments problems and his December, 1962, address to the Economic Club on his new tax and budget program were also well regarded in the business community. But in all these appeals and appearances the President was explaining rather than altering his policies.

Particularly in the summer of 1962, many of his efforts were poorly received. He did not refrain, at a peacemaking White House Economic Conference in May, from chastising American bankers who had endangered our gold supply by telling their European counterparts that Kennedy's deficits were sure to bring inflation. Some businessmen thought the repeated mention of profits in his Chamber of Commerce address (some twenty times in a five-page speech) was designed to make them look greedy. Still others resented his Yale Commencement address labeling as myths most of their cherished concepts. His request that the administration-business dialogue move on "to a . . . difficult . . . confrontation with reality" fell largely on deaf ears in the business community. General Eisenhower, among others, said that the President was saying, "Business, get friendly—or else!" Nothing could have been further from the truth.

But it was true that John Kennedy, merely to placate unreasoning opponents, had no intention of displacing their favorite targets in the administration with business appointees lacking breadth (unlike McNamara, McCone, McCloy, Hodges, Day, Dillon and other business-men whom he appointed and admired), or relaxing his enforcement of the antitrust laws (most indictments, he pointed out, stem from complaints by other businessmen), or preventing all further budget deficits (which would have weakened the economy and depressed the stock market). Above all, he intended to find out whether it was possible to pursue a rational national economic policy in the public interest instead of one based on the myths and pressures of private interests—business, labor or otherwise.

A British cartoon at the height of the business-administration clash showed one irate American executive saying to another: "This guy Kennedy thinks he is running the country!" That caption was correct. He did—and he was.

CHAPTER XVIII

❦

THE FIGHT FOR EQUAL RIGHTS

I N 1953 John Kennedy was mildly and quietly in favor of civil rights legislation as a political necessity consistent with his moral instincts.

In 1963 he was deeply and fervently committed to the cause of human rights as a moral necessity inconsistent with his political instincts.

Of all the national ills which he finally brought to the attention of the nation—not merely that of one branch of government or one wing of his party, but that of the entire nation—none had been more studiously avoided in the past than the evils of racial discrimination. Of all the efforts he made as President none was more important or more bitterly resisted than his effort not only to make such discrimination illegal but to make his white countrymen understand that it was wrong. He was revered in many Negro homes and reviled in many white Southern homes as the first President, in the words of Richard Rovere, "with the conviction that no form of segregation or discrimination is morally defensible or socially tolerable."

In 1963 the Negro revolution in America rose more rapidly than ever before. John Kennedy did not start that revolution and nothing he could have done could have stopped it. But in 1963 he befriended and articulated its high aspirations, and helped guide its torrential currents. He was not forced into this position by circumstances beyond his control, as many have written. On the contrary, the sympathy he displayed, the appointees he assembled, the courage he demonstrated in placing himself at the head of that revolution, all encouraged a climate for reform and a reason for hope within the Southern Negro leadership. Their new efforts and pressures would probably not have been risked had there been a different attitude in the White House and in the Department of Justice.

Contrary to some reports, Kennedy was not converted to this cause by the eloquence of some persuasive preacher or motivated by his own membership in a minority group. John Kennedy's convictions on equal rights —like his convictions on nearly all other subjects—were reached gradually, logically and coolly, ultimately involving a dedication of the heart even stronger than that of the mind. As a Senator he simply did not give much thought to this subject. He had no background of association or activity in race relations. He was against discrimination as he was against colonialism or loyalty oaths—it was an academic judgment rather than a deep-rooted personal compulsion. He voted for every civil rights bill coming before him as Congressman and Senator more as a matter of course than of deep concern. Although he joined in sponsoring several such measures, he regarded the school desegregation question as "a judicial problem, not a legislative one . . . and for the courts to interpret as they see fit." His statement of support for Eisenhower's intervention with troops in the Little Rock schools in 1957 was more impassive than impassioned. Even in addressing Negro audiences he was more likely to talk about the general problems of education, unemployment and slum housing than to focus directly on the race issue.

He was angered in one conference committee when a Southern Senator made a slurring reference in the presence of Negro Congressman Dawson, but he found the approach of many single-minded civil rights advocates uncomfortable and unreasonable also. As the first member of either house of Congress from any New England state to appoint a Negro to his staff (Mrs. Virginia Battle, a secretary in his Boston office)—as a leading speaker for the United Negro College Fund—as an advocate of curbs on filibusters—he was not being hypocritical, but neither was he being nonpolitical.

In fact, when he talked privately about Negroes at all in those days, it was usually about winning Negro votes. He talked privately that way about every group—Poles, farmers, Jews, veterans, the aged, suburbanites or any other. To him Negroes were no different from anyone else. He did not treat them differently, look at them differently or speak of them differently. They were not set aside as a Special Problem or singled out as a special group—he simply sought their votes along with those of everyone else.

Politics, in fact, helped to deepen his concern. He was a good politician—and in the 1960 convention and election Negroes more than most groups were his political friends and their enemies were often his enemies. As he became a national figure, his compassion for the problems of his "constituents" took in a far larger proportion of Negroes than it had in Massachusetts. Harris Wofford, who had previously worked for the Civil Rights Commission, supplied him with some statistics for the campaign which shocked and offended him. He used them in his opening debate with Nixon (just as, nearly three years later, he would use them in his February, 1963, Civil Rights Message and in his June, 1963, address to the nation):

> The Negro baby born in America today, regardless of the section of the nation in which he is born, has about one-half as much chance of completing high school as a white baby born in the same place on the same day, one-third as much chance of completing college, one-third as much chance of becoming a professional man, twice as much chance of becoming unemployed, about one-seventh as much chance of earning $10,000 a year, a life expectancy which is seven years shorter, and the prospects of earning only half as much.

His assumption of the powers of the Presidency accelerated the change in his outlook. As a strong President, he had no intention of permitting Southern governors and others to defy the courts and his office. He was freedom's spokesman—and he recognized the stain on American freedom which race repression represented. He was concerned about the unemployed and the underpaid, the school dropouts and the slum dwellers—and he realized that Negroes were forced into those categories in greater proportions than all others. Racial discrimination was divisive and wasteful—and John Kennedy believed in national unity and strength. It was irrational and he was logical. It was undemocratic and he was a democrat, even before he was a Democrat. It was an historic challenge, a dangerous and unpopular controversy, the nation's most critical domestic problem—and he was a President determined to meet every challenge and to leave his mark.

Above all, he was motivated by a deep sense of justice and fair play. "I do not say that all men are equal in their ability, their character or their motivation," he declared more than once, "but I say they should be equal in their chance to develop their character, their motivation and their ability. They should be given a fair chance to develop all the talents that they have." His instinctive inability to be bound by artificial and arbitrary distinctions had in 1953 caused him to pay little attention to the Negro as a Negro. In 1963 it caused him to pay little attention to those unwilling to accept his basic commitment to fair play. Simple justice requires this program, he would tell the Congress in concluding his Civil Rights Message of June 19, 1963, "not merely for reasons of economic efficiency, world diplomacy and domestic tranquillity—but, above all, because it is right."

EXECUTIVE ACTION, 1961-1962

A long and difficult Presidential journey had preceded that June, 1963, message, and it began on January 20, 1961, as John Kennedy sat in the cold and frosty stands in front of the White House reviewing the Inaugural Parade. There were, he noted, among all the floats and bands that marched before him, no dark faces in the honor guard of the Coast Guard. That night he placed a call to Treasury Secretary Dillon, whose department had jurisdiction over the Coast Guard. Special recruiting efforts would be required, but the Coast Guard Academy in 1962 would have the first Negro student in its eighty-six-year history.

At his first Cabinet meeting the following week, the President mentioned the incident; and he asked each Cabinet member to examine the situation in his own department. He stressed that he was not interested merely in numbers but in opportunity at all levels—in the Foreign Service, for example, and in the top policy, professional and supervisory positions. Among his own earliest appointees were Associate Press Secretary Andrew Hatcher and Housing and Home Finance Administrator Robert Weaver, both "firsts" for their race.

During the next one hundred and the next one thousand days, the President's admonition was heeded. For the first time Negroes were named as ambassadors to European as well as to African nations, as United States Attorneys and as a Commissioner of the District of Columbia. (The U.S. Marshal for the District of Columbia was the first Negro in that position since Frederick Douglass nearly a century earlier.) More Negroes were appointed to top Federal jobs than at any time in history—including a Deputy Assistant Secretary of State, an Assistant Secretary of Labor and members of several boards and commissions. The number of Negroes serving in top professional or supervisory positions multiplied in most departments. In the Department of Justice, for example, the number of Negro attorneys rose from ten to more than seventy. Some of these new appointees were promoted from within. Others were invited through special recruitment programs and regional conferences undertaken by the Civil Service Commission, Foreign Service and other agencies.

Kennedy also appointed five lifetime Federal judges from Negro ranks, more than any other President in history, including the first two to be named district judges in the continental United States. He named the nation's (and NAACP's) leading Negro lawyer, the brilliant Thurgood Marshall, to the Court of Appeals. He named three others, including the first Negro woman jurist (Mrs. Marjorie Lawson, his early campaign aide), to the District of Columbia bench—altogether nearly half the Negro judges ever nominated by the White House. (The appointment of judges in the South whose records were not always pleasing to the President was not, it should be emphasized, the result of a *quid pro quo* with Southern Senators, although the operation of "Senatorial courtesy" limited his choice in one state rather severely. No names were forwarded by the Department of Justice to the President until investigation indicated that the prospective judges would abide by the Constitution and Supreme Court decisions. At least two mistakes of judgment were made in this process. But those judges on the whole, said the President, "sharing, perhaps, as they do, the general outlook of the South, have done a remarkable job in fulfilling their oath of office.")

Early in the transition Kennedy had asked Vice President Johnson to head his committees on nondiscrimination in government contracts and employment and to review how their powers could be strengthened. A new Executive Order in March combined the old Committees on Government Contracts and Employment into a single President's Committee on Equal Employment Opportunity. Its extended jurisdiction and sanctions covered some twenty million employees, a sizable proportion of the labor force. It had more power, personnel and funds than its predecessors. With simplified complaint procedures and regular reports, it adjudicated several hundred more cases in its first eighteen months than its predecessors had handled in six years. Through voluntary "Plans for Progress" it covered plants and unions not included in the Executive Order. (Because these plans were conceived and advanced by a persuasive Southerner, Robert Troutman, the President had to ward off the suspicions of civil rights advocates convinced they were meaningless and eventually had to accept Troutman's resignation. But the success of the idea vindicated his confidence in Troutman.)

No contracts were canceled. From time to time the President and Attorney General were dissatisfied with the committee's pace and skeptical of its glowing statistics. But major breakthroughs were made—in textile mills where Negroes had only been sweepers, in aircraft plants where they had been told not to apply, in thousands of new jobs and supervisory positions.

In all this whirlwind of activity—in the areas of Negro voting rights and education as well as employment—one ingredient was missing: legislation. It was missing throughout 1961, except for a largely routine extension of the Civil Rights Commission. It was confined in 1962 to two efforts in the voting rights area—the prevention of discriminatory literacy tests and the abolition by constitutional amendment of poll taxes. Hope for the first measure was lost in the Senate when failure to obtain even a majority vote for cloture (which requires a two-thirds vote) made two facts abundantly clear: (1) that it could not pass without virtually unanimous Republican support, which was not forthcoming; and (2)

that a filibuster would kill most of the President's other legislative proposals, including those which could provide better housing and more jobs
for both Negro and white. The ban on poll taxes in Federal elections,
which had been sought for twenty years and for which the President had
cast one of his first votes as a freshman Congressman in 1947, finally
passed both houses, was pushed by the President and Democratic National
Committee in the state legislatures, and became the Twenty-fourth
Amendment to the Constitution. The number of Negroes and less affluent
whites enabled to vote by that measure alone, the President believed,
could make a difference in his 1964 re-election race in Texas and
Virginia.

But for two years no other civil rights measures were sought or enacted. Bills originating in the Congress were endorsed by administration
witnesses, thus technically fulfilling the pledges of the 1960 platform,
but none of these was adopted or pressed by the President as his own.
The reason was arithmetic. The August, 1960, defeat of civil rights
measures in the more liberal Eighty-sixth Congress—as well as the voting
patterns in January of 1961 in the Rules Committee fight in the House
and the cloture rule fight in the Senate—all made it obvious that no
amount of Presidential pressure could put through the Eighty-seventh
Congress a meaningful legislative package on civil rights. The votes were
lacking in the House to get it through or around the Rules Committee.
They were lacking in the Senate to outlast or shut off a filibuster. In
view of solid Southern Democratic intransigence, greater Republican
and Western Democratic support was required, and with no broad public
interest in such legislation outside of the various civil rights organizations, that support was not obtainable.[1]

The choice confronting the President was clear. He could put forward
and fight for bold proposals anyway, without any prospects for their
passage, and with some risk of jeopardizing other legislation, or he could
accept criticism for failing to carry out the platform by confining himself to an expansion of executive actions, as his campaign speeches had
in fact emphasized.

It was not an easy choice. The President knew that legislative proposals had been promised and expected. He knew that the token gradu-
alism of the preceding years was insufficient. "But a lot of talk and no
results will only make them madder," he said to me after one civil rights
delegation had left his office. "If we drive Sparkman, Hill and other moderate Southerners to the wall with a lot of civil rights demands that can't
pass anyway, then what happens to the Negro on minimum wages,

[1] An attempt by the President in 1961 merely to strengthen the Civil Rights
Commission by giving it a long-term extension failed to win a third of the Republican votes needed on the House Judiciary Committee.

housing and the rest?" To solidify the conservative coalition—by presenting an issue on which Southerners had traditionally sought Republican support in exchange for Southern opposition to other measures—could doom his whole program. To provoke a bitter national controversy without achieving any gain would divide the American people at a time when the international scene required maximum unity.

There was no "deal" with Southern Congressmen. There was no disagreement with Negro leaders over the need for legislation. There was no indifference to campaign pledges. But success required selectivity. Kennedy had won the Presidency by attacking Nixon, not Eisenhower, and by taking on Humphrey in Wisconsin, not South Dakota. He would take on civil rights at the right time on the right issue. "When I believe we can usefully move ahead in the field of legislation," said the President at his news conference, "when I feel that there is a necessity for Congressional action, *with a chance of getting that Congressional action*, then I will recommend it."

Negro leaders also talked of by-passing the Congress, which had historically been more of a burial ground than a battleground for civil rights legislation. They also talked of promoting equal voting, education, employment and other opportunities through increased executive effort. NAACP Chairman Roy Wilkins presented to me in February, 1961, at the President's request, a sixty-one-page memorandum which offered new areas for executive action. Martin Luther King presented a still longer document. Both talked in terms of an across-the-board Executive Order or "Second Emancipation Proclamation" on or before the hundredth anniversary of the first.[2]

These leaders could not, however, publicly accept the President's decision not to wage a losing fight for legislation. None of them thought a bill could pass, but they had to respond to their constituencies, and they seemed to weigh the disadvantages of defeat less heavily than did the President. King wanted more "fireside chats." Wilkins complained of "supercaution." Like the abolitionists a hundred years earlier, they accused their President of vacillation, equivocation and retreat.

But relations remained cordial and close. The President, the Attorney General, Assistant Attorney General Burke Marshall, Assistant White House Counsel Lee White and Democratic National Committee Deputy Chairman Louis Martin were constantly in touch with Negro leaders. The latter knew they had a President willing to listen and learn. When

[2] In time, the Executive Orders and actions taken on housing, employment, education, Federal administration and other public activities were the equivalent of such a Proclamation and may have accomplished more. Space does not permit an adequate listing of the many efforts initiated by the Department of Justice in particular; and because of the President–Attorney General relationship, more of these efforts proceeded outside the purview of my office than was true of most domestic matters.

Wilkins and a delegation pressed him for legislation, they were impressed by both the charm and the tenacity with which he refused to change his course, and by the candor with which he welcomed their pressure "to off-set pressures from the other side." On Lincoln's Birthday (traditionally celebrated only by Republicans) the President in 1963 held a large White House reception for more than a thousand Negro leaders and civil rights champions. Their displeasure with his strategy was in some measure alleviated because he treated them with dignity—not with condescension, and not as people deserving any preferential status, but with the same respect and recognition that he offered to every American citizen. Most Negro leaders were shrewd judges of which politicians cared deeply about their values and which cared chiefly about their votes—and while Kennedy may have initially been more influenced by the second concern, by the 1960's the first had become more and more important to him.

Negro leaders were satisfied, moreover, that he really did intend to achieve far more by mobilizing the full legal and moral authority of the Presidency than had been achieved in any previous period. The burden of carrying forward the fight for civil rights, accelerated by the Supreme Court desegregation decision of 1954, had in the preceding years rested largely on the Judicial Branch (although President Truman's Executive Order desegregating the armed forces had been a notable earlier gain). The Legislative Branch had made small but significant contributions in 1957 and 1960. Now in 1961 the full powers of the Executive Branch were enlisted in the cause as never before—through litigation, negotiation, moral suasion, Executive Orders and Presidential actions and directives.

Perhaps the most important change was the President's prompt and positive endorsement in public of the equal rights principle in general and the Supreme Court's desegregation decision in particular. Minor gains—which seem so unimportant now—helped set a whole new tone in that very different era. For example, administration officials refused to speak before segregated audiences, and (with some exceptions) made known their boycott of segregated private clubs. (Arthur Krock fumed that the rules of Washington's exclusive Metropolitan Club were none of the President's business. When he later fumed that the administration was deliberately excluding from this country Congolese rebel leader Moise Tshombe, the President told the Gridiron Club that he would invite Tshombe to the United States if Krock would then invite him to the Metropolitan Club.) In a note of irony, the Civil War Centennial Commission under U. S. Grant III had to be told to use only nonsegregated facilities. U.S. Employment Offices were told to refuse "for whites only" job orders. Federal employee unions and recreation associations were told that those practicing race discrimination would not be recognized. The faces in the press club dinners addressed by the President were no longer all-white—neither were the faces in his Secret Service retinue or among the White House drivers. He refused to seek out a Negro child for the White House nursery school or to disclose the race or any other aspect of those who attended. But the popularity during the school's second year of Andrew Hatcher's son was evidence, he said, that color blindness is natural at an early age. (Even the Washington Redskins football team, playing in a Federally financed stadium, was persuaded that it could win more games by acquiring some Negro talent—and it did both.)

In a mid-1961 news conference, without endorsing all the tactics of the "Freedom Riders" who chartered integrated bus trips into Dixie to test the desegregation of interstate travel facilities, the President endorsed their right to cross any and all state lines free from interference. The Freedom Riders situation—including the unchecked violence of Alabama mobs that burned buses and stormed churches—was a hint of the chaos to come. It tested the determination and patience of not only the President but the Attorney General, whose deepening convictions and unceasing effort in the civil rights area played a major role in all the events related hereafter.

It also tested their ingenuity, for there was no clear-cut Federal solution. "The Kennedys," as they would thereafter be lumped in the South, dispatched six hundred deputy U.S. marshals to Alabama to protect the Freedom Riders, shamed Southern governors and mayors into enforcing law and order, brought suit against police officials and Klansmen interfering with interstate traffic or permitting violence against the travelers, initiated action before the Interstate Commerce Commission to enforce integration in the restaurants, waiting rooms and rest rooms at interstate rail and bus terminals, and prodded the major rail and bus lines into ending segregation for all terminals and passengers. Using Federal airport and other aviation funds as leverage, fifteen air terminals were also desegregated, two after legal action. By the end of 1962 enforced segregation in interstate transportation, theoretically outlawed by the Supreme Court back in 1950, had finally ceased to exist, and a Negro could travel for the first time from one end of the country to the other without seeing "White" or "Negro" signs in the waiting rooms.

Meanwhile the President tackled voting rights. He was convinced that enfranchising the Negroes in the South—where less than 10 percent were registered in many counties, compared to two-thirds of the Negroes in the North—could in time dramatically alter the intransigence of Southern political leaders on all other civil rights measures, shift the balance of political power in several states, and immunize Southern politics from the demagogue whose only campaign cry was "Nigger!" Later he was to realize that gaining the vote could not go far enough fast enough to remove a century of accumulated wrongs. But it was an important start. One of his earliest actions in 1961 was to aid Negro tenant farmers evicted for their voting activity in Haywood and Fayette counties, Tennessee. A Federal court order halted their eviction, Federal surplus foods helped them survive in the interim, and looking around at other Southern counties, the Justice Department cited sixteen where Negroes were in a majority but did not have a single registered voter.

Under the limited 1957 and 1960 voting rights laws, less than a dozen cases had been initiated in three years. None had been brought in Mississippi, home state of the Senate Judiciary Committee chairman. Beginning in 1961, more than three dozen were initiated and won in the next three years, with dozens of others in process (including many in Mississippi). Investigations, settlements or court actions were undertaken in practically every Southern county where discrimination prevailed. Many states and counties were voluntarily persuaded to abandon dis- criminatory or segregated registration and voting practices. In others— such as Forrest County, Mississippi, where the local registrar responded to a court order by accepting applications from 103 Negroes and finding 94 of them unqualified, including those with graduate degrees—follow-up court action was required. In still other areas the fear of reprisal was the chief deterrent to Negro registration, and in those areas suits were filed or assurances received against economic, physical, legal or other intimidation. In East Carroll Parish, Louisiana, a series of Federal law- suits enabled Negroes to vote for the first time since Reconstruction. In Macon County, Alabama, newly registered Negroes comprised some 40 percent of the vote—and a racist candidate lost. In other areas Negro candidates emerged for the first time. Private foundations and organizations worked to interest and prepare Negroes for registration once the bars were down. Across the Attorney General's report on two years of voting progress, the President wrote: "Keep pushing the cases."

Under the 1954 decision, the Federal Government was given no right to "push" school desegregation cases. But some suits were initiated to implement court orders, and others already started by private litigants were joined by the Federal Government. Early in 1961 court action was obtained to protect the salaries of New Orleans teachers threatened by the state legislature for teaching integrated classes. The previous year, the Department of Justice had rejected the local Federal judge's request for Federal help. Now all U.S. judges were put on notice that the government was determined to carry out the Constitution and court orders, regardless of the political consequences. Quiet and informal con- sultation with local officials in Atlanta, Little Rock, Memphis, Dallas and other cities helped open those schools to both races without violence.

Negotiations and intervention were effective in the litigation over Prince Edward County, Virginia, where the public schools had shamefully been closed to prevent court-ordered integration (one of the few jurisdictions in the world outside of sub-Sahara Africa not offering free elementary education to all, the Attorney General pointed out—the President literally shook his head with incredulity when told of this situation, and continually pressed to end it). The Department of Justice helped arrange for the reopening of the schools and for the provision of temporary classes in the interim. An administrative order ended the Federally financed segregation of schoolchildren living on Federal bases.

A variety of other executive actions and orders barred segregation or discrimination in the armed forces Reserves, in the training of civil defense workers, in the off-base treatment of military personnel, in Federally aided libraries and in the summer college training institutes of the National Science Foundation and National Defense Education Act. The Department of Justice brought suits to end segregation in Federally financed hospitals; it filed "friend of the court" briefs on behalf of nondiscrimination in employment and public accommodations; and it brought police brutality prosecutions in all parts of the country.

Some of these moves were taken quietly to reduce resistance, some were made with fanfare to set an example. Some were taken in response to crises, some to initiate progress. The President still looked for the least divisive approach—but the walls of segregation were steadily leveled.

On the day after Thanksgiving, 1961, following a long day of meetings at Hyannis Port on trade, defense and other matters, the President, the Attorney General, Burke Marshall, O'Brien, O'Donnell and I met to reassess this approach. The President was generally satisfied with its progress. The literacy test and poll tax measures were to be sent up in January. The rate of executive actions was to be accelerated. The most difficult question was the timing of a long-promised Executive Order banning discrimination in Federally financed housing.

During the campaign the President had made much of Eisenhower's refusal to implement "with the stroke of the pen" a Civil Rights Commission recommendation that such an order be issued. But once in office he moved cautiously. He waited until Congress acted on the nomination of Robert Weaver, who had previously spearheaded the drive for such an order, as head of the Housing and Home Finance Agency. Then he waited until Congress acted on his housing bill, of immense importance to Negro families in the low- and middle-income brackets. That bill, to be administered by Weaver, was dependent on Southern sponsorship and support in both the House and Senate. Then he waited for a full-scale report on housing from the Civil Rights Commission and for a more carefully drafted Executive Order to be prepared by the lawyers.

Meanwhile he gave first priority to the Executive Order on employment and to administrative actions on voting, education and other areas.

But now it was late November. The order had been largely drafted, its remaining issues refined if not resolved. Civil rights groups were clamoring for the promised stroke of the pen. A new dilemma, however, had arisen. An important item in the 1962 legislative program was to be the elevation of the HHFA to Cabinet status as a Department of Urban Affairs. Weaver was to become the first Negro Cabinet member in history. The special concerns of the 125 million people living in urban and suburban areas were to receive the same representation at the Cabinet level as those of the thirteen million on the farm. Passage of the measure would be difficult. Its only hope rested with the two relatively moderate Alabamans who handled housing legislation in their respective chambers, Senator John Sparkman and Congressman Albert Raines. But their support, and that of their Southern colleagues, would not be possible if the Housing Order were issued first.

The President believed that the achievement of Weaver's elevation, as well as the substantive values of the bill, were of sufficient importance to merit another delay. He would not renege on his commitment to issue the order, he said. But if the Urban Affairs bill could be passed promptly, the order would not be issued until a decent interval had elapsed—long enough for Congress to adjourn and be unable to protest, and possibly long enough for its Southern supporters to be re-elected, but in no event stretching beyond the end of the year.

Weaver preferred the order to the departmental bill, but he agreed that, if the President's strategy could obtain both, more delay was not intolerable. The plan was derailed, however, when the House Rules Committee, reverting to its old role as chief legislative roadblock, killed the Urban Affairs bill by a 9-6 margin. The Southern members who customarily supported the administration joined all Republican and Dixiecrat members in voting "no." The bill was dead in the Congress and the President was alive with indignation. "Imagine them claiming," he said to me over the phone, talking a little louder and even faster than usual, "that this bill was bad bureaucratic organization. They're against it because Weaver's a Negro and I'd like to see them say it." He asked me to have the measure redrafted—this time as a reorganization plan, which by law could be blocked only by a roll call. He also decided to state flatly— in answer to a planted news conference question—his intention to name Weaver to the new post. "Obviously," he said, "if the [bill] had been passed, Mr. Weaver would have been appointed. It was well known on the Hill. The American people might as well know it." To the charge that his strategy was based on partisan politics as well as principle, the President would have privately pleaded guilty.

The strategy backfired. It was more combative, more partisan and more obvious than his usual legislative approach—"so obvious it made them mad," the President later commented. Instead of putting Republicans on the spot as intended, it hardened the GOP-Dixie coalition's resistance. Instead of being a political master stroke, it produced new excuses to vote the measure down—partly because of the limitations inherent in the reorganization-plan method and partly because of a tangle in the legislative signals.

The Republicans attempted to protect themselves with Negro voters by announcing, as the President described it with a touch of sarcasm, that they were

> now ready to support [Weaver] for any Cabinet position he wishes. . . . I considered him admirably qualified for this particular position because he has had long experience in it. While I am sure he is grateful for those good wishes for a Cabinet position where there is no vacancy, I think he feels . . . that this country would have been better served to have voted for an Urban Department, and permitted him to continue his service in that capacity.

The fact remained that the Urban Affairs bill was lost, and any immediate issuance of the Housing Order would be attributed to petty spite. The President bided his time, uncertain about the economy, uncertain about naming Weaver to succeed Ribicoff or naming Hastie to the Supreme Court and uncertain whether issuance in the brief period between adjournment and election would look too partisan. His desire was to make a low-key announcement that would be as little divisive as possible. He found the lowest-key time possible on the evening of November 20, 1962. It was the night before he and much of the country closed shop for the long Thanksgiving weekend. The announcement was deliberately sandwiched in between a long, dramatic and widely hailed statement on Soviet bombers leaving Cuba and another major statement on the Indian border conflict with China.

The order's terms had been finally settled by the President in a meeting the night before with Justice and White House aides. To prevent its being tied up in a long legal battle and for other complex reasons (including no control over a key banking agency), the order provided only for voluntary efforts with respect to housing already built and housing financed by conventional bank mortgages. To enforce it, a new committee was established in the executive offices under Pennsylvania's retiring Governor, David Lawrence. The predicted disruptions and decline in home-building and Federal financing never materialized.

MISSISSIPPI

The Housing Order had also been delayed by the priority given another racial issue in the fall of 1962. The issue originally pitted Negro applicant James Meredith against the all-white University of Mississippi. It eventually and unavoidably pitted the state of Mississippi against the United States. It was termed at the time the most serious clash of state versus Federal authority since the end of the Civil War; and its favorable resolution upheld not only the principle of equal rights and the sanctity of law but also the paramount powers of the Presidency.

Well over a year earlier, Meredith had attempted to enroll in the tax-supported public university located at Oxford in his native state. A long series of court rulings, all the way up to the Supreme Court, ordered his admission and an end to official resistance. When open and avowed defiance continued in a manner unprecedented for a century, the United States Court of Appeals for the Fifth Circuit—consisting of eight Southern jurists—found Mississippi's Governor Ross Barnett and Lieutenant Governor Paul Johnson guilty of contempt for blocking Meredith's admission. The judges, their patience exhausted, then directed the Federal Government to enforce the court's order and to put down what bordered on rebellion.

The President and Attorney General accepted this responsibility and moved steadily but cautiously to meet it. They hoped to avoid either force or violence in the most thoroughly segregated, bitterly prejudiced state in the Federal Union. They hoped to avoid making a martyr out of Governor Barnett, who was rumored to be planning a Senate race against the more thoughtful and soft-spoken John Stennis. They hoped to persuade Mississippi officials—and ultimately did persuade the university officials—to comply peacefully and responsibly with the law. They hoped, finally, to prove that many steps lay between inaction and the use of Federal troops—including a few, many or a full squadron of U.S. marshals (including deputies, border patrolmen and Federal prison guards) especially trained for such situations.

In late September of 1962 matters came rapidly to a head. Nearly every day of the last ten days of the month a new effort was made—in court, at the university, at the State College Board, at the Governor's office or with the Governor privately by telephone. Each day the number of marshals accompanying Meredith grew larger. Each conversation with Barnett grew sharper. Bob Kennedy and his brilliant Assistant Attorney General Burke Marshall led the fight, thus re-emphasizing that it was not John F. Kennedy whom Barnett defied but the majesty of the United States Government.

Finally, on Sunday, September 30, Barnett recognized the inevitable. The President had issued a proclamation and Executive Order preliminary to federalizing the Mississippi National Guard and deploying other troops. He had announced a nationwide TV address for Sunday night. In a series of secret telephone conversations with the Attorney General and the President, Barnett suggested that he be permitted to stand courageously in the door of the school and yield only when a marshal's gun was pointed at him. But that little drama would have risked violence from menacing groups of students, sheriffs, state police and hangers-on who gathered for each such confrontation. Still trying to save face, the Governor then proposed that Meredith be spirited quickly and quietly onto the campus that very day, Sunday, before the President's speech. Inasmuch as it had been assumed that the speech would announce Federal action for Monday, the Oxford campus would be deserted for the weekend, the Governor could pretend ignorance and he then would protest vehemently from his office at Jackson. A large force of state police would assure the safety of Meredith, Barnett promised, with no need for National Guardsmen or other forces. The Kennedys agreed to the plan as a means of avoiding Barnett's arrest and a troop deployment but, unwilling to rely wholly on Barnett's word, they kept troops on a stand-by basis in Memphis and equipped Meredith's guard of deputy marshals with steel helmets and tear gas.

It was my misfortune to have been hospitalized that week with an ulcer. I had expressed my suggestions on the crisis in a memorandum to the President on Friday, received his instructions on a possible speech for national television Saturday, and left the hospital a day early on Sunday in response to his call that I "had better get down here." I never returned to the hospital. In fact, none of us gathered at the White House that Sunday afternoon would reach bed until 6 A.M. Monday morning.

I arrived to find the President—accompanied by the Attorney General, Marshall, O'Donnell and O'Brien—pacing the floor of the Cabinet Room, where a direct phone link to Oxford was being maintained. His speech had been set for 7:30 P.M. Sunday night, and by the time that hour arrived Meredith, escorted by state police and university officials, had been driven safely to a men's dormitory on the campus. But the President was still skeptical of Barnett's pledge. "We can't take a chance with Meredith's life," he said to his brother, "or let that ——— make the Federal Government look foolish." He postponed his talk until 10 P.M. The possibility of domestic violence made him more anxious than usual. He carefully rewrote his speech to make it clear that the government was merely carrying out the orders of the court in a case it had not brought and was not forcing anything down the throats of Mississippians on its own initiative.

Meanwhile a squad of U.S. deputy marshals—which in the end reached 550—took up guard positions near the university administration building, deliberately staying away from Meredith's unpublicized quarters. It was not an army. All were civilians, most were from the South, and many worked in Immigration or other Justice Department offices unaccustomed to armed combat. But they were well disciplined under the leadership of Chief Marshal James McShane and Deputy Attorney General Nicholas Katzenbach. Throughout the night these men and other Justice officials on the scene maintained direct telephone contact with the "Command Headquarters" set up in the Cabinet Room, because of the camera crews working in the President's office.

By 10 P.M., when the President went on the air, Barnett had already issued his statement, claiming that Meredith had been sneaked in "by helicopter" without his knowledge. His aides informed the White House that no further forces would be required. But the two hundred state police he provided had suddenly vanished without notice at the first sign of tension, returning only after a bitter protest to the Governor's office from the Attorney General. Now an ugly mob was gathering around the band of marshals as the President began to speak.

The speech, its first rough draft prepared the night before in the hospital but its final text completed by the President only shortly before air time, began with a quiet statement of fact and hope:

> The orders of the court in the case of *Meredith versus Fair* are beginning to be carried out. . . . This has been accomplished thus far without the use of National Guard or other troops.

The President then gave a brief but eloquent summation on "the integrity of American law":

> Our nation is founded on the principle that observance of the law is the eternal safeguard of liberty. . . . Even among law-abiding men, few laws are universally loved, but they are uniformly respected and not resisted. Americans are free to disagree with the law, but not to disobey it. . . . My obligation . . . is to implement the orders of the court with whatever means are necessary, and with as little force and civil disorder as the circumstances permit.

Reviewing the circumstances of the case, he emphasized the Southern backgrounds of the Federal judges, commended other Southern universities that had admitted Negroes and pointed out that only Mississippi's failure to do likewise had brought the Federal Government into the picture. Reminding his Mississippi listeners of that state's history of patriotic courage, he concluded with an appeal to the students of the university, the people who were most concerned.

> You have a great tradition to uphold, a tradition of honor and courage. . . . Let us preserve both the law and the peace, and then, healing those wounds that are within, we can turn to the greater crises that are without, and stand united as one people in our pledge to man's freedom.

The great majority of students, however, did not hear or heed the President's appeal. Nor did the great majority of the more than 2,500 roughnecks who began attacking newsmen and marshals—even as the President was speaking—have any connection with the university. Roughnecks and racists from all over Mississippi and the South had been gathering in Oxford, carrying clubs, rocks, pipes, bricks, bottles, bats, firebombs—and guns. The marshals responded with tear gas but kept their pistols in their holsters. The Attorney General's continuing efforts to enlist the effective help of university officials—including the popular and successful football coach—were in vain. The arrival of the local Mississippi National Guard unit only enraged the Guard's fellow Mississippians further. As rioting raged through the night, a newsman and a townsman were shot dead, two hundred marshals and Guardsmen were injured, vehicles and buildings were burned, campus benches were smashed to provide jagged concrete projectiles, a stolen fire engine and bulldozer tried to batter their way into the administration building and frenzied attackers roamed the campus. But the Governor had failed to reassign the state police in force; and the President, who had previously thought it best to deal with Barnett chiefly through the Attorney General, angrily took the phone and demanded of the Governor that he send his police back. He interrupted each of Barnett's drawled excuses and explanations. "Listen, Governor, somebody's been shot down there already and it's going to get worse. Most of it's happened since those police left and I want them back. Good-bye." He slammed down the phone.

Barnett had whined, grumbled and equivocated, afraid that his compatriots knew he had "sold out," begging that Meredith be withdrawn, but finally agreeing to send the two hundred state troopers back. More crucial time passed, however, before fifty showed up to stay. In a new statement, which reversed his earlier statement of merely indignant submission, the Governor proclaimed that Mississippi would "never surrender." Perhaps he reasoned that mob action could achieve his aims without placing him directly in contempt of court.

The marshals—bloodied, unfed and exhausted—obeyed orders to use only the minimum tear gas necessary to protect lives and to refrain from returning fire. But their telephoned reports to the President and Attorney General expressed concern about snipers in the dark and uncertainty as to how much longer they could hold out even with National Guard help. The President, terribly disheartened by news of increasing violence, especially against the Federal marshals, and concerned lest the mob run rampant, find James Meredith and lynch him, ordered into action the troops standing by in Memphis. Their response was agonizingly slow. Each time he called the Pentagon the troops were "on their way." Each new call from Oxford asked desperately where they were. His temper rising, the President insisted on talking directly to the Army commander on the scene. An elaborate Army communication system failed to function, and the President received his reports from Katzenbach dropping dimes into a pay phone in a campus booth.

We were all tired and hungry now, with an almost helpless feeling about getting the troops there in time to relieve the hard-pressed defenders. The President looked drawn and bleak. He refused to accept our suggestion that he had done everything he could. Through the long night of waiting and telephoning, he cursed himself for ever believing Barnett and for not ordering the troops in sooner. At least one of the two deaths, he believed at the time, might have been prevented had the Army arrived when he had thought it would. Finally, after 5 A.M., he called his wife in Newport, awakening her with a dismal account of the night's happenings, and then obtained a few hours of sleep. In the morning he ordered a full report on the timing of each call placed from the White House to the Pentagon, the time such orders were implemented and an accounting for each minute in between.

Once the flow of troops began, it gushed forth in what were soon needless numbers of up to twenty thousand. The mob was dispersed; the town was quieted; some two hundred troublemakers were arrested (only twenty-four of them students at the university); and Barnett issued still another statement, this one opposing violence. Early the next morning Meredith, accompanied by a group of marshals (at least one of whom would be guarding him constantly thereafter) but not, at the President's insistence, by Army troops, officially registered and began, to the jeers and catcalls of his fellow students, his own ordeal of perseverance.

Governor Barnett, embarrassed by the revelation that he had double-crossed his own segregationist supporters by conniving in Meredith's admission on Sunday, sought to blame "trigger-happy" marshals for starting the trouble, a charge echoed not only by some Senators but by some university officials who knew better. The Governor ignored the injuries suffered by eight marshals before the tear gas was fired in self-protection, the thirty-five marshals shot and the more than 150 others requiring medical treatment. He claimed that the state police gas masks were not suitable for tear gas. And he complained, just as the rest of the world marveled, that the Federal Government had arrayed thousands of troops and spent several hundred thousands of dollars to obtain the admission of one otherwise obscure citizen to the university.

But "this country cannot survive . . . and this government would unravel very fast," said the President, "if . . . the Executive Branch does not carry out the decisions of the court . . . [or] had failed . . . to protect Mr. Meredith. . . . That would have been far more expensive." The cost of the Meredith incident, he reasoned, could be spread over all the other incidents avoided in the peaceful admissions that would follow. "I recognize that it has caused a lot of bitterness against me," he added. "[But] I don't really know what other role they would expect the President of the United States to play. They expect me to carry out my oath under the Constitution, and that is what we are going to do."

He sought to heal "those wounds that are within." He resisted a Civil Rights Commission recommendation that he shut off all Federal funds to Mississippi, regardless of whether they aided whites or Negroes, integrated or segregated activities, believing that no President should possess the power to punish an entire state. (This is not the only situation in which the free-wheeling Civil Rights Commission proved to be a somewhat uncomfortable ally in this struggle.) He urged through Burke Marshall that an indignant Court of Appeals punish Barnett's contempt by fine instead of by the martyrdom of arrest and imprisonment. He urged other states to realize that all court orders would be carried out and that resistance served no purpose other than their own economic harm. He was pleased that quiet preparations with South Carolina leaders, as well as the force of example in Mississippi, helped facilitate the peaceful admission to Clemson University of its first Negro student. But he knew that the Mississippi battle was not an end but a beginning—that his relations with the South would never be the same—and that still harsher crises and choices lay ahead in 1963.

ALABAMA

The Negro revolution had built rapidly in the several years preceding 1963 for many reasons. Negroes who served side by side with whites in World War II and Korea were less willing to accept an inferior status back home. They were more likely to get an education through the "GI bill of rights." Those leaving the mechanized farms for Southern cities found strength in numbers. Those displaced by automation in the factories were hungrier—so were those who had seen a different world on TV—so was a whole new generation of proud, unfrightened Negro youngsters. Even the rise of nationalism in Africa sparked interest in their own lack of freedom. But white political and business leaders were hostile or indifferent, particularly but not exclusively in the South. Denied communication, impatient with litigation, the Negroes revived the familiar weapon of minority protest: demonstration.

"The fires of frustration and discord," the President would say in June, "are burning in every city, North and South, where legal remedies are not at hand." They burned in Philadelphia, Pennsylvania, and Philadelphia, Mississippi; in Cambridge, Massachusetts, and Cambridge, Maryland; in Shreveport, Clinton and nearly a thousand other cities— through demonstrations, marches, picket lines and mass meetings. But the hottest flames that seared the nation's conscience were those spreading in the state of Alabama and particularly in the city of Birmingham.

Birmingham—"the most thoroughly segregated big city in the U.S.," according to the Rev. Martin Luther King—had long been considered by civil rights groups to be a prime target for "nonviolent resistance." Inasmuch as the city's ardent segregationist Police Commissioner, T. Eugene "Bull" Connor, was a candidate for mayor, King was persuaded by the Attorney General to delay his move until after the April 2, 1963, election. But after April 2—despite a legal struggle for power growing out of Connor's defeat—King's carefully prepared campaign could be delayed no longer. Parades, petitions, boycotts, sit-ins and similar demonstrations by an increasingly aroused Negro community followed daily. Bull Connor and his men met them daily—with police clubs, police dogs, fire hoses, armored cars and mass arrests. More than 3,300 Negro men, women and children, most of them trained in passive resistance, were hauled off to jail, including King himself. His wife, fearful for his safety on Easter Sunday when her husband was held incommunicado, telephoned the President and was heartened by his reassurance.

"The civil rights movement," the President often said thereafter, "should thank God for Bull Connor. He's helped it as much as Abraham Lincoln." But news photographers deserve a share of this credit. Front-page pictures of Connor's police dogs savagely attacking Negroes, of fire hoses pounding them against the street, of burly policemen sitting on a female demonstrator, aroused the nation and the world. Previously timid Negroes were spurred into action in their own cities. Previously indifferent whites were shocked into sympathy. And President John Fitzgerald Kennedy, recognizing that the American conscience was at last beginning to stir, began laying his own plans for awakening that conscience to the need for further action.

Because he said little publicly, because he still sought the least divisive answers, because he still relied on reason and persuasion, most of the Negro leaders complained about the administration's attitude toward Birmingham. They were angry at the Kennedys for requesting a moratorium on demonstrations while an agreement was worked out

and the city government settled. They resented the Kennedys' questioning their use of small children in demonstrations which subjected them
to possible injury as well as jail. They were suspicious of Burke Marshall
and other Justice aides who had been striving for more than a year
to negotiate privately some peaceful progress in that troubled community.

Above all, civil rights leaders impatiently demanded that the President "do something" as he had in Mississippi. But troops had been sent
to Mississippi because Federal court orders were defied by both officials
and mobs. No Federal court orders had been broken by Bull Connor, nor
were any crowds massed in Birmingham other than Negroes. Segregated
lunch counters and an all-white police force were not contrary to
Federal law. Even passage of the civil rights bill then pending would
have been of little value; and the White House and Department of
Justice began at this time their deliberations on further legislation.
There were recurring suggestions that the President should personally
appear in Birmingham and take a Negro child by the hand into a school
or lunch counter. But that suggestion badly confused the physical presence of the President with the official presence of his powers. It would
have demeaned the dignity of the office by relying on the same kind
of dramatic stunt and physical contest that was staged by those Southern governors who "stood in the doorway."

The best that could be done in Birmingham was to initiate an investigation of voting rights, file a brief in a pending case against segregation, stay on the alert for official violations of the old civil rights
statutes and work, as the President said, "on getting both sides together
—to settle in a peaceful fashion the very real abuses too long inflicted
on the Negro citizens of that community." That was not enough to
satisfy either the President or his critics. But it was all he had the
power to do under the laws then prevailing in our Federal-state system.

In private conversations with the President and Attorney General,
Negro leaders understood this. They understood also the need to confine
their own charges to the provable and their objectives to the obtainable.
But their public stance was invariably different. The NAACP had lost
members when the Rev. King seized the initiative in the South. King
had lost prestige when he stayed only two days in jail in Albany, Georgia.
All the Negro spokesmen and action groups were competing for leadership, for followers and necessarily for headlines—and none of them intended to be outdone by any of the others in Birmingham, Alabama. They
also believed that the greater the crisis, the greater was their bargaining
power with Southern officials and their "creative pressures" on President
Kennedy.

Finally, early in May, Burke Marshall convinced Birmingham's more
responsible business leaders that racial harmony was better for them

than chaos. Changes in employment opportunities and public facilities were offered. The new Mayor promised a more moderate approach; Negro leaders suspended demonstrations; and the President expressed hope at his news conference for continued cooperation and progress. Asked if that settlement might be a model, he replied, "We will have to see what happens in Birmingham over the next few days."

Three days later he had his answer. With my sons and a group of neighbors, I was playing softball on the ellipse south of the White House on Sunday afternoon, May 12. The police asked us to clear the area for a landing by the President's helicopter. Surprised that he would be returning early from his weekend retreat in the country, I learned the reason as soon as I was home. He had been trying to reach me by phone. Late the previous night a Birmingham Negro home and hotel had been devastated by bombs. Fear, anger, rioting and counterrioting had taken over. By the time I reached the White House the President and Attorney General had decided on a new course of action. Some three thousand troops were being dispatched to bases near Birmingham. At 9 P.M. the President broadcast over all networks a brief but strong statement of warning. Then, as the Attorney General talked with Rev. King by telephone, the President waited in his office for telephoned reports on the prospects for renewed violence. (Idly switching the channels on his TV set in search of news about the crisis, he came across a new political satire show which ribbed current political figures and failings, including a few of his own. Between telephone calls, he relaxed and chuckled appreciatively at each skit until the show ended.)

Tensions also eased in Birmingham. Alabama's Governor George Wallace challenged the legal basis of the troop directive on the grounds that his state police were capable of maintaining order. But the President had already suffered once the consequences of being too quick to accept such assurances and too slow to move in troops; and he responded firmly that his authority to suppress domestic violence gave him full discretion as to how and when that authority should be exercised.

Even as Birmingham returned fitfully to the terms of the agreement that Marshall had negotiated, Kennedy and Wallace were moving steadily toward another confrontation which threatened to resemble that in Mississippi. On that long night in the previous September, after the Federal troops had finally arrived in Oxford and guaranteed Meredith's safety, the President had wearily asked his brother whether there would be "any more like this one coming up soon." Bob Kennedy had replied that he could look forward to losing at least one more state's electoral votes—Alabama. A University of Alabama lawsuit similar to the *Meredith* case, he said, would reach the same critical stage in the spring of 1963. "Let's be ready," said the President grimly.

That same September night Alabama's Wallace was also planning to be ready. Early the next morning he had warned that Alabama would never yield on segregation in education. He was publicly pledged to "stand in the doorway" of any schoolhouse under court order and defy the Federal Government to remove him. The Justice Department, in preparation for the eventual clash, began an intensive campaign of contacts with Alabama educators, editors, clergymen, business and other community leaders, hoping to build a climate that had not been possible in Mississippi.

In May of 1963 the President added his weight to this effort. Less than a week after the Birmingham bombings, he made a one-day trip to Tennessee and Alabama, saluting the ninetieth anniversary of Vanderbilt University and the thirtieth anniversary of the TVA, but in addition reminding his listeners of their roles and responsibilities as citizens. At Muscle Shoals, Alabama, in the presence of Governor Wallace, he cited the TVA and other popular Federal efforts to show that the Federal Government was not "an outsider, an intruder, an adversary . . . [but] the people of fifty states joining in a national effort to see progress in every state." In building the TVA, he said, Nebraska's Norris and New York's Roosevelt "were not afraid to direct the power and purpose of the nation toward a solution of the nation's problems." Even Governor Wallace could not have missed the meaning.

At Vanderbilt the President's remarks were again directed to the point:

> . . . liberty without learning is always in peril; and learning without liberty is always in vain. . . .
>
> Any educated citizen who seeks to subvert the law, to suppress freedom, or to subject other human beings to acts that are less than human, degrades his heritage, ignores his learning and betrays his obligations.

Bull Connor may have felt these words did not apply to him. But George Wallace made clear at a press conference that he had heard the message—had heard it again on the President's plane—and had rejected it.

Alabama was now the only state in the Union without a desegregated state university. The court decisions on two Negro students were final—the university was willing to admit them—prominent Alabamans urged Wallace not to resist—but the Governor was apparently determined on a theatrical show for home consumption. This time each White House move was based on the Mississippi experience. This time the President and Attorney General made certain that troops in nearby Fort Benning were already sitting in helicopters. This time the campus was completely cleared of outsiders, and community leaders spoke out for acceptance. And this time the defiant Governor knew, from Mississippi's experience, that no amount or kind of defiance could succeed.

In two press conference statements, the President expressed the hope that troops would be unnecessary—that all Alabamans would recognize that law "is not a matter of choice"—and that the way to avoid troops was to abide by the law. He also expressed to the Attorney General in our meetings his hope that Wallace would not have to be physically pushed or arrested, thus gaining the martyrdom he sought. As the day of decision neared, the President advised the Governor to stay away from the campus at Tuscaloosa. Wallace rejected the advice.

On June 11, 1963, in a knowingly empty and foolish gesture, Governor Wallace appeared in the doorway of the university registration building, replied to Katzenbach's reading of the President's proclamation by reading one of his own, and made no objection as the two Negro students were taken to their dormitories. The President had been watching their "confrontation" on TV. As previously planned, he promptly federalized the Alabama National Guard. Less than three hours later, Wallace stepped back from a second confrontation with Katzenbach and the Guard commander, and the two students were registered without incident.[3]

THE KENNEDY MANIFESTO

That day, June 11, 1963, marked the end of the state governments' overt resistance to college desegregation. It also marked the beginning of the Federal Government's full-scale commitment to the fight against all discrimination. Kennedy had contemplated a nationally televised address in the event of trouble at Tuscaloosa. When that trouble vanished, he decided at the last moment to address the nation anyway while attention was focused on the subject.

Trouble had not been confined to Birmingham and Tuscaloosa. A white Baltimore postman on a "freedom walk" to Mississippi had been found slain on an Alabama road. A Negro sit-in demonstrator in Jackson had been slugged to the floor, kicked in the face, stomped on again and again—and arrested for disturbing the peace. Rioting by both Negroes and whites in Lexington, North Carolina, had killed one and injured others. The nonviolent passive resistance strategy emphasized by

[3] Two days later, another Negro registered at the university's Huntsville branch without the Governor's even bothering to show up; and a few days earlier another Negro had enrolled without incident at the University of Mississippi at Oxford. Even more marked was the contrast with the situation prevailing some seven years earlier at the same University of Alabama, where a mob of students had driven a Negro coed off the campus in three days, while the Federal Government thought it best to "avoid interference."

Martin Luther King was not deeply rooted in Negro traditions, and there were signs that it might soon give way to a more violent strategy uncontrolled by responsible leaders. The essence of Kennedy's civil rights strategy since inauguration had been to keep at all times at least one step ahead of the evolving pressures, never to be caught dead in the water, always to have something new. Now, in Jackson, Danville, New York and scores of other cities and states, "the events in Birmingham and elsewhere," as he said, had "so increased the cries for equality that no city or state or legislative body can prudently choose to ignore them. . . . Where legal remedies are not at hand . . . redress is sought in the streets, in demonstrations, parades and protests which create tensions and threaten violence and threaten lives."

The President did not regard this as a Federal problem only. With the Vice President and Attorney General he had met with union leaders and businessmen—theater owners, restaurant operators, department store executives and others—asking them to drop racial bars in employment and service. On June 9 he had asked the nation's mayors, gathered in conference in Honolulu, to improve their practices and ordinances.

But his first Civil Rights Message in February, 1963, had already signaled a shift in his thinking about civil rights legislation. That message called for an expansion of the role of the Civil Rights Commission, enabling it to serve as a clearinghouse for information and assistance to local communities. It called for technical and economic assistance to school districts in the process of desegregation. It called for a variety of improvements in the voting rights laws: abolishing literacy tests for those with a sixth-grade education, prohibiting the application of different standards to different races and speeding up the registration of voters in contested areas. It spoke up strongly for equal rights in all areas and reviewed the steps taken under executive authority. The message was not in response to any crisis or particular pressure but a product of the President's own initiative and a part of his regular legislative program. It was well received by Negroes, who were listening. It was virtually ignored by the Congress and the rest of the country, who were not listening.

But by June 11 the country was listening—and the bills previously proposed were insufficient. Unlike the situation prevailing in 1961 and 1962, public interest in civil rights legislation made Congressional passage appear at least possible. For several weeks the White House and Justice Department had been preparing a new package. The President's decision to go ahead definitely on a sweeping bill had been made on May 31, over the opposition of some of his political advisers who saw both Congressional and electoral defeat. Democratic leaders were being consulted. Republican support was being rounded up. The details of the program had not yet been concluded. No address to the nation had been written. But the President at the last minute decided that June 11 was the time and 7 P.M. the hour.

Having assumed that the tranquil resolution at Tuscaloosa that afternoon would make a speech unnecessary, I did not start a first draft until late in the afternoon or complete it until minutes before he went on the air. There was no time for a redraft. "For the first time," said the President to me in my office afterward, "I thought I was going to have to go off the cuff." He did, in fact, wholly extemporize a heartfelt conclusion.

But in a larger sense the June 11 speech had been in preparation by the President himself for some time. It drew on at least three years of evolution in his thinking, on at least three months of revolution in the equal rights movement, on at least three weeks of meetings in the White House, on drafts of a new message to Congress, and on his remarks to the mayors June 9 as well as on the February Civil Rights Message. An opening reference to the University of Alabama provided the springboard. The announcement of new legislation provided the substance. But the moving force of that address was the unequivocal commitment of John Fitzgerald Kennedy, his office and his country "to the proposition that race has no place in American life or law."

Warning of the "rising tide of discontent that threatens the public safety," he stressed that the nation's obligation was to make this "great change . . . peaceful and constructive for all." He outlined the legislation he would send to the Congress, but stressed that "legislation cannot solve this problem alone. It must be solved in the homes of every American." He paid tribute to those cooperating citizens, North and South, who acted "not out of a sense of legal duty but out of a sense of human decency."

This was not, he said, a sectional issue, nor a partisan issue, nor even "a legal or legislative issue alone."

It is better to settle these matters in the courts than on the streets, and new laws are needed at every level. But law alone cannot make men see right.

We are confronted primarily with a moral issue. It is as old as the Scriptures and is as clear as the American Constitution. . . .

Now the time has come for this nation to fulfill its promise. . . . We face a moral crisis as a country and as a people. It cannot be met by repressive police action. It cannot be left to increased demonstrations in the streets. It cannot be quieted by token moves or talk. It is a time to act. . . . Those who do nothing are inviting shame as well as violence. Those who act boldly are recognizing right as well as reality.

No President had ever before so forcefully recognized the moral injustice of all racial discrimination, and no President could ever thereafter ignore his moral obligation to remove it.

The Kennedy commitment was designed to preserve the fabric of our social order—to prevent the unsatisfied grievances of an entire race from rending that fabric in two. But it also stirred deep antagonisms. In Jackson, Mississippi, a few hours after Negro leaders had hailed Kennedy's talk as a second Emancipation Proclamation, one of their number, Medgar Evers, was assassinated. On Capitol Hill the following day a special caucus of Southern Senators vowed to block any civil rights legislation. A routine expansion of Area Redevelopment, expected to pass comfortably, was defeated in the House by a five-vote margin with fifty-four Southern Democrats voting against it. Republicans talked openly of a Northern white "backlash" that would down both Kennedy and his civil rights bill.

But the President had not pledged his prestige and power either lightly or suddenly. His concern had deepened as the crisis heightened. His strategy had altered as the selective approach—emphasizing executive power and voting rights—proved insufficient. His obligation was not to the Negroes but to the nation. Just as he had believed in earlier months that the best interests of the nation required him to avoid a losing, bruising legislative battle, so now he believed that the national interest required him to try. Not content with a bill and a speech, he immediately resumed the hard, practical job of creating the political, legislative and educational climate that would transform the bill into law and the speech into a new era of racial justice.

THE KENNEDY CIVIL RIGHTS BILL

On June 19 President Kennedy sent to the Eighty-eighth Congress the most comprehensive and far-reaching civil rights bill ever proposed. It codified and expanded the pattern his executive actions had already started. It was accompanied by a message as forceful as his June 11 manifesto. It was to differ only slightly from the Civil Rights Act enacted by that Congress the following year. But it was different in several respects from the bill we had first discussed with Justice the previous month.

With the backing of the Vice President, a Community Relations Service had been added to work quietly with local communities in search of progress. (Negro Congressmen had urged that the words "mediation" and "conciliation" had an "Uncle Tom" air about them and should be stricken from the title.) The Vice President, once the decision was final to go ahead with a bill, had also strongly backed the President's addition to the message of new and supplemental programs for job training, vocational education and literacy skills. Added at the suggestion of Congressional leaders was a broad authorization to withhold Federal funds from any program or effort that practiced racial discrimination—thus denying to obstructionist or irresponsible Congressmen their familiar practice of offering nondiscrimination amendments to programs they hoped to defeat. By leaving the cut-off discretionary, the President sought to avoid terminations which punished Negroes for white violations.

The President, aware of the emotions surrounding the initials FEPC, decided finally to omit it from the bill but to endorse a pending FEPC measure in his message. In addition, his Committee on Equal Opportunity under the Vice President was to be given statutory authority and increased jurisdiction.

The two principal features of the bill, in addition to those proposed back in February, had been included from the outset of our discussions:

1. The first was a ban on discrimination in places of public accommodation—including hotels, restaurants, places of amusement and retail stores—with a "substantial" effect on interstate commerce (thus excluding what came to be known as "Mrs. Murphy's boardinghouse"). This kind of discrimination more than any other had been the object of Negro sit-ins, pickets and demonstrations. Like Lincoln's Proclamation taking slaves away from owners, this proposal was condemned as a violation of property rights. But the President reminded the Congress that "property has its duties as well as its rights." (Two years earlier in Paris, he had expressed anger and chagrin upon learning that the two dark-skinned domestics who accompanied him, after being served their meals in a private dining room of their own at the Quai d'Orsay Palace by liveried footmen in wigs and knee breeches, had then crossed the Seine to visit a French lady's maid of their acquaintance, only to be turned away at the hotel door because of their color.)

2. The second basic provision gave authority to the Attorney General to seek desegregation of public education on his own initiative when a lack of means or fear of reprisal prevented the aggrieved students or their parents from doing so. This was the essence of the old Title III supported by Senator Kennedy in 1957 but stricken from that year's bill before passage. A lack of adequate education is one root of other Negro problems, the President said, and the implementation of the Supreme Court's decision cannot be left solely to those who lack the resources to bring suits or withstand intimidation. "The pace is very slow. Too many Negro children entering segregated grade schools at the time of the Supreme Court's decision nine years ago will enter segre-

gated high schools this fall, having suffered a loss which can never be restored."

A host of other proposals had been suggested to the President, but he was looking for a law, not an issue. This Congress and future Congresses could amend and improve his effort. He wanted a package unencumbered by any provisions that went beyond the clearly legal, reasonable and necessary—because he wanted it to pass.

He was asking Congress to swallow a pill many times larger than those it had previously refused to swallow. This was no grandstand play for a lost cause or a political effort. He was not interested in a "moral victory" on a legislative issue—he wanted a legislative victory on a moral issue. Despite the odds and despite the opposition, he set out to get the best bill possible at the earliest time possible. The thrust of his argument was that the country could take no other course, that the Congress had no other choice and that the Republicans—upon whose votes House Rules Committee and Senate cloture approval depended— had no higher obligation.

The basic legislative tactics remained relatively unchanged from our May discussions. One omnibus bill, which included the February proposals as well as the new ones, would be sought instead of several separate measures. Bipartisan sponsorship would be sought to the extent possible—resulting in Democrat Mansfield's introducing the whole bill and simultaneously cosponsoring with Republican Dirksen the same bill minus the public accommodations sections (to which the Republican leader was opposed). The President had considered delivering the message in person before a joint session, but the June 11 speech made that unnecessary. His objective was passage of the bill that year without any loss of priority to the tax-cut bill. Faster economic growth would provide far more jobs for Negroes than FEPC, and a new recession would hit Negroes hardest of all. There was little point, said the President, in gaining entrance to a lunch counter "if you didn't have a dime for a cup of coffee." One out of every seven Negro teen-agers in the labor force was unemployed, a source of both frustration and friction; and his economic measures could not be set aside as irrelevant to the racial crisis.

The one tactical paragraph of his message which received as much careful attention as the portions dealing with legislation concerned the problem of continued Negro demonstrations. Southerners and Republicans warned that further pressures would surely defeat the bill. Negroes warned that they would not give up their chief weapon. They talked of a "massive march" on the Senate and House galleries. The President—as stern in the message as he had been in his private talks with Negro leaders—was careful not to decry the value of peaceful demonstrations:

> But *as feelings have risen in recent days*, these demonstrations have increasingly endangered lives and property, inflamed emotions and unnecessarily divided communities. They are not the way in which this country should rid itself of racial discrimination. *Violence is never justified; and, while peaceful communication, deliberation and petitions of protest continue, I want to caution against demonstrations which can lead to violence.*
>
> This problem is now before the Congress. . . . *The Congress should have an opportunity to freely work its will.* [The italicized portions were personally added by the President to the final draft.]
>
> I . . . ask every member of Congress to set aside sectional and political ties, and to look at this issue from the viewpoint of the nation. I ask you to look into your hearts—not in search of charity, for the Negro neither wants nor needs condescension—but for the one plain, proud and priceless quality that unites us all as Americans: a sense of justice.

The President did not rely on eloquence alone. "It is clear," he had written to Eisenhower June 10, "that such a measure cannot pass either house without substantial bipartisan support." He kept Eisenhower—who was sympathetic but not enthusiastic about the legislative approach—fully informed. Along with the Vice President, he consulted frequently with the leaders of both parties, once with Republican leaders Dirksen and McCulloch alone to brief them on the need for the bill and its details. Bob Kennedy and Burke Marshall held a series of Capitol Hill briefings to which all Democratic Senators, and all but the Deep South Congressmen, were invited. The decision to send a bill, the President stressed to each group, was final, but their comments and suggestions for its contents were welcome. While he would not drop the public accommodations section as Dirksen preferred, or extend it still further under the Fourteenth Amendment as other Republicans preferred, he included the Fourteenth Amendment as additional constitutional grounds and accepted other GOP suggestions for improvement. Assistant Attorney General Norbert Schlei and I reviewed the bill with Dirksen and other Republicans before it was printed in final form. The Illinois Senator, accepting "an idea whose time has come," proved to be constructive and cooperative.

Special attention in the House focused on William McCulloch of Ohio, the key Republican on the House Judiciary Committee and a respected conservative. McCulloch's constituency might normally have

been considered too rural and Republican to have made him a champion
of Negro rights, but his conscience responded to the reason of the administration and to the realities of the situation.

The President wanted not only a bill which dealt effectively with
the problems of discrimination in voting, public accommodations, educational and other public institutions, Federal programs and employment, but also a bill which reflected a bipartisan approach and a
national consensus which the nation would accept and obey. The test
of whether this was possible came in the House Judiciary Committee.
A subcommittee considering the bill under the chairmanship of Congressman Celler, split along bipartisan lines, reported out an expanded
bill which appeared to be stronger and had the unyielding support of
the civil rights groups, but which in fact included provisions that were
of doubtful constitutionality and contained the seeds of more turmoil
than solutions. Southern Democrats gleefully joined Northern liberal
Democrats in giving the bill more weight than the House Rules Committee and full House membership were capable of carrying. The
President had the choice of either making this new version the official
Democratic bill, which would have increased enormously his prestige
and influence with liberal and civil rights groups, or risking an all-out
effort to re-create the badly damaged bipartisan consensus. He chose the
latter course.

Recognizing that the liberal Democrats on the committee were under
great pressure from the civil rights organizations, including church
groups and organized labor, to support the new version, he agreed that
the administration would take on as much as possible the burden of
going back to a bipartisan bill. For this purpose the Attorney General
came before the full committee. He testified in direct fashion that many
of the changes were unenforceable, unconstitutional or undesirable;
that only a bipartisan bill could pass; and that a compromise, which
he outlined, should be adopted by the committee. But this was not
enough. To enlist behind the compromise the full committee's liberal
Democrats, who were suspicious that the Republicans would seek to
outmaneuver them and who were under public pressure to stay with
the subcommittee bill, the President had to intervene personally. In a
series of White House meetings and phone calls, he discovered that, to
do this, he would have to get a commitment of House Republican support for the compromise, lasting through the Rules Committee and on
the floor. For this he needed a commitment from Minority Leader
Halleck and the rest of the Republican leadership in the House, as well
as Congressman McCulloch. To enable him to make his own commitment on a bipartisan approach to the Republican leadership, he first
had to persuade enough liberal Democrats on the committee to follow

his lead, and that required another late-night meeting at the White House. It was a difficult juggling act, but in the end Halleck, aided by McCulloch, told the President that the votes would be there. Right-wing Republicans accused Halleck of appeasing the enemy and placed a furled umbrella on his desk, but the committee reported out the new compromise version, after a dramatic meeting, on October 29, 1963. (The commitment to Kennedy from both Republicans and Democrats which that vote entailed would make possible House passage of the compromise bill in December of that year.)

The President, discouraged by the months of hearings and maneuverings, then pressed the committee to get its report to the House Rules Committee. It arrived there on November 21 as he left for a speech-making tour in Texas.

Meanwhile, in the Senate, where the Attorney General patiently spent one day after another answering Senator Ervin's questions on the Constitution, a real test awaited floor debate. The President hoped—but never with much confidence—that a "Vandenberg" would emerge among the Southern Senators, a statesman willing to break with the past and place national interests first. Despite idle speculation that Arkansas' Fulbright might play such a role, no Southern solon came forward to place the judgment of history ahead of his continued career.

THE CLIMATE FOR CHANGE

Passage of his bill, the President knew, required appeals to more than the Congress; and a peaceful revolution required more than passage of his bill. Its enactment, his message made plain,

> will not solve all our problems of race relations. This bill must be supplemented by action in every branch of government at the Federal, state and local level. It must be supplemented as well by enlightened private citizens, private businesses and private labor and civic organizations.

To enlighten and encourage those citizens, the President, accompanied by the Vice President and Attorney General, embarked on an unprecedented series of private meetings in the White House—seeking to enlist the cooperation and understanding of more than sixteen hundred national leaders: educators, lawyers, Negro leaders, Southern leaders, women's organizations, business groups, governors, mayors, editors and others, Republicans as well as Democrats, segregationists as well as integrationists. He briefed them not only on the bill but on their responsibilities beyond the bill. He had neither funds nor sanctions to induce their assistance, but he offered Presidential leadership.

He pressed for action from the leaders of the American labor movement, some of whom had long given lip service to civil rights but had excluded Negroes from many craft unions, or forced them into segregated locals or seniority systems, or denied them the required apprenticeship training. He pressed for action from clergymen of all faiths, certain they would "recognize the conflict between racial bigotry and the Holy Word." What about racial intermarriage? asked one minister. "I am not talking about private lives," replied the President, dismissing this familiar bugaboo, "but public accommodations, public education and public elections." He pressed for action from the blue-ribbon Business Council (noting later in a caustic aside that it was the only audience not to rise to its feet upon the entrance of the President of the United States).

The over-all response made Kennedy proud of his country. The citizen "lobby" on behalf of the bill—led particularly by religious groups and supported by editorial writers usually poles apart—was massive and effective. Even more striking was the voluntary removal of segregation signs and practices in chain stores, theaters and restaurants. Southern mayors and chambers of commerce began talking with Negro leaders. Employers and unions, North and South, began lowering racial bars. The nation's clergy were goaded into effective action on a major moral issue which had long preceded Kennedy's leadership. Progress was slow and insufficient, but, compared to the previous hundred years, rapid and gratifying.

Federally sponsored apprenticeship programs opened the building trades to more Negroes. James Meredith received his degree. The Prince Edward County, Virginia, schools were reopening on a voluntary basis. "We, as a country, are doing well . . . passing through a very grueling test," said the President. But not everyone passed the test. Alabama's Governor Wallace, hoping to re-enact another summit in the doorway, turned Negro children away from newly integrated schools in Birmingham and two other cities, first with state troopers, then with his National Guard. When Kennedy federalized the Guardsmen once again and simply returned them to their quarters, Wallace backed down as before.

But the Governor's example of defying the law and oppressing Negro children was not lost on his fellow Alabamans. Many white students boycotted the schools. A white man threw a rock at two Negro girls on their way to school. Four days after Wallace's performance, a bomb planted in a Birmingham Negro church killed four little girls in Sunday school, another Negro youth was shot dead by a Birmingham policeman and still another by two white boys. Almost all the warnings about violence in 1963 had been directed at Negroes, yet almost all the victims had been Negroes. "I deplore violence," said George Wallace.

The President sent FBI bomb specialists to the city and left no doubt whom he held at least indirectly responsible. "Public disparagement of law and order has encouraged violence which has fallen on the innocent." He conferred with Negro and white leaders from Birmingham, dispatched General Kenneth Royall and Colonel Earl Blaik as a special negotiating team, and obtained pledges of cooperation from all sides.

In the space of a few months President Kennedy had made the Negroes' troubles his troubles and their problems his priority. Their assailants were attacking him. Their overwhelming endorsement, combined with continued white resentment, the President was told, created the danger of political division along racial lines. "I would doubt that," he said. "I think the American people have been through too much to make that fatal mistake. . . . Over the long run we are going to have a mix. That will be true racially, socially, ethnically, geographically, and that is really, finally, the best way." (A recording of the last two sentences, taken out of context, appeared in the radio commercials of Southern segregationist candidates warning of intermarriage.)

At times there was still grumbling from Negroes, and it was not confined to extremist leaders such as Malcolm X or intellectuals such as James Baldwin. Many of the more genuine and practical leaders failed to understand that Kennedy had to work simultaneously on his tax bill, on the Test Ban Treaty, on the threat of a railroad strike and on Vietnam—in their interest as well as the interest of all Americans. When he did not cancel his European trip in June, some complained that he was interrupting his attention to their problems. But the President valued the trip partly because it did interrupt the nation's attention to this problem. Too much attention, he believed, could accelerate demands and expectations more rapidly than they could be fulfilled, and thereby increase tensions during a long, hot summer.

The summer was, in fact, cooler than the President had feared. The influence of extremist groups in the Negro community dwindled; one civil rights leader was privately persuaded to reject some Communists who had infiltrated his movement; and the President in turn rejected the claims of the Wallaces and Barnetts that the whole civil rights movement was Communist-inspired. It was not surprising, he said, that the nation's few Communists would attempt to "worm their way into those movements. . . . But I must say that we looked into this matter with a good deal of care. We have no evidence that any of the leaders of the civil rights movements in the United States are Communists."

Asked at a late summer news conference about the diminution of demonstrations, he emphasized that a period of calm should be used to advance progress and not be regarded as the end of the effort. With considerable candor, he explained that demonstrations had subsided partly because of the progress under way and "partly because . . . the responsible Negro leadership . . . realizes that this is a long-drawn-out task . . . and a quick demonstration in the street is not the immediate answer. . . . In some cases . . . particularly in their extreme form . . . [or] fringe actions . . . they were self-defeating."

But those opposed to demonstrations could take little comfort from his words. "Some of the people," he said at another news conference, "who keep talking about demonstrations never talk about the problem of redressing grievances. . . . You can't just tell people 'Don't protest,' but still keep them out of your store." The massive march on Washington earlier mentioned had been altered. Instead of a menacing sit-in in the legislative galleries—which he had strongly opposed—it was to be a peaceful assembly on the Washington Monument grounds, marching from there to the Lincoln Memorial. Kennedy worked through the Department of Justice, personal intermediaries and such friendly sponsors as Walter Reuther to make the planning as responsible and effective as possible. While he shared some of the trepidation of those officials who forecast disaster, he was ahead of his team in endorsing the project and recognizing the necessity for its success without turning it into a Federal undertaking. Washington and Park Police and Federally financed facilities were made available. The project was still under fire as a high-pressure, explosive demonstration. But the President termed it "a peaceful assembly calling for a redress of grievances . . . and that is in the great tradition."

As August 28, the day of the march, neared, the President was concerned about how peaceful an assembly it would be. The American Nazi Party threatened a countermarch, the Black Muslims opposed the march, and at least one of the Negro student leaders prepared to denounce the "inadequacies" of the President's bill. Thousands of extra police were to be on hand, with four thousand troops standing by across the river. Many Washingtonians, fearing trouble, said they would stay home that day. Some Congressmen wanted protection for the Capitol. The President made it clear that he would be in his office. Aware of the hard political fact that a crowd of 230,000 is capable of many reactions, he declined to appear before the march. Nor did he want to meet its leaders in advance of their reports, agreeing to see them instead at day's end.

On August 28 all went well. Kennedy marveled, as the world marveled, at the spirit and self-discipline of the largest public demonstration ever held in Washington. Participants from every state and race, arriving by every means of transportation, maintained dignity with enthusiasm, sang, chanted and listened patiently to hours of entertainment and exhortation. The most impassioned oratory from the steps of the Lincoln Memorial was delivered by Martin Luther King.

"I have a dream," he cried over and over, describing the day when harmony and equality would prevail.

"I have a dream," said the President to King as he greeted the group's leaders at the White House. His dream was theirs. He had been deeply touched by the proceedings and was full of admiration for march leader A. Philip Randolph. Their cause, he said, had been advanced by the moving but orderly events of the day. Then, around a table of coffee and sandwiches, he brought them back to the harsh world of legislative committees, compromises and constituent pressures. He doubted that any votes in the Congress had been changed. He doubted that any segregationists had been converted. But he felt that the march had helped to unite the adherents of civil rights more closely; and merely the absence of violence in such a huge and restless throng had awakened new interest and won new adherents in white America.

Polls showed a majority in white America in favor of the Kennedy bill, but they also showed a majority feeling that Kennedy was pushing too fast. Signs of a white "backlash" in Northern suburbs were widely discussed. A poll in California reportedly showed outspoken liberals privately opposed to integration in their neighborhoods and schools. A Lubell survey in Birmingham of white voters for Kennedy in the 1960 election could find only one willing to support him again. Governor Terry Sanford acknowledged that even moderate North Carolina would be lost if the election were in November, 1963. "K.O. the Kennedys" became a slogan for the Mississippi gubernatorial election that fall. Right-wing Republicanism under Barry Goldwater was in the ascendancy. Vitriolic mail poured into the White House every day. Reviewing a speech for Andrew Hatcher's delivery to key Negro audiences, the President came upon a passage describing him as "determined to pass the best bill possible, however it may affect him politically, whatever abuse he may receive from any sector or section of the country." He paused, smiled and wrote in the words: "and he has received some."

Kennedy was not unaware of the strain his stand had placed on his party and on his own political prospects. "Obviously it is going to be an important matter" in 1964, he said. "It has caused a good deal of feeling against the administration. . . . I am not sure that I am the most popular political figure . . . today in the South, but that is all right." He had no doubt that polls showing white discontent were accurate. But "you must make a judgment about the movement of a great historical event . . . after a period of time. . . . Change always disturbs. . . . I was surprised that there wasn't greater opposition. I think we are going at about the right tempo."

At times he found it hard to believe that otherwise rational men could be so irrational on this subject. (He was even surprised to find deep feelings against Negroes' sitting beside whites at a lunch counter. To him that seemed the least controversial part of his bill.) Those who thought he was pushing too fast seemed to think he was taking something away from whites and giving it to Negroes, he said; and he explained over and over that he sought for the Negroes not preference but equality, not special privilege but opportunity; he sought not to drag down white standards but to raise Negro standards.

Privately he confided to a Negro leader that "this issue could cost me the election, but we're not turning back." Publicly he remained cautiously optimistic. The people in time will face up to the truth, he said, and the Republicans will live up to their legacy as the party of Lincoln. He realized that he could never pick up enough Negro and liberal votes (in addition to those he already had) to offset the votes this issue would cost him in the North as well as the South. But he still thought that he would win re-election—that local candidates would be hurt more than the national ticket—that passage of the bill would cool tempers off and let other issues rise—and that the explosive costs of inaction would have been even greater than those of any action he had taken.

> This particular crisis . . . has come and we are going to deal with it. . . . We just have to wait and see what political effect they have. But I think the position of the administration is well known —and I expect it will continue to follow the same course it has followed in the past.

While he himself did not indulge in comparisons, he was not averse to those who called his speech and bill "the Second Emancipation Proclamation." Like the first, it had confronted the issue of the black man's freedom in a white man's society out of necessity as well as belief. Like the first, its reliance on reason and reconciliation had won it enmities on both sides. And like the first it, it was far-reaching in effect and fanatically opposed, but only the beginning of an era. "That Proclamation," wrote John Kennedy on its centennial in 1963, "was only a first step—a step which its author unhappily did not live to follow up."

PART FIVE

President Kennedy
and the World

CHAPTER XIX

THE OLIVE BRANCH

JOHN KENNEDY'S APPROACH to foreign affairs was very different from his approach to domestic problems. "The big difference," he remarked early in his term, "is between a bill being defeated and the country being wiped out." Foreign affairs had always interested him far more than domestic. They occupied far more of his time and energy as President. They received from him far more attention to detail, to the shaping of alternatives, to the course of a proposal from origin to execution. They tested far more severely his talents of judgment and execution, with far less emphasis on budget and legislative planning and far more occasions for reacting to unforeseeable and uncontrollable events. They were the object of a far greater change in his own attitudes, as he learned by experience, grew in wisdom and mastered those complexities he had previously oversimplified. As I have earlier made clear, I was not involved in the multitudinous problems of day-to-day foreign policy to the extent I was in domestic, and the accounts which follow are influenced in part by the accident of what I was near or what the President discussed with me. They are distorted also in the sense that more space is afforded the dramatic and the public when much of Kennedy's best work in foreign policy was undramatic or secret.

The final difference in the Kennedy treatment of foreign and domestic affairs was the relative influence of Congressional and public opinion. His foreign policy actions were still constrained within bounds set by those forces, but they operated more indirectly than directly and his own powers of initiative and decision were much wider. He was, to be sure, concerned in his first year about public complacency over the nation's perils. "It was much easier," he remarked, "when people could see the enemy from the walls." And he reasoned that he could no more meet foreign problems at the expense of his domestic political support than he could woo that support at the expense of our interests abroad— for a show of weakness in either arena would be reflected in the other. Nevertheless he refused to subordinate international considerations—on aid and trade, for example—to every provincial pressure arising in the Congress or electorate.

Some said that Kennedy's bipartisan emphasis in foreign policy was the result of his narrow election margin. But even had he been elected overwhelmingly, his foreign policy *objectives,* as distinguished from his *methods,* would not, I believe, have differed radically from those of his Republican predecessor. He still would have assigned many of the most controversial slots in national security to Republicans to diminish partisan division. His narrow margin of effective Congressional support, a by-product of that close election, did hamper his efforts on foreign aid and lesser problems. But a rash of hot-tempered and uninformed speeches on the Hill when an American plane was hijacked to Cuba caused him to remark privately on the Constitution's wisdom in not entrusting foreign policy wholly to the Legislative Branch.

In one respect his approaches to domestic and foreign affairs were the same—an emphasis on the factual, the rational and the realistic. As a Senator in 1954, he had assailed in a magazine article the "myths" which "surrounded . . . American foreign policy," including

> the untouchability of national sovereignty; the existence of in-
> herently good, bad or backward nations . . . the impairment of an
> aggressor's military power by refusing him our diplomatic recog-
> nition . . . myths . . . that the democratic way of life . . . will in-
> evitably be the victor in any struggle with an alien power . . .
> [and] that other Allies owe homage and gratitude to the United
> States and all of its views at all times.

As President-elect in 1960-1961, he surprised Dean Rusk, said the Secre-
tary, "by the extent to which he wanted to look at everything from the beginning, the ground up . . . the origins."

As President he sought to keep himself and his country attuned to all the new developments: space exploration, the Common Market, the emerging nations, the scientific revolution and the strains within the Communist bloc. He insisted on making careful distinctions—between different kinds of Communist countries, for example, or between differing stages of development in various Latin-American countries—instead of lumping superficial similarities under one label. In Laos and Vietnam, as later illustrated, he believed there were no "right" answers, only prob-

lems to be managed instead of solved. In a notable address at the University of Washington in the fall of 1961, he struck a much less zealous note than the candidate of twelve months earlier:

> We must face the fact that the United States is neither omnipotent nor omniscient . . . that we cannot impose our will upon the other 94 percent of mankind—that we cannot right every wrong or reverse each adversity—and that therefore there cannot be an American solution to every world problem.

Above all, he believed in retaining a choice—not a choice between "Red and dead" or "holocaust and humiliation," but a variety of military options in the event of aggression, an opportunity for time and maneuver in the instruments of diplomacy, and a balanced approach to every crisis which combined both defense and diplomacy. This approach was reflected in the contrapuntal phrases for which he had a penchant:

> Let us never negotiate out of fear, but let us never fear to negotiate.
>   —*Inaugural Address*, 1961

> On the Presidential coat of arms, the American eagle holds in his right talon the olive branch, while in his left he holds a bundle of arrows. We intend to give equal attention to both.
>   —*First State of the Union Message*, 1961

> Our policy must blend whatever degree of firmness and flexibility is necessary to protect our vital interests, by peaceful means if possible, by resolute action if necessary. . . . While we do not intend to see the free world give up, we shall make every effort to prevent the world from being blown up.
>   —*University of North Carolina*, 1961

> We must face up to the chance of war, if we are to maintain the peace. . . . Diplomacy and defense are not substitutes for one another. . . . A willingness to resist force, unaccompanied by a willingness to talk, could provoke belligerence—while a willingness to talk, unaccompanied by a willingness to resist force, could invite disaster. . . . While we shall negotiate freely, we shall not negotiate freedom. . . . In short, we are neither "warmongers" nor "appeasers," neither "hard" nor "soft." We are Americans.
>   —*University of Washington*, 1961

Those accustomed to thinking only in black and white terms were displeased or confused by this approach. One chronicler accused him of fanning the flames of the cold war, another of being blind to the threat of Communism. One critic called his Inaugural and first State of the

Union addresses alarmist, another naïve. Two reporters who interviewed him for an hour on foreign policy, comparing separate memos later, discovered that one had thought him rather tough and uncompromising and the other rather hopeful for agreement. Still others attributed his many-sided approach to a desire to please everyone, to a tendency to compromise or to too many advisers. "You cannot be both Chamberlain and Churchill," advised a columnist;[1] and a religious spokesman— pleased with Kennedy's efforts on disarmament, but displeased with his emphasis on defense—advised him: "Don't try to do two opposite things at once." To which the President replied, with an analogy to the rhythmic expansion and contraction of the heart: "All of life is like that—systole and diastole."

HIS ATTITUDE TOWARD WAR AND "WINNING"

John Kennedy had seen the ugly side of conventional war—in England with his father, in the South Pacific with his crew, at memorial services for his brother and brother-in-law, and on Congressional trips to Asia and the Middle East. But nuclear war could not be weighed by the same units of measure. "Because of the ingenuity of science and man's own inability to control his relationships with one another," he said, "we happen to live in the most dangerous time in the history of the human race. . . . The world has long since passed the time when armed conflict can be the solution to international problems."

He was acutely aware of the responsibility of governing in a world where both the United States and its chief adversary could destroy each other's society in a matter of minutes. "That changes the problem," he said.

> It changes all the answers and all the questions. I don't think many people really understand the change. . . . When that day comes, and there is a massive exchange, then that is the end, because you are talking about . . . 150 million fatalities in the first eighteen hours.

That would be the equivalent for this country of five hundred World War II's in less than a day.

John Kennedy was not obsessed with these fatality figures. He often cited them in public, but they induced in him no panic or paralysis of will. He was still willing to face the ultimate risk of nuclear war to

[1] Ignoring Churchill's advocacy of negotiations to prevent needless conflict and Kennedy's rejection of appeasement. It might be noted, however, that two other columnists, who regarded each other as "hard" and "soft" respectively, were asked unbeknownst to each other to contribute drafts, which were then blended, for the last speech quoted above.

prevent defeat by nuclear blackmail. He neither shrank from that risk nor rushed out to embrace it. Much has been made of the fact that, after his Vienna meeting with Khrushchev, he received a highly secret, high-level briefing on the effects of a nuclear exchange. But this briefing was customary. Obviously it was not the basis of Kennedy's earlier decision on fallout shelters, as claimed; and, to me, sitting across from him during the briefing, he did not appear "transfixed" or show any of the other reactions of stress reported in some stories.

That briefing confirmed, however, the harsh facts he already knew: (1) that neither the Soviet Union nor the United States could "win" a nuclear war in any rational sense of the word; (2) that, except to deter an all-out Soviet attack, our threat of "massive retaliation" to every Communist move was no longer credible, now that it invited our own destruction; and (3) that a policy of "pre-emptive first strike" or "preventive war" was no longer open to either side, inasmuch as even a surprise missile attack would trigger, before those missiles reached their targets, a devastating retaliation that neither country could risk or accept. Nor had either country developed a reliable defense against missiles or even the prospects of acquiring one, despite claims on both sides to the contrary. No matter who fired first or was annihilated last, "there will not be 'winners,' " remarked the President. "So we have to proceed with . . . care in an age when the human race can obliterate itself."

A favorite Kennedy word from my earliest association with him was "miscalculation." Long before he read Barbara Tuchman's *The Guns of August*—which he recommended to his staff—he had as a student at Harvard taken a course on the origins of World War I. It made him realize, he said, "how quickly countries which were comparatively uninvolved were taken, in the space of a few days, into war." Their leaders were talking as their successors are now, he added, about military strength keeping the peace, but strength alone failed to work. In 1963 he would cite the 1914 conversation between two German leaders on the origins and expansion of that war, a former chancellor asking, "How did it all happen?" and his successor saying, "Ah, if only one knew." "If this planet," said President Kennedy, "is ever ravaged by nuclear war—if the survivors of that devastation can then endure the fire, poison, chaos and catastrophe—I do not want one of those survivors to ask another, 'How did it all happen?' and to receive the incredible reply: 'Ah, if only one knew.' "

He had also considered the origins of World War II and admired the work of British historian A. J. P. Taylor. "Hitler," said Kennedy, "thought that he could seize Poland, that the British might not fight [or] . . . after the defeat of Poland, might not continue to fight." And then in

Korea, he added, the North Koreans "obviously . . . did not think we were going to come in and . . . we did not think the Chinese were going to come in . . . as we moved to the north." Thus "three times in my lifetime," he told the nation at the time of the Berlin crisis,

> our country and Europe have been involved in major wars. In each case serious misjudgments were made on both sides of the intentions of others which brought about great devastation. Now, in the thermonuclear age, any misjudgment on either side about the intentions of the other could rain more devastation in several hours than has been wrought in all the wars of human history.

His critics charged that this kind of talk was in pursuit of a "no-win" policy. Kennedy, however, believed that such traditional slogans as "unconditional surrender" and "no substitute for victory" no longer had meaning. "A total solution," he said, "is impossible in the nuclear age." Nor did he even assert that the cold war could be "won" in the traditional sense. He did not expect it to be lost. He simply desired to dampen it down, to outlast it, to make it possible for the long-run forces of liberty and truth to work their way naturally and peacefully, to prevent the cold war from monopolizing our energies to the detriment of all other interests. "Without having a nuclear war," he said, "we want . . . to permit what Thomas Jefferson called 'the disease of liberty' to be caught in areas which are now held by Communists."

He saw no early end to the ideological struggle, or to economic, scientific and political competition with the Communists. The competition would not produce the kind of celebrated "victory" our traditions had prepared the American people to expect, only at best a long, slow process, he said, of evolution "away from Communism and toward national independence and freedom. . . . But if freedom and Communism were to compete for man's allegiance in a world at peace, I would look to the future with ever-increasing confidence."

HIS ATTITUDE TOWARD COMMUNISM AND COEXISTENCE

If those charging him with a "no-win" policy meant to say that he was not determined to drive the partisans of Communist ideology from the face of the earth, that charge was correct. He sought to halt the external expansion of the Soviet regime, not its internal philosophy and development. He regarded Communist aggression and subversion as intolerable, but not Communism itself. "What your government believes," he wrote to Khrushchev in 1961, "is its own business; what it does in the world is the world's business."

Nothing in his term altered his view of Communism's ruthless ambitions. Those he was determined to oppose. But different ideological interests alone did not justify endangering our common biological interest. Khrushchev's first private letter compared the world to Noah's Ark, where both the "clean" and the "unclean" wanted it to stay afloat, regardless of who listed himself with each group. Kennedy replied that he liked that analogy, that whatever their ideological differences, their collaboration was essential to prevent another war destroying everything. At the height or close of every crisis—in Berlin, Southeast Asia and Cuba—he sought to be in touch with Khrushchev, to return to the path of accommodation, to prevent violence and distrust from reproducing themselves.

From his Inaugural onward, he referred to Communists not as "our enemies" but as "those who would make themselves our adversary." Theodore Roosevelt's maxim of "Speak softly and carry a big stick," he said, was "a very good standard for us all." "Our words need merely to carry conviction, not belligerence," he wrote for his 1963 address in Dallas. "If we are strong, our strength will speak for itself. If we are weak, words will be of no help."

In 1963, his words at American University—backed by strength in the Cuban missile crisis—held out an olive branch to the Communist system. "We find Communism," he said,

> profoundly repugnant as a negation of personal freedom and dignity. But we can still hail the Russian people for their many achievements. . . . No government or social system is so evil that its people must be considered as lacking in virtue. . . . World peace . . . does not require that each man love his neighbor . . . only that they live together in mutual tolerance, submitting their disputes to a just and peaceful settlement.

To the editor of *Izvestia* in 1961 he had been even bolder:

> If the people of any country choose to follow a Communist system in a free election, after a fair opportunity for a number of views to be presented, the United States would accept that. What we find to be objectionable . . . is when a system is imposed by a small militant group by subversion. . . . If the Soviet Union were merely seeking to . . . protect its own national security, and permit other countries to live as they wish . . . then I believe that the problems which now cause so much tension would fade away.

To the extent that Western defense and diplomacy could influence the evolution of Communist policy, he hoped to prevent the dominant force of that policy from being located in Peking instead of Moscow, from being shaped by the followers of Stalin instead of Khrushchev, and from seeking external instead of internal expansion. He knew that Moscow, like Peking, believed in the world-wide triumph of Communism; and that Khrushchev, like Stalin, could be expected to exploit every fair and foul means of advancing those ambitions. But he hoped that in time American and Allied power and policy could persuade Moscow and Khrushchev that no safe or cheap route was open to world domination, that all channels were open for true negotiation, that any real grounds for the Soviet Union's fears could be peacefully removed, and that realistic, effective steps to accommodation—enabling Moscow to devote more energies internally—would advance the interests and security of both sides.

HIS ATTITUDE TOWARD NEGOTIATIONS

In this context, the President believed more strongly than some of his subordinates that "we have nothing to fear from negotiations . . . and nothing to gain by refusing to take part in them." Specific negotiations were needed to reduce specific areas of confrontation. He did not share the belief that no reasonable negotiations with the Soviets were possible and that no agreements reached would be kept, though he harbored no illusions about Communist good faith. Neither did he share the "illusion that negotiations for the sake of negotiations always advance the cause of peace. If for lack of preparation they break up in bitterness . . . if they are made a forum for propaganda or a cover for aggression, the processes of peace have been abused."

He carefully defined limits within which negotiations could take place. "We cannot," he said, "confine our proposals to a list of concessions we are to make," abandon our commitments to the freedom or security of others, or negotiate while the air is full of threats. (He briefly worried in 1961 that he might be making too many speeches about the virtues of negotiations and the horrors of nuclear war. To one writer he expressed the prophetic fear that an actual nuclear confrontation might be required before Khrushchev understood that Kennedy's conciliation would not permit humiliation. "If he wants to rub my nose in the dirt," said the President, "it's all over.") On the other hand, he did not believe in advancing meaningless, unattainable or obviously unacceptable proposals, or in deliberately taking ambiguous or flabby positions.

He strongly objected to what Dean Rusk aptly called the "football stadium psychology" of diplomacy, in which someone wins or loses each day. "Negotiations," said the President, "are not a contest spelling victory or defeat." If they succeed because both sides regard their agreement as an improvement, that can hardly be called an American victory. If they fail because the only agreement possible would have damaged our interests, that can hardly be called a defeat. If they continue in seemingly endless, pointless talks, that is usually better than a battle. Indeed, the most successful diplomacy, in his view, was more often dull than dramatic. Drama usually came with what he called "collision courses," direct confrontations—and "You can't have too many of those, because we are not sure on every occasion that the Soviet Union will withdraw." Nuclear devastation could be accomplished instantly, but peace, he said, was a long haul, "the sum of many acts."

He undertook such acts in his first months as President. Responding to Khrushchev's dropping of the U-2 incident and release of the RB-47 fliers, Kennedy removed restrictions on the importation of Soviet crabmeat, proposed a pact on more consulates and sought broader Soviet-American exchanges in science and culture. Later Khrushchev would release U-2 pilot Gary Powers in exchange for convicted Soviet spy Rudolf Abel. These were all small steps, but others would follow.

In a letter to Khrushchev as well as in a talk with his son-in-law, Kennedy urged a policy of patience and perseverance at Berlin, suggesting that neither side knew what future events or evolution might someday unify Germany without endangering either side. More broadly applied, that was a key to his own philosophy. He did not think it possible to achieve in his administration a sweeping settlement of East-West divisions. But he did hope that small breakthroughs could lead to larger ones, and that brick by brick a *détente* could be built, a breathing spell, a "truce to terror" in which both sides could recognize that mutual accommodation was preferable to mutual annihilation.

THE INSTRUMENTS OF PEACE

In the Presidential seal woven into the design of the carpet in his office, Kennedy pointed out in a speech, the eagle faced toward the olive branch of peace. In the older design of that seal on the ceiling, the eagle faced toward the arrows of war. A later chapter relates Kennedy's strengthening of those arrows. But, as the foregoing pages make clear, his objective was peace; and he strengthened this nation's olive branch in his efforts on disarmament, the United Nations, outer space and aid to less fortunate peoples.

1. *Disarmament*

The new United States Arms Control and Disarmament Agency —the first full-scale, full-time research and planning agency of its kind in the world—grew out of Kennedy's campaign complaint that fewer than one hundred scattered men in government were working on disarmament. Established in 1961 with a lot of legwork by one Republican, John McCloy, and headed by another, William Foster, it weathered Congressional opposition—and some foolish wrangling over its name— to symbolize the combination of scientific, legal, military and diplomatic talents needed to develop concrete disarmament proposals. While the agency was not an unmitigated success, and had little to do with the disarmament steps taken, it provided useful studies of small and immediate problems, such as joint measures to prevent surprise attacks, and large, long-range problems, such as the economic adjustments necessary when all arms production ceases. A religious leader complained to the President that the prestigious businessmen in the Agency's leadership had no background in the professional peace movement. But the President pointed out that Pentagon and Congressional opposition would not be changed by long-time believers, and added: "You believe in redemption, don't you?"

The President underwent a degree of redemption on this subject himself. His initial interest in disarmament was largely for propaganda reasons—a desire to influence neutral and "world opinion." He told his disarmament planners, as they were preparing for the spring, 1962, Geneva Disarmament Conference, that he wanted them to meet the sweeping, oversimplified Soviet proposals with counterproposals that were "not so complex and cautious as to lack all force and appeal." But he increasingly recognized that there was no ultimate security in armaments, that tensions and danger were rising even as our nuclear stockpiles rose. Gradually and still skeptically he began to believe that disarmament was really achievable, that the money he was putting into the arms race could someday go into health and education, and that his administration's own plan, formulated with considerable White House prodding of the new Agency, was a good beginning toward a goal he did not expect to achieve in his political lifetime.

Seeing no reason why the Russians should be permitted to monopolize the label of "general and complete disarmament," the President adopted that unrealistic title for his own, despite the fears of those who thought even the phrase was a Communist plot. The American plan differed sharply from the Soviet plan—particularly in its call for inspecting whatever arms each nation might have retained, not merely those it destroyed. It was also more realistic and specific than the Soviet plan in calling for an advance to complete disarmament by stages and for a parallel build-up of new peace-keeping institutions to police it. At Vienna the Kennedy-Khrushchev talks on this topic were their least illuminating. This was partly due to the fact that the U.S. did not yet have a plan of its own and neither man seemed too familiar with the

Soviet plan. But it was largely due to the fact that Khrushchev talked grandly of general and complete disarmament—as a millennium when inspection would be unimportant, and compared to which a nuclear test ban was already unimportant—without ever saying how that millennium could be reached.

To the leaders of a closed society as obsessed with secrecy as the Soviet Union, the whole notion of outside inspection of their country was unexplainable. "A totalitarian system cannot accept the kind of inspection which really is desirable . . . because [it] must exist only in secrecy," said the President in his candid three-man TV interview; and then he added significantly: "The camera, I think, is actually going to be our best inspector." He may have been referring to the U-2 aerial surveys of Cuba. But it was also increasingly public knowledge that, even though U.S. planes no longer violated Soviet air rights, high-orbiting space satellites were covering all parts of the globe. Observation from outer space was as legitimate as observation from the high seas. But it was vastly more effective and placed all arguments about inspection and secrecy in a somewhat different light.

To the President's surprise, Soviet negotiators in the fall of 1961 accepted—with one very major exception on the inspection of retained arms—a new U.S. "statement of principles" on disarmament as a joint declaration. In doing so, they conceded several points they had long opposed. But "all issues of principle are not settled," said the President, and

> principles alone are not enough. It is therefore our intention to challenge the Soviet Union, not to an arms race, but to a peace race: to advance together step by step, stage by stage, until general and complete disarmament has actually been achieved. . . .
>
> Today . . . every man, woman and child lives under a nuclear sword of Damocles, hanging by the slenderest of threads, capable of being cut at any moment by accident or miscalculation or madness. . . . Unless man can match his strides in weaponry and technology with equal strides in social and political development, our great strength, like that of the dinosaur, will become incapable of proper control, and man, like the dinosaur, will vanish from the earth.

2. *The United Nations*

These remarks were contained in John Kennedy's address to the United Nations General Assembly in September, 1961. It was a critical moment in the life of that body, the most critical in its sixteen-year history. The Soviet Union, angered in particular by the UN peace-keeping operation in the Congo, was slowly strangling the organization financially, disrupting its progress and insisting upon three Secretary Generals instead of one, each representing a different bloc (East, West and neutral), and each empowered to block the others.

The application of this principle, known as the Troika (a Russian wagon drawn by three horses abreast), would have permanently crippled the United Nations. It stemmed from Khrushchev's anger at Secretary General Dag Hammarskjöld, "who poses as a neutral person. . . ." There are neutral nations but no neutral men, he told the President at Vienna, and the events in the Congo taught the Soviet Union a lesson —that the UN could act against the interests of individual states. The Soviet Union did not seek control over the organization, he said, but it did not wish the United States to have such control either. The United States had a majority in the UN, but times may change, he went on. The UN is not a parliament and the rule of majority has no place there. With a three-man Secretariat no one would be able to pursue a policy prejudicial to any other side.

At the time there seemed little reason to believe that the Chairman could succeed in displacing Hammarskjöld and amending the UN Charter. On the contrary, Hammarskjöld daily was making the UN a more meaningful, powerful instrument. But on the morning of Monday, September 18, 1961, as Kennedy boarded "Air Force One" at Cape Cod to return to Washington, he was handed a grim message. Dag Hammarskjöld had been killed in a plane crash in the Congo. The President had not known the Secretary General well, but he admired his courage and skill. "I hope that all of us recognize," he said, "the heavy burdens that his passing places upon us."

Only three days earlier he had tentatively decided to address the opening of the General Assembly on September 25. Now it was suggested in some quarters that he wait until the dust settled. The atmosphere at the UN was dispirited and disorganized. The Soviets were insisting that they would veto even an Acting Secretary General until a Troika was installed. The Congo operation was at a standstill. The last session had been at times turned into a circus by the antics of Khrushchev and Castro. And now rising tensions in much of the world—over Berlin, nuclear testing, Southeast Asia, Bizerte and elsewhere—cast doubt upon the UN's future.

But the President believed the UN had to have a future. He hoped he could help to rekindle its hope. Brushing aside suggested gimmicks for the contents of his speech—e.g., "The Agenda of Man" or "A World Bill of Rights"—he decided to speak forcefully (although not for an hour, which he was told was customary) on the real issues confronting the Assembly and the world: a stronger UN with no Troika—disarmament and a nuclear test ban—cooperation on outer space and economic development—an end to colonialism in the Communist empire as well as in the West—and a recognition of the Communist threats to peace over Berlin and Southeast Asia. He wanted the United States to initiate concrete proposals for UN efforts and to include them in his remarks.

Several days later, the speech was written and rewritten over an intensive weekend at Hyannis Port. I worked with the President at his cottage, on the phone and, finally, on his plane as it flew in heavy fog from Cape Cod to New York. Because both the Presidential and passenger cabins were crowded and noisy, we squatted on the floor in the bare passageway between the two, comparing and sorting pages. He suggested that we each write a peroration and then take the best of both. In New York he read the latest draft aloud to Rusk and his UN team—an unusual practice for him—and then made his final revisions that night.

The next morning, as he strode to the rostrum in that great hall, the Secretary General's chair was empty and the air seemed heavy with gloom. The President began softly:

> We meet in an hour of grief and challenge. Dag Hammarskjöld is dead. But the United Nations lives on. His tragedy is deep in our hearts, but the task for which he died is at the top of our agenda. . . .
> The problem is not the death of one man; the problem is the life of this organization. . . . For in [its] development . . . rests the only true alternative to war, and war appeals no longer as a rational alternative. . . .
> So let us here resolve that Dag Hammarskjöld did not live, or die, in vain. Let us call a truce to terror. . . .

The UN, said the President, was "both the measure and the vehicle of man's most generous impulses." It needed to be strengthened, not defied.

> However difficult it may be to fill Mr. Hammarskjöld's place, it can better be filled by one man rather than by three. Even the three horses of the troika did not have three drivers, all going in different directions. . . .
> To permit each great power to decide . . . its own case would entrench the Cold War in the headquarters of peace. . . . As one of the great powers, we reject it. For we far prefer world law,

in the age of self-determination, to world war, in the age of
mass extermination.

He reviewed the pending issues and proposals, and then closed with
unusual feeling in his voice:

> However close we sometimes seem to that dark and final
> abyss, let no man of peace and freedom despair. For he does
> not stand alone. . . .
> Together we shall save our planet or together we shall perish
> in its flames. Save it we can, and save it we must, and then
> shall we earn the eternal thanks of mankind and, as peace-
> makers, the eternal blessing of God.

The subsequent success of the sixteenth session of the United Nations General Assembly could hardly be attributed to the President's
address. Skillful negotiations, conducted chiefly by Ambassador Stevenson, played a major role. But the President had provided a fresh impetus when it was badly needed. The Troika was rejected, U Thant
was installed as Acting Secretary General and the integrity of his office
was reinforced. Despite a double standard on India's seizure of Goa,
and the growing dangers of an irresponsible Assembly majority, composed of new members who had not participated in drafting the Charter,
the UN remained active, and so did U.S. influence within it. No Soviet
initiative succeeded over our opposition, yet the reverse was frequently
true. In fact, by obtaining a decision that Red China's admission came
under the "important question" category requiring a two-thirds vote,
that admission—in the absence of a change of manner in Peking—
was made all the more difficult.

But a new UN crisis loomed almost immediately—a financial crisis.
To ease the deficit caused by the Soviets, French and others default-
ing on their special assessments for the Congo and other peace-keeping operations, a stopgap emergency bond issue was decided upon. The
President pledged that his government would purchase up to $100 mil-
lion. It was, he recognized, in this country's interest. The loan would be
paid back out of the regular UN membership assessments, to which the
Communists were contributing proportionately; and any vacuum caused
by the bankruptcy and disintegration of the UN in such areas as the
Congo would surely lead in time either to a big-power confrontation or
a far more costly U.S. operation.

Nevertheless the Congress was hard to convince. Some members
complained about various UN actions. ("No policeman is universally
popular," said the President to the Congress, "particularly when he uses
his stick to restore law and order on his beat.") Others complained

about the "one country–one vote" principle diminishing our influence. ("Have they ever stopped to consider," mused the President, calling me from his plane about an anti-UN speech by Senator Jackson that he wanted me to check before he returned from a trip, "what our influence would be compared with India, China and Russia if votes were weighted according to population?") Some complained about the cost. (This bill represents, said the President, an investment of one-tenth of one percent of our budget, compared to the 50 percent going for defense.) Others complained about even belonging to so weak and dissonant an organization. (They "would abandon this imperfect world instrument," said the President, "because they dislike our imperfect world.") With considerable White House help the bill passed; and though its financial crisis was only postponed, the United Nations survived.

The President did not regard the UN as a substitute for American action on matters where he bore primary responsibility for our security. The small and neutralist nations—always desperate to avoid war and often gullible to oversimplified Soviet propaganda (such as a "free city" in West Berlin without Western protection, or equating the Cuban missile bases with American overseas installations)—could not be relied upon, in his opinion, to settle major disputes, even if the UN had the power to assume jurisdiction. The great powers had to settle their own confrontations. Nor could the UN do much about Communist subversion and infiltration, or impose effective disarmament, or provide its own military deterrent to major aggression.

But it was, said the President, "primarily the protector of the small and the weak, and a safety valve for the strong." A small nation's blowing off steam in the General Assembly was obviously preferable to its blowing up cities elsewhere. The executive actions of the UN Secretary General—far more than the noisy clashes in the Assembly—could help settle, confine or cool off brush-fire wars among the smaller nations and prevent them from turning into major conflagrations. No single outside government could intervene in such cases as safely, impartially or effectively. In the UN's exercise of this capacity—in West New Guinea, in Yemen, in the Congo—Kennedy was willing to give it every support, including military transports. And over the very long run it could be developed, he hoped (without too much expectation), into "a genuine world security system."

3. *The Space Effort*

In his 1961 address to the United Nations, the President called for peaceful cooperation in a new domain—outer space. "The cold reaches of the universe," he said, "must not become the new arena of an even colder war." In both his Inaugural and first State of the Union addresses that year, he had called for East-West cooperation "to invoke the wonders of science instead of its terrors. Together let us explore the stars."

But the Soviets had brusquely rejected the suggestion. They had little incentive to cooperate with an American space program which lagged far behind their own—not in the number and variety of scientific studies but in the all-important capacity to lift large payloads into orbit. With their more powerful rocket boosters—developed originally to launch more massive nuclear warheads before they learned the technique of the small hydrogen bomb—the Soviets in 1957 were the first to launch a space satellite, then the first to put living animals into orbit. The Eisenhower administration, despite prodding from Majority Leader Johnson, started its own program slowly and tardily, with much scoffing and skepticism from Republican officials about the meaning of the Russian effort. President Truman had also cut back the infant American space program started after the war with the help of German scientists.

John Kennedy had borne down hard on this space gap in the 1960 campaign. To him it symbolized the nation's lack of initiative, ingenuity and vitality under Republican rule. He was convinced that Americans did not yet fully grasp the world-wide political and psychological impact of the space race. With East and West competing to convince the new and undecided nations which way to turn, which wave was the future, the dramatic Soviet achievements, he feared, were helping to build a dangerous impression of unchallenged world leadership generally and scientific pre-eminence particularly. American scientists could repeat over and over that the more solid contributions of our own space research were a truer measure of national strength, but neither America nor the world paid much attention.

After the election, a top-notch transition task force under Jerome Wiesner had warned Kennedy that the United States could not win the race to put a man in space. Others expressed concern that a Soviet space monopoly would bring new military dangers and disadvantages to the West. Our own rocket thrust was adequate for all known military purposes, but no one could be certain of its future uses. Other nations, moreover, assumed that a Soviet space lead meant a missile lead as well; and whether this assumption was true or false, it affected their attitudes in the cold war.

Before his first hundred days in the White House were out, Kennedy's concern was dramatically proven correct. Moscow announced on April 12 that Cosmonaut Yuri Gagarin had completed an orbital flight around the earth in less than two hours. As the Soviet Union capitalized on its historic feat in all corners of the globe, Kennedy congratulated Khrushchev and Gagarin—and set to work.

He had already sharply increased the budget request for development of the large Saturn rocket booster; and he had already revitalized the National Space Council, with the Vice President as Chairman, to expedite progress with less military-civilian quibbling. But that was not enough. Nor was he reassured on the day after the Gagarin announcement when National Aeronautics and Space Administrator James Webb brought in a desk model of the U.S.-designed capsule soon to carry an American astronaut into space. Eying the Rube Goldberg-like contraption on his desk, Kennedy speculated that Webb might have bought it in a toy store on his way to work that morning.

To gain some immediate answers, he asked me to review with Wiesner that same day—in preparation for an interview he had granted for that evening—the outlook in NASA and the Budget Bureau on next steps in the space race. NASA reported that the dramatic big-booster steps still to come might include, in possible order of development, longer one-man orbits, two men in a spacecraft, an orbiting space laboratory, a fixed space way station, a manned rocket around the moon and back, a manned landing on the moon and return, manned exploration of the planets and a fully controllable plane for space travel. For any of the early items on this list, said the scientists, America's prospects for surpassing the Soviets were poor because of their initial rocket superiority. Our first best bet to beat them was the landing of a man on the moon.

The President was more convinced than any of his advisers that a second-rate, second-place space effort was inconsistent with this country's security, with its role as world leader and with the New Frontier spirit of discovery. Consequently he asked the Vice President as Chairman of the Space Council to seek answers to all the fundamental questions concerning the steps we could or must take to achieve pre-eminence in space—in terms of manpower, scientific talent, overtime facilities, alternative fuels, agency cooperation and money. Intensive hearings were held by the Council. The details of a new space budget were hammered out by Webb and McNamara. On the basis of these reports, the President made what he later termed one of the most important decisions he would make as President: "to shift our efforts in space from low to high gear." In his special second State of the Union Message of May, 1961, he included a determined and dramatic pledge: to land a man on the moon and return him safely to earth "before this decade is out."

He was unwilling to promise a specific year, and referred to "this decade" as a deadline he could later interpret as either 1969 or 1970. James Webb, in fact, gave him visions of a late 1968 moon trip as a triumphant climax to his second term. (Under the level of support previously provided, the flight would not have been accomplished before the middle 1970's, if at all.) Whatever the date, the purpose of the pledge was to provide a badly needed focus and sense of urgency for the entire space program. The lunar landing was not the sole space effort to be undertaken; but it was clearly one of the great human adventures of modern history.

"No single space project in this period," the President told the Congress, "will be more impressive to mankind or more important . . . [or] so difficult or expensive to accomplish." It would require, he said, the highest kind of national priority, the diversion of scientific manpower and funds from other important activities, a greater degree of dedication and discipline, and an end to all the petty stoppages, rivalries and personnel changes long troubling the space program.

> In a very real sense, it will not be one man going to the moon . . . it will be an entire nation. For all of us must work to put him there. . . . This is not merely a race. Space is open to us now; and our eagerness to share its meaning is not governed by the efforts of others. We go into space because whatever mankind must undertake, free men must fully share.

The routine applause with which the Congress greeted this pledge struck him, he told me in the car going back to the White House, as something less than enthusiastic. Twenty billion dollars was a lot of money. The legislators knew a lot of better ways to spend it. Seated to the side of the rostrum, I thought the President looked strained in his effort to win them over. Suddenly he departed extensively from his prepared text—the only time he ever did that in addressing the Congress—to express his awareness of the responsibility they faced in making so expensive and long-range a commitment. "Unless we are prepared to do the work and bear the burdens to make it successful," he said, there is no sense in going ahead. His voice sounded urgent but a little uncertain.

The Congress by nearly unanimous vote embraced what the President called this "great new American enterprise," aided by the successful shot of Commander Alan Shepard into space (although not into orbit) a few weeks earlier. The space budget was increased by 50 percent in that year. The following year it exceeded all the pre-1961 space budgets combined. Major new facilities sprang up in Houston, Texas, Cape Canaveral (now Cape Kennedy), Florida and elsewhere. Research produced for or from U.S. space launchings introduced advancements in dozens of other fields, ranging from medicine to metal fabrication. With the orbital flight of Colonel John Glenn in February, 1962, an instrumented flight past Venus later that year, and the use of a Telstar satellite to relay TV programs (including a Presidential news conference), the acceleration and expansion of America's space program began to gain ground.

The United States was still not first, said the President. He was not lulled by a variety of seemingly indifferent statements from Chairman Khrushchev, including the suggestion at Vienna that the U.S. could better afford to go to the moon first and then the Soviet Union would follow. Nor was he deterred by a swelling chorus of dissenters at home. After each striking Soviet success, he noted, there were demands that we do more on a crash "Manhattan Project" basis. After each American astronaut's flight, there were demands that the world recognize our pre-eminence. But during the long intervals between flights, there were demands—sometimes from the same political and editorial sources—that our space budget be cut back and our timetable slowed down. Taxpayers complained about the cost. Scientists complained that more important activities were being slighted. Republicans began dipping into such phrases as "boondoggle" and "science fiction stunt."

But the President, once started, was not backing out. To those who said the money could better be spent relieving ignorance or poverty on this planet, he pointed out that this nation had the resources to do both but that those members of Congress making this point seemed unwilling to vote for more welfare funds, regardless of the size of the space program. To those who criticized concentration on the moon shot, he pointed out that this was a focal point for a broad-based scientific effort, and that some sixty other unrelated projects comprised nearly one-quarter of the space budget. To those who argued that instruments alone could do the job, he replied that man was "the most extraordinary computer of them all . . . [whose] judgment, nerve and . . . [ability to] learn from experience still make him unique" among the instruments. To those who feared that the publicity given our launchings would cost us heavily in the event of failure, he replied that this risk not only demonstrated our devotion to freedom but enhanced the prestige of successes which might otherwise be written off as second-best.

He was concerned, to be sure, about risks to the astronauts' lives; and he made clear at the outset that, "Even if we should come in second . . . I will be satisfied if, when we finally put a man in space, his chances of survival are as high as I think they must be." He was also concerned about the program's effect on our nation's supply of scientists and engineers, and voiced new urgency for his higher education and other personnel development programs. He was concerned, finally, about waste and duplication in the space effort, and kept his Budget Director, Science Adviser and Space Council riding herd on the rapidly growing NASA complex (although not, he admitted, very successfully).

But he never relinquished that goal, "not simply to be first on the moon," as he put it, "any more than Charles Lindbergh's real aim was to be the first to Paris," but to strengthen our national leadership in a new and adventuresome age. In September of 1962, at Rice University in Houston, his most notable address on the subject summed up all the reasons why this nation must "set sail on this new sea." The exploration of space will go ahead whether we join it or not, he said; and just as the United States was founded by energy and vision, and achieved world leadership by riding the first waves of each new age—the industrial revolution, modern invention and nuclear power—so this generation of Americans intends to be "the world's leading space-faring nation." His remarks revealed much of his general outlook on life as well as on space:

> But why, some say, the moon? . . . And they may well ask, why climb the highest mountain? Why, thirty-five years ago, fly the Atlantic? Why does Rice play Texas? [A traditional, but almost inevitably more powerful, football rival.] . . .
>
> We choose to go to the moon in this decade, and do the other things, not because they are easy but because they are hard; because that goal will serve to organize and measure the best of our energies and skills. . . .
>
> Many years ago the great British explorer George Mallory, who was to die on Mount Everest, was asked why did he want to climb it, and he said, "Because it is there."
>
> Well, space is there, and . . . the moon and the planets are there, and new hopes for knowledge and peace are there.

Kennedy's accelerated space program also served as a useful aid to American foreign policy. Other nations cooperated in tracking our space vehicles and benefited from our weather, navigation and communications satellites. Many instituted space research programs in conjunction with our own. But it was not until after the orbital flight of John Glenn in 1962 that the Soviet Union for the first time showed any interest in space cooperation.

The Glenn flight was a turning point in many ways. Ten times it had been postponed. Frequently during the five-hour, three-orbit trip unforeseen dangers threatened to burn Glenn alive. The President, who enjoyed talking with each astronaut immediately upon the latter's safe return, personally liked Glenn immensely. Indeed, he found all the astronauts to be a remarkably competent and personable group. He did not approve of the rights granted them by his predecessor to make large profits through the exploitation of their names and stories while still in military service; nor did he want the period or frequency of their parades and speech-making to reach a level interfering with their work. But he recognized that their courage and achievement merited special honors. "The impact of Colonel Glenn's magnificent achievement," he said, after Glenn was safely down, having watched his flight most of the day on TV, "goes far beyond our own time and our own country. We have a long way to go. We started late. But this is the new ocean, and I believe the United States must sail on it."

At Vienna Khrushchev—dismissing the importance of scientific coordination on launchings which he asserted were undertaken primarily for prestige—had said cooperation was impossible anyway because he did not want his rockets observed. In a later interview he had compared space progress with the evolution of insects, with his nation in the flying stage and the Americans merely jumping. But among the many cables from heads of state pouring in after the Glenn flight was a Khrushchev message extending not only congratulations but new interest in cooperation. There had been no such response, noted Kennedy, to similar proposals in his Inaugural, State of the Union and United Nations addresses. "But we . . . now have more chips on the table . . . so perhaps the prospects are improving."

The President's letter to Khrushchev on specific areas of cooperation largely repeated the proposals set forth over a year earlier in his first State of the Union: a joint weather satellite system, communications satellite coordination, an exchange of information on space medicine, cooperative tracking arrangements and other, less dramatic areas. The Soviet response was limited. Communist suspicions and secrecy were hard to dent, and negotiations proceeded slowly. Some of Kennedy's own advisers complained that too much cooperation instead of competition would dampen Congressional interest and appropriations. But the limited arrangement finally reached—and as of this writing never implemented by the Soviets—was at least a small first step toward fulfillment of the vow he made at Rice about space:

> . . . that we shall not see it governed by a hostile flag of conquest, but by a banner of freedom and peace . . . not . . . filled with weapons of mass destruction, but with instruments of knowledge and understanding . . . for the progress of all people.

4. Foreign Aid and the Peace Corps

John Kennedy's concept of peace meant more than an absence of war. It required a stable community of free and independent nations, free from the unrest and strife on which Communism fed. It required those nations blessed with plenty to help those weakened by want. He gave top priority upon entering the White House to America's programs for the new and developing nations. "The great battleground for the defense and expansion of freedom today," he said, is the whole southern half of the globe—Asia, Latin America, Africa and the Middle East—the lands of the rising peoples. Their revolution is the greatest in human history. They seek an end to injustice, tyranny and exploitation. More than an end, they seek a beginning.

He regarded a revitalized program of economic aid as the principal instrument with which we could help them begin. It was not only a matter of idealism or generosity. These vast undeveloped continents were, in the absence of a major war, the crucial point of conflict between East and West. The modernization and maturity of their societies would strengthen our own security. He recognized that each of the poor nations (not all of them could even be called "developing," although that was the official term used to avoid "backward" or "undeveloped") was in a different stage, faced with different problems; and he emphasized that no amount of American aid would be effective unless the recipient nation mobilized its own resources under a long-range economic plan. But his efforts to obtain that kind of self-help and self-reform by the recipient nations were only partially successful. So were his efforts to obtain a larger cooperative effort by the other industrialized nations. And so, finally, were his efforts to obtain a thoroughgoing reorganization and long-term financing in the American aid program.

Each year, as previously recounted, the Congressional opposition to foreign aid increased—and each year the President's indignation increased with it. "They try to sound so noble talking about setting an example with our own people first," he said to me one evening. "What does medical care for the aged mean in countries with a life expectancy of forty? Who's impressed by our education programs if most of them are illiterate and never went to school? I'm all for helping the distressed areas and the unemployed, but these people are concerned about just living." Frequently, in press conferences and public speeches, he expressed that same indignation in terms he hoped the Congress and country would understand:

> It is hard for any nation to focus on an external or subversive threat . . . when its energies are drained in daily combat with the forces of poverty and despair. It makes little sense for us to assail . . . the horrors of Communism, to spend $50 billion a year to prevent its military advance—and then to begrudge spending . . . less than one-tenth of that amount to help other nations . . . cure the social chaos in which Communism has always thrived.

To be sure, some important gains were achieved in this country's program: a more streamlined Agency for International Development

(AID) in place of the previous conglomeration (although he later regretted the new title as an unhelpful gimmick), a shift in emphasis from military to economic assistance and from grants to loans, new incentives for private investment, and at least a degree of long-term, country-by-country planning, with emphasis on those nations able to organize their own assets and in time stand up on their own. Although delays and deficiencies in the program's leadership in 1961-1962 lost much of the momentum sought in his first foreign aid message to the Congress, he found in David Bell the AID program's ablest administrator in many years. At the United Nations he helped launch an international "Decade of Development." But the scale of the assistance effort by this and the other prospering countries (whom he tried to spur to greater heights) was not enough to prevent the gap between rich and poor nations from widening, to the despair of their citizens and to the despair of John Kennedy.

He had more success with two specialized efforts. The "Food-for-Peace" program, initiated by a Hubert Humphrey amendment during the previous administration, had been limping along, caught in a cross fire between Agriculture and State, and regarded as an outlet for farm surpluses rather than American generosity. Kennedy set up an independent Food-for-Peace office in the White House under George McGovern (and later Richard Reuter), secured legislation authorizing its expansion, and within eighteen months shipped more food abroad than Herbert Hoover and his associates had shipped in ten years of relief to the victims of World War I. Preferring to pay for transporting food otherwise stored at the taxpayers' expense, he nearly doubled the program's previous volume, with such new uses as school lunch programs and food-for-wages projects in more than eighty countries. Some of the food was donated in order to combat famines and floods in the Congo, Kenya, Vietnam and elsewhere, some of it was given to local schools and relief agencies, some of it was delivered under long-term credit arrangements, and some of it was paid for in local currencies. The program was a marked success.

But Kennedy was proudest of a unique institution he had advocated in his 1960 campaign, created in his first hundred days and staffed in the field with Americans motivated only by the kind of dedication he had urged—the Peace Corps. The Peace Corps was a cadre of several hundred, later several thousand, mostly youthful volunteers carrying American energy and skills directly to the people of the poor nations. They lived with those people in their villages, spoke their languages, helped them develop their natural and human resources, and received no compensation other than the satisfaction of helping others. The Peace Corps became in time—at least in the developing nations—the most stirring symbol of John Kennedy's hope and promise.

Its formation, however, was not untroubled. Liberals demeaned it as a gimmick. Conservatives dismissed it as a nonsensical haven for beatniks and visionaries. Communist nations denounced it as an espionage front. Leaders in many of the neutral nations most in need of it heaped resentment and ridicule upon it. And its own backers threatened to dissipate its momentum by talking, even before it was started, of a UN peace corps and a domestic peace corps and a dozen other diversions. In 1961, in both the House and the Senate, Republican opposition on the key roll-call votes was strong.

But the President—and his energetic, idealistic brother-in-law, Peace Corps Director Sargent Shriver—built carefully and persistently. They pledged that the Peace Corps would be nonpolitical in world as well as domestic affairs. They made clear that it would go only where specifically invited. Attempts by the CIA to use or infiltrate it were stoutly and successfully resisted. Shriver, with the persuasion that only a member of the family could muster, induced the President to reverse his decision to put the Peace Corps under the far less popular AID. Applicants were carefully screened and thoroughly trained. Misfits were promptly weeded out. Peace Corps country and regional directors were unusually well qualified. Its mission was described by the President in practical, matter-of-fact tones, leaving the zeal to Shriver.

In time, its birth pangs and growing pains gave way to flourishing health. Each year the Peace Corps appropriation grew larger and the opposition diminished. Each country with Peace Corps volunteers asked for more. When a postcard from a volunteer in Nigeria was distorted into a major incident, the President penned a handwritten note of reassurance to the young lady involved and asked that it be hand-delivered to her upon her arrival back in this country. With surprisingly few errors and incidents, these volunteers—who became better known outside of a host country's capital city than any American diplomat, and who worked as teachers, doctors, nurses, agricultural agents, carpenters and technicians of all kinds at all levels—served as this nation's most effective ambassadors of idealism. They also brought back to this country an unusually well-grounded understanding of life in the backwoods of the world.

A special bond grew up between the President and the Peace Corps volunteers. Today they are known in some areas as "Kennedy's children" —and that term comes close to describing how he and they felt about each other. He was truly, one Peace Corpsman would later write, "*the* volunteer." And the Peace Corps volunteers, said the President—who met with groups of them every chance he could get—represented the highest response to his Inaugural injunction to "ask not."

5. *The Alliance for Progress*

His Inaugural Address had contained another phrase from the campaign—a new "alliance for progress"—*Alianza para el progreso*. No continent was more constantly in the President's mind—or had a warmer appreciation of his efforts—than Latin America. Many Africans, to be sure, had a special regard for John Kennedy—because of his civil rights efforts, his Senate speech on Algeria, his lead-off appointment of the crusading Mennen Williams as Assistant Secretary of State for African Affairs, his initiative to achieve better treatment and housing for their diplomats in Washington, his enthusiasm for the African independence movements, and his bold support of Adoula in the Congo, the Angolans against Portugal and the Volta Dam project in Ghana. Many Latin Americans, in contrast, were initially skeptical of Kennedy's early promises, which sounded familiar, and dubious about his early emphasis on anti-Communism and Castro and his failure to put one man in charge of hemispheric policy. But in time they realized he meant what he said when he called their continent "the most critical area in the world."

Both the name and the essence of the Alliance for Progress first publicly appeared in the text of a Kennedy election campaign speech in Tampa, Florida. With time running short, he dropped the phrase and a proposed program from his actual delivery, assuring reporters later that he stood by the full text. The plight of our Latin-American neighbors was, in fact, a favorite theme throughout his campaign— this nation's failure to relieve their poverty, the favors we bestowed upon their military dictators, the neglect of the entire continent in U.S. student exchange, Voice of America, economic development and other programs. He talked one night on the *Caroline* of concentrating on Latin America during his first months in office; and he requested suggestions for a policy label as meaningful for the sixties as Roosevelt's "Good Neighbor Policy" had been for the thirties. I suggested *"Alianza,"* assuming that it had broader meaning than "alliance" because it was the name of an insurance cooperative organized by some of our Mexican-American supporters in Arizona. A Cuban refugee and Latin-American expert in Washington, Ernesto Betancourt, suggested through Goodwin the addition of *"para el progreso"* (although for some time we mistakenly dropped the *"el"*). The candidate liked it—and the Alliance for Progress was born.

The official birth date, however, was March 13, 1961, when the President convened, in the East Room of the White House, the ambassadors from Latin America. The ten-point program which he unveiled in that address under the Alliance for Progress label had its roots in the undelivered portion of his Tampa speech, his January State of the Union speech and his December, 1958, speech in San Juan, Puerto Rico. The Alliance was legislatively launched following the East Room speech—which was broadcast in Spanish, Portuguese, French and English throughout the hemisphere by the Voice of America—when he sent a special message to Congress requesting funds.

In each of these speeches and messages the emphasis was the same: on the need for more self-help as well as American help, for ending injustice as well as poverty, for reform as well as relief.

> Our unfulfilled task is to demonstrate . . . that man's unsatisfied aspiration for economic progress and social justice can best be achieved by free men working within a framework of democratic institutions. . . . Let us once again transform the [Western Hemisphere] into a vast crucible of revolutionary ideas and efforts.

The *Alianza*, he added a year later to a similar gathering, "is more than a doctrine of development. . . . It is the expression of the noblest goals of our society."

During the course of that first year, funds had been provided by the Congress. An August meeting of the Inter-American Economic and Social Council at Punta del Este, Uruguay, had adopted the official charter of the *Alianza para el Progreso*. A host of New Frontiersmen—including Berle, Schlesinger, Goodwin, Stevenson, Dillon and others, in addition to the usual foreign policy and foreign aid officers—had advised on policy or attended conferences south of the border, producing some dismay among the State Department professionals and some disarray in the continuity of policy, but more activity and interest in Latin America than that region had ever seen. The debacle at the Bay of Pigs had temporarily soured relations, but after his first bristling reaction, the President had once again stressed positive goals. He had begun work on a coffee stabilization agreement, sent more Peace Corpsmen south than to any other continent, increased Food-for-Peace shipments, created a new training institute, appointed a separate Alliance for Progress coordinator in the AID program (Puerto Rican leader Teodoro Moscoso) and made a dozen other beginnings.

But the Alliance was slow getting started, and not without reason. With a rate of infant mortality nearly four times our own, a life expectancy less than two-thirds of our own, a per capita annual product less than one-ninth of our own, an illiteracy rate of 50 percent, a lack of schools and sanitation and trained personnel, runaway inflation in some areas, shocking slums in the cities, squalor in the countryside, and a highly suspicious attitude toward American investments, where were we to begin? The task, said the President, was "staggering in its dimen-sions," even for a ten-year plan; and in the months that followed he was himself staggered by its sheer size. He felt "depressed," he said at one news conference, using a word rare in his vocabulary,

> by the size of the problems that we face . . . the population in-creases, the drop in commodity prices . . . serious domestic prob-lems. . . . The Alliance for Progress . . . has failed to some degree because the problems are almost insuperable, and for years the United States ignored them and . . . so did some of the groups in Latin America. . . . In some ways the road seems longer than it was when the journey started. But I think we ought to keep at it.

He kept at it. But what disturbed him most was the attitude of that 2 percent of the citizenry of Latin America who owned more than 50 percent of the wealth and controlled most of the political-economic ap-paratus. Their voices were influential, if not dominant, among the local governments, the armies, the newspapers and other opinion-makers. They had friendly ties with U.S. press and business interests who re-flected their views in Washington. They saw no reason to alter the ancient feudal patterns of land tenure and tax structure, the top-heavy military budgets, the substandard wages and the concentrations of capital. They classified many of their opponents as "Communists," considered the social and political reforms of the *Alianza* a threat to stability and clung tenaciously to the status quo. Kennedy at all times kept the pressure on—stirring the people in his trips to Mexico, Colom-bia, Venezuela and Costa Rica, using what influence he had through the OAS and AID to give preference to those governments willing to curb the holdings and privileges of the elite. It was a revolution, he said over and over, and "those who make peaceful revolution impossible will make violent revolution inevitable."

The President and his advisers were less consistent, however, on their attitude toward military takeovers. Kennedy deplored the arrest of fellow Presidents with whom he had visited, the suspension of civilian rule and the consequent interruptions in the progress of the *Alianza*. "We are opposed to military coups," he said, "because we think they are self-defeating . . . for the hemisphere." He recognized, however, that the military often represented more competence in administration and more sympathy with the U.S. than any other group in the country. To halt work on the Alliance in every nation not ruled by a genuine democ-racy would have paralyzed the whole program. Some military usurpers in Latin America, moreover, like those in Burma and Korea, were neither unpopular nor reactionary; and those able and willing to guide their countries to progress he wanted to encourage. Unfortunately, he had learned, many of the more progressive civilian governments in Latin America (as elsewhere) were less willing or less able to impose the necessary curbs on extravagant projects, runaway inflation and political disorder. They were more likely to frighten away local and foreign investments and to ignore the less vote-worthy rural populations.

A succession of military coups in Latin America thus presented a puzzle. To try to prevent them by sending in the Marines, he said, "is not the way for democracy to flourish." He attempted to impose conditions—such as free elections within a specified period and adherence to constitutional forms—but his policy was neither consistently applied nor consistently successful. Both economic aid and diplomatic relations were cut off, restored or not cut off without any discernible pattern in a situation which itself had little discernible pattern.

A special case was that of the Dominican Republic, where the May, 1961, assassination of long-time military dictator Trujillo (whom Kennedy had excluded from all *Alianza* arrangements) produced endless unrest and dissension. The advice of American diplomats and the sight of American warships helped keep the Trujillos out and bring a democratic government in. But the first legitimately elected President in a generation, Juan Bosch, proved too weak to prevent the continuation of coups and countercoups.

The opposite threat to a military coup was takeover by the followers of Castro or Communism. Kennedy sought joint action against the exportation of weapons and agents from Cuba to the rest of Latin America. He succeeded in increasingly isolating Castro politically and economically from his neighbors. He had under study in 1963 a possible new document to modernize the Monroe Doctrine as a declaration against further Communist penetration of the hemisphere. But he also recognized more clearly by 1963 that "the big dangers to Latin America are . . . unrelated to Cuba . . . [including] illiteracy, bad housing, maldistribution of wealth, balance of payments difficulties, the drop in the price of their raw materials . . . [and] local Communist action unrelated to Cuba." "If the Alliance is to succeed, we must . . . halt Communist infiltration and subversion," he said in Miami on November 18 of that year, but ". . . these problems will not be solved simply by complaining about Castro [or] Communism."

Despite these many problems, the Alliance made progress, and Kennedy was greeted wildly on his trips below the border. Jacqueline generally accompanied him; and her presence, he remarked before one trip, was insurance of both a big crowd and safe treatment. He received both. He was pleased by the enthusiasm that greeted her, and saddened that the entire continent should regard with astonishment her willingness to be kissed on a visit to a home for orphans. Near Bogotá, Colombia, in

1961, the President stood in an open field to dedicate a future *Alianza* housing project. Little more than a year later, he received a grateful letter from the head of the first family to be housed in that project, Señor Argemil Plazas García, concluding "We are very happy to . . . no longer be moving around like outcasts. Now we have dignity and freedom."

Greater dignity and freedom had also been accorded to one out of every four school-age children in Latin America with an extra food ration, to tens of thousands of farm families resettled on their own land, and to thousands of others with new housing or new schoolrooms or new textbooks. More important in the long run were the beginnings of long-range reform: the creation of central planning agencies, slightly improved tax laws and administration, some improvements in land use and distribution, the submission of detailed development programs to the OAS, and greater local efforts to provide education, housing and financial institutions. Ten of the nineteen nations surpassed Alliance targets in annual economic growth.

Nevertheless reality did not match the rhetoric which flowed about the Alliance on both sides of the Rio Grande; and the President had constantly to answer the skeptics and doubters. "Despite dangers and difficulties . . . the obstacles, the resistance . . . the pace," he said on November 18, 1963, "I support and believe in the Alliance for Progress more strongly than ever before. . . . I do not discount the difficulties . . . but . . . the greatest danger is not in our circumstances or in our enemies but in our own doubts and fears."

THE APPROACH TO DIVERSITY

Among those complaining about the *Alianza* in both North and South America were those objecting to Kennedy's willingness to aid nationalized industries and to aid nations expropriating (for compensation) American-owned industries. This was not only a problem in Latin America. Similar opposition was encountered to his aid projects in India (the Bokaro steel mill), Ghana (the Volta Dam project) and elsewhere. Hostility in the Congress to aiding many of these countries was further heightened by their pursuit of foreign policies as inconsistent with ours as their domestic economics. Many of them sought aid from the Soviets as well as from the Americans. Many former colonies automatically adopted anti-Western postures.

The President shared in the irritation caused by neutrals who loudly condemned America's defense of Vietnam but looked the other way when India seized Goa or merely wrung their hands when China invaded India. He was not blindly courting the neutrals at any cost. He had supported the Angolan nationalists against Portugal only after the Afro-Asians toned down their UN resolution;[3] and he had authorized U.S. participation in the Volta Dam project, in one of his very closest decisions, only after attaching strict economic conditions. He was particularly angry when the 1961 conference of neutrals at Belgrade, asserting to speak for "the conscience of mankind," passed the usual resolution against Western colonialism but timidly failed to condemn the Soviets for suddenly resuming nuclear testing. His anger was reflected in a statement issued at that time upon the signing of the foreign aid bill. The administration of the bill, said Kennedy coldly, "should give great attention and consideration to those nations who have *our* view of the world crisis." But the anger passed, and he was soon explaining that

> Our view of the world crisis is that countries are entitled to national sovereignty and independence. That is all we ever suggested. That is the purpose of our aid. . . .. That is a different matter from suggesting that, in order to be entitled to our assistance . . . they must agree with us, because quite obviously these people in the underdeveloped world are newly independent, they want to run their own affairs, they would rather not accept assistance if we have that kind of string attached to it.

He did not insist that every nation be marked as either Communist or anti-Communist, or even be interested in the cold war. Neutralism he said, had been "part of our own history for over a hundred years," and he regarded its practice by many struggling new nations as "inevitable" rather than "immoral" (the term once applied by John Foster Dulles). "We shall not always expect to find them supporting our view," the President had said in his Inaugural. "But we shall always hope to find them strongly supporting their own freedom." Allies such as Pakistan at times complained that he was equally friendly with neutrals such as India. But inasmuch as the purpose of our alliances was to preserve the independence and safety of nations, he saw no reason to treat less favorably any nation in which that purpose was best served by a course of nonalignment. The Soviets had long wooed the neutrals assiduously and Kennedy had no desire to withdraw from the competition. European Allies also complained early in 1961 when he quietly abandoned the State Department's former policy of referring all new foreign aid applicants from Africa to their former masters first—and ·complained even more when Mennen Williams endorsed the slogan of

---

3 Nevertheless the Portuguese thereafter tried every form of diplomatic blackmail to alter our position on Angola, using as a wedge our country's expiring lease on a key military base on the Portuguese Azores Islands. The President finally felt that, if necessary, he was prepared to forgo the base entirely rather than permit Portugal to dictate his African policy.

"Africa for Africans." "I don't know who else Africa should be for," commented the President drily.

Nor did he try to fix an aid recipient's domestic policy. Although he did seek basic reforms in the efforts of other countries to make use of our funds, he knew that our own system could not be universally imposed or accepted in a world where most of the people "are not white . . . are not Christians . . . [and] know nothing about free enterprise or due process of law or the Australian ballot." All must adopt their own system, and their freedom to do so was the heart of his policy. Without specifically contradicting Wilson's phrase of "a world made safe for democracy," he began in 1963 to refer in his speeches to "a world made safe for diversity." That single phrase summed up much of his new thinking in foreign policy.

In time most of the neutralist leaders came to respect Kennedy's concepts of independence and diversity and to respect the man who put them forward. They recognized that a subtle shift in attitude had aligned the United States with the aspirations for social justice and economic growth within their countries—that land distribution, literacy drives and central planning were no longer regarded in the U.S. as Communist slogans but as reforms to be encouraged and even specified by our government—that this nation's hand was now more often extended to leaders with greater popular backing and social purpose than the "safe" right-wing regimes usually supported by Western diplomats—and that the United States had a President who both understood and welcomed the nationalist revolution and believed that the most relevant contributions from his own country's experience were not its concepts of private property or political parties but its traditions of human dignity and liberty.

The student groups, the trade unions and the nationalist parties of Africa, Asia and Latin America began to soften their anti-American slogans. Their UN delegations began voting more often with ours. Guinea's Premier Sékou Touré, once written off as a pro-Soviet, assailed the Communist embassies for plotting in his country and welcomed U.S. AID and Peace Corps delegations. Even Indonesia's Sukarno, Ghana's Nkrumah and Egypt's Nasser at times softened their denunciations of American imperialism when that kind of rhetoric seemed less helpful either at home or in the Afro-Asian world.

These were at times uncomfortable friends for an American President, and the Congress was critical of continuing aid. But Kennedy believed that his policies had enabled him to retain some influence on the actions of these neutrals and caused their leaders to exercise some restraint. Kennedy's personal prestige helped induce Sukarno to free a CIA pilot downed years earlier in an attack on his government. It helped persuade Nasser to hold back anti-Israel fanatics in the Arab League. Nasser liked Kennedy's Ambassador, John Badeau, and he liked Kennedy's practice of personal correspondence (Kennedy put off, however, an invitation for a Nasser visit until improved relations could enable him to answer the political attacks such a visit would bring from voters more sympathetic with Israel). Sukarno liked the Peace Corps, and— despite a bruising verbal exchange with the Attorney General—he hoped for a visit from the President. To dismiss or denounce these men for every foolish thing they said or did, to cut off our aid or food shipments every time they aroused our displeasure, Kennedy said, would only play into the hands of the Communists.

He was also desirous of using our aid and trade policies "to develop whatever differences in attitude or in tempo may take place behind the Iron Curtain," specifically in Poland and Yugoslavia. The Communist bloc was not a monolith in the sixties, if it ever had been, and he wanted to encourage every nationalist strain present. Relations with the Poles and Yugoslavs fluctuated, but that was better than a posture of complete hostility on their part. He was willing to take the political heat of welcoming Yugoslav President Tito to the White House, even though Tito's relations with Moscow had improved; he acted swiftly to send medical aid to the victims of an earthquake at Skopje; he greeted a Polish boys' choir in the flower garden; he sought economic aid for both countries; and he fought with the Congress over his insistence that it grant both countries the same tariff treatment it gave to all others. He fully sympathized with his Ambassador to Yugoslavia, George Kennan, who resigned because of the "contradictory, unproductive and unsatisfactory" mishmash the Congress had made out of Kennedy's Yugoslav policy.

All in all, this was a sophisticated approach to foreign affairs: helping some Communist nations but not others, befriending neutrals as well as allies, financing socialist projects as well as private, aiding some revolutionaries and some reactionaries, and approving of some one-party governments but not of others. It was too sophisticated an approach for those elements in the country and Congress whose solution to all problems continued to be the withholding of our aid on grounds of misbehavior. "These countries are poor," the President stressed once again in his final news conference of 1963, "they are nationalist, they are proud, they are in many cases radical. I don't think threats from Capitol Hill bring the results which are frequently hoped. . . . I don't regard the struggle as over and I don't think it's probably going to be over for this century." Then he summed it all up rather simply: "I think it is a very dangerous, untidy world. I think we will have to live with it."

CHAPTER XX

THE WORLD LEADER

THE ELECTION in 1960 of an American President young enough to be their son was greeted by most of the world's other leaders with mingled misgivings and curiosity. At least two of them—West Germany's Konrad Adenauer and Free China's Chiang Kai-shek—had been almost openly pro-Nixon. The Soviet Union's Nikita Khrushchev had dismissed both candidates as "a pair of boots—which is the better, the right or the left boot?" But friendly, unfriendly and neutral leaders alike sought in 1961 to learn more about John Kennedy. To assert his own position, to allay their suspicions and to "begin anew the quest for peace," he set out promptly to improve the channels of communication.

Khrushchev made plain to U.S. Ambassador Llewellyn Thompson in Moscow his interest in meeting with Kennedy as soon as possible and sent him a cordial message upon his inauguration as he had upon his election. Promptly thereafter, in a gesture designed to renew Soviet-American communications, clogged since the Paris Summit failure, he released two downed U.S. airmen imprisoned virtually incommunicado since the previous summer. "This action," said Kennedy, announcing the heartening news in a low-key, matter-of-fact manner at his first news conference, "removes a serious obstacle to improvement of Soviet-American relations." Without calling it a *quid pro quo*, he made clear that U-2 and other aircraft flights over the Soviet Union would not be resumed.[1]

On February 11 the President assessed our relations with the Soviets

1 He had previously decided against the flights anyway on the grounds that the results were no longer worth the risk. He was genuinely disturbed on the four occasions during his term when mechanical or other failures caused accidental penetration of Soviet air space, and he instigated the adoption of more rigid safeguards.

in a lengthy White House meeting with Rusk, Bundy and four experts who had served as Ambassadors to Moscow: Thompson, whom he continued in that position; Charles "Chip" Bohlen, whom he continued as the State Department's Russian expert; George Kennan, whom he made Ambassador in the sensitive listening post of Yugoslavia; and Averell Harriman, whose first post under Kennedy was Ambassador at Large. None of these men, least of all the President, wanted a formal "summit" conference between the two heads of government. While such a conference, in Kennedy's long-held view, might be necessary when war threatened, or useful as "a place where agreements . . . achieved at a lower level could be finally, officially approved . . . a summit is not a place to carry on negotiations which involve details." Those had to be conducted through quieter channels and by full-time experts. Summitry raised undue hopes and public attention, thus producing unjustified relaxations, disappointments or tensions. It injected considerations of personal prestige, face-saving and politics into grave international conflicts.

But the February 11 discussion distinguished between a personal, informal meeting with the Soviet leader and a summit with serious negotiations. It would be useful, all agreed, for the President to size up Khrushchev, to find out face to face his views on a test ban and other issues, to gain a firsthand impression against which he could then judge Khrushchev's words and deeds, and to make more clear and precise than his letters could do or his predecessor had done the vital interests for which this nation would fight. It was Kennedy's "basic premise," as he later described it at a news conference, "that the channels of communication should be kept very widely open," to "lessen the chance of danger," to prevent the kind of miscalculation which had led to three wars in his lifetime, and to achieve the kind of understanding which could prevent a nuclear war and in time abate the cold war.

Consequently, when Thompson returned to Moscow he carried with him a letter expressing hope for such a meeting. It was not inspired, as some believed, by Kennedy's later setback at the Bay of Pigs; nor did the President entirely agree with those who thought that incident cast a shadow over the conference. He thought on balance that it provided all the more reason for the Soviet Chairman to be disabused of any misapprehension that Kennedy was either reckless or weak of will. "I had read his speeches and his published policies," the President said.

> I had been advised on his views. I had been told by other leaders of the West . . . what manner of man he was. But . . . it is my duty to make decisions that no adviser and no ally can make for me . . . to see that these decisions are as informed as possible, that they are based on as much direct, firsthand knowledge as possible. . . . At the same time, I wanted to make certain Mr.

Khrushchev knew this country and its policies . . . to present our views to him directly, precisely, realistically, and with an opportunity for discussion and clarification.

VIENNA

The Kennedy-Khrushchev meeting in Vienna on June 3 and 4, 1961, was neither a victory nor a defeat for either side. It was, as the American President hoped, useful. It was, as the Soviet Chairman later reported, necessary. It was not, both would have agreed, a turning point of any kind.

In preparation for the meeting, Kennedy devoted both office and spare time to a review of all previous conversations held with Khrushchev, interviewed those who had met him, studied his personal ways as well as his policies and conducted intensive surveys of all the nuances and background of every issue likely to come up. In Paris the night before and on the plane en route to Vienna he continued to study right up to the last minute.

Some skeptics had been fearful that Khrushchev had sought the meeting in order to create another international incident. Such was not the case. Both men were unyielding but courteous. Both argued vigorously but civilly. Generally, Kennedy carried the conversational initiative, introducing topics, keeping them specific, bringing straying discussions back to the question and pressing Khrushchev for answers. Khrushchev usually talked at much greater length. Kennedy usually talked with much greater precision. Both often cited history and quotations, although Khrushchev's language was far more colorful and lively. Between the two men, despite the divergence of their views, a curious kind of rapport was established which was to help continue their dialogue in the months and years that followed.

Three meals presented the only real opportunity for idle personal conversation. Kennedy was the host for lunch on the first day at the American Embassy. Khrushchev hosted the second in the Soviet Embassy. A splendiferous dinner and after-dinner ballet at Vienna's glittering Schönbrunn Palace were arranged by the Austrian Government for the evening in between. (The President almost sat in Mrs. Khrushchev's lap through a mix-up in seating directions, and the Chairman kept Jacqueline amused with almost nonstop humor and a promise to send an offspring of the dogs flown in space.)

During these meals the conversation was light. When Kennedy, lighting up a cigar, dropped the match behind Khrushchev's chair, the latter asked, "Are you trying to set me on fire?" Reassured that this was not the case, he smiled: "Ah, a capitalist, not an incendiary." Kennedy noted that not one of the top capitalists of industry and finance whom Khrushchev had met in 1959 had voted Democratic in 1960. "They are very clever," responded Khrushchev, certain it was all a trick. When Khrushchev said that the medal he was wearing was for the Lenin Peace Prize, Kennedy retorted with a smile: "I hope you keep it."

Khrushchev chatted about his country's need for fertilizer and corn, its new emphasis on submarines instead of surface craft and the President's special message to Congress the previous month. It was clear that he had read—or had been briefed on—all Kennedy's major speeches and messages, and a good many obscure Congressional debates as well. Kennedy's defense requests, he said, put pressure on him to increase his forces, just as both of them were under pressure from their scientists and military to resume nuclear tests. "But we will wait for you to resume testing and, if you do, we will."

The Soviet leader also made clear his belief in summitry. If the heads of state cannot resolve problems, how can officials at a lower level? He liked as much personal contact as possible, he said, no matter how able one's ambassadors might be—just as natural love is better than love through interpreters. While it was difficult for both of them to speak on behalf of their "jealous" allies, the President would surely not be concerned by objections from an ally such as tiny Luxembourg—and Russia, too, had allies "whom I do not wish to name" but who, "if they were to raise a belligerent voice, would not frighten anyone."

Describing the historic space orbit of Soviet Cosmonaut Gagarin, Khrushchev said they had feared the psychological effects of such a flight on Gagarin's ability to take over the controls. Consequently they gave him sealed instructions coded in such a way that only a normal person could decode them. He was even more doubtful, he said, about going to the moon. Perhaps the two nations should go together, the President suggested. Khrushchev first replied in the negative, but then added half-jokingly: "All right—why not?"

The Chairman said he had respected Kennedy's predecessor. He was almost sure that Eisenhower had not known about the U-2 flight deliberately designed to sour Soviet-American relations but had taken the responsibility in a spirit of chivalry. Eisenhower's trip to the U.S.S.R. had necessarily been canceled, but he hoped Kennedy would come "when the time is ripe. . . . The road is open." Then he could see whomever and whatever he liked. For the Soviets were unafraid for their system. But Mr. Nixon, Khrushchev said, had thought he could convert the Soviet people to capitalism by showing them a kitchen that never existed, even in the U.S. "I apologize for referring to a citizen of the United States," he said, "but only Nixon could think of such nonsense."[2]

[2] Earlier he had joked about what an insult it was to Soviet Foreign Minister Gromyko to say he looked like Nixon.

The Soviet people admire the American people and their techno-logical success, Khrushchev went on, and had decorated American engi-neers who helped them build their country after the Revolution. One of them, he said, had later visited the Soviet Union and mentioned that he was building houses in Turkey. Of course, the Soviets knew "that in fact he was building bases there—but this is a matter for his own conscience." Toasting the President's health, he envied his youth. "If I were your age, I would devote even more energy to our cause. Never-theless, even at sixty-seven, I am not renouncing the competition."

In his toast at the second luncheon, with both men more preoccupied by the gravity of their problems, Khrushchev said he would "raise my glass to their solution. You are a religious man and would say that God should help us in this endeavor. For my part, I want common sense to help us."

Kennedy's toasts at both luncheons were confined to expressions of hope for peace and understanding and to a recognition of the special obligations which rested upon the two leaders. "I hope we will not leave Vienna," he concluded on the second day, "a city that is symbolic be-cause it indicates that equitable solutions can be found, with a possi-bility of either country being confronted with a challenge to its vital national interests."

The talks themselves began with the two men recalling their brief introduction at a Senate Foreign Relations Committee meeting during Khrushchev's 1959 tour of the United States. The President mentioned that the Chairman had commented on the then Senator's youthful ap-pearance, adding that he had aged since then. Khrushchev doubted that he had really said that, because he knew that young people want to look older and older people like to look younger. In his own youth, he added, he was offended when someone misjudged his age because of his youth-ful appearance, but he began to gray at twenty-two and that ended the problem.

The President immediately turned to his central thesis of the two major nuclear powers avoiding situations which committed their vital interests in a direct confrontation from which neither could back down. Time and again he returned to that point during the two days of talks. Khrushchev complained that John Foster Dulles had wanted to liqui-date Communism. Kennedy replied that the real problem was the Soviet attempt to impose Communism on others. Not true, said Khrushchev, they expected it to triumph as a social development. The Soviet Union was against imposing its policy on other states. As feudalism gave way to capitalism, so the latter was being challenged by Communism.

Historical inevitability is not demonstrated by a minority's seizing power against the will of the people, replied the President, even if they are called "wars of liberation." The death of systems such as feudalism and monarchy had brought wars in the past, and today both our countries would suffer in a new world war. The competition of ideologies should be conducted without affecting the vital security interests of the two countries; and he repeated his view of the dangers of miscalculation.

At this Khrushchev bristled. He did not like the term miscalculation or the President's repeated usage of it, he said. Was the President saying that Communism should exist only in Communist countries, that its development elsewhere would be regarded by the U.S. as a hostile act by the Soviet Union? The United States wants the U.S.S.R., he said, to sit like a schoolboy with hands on the table, but there is no immunization against ideas. Even if he should renounce Communism, his friends would ostracize him but the doctrine of Communism would keep on developing. He didn't even know who some of the indigenous Communist leaders were, he said; he was too busy at home. Smiling again, he suggested that the Germans be blamed for producing Marx and Engels. It was Soviet policy, he repeated, that ideas should not be imposed by war or arms.

Mao Tse-tung, the President interjected, has said that power was at the end of a rifle. No, replied Khrushchev, Mao could not have said that. He is a Marxist and Marxists have always been against war. In any event, said the President, miscalculation simply referred to an erroneous prediction of the other side's next move. It applied equally to all countries. He had made a misjudgment earlier at the Bay of Pigs. Khrushchev had to make many judgments about the West. The whole purpose of their meeting was to introduce more precision into those judgments.

Khrushchev gave no ground on this or any other point. He returned time and again to the thesis that the Soviet Union could not be held responsible for every spontaneous uprising or Communist trend. Nasser, Nehru, Nkrumah and Sukarno, he pointed out, had all said they wanted their countries to develop along Socialist lines. But what kind of Socialist was Nasser when he kept Communists in jail? Nor did Nehru favor the Communist Party in India. Nevertheless the Soviet Union helped them all and that was proof of its policy of noninterference. He predicted a popular overthrow of the Shah of Iran but asserted that Russia would have nothing to do with it. The Cubans turned against the United States, he said, because capitalist circles supported Batista. The Bay of Pigs landing only increased Cuba's fears that the Americans would impose another Batista. Castro was not a Communist but U.S. policy could make him one, said Khrushchev, adding that as a Communist himself (not a born Marxist, he said, but the capitalists had made him one) he could not foretell which way Castro would go. And if the United States felt itself threatened by tiny Cuba, what was the U.S.S.R. to do about Turkey and Iran?

Cuba alone was not regarded as a threat, replied the President, making clear he held no brief for Batista. It was Castro's announced intentions to subvert the hemisphere that could be dangerous. Had Castro been selected by a free choice and not interfered with the choice of others, the U.S. might have endorsed him. What would Khrushchev's reaction be to a pro-Western government in Poland, which might well be the result of a free election?

It was disrespectful of the President, said Khrushchev, to talk that way about Poland, whose election system was more democratic than America's. In the United States we have a choice, said Kennedy. U.S. political parties, responded the Chairman, are only for the purpose of deluding the people. There is no real difference between them. And what about the U.S. support of reactionary, undemocratic regimes —Nationalist China, Pakistan, Spain, Iran, Turkey, and the oppression of colonies? The Shah of Iran said that his power was given to him by God. Everybody knew how this power was seized by the Shah's father, who was not God but a sergeant in the Iranian Army. The arms America gave to China after World War II to fight the Communists, he said, were not successful because the troops wouldn't fight against the people. Chiang Kai-shek became a sort of transfer point for American arms to Mao Tse-tung. The U.S. should beware of setting a precedent of intervening in the internal affairs of other countries.[3] Once, said the Chairman, the United States was a leader in the fight for freedom, so revolutionary in its creation that the Russian czar refused to recognize it for twenty-six years. Now the United States refused to recognize New China, indicating how things had changed.

The President, in replying, did not pretend that all our allies were as democratic as the United States. Some of our associations are for strategic reasons, he said, citing Yugoslavia (to Mr. K.'s discomfort) as well as Spain. But he recognized, he said, the advantage of those on the side of change. He was for change and was elected in the 1960 campaign on the basis of advocating change. He had supported Algerian independence as a Senator. He had incurred the wrath of Portugal and other allies for supporting self-determination in their colonies. The independence movement in Africa was unmistakable, unprecedented and a tribute to peaceful change. But the "wars of liberation" Khrushchev had endorsed in January did not always reflect the will of the people and they might dangerously involve the great powers.

The United States, replied Khrushchev, suffers from delusions of

[3] The President resisted the temptation, he later told me, to cite at this point Khrushchev's "precedent" in Hungary.

grandeur. It is so rich and powerful that it believes it has special rights and can afford not to recognize the rights of others. The Soviet Union cannot accept the thesis of "don't poke your nose" because whenever the rights of people are infringed upon, the Soviet Union will render assistance.

But he stuck to his story that his country opposed interference in the choice of local populations. The Communists have had great experience in fighting guerrilla warfare, he said. If guerrilla units should be sent from the outside and not be supported by the people, that would be a hopeless undertaking. But if guerrilla troops were local troops belonging to that country, then every bush was their ally.

He had not been authorized or requested to speak on Red China's behalf, Mr. K. said twice, but he wanted to make clear his own belief that Red China belonged both in the UN and on Formosa. No, said the President, withdrawal of American forces and support from Formosa would impair our strategic position in Asia. That proves that Red China will have to fight for Formosa, said Khrushchev, and that was a sad thing. It forced him to doubt America's sincerity about peaceful co-existence. Kennedy might even occupy Crimea and say that this would improve his strategic position. That would be the policy of Dulles. Times had changed and this was doomed to failure. Were he in Red China's position, he said, he already would have fought for Formosa. After the Revolution Russia had fought off stronger countries similarly interfering in her territory. Like colonial battles for liberation, he added, such wars were not aggressive, they were holy wars.

Three specific substantive issues dominated the discussion: Laos, a nuclear test ban and Berlin. On the subject of Laos, as noted in a later chapter, Kennedy's persistence helped pin Khrushchev down on their only substantial agreement, a small but unexpected gain. Khrushchev claimed that the President had ordered and then rescinded a landing of U.S. Marines in Laos. There was no such order, said the President. The Chairman said he had assumed it from press reports.

His administration did not want to increase U.S. commitments but decrease them, said Kennedy. There was no point in raking over the past history to which both sides might have some objections. That was not an issue in Vienna. Very well, said Khrushchev, but Kennedy could not avoid responsibility by saying all the commitments were made before he took office. The Soviet Union had rescinded all the unreasonable decisions made by the previous governments. By overruling Molotov on Austria, for example, he had made a peace treaty possible. Westerners, he went on, were much better than Easterners at making threats in a refined way, talking about "commitments" and hinting at Marines. But the law of physics says that every action causes counterreactions. Nevertheless, he agreed finally that Laos was not worth a war to either power, that a government both sides could accept was called for and that the cease-fire should be observed.

On banning nuclear weapons tests there was no agreement. Any more than three on-site inspections a year would be for espionage purposes, said Mr. K., adding his belief that that was what the Pentagon had wanted all along—and that Eisenhower's open-skies proposal was a part of that scheme. Moreover, he said, events that year in the Congo had taught the Russians that no UN neutral or other third party could be trusted to inspect their actions without being subject to a veto. If the United States wanted him to be fired, he joked, it should pursue that line.

The President asked him whether he believed it was impossible to find any person strictly neutral between both countries. The Chairman answered in the affirmative. In that case, said Kennedy, the Troika veto would leave both sides uncertain whether the other was secretly testing, and the Senate would never approve such a treaty. Then let us have complete disarmament, said Khrushchev, and the U.S.S.R. will drop the Troika and subscribe to any controls as developed by the U.S. without even looking at the document. Almost any other measure would be a better beginning than a nuclear test ban, and he listed the prohibition of nuclear weapons, their manufacture and military bases.[4]

Russia's alleged fear of espionage, replied the President, will pale in comparison to the problem of a half-dozen other countries developing nuclear weapons while disarmament talks drag on. He cited a Chinese proverb that a journey of a thousand miles begins with one step, and urged Khrushchev to take that step. Apparently you know the Chinese very well, said the Chairman, but I, too, know them quite well. You might get to know them even better, the President shot back. I already know them very well, concluded Khrushchev.

The grimmest talks were on Germany and Berlin. As noted in a subsequent chapter, Khrushchev was belligerent, Kennedy was unyielding. It was this portion of the conference that most sobered the President.

"I did not come away," he later said, "with any feeling that . . . an understanding . . . —so that we do not go over the brink . . . —would be easy to reach." To more than one newsman he described Khrushchev's demands and his own determination not to give in. If Khrushchev had meant what he said about Berlin, the prospects for nuclear war were now very real—for Kennedy had meant what he said. He was discouraged also that Khrushchev clung to all the old myths—about inspection as the equivalent of espionage, about West Germany as a source of danger, about the United States as a supporter of colonialism and about Kennedy as a tool of Wall Street.

4 At this point Gromyko corrected the interpreter, possibly for policy reasons, saying that the Chairman had not mentioned manufacture—but Khrushchev said he had.

The Soviets and ourselves give wholly different meanings to the same words—war, peace, democracy, and popular will. We have wholly different views of right and wrong, of what is an internal affair and what is aggression, and, above all, of where the world is and where it is going.

With less than six months to prepare for a possible nuclear war over Berlin, he wanted no newsman or citizen to be under any impression that the complacency he had battled so long could be tolerated any longer, or that there were any easy, magic ways to deflect the Soviet drive. He wanted Congress, dawdling on his foreign aid and related programs, awakened to support his next moves. He wanted no one to think that the surface cordiality in Vienna justified any notion of a new "Spirit of Geneva, 1955," or "Spirit of Camp David, 1959." But he may have "overmanaged" the news. His private briefings of the press were so grim, while Khrushchev in public appeared so cheerful, that a legend soon arose that Vienna had been a traumatic, shattering experience, that Khrushchev had bullied and browbeaten the President and that Kennedy was depressed and disheartened.

In fact, as several newsmen would later report on the basis of Khrushchev interviews, the Soviet Chairman had found Kennedy "tough," especially on Berlin. He liked the President personally, his frankness and his sense of humor—but Eisenhower had been more reasonable, he said, and, until the U-2 incident, easier to get along with.

Actually, neither Kennedy nor Khrushchev emerged victorious or defeated, cheerful or shaken. Each had probed the other for weakness and found none. Khrushchev had not been swayed by Kennedy's reason and charm, nor had Kennedy so expected. Kennedy had not been panicked by Khrushchev's tough talk—and had Khrushchev so expected, he learned differently. ("We parted," he told a reporter, "each sticking to his own opinion.") There was no progress toward ending the cold war— and neither had expected any. But each made a deep and lasting impression on the other. Each was unyielding on his nation's interests. Each had seen for himself, as a leader must, the nature of his adversary and his arguments; and both realized more than ever the steadfastness of the other's stand and the difficulty of reaching agreement.

CONTINUED CONTACTS

The President, after a one-day stopover in London for a report to Macmillan, a family christening and a dinner with the Queen, returned to Washington for his own report to the American people. The speech was hammered out overnight in the plane and during the few hours he was back in the White House, with less time for the usual departmental clearances and cautions. The words "sober" and "somber" appeared often in a very candid text.

I will tell you now that it was a very sober two days. There was no discourtesy, no loss of tempers, no threats or ultimatums by either side; no advantage or concession was either gained or given; no major decision was either planned or taken; no spectacular progress was either achieved or pretended. . . .

. . . neither of us tried merely to please the other, to agree merely to be agreeable, to say what the other wanted to hear. . . .

Our views contrasted sharply but at least we knew better at the end where we both stood. . . .

At least the channels of communication were opened more fully . . . and the men on whose decision the peace in part depends have agreed to remain in contact.

But contact never again included a personal meeting. In September of that same year, as tensions mounted, and as the conference of neutral nations at Belgrade called for a summit, Khrushchev—who enjoyed the personal and national prestige of the summit spotlight—said publicly he was willing to have a new meeting. Similar suggestions were from time to time made by the Soviet Chairman both privately and publicly during the following two years, especially in 1963 after the signing of the Test Ban Treaty and in 1962 before the U.S. resumed nuclear tests. Prime Minister Macmillan of Great Britain also kept hoping for a summit of the three nuclear powers, and pressed Kennedy particularly hard early in 1962.

But the President stood fast. He told Macmillan that they should wait for some definite progress. He told Khrushchev—who often seemed to agree that a fruitless get-together would be a mistake—that they should wait until some specific breakthrough could be agreed upon. He proposed privately in early 1962 that such a meeting be held to conclude a test-ban treaty, but no agreement on a treaty was possible at that time. He told his negotiators at the Moscow meeting in July, 1963, that they could commit him if necessary—but he avoided it when it was not necessary. He told the press that he would go to a summit "to ratify an agreement . . . [or] if we were on the brink of war . . . [or] if I thought it was in our national interest." But he had no need for another personal size-up, retained all his earlier objections to formal summit diplomacy, and achieved solid agreements in 1963 "through skilled negotiators, and that is really the best way unless there is an overwhelming crisis . . . or some new factor." Asked at a spring 1962 press conference about written reports that he would eat his words, he replied: "I'm going to have a dinner for all the people who have written it, and we will see who eats what."

Similarly he resisted all Khrushchev's hints about a visit to the Soviet Union, despite talk of an exceedingly warm welcome from the Russian people and bear-hunting with the Chairman. After the nuclear test ban and other agreements had been reached in 1963, such a trip became possible; but in 1961-1962 he would not go while the two powers were in dangerous conflict over Berlin and Cuba. When events permitted it, he wrote the Chairman, he would take great pleasure in such a visit, for he had visited the Soviet Union in 1939 very briefly and would look forward to seeing the changes that had occurred since then.

The two men remained in active, personal contact without another meeting. The means was a unique, private correspondence initiated by Khrushchev by a letter sent September 29, 1961, from his Black Sea resort. Although the publication of this correspondence could no longer affect the power or plans of either man, it is important that future Soviet leaders feel free to make private proposals via this channel without fear of their future use. Consequently I shall confine myself to a discussion of the nature and purpose of these messages and quote no passages from Khrushchev's letters which involve any substantive proposals.

Khrushchev had planned to write, his first letter said, earlier in the summer after Kennedy's meeting in Washington with his son-in-law and a Soviet press officer. But Kennedy's July speech to the nation on Berlin had been so belligerent in its nature that it led to an exchange of militant actions taken, he said, under pressures in both countries which must be restrained. He emphasized almost pridefully the special burdens resting on their shoulders as the leaders of the two most influential and mighty states. It might be useful to have a purely informal, personal correspondence, he wrote, which would by-pass the foreign office bureaucracies in both countries, omit the usual propaganda for public consumption and state positions without a backward glance at the press. If Kennedy did not agree, he could consider that this first letter did not exist. The Chairman in any event would not refer to the correspondence publicly. The letter, which had opened "Dear Mr. President," was signed: "Accept my respects, N. Khrushchev, Chairman of the Council of Ministers of the U.S.S.R."

The letter was not delivered through the usual diplomatic channels, and its arrival caused both sensation and speculation among the handful of advisers whom the President informed of its existence. The proposed correspondence fitted Kennedy's idea of open channels of communication. Possibly it could lessen the danger of a showdown on Berlin while hopeful letters were being exchanged. But he knew that it had its dangers. A strongly negative U.S. reply on Berlin might precipitate Soviet action.

A strongly positive reply might be privately shown to the Germans and French as proof that we were conspiring behind their backs. If Kennedy revealed the correspondence to the leaky Alliance, it would be shut off. If he did not, Khrushchev might use it to split the West. "The answer to this letter," said Ambassador Bohlen, "may be the most important letter the President will ever write."

Some two weeks later the President completed his reply at Cape Cod. Like Khrushchev, he opened with a chatty note about his retreat, the children and their cousins, and the opportunity to get a clearer and quieter perspective away from the din of Washington. He welcomed the idea of a private correspondence, though making clear that the Secretary of State and a few others would be privy to it. A personal, informal but meaningful exchange of views in frank, realistic and fundamental terms, he wrote, could usefully supplement the more formal and official channels. Inasmuch as the letters would be private, and could never convert the other, they could also, he added, be free from the polemics of the "Cold War" debate. That debate would, of course, proceed, but their messages would be directed only to each other.

In this letter as in others that followed, the President picked out points in Khrushchev's letter with which he could agree, sometimes re-stating them or interpreting them more to his own liking. By Kennedy's standards, his was a long letter—nearly ten pages single-spaced—but not nearly so long as Khrushchev's. He kept his letter cordial and hopeful, with a highly personal tone and repeated first-person references (which were rare in his speeches). He agreed with the Chairman's emphasis on their special obligation to the world to prevent another war. They were not personally responsible for the events at the conclusion of World War II which led to the present situation in Berlin, he added, but they would be held responsible if they were unable to deal peacefully with that situation.

Having opened with "Dear Mr. Chairman," he closed with best wishes from his family to Khrushchev's and the expression of his deep hope that, through this exchange of letters and otherwise, relations between the two nations might be improved, making concrete progress toward the realization of a just and enduring peace. That, he said, was their greatest joint responsibility and their greatest opportunity.

In the two years that followed, this correspondence flourished, even when its existence became known after the Cuban missile crisis. At times separate letters arrived from Khrushchev almost simultane-ously on different topics. Substantively the correspondence accom-plished very little that was concrete, if the special letters exchanged over the Cuban missile crisis are excluded. The arguments exchanged—on Laos, nuclear testing, Cuba, Vietnam and Berlin—did not differ in essence, though they did sometimes in tone, from the arguments their envoys or even speeches exchanged. On more than one occasion Kennedy had to remind the Chairman that this private and informal channel of communication should not be used to repeat the usual arguments and assertions normally reserved for public debates and propaganda. While this was not, he made clear, a substitute for a genuine negotiating forum, it should be used to identify more clearly the areas of agreement and disagreement, not to cast blame, repeat slogans or argue history, personalities and press reports.

Khrushchev's letters varied. At times they were even tougher than his public statements. Some seemed to have been drafted by an aide and contained the usual bargaining positions. Others were more candid, colorful, anecdotal and lengthy, placing more emphasis on his personal responsibilities and activities. Those, we were certain, he dictated himself. His references to American press reports and Congressional debates often showed surprising knowledge of detail. His illustrations were often amusing. The U.S.-U.S.S.R. deadlock on Berlin, for example, he compared to two stupid and stubborn goats head to head on a narrow bridge across an abyss, neither giving way and both falling to their doom. De Gaulle's influence over Adenauer was compared to the Russian peasant who caught a bear barehanded but could neither bring it back nor make the bear let loose of him. When Khrushchev's language was sharp, it was nevertheless courteous, usually placing blame not on Kennedy but on "certain circles" and "hotheads" in the United States and the West.

Kennedy's letters were also cordial, but shorter, more direct and—despite the lack of concrete results—among the most persuasive he had ever written. He kept Khrushchev peppered with appealing arguments to answer, with reasons for delaying a German peace treaty and with hope for an ultimate agreement. The correspondence avoided the harsh atmosphere of Vienna, where both men had felt that all appeals had been exhausted and that a showdown was next.

Inasmuch as Khrushchev was told that our Secretary of State and Ambassador to Moscow were informed of the correspondence, we speculated about whether he continued to use this private channel—for a time with a cloak-and-dagger atmosphere of delivery—to keep it from someone in *his* government, possibly someone in the Presidium or military. On the one occasion when I served as contact, Khrushchev's courier—a lesser Soviet functionary in Washington, Georgi Bolshakov, who handed me a folded newspaper containing the letter, already translated, as we met and walked in downtown Washington—emphasized to me that the letter's proposal (a minor but hopeful Berlin concession) was personally that of the Chairman. Khrushchev believed, he said, that his best efforts came from his own pen, not from Foreign Office experts "who specialized in why something had not worked forty years ago"—and he assumed Kennedy operated on the same basis.

There were, of course, the usual formal letters and diplomatic notes as well. The State Department experts expressed their traditional doubts about any avoidance of their normal channels. Eisenhower had also corresponded with Zhukov, Bulganin and Khrushchev; but those letters were recognized as a formal, governmental correspondence and were usually public. Kennedy rejected all advice that he terminate the correspondence; and the familiarity of this private channel facilitated, in my opinion, the exchange of letters that ended the Cuban missile crisis.

The letters also enabled both men to judge the other more accurately. Khrushchev told Salinger and others that he had acquired a healthy respect as well as a personal liking for Kennedy, despite their differences. He told Castro, according to one source, that "Kennedy is a man you can talk with." He appreciated Kennedy's undemagogic approach and—certainly after October, 1962—believed in his determination.

Kennedy in turn wholly rejected the popular images of Khrushchev as a coarse buffoon or lovable figure. The Chairman, in his view, was a clever, tough, shrewd adversary. "A national inferiority complex," said JFK, "makes him act extra tough at times." But Khrushchev was aware, Kennedy believed—certainly after October, 1962—of the caution with which they must both move in an age of mutual nuclear capability. He found the Chairman admirably uninterested in arguing over matters too small to concern him or too large to be changed. Khrushchev, he noted, shared some of his own complaints of internal pressures from the military, from other politicians and from associated countries. He was interested in Harriman's report, after a visit to Moscow in 1963, that the Soviet Chairman—unlike Stalin, whom Harriman had also known—was willing to walk openly among the people, appeared to share a mutual affection with them, and maintained a stern dictatorial discipline without the Stalinist atmosphere of terror. Asked his evaluation of Khrushchev's political status, the President replied simply: "I don't think we know precisely, but I would suppose he has his good months and bad months—like we all do."

The President's contacts with the Soviet Union were not confined to Khrushchev. He talked regularly with Soviet Ambassador (as of early 1962) Dobrynin, who combined a more genial attitude than his predecessor with a more sophisticated understanding of Western ways and a closer rapport with the Chairman. Dobrynin also saw Thompson and Rusk regularly, and talked with the Attorney General and White House aides. A variety of special trips to Moscow—by Rusk, Harriman, Salinger, McCloy, Udall and others—added to the increased exchange of views.

The President met on several occasions with Khrushchev's son-in-law, Aleksei Adzhubei, editor of *Izvestia* and a member of the Central Committee. ("He combines," said the President, "the two hazardous professions of politics and journalism.") Welcoming Adzhubei and his wife to his January 31, 1962, news conference in his first opening statement, he then devoted the second, as previously planned, to praising the Punta del Este OAS session for denouncing Marxism-Leninism in this hemisphere. Answering a query about a Republican Congressman's attack on Salinger's trip to Moscow, he commented: "I'm sure that some people in the Soviet Union are concerned about Mr. Adzhubei's visits abroad" (undoubtedly an accurate surmise).

Adzhubei was a useful if sometimes arrogant channel to the Chairman, and the possessor of an excellent sense of humor.[5] His most valuable role, however, was as a channel to the Russian people. Under an agreement inspired by Salinger, Adzhubei was granted late in 1961 an exclusive two-hour interview with the President and published it in full, subject to check by our Russian-language experts, on the front page of *Izvestia*. It was the first time in history that the Russian people had been directly and fully exposed to an American President's views on Soviet policy—and Kennedy mixed incisive reason with quiet reproof.

Adzhubei, representing both of his hazardous professions, made a speech out of most of his previously prepared questions and another speech in response to most answers. "He is afraid," said the President afterward, "that his colleagues on the Central Committee won't think so much of his scoop when they see what he has to print on the front page."

What *Izvestia* had to print was Kennedy's statement that the great threat to peace "is the effort by the Soviet Union to communize . . . the entire world . . . [and] to impose Communism by force"; that the Soviet Union had resumed nuclear tests even while its representatives were at the bargaining table; that if it would look "only to its national interest and to providing a better life for its people," all would be well. Emphasizing the threats posed by Soviet moves in Berlin and elsewhere, he stressed constantly his desire for peace, his sympathy with Russian losses in World War II and his desire to work out a solution in Central Europe which would end all fears for both sides. "Our two peoples have the most

[5] During a long dinner he accepted in good grace all the anti-Communist jokes I had heard, and supplied a few of his own from their "Armenian Radio"; and the following day, when we flew together on a Presidential staff plane, he responded to my suggestion that he was now in the hands of the U.S. Air Force with the smiling reply: "I know they will not deliberately crash the plane with Kennedy's Assistant aboard!"

to gain from peace," he said, speaking to the larger Russian audience without forgetting his American and Allied readers also.

He reassured the Russians that West Germany would not be armed with nuclear weapons, expressed hope for more Soviet-American trade in calmer times and exposed the fallacies in the Soviet position on disarmament. He was at his best when asked to imagine how he would look at West Germany if he were a veteran of the Soviet Navy instead of the American:

> If I were a Soviet veteran, I would see that West Germany has only . . . a fraction of the Soviet forces . . . [all] under the international control of NATO . . . and [poses] no . . . military threat now to the Soviet Union. . . . Then I would look at the power of the United States . . . and I would say that the important thing is for the Soviet Union and the United States not to get into a war, which would destroy both of our systems. So as a Soviet veteran, I would want the Soviet Union to reach an agreement with the United States which recognizes the interests and the commitments of the United States as well as our own, and not attempt to enforce singlehandedly a new situation . . . which would be against previous commitments we had made. . . . I would feel that the security of the Soviet Union was well protected, and that the important thing now is to reach an accord with the United States, our ally during that second war.

The interview, faithfully reprinted, was reported by our embassy to have caused quite a stir in Moscow. Those unable to buy newspapers clustered around the outdoor bulletin boards where the front page was tacked up. Among those who purchased the paper, reported my brother Tom, a Deputy Director of USIA, after his visit to Moscow with Salinger several months later, many still carried well-worn copies in their pockets for cautious reference. Kennedy had come through loud and clear.

Kennedy and Salinger then moved to carry communication with the Russian people still further. Agreement was reached early in 1962 on a TV exchange between Kennedy and Khrushchev. Each was to tape a film in his own office, without limitation as to subject matter and supplying his own translator's "voice-over." Films would then be exchanged one week ahead of their joint showing in both countries without either having an opportunity to answer or edit the other's remarks. The order of appearance was up to the home country's government. Kennedy was pleased. The American people, he noted, had far more TV sets than the Russians, but they also had far more exposure to the opposing point of view.

The show was scheduled for March 25, 1962, to be announced March

15, to be filmed March 8. I began working on the President's script on March 7. No cold war polemics were to be included, but America's position on disarmament, wars of liberation and similar issues was to be set forth frankly. The chief emphasis was on our desire for peace, our friendship for the people of the Soviet Union and our common interests. The President hoped to use a few Russian words, to invoke the magic name of FDR and to ask the Soviets to reverse the course that Stalin had started.

That very evening one of Khrushchev's private messages arrived. He was deeply offended, he said, by the President's address a few days earlier announcing that the United States was resuming full-scale nuclear tests. The TV exchange was off. Bolshakov told me a few days later that his government had been obligated to say a few harsh words. But these were comparatively low-key, he said. The Chairman still liked the President and the TV exchange would be held later. It never was.

THE WESTERN ALLIANCE

Kennedy had set out early in 1961 to establish personal contacts not only with his chief adversary but with his chief partners in the Atlantic Alliance. The Western leader whom he saw first, liked best and saw most often—four times in 1961 alone, seven times altogether—was British Prime Minister Harold Macmillan. They did not always see eye to eye. Macmillan was more eager for summits with Khrushchev and less eager to prepare for war at West Berlin. He was not sure whether his government could go along with American plans for NATO conventional forces; and Kennedy knew his government couldn't go along with Great Britain's recognition of Red China. From time to time, the President had to discourage the Prime Minister's temptation to play the role of peacemaker between East and West. And at least once Macmillan was briefly but violently angry—when he thought Kennedy's offer of American Hawk missiles to Israel had displaced a British sale.

But no differences of opinion or age prevented the two leaders from getting along famously. Each recognized in the other a keen understanding of history and politics—both international and domestic. Kennedy regarded Macmillan as a reliable ally, cooperative on issues that were difficult for him back home—such as the 1962 nuclear test resumptions. He enjoyed the Briton's amiable conversation and style, his often eloquent letters, their frequent talks by transatlantic phone and his delightful sense of humor. (He enjoyed retelling Macmillan's version of how Eisenhower "wouldn't let Nixon on the property.") A fondness developed between them which went beyond the necessities of alliance. A Washington luncheon in the spring of 1962, for example, was devoted mostly to a relaxed discussion of books and politics. Told after the Nassau agreement described below that he was "soft" on Macmillan, Kennedy replied: "If you were in that kind of trouble, you would want a friend."

This relationship was enhanced by the close personal ties and mutual respect linking Kennedy and Macmillan's Ambassador to the United States, David Ormsby-Gore. The Ambassador knew both the President and the Prime Minister so well that he was ideally equipped to interpret or even predict each one's reaction to the other's proposals. Cousin to the late Kathleen Kennedy's titled husband (who had been killed in the war), he was a long-time friend and contemporary of John Kennedy; and when in mid-1961 he was assigned to Washington, his handwritten note of delight pleased the President enormously. They saw each other frequently, on both a personal and official basis. Indeed, the President often consulted with or confided in the British Ambassador as he would a member of his own staff. "I trust David as I would my own Cabinet," he said.

Ormsby-Gore's advantage was heightened by the President's lesser confidence in the other two leading ambassadors of the Alliance, Wilhelm Grewe from West Germany and Hervé Alphand from France. Kennedy regarded both as extremely competent diplomats (although he was amused on one occasion when the social-minded Alphand chose Jacqueline as his pipeline for a message); and certainly the frequency of four-power ambassadorial meetings in Washington in 1961, principally on Berlin, was unprecedented. But he found Ormsby-Gore far more likely to know the thinking of his principal and far less likely to spill secrets and complaints to favored newsmen.

The other leader of a Western power most in contact with Kennedy was West Germany's Konrad Adenauer, eighty-five. Kennedy altered the Dulles policy of regarding the Chancellor as our principal European adviser and Adenauer knew it. Their differences on whether to negotiate with Khrushchev and how closely to follow De Gaulle were important and unresolved. The age barrier was formidable. "I sense I'm talking not only to a different generation," the President told me, "but to a different era, a different world." He found Adenauer hard to please and hard to budge, and his government hard put to keep a secret. The old Chancellor was constantly in need of repetitious reassurances of our love and honor. Yet Kennedy had a genuine liking and a deep respect for Adenauer. He admired what he had accomplished, and enjoyed his wit. Although Adenauer never seemed to feel fully confident of Kennedy, he respected the firm U.S. stand at Berlin in 1961 and at Cuba in 1962.

Charles de Gaulle and John Kennedy met only during their Paris talks in 1961. Their personal rapport on that occasion surprised them as well as everyone else. The President was fascinated by De Gaulle's role in previous history and his focus on future history. During a glittering white-tie dinner at Versailles Palace, he quizzed the General on his recollections of such former associates as Churchill and Roosevelt. Churchill, said De Gaulle, concerned himself only with short-range aims. "Like all Englishmen, he was a merchant, and bargained with Russia by giving concessions in the East in return for a free hand elsewhere. A fighter, he could on some days be extremely interesting and on others totally impossible." Roosevelt was always the charming aristocrat, said the General, an exceptional war leader who did have long-range views but often the wrong ones, as in the case of Russia. Despite "much superficial appearance of mutual affection," he said, FDR and Churchill basically did not see eye to eye.

"Of the two whom did you prefer?" asked Kennedy. The General's answer intrigued him. "I quarreled violently and bitterly with Churchill but always got on with him. I never quarreled with Roosevelt and never got on with him." When Kennedy remarked that both Churchill and Macmillan must have inherited some of their qualities from their American mothers, De Gaulle replied grandly that "pure English blood does not seem capable of producing a really strong man"; and he cited the cases of Disraeli and Lloyd George as well as Churchill.

Kennedy had prepared for his meeting with this "great captain of the West," as he called him—in a successful appeal to De Gaulle's known vanity—by reading selections from the General's Memoirs, which he later quoted back to him. There he found the basic convictions which the French President had maintained for nearly twenty years, and with which he would shock a strangely unprepared Western world in 1963: (1) a determination "to assure France primacy in Western Europe" and to block the efforts of the Anglo-Saxons (Britain and the United States) "to relegate us to a secondary place"; and (2) a belief in unifying all of Europe, including a disarmed Germany, and eventually a reconciled Russia, but never, never Great Britain. (Unification, moreover, could proceed only so far inasmuch as the only ultimate reality was the nation-state.) Britain—as proven by Churchill's rejection of his plea for an accord in 1945—was an island more interested in the open sea than in Europe, he felt, both a cause and an agent of "the United States's desire for hegemony" in Europe and Europe's former colonies.

"I was almost startled," Ambassador Gavin would remark later, "by the cold hardness of his unqualified statement that the U.S. should stay out of the affairs of Europe . . . only bringing its weight to bear in case of necessity." Kennedy was not startled. In 1961 he had read it in De Gaulle's Memoirs and heard it from De Gaulle's lips. Yet their talks, he said, "could not have been more cordial and I could not have more confidence in any man. I found General De Gaulle . . . a wise counselor for the future . . . far more interested in our frankly stating our position . . . than in appearing to agree." He did not share the view that the General was merely a nineteenth-century romantic with nostalgic yearnings for the past. But he did share the view that the French President could be irritating, intransigent, insufferably vain, inconsistent and impossible to please.

De Gaulle, for example, talked often of the need to reorganize NATO. Kennedy saw merit in this, in view of the vastly changed conditions since the Organization was formed. The French Foreign Office, during my diplomatic scouting trip in advance of the President's arrival in Paris, repeatedly suggested that, inasmuch as De Gaulle was not the type to make requests, Kennedy should ask him how he wanted to reorganize NATO. (Obviously De Gaulle's own subordinates did not know.) Kennedy did ask, but he received only vague generalities in reply. The General did tell Kennedy that he believed in uniting the Allies for swift, effective responses to every Communist move in Berlin. But within two months his nonparticipation and opposition on everything proposed were making such a stance impossible. He also told Kennedy that he had been frustrated by Eisenhower's habit of agreeing in principle but never following through, and that increased political and military consultations were required. Kennedy was no more willing than Eisenhower to accept De Gaulle's scheme for a three-man directorate in which France spoke for all nations of continental Western Europe. But he agreed to more meetings between the two of them and to closer consultation at the Foreign Secretary and Chief of Staff level.

Yet nothing came of this agreement either. De Gaulle's answers to Kennedy's letters on nuclear problems and Berlin negotiations were sharp, evasive or both; attempted telephone contact broke down as both men overwhelmed the interpreters; and all invitations to talk again with the General or with his representative were politely put aside. In September, 1962, for example, De Gaulle sent word through Alphand that he liked Kennedy, liked their last meeting and would like to meet him again, but inasmuch as solid agreements on a long list of issues seemed unlikely, the time was not yet right. (The message strongly resembled Kennedy's own refusals to meet at the summit with Khrushchev.) Late in 1963 the General did tentatively agree to come in March of the following year. Ambassador Alphand suggested Palm Beach. "But I'll be damned," said Kennedy, "if I'll show De Gaulle the worst side of American life. Cape Cod is where I'm really from, and it can't be any more gloomy in March than Colombey-les-deux-Églises" (where De Gaulle stays).

De Gaulle's inconsistencies of policy and position were regarded by Kennedy with some irony. The General favored neutralism in Southeast

Asia (where he was powerless) but not in Africa (where he wasn't). He believed in stout Allied resistance to the Communists, but constantly provoked divisions that could only weaken that resistance. He felt free to divide the Alliance politically because it protected him militarily. He wanted to be a leader in NATO, but withdrew his forces from it. He assumed to speak for the Common Market, but constantly hampered it. "Unlike us," said Kennedy privately, more in wonder than in irritation, "he recognizes the Soviet position on the Oder-Neisse, trades extensively with the East Germans and accepts the division of Germany—and yet he has persuaded the West German Government that he is more pro-German and anti-Communist than we." De Gaulle refused to sign the Test Ban Treaty, to pay his back UN assessments or to take part in disarmament talks. Indeed, he seemed to prefer, observed Kennedy, tension instead of intimacy in his relations with the United States as a matter of pride and independence.

Despite these differences, the two men retained a consistent admiration for each other. De Gaulle in 1961 toasted Kennedy's "intelligence and courage" with unaccustomed warmth. He was smitten with Jacqueline, warned her to beware of Mrs. Khrushchev at Vienna, and was touched by the Kennedys' hand-picked gift of an original letter from the Washington-Lafayette correspondence. He was reported to be deeply impressed by "the real stuff" in an American President calmly prepared to exercise his nuclear responsibilities. "I have more confidence in your country now," said De Gaulle when Kennedy departed Paris. (According to one veteran diplomat with us who had observed the General's attitude toward Roosevelt, Truman and Eisenhower, that was no exaggeration but very faint praise.)

JFK in turn could not help but admire De Gaulle's single-minded determination and progress in restoring the glory and grandeur of a country geographically smaller than Texas, his ability to convert French weaknesses into strengths, and his majestic command of language, presence and character. Publicly he maintained that

> if trouble comes, General De Gaulle, as he has in the past, will definitely meet his responsibility. . . . We do not look for those who agree with us but for those . . . who are committed to the defense of the West. I believe General De Gaulle is. So we will get along.

The truth is that Kennedy himself did not look upon either the Alliance or Atlantic harmony as an end in itself. He cared about the concrete problems which the Alliance faced, such as Berlin, trade negotiations and the American balance of payments. But he felt that State Department tradition had led us to think of every problem of foreign policy in terms of the Western Alliance when it was no longer as central to all our problems as it once had been, and when Europe's own strength had caused it to assert its views more independently. He tended to look upon the rest of the Alliance in somewhat the same light as he looked upon the Congress—as a necessary but not always welcome partner, whose cooperation he could not always obtain, whose opinions he could not always accept and with whom an uneasy relationship seemed inevitable. As the Cuban missile crisis illustrated, he was at his best when his responsibilities did not have to be shared.

He quoted Napoleon as having said that he won all his successes because he fought allies—and Churchill as having said that the history of any alliance is the history of mutual recrimination—and obviously he agreed with both of them. The prolonged, fruitless consultations on Berlin in 1961, and the constant criticisms emanating from unnamed sources in Allied capitals, often annoyed him. He noted sarcastically that NATO members who complained about U.S. "interference" in European security still expected the U.S. to bear the brunt of NATO military outlays while they failed to meet their quotas. ("A coherent policy," he said, "cannot call for both our military presence and our diplomatic absence.") He could not please both Macmillan and De Gaulle on the pace of Berlin negotiations and recognized that displeasing them both was better than trying to please either.

Yet he recognized that the preservation of Allied unity, like the passage of his legislative program, was indispensable to the achievement of his aims. Consequently, he labored tirelessly to win support in the Alliance as he did in the Congress. While he had devoted more time as Senator to Latin America, Africa and Asia (and continued as President to give those areas unprecedented attention), he recognized— as he showed in the Berlin crisis—that Western Europe was this nation's foremost area of "vital interest." While some charged him with downgrading NATO, his emphasis on conventional force to meet Communist "nibbling"—as a substitute for total reliance on the American nuclear umbrella—actually gave the full NATO membership a more important role than it would otherwise have played. His opposition to individual nuclear deterrents, while unpopular among some allies, helped in part to hold the Alliance together. He recognized—in his 1961 Paris address, among others—that Western Europe was no longer an uncertain dependent but an increasingly productive, united and influential equal. On July 4, 1962, in a "Declaration of Interdependence" address from Independence Hall in Philadelphia, he looked forward to a "concrete Atlantic Partnership, a mutually beneficial partnership between the new union now emerging in Europe and the old American union founded here 175 years ago."

In both 1961 and 1962 he expressed the hope that Western Europe would "play [its] role in this great world struggle, as we have done it . . . not look inward and just become a rich, carefully secluded group." He encouraged—even though it created problems for American business —Europe's economic and political integration, including the adherence of Great Britain to the Common Market.

His chief concern was the necessity of maintaining Western unity in the face of specific Communist threats. "If there is one path above all others to war," he said in his 1961 address on Berlin, "it is the path of weakness and disunity." He did not expect the Alliance to hold tight on Vietnam, the Congo, Cyprus or similar side issues. But he was determined to hold it together on any major confrontation with the Soviet Union.

TROUBLE IN THE ALLIANCE, 1963

The Alliance held when war threatened at Berlin and again in the Cuban missile crisis. But Kennedy's success at Cuba caused Khrushchev to revise his plans for Berlin. The balance of power became more stable; the superiority of our deterrent was hailed; and the Western Europeans, unduly confident that their danger was over, promptly indulged in what the President called "the luxury of dissension" and displayed a not unnatural resentment of their powerful American guarantor.

The initial, and possibly avoidable, trouble came in a chain of events sparked by the Kennedy-McNamara decision to cancel all further work on the Skybolt air-to-ground missile. The high cost of this highly complex weapon, compared to Polaris and Minuteman missiles, could not be justified once more reliable means had been developed to do the same job. But this decision stunned not only the Air Force and its manned bomber partisans in the Congress but Great Britain as well. For that country had planned with our assent to purchase Skybolt missiles as the best available means of remaining a nuclear power. A 1960 Macmillan-Eisenhower agreement that the U.S. would make Skybolt available if produced was interpreted by the British as a promise to produce. Now Kennedy had decided that it was not worth producing.

Unfortunately preoccupation with the Cuban and India-Chinese crises postponed all White House decisions on the defense budget until late in 1962, too late for an orderly consideration of the problems created by Skybolt's demise. The President—who saw no point to a small independent British deterrent anyway—mistakenly assumed that it was largely a technical and not a political problem. He paid comparatively little attention after McNamara promised to see British Defense Minister Thorneycroft and "work it out." After Cuba, it seemed a small problem. All problems did. Later Kennedy would wonder aloud why his Ambassador to London, David Bruce, or Macmillan's Ambassador to Washington, David Ormsby-Gore, or Macmillan himself, or Rusk, or *someone,* had not warned both sides in advance of the storm. But no doubt Macmillan wondered why Kennedy had not called him; and Rusk, after warning Kennedy in November of the possible British reaction, deferred to McNamara.

The storm, when it broke, threatened a rift in Anglo-American relations. It posed a major political crisis for Macmillan's already shaky government. McNamara had alerted Bruce, Thorneycroft and Ormsby-Gore in November but postponed until mid-December his trip to London to break the news definitely. Then he frankly stated at the London airport that Skybolt was on its way out, and refused to present an alternative that would keep alive a separate British deterrent. This led to an angry outburst from Thorneycroft, which promptly appeared in the British press. McNamara was surprised—not only by the outburst but by the British Government's failure to face up to the problem during the preceding month, and even during the previous fourteen months which had witnessed recurring doubts about Skybolt. He had expected them to propose an alternative, probably Polaris, which we could then negotiate. But the British, under pressure from their own air force and defense contractors, preferred to take their stand on Skybolt, hoping that delay would pressure Kennedy into keeping it.

In previous years Macmillan—despite cautions from his scientists and in answer to attacks from anti-American and antinuclear members of Parliament from both parties—had extravagantly praised the Skybolt agreement as the key to Britain's "special relationship" with the U.S. He had canceled Britain's own missile program entirely. Now British press and politicians complained with some justification that the Americans had been tactless, heavy-handed and abrupt, that the U.S. was revealing either an insensitivity to an ally's pride and security concerns or a desire to push her out of the nuclear business. Latent resentment of Kennedy's refusal to consult more on the Cuban missile crisis boiled to the top. Some charged that the Skybolt system was not really a failure, and that the U.S. was threatening cancellation to force Britain to fulfill its troop quota in Western Europe.

A largely symbolic meeting between Kennedy and Macmillan—their sixth—had already been set for late December in Nassau in the Bahamas (Kennedy having rejected another Bermuda meeting on the grounds that its midwinter climate was too undependable for relaxation). There was little relaxation at Nassau. The two leaders talked briefly and with essential agreement on the next steps for the Congo, India, test-ban negotiations and conventional forces. But the nuclear issue prolonged their sessions. Kennedy adamantly refused to retain the full Skybolt cost in his Budget, ignoring the suggestion that he keep it alive until Britain's Common Market negotiations were settled. His public commitment to abandon it and his plans for the tax-cut Budget made that impossible. Macmillan was equally adamant and both eloquent and emotional as well. He was like a ship that looks buoyant but is apt to sink, he said. Did Kennedy want to live with the consequences of sinking him? He warned that the collapse of his government on this issue could bring to power a more anti-American, more neutralist group from either party.

Like his Republican predecessor, Kennedy had a soft spot for Macmillan; and he had already decided that the bipartisan nature of our "special relationship" with the British required him not to send the Prime Minister home without some substitute for the missiles Eisenhower had promised. "Looking at it from their point of view—*which they do almost better than anybody*," he remarked to me later, "it might well be concluded that . . . we had an obligation to provide an alternative." A political crisis in England could upset plans for its accession to the Common Market or even the agreement—made simultaneously in 1960 with the Skybolt agreement—to provide a Polaris submarine base for the U.S. in Scotland.

If the British still had faith in Skybolt, said the President, the project could proceed—and they need pick up only half of the development costs.[6] No, said Macmillan, he now accepted U.S. evidence on the missile's performance. Perhaps, said the President, a joint study could be commissioned on how to fill the Skybolt gap. No, said Macmillan, he needed something more definitive; and he cited an angry letter he had received from 137 members of Parliament from his own party. Possibly, said the President, the Royal Air Force could be adapted to use our shorter-range Hound Dog air-to-ground missile. No, said Macmillan, that won't work.

Obviously Macmillan would be satisfied only with some arrangement on Polaris missiles, and Kennedy was unwilling to provide them on unconditional bilateral terms. No real thought had been given to a new Polaris arrangement. Under Secretary George Ball, representing the State Department at Nassau, strongly reflected the department's view that any offer of Polaris outside of a NATO multilateral framework would be regarded as fresh evidence of pro-British discrimination and indifference to nuclear "proliferation." It would sharply contrast with Kennedy's decisions earlier in the year not to aid the French nuclear force and not to give land-based medium-range missiles to NATO. The President, moreover, considered nuclear proliferation—the development

6 Instead of 100 percent as the original agreement had provided in the case of an adverse American decision. The President was unenthusiastic about the budget aspects of this proposal, but he and Ormsby-Gore had worked it out on the plane going down.

of nuclear capabilities by more countries, even allies—as a most dangerous development. It would increase instability in the balance of power, divisions within the Alliance, the difficulties of disarmament, the diversion of Alliance funds from ground forces, the dangers of accidental or irrational nuclear war, and a duplication of targeting with inconsistent strategies. It raised the possibility of an ally's triggering a nuclear exchange in the expectation that our deterrent would necessarily come to their aid. The French were already developing their own nuclear "*force de frappe,*" too small to deter the Soviets but large enough to provoke an attack. The West Germans, who had formally renounced nuclear arms, were under pressure in some quarters to be equal with the French and British. And a nuclear-rearmed Germany, the President knew, would be regarded as intolerable by the Soviets and all Eastern Europe.

In this context, proposals for a NATO nuclear force had been under study since first publicly aired by Eisenhower's Secretary of State Christian Herter in 1960. Kennedy, in a May, 1961, address at Ottawa, had pledged to the NATO command five Polaris submarines, which would remain under U.S. control. At the same time he had talked vaguely of an eventual "NATO seaborne force, which would be truly multilateral in ownership and control, if this should be desired and found feasible by our allies, once NATO's nonnuclear goals have been achieved." That deliberately left the initiative with our allies to come forward with a feasible plan and first to fulfill their conventional force quotas. Inasmuch as he doubted that they would do either, Kennedy had at that time paid little further attention to the matter. Certainly it was to have no priority until after further steps toward European unity—especially British membership in the EEC—had been taken.

But at Nassau the pressure was on Kennedy to come forward with some plan "to meet our obligation to the British," as he put it. He finally offered Polaris missiles (not submarines or warheads) to Macmillan in the NATO context. The Nassau Pact of December, 1962, declared that the British-built submarines carrying these missiles—except when "supreme national interests are at stake"—would be assigned to the NATO command and, upon its development, to a multilateral NATO nuclear force. NATO, in short, was to have two elements, one nationally directed and manned, the other internationally owned and "mixed-manned" by nationals of member governments. By calling both elements "multilateral," the Nassau communiqué caused some confusion, and thereafter we reserved the term for the second element, which became known as the MLF. But because both sides were uncertain of just what was meant and wanted, in the absence of both State Department experts and an agreed U.S. position, the communiqué contained other deliberate ambiguities; and it was thereafter read with different interpretations and emphasis by the British, the State Department and the Pentagon.

The merit of a multilateral force, as distinguished from a series of independent nuclear forces, was obvious. Nevertheless, from that hopeful day in Nassau forward, the concept of MLF was a source of confusion and dissension within the Alliance. The Nassau Pact itself showed signs of hasty improvisation and high-level imprecision, of decisions taken by the President in Nassau before he was ready to take them in Washington, of excellent motivation and poor preparation. The pact was accompanied by an offer to the French "similar" to Kennedy's offer to the British, but the French promptly rejected it. The MLF idea envisioned an all-NATO force; but the British began to back away from it, the Greeks and Turks couldn't afford it, the Italian elections avoided it, only the Germans clearly wanted it, and the prospect of an exclusive German-American force was not appealing, particularly if the Germans' real desire, as many supposed, was to ease out in time the American veto on the nuclear trigger. In this country, MLF had no warm backers in the Congress and few in the military. It presented major legal and legislative problems on the disclosure of nuclear information, the custody of nuclear warheads and—until a surface fleet was substituted—the use of nuclear-powered submarines.

The decisions taken at Nassau had been put forward for many reasons:

1. To prevent an independent West German nuclear force—yet they led to cries on both sides of the Wall that we were needlessly placing Germans too close to our force.

2. To minimize this country's preferential treatment of Great Britain —yet they seemed in some quarters only to emphasize it.

3. To meet charges of an American nuclear monopoly—yet, by retaining an American veto, the MLF concept produced fresh attacks upon that monopoly.

4. To strengthen Western Strategic defense forces—yet no one denied that the real purpose of MLF was political and that it could increase those forces by no more than 1 or 2 percent.

Gradually in 1963 the MLF proposal fell from the top of the President's agenda toward the bottom. He would not remove it altogether from his agenda. He understood the desire of allies who lived in the shadow of Russia's medium-range missiles to join the prestigious "nuclear club" and to have some voice in decisions affecting their security. He did not make a fetish out of national sovereignty, and was willing to accept more direct European participation in the nuclear deterrent to prevent a proliferation of national nuclear forces. Judging from the reaction in Europe, MLF was apparently not the answer. But "there are shortcomings to every proposal," he said, "and those who do not like our proposal should suggest one of their own."

He wanted the Europeans to decide whether or not they wanted an MLF in their own interest, not to accept it as a favor to the United States or because he had coerced them—that would only renew their complaints. Total abandonment of the effort, he felt, would renew French charges against the unreliable American monopoly and West German pressures to obtain their own nuclear force. Moreover, many of the State Department professionals, enthusiastic about MLF as an instrument for European integration, were optimistic about its acceptance. They pushed it harder than the President intended, in the belief that Western Europe would embrace it if we did. Kennedy, while still backing MLF within the Alliance, was increasingly skeptical. "How does it feel," he asked one chief advocate, "to be an admiral without a fleet?" The very issue giving rise to the plan—the distribution of nuclear decision-making —was also its most insurmountable difficulty. "To do something more than merely provide . . . a different façade of United States control," he said candidly, "will require a good deal of negotiation and imagination. . . ."

The negotiations continued intermittently throughout 1963, but showed no burst of imagination that impressed him. To Richard Neustadt, whom he commissioned to write a comprehensive account of the Skybolt-Nassau-MLF affair (in his most serious organized effort to meet his responsibility to future historians as well as to review the adequacy of his policy-makers and methods), he expressed his growing doubts:

> There is no "Europe." I understand their objection to my speaking for them on nuclear matters, but who's to be my opposite number? I can't share this decision with a whole lot of differently motivated and differently responsible people. What one man is it to be shared with—De Gaulle, Adenauer, Macmillan? None of them can speak for Europe.

Since 1958, however, General Charles de Gaulle did presume to speak for Europe—at least for continental Western Europe. The Cuban missile crisis and its outcome enabled De Gaulle to argue that Berlin and Western Europe were no longer in real danger from a chastened Khrushchev, that nuclear, not conventional, forces made the difference and that the defense of Europe had "moved into second place" in American military priorities.[7] Nassau enabled De Gaulle to argue that continental

---

[7] Does he suggest, said the President, "that what happened at Cuba proved that the United States might not defend Europe? That is a peculiar logic. If we had *not* acted in Cuba, [would] that . . . have proved we would defend Europe? . . . The United States over the last . . . twenty years has given evidence that its commitments are good. Some [Europeans] . . . may not believe that commitment, but I think that Chairman Khrushchev does—and . . . he is right."

Europe's chances for nuclear independence were about to be submerged in the Atlantic Alliance, that Europe was being asked to pay part of the cost of America's deterrent, and that Macmillan (with whom he had met only a few days earlier at Rambouillet and who had not offered *him* any nuclear assistance) had chosen to tie "insular, maritime" Britain to the United States instead of to Europe. Further emboldened by continuing weakness in this country's balance of payments position, he moved with more speed than tact—beginning with a caustic January, 1963, press conference—(a) to reject the Polaris offer and the MLF concept, insisting once again on an independent French nuclear force; (b) to veto Britain's entry into the Common Market, just as the long negotiations for that entry neared success, suggesting that Britain was too closely tied to the United States; (c) to sign with Adenauer a new treaty of unity, thus implicitly tying West Germany to his position; (d) to withdraw still more French forces from NATO; and (e) to frustrate the efforts of the Common Market countries to proceed more quickly to political integration.

In his famous press conference as in subsequent statements in defense of these bombshells, De Gaulle cleverly played on European resentment of both the American nuclear monopoly and the influence in Europe's affairs of our massive military, economic and political presence. He also appealed to European pride in refusing to rely on a distant nation for the means and decisions of survival and to European suspicions that England and America wished to dominate. He exploited European fears that the U.S. would not risk its cities to save theirs, that Kennedy's nagging about nonnuclear forces meant a weakening of our nuclear commitment and that Kennedy's stance at Cuba proved the danger of a Soviet-American deal or war in which Western Europe could be sacrificed. He appealed to European complacency and parsimony to forget the build-up of ground troops and rely on the French nuclear force's presence to convince Moscow that the American nuclear force would be dragged in. Now that America, too, was subject to attack, said De Gaulle, "no one in the world—*particularly* no one in America—can say if, where, when, how and to what extent the American nuclear weapons would be used to defend Europe."

The angry initial reaction in the United States and Great Britain was due in part to surprise—not at De Gaulle's attitudes, which were old, but at his tactics, his willingness to act so abruptly, brazenly and brutally, and with so little notice to his allies, when he might have blocked all the same efforts more subtly and gradually. De Gaulle had originally taken the position that Britain belonged in the Common Market. The American Embassy in Paris had recently reported that the French were resigned to U.K. membership in the Common Market. Even after Nassau,

De Gaulle's Foreign Minister had flatly stated that "no power on earth could keep Britain out of the Common Market." (It was later speculated that this may not have applied to the General.) At Nassau Macmillan had assured Kennedy that nothing more than a dispute on agriculture stood between his somewhat dilatory negotiators and admission to the Common Market.[8]

Macmillan had also argued to Kennedy that De Gaulle, as a believer in national deterrents, would have no objection to a U.S.-U.K. deal on Polaris. The General himself, less than two *weeks* before he slammed the door on JFK's "similar" Polaris offer, had indicated that it would take two *months* to evaluate. Moreover, wholly apart from the events at Nassau, optimism in Washington on the prospects for European integration had long been on the rise. This was partly because the administration's deep admiration for such advocates as Spaak and Jean Monnet had produced a false expectancy that their logic would prevail. It was also because De Gaulle's own political position the previous year had seemed so shaky, after the loss of Algeria, that much of the State-CIA-White House speculation had been not how he would block Western unity but who or what would succeed him.[9]

De Gaulle's tactics, however, had often surprised even his own Cabinet with their unexpected turns. Thus Kennedy was briefly startled early in 1963 by a foreign intelligence report of doubtful authenticity. "Rumors from regular and reliable sources" maintained that De Gaulle and the Soviet Union had made or were about to make a secret deal, calling for a demilitarized Central Europe, including all Germany, Greece and Turkey, the progressive withdrawal of American troops from France as well as Germany, and a recognition of the Oder-Neisse line. The report was sufficiently consistent with the needs and desires of both Khrushchev and De Gaulle—to spite the U.S. and dominate Europe "from the Atlantic to the Urals" (a favorite De Gaulle phrase)—to deserve checking. Fortunately it proved groundless; but this possibility motivated many of Kennedy's inquiries in the round of meetings that followed.

Commissioning papers by David Bruce and Dean Acheson, summoning to a series of lengthy conferences in January and February all the ambassadors and experts on the West, the President explored, probed and reappraised. On the basis of these meetings, he decided that no basic change in strategy was required for four reasons:

1. Even the proudest and most suspicious Europeans refused to join in De Gaulle's attacks on NATO and the Americans, whose ties they valued and whose association was preferable to Russia's in the long

8 Although the evidence is strong that De Gaulle virtually told him to expect a veto when the two met at Rambouillet.

9 I was witness, for example, to a very large wager by a high-ranking New Frontiersman that John Kennedy would be President long after De Gaulle.

years before De Gaulle's dreams could be realized. Nor would their interest in European unity be satisfied by a paternalistic De Gaulle-Adenauer domination.

2. De Gaulle's goal of a united Europe enveloping a reconciled Germany was Kennedy's goal as well. They fundamentally disagreed over means and over Anglo-American participation; but "the unity of freedom," said the President,

> has never relied on uniformity of opinion. . . . Whatever success we may have had in reducing the threat . . . to Berlin, we pay for by increased problems within the Alliance. . . . [On] those questions that involve the atom . . . there are bound to be differences of opinion—and there should be, because they involve life and death.

Moreover, contrary to press talk about De Gaulle's "Grand Design" frustrating Kennedy's "Grand Design," Kennedy had never looked upon either MLF or British entry into the EEC as pillars of American policy. Nor had he regarded the pace, process and personalities of European integration as matters for us to decide.

3. Although he quietly withdrew an earlier arrangement to sell nuclear-powered Skipjack submarines to France, any effort to punish the General, to trade insults with him or to compete with him for the allegiance of Germany and others would only play into De Gaulle's hands. No previous American President had been able to curb De Gaulle's disrespect for NATO and insistence on his own nuclear force; and all the proposals to isolate him now by new military or economic arrangements with others, or withdrawals of American pledges, would only retard long-range progress toward Atlantic Partnership.

4. Finally, he saw no value in appeasing De Gaulle by offering him nuclear weapons on his terms. A year earlier, despite the General's repeated assertion that France was asking (and offering) nothing, the President—at the urging of the Pentagon and our Ambassador in Paris, and over the opposition of most White House and State Department advisers—had re-examined this nation's opposition to aiding the French nuclear development. He had decided then that such aid would not win General De Gaulle to our purposes but only strengthen him in his. While minor military benefits might have been received in return, the General's desire to speak for all Europe, free from British and American influence, would not have been altered. His desire to be independent of NATO, and to form a three-power nuclear directorate outside of NATO, would only have been encouraged. And the West Germans, more pointedly excluded than ever, would surely have reappraised their attitude toward the Atlantic Alliance and toward the acquisition of their own nuclear weap-

ons. "I do not believe it is in the interest of the United States," the President wrote to a prominent critic in February, 1963, who demanded that he give France nuclear weapons (thus enabling De Gaulle's tiny force to trigger our own),

> to view the possession of a nuclear arsenal as a legitimate and desirable attribute of every sovereign nation. . . . If we are to be caught up in a nuclear war, should we not have a voice in the decision that launches it? Is not my first responsibility . . . to protect the interests of the United States?

Nevertheless he had been prepared after Nassau to open full discussions with De Gaulle on nuclear matters, to recognize France as a nuclear power and to provide assistance on weapons, and perhaps even on warheads, if the French aligned their force with NATO under something like the Nassau formula. He would similarly be prepared later in 1963—after the atmospheric Test Ban Treaty had been signed—to help France with techniques of underground testing in exchange for her signature on that treaty. But De Gaulle's negative response on both occasions—no doubt heightened in January by his suspicions of MLF—made serious negotiations impossible.

In short, concluded the President, little could have been done to avert De Gaulle's actions and little should be done in response. It was an uneasy conclusion, which he privately re-examined often. But as Western Europe and Red China became stronger and less dependent on their respective big-power backers, he decided splits within both the East and West camps had become inevitable; and lower tensions after Cuba had been certain to widen those splits. He had no desire to raise tensions and reunite the Communists to patch over Western splits.

A decision not to change American strategy, however, did not mean total inaction. Kennedy began wooing more Europeans more assiduously, expressing sympathy for their desire for a larger voice in East-West and nuclear affairs, and paying particular attention to the West Germans. Aware that history would look kindly on the reconciliation of France and Germany, he rejected all suggestions that he pressure Adenauer into choosing between the U.S. and France or putting off ratification of the new French-German Treaty of Friendship. But he did encourage moves in Bonn to associate its ratification with a preamble restating, much to De Gaulle's discomfiture, Germany's pledge to NATO and Atlantic unity.

He also proceeded with MLF negotiations, leaving the door open to France and to an eventual all-European nuclear force, which would be aided but not restricted by the U.S. and represented on a two-man (U.S. and Europe) Western nuclear directorate. The May, 1963, NATO meetings created an inter-Allied nuclear force (not

an MLF, but British bombers and five American Polaris submarines, retained in their national force structures, under NATO command).
Arrangements were made for European military officers to participate
more fully and equally in nuclear target planning at SAC headquarters
in Omaha. He also sought to strengthen the dollar against further balance of payments weaknesses, and pushed ahead on tariff negotiations
under the Trade Expansion Act, on consultations for monetary reform
and on other small, steady steps in building Atlantic ties. Progress was
slow; but in a long evolutionary process altering the basic structure of
the world's political architecture, the United States could afford to be
patient. The long-range movement, he felt, was irreversible.

Kennedy's most striking and successful answer to De Gaulle—and
one he came perilously close to calling off—was his June, 1963, trip to
Western Europe and particularly West Germany. Hailed as even De
Gaulle had not been hailed on his earlier triumphant tour, the President
summed up the purpose of his trip promptly upon his arrival at the
Bonn airport:

> I have crossed the Atlantic, some 3,500 miles, at a crucial
> time in the life of the Grand Alliance. Our unity was forged in a
> time of danger; it must be maintained in a time of peace. . . .
> Economically, militarily, politically, our two nations and all the
> other nations of the Alliance are now dependent upon one an-
> other. . . .
> My stay in this country will be all too brief, but . . . the United
> States is here on this continent to stay so long as our presence is
> desired and required; our forces and commitments will remain,
> for your safety is our safety. Your liberty is our liberty; and any
> attack on your soil is an attack upon our own. Out of necessity,
> as well as sentiment, in our approach to peace as well as war, our
> fortunes are one.

Two days later, in the historic Paulskirche in Frankfurt where the
first German Assembly had been born, he expanded the theme of Atlantic Partnership in one of the most carefully reworked speeches of
his Presidency. The Western Allies, he said, faced not only common
military problems but similar internal economic problems. They were
bound not only by threat of danger but shared values and goals.

> It is not in [the U.S.] interest to try to dominate the European
> councils of decision. If that were our objective, we would prefer
> to see Europe divided and weak, enabling the United States to
> deal with each fragment individually. Instead, we look forward
> to a Europe united and strong, speaking with a common voice,

acting with a common will, a world power capable of meeting world problems as a full and equal partner. . . .

The United States will risk its cities to defend yours because we need your freedom to protect ours. . . . Those who would doubt our pledge or deny this indivisibility, those who would separate Europe from America or split one ally from another, would only give aid and comfort to the men who make themselves our adversaries and welcome any Western disarray.

Restating these convictions throughout West Germany, Italy and on European television, and in effective private talks with leaders in those countries and with Macmillan in England, he left the continent the following week convinced—on the basis of citizen, leader and press responses—"that our commitment and its durability are understood."

Back on his own side of the Atlantic, earlier in 1963, another Allied leader had brought Kennedy headaches, Canada's erratic John Diefenbaker. But the President, while concerned about his relations with Canada, was less concerned about Diefenbaker. Having troubled himself to learn more about Canada than any previous American head of state, wrote one Canadian observer, Kennedy "expected more of us than his predecessors ever had." With Diefenbaker his expectations had swiftly vanished.

Their difficulties had begun long before 1963. The Canadian Prime Minister, who embraced anti-Americanism both as a personal view and as a political tactic, was annoyed when his rival, Lester Pearson, talked privately with Kennedy at the White House dinner for Nobel Prize winners. A Diefenbaker-Kennedy meeting in May of 1961 had proceeded harmoniously; but Kennedy had inadvertently left behind one of the staff papers he had been using. Diefenbaker not only expropriated the paper but threatened to expose it publicly, claiming that it referred to him as an s.o.b. (Apparently this was a typically illegible reference to the OAS, which the President was urging Canada to join. "I couldn't have called him an s.o.b.," commented Kennedy later. "I didn't know he was one—at that time.") Kennedy was his sternest when threatened.[10] To Diefenbaker's threat he replied simply: "Just let him try it."

In 1963 Diefenbaker and his government not only refused to fulfill their commitments on the location of nuclear warheads on Canadian soil but, in a Parliamentary debate, consistently misrepresented both their position and that of the United States. The Cuban missile crisis had reemphasized to all the vital importance of rapid readiness to North American defenses; and the State Department, obtaining clearance from the

10 "I didn't get here by taking that kind of stuff from anybody," he had warned one former friend who said he would raise new health issues if not given his way on a personal matter.

White House but not from the President, issued a press release making clear the inaccuracy of Diefenbaker's claims about the American request and his response. Kennedy "hit the roof" when he read it in the newspapers—and Diefenbaker hit the ground. His government fell. The President had been anxious to help Harold Macmillan when he had a domestic political crisis that had stemmed partly from U.S. action, but he had no similar sympathy for Diefenbaker. New Canadian elections were held; Pearson was elected; and a nuclear warhead agreement was promptly reached.

CONTACTS WITH OTHER WORLD LEADERS

Pearson was not the only opposition leader with whom the President had friendly contacts. He was particularly fond of Britain's Hugh Gaitskell and West Germany's Willy Brandt. With all chief executives and opposition leaders he could talk politics, theirs and his. He privately weighed and analyzed these men as he had his fellow American politicians in the 1960 quest for the nomination, sometimes even comparing a foreign chief to some similar Democratic leader. He understood, as few do, the fact that not only geography but domestic political pressures often accounted for the differences in foreign policy expressed by other nations' leaders. With few exceptions, foreign politicians soon recognized the impact of his popularity on their own elections. A visit to the White House had long been considered a necessity by the leaders of both parties in many a country. Now the younger politicians in particular imitated Kennedy's style, analyzed his campaign techniques or permitted their publicists to call them "another Kennedy."

At an average of more than one a week in his first year in office, and frequently thereafter, Kennedy met personally with his fellow heads of state and chief executives, visiting eleven in their countries and receiving more than fifty presidents, prime ministers and royal leaders in the White House. He prepared for each of those meetings—whether it was the President of France or Togo—with a searching inquiry into all available facts about the other country, its politics, its problems and its personalities. Citing their local statistics from memory, quoting from their writings or their history without notes, he left his hosts and visitors both pleased and impressed. (West Berlin's Mayor Willy Brandt, for example, could not get over Kennedy's knowledge of East Berlin's Mayor: "He asked me whether Ebert's other son was also a Communist. Ebert's other son! I didn't even know he had another son!")

With his own travels limited, Kennedy maintained a voluminous correspondence with other national chiefs—met separately with an even greater number of foreign secretaries, finance ministers and other officials—sent his wife, his brother Robert, the Vice President and others on foreign visits—encouraged State Department officials to deal with their counterparts firsthand on special crises instead of through letters and ambassadors—and improved our relations with Japan through annual joint Cabinet sessions. The principal effort in this unprecedented concern for the care and feeding of foreign egos was the White House visit. Each visiting dignitary was brought upstairs to the Kennedys' private quarters (JFK picking up Caroline from her nap, for example, to show her to King Saud of Saudi Arabia) and shown the Indian paintings and the French furniture in which both Kennedys took pride. Noticing the deplorable condition of the limousine to which he escorted one prime minister, he found it had been rented from a funeral parlor and promptly ordered new arrangements. Impressed by the honor guard lining the avenues in Paris, he installed a similar plan for state dinners at the White House. Convinced that Andrews Air Force Base was a dreary place to begin an official visit, he instituted arrivals by helicopter south of the White House.

The unprecedented flood of high-ranking dignitaries to Washington required less use of the three-day "state visits," with all the frills and fixings, and more use of one-day "working visits," with merely a lunch at the White House, as well as more two-day compromises under either label. Nearly always more interested in these talks than in small talk with many Congressmen, he usually kept his foreign visitors overtime, even when other crises pressed. His interest in their problems and politics, his broad knowledge of their needs and views, his wit and charm, and the uniquely hospitable treatment lavished by both Kennedys —glittering White House dinners with menus personally reviewed by the President, dazzling artistic performances and gifts tailored to the recipient's interests—all helped establish warm ties between Kennedy and his fellow leaders.

This was particularly true and important with the leaders of the new and developing nations, especially in Africa. They liked his efforts on immigration, disarmament, foreign aid, the Congo, Laos and especially civil rights. (Kennedy, in fact, took special pains to send his civil rights address with a personal letter to every African head of government.) They particularly liked his personal grasp of their aspirations and anxieties. Even Ghana's Nkrumah, who blamed the United States for the assassination of former Congolese Premier Lumumba and the subsequent collapse of Nkrumah's vision of Pan-African power, was delighted with the American President. To the President of the Sudan Kennedy presented a specially made hunting rifle, and was told with a grateful smile: "In my country there are thirteen million people and a hundred million wild animals." Accepting Haile Selassie's plaudits on civil rights, he steered him to meetings with Roy Wilkins and the Attorney General. Of newly independent Tanganyika's Julius Nyerere, one of his fellow leaders he most liked, he inquired with a smile, "Tell me, how does it feel to be the first Catholic President of a great country?"

He was particularly interested in those figures already living in the history they helped to write—De Gaulle, Adenauer, Haile Selassie and India's Jawaharlal Nehru. Kennedy and Nehru, for all their differences in age, culture and policy, shared much in common: an intellectual bent, a wry sense of humor, a preference for clear disagreements instead of diplomatic generalities and an affection for Kennedy's Ambassador, J. Kenneth Galbraith ("Although," said the lanky professor to the President, "I don't see how you trust me to deal with the Prime Minister of India when you wouldn't consider me competent to handle political problems in Dorchester, Massachusetts"). Greeting Nehru at Newport in the fall of 1961, Kennedy and Galbraith drove him by the enormous homes in that wealthy resort, the President remarking, "I wanted you to see how the average American lives"—to which Nehru, equally dead-pan, replied, "Yes, I've heard of your 'affluent society' " (the title of a Galbraith book).

Kennedy persuaded Nehru on that occasion to recognize in their communiqué the need for Western access to Berlin. But otherwise that meeting convinced him that Nehru would never be a strong reed on which to rely and that India's potential role in world affairs had been overestimated by its admirers. The Prime Minister seemed to him overtired, requiring a great effort to interest himself deeply in any problem. Astonished when Nehru later chose to visit Disneyland, he decided that he had accepted too readily the Prime Minister's request for a "private" visit with no pretentious ceremony or crowds. The intimacy of upstairs in the Mansion (where a furiously smoking fireplace nearly drove them out) had been a little too private for a major world figure.

Whatever their differences, the President liked Nehru. At a news conference shortly after the Prime Minister's departure, annoyed by a question on whether he had found "pro-Communist" tendencies in the Indian leader, Kennedy said he knew of "no rational man . . . who holds that view"; and he went on to defend Nehru's commitment to individual liberty and to national independence.

He was critical of Nehru's use of the Western-hating Krishna Menon and his blatant seizure of the tiny Portuguese enclave of Goa in late 1961. But the following year, when Nehru's daughter paused briefly in Washington on an unofficial lecture tour, she was astonished to receive a personal call from the President. He warned her that newspaper interviewers across the country would try to pit her against the Congress, which was then considering a slash in Indian aid funds because of the

Goa incident. Introducing her to his own technique of preparing for press conferences, he proceeded to fire at her the toughest questions she might be asked on her tour.

Kennedy's own press conference answers and public statements when traveling outside his own country—and those statements and speeches at home which affected foreign countries—were beamed not only to government leaders but also to their constituents. "He talked," said Averell Harriman, "over the heads of government to the hearts of people." He particularly enjoyed talking on several occasions to foreign students on the White House lawn; and he sounded more pleased than miffed when he returned from one such encounter to tell me that his tie clasp and handkerchief had been lost when the crowd swarmed around him. (The two Indonesian students who had taken them returned them the next day.)

His trip to Western Europe in the summer of 1963 was criticized by Washington columnists on the grounds that his host governments in Germany, England and Italy were all in a stage of transition which made negotiations difficult. But Kennedy's primary purpose was not to negotiate with governments but to talk to their publics in the wake of De Gaulle's charges against the U.S. His trip was concerned, he said, with "the relationship between the United States and Western Europe. . . . This is a matter of the greatest importance to us and, I hope, to the *people* [of Europe]."

He returned from that trip exhilarated by the feeling that he had reached the general public, particularly the younger generation. He realized that he had enjoyed on that trip several advantages unrelated to the force of his foreign policy ideas: the contrast between his youthful vitality and the weary pessimism of most older leaders—the adoption of all the old Kennedy campaign techniques, including advance men, motorcades, outdoor rallies, local humor and maximum television coverage— the combined appeal of his own victory over religious intolerance and his fight against racial injustice—and an identification with the kind of cultural and intellectual excellence which appealed to European traditions.

He took satisfaction nevertheless in the belief that his tour had gained increased respect for the nation as well as the man. He did not feel that "world opinion" was either an identifiable fact or a reliable force. Nor was he willing

to base those decisions which affect the long-run state of the common security on the short-term state of our popularity in the various capitals of Europe. . . . We are going to have disagreements. . . . But . . . whenever the United States has a disagreement with a foreign country, it is a mistake always to assume that the

United States is wrong, and that—by being disagreeable to the United States—it is always possible to compel the United States to succumb. . . .

I think too often in the past we have defined our leadership as an attempt to be rather well regarded in all these countries. The fact is you can't possibly carry out any policy without causing major frictions. . . . What we have to do is to be ready to accept a good deal more expression of newspaper and governmental opposition to the U.S. in order to get something done. *I don't expect that the U.S. will be more beloved, but I would hope that we could get more done.*

America's role as world leader, he observed, often involved it in disputes between its friends and allies. Our support—and occasionally our services as a mediator—were sought by both sides; and the likelihood of both being pleased with our stand was remote. In the Middle East and on the Indian subcontinent, his efforts to restore harmony were diligent, often suspect on both sides and largely unsuccessful. But a temporary success of sorts was registered in 1962 in the territory of West New Guinea, the subject of a bitter dispute between the Netherlands and Indonesia. To avoid a war which the Dutch had no desire to fight and which the Indonesians had every intention of winning with massive Soviet backing—and to strengthen the position of the Indonesian moderates, the only hope against an ultimate Communist takeover in that country—Kennedy made available the brilliant diplomatic services of Ambassador Ellsworth Bunker as a UN mediator. Some American diplomats, more concerned with complaints from the Dutch and Australians than with the resultant rise in our standing with some of the Asian neutrals, did not support this effort with any enthusiasm. But "our only interest," said the President, "is . . . a peaceful solution which we think is in the long-range interests of [all concerned]. The role of the mediator is not a happy one; [but] we are prepared to have everybody mad if it makes some progress."

Despite this refusal to give priority to America's popularity in world opinion, he never discounted the practical effect of popular respect for American ideals on the cooperation of other leaders, on the maintenance of our overseas installations and on resolutions in the UN and OAS. The competition with the Soviets was not on the material and military level only, and even military actions required the support of other peoples. While America's interests were more important than her image, at times they were affected by it. Thus, in the developing world in particular—and aided by a greatly improved USIA program under Murrow, by a more active and attractive UN posture under Stevenson and by a growing, energetic Peace Corps under Shriver—Kennedy set out to change "the stereotype view of the United States . . . — about fifty years old . . . Marxist oriented . . . [and unaware of] the tremendous changes which have taken place in the United States . . . the cultural efforts . . . the intellectual efforts."

He succeeded beyond his own expectations in dispelling the notion that the United States was unconcerned, conservative and committed to the status quo. USIA surveys in Western Europe in 1963—on the heels of the Skybolt controversy and De Gaulle's attacks—showed a higher proportion of approval for American foreign policy, even in France, than at any time in the eight-year history of these surveys. A poll by *Asia Magazine* found him well ahead of Nehru as "the most admired world figure today." The reports of Peace Corps men in Africa and the mail he received from Eastern Europe all indicated a personal breakthrough of international significance in those areas. His receptions in Latin America were particularly unforgettable (as was his anger upon discovering that the White House social officer was sending down the Presidential china for his every meal). The exuberance of the crowds yelling *"Viva!"* soon caused him to join in. At first the notion of men embracing him with the traditional Latin-American *abrazo* embarrassed him, and his visits began with a stiff handshake at the airport. But by the time he departed from that same airport he was exchanging *abrazos* with as much gusto as his hosts. Those Latin-American trips were also aided by the expert work of State Department interpreter Donald Barnes, for elsewhere Kennedy had constant problems with lifeless translations of his rhetoric, requiring him on his 1963 German trip to borrow Adenauer's interpreter for his important Frankfurt and Berlin speeches.

I have many vivid memories of those Kennedy overseas trips—the smiles and tears on the faces of West Berliners, the crowds running up to our motorcades in Naples and San José, the dazzling effect of Jacqueline Kennedy on presidents and peasants, her husband's stealthy gaze at the magnificent Cologne Cathedral dome in the midst of a prolonged prayer, the laughter among West Germans understanding his quips before they were translated, the regal splendor of the state dinners at Schönbrunn and Versailles and his ornate quarters at the Quai d'Orsay Palace in Paris. (As I reported to him on my findings, he suggested I speak softly in the middle of the room, adding: "Or don't you think our oldest and closest ally could be capable of 'bugging' my bedroom?")

"One of the most moving experiences" of his life, in his words, was his 1963 journey to Ireland. Although he had privately kept an eye on Ireland's hopes for a U.S. sugar quota from the Congress, his earlier interest in the land of his forebears was largely literary and political. His companions on a youthful visit there to his sister Kathleen, his mother told me, were mostly English or "Anglo-Irish."

But in 1963 he discovered in full measure the joys of the country and its people. The first outsider ever to address a joint assembly of both houses of the Irish Parliament (holding its first session on television), he delivered a major foreign policy address on the role of the little nations; and it filled that island with pride.[11]

To his third cousin, Mary Kennedy Ryan, he expressed gratitude for the hot tea, the delicious salmon (asking if it had been illegally poached), the blazing fire and the fact that "some of the Kennedys missed the boat and didn't all go to Washington." At Cork he introduced all the Irish aides traveling with him, claiming that Dave Powers' local cousins looked less Irish than Dave. Simultaneously awarded honorary degrees by the rival National University of Ireland and Dublin's Trinity College (an institution less favored by the Irish Catholic hierarchy), he said he felt equally part of both, "and if they ever have a game of Gaelic football or hurling, I shall cheer for Trinity and pray for National." Wholly fascinated by his talk with the aged wife of Ireland's President De Valera, he quoted in his farewell talk at Shannon airport a poem she had taught him, promising like the poet "to come back and see old Shannon's face again."

He was so pleased with the specially designed O'Kennedy coat of arms, with an added strong arm holding both an olive branch and arrows, that his wife had it made into a seal ring for him. Not much of a ring wearer, he kept it in his desk, but one day he told her with a mischievous smile: "I used my Irish seal on a letter today—to the Queen of England!"

[11] An eloquent quotation from David Lloyd George, on the contribution of small countries, he diplomatically attributed only to "one of the great orators of the English language"; but a reference to the Atlantic as a "bowl of bitter tears" was attributed by name to James Joyce, whose books had once been denounced in Dublin.

CHAPTER XXI

THE BERLIN CRISIS

IN A 1959 INTERVIEW Candidate Kennedy predicted that Berlin in time was certain to be a harsh "test of nerve and will." He could not then have known that his own will and nerve would be so harshly tested so soon in that beleaguered city.

Military and diplomatic agreements near the close of the Second World War left Berlin one hundred miles within the East German territory controlled by Soviet troops, with no specific guarantees of Western access, and with a four-power administration of the city itself. In 1948, a series of Soviet actions had split the city into Soviet-occupied East Berlin and Western-occupied West Berlin. For ten years East Berlin and East Germany were increasingly cut off from their Western counterparts. Then, in 1958, Khrushchev demanded a German peace treaty, permanently legitimatizing the division and ending all Allied occupation rights inside East German territory. That demand, and the explosion of the Paris Summit Conference of 1960, made it clear that Berlin and Germany would top the Soviet Chairman's agenda for discussions with Eisenhower's successor.

Kennedy's own foreign policy interests in the Senate had concentrated more upon Asia, defense and Eastern Europe. To gain new preparation and perspective, he commissioned early in 1961 a special report on Berlin from former Secretary of State Dean Acheson. In an interim report in April, Acheson warned that a crisis was likely in 1961, that the Allies were divided and the neutrals unhelpful, that the West was unprepared to counter effectively any Soviet interruption of access, and that West Berlin's importance might require us to use all-out force to maintain the three basic American objectives: (1) the freedom of the people of West Berlin to choose their own system; (2) the presence of Western troops so long as the people required and desired them; and (3) unimpeded access from the West to the city across the East German *Autobahn,* air lanes and canals.

Khrushchev had once talked of April, 1961, as his latest deadline on Berlin, and he vowed on January 6 to "eradicate this splinter from the heart of Europe." But the decision to meet with Kennedy at Vienna in June deferred all action until that time. The President, in his pre-Vienna studies and in his talks with Adenauer in Washington and De Gaulle in Paris, recognized more clearly than ever that West Berlin was the touchstone of American honor and resolve, and that Khrushchev was certain to use it to test Allied unity and resistance.

Inasmuch as all three of the basic American objectives stated by Acheson were peacefully if uncomfortably part of the status quo, and the Vienna meeting was not a negotiating session, Kennedy intended no new Berlin proposals at Vienna. But he was not surprised when, at the close of their first day's talks, Khrushchev mentioned almost casually the need to discuss Berlin on the second: The main problem is a peace treaty, he said. If the United States refuses to sign it, the Soviet Union will do so and nothing will stop it. On that harsh note they went to dinner, and on that harsh note Khrushchev introduced the subject the following day. A formal ending to the Second World War was already overdue, he said. Only a treaty or separate treaties recognizing the permanent existence of two Germanys could be signed. Aware that neither the West Germans nor any Western Ally could sign such a treaty, he said the Soviets would sign one with East Germany alone if, along with the aggressive, revenge-seeking West Germans, the Americans stood aloof. Then the state of war would cease and all commitments stemming from Germany's surrender would become invalid, including occupation rights and access to Berlin and the corridors. West Berlin would be preserved as what he called a "free city," but its links to the outside world would be turned over to the "sovereign" East Germans.

Such frankness was appreciated, replied Kennedy. Berlin was no Laos. It was a matter of the highest concern to the United States. Our national security was involved. If we accepted the loss of our rights in Berlin, no one would have any confidence in our commitments or pledges. Our leaving West Berlin would result in the United States becoming isolated. It would mean abandonment of the West Berliners and all hope for German reunification, abandonment of America's obligations and America's allies. Our commitments would be regarded as mere scraps of paper.

This was a significant answer, for it indicated Kennedy's determination to make this not only a question of West Berlin's rights—on which U.S., British, French and West German policies were not always in accord—but a question of direct Soviet-American confrontation over a shift in the balance of power. Khrushchev, however, was equally tough. He was very sorry, he said, but he had to assure Kennedy that no force in the world could prevent the U.S.S.R. from signing a peace treaty by the end of the year. No further delay was possible or necessary. The sovereignty of the German Democratic Republic (East Germany) would have to be observed. Any violation of that sovereignty would be regarded by the U.S.S.R. as an act of open aggression against a peace-loving country with all the consequences ensuing therefrom. If East German borders—land, air or sea borders—were violated, they would be defended. If the United States wanted to start a war over Germany, let it be so; perhaps the U.S.S.R. should sign a peace treaty right away and get it over with. That is what the Pentagon had been wanting. But any madman who wants war, he said, should be put in a strait jacket.

Would such a treaty block access to Berlin? asked the President to make certain. It would. But the United States would not give up its rights, the President stressed again. Mr. K. should consider the responsibilities both of them had.

Why does America want to stay there? asked Khrushchev. President Eisenhower had agreed that the situation in Germany was abnormal, but wanted a delay because American prestige was involved. Now Kennedy wanted to become master to protect his position.

No, said Kennedy, we are not talking about my nation going to Moscow or the Soviet Union coming to New York. We are talking about the United States staying in Berlin, where it has been for fifteen years. He had not, he said firmly, assumed the office of the Presidency to accept arrangements totally inimical to American interests.

In an added private session after lunch, with only the interpreters present and the words of both men sharpening steadily, Khrushchev insisted that he, too, could not shirk his responsibility as prime minister, that the U.S. position was based not on legal rights but on a desire to humiliate the U.S.S.R.—and this he could not accept.

There is a difference, said the President, between the Soviets' merely signing a treaty and their turning Western rights over to the East Germans to be terminated. Denying the West its contractual rights would be a belligerent act. A face-saving interim agreement might be reached to cover the next six months, answered Khrushchev, but the U.S.S.R. could no longer delay. Any continued Western presence inside East Germany after a treaty had ended the war would be illegal, humiliating and a violation of East Germany's borders—and those borders

would be defended. Force would be met by force. The U.S. should prepare itself for that and the Soviet Union would do the same. If the
United States wanted war, that was its problem. The U.S.S.R. would have
no choice other than to accept the challenge. The calamities of a war
would be shared equally. The decision to sign a peace treaty in December
(unless there was an interim six months' agreement) was firm and
irrevocable.

"If that is true," observed the President, "it will be a cold winter."
But it was an even hotter summer. The official Soviet *aide-mémoire*
handed him at the close of the talks, which restated the same arguments and proposals in more formal and less belligerent language, confused the question of deadlines. It referred only to a six months'
period in which the two German sides could discuss differences, and
otherwise omitted the "end of the year" references used by Khrushchev.
But the Soviet Chairman, in his first speech on Vienna, again stressed
his intention of "freeing" West Berlin from its "occupation regime . . .
this year." East German boss Ulbricht announced that the treaty would
soon enable him to close West Berlin's refugee centers, radio station and
Tempelhof Airport. It was widely predicted on both sides of the Iron
Curtain that Khrushchev would call a German peace conference following the Communist Party Congress in October. That left Kennedy and
the West with very little time.

The President's first and most basic decision was that the preservation of Western rights in West Berlin was an objective for which the
United States was required to incur any cost, including the risk of
nuclear war. It was reported by some that he was obsessed by the fear
that he might be ordering his country's semiextinction. He was, in fact,
calmly convinced that an unflinching stand for West Berlin's freedom
would, in the long run, lessen the prospects for a nuclear war, while
yielding on West Berlin would only weaken the future credibility of our
defenses. Asked at a July news conference about a report that the Soviet
Ambassador, departing Washington for a new post, had sneered that
"when the chips are down, the United States won't fight for Berlin,"
Kennedy replied matter-of-factly: "We intend to honor our commitments."

His second basic decision was to take complete charge of the operation. For months he saturated himself in the problem. He reviewed and
revised the military contingency plans, the conventional force build-up,
the diplomatic and propaganda initiatives, the Budget changes and the
plans for economic warfare. He considered the effect each move would
have on Berlin morale, Allied unity, Soviet intransigence and his own
legislative and foreign aid program. He talked to Allied leaders, to
Gromyko and to the Germans; he kept track of all the cables; he read

transcripts of all the conferences; and he complained (with limited success) about the pace at the Department of State, about leaks from Allied clearances and about the lack of new diplomatic suggestions.

His most frustrating experience—and one which to him demonstrated the need for more expeditious management within the Department of State as well as the difficulties and delays of seeking agreed Allied positions—arose from his desire to send a prompt and freshly worded reply to the Soviet *aide-mémoire*. That reply was to be the first full official statement of the Western position on West Berlin since his assumption of office. He awaited the State Department's draft. Weeks went by. The simultaneous Soviet *aide-mémoire* on nuclear testing was answered, but this country remained officially silent on West Berlin. Finally, a month having lapsed, the President asked for the latest proposed draft of the reply to review at Hyannis Port over the Fourth of July weekend. He found, to his dismay, not a clear, concise response which all Americans, Germans and Russians could understand, but a compilation of stale, tedious and negative phrases, none of them new. The whole document could have been drafted in one-quarter as much time and with one-tenth as many words. He asked me to produce that afternoon a shorter, simpler version. Then he learned that the latter could not be substituted for the formal note without starting all over again with inter-Allied and interdepartmental clearances. But he used it anyway as a Presidential statement in "explanation" of the official text. Even then, two more weeks elapsed before that official note was ready on July 18.

By July 18 he was ready with his more detailed decisions on this nation's over-all response. Khrushchev had repeatedly emphasized at Vienna that, if there were military action over Berlin, it would have to be initiated by the United States. Obviously he did not believe that Kennedy would start a nuclear war over traffic controls on the *Autobahn*. For West Berlin, entirely surrounded by East German territory, was peculiarly vulnerable to seizure or strangulation by Communist troops. If Western access routes were to be blocked upon the signing of a treaty— by an East German sentry, a squadron, a battalion or more—years of over-reliance on massive nuclear retaliation had left the West unable to counter the Communist forces with its own nonnuclear power. That left few alternatives other than nuclear war or practically nothing—or, as the President put it, "holocaust or humiliation."

Upon Kennedy's return from Vienna, he had intensively reviewed the Berlin military contingency plans prepared by NATO and the Joint Chiefs of Staff. In the event of blocked access, under these plans, a series of military "probes" down the *Autobahn* would be attempted. But with the West lacking both the intention and the capacity to wage a conventional war on the ground, these probes were too small to indicate a serious intent and would surely be quickly contained by the Soviets or even by the East Germans alone. Then the plans called for nuclear weapons. In short, said the President, "We go immediately from a rather small military action to one where nuclear weapons are exchanged, which of course means . . . we are also destroying this country." Little time or opportunity would be allowed for either side to pause, talk, reconsider or judge the other's intentions. If we can't remove the fuse from the bomb of global catastrophe, said one Berlin planning paper, at least we can lengthen it.

Kennedy regarded the existing strategy as a weak and dangerous position. The imbalance of ground forces which the two sides could readily deploy in the area was an excessive temptation to Khrushchev to cut off access to West Berlin so gradually that we would never respond with a nuclear attack. "If Mr. Khrushchev believes that all we have is the atomic bomb," he said, "he is going to feel that we are . . . somewhat unlikely to use it."

The President sought therefore to fill that gap with a rapid build-up of combat troops in Central Europe—with a contingent large enough to convince Khrushchev that our vital interests were so deeply involved that we would use any means to prevent the defeat or capture of those forces. This required a force large enough to prevent any cheap and easy seizure of the city by East German guards alone, which would weaken our bargaining power—and large enough to permit a true "pause," a month instead of an hour before choosing nuclear war or retreat, time to bring up reserves, to demonstrate our determination, to make a deliberate decision and to communicate at the highest levels before the "ultimate" weapons were used.

Only in this way, Kennedy was convinced, could Khrushchev be dissuaded from slowly shutting off West Berlin. Such a commitment, moreover, would bolster Western will with a reminder that Americans were there to stay. And if Khrushchev were counting on Allied disunity and timidity in the face of a nuclear threat, a similar increase in ground forces by other Western nations, he argued (they did not all listen), would increase the nuclear credibility of NATO as a whole.

The precise nature and numbers of this build-up are discussed in the next chapter. Except for a military-civilian dispute over whether economic and political action should precede any major military response, and some Air Force grumbling over being given a nonnuclear role, there was in the summer of 1961 little disagreement within the administration over the necessity of this approach. There was internal agreement also on the steps needed to improve the dangerously rigid military contingency plans, to strengthen the readiness of West Berlin with stockpiled supplies and airlift preparations and to use economic sanctions against East Germany if access were cut off. But there was sharp disagreement within the administration as well, and it centered on two interrelated issues: (1) whether the President should declare a national emergency; and (2) whether a prompt offer to negotiate should accompany the military build-up. Dean Acheson, in his final report, had recommended an affirmative answer to the first question and a negative answer to the second; and his view initially prevailed in the Departments of Defense and State.

Khrushchev will be deterred, argued Acheson, only if he believes the United States is sufficiently serious about Berlin to fight a nuclear war —and he does not believe that now. While a conventional force build-up would, however paradoxically, contribute to that impression, we could not risk Khrushchev's believing that we were limiting ourselves to a conventional war. A declaration of national emergency would enable the President to call up one million Reserves, extend terms of service, bring back dependents from Europe, and impress our allies, our citizens and, above all, Mr. K., with the gravity with which we regarded the situation. Increasing draft calls alone, added General Lemnitzer, could not produce enough trained men before the end of the year.

But to rebuild Allied confidence in his leadership after the Bay of Pigs, said Kennedy, he could not afford to overreact. A national emergency declaration was an ultimate weapon of national alarm and commitment. Such declarations, he reasoned, could not be frequently declared or easily rescinded; and without underestimating the seriousness of the Berlin threat, it might be better to await an actual Soviet treaty or move against access. Khrushchev's ability to turn the pressure off and on in Berlin and a half-dozen other spots required the United States to prepare a long-haul global effort, not constant "crash" programs for what might be, he said, "a false climax." The foreign aid, space and domestic measures required for that long haul would be endangered by the extensive new budget and tax requests envisioned in the national emergency declaration.

He liked, moreover, the advice cabled from our embassy in Moscow that the Soviet mind was more likely to be impressed by substantial but quiet moves that did not panic our allies. Other Soviet experts also counseled that dramatic gestures would impress the Soviets less than a long-range build-up in our readiness. This was in keeping with Kennedy's own philosophy: a decision to go all the way can afford to be low-key because it is genuine, while those who loudly flail about are less likely to frighten anyone. Fanfare at an early stage, added his intelligence advisers, would make the Soviets feel compelled to respond with a strong public posture and military measures of their own, and make their negotiating position more rigid.

Gradually the President brought McNamara, Rusk and others around to his view. The Defense Secretary agreed that a more gradual and orderly build-up could be achieved through a quick but quieter Congressional Resolution. On the afternoon of Wednesday, July 19, meeting at 3 P.M. with a small group of us in his living quarters on the second floor of the Mansion, the President put the finishing touches on his plan. After six weeks of intensive meetings, he stated each decision in firm, precise tones. The additional military budget requests would total $3.2 billion rather than $4.3 billion. The Congress would be asked to provide stand-by authority to call up the Reserves, rather than an immediate mobilization. Draft calls would be more than tripled, West Berlin would be readied, Allied agreement on economic sanctions would be sought, a temporary tax increase would be requested (this decision, as previously noted, was later reversed) and no declaration of national emergency would be proclaimed.

The same advisers and the President then met at 4 P.M. in the Cabinet Room with a larger group in a formal National Security Council session. The decisions just concluded were "decided" for the record. Acheson questioned caustically the changes in his recommendations; and to the delight of the President—who enjoyed an articulate clash—Secretary McNamara, who had been finally converted to these changes only the previous day, undertook their defense with equal fervor.

The President also decided, contrary to Acheson's paper and the initially prevailing view among his advisers, that the West should "lean forward" on negotiations. Here again some of the Kremlinologists had been influential, suggesting that the Soviets would be impressed by firmness in our negotiating position, not by our staying away from all talks. Acheson counseled that Khrushchev would accept nothing reasonable and would interpret all offers as weakness. The United States, replied the President, cannot leave the diplomatic initiative to a Soviet-sponsored peace conference. "We do not intend to leave it to others," he said later, "to choose and monopolize the forum and the framework of discussion." His hopes for a world-wide propaganda campaign—on "self-determination" for West Berlin and on the contrast between the two Germanys— would surely fail if only the Soviets had a "peaceful" solution. He had no intentions of lulling the West into believing that a meeting at the negotiating table reduced all danger. But he did have hopes of persuading Khrushchev to postpone his treaty as long as alternatives were being actively explored.

Before Khrushchev could be presented with any agreed-upon new ideas, however, the West had to produce some new ideas and agree upon them—and neither had happened by mid-July. Indeed, the difficulty of finding any new ideas which could be sold to all concerned would remain throughout Kennedy's term. The French were against all negotiations;

the British were against risking war without negotiations; and the Germans, as their autumn elections drew nearer, were against both of these positions and seemingly everything else. The necessarily generalized passages dealing with diplomatic approaches were thus the weakest parts of the President's July 25 TV address. Nevertheless, by underlining our willingness to talk "with any and all nations that are willing to talk, and listen, with reason"—our willingness "to remove any actual irritants in West Berlin [though] the freedom of that city is not negotiable"—and our willingness to submit the legality of our rights to "international adjudication" and our presence in West Berlin to a free vote among its people, he at least struck in a few moments more positive notes than he had been able to obtain in seven weeks from the American and Allied diplomats. Nevertheless, these were comparatively weak initiatives.

It was not, however, a weak speech. Its delivery was hampered by an overcrowded, overheated office. Its domestic economic references were out of place. Its civil defense references were out of perspective. But its basic message was firm and urgent without resort to threats or fear. I had completed the first draft over the weekend. All day Monday and Tuesday successive drafts were reviewed and revised by the President and his aides. General Taylor suggested the paragraph:

> I hear it said that West Berlin is militarily untenable. And so was Bastogne. And so, in fact, was Stalingrad. Any dangerous spot is tenable if men—brave men—will make it so.

Murrow suggested the phrase: "We cannot negotiate with those who say, 'What's mine is mine and what's yours is negotiable.'" Bundy suggested passages recognizing "the Soviet Union's historical concerns about their security in Central and Eastern Europe" and the "enormous losses . . . bravely suffered [by] the Russian people . . . in the Second World War." Journalist Max Freedman suggested the basis for an eloquent peroration. I added a sentence used by the President in his July 19 meeting: "We do not want military considerations to dominate the thinking of either East or West." The State Department added a reminder to our NATO Allies: "The solemn vow each of us gave to West Berlin in time of peace will not be broken in time of danger. If we do not meet our commitments to Berlin, where will we later stand?"

Finally, with all changes and clearances completed and coordinated along the lines of the President's instructions, I took his reading copy for the 10 P.M. talk over to the Mansion around eight o'clock. I found the President sitting up in bed, a hot pad behind his back, scribbling out a personal note with which to close.

> When I ran for the Presidency of the United States, I knew that this country faced serious challenges, but I could not realize,

nor could any man realize who does not bear the burdens of this office, how heavy and constant would be those burdens. . . . In these days and weeks I ask for your help, and your advice. I ask for your suggestions, when you think we could do better. All of us, I know, love our country, and we shall all do our best to serve it. In meeting my responsibilities in these coming months as President, I need your good will, and your support and, above all, your prayers.

It was a somber close for a somber speech—a speech more somber, in fact, than the American people were accustomed to accept, more somber than any previous Presidential speech in the age of mutual nuclear capabilities. "West Berlin has now become," he said,

> the great testing place of Western courage and will, a focal point where our solemn commitments . . . and Soviet ambitions now meet in basic confrontation.
>
> We cannot and will not permit the Communists to drive us out of Berlin, either gradually or by force. For the fulfillment of our pledge to that city is essential to the morale and security of Western Germany, to the unity of Western Europe, and to the faith of the entire free world. . . . It is as secure . . . as the rest of us, for we cannot separate its safety from our own. . . . We will at all times be ready to talk, if talk will help. But we must also be ready to resist with force, if force is used upon us. Either alone would fail. Together, they can serve the cause of freedom and peace. . . .
>
> To sum it all up: we seek peace, but we shall not surrender. That is the central meaning of this crisis, and the meaning of your government's policy. With your help, and the help of other free men, this crisis can be surmounted. Freedom can prevail, and peace can endure.

Khrushchev, as he later wrote Kennedy, regarded the speech as belligerent. He had previously increased the Soviet military budget and put on his old uniform to talk loudly about destroying the aggressors. Yet he professed—to John McCloy in a private talk and to Kennedy in their later correspondence—to be angry at the increases in the American military budget and the reinforcements sent to West Berlin. He called these moves military hysteria. Inwardly he may well have been angry that Kennedy was not backing down, and that the West had failed, as he had also failed, to come forward with any new negotiating proposals. His own prestige had been heavily engaged—by pressures from the East German and other Eastern European regimes to stabilize German frontiers and remove the Berlin "splinter," and by pressures from the more militant voices within the Communist camp to make good on his vow to "rebuff" those violating East German sovereignty.

Seeking to exploit disunity in the West, Khrushchev that summer had alternated between reasonable and intimidating postures, talking menacingly one day about the "shambles" in which a nuclear war over Berlin would leave Western Europe, suggesting sweetly the next day that token American and Russian troops could stay in West Berlin under a UN solution, then warning on another day that Italian orange groves, Greek olive orchards and the Acropolis would be destroyed if the West forced a war.

In mid-August a crisis within the crisis came dangerously close to the flash point. The Communists had for some years, over Western protest, gradually increased the legal—and in some cases physical—barriers between West and East Berlin, including temporary closings of most crossing points, special traffic and entry permits and a prohibition against West Berliners working in East Berlin. Sensing that they were gradually becoming imprisoned, East Germans and East Berliners poured increasingly across the dividing line between East and West Berlin, the principal hole in the Iron Curtain. By the summer of 1961 some 3.5 million had left their homes and jobs for the refugee centers and airports of West Berlin, draining the already depressed East German economy of its lifeblood and dramatizing to all the world their choice of freedom over Communism. In August, as the fear of war or more repression increased, the daily flow of refugees rose from the hundreds to the thousands. Khrushchev's response on August 13—due possibly in part to Kennedy's speech and to De Gaulle's veto of four-power negotiations, but certainly due primarily to the hemorrhage of East German manpower—was the Wall.

The Berlin Wall—sealing off the border between the two cities with a high, grim barrier of concrete and barbed wire, separating families and friends, keeping East Germans in, free Germans out and Western access to East Berlin on a more limited basis—shocked the free world. Kennedy promptly turned to his aides and allies for advice; but there was little useful they could say in such a situation.

All agreed that the East German regime had long had the power to halt border crossings, was bound to do it sooner or later and had at least done so before the West could be accused of provoking it. All agreed also that the Wall—built on East German territory, the latest and worst in a twenty-three-year-long series of such actions in the Soviet-administered zone—was illegal, immoral and inhumane, but not a cause for war. It ended West Berlin's role as a showcase and escape route for the East, but it did not interfere with the three basic objectives the

West had long stressed: our presence in West Berlin, our access to West
Berlin and the freedom of West Berliners to choose their own system.
Not one responsible official—in this country, in West Berlin, West Germany or Western Europe—suggested that Allied forces should march
into East German territory and tear the Wall down. For the Communists,
as General Lucius Clay later pointed out, could have built another,
ten or twenty or five hundred yards back, and then another, unless
the West was prepared to fight a war over extending its area of vital
interest into East Berlin. Nor did any ally or adviser want an excited
Western response that might trigger an uprising among the desperate
East Berliners—that would only produce another Budapest massacre.

The President was nevertheless convinced that some response was
required—not to threaten the Communists for their blatant admission
of failure but to restore morale among the shocked and sickened West
Berliners. Our contingency plans had been prepared for interference
with our access to West Berlin, not emigration from the East. Our intelligence estimates, although recognizing that the Communists would
have to control their loss of manpower, had offered no advance warning of
this specific move. Kennedy thus had to improvise on his own; and
meanwhile crucial time—too much time—went by.

Finally, to test Communist intentions and demonstrate our own, he
dispatched an additional contingent of fifteen hundred American troops
down the *Autobahn,* riding in armored trucks through the East German
checkpoints to West Berlin. Obviously fifteen hundred more troops could
not hold the city against a direct Soviet attack, he said, but "the West
Berliners would benefit from a reminder of [our] commitment . . . at
this time," and the Soviets would recognize the troops as "our hostage
to that intent." It was his most anxious moment during the prolonged
Berlin crisis, his first order of American military units into a potential
confrontation with Soviet forces. Postponing his usual weekend change
of scenery to the Hyannis Port White House, he kept his military aide
in constant touch with the convoy's commander. When the first group
of sixty trucks turned unimpeded into West Berlin, he felt that a turning
point in the crisis had been reached.

Simultaneously he dispatched Vice President Johnson to address the
people of West Berlin, to rally their hope and their will, and to restate
this nation's commitment in the language (personally approved by the
President) of our most solemn pledge: "our lives, our fortunes, our sacred
honor."

Accompanying Johnson—and returning to West Berlin shortly thereafter for a prolonged stay as Kennedy's personal emissary—was retired
General Lucius Clay, a hero to West Berliners. Clay had been in command in 1947 when a Soviet land blockade of West Berlin had required

a massive Western airlift. A constant spur to Allied effort and a beloved symbol to West Berliners, Clay's presence was highly valued by the President despite his tendency to be something of an alarmist in his private cables, sometimes hinting he might resign unless his requests were granted. "He's a conservative Republican doing a good job on a thankless assignment and staying publicly loyal under a Democratic administration," remarked the President. While he was not always happy with Clay's failure to distinguish our "vital rights" in West Berlin from our grievances in East Berlin, he nevertheless fully understood the General's tendency at times to act without waiting for unanimity in his instructions from Washington, General Norstad and Allied representatives in Berlin.

The basic objective of the military, the Johnson and the Clay missions was to rekindle hope in West Berlin. Its spirit had been damaged by the Wall, its role altered, its future as the ultimate capital of a reunited Germany darkened. Khrushchev predicted that it would soon be a dying, withering city. Many Westerners as well saw little prospects of inducing new industry and labor to locate there or even inducing its present residents to remain. Some urged its complete incorporation into West Germany; but Kennedy felt that that would close out all hope of ever reuniting the city, and merely provoke the Soviets into further acts with no real gain for the West. Instead, starting with these three missions, a major effort was made under Walt Rostow to maintain and increase the viability of West Berlin—to enhance its economic, educational and cultural roles—to attract young families, new investments and world understanding. That effort succeeded, and in the years that followed West Berlin not only survived but flourished.

The Wall, however, remained—and it was an ugly source of tension. At one stage Western and Soviet tanks and troops faced each other across the barricade until the Soviets drew back. American tests of our rights to enter East Berlin—and to ignore Red warnings about keeping Westerners one hundred meters away from the Wall in West Berlin—were all successful. But no one knew when either side, convinced that the other would back down, might precipitate a situation from which neither could back down. The Soviet resumption of nuclear testing in September added to the atmosphere of belligerence.

Rapidly building Western ground troop strength (although never to the level desired, because of the failure of our allies to increase their forces proportionately), drastically revising the Berlin contingency plans to permit a wider choice of response, the President speculated as to when the great confrontation would come, when a Soviet-German peace treaty would be signed and when a move would be made to cut off access. But the confrontation never came. The December, 1961, deadline passed without any treaty. Slowly, imperceptibly, the tides of crisis receded. From time to time they would rise suddenly again, with an incident at the Wall or on the access routes. The most serious was a deliberate Soviet test in the early months of 1962 on the air corridors from West Germany to West Berlin. Chaff was dropped to upset our radar, Soviet planes buzzed our own, and the Soviets seemed to be trying in every way possible to harass the Alliance into disunity and defeat. But under the revised contingency plans and the cool leadership of General Norstad, all flights proceeded, fighter aircraft were added, and Communist bloc nations were warned that stoppage would bar their planes from NATO countries. In time the intereference ended, and the tides of crisis once more receded.

They receded in part, we must assume, because Khrushchev recognized more clearly that turning access over to the East Germans was a highly dangerous venture—and in part because the ending of East German emigration eased the pressure on him for immediate action. But they also receded because Kennedy finally succeeded in getting his side ready to talk as well as fight, in changing the East-West confrontation to one of words instead of weapons. "Winston Churchill," observed the President, "said it is better to jaw, jaw than war, war, and we shall continue to jaw, jaw and see if we can produce a useful result. . . . That [is] the purpose . . . in calling up 160,000 men [and] adding billions of dollars to our defense budget . . . not to fight a nuclear war."

To jaw, jaw, however, Kennedy had to overcome stout resistance within his own administration and within the Western Alliance; and it must be said that he never fully succeeded with either. Our diplomatic posture improved far more slowly than our military posture. The "old German hands" in the State Department were not—as some charged—loyal only to the old Dulles-Adenauer line. But in contrast to those experts on Soviet affairs who thought that at least one of Khrushchev's chief aims was security in Eastern Europe and that new Western proposals should be put forward, they basically believed that the real Soviet aim in this situation was to destroy the Western Alliance; that any willingness to negotiate on anything other than obviously unattainable proposals was a sign of weakness; that there was nothing to negotiate about since the Soviets had no legitimate interests in Central Europe that we could concede and the West wanted no changes that the Soviets could accept; and that any revision in the old, oft-rejected "Western Peace Plan" would be regarded by the West Germans as a sellout. Thus the department was slow to respond to the President's request for new proposals and slow to reflect his views in talking with its Allied counterparts.

In West Germany two fears prevailed: fear that the Allies would not stand firm and fear that they would. Welcoming concessions when war threatened, said our embassy in Bonn, the West Germans would later grumble that the West could have done better. The Adenauer government—described as "deeply neurotic" by one of its American admirers, and suspicious that the new contingency plans were a weakening of nuclear resolve—had not brought the German people face to face with the realistic choices. It was a hotbed of rumors, none of them true, that the West knew of the Wall in advance, for example, or had concluded a secret pact at German expense.

In France, General De Gaulle supported Adenauer with variations on the same theme. Unlike the German Chancellor, he saw no practical purpose in talking about reunifying the two Germanys or recovering from Poland the disputed territory east of the Oder-Neisse line. But he was convinced that Khrushchev was bluffing, that there was no real crisis, that an early showdown would prove it, that conventional forces were unnecessary and that political overtures would be harmful. Inasmuch as West Berlin was a three-power responsibility, Kennedy had proposed four-power ministerial talks when Gromyko came to New York for the UN session in September, 1961. De Gaulle objected to any such talks until the West had a new position—and he objected to any new position. The British, on the other hand, who were as uncooperative as the French on military preparations (but for different reasons), let it be known that they were only too eager to make major negotiating concessions—and this simply encouraged Khrushchev to be tougher, in Kennedy's view.

The President decided, therefore, that the United States would jaw, jaw on its own as a self-appointed agent for the Alliance. Theoretically we were to engage, not in "negotiations," but in "exploratory talks to see whether serious negotiations could be undertaken." De Gaulle opposed even this approval, and caused the first split (14 to 1) NATO communiqué in history. Adenauer was persuaded by Kennedy to give it his grudging approval, but the German Foreign Office continued to leak and then disparage each new suggestion that was put forward. Yet neither the West German nor any other ally's response to the crisis had incurred an added military and financial burden proportionate to our own, the President often pointed out, and he had to restrain his public comments about those nations "who speak with [such] vigor now. It is not difficult to . . . say 'Oh, well, you shouldn't do this or that' . . . but *we* carry the major military burden." Adenauer had expressed concern about the dangers of "undue optimism," he added, but that was *one* danger unlikely to arise.

Kennedy recognized that he would only encourage Khrushchev's ambitions if the Alliance were badly split, and that he could not conclude any settlement which the West Germans were convinced was a sellout. But he was equally persuaded that failure on the diplomatic front meant a return to the military front. Between this Scylla and

Charybdis he proceeded somewhat unsteadily for more than a year. "It's not easy," he candidly told his news conference.

> The United States is attempting to carry on negotiations for several powers. All of them have different ideas how it ought to be done, and we have to . . . present a position which has some hope of working out. . . . There is daily consultation . . . but . . . it takes a long time. . . . [The] necessity to debate these matters publicly . . . even before they become our official position . . . makes it very difficult to carry on any negotiations with the Soviet Union.

Yet the talks were carried on—in New York, Moscow, Geneva and Washington, in meetings between Rusk and Gromyko, Thompson and Gromyko, Rusk and Dobrynin, and Kennedy and Gromyko. Proposals were discussed in the Kennedy-Khrushchev letters and in Kennedy's meetings with Adzhubei. But no real progress was made. With all the overlapping U.S. and Allied machinery bogged down in disagreement and detail, few initiatives were forthcoming. Many of those came from the White House or from outside advisers such as Acheson; and even these, the President thought, were dissipated or discounted by the time they had gone through the bureaucratic and inter-Allied mills. Objections, amendments, delays and referrals to one group or another seemed to block every proposed plan and nearly every Soviet-American meeting. If the White House and State Department agreed, one or more Allies disagreed; and if all were agreed, the Soviets disagreed. Indeed, one of the most useful lessons to Kennedy in the entire episode was the folly of pressing upon the Germans and other Allies solutions which were not really negotiable anyway.

The talks nevertheless served the purpose of defining the U.S. position more precisely, making clear what we would and would not fight for or talk about. By stressing that his essential objectives were carefully limited, Kennedy thereby stressed that his commitment to defend them was unlimited. Our real concern, he indicated to the annoyance of Adenauer and the "hard-line" diplomats, was the continuation of our access and other rights—not whether the Soviets signed a treaty with a regime of their own creation, not whether Russian or East German sentries stamped Western papers on the *Autobahn,* and not even whether East Germans were represented at the conference table or in an International Access Authority. Nor would he close his eyes to the facts of life that would keep Germany divided for some years to come, the Ulbricht regime in control in the East, its present Eastern boundaries permanent, and Eastern Europe in fear of German military might, particularly nuclear weapons. He was willing to curtail certain of the American "irritant" activities within West Berlin which were in fact nonessential. He was willing to recognize the historic and legitimate interests of the nations of Eastern Europe in preventing future German aggressions. Could an accommodation within this framework obtain a detailed written guarantee of freedom in and access to West Berlin, thus improving our position? he asked. "We are committed to no rigid formula. . . . We see no perfect solution."

Rusk, with a professional preference for four-power ministerial meetings, had initially been undecided about meeting the Soviets alone on this issue. But once he started he tirelessly and skillfully demonstrated the value of using prolonged discussions to avert deadlines and disaster. In three autumn, 1961, talks with Gromyko in New York, he stressed that the West would not sign an agreement giving concessions in exchange for nothing more than its present ill-defined rights. "That," he said, "would be buying the same horse twice." Kennedy, in his subsequent talk with Gromyko, added his own metaphor: "You have offered to trade us an apple for an orchard. We don't do that in this country." Khrushchev, no slouch at figures of speech himself, complained later in a letter that West Berlin for him was not an orchard but a weed of burr and nettle.

Berlin was the principal topic of the Kennedy-Khrushchev letters. The initiation of the correspondence in September, 1961, helped cool off the crisis; and while Khrushchev's subsequent letters on the subject fluctuated in tone, the President always managed to find some passage with which he could associate himself to keep the Chairman's hopes alive. He wrote Khrushchev that an East German peace treaty, by convincing the West German people that peaceful reunification was impossible, might well give rise to the very kind of nationalism and tension that Khrushchev most feared. He pointed out the discrepancy between Khrushchev's stated wish not to exacerbate the situation and Ulbricht's savage bluster. He asked the Soviet Chairman to be as realistic in recognizing the West's continued presence in West Berlin as Khrushchev wanted him to be in recognizing that no all-Berlin or all-German solution was immediately possible.

During 1961-1962 the President interested himself in a variety of negotiating proposals: an updated version of the 1959 "Western Peace Plan," adjudication by the World Court, an all-Berlin free city, parallel Western and Communist peace conferences, a five-to-ten-year *modus vivendi*, the use of Berlin as a UN headquarters, a Central European security plan, an International Access Authority, a ten-point mutual declaration and others. Most failed to survive copious Allied study and deliberate French and German leaks. The result, as Prime Minister Macmillan commented to him, was that he had little that was specific to offer the Russians, "hardly the soup course and none of the fish." The Germans, prodded by De Gaulle, became angry all over again in the spring of 1962, wrongfully charging that the Americans were not reporting all their proposals and complaining about those that were reported. Our error, JFK later acknowledged, was in trying to push the Germans to accept ideas in which he could not interest Khrushchev anyway.

Nevertheless the contacts and exchanges continued. Kennedy often likened the problem to that of Austria, where several years of fruitless bargaining had suddenly produced a Soviet-Western agreement after Khrushchev took over. But even in 1963, after the Cuban missile crisis and the nuclear Test Ban Treaty had helped change the bargaining atmosphere, no agreement was reached or in sight. Khrushchev did, however, remove his pressure and halt his threats; and the President believed that our demonstrated willingness to talk—by holding out the possibility of a reasonable settlement, by treating the Soviet Union as a great power and by making clear to the world that the intransigence was not on our side— had contributed in its own way to the peaceful defense of West Berlin. "Jaw, jaw" for its own sake had been helpful and effective, and Kennedy was not pushing for any new solutions now that the pressure was off.

In 1963 the Wall was still there, but the East Germans had initiated proposals for openings in exchange for trade. West Berlin was still a city in danger, an island of freedom and prosperity deep within imprisoned East Germany. And incidents still occurred—including an unseemly squabble in the fall of 1963 over whether Western troops at the *Autobahn* checkpoints needed to dismount or lower their truck tailgates to be counted. But access to West Berlin remained free—West Berlin remained free—and neither a devastating nuclear war, nor a collapse of the Western Alliance, nor a one-sided treaty of peace had taken place as once feared. "I think [the Communists] realize," said President Kennedy, "that West Berlin is a vital interest to us . . . and that we are going to stay there."

The West Berliners also realized it. They gave John Kennedy the most overwhelming reception of his career on the twenty-sixth of June, 1963. The size of the crowd, their shouts and the look of hope and gratitude in their eyes moved some in our party to tears—even before we surveyed the Wall. The President—who would later remark that his trip had given him a far deeper understanding of the necessity of ultimate reunification—was moved to extemporaneous eloquence. "When I leave tonight," he told a trade union conference, "the United States stays." "You are now their hostages," he said to the American troops stationed in the city, "you are . . . the arrowhead." And at a luncheon given by Mayor Brandt at Berlin City Hall, he offered a toast "to the German people on both sides of the Wall [and] to the cause of freedom on both sides of the Wall."

It was on the platform outside that City Hall—from where I could see only a sea of human faces chanting "Kenne-dy," "Kenne-dy" as far as my vision could reach—that he delivered one of his most inspired and inspiring talks:

> Two thousand years ago the proudest boast was "Civis Romanus sum." Today, in the world of freedom, the proudest boast is "Ich bin ein Berliner."
>
> There are many people in the world who really don't understand, or say they don't, what is the great issue between the free world and the Communist world. Let them come to Berlin. There are some who say that Communism is the wave of the future. Let them come to Berlin. . . . And there are even a few who say that it is true that Communism is an evil system, but it permits us to make economic progress. "Lasst sie nach Berlin kommen."
>
> Freedom has many difficulties and democracy is not perfect, but we have never had to put a wall up to keep our people in. . . .
>
> We . . . look forward to that day when this city will be joined as one—and this country, and this great continent of Europe—in a peaceful and hopeful globe. When that day finally comes, as it will, the people of West Berlin can take sober satisfaction in the fact that they were in the front lines for almost two decades.
>
> All free men, wherever they may live, are citizens of Berlin, and, therefore, as a free man, I take pride in the words "Ich bin ein Berliner."

As we departed that evening to fly over East Germany to Ireland, the President was glowing from his reception. It would make all Americans recognize that their efforts and risks had been appreciated, he said. He would leave a note to his successor, "to be opened at a time of some discouragement," and in it he would write three words: "Go to Germany."

He came into the cabin of "Air Force One" with a look of pride and pleasure that reflected more, I believe, than that day's tributes. It reflected satisfaction that he had done what had to be done, despite dangers and detractors, to keep that city free. As he sat down across from me, weary but happy, he said, "We'll never have another day like this one as long as we live."

CHAPTER XXII

THE ARROWS

O F ALL the Churchill phrases John Kennedy liked to quote, his favorite was: "We arm to parley." Kennedy believed in arming the United States to provide bargaining power and backing for disarmament talks and diplomacy. He also believed in 1961 that urgent steps were required to make certain that "our arms are sufficient beyond doubt."

His task was made more difficult by the fact that his predecessor was a justly renowned general who believed that our arms were sufficient beyond doubt. "I've spent my life in this," President Eisenhower had snapped in answer to a 1960 press conference question on defense, "and I know more about it than almost anybody, I think, in the country. . . . Defense has been handled well and efficiently." Later, in 1963, complaining of Kennedy's large military expenditure increases, he would declare that "the defense budget I left behind provided amply for our security."

But John Kennedy had a different view. As a student author in 1940 he had written: "We must always keep our armaments equal to our commitments." As a Senator in the 1950's he had grave doubts that we had done so, and had strongly opposed the "New Look" weakening of Army manpower and the overreliance on "massive retaliation." As a candidate in 1960 he had repeatedly called for strengthening our nuclear and conventional forces. As President-elect he fired off a list of questions to his new Secretary of Defense following our late December, 1960, budget and program review:

> Should there be a supplemental Defense Budget . . . additional funds now for Polaris, Minuteman and Atlas missiles . . .

an air alert . . . continental defense . . . modernization of conventional forces . . . airlift capabilities . . . ?

[We] will have to undertake a basic re-evaluation of our defense strategy, targets and capability . . . the place of manned aircraft . . . aircraft carriers . . . present troop strength . . . bases abroad . . . the overlapping of services and missions . . . the coordination of intelligence functions . . . command and control systems, particularly with regard to the authority to use nuclear weapons . . . the role of the Reserves and the National Guard . . .

At the same time he gave McNamara his first basic policy change: "Under no circumstances should we allow a predetermined arbitrary financial limit to establish either strategy or force levels." Our strategy was to be determined by the objectives of our foreign policy. Our force levels were to be determined by the necessities of our safety and commitments. His Budget Director and White House aides were to work with McNamara on providing whatever had to be provided at the lowest possible cost. "Like any other investment," Kennedy had said of defense spending in 1960, "it will be a gamble with our money. But the alternative is to gamble with our lives."

Less than a week after the new administration had come into office, McNamara reported to the Cabinet and then in detail to the President what he had found in the Pentagon:

1. A strategy of massive nuclear retaliation as the answer to all military and political aggression, a strategy believed by few of our friends and none of our enemies and resulting in serious weaknesses in our conventional forces.

2. A financial ceiling on national security, making military strategy the stepchild of a predetermined budget.

3. A strategic nuclear force vulnerable to surprise missile attack, a nonnuclear force weak in combat-ready divisions, in airlift capacity and in tactical air support, a counterinsurgency force for all practical purposes nonexistent, and a weapons inventory completely lacking in certain major elements but far oversupplied in others.

4. Too many automatic decisions made in advance instead of in the light of an actual emergency, and too few Pentagon-wide plans for each kind of contingency. The Army was relying on airlift the Air Force could not supply. The Air Force was stockpiling supplies for a war lasting a few days while the Army stockpiles assumed a war of two years.

As a result, reported the Secretary, he could not answer all the President's questions until some basic analyses had been worked out.

He requested detailed answers to ninety-six questions of his own (which rocked the Pentagon and became known as McNamara's ninety-six trombones). But for the present neither the overformalized NSC apparatus nor the rivalry-ridden, disorganized Pentagon was geared to provide precise answers. He had seen enough, however, to support the President's announcement in his first State of the Union Message of plans for an increase in airlift capacity and an acceleration of Polaris; and he was agreeable to that message's direction that the Secretary of State "reappraise our entire defense strategy—our ability to fulfill our commitments —... and the adequacy, modernization and mobility of our present conventional and nuclear forces."

No incoming President had ever undertaken a more searching reexamination of the defense establishment; and Kennedy wanted it in a month. "We are trying to telescope a lifetime's work into twenty days," remarked McNamara. But he compared it with an architect designing a new house without starting all over with the concept of housebuilding.

Before the month was out, the report was in. In a succession of meetings with his White House (Bundy, Wiesner, Sorensen), Defense (McNamara, Gilpatric and Comptroller Charles Hitch) and Budget Bureau teams, the President hammered out a series of drastic revisions in nearly every part of the defense budget. He added nearly three billion dollars in appropriations, offsetting this in part by the elimination of obsolete or duplicative programs. The Special Presidential Message to the Congress on March 28 containing these revisions was remarkable for two characteristics. One was the first full statement of a coherent national defense doctrine for the age of mutual nuclear capabilities:

1. The primary purpose of our arms is peace, not war. . . . The basic problems facing the world today are not susceptible to a military solution. Neither our strategy nor our psychology as a nation, and certainly not our economy, must become dependent upon the permanent maintenance of a large military establishment. . . .

2. Our arms will never be used to strike the first blow in any attack. This is not a confession of weakness but a statement of strength. . . . We must offset whatever advantage this may appear to hand an aggressor by . . . increasing the capability of . . . that portion of our forces which would survive the initial attack. . . .

3. Our arms must be adequate . . . without being bound by arbitrary budget ceilings. . . .

4. Our arms must be subject to ultimate civilian control and command at all times, in war as well as peace . . . including all

decisions relating to the use of nuclear weapons, or the escalation of a small war into a large one. . . .

5. Our strategic arms and defenses must be adequate to deter any deliberate nuclear attack on the United States or our allies. . . .

6. The strength and deployment of our forces in combination with those of our allies should be sufficiently powerful and mobile to prevent the steady erosion of the free world through limited wars; and it is this role that should constitute the primary mission of our overseas forces. . . .

7. Our defense posture must be both flexible and determined . . . our response . . . suitable [and] selective . . . permitting deliberation and discrimination as to timing, scope and targets. . . .

8. Our defense posture must be designed to reduce the danger of irrational or unpremeditated general war. . . .

CIVILIAN CONTROL

The other remarkable feature of this and subsequent statements of military policy was their reflection of civilian control. "The Secretary of Defense and I," said the President in his message, "have had the earnest counsel of our senior military advisers. . . . But I have not delegated to anyone else the responsibilities for decision which are imposed upon me by the Constitution." In the crisis-filled months and years that followed, with the exception already noted at the Bay of Pigs, he exercised his full authority as Commander in Chief.

More than ever before, defense policy was integrated with foreign policy. No problem in the present world-wide struggle, the President told the Air Force Academy, is purely military or political. Nor do we have separate policies on defense, disarmament, diplomacy and foreign aid—"they are all bound up together in one . . . over-all national security policy." Settling an old Pentagon debate, he issued an unprecedented directive to the Joint Chiefs asking them to base their advice not on narrow military considerations alone but on broad-gauged political and economic factors as well.

In the determination of military budgets and strategy, Kennedy and McNamara were no longer mere arbiters of rival service requests. They became originators, planners and analysts, setting up task forces, sending out questionnaires, insisting on alternatives, hard facts and precise comparisons. Instead of unifying the services into one body, as long urged but bitterly resisted, they unified their effort. They did this by aligning the budgets, force levels and strategy of the three branches for the first time, cutting across traditional service lines to budget according to function for Strategic Retaliatory Forces, Continental Air and Missile Defense Forces, General Purpose Forces, Airlift and Sealift Forces and the Reserve and National Guard Forces. A new unified Strike Command, for example, combined combat units of the Strategic Army Reserve, the Tactical Air Command and supporting airlift under an Army general and an Air Force lieutenant general. The size of our Polaris force was no longer settled by the size of the Navy's shipbuilding budget but by our over-all strategic need and the contributions of other forces. The number of overlapping weapons systems was reduced— by providing, for example, a new TFX aircraft for both Navy and Air Force use. In time other vested interests gave way to modernization, as the strategic emphasis was shifted from bombers to missiles, vulnerable overseas missile bases were replaced with Polaris submarines, and jet airliftable troops deployed in this country were considered part of the forces available to a foreign front.

Contrary to complaints that he was by-passing his military advisers in these drastic alterations, Kennedy met regularly if not frequently with the Joint Chiefs of Staff. But the President centralized military decision-making in the office of his civilian Secretary. McNamara relied not only on the Joint Chiefs but also—to the despair of the military cliques and their special pleaders in the press and Congress—on a brilliant array of civilian aides, young men free from interservice bias who thought in terms of costs and options and management control. These "Whiz Kids," as they were nicknamed, supplemented the military experience of the generals and admirals with economic, political and other analyses. "We have gone pretty far afield," complained one Congressman, "when we absolutely ignore the thinking of men who came up the hard way from second lieutenant on up to wearing a galaxy of stars on their shoulders" in favor of men "who believe we can settle all by a computer or a slide rule." "We read every day," said a general sarcastically to a Congressional committee, "about how fortunate we are to have the civilian competency which is being brought into the government; and as a simple military man I accept these profound decisions as being made in great wisdom."

The President was not unmindful of his relations with the military. He addressed the three major service academies, the Veterans Day services at Arlington Cemetery and the assembled brass at the Pentagon. He toured military installations and watched demonstrations from coast to coast. He protected the military from Congressional badgering, sought to move younger men into command positions and gained the admiration of many officers resentful of his rejection of their projects.

But communications between the Chiefs of Staff and their Commander in Chief remained unsatisfactory for a large portion of his term. Enjoying a popular novel, *Seven Days in May*, about a fictional attempt by a few military brass to take over the country, the President joked, "I know a couple who might wish they could." His favorite among those Chiefs whom he inherited was Marine Commandant David Shoup, whose infrequent comments were always crisp, thoughtful and broad-minded. ("I don't think that you have to hate to be a good fighter," Shoup told Senate investigators. "I've made more than a hundred speeches and I've never mentioned the word Communism.") But with this exception, the President was convinced after the Bay of Pigs that he needed military advice that neither Bundy's civilian staff nor the holdover Chiefs of Staff were able to give.

Nor were his three military aides in the White House expected to serve in this capacity. They worked primarily on White House ceremonies and operations, warily watching each other to make certain that no other branch received a preference. Chester Clifton and Tazewell Shepard were particularly competent, useful and loyal aides from the Army and Navy respectively. But parochialism was automatically built into the White House military aide establishment, as demonstrated by Air Force Aide Godfrey McHugh late in 1962. The President was resting in Palm Beach after painfully satisfying the British at Nassau about the termination of the Skybolt missile. An Air Force spokesman in Washington thereupon loudly announced a supposedly successful test of the Skybolt, to the embarrassment and anger of both governments. The President was mentally vowing that heads would roll when suddenly General McHugh breathlessly burst in with the Air Force announcement in his hands. "Mr. President! Mr. President!" he shouted (or so the President enjoyed telling it later). "Did you hear the good news about Skybolt?"

To fill an obvious gap, the President in mid-1961 persuaded the ablest soldier-statesman available, General Maxwell Taylor, to join the White House staff as "military and intelligence adviser and representative." Taylor's frank and incisive speech, his intellectual depth and his emphasis on a range of military capabilities fit perfectly with the thinking of Kennedy and McNamara. The President had never met Taylor before 1961, but had in fact long considered him for several posts in the administration.

Some members of the military hierarchy—and their friends in the Congress and press—were not pleased at this insertion of a new figure between the Chiefs and the Commander in Chief. But terms terminate, Chiefs change and in time Taylor himself was Chairman of a Joint Chiefs of Staff which included only one of the holdovers Kennedy inherited: David Shoup.

Compatibility with the President's thinking was as important in the Joint Chiefs, Kennedy believed, as in the head of any civilian department. He strongly opposed a bill which would have lessened a President's appointive freedom by fixing the tenure of all Chiefs at four

years. "Any President," he said, "should have the right to choose carefully his military advisers." Privately he told me he would veto the bill
if it passed; and, in a demonstration of his conviction and authority,
he broke precedent by failing to reappoint Admiral George Anderson to
a second term as Chief of Naval Operations and by extending Air Chief
LeMay's term for only one year. Anderson had overstepped the bounds
of dissent with Kennedy and McNamara on more than one issue, and
the meaning of his departure was not lost on his fellow brass; but his
many backers in the Congress were unable to make out a case of martyrdom when Kennedy put his considerable talents to use by naming him
Ambassador to Portugal.

Kennedy and McNamara were also determined that civilian control
be maintained in the event of emergency. In order to lessen the chances
of unauthorized or accidental war—in order to permit the kind of deliberate and selective response which might end or limit even a nuclear war
—and in order to preserve a clear authority capable of giving recognized
messages to our citizens, servicemen and enemies at a time of pandemo-
nium—they steadily improved the reliability and survivability of the
command and control system. They initiated, among other steps, a
safer missile design, improved warning systems, clearer centralization of
authority in the President, better wartime protection of the President
and his potential successors, new airborne and seaborne command posts
for the President and others, alternate communication channels, electronic remote-control locks on nuclear weapons, and an improved series
of checks on mechanical and human failure from the White House on
down to the B-52 pilot.

Both at his desk and on some of his many trips to military installations about the country, the President sometimes tested the speed and
reliability of the communications network. Startled officers in the Pentagon War Room or in a remote SAC base would pick up seldom-used
phones to hear him say, "This is President Kennedy. I'm just checking
communications. How are things going up your way?" He remained
slightly suspicious, however, of the value and purpose of all the special
telephones. He and I were both startled early in his first year when the
ring of a previously unnoticed phone in his bedroom interrupted our
conference. The woman on the other end, certain she had called the
animal hospital, was not easily persuaded by the voice saying, "No,
this is John Kennedy. . . . No, this really is President Kennedy."

THE NUCLEAR DETERRENT

In three years Kennedy's build-up of the most powerful military force in
human history—the largest and swiftest build-up in this country's peace-

time history, at a cost of some $17 billion in additional appropriations—provided him, as he put it, with a versatile arsenal "ranging from the most massive deterrents to the most subtle influences." The most massive deterrent was our strategic nuclear force. Beginning with that first Defense Message of March, 1961, the President sharply increased the production and development of the submarine-launched Polaris and the underground Minuteman missiles. By emphasizing the survivability of these weapons, he emphasized both the futility of any attempt to find and knock them out and their second-strike, nonprovocative, time-granting nature. (They were in sharp contrast, for example, with the vulnerable Jupiter missiles located near the Soviet Union in prior years, easy targets requiring hair-trigger Presidential decisions.) Having warned in the campaign against "tempting" Soviet leaders "with the possibility of catching our aircraft and unprotected missiles on the ground in a gigantic 'Pearl Harbor,'" he placed more nuclear-armed bombers—our chief deterrent until the long-range missile program was completed—on a stand-by fifteen-minute alert basis.

Even more reassuring than these increases was a clearer definition of exactly what was meant by, and needed for, "deterrence," namely: a nuclear force sufficiently large and secure (1), in general, to give any rational decision-maker in the enemy camp the strongest possible incentive not to launch an attack by denying him all prospect of victory or even survival and (2), specifically, under the most pessimistic assumptions, to enable that portion of our force which could survive the most serious possible attack to destroy (a), if necessary, the aggressor's cities and population and (b) enough of his remaining military strength, while still retaining some reserve of our own, to convince him that he could neither complete our destruction nor win the war.

How was this point of deterrence to be determined in concrete figures? asked the skeptics. All the factors contained variables and uncertainties. But, within a reasonable range, McNamara made the first systematic effort to calculate this level on the basis of our best estimates of the size and nature of Soviet attack forces and the performance capabilities of our own retaliatory forces. The estimates used in these calculations were based on public information, reports from Soviet defectors and modern as well as traditional intelligence methods.

In our budget review sessions, McNamara in effect acknowledged that he was agreeing to a nuclear force above the level of pure deterrence, but that the additions could be justified as forces to limit the Soviet's ability to do further damage should deterrence fail. He and Kennedy agreed, however, that to go further and seek a "first-strike" capability—designed theoretically to render the enemy incapable of damaging us severely, the kind of capability advocated in some Air

Force quarters—was not only unnecessarily expensive and provocative but not really feasible. An enemy could always protect or conceal enough missile power to inflict at least thirty to fifty million fatalities on this country, especially by using more submarine-launched missiles. And he could easily offset our attempts to outbuild him by increasing his own forces as he saw ours grow.

Recognizing the infeasibility of a pre-emptive first-strike or full "counterforce" capability, Kennedy and McNamara could see as no one else could the insecurity of an endless, unlimited arms race, and the waste of indiscriminately adding tens of billions of dollars' worth of nuclear weapons as requested by the individual service Chiefs. "There is a limit to how much we need . . . to have a successful deterrent," said the President. "When we start to talk about the megatonnage we could bring into a nuclear war, we are talking about annihilation. How many times do you have to hit a target with nuclear weapons?" He looked forward to a leveling off of defense spending and the allocation of more funds to domestic needs.

But these same calculations of deterrence also enabled Kennedy and McNamara to see clearly the folly of unilateral disarmament, and the irrelevance of complaints that we already had enough to "overkill" every Soviet citizen several times. Because our safety as a second-strike nation required a great enough force to survive a first strike and still retaliate effectively, and because our strategy required enough weapons to destroy all important enemy targets, there was no absolute level of sufficiency. The concept of deterrence, moreover, required not only superior forces but a degree of superiority that would, when made known—and the Kennedy administration took unprecedented steps to make it known—convince all Allies and adversaries of that fact.

THE MISSILE GAP

This same problem of determining how much is enough in comparison with a secret, aggressive society produced the issue known as the "missile gap." That controversy, which rose rapidly on the political scene following the successful Soviet missile tests in 1957, can now be put into perspective:

• Contrary to the charges made by some Democrats in 1960, the Eisenhower administration's official intelligence estimates of Soviet missile prospects were not revised downward for political or budgetary reasons.

• Contrary to the charges made by some Republicans in 1961, Democratic alarms in previous years about a coming "missile gap" had been sounded in good faith and with good reason. The gap prediction was not the fictitious invention of either deceitful politicians or budget-hungry Air Force officers who knew their fears were exaggerated. It was largely the result of honest error by both military and civilian officers; and it was spread by Republican officials as well as Democratic Senators and nonpartisan columnists.

• Eisenhower was right in downgrading the "missile gap" dangers in 1960; Kennedy was right in stepping up our missile program in 1961. In fact, the high-priority missile build-up undertaken by both Presidents, prodded by these fears which proved unfounded, prevented the opening of any gap.

Much of the controversy stemmed from different definitions of the same phrase. While "missile gap" to some implied a comparison of each country's current missile efforts, to others it referred to the future. While some talked about intercontinental ballistic missiles (ICBMs) only, others talked about all missiles. While some compared sheer numbers, others proposed a more realistic equation of technology, vulnerability, delivery systems and the advantage lying with the aggressor.

If the phrase referred to the Soviets' lead in 1957 in rocketry and engine thrust, to their capacity to convert that lead into the world's first sizable force of ICBMs, or to the *total* number of missiles of all sizes and ranges targeted by either side, then clearly a "missile gap" did exist at one time. But if the phrase referred to a Soviet missile-based over-all military superiority capable of reducing on first strike America's re-taliatory capacity to an insignificant level, then clearly no such "missile gap" ever existed.

Yet even that latter gap might have existed, and concern with it was not incomprehensible. The successful Soviet missile test in 1957, their subsequent space exploits, Khrushchev's claim that missile mass production was under way, and his new belligerence and fondness for nuclear blackmail, all seemed to confirm the worst fears of the U.S. intelligence experts in the late 1950's. They assumed that the Soviets would seek a superior first-strike force, since they had the industrial and technological capacity to do so. These fears were repeated by a series of secret and public reports by impartial commissions, leaked to column-ists and Congressmen and variously supported by the testimony of sev-eral top generals. President Eisenhower and his Secretaries of Defense stated that it was probable that the Soviets were ahead in some areas of long-range ballistic missile development, at least in numbers; and the House Appropriations Committee, after listening to Secretary Mc-Elroy in closed session in 1959, indicated that its information forecast a possible three-to-one Soviet lead by the end of 1962.

But before all U-2 flights were ended on May 1, 1960, their photog-raphy indicated that Khrushchev had been bluffing. Apparently his first

ICBM had been too costly, too cumbersome and too vulnerable a weapon for mass production and deployment. He had settled, instead, for a very few of those missiles while pushing ahead on the deployment of medium-range missiles aimed at Europe and the development of a better ICBM.

But 1960 was a campaign year. Republican attempts to downgrade the issue were looked upon with suspicion. All the evidence available to Kennedy, and to those Senators on whose efforts he drew, indicated a dangerous situation. In his primary and fall campaigns he referred sparingly and for the most part cautiously to the Soviet missile "advantage," avoiding precise dates and numbers, quoting nonpartisan experts and emphasizing that the United States was still the stronger military power although danger lay ahead. The conflicting claims over dates and numbers, he said, were differences of degree which he preferred to avoid: "I say only that the evidence is strong . . . that we cannot be certain of our security in the future any more than we can be certain of disaster. . . . If we are to err in an age of uncertainty, I want us to err on the side of security."

All the U-2 evidence was in before the Kennedy-Nixon campaign began. But it was never made available to Kennedy in the CIA and military briefings arranged for him. Late in August he flew to Strategic Air Command headquarters in Omaha for a briefing arranged by the administration. Almost immediately it was apparent that he was not to be given a full-scale top-secret fill-in on Soviet-American missile and bomber strength. Somewhat angrily Kennedy insisted that he had had more access to information merely as a member of the Senate Foreign Relations Committee—and that if the Air Force was that complacent, he would remember it at appropriation time the following year.

When Kennedy and McNamara took office, their first review of the National Intelligence Estimates revealed not one but several estimates —and these were likely to coincide in the case of the military intelligence representatives with the strategic views and roles of their respective services. The Air Force estimate, for example, of Soviet missiles then in being was far higher than that of the Navy. While they searched for better answers, the Secretary of Defense—new to the perils of the Washington press corps—stumbled over the ill-defined meaning of "missile gap" in a background press briefing, causing a new controversy as to whether he had admitted that no such gap existed. But before the summer was out the picture was clear.

The new 1961 estimates did suggest a "gap" favoring the Soviet Union in raw numbers of ballistic missiles then in operation; but the quantities of long-range missiles on both sides were so small compared to our bomber force that this "gap" had no serious military significance. Even this estimate was later revised downward, and the build-up undertaken by the Kennedy administration helped make certain that no gap would ever subsequently open.

CIVIL DEFENSE

Kennedy's error in 1960 on the "missile gap" had been the result of the public's being informed too little and too late—even after the facts were certain—about a danger which he had in good faith overstated. His error in 1961 on civil defense, however, was in giving the public too much information too soon—even before his program was certain —about a danger which with good reason he understated.

John Kennedy's views on civil defense, unlike most of his views as man and President, were too quickly formed. He did not, to my knowledge, ever talk about the subject as a Senator or candidate. It was not mentioned in his Inaugural or State of the Union addresses. It was ignored in his March 28 Defense Message, despite all the attention that message paid to continental defense. It was not stirred by intermittent and unreliable reports that the Soviet Union was starting a vast fallout shelter program.[1]

Nor was the President influenced by the zealous advocacy of his Director of the Office of Civil Defense Mobilization, Frank Ellis. After rendering effective political support in Louisiana, Ellis had finally settled for the OCDM job. Hoping to make it more meaningful, he publicly appealed for more funds than Kennedy allotted him, and vigorously sought ways to alert the public to the importance of civil defense. Upon learning that Ellis planned to fly to Rome to seek a testimonial from the Pope in behalf of the Ellis plan to install a fallout shelter in every church basement, the President gently suggested that it would be a mistake to bother the Pope at that time.

But more serious mistakes lay ahead. It is often said that Kennedy's decision to push civil defense was the result of the Berlin crisis. In fact, it came during the five weeks of agonizing reappraisal between the Bay of Pigs in April and his second State of the Union Message in May. A study by Carl Kaysen of the White House staff made clear that the current effort was based on outmoded concepts, that its budget was a waste, and that the United States should either face up to the problem in a serious way or forget it. It was not in John Kennedy's nature to forget it. Facing up to it was consistent with the note of added ur-

[1] Adzhubei told me that fall the latest advice to Russians on the subject from the "Armenian Radio":
Q—What should I do if a nuclear bomb falls?
A—Cover yourself with a sheet and crawl slowly to the nearest cemetery.
Q—Why slowly?
A—To avoid panic.

gency and effort he wished to sound to the Congress. His obligations as President did not permit him to ignore the protection of human lives while protecting our weapons of war. He did not expect an attack, but he was always aware of the danger of escalation, miscalculation or accidental war. Nor was he unmindful of the fact that New York's Governor Nelson Rockefeller, who appeared then to be his most likely opponent in 1964, was criticizing the administration's "complacency" on civil defense in much the same terms Kennedy had applied to the "missile gap" in earlier years.

His May 25 address to the Congress thus called for shelters as a new form of "survival insurance" against the hazards of radioactive fallout. Partly as a matter of more efficient government organization, he transferred jurisdiction over civil defense from Ellis to McNamara. A long and difficult negotiation between the two men on the terms of the transfer, mediated by the Budget Bureau with my help, had not yet been completed by the time of the President's speech. Ellis was willing to have only the shelter program transferred to Defense, McNamara wanted full responsibility or none. To obtain the agreement of both men to the language in Kennedy's announcement, I carefully worded that portion of the President's message to read somewhat ambiguously: "I am assigning responsibility for this program to . . . the Secretary of Defense." Each man assumed this meant I had decided he was right. But shortly thereafter all civil defense functions were moved to Defense, the OCDM was reorganized into the Office of Emergency Planning, and Ellis resigned to accept a judgeship.

The May 25 plea for a new Federal effort was strong in comparison with past Presidential statements but cautiously worded. The President emphasized that it was insurance "we could never forgive ourselves for foregoing in the event of catastrophe." A new plea for civil defense was thus logically included in his TV address on the Berlin crisis some two months later. But this speech, unlike that in May, was delivered in a context of clear and present danger. It had the anxious attention of the nation to a far greater degree. It was concerned with a possible nuclear war over Berlin that very year, not simply an accidental attack at some speculative time. And its concluding advice on civil defense was couched in particularly ominous tones:

> In the event of an attack, the lives of those families which are not hit in a nuclear blast and fire can still be saved—*if* they can be warned to take shelter and *if* that shelter is available. . . . The time to start is now. In the coming months, I hope to let every citizen know what steps he can take without delay to protect his family in case of attack. I know that you will want to do no less.

The President's aim was to bestir a still slumbering public; and he succeeded beyond his own expectations and desire. The civil defense "balloon" not only went up, it disappeared from sight. Shelter manufacturers reported a surge in sales at $1,500 each (and some did their best to keep fears at a peak). Local civil defense officers were besieged with inquiries. Saving one's family from fallout became the individual citizen's contribution to foreign policy. Scientists and pseudoscientists debated how many could survive a nuclear war with or without shelters, how long they would have to remain underground and what life would be like when they emerged. Clergymen debated whether man's ethical values required him to accept death like a cinder or life like a mole. Woman's-page columnists offered handy advice on foods to stock, clothes to bring and books to read. Merchants quickly sold home survival kits, ration packs, sandbags, periscopes, and phony fallout suits and salves. A national controversy raged over whether those who had provided for their own survival could shoot less diligent neighbors demanding access, or whether those barred from a shelter would block up its air shafts. Parents warned their children not to reveal the whereabouts of their shelters. Do-it-yourself became save-only-yourself.

Jingoist groups thrived on the level of near-hysteria which was reached—at least in some parts of the country—as increased discussion only made it obvious that no program could save everyone. Some shelter owners, believing the claims of *Life* magazine and others that shelters could enable 90-97 percent of the population to survive a nuclear attack, said it would be "just another war." Pacifist organizations assailed shelters as though they were a substitute for our efforts on peace. Local civil defense officials proved in some cases to be overzealous or confused.

The confusion and panic were aggravated by the Kennedy administration's lack of a comprehensive shelter program, a clear-cut shelter policy or even an authoritative voice placing the whole problem in perspective. Only the President could supply that voice. But the President was uncertain; and his advisers, like the country, were divided. All agreed that any effort that might save millions of lives was worthwhile. But should it be family shelters or community shelters—receive high budget priority or a more limited investment—be under national or local control? He had spoken of shelter against fallout, but nuclear scientist Edward Teller told him that, for a mere $50 billion, the nation could protect itself against even nuclear blast by burrowing deeper and deeper as the Soviet weapons grew larger. There were political pressures on every side; and the President, aware of the different effects his own two statements had caused, and conscious of his obligations to save Americans in the future and unite them in the present, resisted suggestions for a new "fireside chat." He wanted no more said until our program was ready, and he wanted that program weighed carefully. Having created this laboring mountain, he was reluctant to bring forth a mouse; but he was even more unwilling to let the mountain over-shadow his over-all policy.

The chief focal points of the debate within the administration were the proposals for shelter legislation and a public information booklet. In time both were toned down to a low-key level. The legislation in 1962 simply requested a long-range program of Federal incentives for the construction of community shelters in schools, hospitals, libraries and similar public centers, the cost to be shared by state and local governments and nonprofit institutions. These would supplement the sixty million existing shelter spaces identified in a quietly successful Defense Department survey, but made no pretense of covering everyone or offering protection against blast and firestorm.

The original draft of the Federal booklet contained terrorizing pictures, fatuous assurances, useless instructions and an expectation of nuclear war. It even praised the "new market for home shelters . . . in keeping with the free enterprise way." It was scrapped in favor of a blander, more realistic pamphlet, which deleted references to shelters as part of our national defense, inserted material on how grim a post-attack world would be and made a series of similar alterations. Instead of being sent to every American household as first planned, it was simply made available in post offices and local civil defense offices for those who requested it.

The internal administration debate over the bill and the booklet helped clarify the President's own mind. Civil defense, as he had said in May, was simply a matter of insurance, not deterrence. It had no direct bearing on either defense or disarmament and was not a new weapon in the cold war. No reasonable shelter program could help discourage an enemy attack, prevent an unacceptable loss of life or strengthen this nation's position at either the summit or the brink. But neither was such a program provocative, cowardly or unnecessary. He still bore the responsibility in an age of thermonuclear weapons for the lives of 180 million Americans and the survival of this nation as a nation. Nuclear war was improbable but not impossible—"And I don't want the survivors, if there are any," he said ruefully to me one day, "to say we never warned them or never did anything to save at least some of their families while there was still time."

He did not give the shelter bill a top priority—reducing it in 1963 from the level of a major Presidential message to a departmental request —but he continued (in vain) to put it forward. "When the skies are clear," he told his news conference in 1962, noting that public interest

had subsided almost as suddenly as it had spurted upward, "no one
is interested. . . . Then, when the clouds come—[and] after all, we have
no insurance that they will not come— . . . everyone will wonder, why
wasn't more done? I think the time to do it is now."

THE RESUMPTION OF NUCLEAR TESTING

The fallout shelter controversy in the summer of 1961 was heightened
by new fears of nuclear testing in the atmosphere. Since 1956, when he
had followed the lead of party nominee Adlai Stevenson, Kennedy had
believed—as he said at that time—that "the United States should take
the leadership in bringing these tests to an end." In 1959, as a Senator
and national contender, he had strongly opposed Governor Rockefeller's
call for resuming underground testing, which along with all other tests
had been suspended on both sides while negotiations at Geneva sought
a formal test-ban treaty. In 1960, as a candidate, he had pledged not to
resume testing in the atmosphere first and not to test underground
until he had had time "to exhaust all reasonable opportunities" for agreement. In January, 1961, his first announcement at his first Presidential
news conference had disclosed the commissioning of a special group to
prepare a new bargaining position and an actual draft of a reasonable
and effective treaty. His private belief was that a better prepared, more
reasonable U.S. position in 1960 would have secured a test-ban treaty
then, and he regarded this as the most promising area for him to begin
"anew" with the U.S.S.R.

But when he sent Arthur Dean to Geneva in the spring with a new
treaty, carefully designed to meet all legitimate Soviet objections, he
found that the Soviet position had moved still further away from ours.
Events in the Congo, they argued, had convinced them that they could
not rely on international operations governed by either a neutral or a
majority, and no test-ban inspection system in which they did not reserve a veto would be acceptable.

At Vienna Khrushchev insisted to Kennedy that no neutral could
be trusted not to authorize American spying, that more than three on-site
inspections a year of seismic disturbances would be espionage, and that
the whole subject should be relegated to an unimportant part of his
elusive disarmament plan. Kennedy pressed him hard on the dangers
of other countries developing nuclear arsenals; but Khrushchev, while
agreeing that there was some logic in this, stated that the fact that
France simply spat on the Geneva negotiations and continued testing
proved his point.

The Soviet Chairman did state at Vienna, however, that his country
would wait for the United States to be the first to resume testing.

Gromyko said the same to Rusk. Both agreed with Kennedy that the negotiations at Geneva should continue. The President told his news conference that "the stakes are too important for us to abandon" the effort. In August he asked Dean to return to Geneva for one more try, "with our hopes and prayers, and I believe with the hopes and prayers of all mankind." He asked Dean to outsit, outtalk and outlast the Russian negotiators (in what Dean had once privately called "the bladder technique" of diplomacy) until he could find out for certain whether any glimmer of progress was possible.

But ever since he had taken office, Kennedy had been pressured to authorize a resumption of U.S. testing. Renewed American testing, according to the military and the Teller wing of the scientific community, was indispensable to the development of new nuclear weapons. It would provide a necessary hedge against the possibility that the Soviets were secretly testing underground. The Joint Chiefs urged him in February to resume testing if no agreement could be reached after sixty days of negotiations (implying that they agreed to his test-ban proposals only if he agreed with their position). They were for atmospheric testing; the Defense Department was for underground testing; the State Department was for putting off a decision; and a variety of nuclear scientists said that no agreement was in sight, the moratorium had dangerously slowed our technical progress and the United States should test while continuing to talk.

A Gallup Poll in July, 1961, showed public support, by more than a two-to-one margin, for America's resuming testing on its own. The Joint Atomic Energy Committee of the Congress, almost always a force for bigger and better bombs, favored resumption. Similar pressures came from various parts of the Congress and press. Dr. Teller maintained publicly that the Soviets had been testing underground steadily since the moratorium began. The President convened in June a special scientific panel to examine the latter possibility and that panel concluded in the negative. Finally, early in August, despite a new recommendation from Maxwell Taylor and the Chiefs that testing be resumed immediately, he decided to order preparations for underground tests but not actually to resume them until it was absolutely clear—not only to him but to the world—that he had done everything possible to obtain a treaty, that the Soviets had not bargained in good faith or really wanted such a treaty, and that the security of the free world required this country to test.

At both Vienna and Geneva it had seemed to Kennedy at times that the Soviets were attempting to goad us into resuming testing first. The appealing logic of the U.S.-U.K. proposals seemed only to make them more indignant. Nevertheless, asked at his August 30 news conference about continued Soviet objections, the President refused to acknowledge the cause as hopeless. Shortly after his return to the White House that afternoon, he was handed the grim news: the Soviets had announced a resumption of atmospheric tests.

His first reaction is unprintable. It was one of personal anger at the Soviets for deceiving him and at himself for believing them. For their tests had obviously been under secret preparation even before Vienna and throughout the Geneva negotiations. His second reaction was one of deep disappointment—deeper, I believe, than that caused by any other Soviet action during his tenure.

But anger and disappointment were not panic. As a two-month series of enormous Soviet explosions went forward, Khrushchev boasted of a hundred-megaton bomb.[2] "No super-deep shelter," said the Russian Army newspaper *Red Star*, "can save [one] from an all-shattering blow from this weapon." His hope, Khrushchev told two British visitors, was to shock the West into concessions on Berlin and disarmament. But if that actually was his intention, he was doomed to disappointment.

In a series of emergency meetings which followed the Soviet announcement, Kennedy was the calmest man in the room. His advisers were filled with suggestions, including a "fireside chat" detailing our nuclear superiority, a prompt announcement of our own test resumption, the explosion of a test bomb immediately to show we weren't unprepared, and knocking out the Soviet test site with one well-placed nuclear bomb. But the President, rejecting all these answers, was filled with questions: Why did our intelligence not detect their preparations? What kinds of weapons will they need to test? How thoroughly can we monitor their tests? Can we now maintain our superiority by testing underground only? When should we test and when should we announce it?

One of the most thoughtful pieces of advice, in the President's view, was that of his United States Information Agency Director, Edward R. Murrow. Murrow urged no precipitate action that might throw away this opportunity to consolidate our leadership of the non-Communist world and isolate the Communist bloc. The voices on the right "who today urge you to resume testing immediately," he said, "will tomorrow contend that the decision to do so was merely another belated reaction to Soviet action."

What emerged from these meetings was a controlled and deliberate response that made the most of world-wide antagonisms toward the Soviets without compromising our own freedom to test:

1. On that same night of August 30, a White House statement de-

2 *One* megaton is considered the equivalent—although the comparison is almost meaningless—of one million tons or two billion pounds of TNT explosives; and it is fifty times more powerful than the bomb that destroyed Hiroshima.

nounced the Soviet tests as a hazard to health and peace and as proof of their hypocrisy and duplicity, leaving the United States "under the necessity of deciding what its own national interests require."

2. The following day, after a formal NSC meeting, another statement called the Soviet action "primarily a form of atomic blackmail, designed to substitute terror for reason . . . testing not only nuclear devices but the will and determination of the free world." That statement reassured all allies—and a subsequent full-scale briefing reassured the Congress—as to the adequacy of our nuclear capabilities.

3. Over the Labor Day weekend various statements on and off the record made clear that a hundred-megaton bomb was "far too large for military objectives," and that the United States could make one if desired but could accomplish the same impact with two well-placed ten-megaton bombs.

4. On September 3 Kennedy—joined by British Prime Minister Harold Macmillan—gave Khrushchev a chance to draw back by proposing an immediate three-power ban on atmospheric tests.

5. On September 5, having "taken every step that reasonable men could justify," and having waited until the Soviet bombs were actually exploding to the dismay of people the world over, the President ordered the resumption of underground testing in the United States. Those tests began almost immediately thereafter.

6. In the following weeks, in his talks with spokesmen for the Belgrade conference of nonaligned nations (which had timidly refused to censure the Soviet blasts) and to the General Assembly of the United Nations, he indicted the Soviets for "secretly preparing new experiments in destruction . . . while we were negotiating in good faith in Geneva," defended the necessity and safety of U.S. underground tests, and denounced the use of terror as a weapon "by those who could not prevail either by persuasion or example." He publicly appealed to the Soviets not to test a fifty-megaton bomb which could serve only to pollute the atmosphere, and then announced the explosion when it occurred—as our government had announced most of the Soviet explosions. A White Paper, reviewing the Soviet's negative negotiating position and detailing the fallout effects of the fifty-megaton bomb, was distributed to all UN delegations and others.

7. Finally, as the Soviet test series came to a close on November 2, the President issued a brief statement more carefully rewritten than any of similar size on which I worked. In addition to making clear that their tests had not ended our over-all superiority ("In terms of total military strength, the United States would not trade places with any nation on earth" was deemed by the President to be the most positive way of saying this without being provocative), the President made his

first specific statement on the possibility of this nation's resuming nuclear tests in the atmosphere.

Despite all the cautions and conditions he attached to it—which were aimed at his own military as well as the world (some of the Joint Chiefs, for example, wanted all kinds of tests immediately)—it was widely assumed that the decision had already been made with absolute finality to resume atmospheric tests. It had not. It was, in fact, one of the closest decisions the President ever had to make. While believing he had little choice other than to resume, he at least wanted to keep the door open. He had no intention of being stampeded into so serious an action merely because the Soviets had done so first. He made clear to the Pentagon that preparations to test did not commit him to test; that his personal approval would be required for each test proposed; that no test would be conducted to provide information not strictly essential and otherwise unobtainable; that no test would be undertaken which could not hold fallout to a minimum; and that several of the tests that were proposed would have to be combined, others deferred or held underground and some excluded as unnecessary. Having been told before August 30 how much progress could be made by merely testing underground, he was now skeptical when the same military and scientific authorities told him only atmospheric tests could do the job. He wondered whether our nuclear superiority and weapons development had not already reached the point where they were adequate, regardless of Soviet gains. Inasmuch as Soviet progress had not ended our deterrent, and U.S. tests could not give us a pre-emptive first strike or an anti-missile missile capability, did we need to test? Talk about a neutron bomb which destroyed only people, not buildings, struck him as foolish in the extreme.

He was, moreover, genuinely concerned about fallout: the airborne radioactive debris produced by all atmospheric nuclear explosions which emitted tissue-damaging rays into human bodies and food. He realized that natural radiation hazards would have a far greater impact on present and future generations than several series of U.S. and Soviet tests combined. But he could not accept the bland assurances of Teller and others that there was no danger at all. Even one more case of leukemia, cancer or sterility was an unwelcome responsibility; and he thought it remarkable that extremist groups opposed to fluoridation of urban water supplies could strongly favor this pollution of our air.

One rainy day, seated at his desk, he asked Jerome Wiesner what brought the radioactive particles down on areas not immediately beneath an explosion. "And I told him," said Wiesner, "that it was washed out of the clouds by the rain, that it would be brought to earth by rain, and he said, looking out the window, 'You mean, it's in the rain out there?'—and I said, 'Yes'; and he looked out the window, looked very sad, and didn't say a word for several minutes."

Even after August 30 he repeated his hopes for a test-ban treaty, his hope to get the nuclear "genie back in the bottle." Now he had to decide whether his resumption of atmospheric tests would convince the Soviets that a treaty was necessary or impossible.

An impartial panel of scientists evaluating the Soviet tests concluded that they had made important weapons progress, particularly in the development of larger weapons of low weight and high explosive content. Another long, secretly prepared and intensive Soviet series, based on the findings of the first series, might achieve a breakthrough of dangerous proportions if the U.S. had not meanwhile conducted its own experiments. The Defense Department argued that the improvement in our own capabilities from a new test series, even if not essential to the deterrent, could help provide that extra margin for limiting damage should deterrence ever fail. The unanimous military and scientific opinion was that underground and outer space tests would not be adequate.

Nearly all the principal advisers involved favored resuming atmospheric tests (although a few days before the tests began McNamara startled Rusk and Bundy at lunch by suggesting that they were not really necessary). Wiesner thought the technological arguments about even. Arthur Schlesinger suggested that we agree not to test unless and until the Soviets tested again, and Britain's Macmillan made a similar suggestion. But that meant a return to the pre-August 30 status quo as though nothing had happened. "If they fooled us once," said the President, "it's their fault. If they fool us twice, it's our fault." American scientists could not be kept constantly in a state of readiness with no testing of our own, no commitment from the Soviets and no knowledge of their possible preparations.

Macmillan was eloquent in his pleas to the President to find some way to avoid more testing. He agreed that the West must test if no agreement could be reached. But a new round of testing by both sides, he said, could spur the arms race onto a path "at once so fantastic and so retrograde, so sophisticated and so barbarous, as to be almost incredible," with nuclear weapons ultimately turning up in the hands of all kinds of "dictators, reactionaries, revolutionaries, madmen. . . . Then sooner or later, and certainly I think by the end of this century, either by error or folly or insanity, the great crime will be committed."

Kennedy shared Macmillan's concern. He agreed on the need for a "determined new initiative, a supreme effort to break the log jam" before he ordered atmospheric tests resumed. But how was that new initiative to be launched? Macmillan proposed a summit. Not without evidence that agreement is possible, said JFK. But the Soviets might stir up a new crisis over Berlin if the United States tests, warned Macmillan. They could anyway, said Kennedy. The new disarmament talks opening in Geneva might be wrecked unless the Americans forgo testing, said the Prime Minister. The Soviets would be more likely to attribute such a decision to weakness rather than goodwill, said the President, and make a treaty all the more difficult to reach.

In the end, Macmillan—whose cooperation was essential as our long-time nuclear ally and partner at Geneva, and whose Christmas Island test site was badly needed—loyally supported the President's decision. But it was the leader of his loyal opposition, Labour Party Chief Hugh Gaitskell, who helped shape the final Presidential policy. Gaitskell, whom the President liked immensely, suggested in a letter on February 20 that our tests not begin before the new disarmament conference opened in Geneva on March 14, that they be announced before that date to enable the Soviets to agree to a treaty during the first month of that conference, and that the President make clear that the conclusion of a treaty would call off our tests. The President liked this approach, for he was willing to take whatever disadvantages would accrue from the Soviets' testing last in exchange for the advantages of an enforceable treaty.

Some delicate problems remained. Some urged that he not announce our decision until the day of testing. No, said the President, secret preparations by the United States during the Geneva talks would seem too much like the previous year's Soviet performance. The State Department proposed a test over Nevada immediately after the President's announcement to show there was no indecision, no fear of fallout and no agonizing wait ahead. That made no sense to Kennedy on any of those grounds. Writing Macmillan on February 27, after we had worked on his speech over the holiday weekend at Palm Beach, he stated his intention to make a nationwide TV address on March 1 announcing atmospheric tests beginning April 15, unless an agreement were reached before then. The Prime Minister requested that the speech be given March 2 when the House of Commons would have recessed for the weekend (JFK agreed) and that the Soviets be given until May 3 (JFK changed it to "the latter part of April").

The President's solemn, factual televised address was impressive. He refused to sound so reassuring on the possible dangers of fallout that a future test-ban treaty would seem unimportant. He explained that his own soul-searching had concluded that the overriding dangers were those confronting free world security if the U.S. failed to test. With a painstaking detail which made no effort to oversimplify the facts, he reviewed the results of Soviet tests, the types of American tests needed, the stricter controls he would impose on fallout, the illogic and impossibility of another informal moratorium and the renewed offer to the Soviets of a treaty. He was acting, he stressed, on behalf of all

> free peoples who value their freedom and security and look to our relative strength to shield them from danger. . . .
>
> It is our hope and prayer that these grim, unwelcome tests will never have to be made, that these deadly weapons will never have to be fired, and that our preparations for war will bring us the preservation of peace. Our foremost aim is the control of force, not the pursuit of force, in a world made safe for mankind. But whatever the future brings, I am sworn to uphold and defend the freedom of the American people, and I intend to do whatever must be done to fulfill that solemn obligation.

No Soviet agreement was forthcoming, and the tests began on April 25, 1962. They received as little publicity as the President could "manage." He wanted no pictures of mushroom clouds, no eyewitness reports of each blast, and as little stimulus as possible to picketing and ban-the-bomb parades around the world. The Chinese Communists said the tests showed him to be "more vicious, more cunning and more adventurist than his predecessor"; the Russian news agency Tass called his last-chance offer to the Soviet Union a maneuver "strongly resembling blackmail"; the Young Americans for Freedom denounced him for waiting so long to resume; and the Students for Democratic Action denounced him for deciding to resume at all. But, as the result of Kennedy's careful approach, both domestic and world opinion leaders were generally far more united on the necessity of our tests than they had been a few months earlier and far less critical of the U.S. than they had been of the Soviets.

It was John Kennedy who still had doubts about the value of his test series (although not about the necessity of his decision). He followed the tests closely, regarded their results skeptically and resisted constant pressures to expand them. Privately he speculated that fears of Soviet nuclear test progress might have been akin to previous fears of a Soviet "bomber gap" and "missile gap"; and he continued to ask just how much nuclear power beyond the deterrent level was really necessary. His ever-increasing mastery of these complex questions would enable him to make the most of the test-ban opportunity when it came.

CONVENTIONAL AND UNCONVENTIONAL FORCES

No degree of nuclear superiority and no amount of civil defense shelters would have increased John Kennedy's appetite for nuclear war or his willingness to use nuclear weapons. It was a responsibility he was coolly prepared to meet, if meet it he must. But he deeply believed, as he once privately remarked, that any actual resort to nuclear missiles would represent not the ultimate weapon but "the ultimate failure"—a failure of deterrent, a failure of diplomacy, a failure of reason.

A superior nuclear deterrent, moreover, had a limited military value in the 1960's. It could deter a nuclear attack. It could probably deter a massive conventional attack on a strategic area such as Europe. But it was not clear that it could deter anything else. And for at least a decade the most active and constant Communist threat to free world security was not a nuclear attack at the center but a nonnuclear nibble on the periphery—intimidation against West Berlin, a conventional attack in the Straits of Formosa, an invasion in South Korea, an insurrection in Laos, rebellion in the Congo, infiltration in Latin America and guerrillas in Vietnam.

Khrushchev's speech on January 6, 1961, threatened not to destroy or invade new areas and populations but to impose his system upon them through continued "salami" tactics—through piecemeal expansion of the Communist domain one slice at a time—through limited warfare, subversion or political aggression in areas where our nuclear deterrent was not usable both because our security was not directly in danger and because massive weapons were inappropriate. If we lacked the conventional capacity to withstand these tactics effectively, we could be faced with a choice of launching a virtually suicidal nuclear war or retreating.

Unfortunately, in the 1950's, as the Communists increasingly achieved a military posture that made the threat of massive retaliation less and less credible, the United States had moved increasingly to a strategy based on that threat. Kennedy inherited in 1961 a 1956 National Security Council directive relying chiefly on nuclear retaliation to any Communist action larger than a brush fire in general and to any serious Soviet military action whatsoever in Western Europe. "If you could win a big one," Eisenhower had said, "you would certainly win a little one." Because NATO strategy had a similar basis, no serious effort had been made to bring its force levels up to full strength, and our own Army had been sharply reduced in size.

This doctrine bore little relation to the realities. Frequently, when conferring about some limited struggle, the President would ask, "What are my big bombs going to do to solve that problem?" There was no acceptable answer. Even the tactical nuclear weapons supposedly designed for "limited" wars were not an answer. The Kennedy administration increased the development and deployment of those weapons worldwide, and by 60 percent in Western Europe alone. The President understandably preferred that we hold the edge in such weapons rather than the Soviets. But he was skeptical about the possibility of ever confining any nuclear exchange to the tactical level, and he was concerned about the thousands of such weapons theoretically under his control that were in the hands of lower-level commanders. For some of these "small" weapons carried a punch five times more powerful than the bomb that destroyed Hiroshima. Those ready for use in Europe alone had a combined explosive strength more than ten thousand times as great as those used to end the Second World War. If that was tactical, what was strategic— and what would be the effect of their use in heavily populated Europe on the people we were supposedly saving? Once an exchange of these weapons started, the President was convinced, there was no well-defined dividing line that would keep the big bombs out.

This analysis of our predicament produced the new Kennedy-McNamara doctrine on conventional forces—a more radical change in strategy even than the augmenting and defining of the nuclear deterrent. The essence of this doctrine was choice: If the President was to have a balanced range of forces from which to select the most appropriate response for each situation—if this country was to be able to confine a limited challenge to the local and nonnuclear level, without permitting a Communist victory—then it was necessary to build our own nonnuclear forces to the point where any aggressor would be confronted with the same poor choice Kennedy wanted to avoid: humiliation or escalation. A limited Communist conventional action, in short, could best be deterred by a capacity to respond effectively in kind.

Obviously this doctrine did not downgrade nuclear power. But Kennedy's experiences in Berlin in 1961 and Cuba in 1962 demonstrated to his satisfaction that the best deterrent was a combination of both conventional and nuclear forces. At times, he commented, "A line of destroyers in a quarantine or a division of well-equipped men on a border may be more useful to our real security than the multiplication of awesome weapons beyond all rational need."

The new approach began immediately upon the administration's taking office. It was consistent with the President's Senatorial and campaign speeches on a "military policy to make all forms of Communist aggression irrational and unattractive." It was articulated in books he admired by Maxwell Taylor, James Gavin and the British analyst B. H. Liddell Hart. It was urged by Secretary Rusk as essential to our diplomacy. It was recommended by Secretary McNamara as a part of his build-up of options. It was represented in Kennedy's first State of the Union Message authorizing a rapid increase in airlift. It was emphasized by the ammunition, personnel and other increases in his March, 1961, Defense Message. It was expanded considerably in his May, 1961, special State of the Union Message, in which all his defense recommendations were in the nonnuclear field. It was stressed in his efforts to strengthen local forces through the military assistance program. And it was, finally, the heart and hard core of his military response to the 1961 Berlin crisis.

That crisis, as described in the previous chapter, illustrated as nothing before how useless and dangerous the old "New Look" policy could be. It also caused Kennedy and McNamara to re-examine the traditional American doctrine that the West could not fight a ground war in Europe. Eisenhower had said so publicly. But Kennedy refused to concede that the Warsaw Pact nations in the Soviet Alliance were automatically more powerful in conventional strength than the members of NATO, who had a hundred million more people, twice as large an economy, one-half million more men in uniform, and the capability of placing in time more combat forces on the ground in Central Europe and more tactical bombers in the air. ("We do not believe," said McNamara, "that if the formula $E = Mc^2$ had not been discovered, we should all be Communist slaves.") The President did not hope to defeat an all-out Communist attack on Western Europe by conventional forces alone, but he doubted that the Communists would try an all-out attack since it would guarantee a nuclear response.[3]

To provide the manpower needed for the Berlin crisis, draft calls were doubled and tripled, enlistments were extended and the Congress promptly and unanimously authorized the mobilization of up to 250,000 men in the ready Reserves and National Guard, including the activation of two full divisions and fifty-four Air Force and Naval air squadrons. Some 158,000 men, Reservists and Guardsmen, mostly for the Army, were actually called up; and altogether the strength of our armed forces was increased by 300,000 men before winter. Some 40,000 were sent to Europe, and others were prepared for swift deployment. Six "priority divisions" in the Reserves were made ready for quick mobilization, and three Regular Army divisions engaged in training were converted to full combat readiness.

Along with the manpower, the Berlin build-up provided enough equipment and ammunition to supply the new troops, enough sealift and airlift to transport them and enough airpower to cover ground combat. Some three hundred tactical fighter aircraft, more than 100,000 tons of equipment and several thousand tanks, jeeps, armored personnel carriers and other vehicles were placed in position on the European continent, and still more on "floating depot" ships.

A degree of inefficiency and grumbling not surprisingly accompanied this rapid expansion of conventional forces in late 1961. The mobiliza-

[3] His statement to a magazine interviewer that "a clear attack on Western Europe" might require us to use nuclear weapons first was not new policy, but others read "preventive war" or "pre-emptive strike" overtones into it and he took prompt steps to quash them.

tion of Reservists in peacetime had traditionally been considered politically suicidal. Newsreels containing Kennedy's picture were booed in theaters on newly opened Army bases. Some men called to beef up below-strength units at first lacked uniforms and bedding as well as weapons and equipment. Reservists who had assumed that their contract to serve would never be taken up complained to reporters and Congressmen that the interruption of their lives was unnecessary inasmuch as no fighting had broken out at Berlin. Early in 1962 two privates first class—one who organized protest meetings and disparaged his commanding officer's ban, and another who wrote his Senator, on behalf of seventy-four buddies, attacking Kennedy's "political maneuvers" in giving their jobs to the unemployed—faced court-martial charges. But "in the spirit of Easter Week" the President directed their release.

"I would hope that any serviceman who is sitting in a camp," he had said earlier, recalling his own service,

> however unsatisfactory it may be—and I *know* how unsatisfactory it is—will recognize that he is . . . rendering the same kind of service to our country as an airplane standing on a fifteen-minute alert at a SAC base. . . . We call them in order to prevent a war, not to fight a war . . . to indicate that the United States means to meet its commitments.

His objectives were achieved. The Berlin crisis eased. He could not claim that he had increased NATO ground forces to a level where Soviet forces could be long contained without resort to nuclear weapons. For our NATO Allies, accustomed to relying wholly on the nuclear bombs they hoped we would never use, responded only partially to his request for more troops. But Berlin remained free. And elsewhere in the world—in Greece, Turkey, Iran, Pakistan, Thailand and other nations around the Communist perimeter or in danger of Communist penetration—the emphasis on conventional preparations continued through the training and equipping of local armies with American military assistance as a substitute for American forces.[4]

Throughout his term in office Kennedy's emphasis on conventional forces continued. Some Senators as well as allies alleged that all this attention to nonnuclear responses signaled a dangerous timidity about

---

4 In Latin America, on the other hand, our military aid was often motivated—and used—more for political than security reasons. Even in Iran the Shah insisted on our supporting an expensive army too large for border incidents and internal security and of no use in all-out war. His army, said one government adviser, resembled the proverbial man who was too heavy to do any light work and too light to do any heavy work.

reaching for the nuclear button.[5] And in 1963 Kennedy himself wondered aloud in more than one meeting whether, were it not for Berlin,
any large-scale armies would ever be needed in Europe. But he believed
that his conventional force build-up had helped prevent a confrontation
over Berlin that might otherwise have reached the nuclear level. He
believed that his increased nonnuclear forces had required Khrushchev
to choose at the time of the Cuban crisis between nuclear war and
the withdrawal of his missiles. And he believed that the Communists
would continue their world-wide pattern of crawling under our nuclear
defenses in limited forms of penetration and pressure. To demonstrate
his appreciation of the role played by our troops, he made a special effort
to visit their operations at home and overseas. He did not share, he said,
the sentiment supposedly scrawled on an old sentry box in Gibraltar:

> *God and the soldier all men adore,*
> *In time of danger and no more,*
> *For when the danger is past and all things righted,*
> *God is forgotten and the old soldier slighted.*

UNCONVENTIONAL WARFARE

The scrawl was no doubt illegible because the President varied the verse
slightly each time he quoted it. But he neither slighted our old soldiers
nor lost sight of the need for a wholly new kind of soldier. For even
increased conventional power could not root out the assassins, guerrillas,
insurgents, saboteurs and terrorists who fought the Communist "wars of
liberation." These wars, as the following chapter illustrates, were designed not to liberate but to undermine the newly independent nations
through erosion and exhaustion in the twilight zone between political
subversion and limited military action. A small band of guerrillas, for
example, might tie down ten to fifteen times as many conventional
forces. "We possess weapons of tremendous power," said the President
in 1961, "but they are least effective in combating the weapons most
often used by freedom's foes: subversion, infiltration, guerrilla warfare,
civil disorder." A new kind of effort was required, "a wholly new kind of
strategy," he told a West Point commencement the following year.

Conventional military force alone at the Bay of Pigs, he recognized,
had been used to no avail, in the absence of indigenous support. A
prime lesson of that disaster, he told the nation's editors on April 20,
1961, one day after it ended, was that freedom in the 1960's faced

5 That makes no sense, said Kennedy. Did anyone believe that the Soviet Union's
maintenance of massive land armies cast any doubt on *its* willingness to use
nuclear weapons?

a struggle in many ways more difficult than war . . . [the] struggle . . . taking place every day, without fanfare, in thousands of
villages and markets . . . and in classrooms all over the globe. . . .
Armies [and] modern armaments . . . serve primarily as the shield
behind which subversion, infiltration and a host of other tactics
steadily advance . . . exploiting . . . the legitimate discontent of
yearning peoples [and] the legitimate trappings of self-determination.

The lessons of the Bay of Pigs altered Kennedy's entire approach—to
executive management and foreign policy in general and to conflicts in
the developing nations in particular. I am not referring to any loss of
nerve on his part but to the sweeping changes in procedure, policy and
ultimately personnel that followed that April fiasco. At first, in keeping
with the "Kennedys never fail" doctrine, he had come closer to being
pushed in even deeper, searching for a plan to bring down Castro, emphasizing that "our restraint is not inexhaustible," appealing to publishers to limit certain stories and sounding a strident note of urgency
about improving our paramilitary capacity. But while these public statements were in part deliberately stern to rebuild national unity and
morale, Kennedy's private approach was much more cautious. He placed
more emphasis on the positive path of helping Latin Americans build
more stable and democratic institutions, a policy aimed at isolating
Castro but not removing him. And casting off his own sense of shock
and irritability, he focused his attention less on the bearded nuisance
ninety miles from our shores and more on our world-wide obligations.
    He was unwilling to abandon a capacity for paramilitary action.
But his experience at the Bay of Pigs convinced him that the primary
responsibility for this kind of effort should be transferred from the
CIA to the Pentagon. The CIA, however, retained operating responsibilities as the "department of dirty tricks"; and to improve his oversight of
that agency and its many unbudgeted funds, he reactivated the Foreign
Intelligence Advisory Board under James Killian, tightened White House
review procedures under Bundy and Taylor and, upon the voluntary
retirement of Allen Dulles, searched for his own man to install as CIA
Director.
    Kennedy was never angry at Dulles, who manfully shouldered his
share of responsibility for the Bay of Pigs. Nor did he lose his personal
high regard for the Deputy Director most responsible for that operation,
Richard Bissell, who quietly resigned. But it was clearly time for a
change. Neither Taylor nor the Attorney General wanted the job of
CIA Director. New York Attorney Fowler Hamilton came highly recommended and was nearly nominated, but was finally asked to head the

foreign aid program instead. ("Just tell him," I suggested to the President, "that you meant to say ICA, not CIA.") Other names were reviewed and some were interviewed. "We want someone who won't be too prominent on the social circuit," the President told a group of us suggesting names.

Finally he selected Republican John McCone, Truman's Under Secretary of Air and Eisenhower's Atomic Energy Commission Chairman. It was one of the few Kennedy selections which caused prolonged debate within the White House.[6] McCone was extravagantly praised as a dynamic administrator who would revamp and revitalize all intelligence gathering, and he was excessively assailed as a highly prejudiced Republican who was opposed to academic freedom and coexistence. Neither extreme proved correct. Kennedy liked McCone's keen and quiet achievements and the steady manner in which he carried out his duties.

The President did not doubt either the necessity or the legitimacy of "dirty tricks" when confronted with a covert, conspiratorial adversary in an age of hidden perils. But he believed they should be conducted within the framework of his foreign policy, consistent with his democratic objectives for the developing countries and preceded by more planning and less advertising than preceded the Bay of Pigs. He also believed that the human and psychological side of planning for the cold war in general and "wars of liberation" in particular required a broader effort than those of either the CIA or the Pentagon.

"We cannot," he said, "as a free nation, compete with our adversaries in tactics of terror, assassination, false promises, counterfeit mobs and crises." But we could compete in the political and economic tactics required to gain the support of the countryside in the contested developing nations, turning against the Communists their own slogans of anti-imperialism and anticolonialism, and winning to the cause of independence in each country the young men who would be running it five or ten or fifteen years hence. Assisted by Taylor, Murrow and the Attorney General, he set up a new cold war strategy committee to develop these tactics. He gave orders to train our counterguerrilla corps in a host of civilian techniques and to send tens of thousands of civilian officials to counterinsurgency courses. A Civic Action program was initiated in Latin America training local armies in bridge-building and village sanitation as well as preventing civic disorders.

The specific military burden required to combat Communist guerrillas and insurgents, however, rested with the Pentagon—and it truly "rested." For years this problem had been given a low priority, despite

6 Others included Henry Cabot Lodge as Ambassador to Vietnam, a Boston Federal judge never appointed and Kennedy's final appointment to the Federal Reserve Board.

its prevalence since World War II in Greece, Malaysia, Burma, the Philippines, Laos, Vietnam, Cuba and China. It was the weakest point in the Western armor. Only eighteen hundred men comprised the U.S. Army's Special Forces, and they were preparing for a wholly different kind of action in a general war in Eastern Europe. Their equipment was outmoded and insufficient, unchanged since the Second World War.

Even more than money, the whole antiguerrilla effort needed leadership and ingenuity. President Kennedy, far more than any of his generals or even McNamara, supplied that leadership. Finding little to go on in the Army field manuals, he read the classic texts on guerrilla warfare by Red China's Mao Tse-tung and Cuba's Che Guevara, and requested the appropriate military men to do the same. He was not counting on American guerrillas to win foreign wars; for he knew that guerrillas depended on the local countryside and must be combated primarily by local countrymen. He quoted Mao's phrase: "Guerrillas are like fish, and the people are the water in which the fish swim. If the temperature of the water is right, the fish will thrive and multiply." But the United States, believed Kennedy, could effectively supply training, arms and leadership for this new yet ancient kind of warfare.

At first the top Army generals—accustomed to deploying battle groups and divisions too grand for these mean little messes—were skeptical, if not sullen. Kennedy kept after them. Maxwell Taylor kept after them. Soon the Special Forces—trained at Fort Bragg, North Carolina— were growing rapidly in size, skill and stature, becoming steadily better trained and better equipped. In time, all the services wanted to show how much they were doing in this effort. The Air Force came up with an "Operation Farmgate" program to provide air support for jungle warfare and with new commando-type "Jungle Jim" units. The Navy increased its amphibious and underwater demolition teams and created a fleet of Vietnamese fishing junks to harass Vietcong supply lines. Marine forces, all trained in guerrilla combat, were augmented by fifteen thousand men. Military advisers, instructors and attachés in foreign countries were trained in the language of that country at a far higher rate. Guerrilla and counterinsurgency training was added to the curriculum at the service academies and War Colleges.

But the President's pride was still the Army Special Forces, rapidly growing to a level some five or six times as large as when he took office, although still small both in total numbers and in relation to the need for more. The President directed—again over the opposition of top generals—that the Special Forces wear green berets as a mark of distinction. He wanted them to be a dedicated, high-quality elite corps of specialists, trained to train local partisans in guerrilla warfare, prepared to perform a wide range of civilian as well as military tasks, able to live off the bush, in a village or behind enemy lines. He personally supervised the selection of new equipment—the replacement of heavy, noisy combat boots with sneakers, for example, and, when the sneakers proved vulnerable to bamboo spikes, their reinforcement with flexible steel inner soles. He ordered more helicopters, lighter field radios and—for use by the smaller Vietnamese—a shorter, lighter rifle, with a less powerful kick, which still provided all the range jungle warfare required.

In time, despite continued opposition from much of the top Army brass, the new antiguerrilla forces proved one of his most important military contributions. In South Vietnam they delivered babies, chopped trails, dug wells, prevented ambushes, raised morale and formed effective bands against the Communists. "You can't say enough good things about these men," reported one observer back from that war four years after Kennedy launched the program. "Unfortunately, there aren't enough green hats . . . in Vietnam." More were on the way. But one green hat not in Vietnam that year rested in a place of honor in Arlington Cemetery.

CHAPTER XXIII

❧❦❧

THE CONTINUING CRISES

I T WAS NOT POSSIBLE for John Kennedy to organize his approach to
foreign affairs as arbitrarily as the chapters of this or any book. Military conflicts required more than military solutions. The Communists
exploited genuine non-Communist grievances. The problems of aid and
trade, the need for conventional and unconventional forces, the roles
of allies and neutrals, all were tangled together. Nowhere were these
interrelationships more complex than in those situations in the new and
developing nations which Khrushchev somewhat hypocritically called
"wars of liberation." The extent of U.S. commitment and of Communist
power involvement differed from one to the other, but the dilemma facing John Kennedy in each one was essentially the same: how to disengage the Russians from the "liberation" movement and prevent a
Communist military conquest without precipitating a major Soviet-
American military confrontation.

On Inauguration Day, 1961, three such dilemmas were on Kennedy's
desk, with dire predictions of catastrophe before the year was out: the
Congo, Laos and South Vietnam. In none of these cases were those
predictions fulfilled, even by the end of Kennedy's term. Supporting the
UN in the Congo, seeking a neutral coalition in Laos and trying to
broaden the political appeal of the local regime in Vietnam, he rejected
the purely militaristic and automatically anti-Communist answer to pursue more meaningful objectives in all three countries. While these objectives also remained unfulfilled, their conflicts were at least adequately
managed and confined, partly because of his growing grasp of their
nonmilitary implications, partly because the Sino-Soviet split restrained

as well as aggravated these situations, and partly because of the lessons John Kennedy had learned since the Bay of Pigs.

THE CONGO

The chaos in the Congo would have resembed an implausibly slapstick comic opera were it not for its grim toll of human life. After nearly eighty years of rule by a nation one-eighteenth as large, the former Belgian colony was cast adrift in the summer of 1960 in the name of independence without any solid preparation for independence. Its forces of law and order were lawless and disorderly. Its richest province promptly seceded. Its national capital soon contained almost as many self-proclaimed premiers and presidents as native college graduates. Its power centers were leaderless and its leaders powerless. It was a nation with little sense of nationhood, torn by rivalries between dozens of local political parties and hundreds of tribes. Inflation, graft, tribal friction and unemployment were rampant.

Belgian technicians were driven out and then sorely missed. Blacks massacred blacks as well as whites, and white fought against white to see which black man would prevail. President Kasavubu dismissed Prime Minister Lumumba, who dismissed Kasavubu. Lumumba attacked provincial leader Tshombe for not recognizing the authority of the Central Government, and was in turn arrested by Colonel Mobutu for saying he was the Central Government. Troops holding Lumumba for mutiny mutinied. Unity conferences produced further disunity. And rushing in to fill this gaping power vacuum with advice, technicians, trucks, transport planes and equipment—with troops to follow, if necessary— was the Soviet Union, eager to build a power base in the heart of Africa.

The only effective counter to Communist penetration and domination in the Congo was the United Nations, free from the taints of white supremacy and the appearance of direct big-power intervention. This country's unilateral intervention might have produced a needless, endless jungle war. When, in 1960, the United Nations was asked by the Congolese Government to intervene, the United States supported that effort. By the combination of a Soviet boycott of the operation, a favorable majority in the Assembly and the forceful initiative of the Secretary General, a surprisingly bold UN presence was established.

But tensions were mounting again as John Kennedy prepared to take office. Afro-Asian nations disillusioned by the UN's impartiality threatened to undermine its operation by the withdrawal of their troops. Soviet anger at Hammarskjöld's role was rising.

The Kennedy Congo policy was largely an extension of the Eisenhower policy. Its aim was the restoration of stability and order to a reunited, independent and viable Congo, free from Communist domination and free from both civil war and cold war conflicts. The chief channel of this policy was our support—diplomatic, economic and, to the extent of providing air transport, military—of the United Nations in its effort to pacify the country and reconcile its factions.

Kennedy did not want the Congo to become another Laos, draining American energies and goodwill in a jungle war against Communist-supported local troops. Nor did he want it to become another Cuba, providing Communism with a strategically located military base, vast natural resources and a fertile breeding ground of subversives and guerrillas.

His first move—taken during his first week in office—was to relieve the widespread hunger and human distress that had been created by the collapse of the Congolese economy. From our surplus stocks, he dispatched rice, corn meal, dry milk and other foodstuffs in an emergency airlift.

But little more than two weeks later he faced a sterner test. Patrice Lumumba, the erratic admirer of Ghana's Nkrumah who had served briefly as the Congo's first premier—a man who both used and was used by Soviet ambitions—was assassinated. As Communist and African nationalist mobs turned out to protest in front of Western embassies and even inside the UN chambers, the Soviets savagely demanded the removal of the UN from the Congo and the removal of Hammarskjöld—as an "accomplice and organizer of murders"—from the UN. They quickly recognized Lumumba's old Vice Premier, Antoine Gizenga (much more of a Marxist than Lumumba), as the legitimate head of the Congo, and promised him "all possible assistance and support." The threat of military force was clearly implied.

Kennedy, in an opening statement at his February 15 news conference, pledged support to the United Nations presence, backing to the UN-recognized government of President Kasavubu, and resistance to any government's attempt to intervene unilaterally "in the internal affairs of the Republic of the Congo." "There should be no misunderstanding of the position of the United States," he said, if "any government is really planning to take so dangerous and irresponsible a step."

The Russians, no more eager for a major confrontation there than we, did not take that step. The military logistics and the political balance were both against them. The General Assembly voted to back up the Hammarskjöld effort; and the Gizenga movement and Communist influence began to fade. A new constitution, a broader-based government and a renewed UN economic as well as police-keeping effort in time eased the crisis, despite Hammarskjöld's death; and a new U.S. effort to woo Africa, discussed in an earlier chapter, brought a waning of Khrushchev's influence on the entire continent.

The secession of Moise Tshombe's Katanga Province, however, was a more difficult hurdle. It was always clear to Kennedy that, if the Central Congolese Government fell over this hurdle, Gizenga or some other Communist-backed leader would not be long moving in. Katanga, with less than one-twelfth of the Congo's territory and one-twentieth of its population, produced three-fifths of its revenue and possessed the bulk of its mineral wealth—particularly the rich copper and cobalt mines of the giant Union Minière combine. Tshombe, the province's shrewd leader, used these resources and revenues to enlist help from powerful European investors, to pay white mercenaries in his army and to employ lobbyists in the UN and Washington. White supremacists in the United States Senate praised him as a black anti-Communist hero. Other black African nations, looking upon him as a tool for white neo-colonialism, urged swift action to crush him. West European nations, eager to keep Katanga's copper, cobalt, diamond and uranium mines safe and running, urged a go-slow policy. The African and European desks in Kennedy's State Department reflected a similar split.

Kennedy's own thinking was divided in quite a different way. The unification of the Congo was consistent with over-all American policy in Africa. UN pacification of Katanga was preferable to a bloody civil war that could drag in the other African states on both sides—the black nationalists against the white supremacists—and ultimately drag in the great powers as well. He was concerned, however, that the UN did not have the means to achieve this goal, and he wanted no undertakings launched which would shift the burden of achieving it to direct American action. He recognized the unpopularity in this country of supporting with funds and planes a UN peace-keeping operation that was neither peaceful nor aimed at Communists. He disliked disagreeing with the British, French and other Allies who were more inclined to protect Katanga—although Belgium's Paul Spaak, he felt, had shown great courage and restraint in reversing that nation's encouragement of Tshombe's secession. But backed by his able Ambassador, Edward Gullion, he believed that world peace, the effort to keep Communism out of Africa and our relations with the other African nations were all best served by opposing all tribal secessions in the Congo, and by supporting instead the UN's precedent-setting role as a nation-builder.

For nearly two years, during 1961-1962, the Congo question constantly intruded upon the President's agenda, as a variety of tactics, special missions and subtle shifts in U.S. policy were tried and failed. A series of clashes, cease-fires and conferences of Congolese leaders produced no reintegration, only a continuing drain on the UN's finances and on Kennedy's patience with both sides. By late 1962 the Soviets had begun casting hungry eyes in the Congo's direction once again. India, for both financial and political reasons, threatened to withdraw her troops, which formed the heart of the UN contingent. Tshombe talked cooperation, thus persuading the British and Belgians to hold off the economic sanctions the U.S. requested; but he had both the funds and forces to sit tight. Congolese Premier Adoula, showing little talent for maneuver or political flexibility, was in danger of overthrow or replacement by a more radical regime committed to the conquest of Katanga by force. If the UN would not do it, Communist bloc arms would be sought directly or through Algeria and Ghana.

Both the President and UN Secretary General U Thant had tried in vain a variety of approaches to break the deadlock. The UN now prepared for a greater show of military strength to bring Katanga to terms. U Thant requested from the U.S. additional transport planes and equipment. The Department of State, however—with a somewhat alarmist view of the pace of the deterioration and the prospects of Soviet intervention—proposed to the President that we persuade U Thant to accept in addition a squadron of U.S. fighter aircraft, to be flown by our Air Force, thus ending Katanga's resistance in a hurry. U Thant and the Afro-Asian bloc, the President was told, were so committed to Tshombe's downfall that they would ignore in this case the tradition against using big-power forces in a UN peace-keeping operation.

The most startling feature of this startling proposal was its backing. Many of the "doves" were all for it and most of the "hawks" were highly skeptical. It struck me, in the aftermath of the Cuban success of some two months earlier, as evidence of a desire by the peace-lovers to show their belief in military solutions, too. But the President was skeptical. Sending American combat forces against non-Communist Katanga would be hard to explain to the Congress, the Allies and the American people, he said, unless we could make a better case for the threat of a Communist takeover. The confidence engendered throughout the West by our careful approach to the Cuban missiles might well be lost by a hasty move not yet proven to be necessary.

On December 14, 1962, when it appeared that the proposal would not actually place the air squadron in combat or even under the UN command, he indicated tentative approval—if both Adoula and U Thant would request it. But on December 17, with both of them reported hesitant, and with the air squadron advocates now calling for its combat use under UN direction, he ruled against an immediate move, sought proof of its necessity by authorizing a military survey mission and deferred all decisions until that had been made. In the meantime, he authorized compliance with U Thant's original request for more American planes, trucks and armored personnel carriers.

In an ironic anticlimax, before Kennedy's military mission could complete its report, the UN's new offensive—prematurely launched by Katangan disorders and poor UN communications—swept into Jadotville and ended the resistance. Katanga was reintegrated, Belgium and the Congo were basically reconciled, and the Soviets were left looking in on the outside.

Yet the President knew that the creation of a new nation was just beginning. The economic, educational, administrative, medical and other tasks that lay ahead were formidable. Tribal rebellions were still a danger. Politics were still chaotic. Commerce remained at a standstill.

The United Nations, he strongly believed, should remain "to preserve the gains already made," as he said in his September, 1963, address to the General Assembly.

Let us complete what we have started, for "No man who puts his hand to the plow and looks back," as the Scriptures tell us, ". . . is fit for the Kingdom of God."

LAOS

On the Indochinese peninsula in Southeast Asia, the United States in the 1950's had put its hand to the plow of national independence. President Kennedy, skeptical of the extent of our involvement but unwilling to abandon his predecessor's pledge or permit a Communist conquest, would not turn back from that commitment.

But Kennedy did reverse the policy by which our commitment was met in the tiny kingdom of Laos, which occupied the northwest portion of that peninsula. Here, as in the Congo, the chaos would have reached comic opera proportions but for the tragedy which came with it. The tragedy in Laos, unlike the Congo, was not the excessive loss of human life. Despite constant revolts and civil war, the Laotians were a peaceful people, their many generals commanded few troops and their headlined battles shed little blood. The tragedy of the Laotian conflict was its diversion of money and effort away from the desperate economic problems of Indochina's least developed area. In the years preceding Kennedy's inauguration both American and Soviet funds had been manipulated by rival and unstable factions to serve their own political ends with very little improvement in the lot of the Laotian people.

Wholly uninterested in the cold war, the vast majority of Laotians wanted only to be left alone, as the 1954 Geneva Accords had promised. The United States refused to sign the Accords, but agreed to abide by them. The neutral coalition government in Laos envisioned by those Accords, however, was "immoral" under the Dulles doctrine. The Communists having clearly violated them in both Laos and Vietnam, the United States felt free to do so also. Consequently, the Eisenhower administration spent some $300 million and five years in the hopeless effort to convert Laos into a clearly pro-Western, formally anti-Communist military outpost on the borders of Red China and North Vietnam. Its concentration of support on the nation's right-wing military strong man, General Phoumi Nosavan, helped bring about a series of largely bloodless coups and countercoups which late in 1960 drove neutralist Premier Souvanna Phouma into working with the Soviets and drove the neutralist portion of the army, under Captain Kong Le, into an accommodation with the Communist-led Pathet Lao who controlled the northern sectors of the kingdom. American influence, incompetence and intrigue—including the support of different rival leaders by State, Defense and CIA operatives—only weakened the standing of General Phoumi and his associates among their placid countrymen; and discord between the anti-Communist rightists and the non-Communist neutrals encouraged the Communists to push even further.

As the Kennedy administration prepared to assume office, the situation was deteriorating rapidly. The Soviet Union was airlifting an estimated forty-five tons of arms and ammunition out of Hanoï every day to the Pathet Lao and Kong Le forces, steadily expanding their positions in northeast Laos and on the strategic Plaine des Jarres. The United States was airlifting supplies to General Phoumi's forces further south in the Mekong Valley (the Pathet Lao also held pockets throughout the southern half of the country). The British and French still favored Souvanna Phouma, but he had fled to Cambodia. General Phoumi had committed himself to a new offensive into Pathet Lao territory. His troops, though superior in numbers, American trained and American equipped, gave way to panic upon hearing that the more toughened North Vietnamese might be fighting on the other side.

In short, a Communist conquest of almost every key city in the entire kingdom was an imminent danger. "Whatever's going to happen in Laos," the President-elect said to me in Palm Beach, "an American invasion, a Communist victory or whatever, I wish it would happen before we take over and get blamed for it." In his January 19 conference with President Eisenhower, he asked more questions on this than any other subject. Eisenhower acknowledged that it was the most immediately dangerous "mess" he was passing on. "You might have to go in there and fight it out," he said.

In a round of conferences with his own advisers during his first two months in office, Kennedy devoted more time and task force studies to this subject than to any other. But neither Eisenhower nor the Kennedy advisers had any "right" answers. One early effort was to obtain a guarantee of Laotian security by three neutral neighbors—but they refused to take on the job. Early in March Phoumi's forces were easily driven out of their one forward position—and the moment of decision was at hand.

Essentially, Kennedy decided, he had four choices. One was to do nothing and let the Pathet Lao overrun the country. That he regarded as unacceptable. It would shake the faith of every small nation we were pledged to protect, particularly in Asia, and particularly South Vietnam and Thailand, who bordered Laos on either side. As elaborated below with respect to Vietnam, abandoning one nation to the Communists seemed almost certain to lead to a more costly stand against them somewhere else in Asia.

A second possible course was to provide whatever military backing was necessary to enable the pro-Western forces to prevail. This was in effect the policy he had inherited—and he had also inherited most of the military and intelligence advisers who had formed it. But this course struck Kennedy as contrary to common sense as well as to the wishes of our chief allies. A bastion of Western strength on China's border could not be created by a people quite unwilling to be a bastion for anyone. Even if no other Communist forces intervened, it appeared to require the prolonged deployment of a large American expeditionary force to the mountains and rain forests of the Asian mainland in defense of an unpopular government whose own troops had little will for battle. It had all the worst aspects of another Korean War—the kind of war many Army commanders had vowed they would never fight again without nuclear arms—in a country with no seaports, no railroads, only two mountain "highways" (on dry days) and almost no communications. General Douglas MacArthur, in an April, 1961, meeting with the President, warned him against the commitment of American foot soldiers on the Asian mainland, and the President never forgot this advice.

This led to Kennedy's third choice: accepting a division of the country. But the division of Vietnam and Korea had pointed up the difficulties of defending a long frontier without a large and indefinite commitment of U.S. ground forces. It would bring down upon the President all the cries about turning an area over to the Communists without solving the existing military problem. Moreover, a division would leave the royal capital of Luang Prabang in the north; and the King of Laos would never be willing to abandon the royal palace, which contained the sacred solid-gold palatine of the Laotian people, the Prabang image, regarded as the nation's only true defense. (When captured by the Thais in 1878, the only time it had ever left Laos, the image according to legend brought them such bad luck that it was hastened back to Luang Prabang.)

Kennedy's fourth choice, which he ultimately adopted, was to seek peaceful negotiations to restore a neutral coalition government. There was no need for a military solution. The vital interests of neither the Soviet Union nor the United States would be impaired by a neutralist government, and neither the Red Chinese nor the North Vietnamese were ready to fight a major war against it. Clearly the gentle Laotians themselves, if left alone, showed little interest in fighting. At times both sides would leave the field for a week-long festival, and then return to take up their same positions.

While a negotiated neutral coalition was the only feasible alternative, the President knew it would not be the most popular one. It meant sitting at the conference table with Red China. It meant abandoning not Laos but the previous policy of tying our position to the right-wing forces only. It meant in time supporting as Premier the same Souvanna Phouma, the symbol of neutralism, whom this country had previously condemned. It meant withdrawal of the American military mission, one of a world-wide network which was regarded as almost permanent. It meant, finally, accepting a government with Communist participation, with all the dangers he knew that entailed since the coup in postwar Czechoslovakia.

"I can assure you," the President would say later on this last point, "that I recognize the risks that are involved. But I also think we should consider the risks if we fail . . . what our alternatives are, and what the prospects for war are in that area. . . . There is no easy, sure answer for Laos."

In March, 1961, the fourth choice outlined above certainly provided no easy, sure answer. The President was determined not to start negotiations until the fighting stopped, given our difficult position. In 1954 the Geneva Conference on Indochina had been called while the fighting continued; and the subsequent French defeat at Dienbienphu had made inevitable the Communist gains at that Conference. The Pathet Lao and its backers now favored a repeat performance in 1961, agreeing to a new Geneva Conference but without an end to hostilities. Kennedy insisted that a cease-fire precede negotiations. He warned that the United States would otherwise, however unwillingly, be required to intervene militarily on the ground to prevent the takeover of Laos by force. He saw to it that this message was conveyed to the Red Chinese through the ambassadorial channel in Warsaw; that it was conveyed by the British—after he personally saw Macmillan at Key West—to their Soviet co-chairman of the Geneva Conference; and that it was conveyed by Nehru and Ambassador Thompson to Khrushchev. He conveyed it himself to Soviet Foreign Minister Gromyko in their first meeting at the White House.

To back up the message, preparations were initiated for a seventeen-part, step-by-step plan of increasing military action, moving from military advisers to a token unit to all-out force. The President ordered the loading of Marines in Japan and Okinawa to prepare to move to positions in the Mekong Valley section of Thailand. One unit, complete with helicopters and guerrilla experts, was landed. The Seventh Fleet was alerted. Congressional leaders were briefed. When word of the military planning leaked, Kennedy was unperturbed, believing that it was just as well the Communists knew his intentions.

On the evening of March 23 he opened his news conference with a long and strongly worded statement on our Laotian policy. A large map had been brought in at his suggestion to show the extent of the Communist threat. It is commonly said that that statement was designed to prepare the American people for an invasion of Laos. The President, if not all his advisers, had no such intent. To make this clear, he had carefully reworded the statement first drafted by the departments. His intention was to warn the Communists in unmistakable terms that a cease-fire must precede negotiations ("No one should doubt our resolution on this point")—to alert the American public to the facts of the crisis ("Laos is far away from America, but the world is small. . . . Its own safety runs with the safety of us all")—and to make clear the new American policy of supporting "a truly neutral government, not a Cold War pawn; a settlement concluded at the conference table, not on the battlefield. . . . We will not be provoked, trapped or drawn into this or any other situation; but I know that every American will want his country to honor its obligations." He spoke coolly, quietly, without bombast. Refusing to refer to Laos as a small country, he termed it "three times the size of Austria." In answer to questions he indicated that, far from regarding neutralism as immoral, he would be prepared to continue economic aid to a neutral Laos.

No deadline was set for a cease-fire, though he indicated that "every day is important." In the weeks that followed, the prospects for a cease-fire rose and fell as sporadic fighting continued. The President, in the key strategy meeting of March 9, had agreed to preparations for a military build-up. But he had not agreed, he had emphasized at the time to all present, to giving the final "go" signal. Throughout March and April he calmly withstood pressures to launch the new military effort, believing that Khrushchev might still agree to a cease-fire. The Pathet Lao, shrewdly avoiding any all-out assault, continued to expand and consolidate their position. "With a few more weeks of fighting," the President would admit privately later, "the Communists had every military prospect of picking up the entire country."

A new round of White House talks on Laos took place around the first of May. But these talks had a different ring, due to two intervening factors or events. One was the growing evidence that this nation would be largely alone if we intervened in Laos. The Pentagon talked of landing a SEATO force in which U.S. troops would play only their part. But upon pressing the other SEATO nations hard about the actual extent of their help, the President found the French strongly opposed, the British dragging their feet and most of the others willing to give only token forces, if any. The Laotian people themselves were wholly unenthusiastic, and the Phoumi forces were unwilling to fight very hard for their homeland. Phoumi himself still talked tough, but he and his men seemed both unable and unwilling to engage in many actual exchanges of gunfire.

Second, the Bay of Pigs fiasco had its influence. That operation had been recommended principally by the same set of advisers who favored intervention in Laos. But now the President was far more skeptical of the experts, their reputations, their recommendations, their promises, premises and facts. He relied more on his White House staff and his own common sense; and he asked the Attorney General and me to attend all NSC meetings. He began asking questions he had not asked before about military operations in Laos. He requested each member of the Chiefs of Staff to give him in writing his detailed views on where our intervention would lead, who would join us, how we would react to a massive Red Chinese response and where it would all end. Their answers, considered in an NSC meeting on May 1, looked very different from the operation originally envisioned; and the closer he looked, the less justifiable and definable those answers became. "Thank God the Bay of Pigs happened when it did," he would say to me in September, as we chatted about foreign policy in his New York hotel room on the eve of his UN address. "Otherwise we'd be in Laos by now—and that would be a hundred times worse."

In general, the Joint Chiefs (and most other advisers) accepted without reservation the "falling domino" theory—the premise that an absence of American military intervention would lose Laos, which would move Thailand toward the Communist orbit, which would jeopardize SEATO, which in five or six years would lose all Southeast Asia, and so on down a trail of disaster. But their individual written views revealed all kinds of splits not previously made known to the President. Those whose troops would have to do the fighting were dubious, pointing out the difficulties the Army would encounter in supplying its troops and clearing guerrillas out of the rugged mountains, and warning (somewhat inaccurately, the President later learned) of the crippling effects of dysenteric and other diseases native to the area. The President was also warned that the Communists had the manpower to open another front against us elsewhere in Asia. The majority, however, appeared to favor the landing of American troops in Thailand, South Vietnam and the government-held portions of the Laotian panhandle. If that did not produce a cease-fire, they recommended an air attack on Pathet Lao positions and tactical nuclear weapons on the ground. If North Vietnamese or Chinese then moved in, their homelands would be bombed. If massive Red troops were then mobilized, nuclear bombings would be threatened and, if necessary, carried out. If the Soviets then intervened, we should "be prepared to accept the possibility of general war." But the Soviet Union, they assured the President, "can hardly wish to see an uncontrollable situation develop." At least that was their judgment—and the President had relied on their judgment at the Bay of Pigs.

Earlier the Chiefs had talked of landing and supplying American combat forces through Laotian airports (inasmuch as the kingdom is landlocked). Questioning now disclosed that there were only two usable airstrips even in good weather, that Pathet Lao control of the nearby countryside could make initial landings difficult, and that a Communist bombing of these airstrips would leave us with no alternative but to bomb Communist territory.

If we used nuclear bombs, the President asked, where would it stop, how many other Communist movements would we have to attack, what kind of world would it be? No one knew. If we didn't use nuclear weapons, he asked, would we have to retreat or surrender in the face of an all-out Chinese intervention? That answer was affirmative. If we put more forces in Laos, he asked the Chiefs, would that weaken our reserves for action in Berlin or elsewhere? The answer was again in the affirmative. If neither the royal nor the administrative capital cities fell, and the cease-fire squabble was merely over where the truce was to be signed, would these risks be worthwhile? No one was sure.

Once in, how and when do we get out? he asked. Why cannot air and Naval power suffice? Do we want an indefinite occupation of an unenthusiastic, dark-skinned population, tying up our forces and not those of the Communists? Is this our best bet for a confrontation with Red China—in the mountains and jungles of its landlocked neighbor? Would forces landing in Vietnam and Thailand end up defending those regimes also? Above all, he asked, why were the Laotian forces unwilling to fight for their own freedom? "Experience has taught us," the President said later that May in his second State of the Union,

that no one nation has the power or the wisdom to solve all the problems of the world or manage its revolutionary tides; that extending our commitments does not always increase our security— . . . that nuclear weapons cannot prevent subversion; and that no free peoples can be kept free without will and energy of their own. . . .

He spoke of the world in general but he was thinking of Laos in particular.

Nevertheless he did not alter his posture (which combined bluff with real determination in proportions he made known to *no one*) that the United States would have to intervene in Laos if it could not otherwise be saved. That posture, as communicated by his March 23 news conference, by an order for American military advisers in Laos to don their uniforms and by further preparations to send a contingent to Thailand, helped persuade Khrushchev not to overplay his hand. A military solution—risking a big-power confrontation and the danger of "escalation"—was not in the Soviets' interest either. Moreover, the monsoon season had halted most major military movements. In the late spring of 1961 the crisis eased. A military cease-fire was effected, and a new Geneva Conference began, with the West once again united on the goal of a "neutral and independent" Laos.

East-West agreement on the meaning of that phrase was advanced by the Kennedy-Khrushchev talks at Vienna in early June. Kennedy was very frank. American policy in that region has not always been wise, he said, and he wanted to change it in Laos because that country is of no strategic importance. The Pathet Lao had the advantage of being for change, he admitted, and he could not make a final judgment as to the desires of the people. But the United States nevertheless had treaty obligations under a SEATO protocol. A solution had to be found which could avoid committing the prestige of the great powers, secure and verify the cease-fire (which each side was accusing the other of violating), obtain a government acceptable to both sides and thus draw the fire out of the situation in a way that would be mutually satisfactory. He suggested the use of Burma and Cambodia as examples of "neutral and independent" countries.

At first Khrushchev seemed to brush aside Laos as an unimportant detail, preferring to talk more generally about "wars of liberation" in the old colonial areas, and ranging into a variety of other issues about China, Africa and guerrilla warfare. But patiently and persistently Kennedy brought him back to the specific question of Laos. On the second day of talks he pressed the Soviet Chairman again on both sides' reducing their commitments. Laos, he said, is not so important as to get us as involved as we are. Khrushchev agreed, asserting that his nation had neither obligations nor vested interests in this little country far from Soviet borders. He acknowledged that the cease-fire should be verified, and promised to encourage both sides in the kingdom to get together. Rusk and Gromyko, he said, should be locked in a room and told to find a solution (at which the usually dour Gromyko interjected the point that the Palace of Nations in Geneva is a big place with a lot of rooms).

But the negotiations at Geneva dragged on. The princely leaders of the three factions of Laotians were slow to agree on specifics and quick to walk out in protest. They bogged down trying to list personnel in Souvanna Phouma's new coalition Cabinet in which the rightists and Pathet Lao were to have appropriate representation and the neutralists were to predominate. Arguments broke out over which way various neutralists leaned. From time to time fighting broke out in violation of the cease-fire, and the Pathet Lao nibbled away at more territory. The Red Chinese and North Vietnamese delegates were not only less open to reason than the Russians but more prone to rudeness. Nevertheless, "We will stay at the Conference," said the President patiently, "for as long as we feel there is some hope of success."

Finally on May 15, 1962, after a major Pathet Lao attack across the Mekong Valley on the town of Nam Tha had threatened both the Conference and the Thai border, Kennedy moved once again. He had to show that his March, 1961, talk was no bluff—that he would not permit Laos to be taken into the Communist orbit through military action. On the basis of a decision quickly made and quickly executed, barely going through the formality of asking the Thais to "request" our help under the SEATO Treaty, U.S. Naval forces and two air squadrons were moved to the area. More than five thousand marines and Army combat personnel were put ashore in Thailand and moved up to the Laos border. Australia, New Zealand and Britain sent units as well. At the same time concentrated diplomatic pressure was put on the Soviets, making clear that we still favored a negotiated neutral settlement but wondered if they still controlled events on their side.

The Pathet Lao stopped, convinced that the United States meant business. General Phoumi also stopped, in doubt perhaps after his defeat at Nam Tha that he could ever win the country with his anti-Communist (and apparently antibloodshed) army. The negotiating atmosphere quickly improved. In June a shaky coalition "government of national union" was glued together with its tripartite Cabinet. And in July, after fifteen months of persistence by America's chief negotiator, Averell Harriman, a new Geneva Accord on Laos was signed by fourteen governments—including those of Red China and North Vietnam, whom this country did not officially recognize but who were indispensable to any agreement. Kennedy shortly thereafter recalled the American troops in Thailand, leaving behind the logistic facilities needed for their rapid reintroduction, and resumed economic aid to Souvanna.

The new Accord reflected the preference of all the major powers that Laos should be left to work out its own destiny geographically undivided, politically unaligned, militarily unoffensive and generally unimportant except as a buffer state. It was a precarious agreement, never entirely fulfilled by the Communists. Western military advisers were withdrawn and the Soviet airlift stopped; but North Vietnam continued to provide military support to the Pathet Lao and to use Laotian corridors into South Vietnam. The Pathet Lao, unwilling to meet in a capital patrolled by Phoumi's troops, finally withdrew from Souvanna's government, attacked their former ally, Kong Le, and prevented the International Control Commission from inspecting possible Geneva violations in the areas they controlled. The rightists, resisting Kennedy's suggestions to reduce their troop strength, constantly agitated against Souvanna's inclusion of Communists; Souvanna constantly threatened to quit the government; and Kennedy was constantly calling upon the International Control Commission or the Soviet Union directly to carry out the Geneva mandate. Harriman, talking to Khrushchev twice in 1963, found him less interested in Southeast Asia than previously, possibly reflecting the rise of Red Chinese influence in the area. In the spring of that year it was once again necessary for Kennedy to alert the Seventh Fleet and to stage "war games" in Thailand as a warning against a Communist takeover. Nevertheless, none of the parties involved in Laos, including Red China, seemed willing to push the fighting to a decisive point or to seek control of the country through a violent coup, apparently for fear that such an attempt might bring in the other side.

The Geneva agreement was imperfect and untidy, but it was better than no agreement at all, better than a major military confrontation and better than a Communist conquest. It was more consistent, in short, with this nation's capabilities and interests than the untenable position in which Kennedy found himself wedged in January, 1961. Contrary to the public predictions of many "experts," Souvanna Phouma did not turn out to be a Communist in disguise and his country did not slip quickly behind the Iron Curtain. "We have never suggested that there was a final easy answer in Laos," said the President. "It is a situation which is uncertain and full of hazard. . . . [But so] is life in much of the world."

VIETNAM

Life was certainly uncertain and full of hazard next door to Laos in South Vietnam. There the prospects of a final, easy answer were even more remote. Unlike Laos, Vietnam was a highly populated and productive country ruled by a central government determined to oppose all

Communist aggression and subversion. Unlike the often farcical battles in Laos, the war in Vietnam was brutal on both sides, and the government forces—despite a lack of imaginative and energetic leadership— were sizable, engaged in actual combat and dying in large numbers for their country. Unlike their situation in Laos, the great powers were more firmly committed on both sides in Vietnam, and the struggle was over not merely control of the government but the survival of the nation.

Kennedy's basic objective in Vietnam, however, was essentially the same as in Laos and the rest of Southeast Asia. He sought neither a cold war pawn nor a hot war battleground. He did not insist that South Vietnam maintain Western bases or membership in a Western alliance. As in Laos, his desire was to halt a Communist-sponsored guerrilla war and to permit the local population peacefully to choose its own future. But South Vietnam was too weak to stand alone; and any attempt to neutralize that nation in 1961 like Laos, at a time when the Communists had the upper hand in the fighting and were the most forceful element in the South as well as the North, would have left the South Vietnamese defenseless against externally supported Communist domination. The neutralization of *both* North and South Vietnam had been envisioned by the 1954 Geneva Accords. But when a return to that solution was proposed by Rusk to Gromyko, the latter not surprisingly replied that the North was irrevocably a part of the "socialist camp."

We would not stay in Southeast Asia against the wishes of any local government, the President often said. But apart from that local government's interest, free world security also had a stake in our staying there. A major goal of Red China's policy was to drive from Southeast Asia—indeed, from all Asia—the last vestiges of Western power and influence, the only effective counter to her own hegemony. Southeast Asia, with its vast population, resources and strategic location,[1] would be a rich prize for the hungry Chinese. Kennedy, as shown by his reversal of our policy in Laos, saw no need to maintain American outposts in the area. The Kennedy Southeast Asia policy respected the neutrality of all who wished to be neutral. But it also insisted that other nations similarly respect that neutrality, withdraw their troops and abide by negotiated settlements and boundaries, thus leaving each neutral free to choose and fulfill its own future within the framework of its own culture and traditions. To the extent that this required a temporary U.S. military presence, American and Communist objectives conflicted. The cockpit in which that conflict was principally tested was hapless South Vietnam, but neither Kennedy nor the Communists believed that the

[1] Lying across the air and sea lanes between the Pacific and Indian oceans, it had served as a staging area in World War II for Japanese attacks on the Philippines.

consequences of success or failure in that country would be confined to Vietnam alone.

This nation's pledge to assist and defend the integrity of South Vietnam was first made in 1954. In that year the Geneva Accords divided the country at the 17th Parallel into Communist and non-Communist territories, both sides promising (but neither expecting) an election to reunify the country. The new Republic of South Vietnam, attempting to build a nation on the ruins of nearly a hundred years of colonial rule, Japanese occupation and war with France, faced seemingly insurmountable difficulties. With the majority of the population and industry in the North, with no core of trained or well-known administrators, with four-fifths of its population in a virtually inaccessible and ungovernable countryside, with one million hungry refugees fleeing south from Communist repression, its early collapse was expected. Communists moving north after the Geneva Conference secretly left cadres and arms caches behind to prepare for that eventuality. But American aid, Vietnamese energy and the vigorous administrative talents of South Vietnam's President Ngo Dinh Diem prevented that collapse and in fact produced more economic and educational gains than the North.

Unfortunately, Diem also purged his political opposition, causing many dissidents to go underground, into exile or to the Communists, and causing the local Communists to turn for support to Vietnam's traditional enemies, the Chinese. During the first few years following the Geneva Conference, North Vietnam's leader Ho Chi Minh was content to consolidate his position. But as his own economy faltered in comparison with Diem's, as the latter's political repressions warmed the water in which guerrilla fish could swim, as the militancy of Red China gained ascendancy in his own camp, the "struggle for national reunification," as Ho called it—"to liberate the South from the atrocious rule of the U.S. imperialists and their henchmen"—began in earnest: assassinations in 1957, the training and increased reinfiltration of South Vietnamese insurgents in 1958, the announcement of a planned campaign of "liberation" in 1959 and the formation in December, 1960, of the National Liberation Front of South Vietnam.

In 1961 all the evidence was not yet in on the extent to which the antigovernment forces in the South were the creatures of the Communist North. But it was reasonably clear that many of them were trained in the North, armed and supplied by the North, and infiltrated from the North through the Laotian corridors, across the densely wooded frontier and by sea. The North supplied them with backing, brains and a considerable degree of coordination and control. Their food and shelter were largely provided at night by South Vietnamese villagers, who were sometimes wooed—with promises of land, unification and an end to political corruption, repression and foreign troops—and sometimes terrorized, with demonstrations of kidnaping, murder and plunder, before the guerrillas vanished back into the jungle at daybreak. A considerable portion of the insurgents' arms, American-made, were captured from the South Vietnamese forces.

By early 1961 these "Vietcong" guerrillas, as they were labeled by the government in Saigon, were gradually bleeding South Vietnam to death, destroying its will to resist, eroding its faith in the future, and paralyzing its progress through systematic terror against the already limited number of local officials, teachers, health workers, agricultural agents, rural police, priests, village elders and even ordinary villagers who refused to cooperate. Favorite targets for destruction included schools, hospitals, agricultural research stations and malaria control centers.

The Eisenhower administration—in the creation of SEATO, in statements to President Diem and in commenting on the 1954 Geneva Accords—had pledged in 1954 and again in 1957 to help resist any "aggression or subversion threatening the political independence of the Republic of Vietnam." Military as well as economic assistance had begun in 1954. This country in that year drew the line against Communist expansion at the border of South Vietnam. Whether or not it would have been wiser to draw it in a more stable and defensible area in the first place, this nation's commitment in January, 1961—although it had assumed far larger proportions than when it was made nearly seven years earlier—was not one that President Kennedy felt he could abandon without undesirable consequences throughout Asia and the world.

Unfortunately he inherited in Vietnam more than a commitment and a growing conflict. He also inherited a foreign policy which had identified America in the eyes of Asia with dictators, CIA intrigue and a largely military response to revolution. He inherited a military policy which had left us wholly unprepared to fight—or even to train others to fight—a war against local guerrillas. Our military mission had prepared South Vietnam's very sizable army for a Korean-type invasion, training it to move in division or battalion strength by highways instead of jungle trails. Nor had the United States encouraged a build-up in the local Civil Guard and Self-defense Corps which bore the brunt of the guerrilla attacks.

Under Kennedy the earlier commitment to South Vietnam was not only carried out but, as noted below, reinforced by a vast expansion of effort. The principal responsibility for that expansion belongs not with Kennedy but with the Communists, who, beginning in the late 1950's, vastly expanded their efforts to take over the country. The dimensions of our effort also had to be increased, unfortunately, to compensate for the political weaknesses of the Diem regime.

In that sense, Eisenhower, Ho Chi Minh and Ngo Dinh Diem all helped to shape John Kennedy's choices in Vietnam. His essential contribution—which is reviewed here as the situation then appeared, not to pass judgment on subsequent developments—was both to raise our commitment and to keep it limited. He neither permitted the war's escalation into a general war nor bargained away Vietnam's security at the conference table, despite being pressed along both lines by those impatient to win or withdraw. His strategy essentially was to avoid escalation, retreat or a choice limited to those two, while seeking to buy time —time to make the policies and programs of both the American and Vietnamese governments more appealing to the villagers—time to build an antiguerrilla capability sufficient to convince the Communists that they could not seize the country militarily—and time to put the Vietnamese themselves in a position to achieve the settlement only they could achieve by bringing terrorism under control.

That it would be a long, bitter and frustrating interval he had no doubt. Ultimately a negotiated settlement would be required. But the whole fight was essentially over a return to the basic principles (if not the letter) of an earlier negotiated settlement, the Geneva Accords of 1954. The North Vietnamese and Chinese showed no interest in any fair and enforceable settlement they did not dictate; and they would show no interest, the President was convinced, until they were persuaded that continued aggression would be frustrated and unprofitable. Any other settlement would merely serve as a confirmation of the benefits of aggression and as a cover for American withdrawal. It would cause the world to wonder about the reliability of this nation's pledges, expose to vengeance all South Vietnamese (and particularly those the U.S. had persuaded to stand by their country) and encourage the Communists to repeat the same tactics against the "paper tiger" Americans in Thailand, Malaysia and elsewhere in Asia—until finally Kennedy or some successor would be unalterably faced with the choice he hoped to avoid: withdrawal or all-out war.

Almost immediately upon his assumption of office, Kennedy created a State-Defense-CIA-USIA-White House task force to prepare detailed recommendations on Vietnam. Those recommendations were considered in late April and early May of 1961 simultaneously with the Joint Chiefs' recommendations for intervening in Laos. The two reports, in fact, resembled and were related to each other. Both called for a commitment of American combat troops to Vietnam.

The President—his skepticism deepened by the Bay of Pigs experience and the holes in the Laos report—once again wanted more questions answered and more alternatives presented. The military proposals for Vietnam, he said, were based on assumptions and predictions that could not be verified—on help from Laos and Cambodia to halt infiltration from the North, on agreement by Diem to reorganizations in his army and government, on more popular support for Diem in the countryside and on sealing off Communist supply routes. Estimates of both time and cost were either absent or wholly unrealistic.

Finally, a more limited program was approved. The small contingent of American military advisers was tripled, with officers assigned at the battalion level as well as to regiments, to advise in combat as well as training and to aid in unconventional as well as conventional warfare. American logistic support was increased, and money and instructors were made available to augment the size of South Vietnam's Civil Guard and Self-defense Forces as well as her army. To demonstrate his support, to obtain an independent firsthand report and to make clear to Diem his insistence that Diem's own efforts be improved, the President dispatched Vice President Johnson on a tour of Southeast Asia, including a lengthy stopover at Saigon.

But throughout 1961 the situation in Vietnam continued to deteriorate. The area ruled by guerrilla tactics and terror continued to grow. American instructors—accompanying Vietnamese forces in battle and instructed to fire if fired upon—were being killed in small but increasing numbers. The Vice President's report urged that the battle against Communism be joined in Southeast Asia with strength and determination. The key to what is done by Asians, he said, is confidence in the United States, in our power, our will and our understanding. In late October a new high-level mission to Vietnam, headed by Maxwell Taylor and Walt Rostow, visited Vietnam preparatory to a major Presidential review.

A new set of recommendations proposed a series of actions by the American and Vietnamese governments. Once again, the most difficult was the commitment of American combat troops. South Vietnam's forces already outnumbered the enemy by ten to one, it was estimated, and far more could be mobilized. But many believed that American troops were needed less for their numerical strength than for the morale and will they could provide to Diem's forces and for the warning they would provide to the Communists. The President was not satisfied on either point. He was unwilling to commit American troops to fighting Asians on the Asian mainland for speculative psychological reasons.

Nevertheless, at this moment more than any other, the pressures upon the President to make that commitment were at a peak. All his principal advisers on Vietnam favored it, calling it the "touchstone" of our good faith, a symbol of our determination. But the President in effect voted "no"—and only his vote counted.

The key to his "vote" could be found in his speech on the Senate floor on the French-Indochinese War on the sixth of April, 1954:

> ... unilateral action by our own country ... without participation by the armed forces of the other nations of Asia, without the support of the great masses of the peoples [of Vietnam] ... and, I might add, with hordes of Chinese Communist troops poised just across the border in anticipation of our unilateral entry into their kind of battleground—such intervention, Mr. President, would be virtually impossible in the type of military situation which prevails in Indochina ... an enemy which is everywhere and at the same time nowhere, "an enemy of the people" which has the sympathy and covert support of the people.

That year he had watched the French, with a courageous, well-equipped army numbering hundreds of thousands, suffer a humiliating defeat and more than ninety thousand casualties. Now the choice was his. If the United States took over the conduct of the war on the ground, he asked, would that not make it easier for the Communists to say we were the neo-colonialist successors of the French? Would we be better able to win support of the villagers and farmers—so essential to guerrilla warfare—than Vietnamese troops of the same color and culture? No one knew whether the South Vietnamese officers would be encouraged or resentful, or whether massive troop landings would provoke a massive Communist invasion—an invasion inevitably leading either to nuclear war, Western retreat or an endless and exhausting battle on the worst battleground he could choose.

What was needed, Kennedy agreed with his advisers, was a major counterinsurgency effort—the first ever mounted by this country. South Vietnam could supply the necessary numbers—and would have to supply the courage and will to fight, for no outsider could supply that. But the United States could supply better training, support and direction, better communications, transportation and intelligence, better weapons, equipment and logistics—all of which the South Vietnamese needed, said his advisers, if they were to reorient their effort to fight guerrilla battles.

Formally, Kennedy never made a final negative decision on troops. In typical Kennedy fashion, he made it difficult for any of the prointervention advocates to charge him privately with weakness. He ordered the departments to be prepared for the introduction of combat troops, should they prove to be necessary. He steadily expanded the size of the military assistance mission (2,000 at the end of 1961, 15,500 at the end of 1963) by sending in combat support units, air combat and helicopter teams, still more military advisers and instructors and 600 of the greenhatted Special Forces to train and lead the South Vietnamese in anti-guerrilla tactics.

The Kennedy administration's decision to carry out, with increased aid, this country's long-standing commitment to Vietnam was officially sealed and conveyed in a public exchange of letters between Presidents Kennedy and Diem on December 15, 1961. The wording of both letters was carefully worked out by both governments, although, as noted below, Diem balked at many reforms. Kennedy placed no limits of time or amount on our assistance, noting only that it would no longer be necessary once North Vietnam ceased its aggression. But he did stress throughout the letter that primary responsibility would remain with the people of South Vietnam—that Americans were there only to help them—and that he was "confident that the Vietnamese people will preserve their independence." In other statements he re-emphasized the fact that this remained their war to win, not ours, depending more upon their effort than ours, that it had to be won in the South as a political as well as a military conflict.

This meant, the President wrote Diem in a separate message—also based on the Taylor report—that South Vietnam's military effort would have to be fully mobilized, reorganized and given the initiative; that specific tax, land, education and other social and political reforms would have to be instituted, including a more broadly based national government, improved civil liberties, fewer political restraints and more assistance at the village level; and that without such assurances and cooperation, including joint American participation in key military planning, American support would be useless. The United States could not instill morale in Diem's troops, improve his and their rapport with the villagers, or confer a sense of national identity on the country as a whole. That was up to Diem. But Diem's only noticeable response was a series of anti-American stories in the controlled Vietnamese press.

Kennedy recognized far more clearly than most of his advisers that military action alone could not save Vietnam. As a Congressman back from Indochina in 1951, he had warned that the southward drive of Communism required its opponents to build "strong native non-Communist sentiment within these areas and rely on that as a spearhead of defense rather than upon . . . force of arms." As a Senator in 1954, he had cited the dangers and inaccuracies inherent in the long years of assurances given by French and American officials that the Vietnamese people were truly free and independent.

But as President, unfortunately, his effort to keep our own military role in Vietnam from overshadowing our political objectives was handicapped by the State Department's inability to compete with the Pentagon. The task force report in the spring of 1961, for example, had focused almost entirely on military planning. A five-year economic plan, "a long-range plan for the economic development of Southeast Asia on a regional basis," a diplomatic appeal to the United Nations and other miscellaneous ideas were somewhat vaguely and loosely thrown in to please the President. But there was no concrete definition of the civil effort essential to the success of the military effort, nor was there in the months and years that followed. Economic aid and a rural rehabilitation program were increased. But the guerrillas kept much of the countryside too frightened or hostile to cooperate, repeatedly ambushed health and education workers, and burned schools and other government centers. "You cannot carry out a land reform program," Secretary McNamara said, "if the local peasant leaders are being systematically murdered." No amount of social and economic assistance in South Vietnam would end the ambitions of North Vietnam. American assistance, moreover, was not accompanied by the internal reforms required to make it effective.

A full-scale articulation by the President of this country's long-range political and economic aims for Southeast Asia might have strengthened this neglected nonmilitary side of his Vietnam policy. The Taylor report recommended a major television address. But unwilling to give Vietnam a status comparable to Berlin, the President chose to keep quiet. Even his news conference statements on Vietnam were elusive. Moreover, the new military efforts mounted late in 1961 and early 1962 seemed initially to be paying off. The rapid disintegration taking place in the fall of 1961 was stemmed, especially in the coastal provinces where the Vietcong had threatened to cut the country in two. American helicopters in particular provided a new and effective challenge to the guerrillas. From time to time the building of U.S. forces in the area continued, particularly with the addition of more airpower early in 1963. The President hopefully reported to the Congress in January of that year that "the spear point of aggression has been blunted in Vietnam."

In fact, the neglected civilian side of the effort had already begun to handicap the military side, and in 1963 these handicaps would become evident. Taylor's 1961 report had warned Kennedy—and Kennedy had politely warned Diem—that the people around the Presidential palace in Saigon were often corrupt and ambitious, that Diem's army was weakened by politics and preference, that his treatment of political opponents had stifled the nation's nationalism and that Diem's own lack of popularity in the countryside was handicapping antiguerrilla efforts. The ever suspicious and stubborn Diem had promised reform, but few reforms were forthcoming. American military advice was requested, but it was still often disregarded—in an overexpansion, for example, of

the "strategic hamlet" program which sought to clear areas of all guerrillas and then protect the inhabitants in newly constructed and fortified
settlements. Antiguerrilla tactics were taught but ignored. Funds were
sought for additional Vietnamese battalions, but those battalions were
too stationary, too cautious about going out to meet the enemy. Diem
and his family still meddled deeply in army politics.

As President Diem became more and more remote from the people,
his government was increasingly dominated by an increasingly unbalanced man, the President's brother, Ngo Dinh Nhu. The Catholic
Diem, his brother and his brother's wife—the sharp-tongued Madame
Nhu—were accused of religious persecution by powerful Buddhist
leaders, many of whom for political reasons fanned small instances of
personal discrimination into national crises.

In mid-1963 the picture worsened rapidly. Diem's troops broke up
a demonstration of Buddhists protesting a ban on their banner. Nhu's
Special Forces raided Buddhist pagodas. Pictures of Buddhist monks
burning themselves to death in protest—as well as Madame Nhu's cruel
remarks on the "barbecue show" sacrifice of "so-called holy men"—
brought calls in Congress to cut off all aid. Vietnamese students rioted
against the government. Officials not personally committed to the family
—including Madame Nhu's father, the Ambassador to Washington—
resigned in protest against new repressions. The maintenance of internal security, employing the most arbitrary means and the most
valuable troops, began to occupy the full attention of the shaky Diem
regime. The prosecution of the war inevitably faltered. Nhu was reported
ready to make a secret deal with the North, and both he and his wife
publicly castigated the United States for its efforts to broaden the government and get back to the war.

The religious persecutions deeply offended John Kennedy. "Human
. . . rights are not respected," he pointedly said in his September, 1963,
UN speech, "when a Buddhist priest is driven from his pagoda." He
further bristled when brother Nhu, angered at American interference,
said publicly there were too many U.S. troops in Vietnam. "Any time
the government of South Vietnam would suggest it," said the President,
"the day after it was suggested we would have some troops on their
way home." But while publicly deploring "repressive actions," he at first
paid too little attention to those members of the Congress and American
press—particularly the heavily restricted correspondents in Saigon—
who complained that we were aiding a dictator. He had generally been
more careful than his subordinates to talk of our support for the aspirations of the country, not the individual regime. But sometimes the
national security required this country to aid dictators, particularly in
the newer nations unprepared for true democracy. He knew that we

were dangerously dependent on one man, but there was no simple way to force a broadening of that man's government or the development of more representative civilian leaders without endangering the entire war effort.

By late summer, 1963, he had become more concerned. Growing disunity and disorder within the non-Communist camp in Saigon further handicapped the national war effort. Countering guerrilla warfare, as he had stressed in 1961, was more of a political than a military problem; and a government incapable of effective political action and popular reform would continue to lose ground steadily throughout the country.

In a long letter to Diem, the President reviewed frankly the troubled relations between the two governments. Some of the methods used by some members of your government, he wrote Diem, may make it impossible to sustain public support in Vietnam for the struggle against the Communists. Unless there can be important changes and improvements in the apparent relation between the government and the people in your country, he added, American public and Congressional opinion will make it impossible to continue without change their joint efforts. American cooperation and American assistance will not be given, he stressed, to or through individuals whose acts and words seem to run against the purpose of genuine reconciliation and unified national effort against the Communists.

He urged Diem to ease his censorship and harassment of American reporters in Vietnam—for that, said Kennedy, can only impair our confidence. He emphasized that American officials and officers in Vietnam, while respecting that country's independence, must participate extensively in decisions affecting a situation in which our own resources, and thousands of members of our armed forces, are so heavily committed. The consistent rejection of our advisers' advice, Kennedy knew, had made much of our aid and effort useless.

At the same time—September, 1963—he was surprisingly candid in two television interviews. He agreed with one reporter that we had become locked into a policy from which it was difficult to shift. He told another that we were attempting to use our influence to persuade the Diem government to take the steps necessary to gain popular support, although "we can't expect these countries to do everything the way we want." To another he was even more explicit, stating that Diem could regain the support of the people and win the war only

with changes in policy and perhaps with personnel. . . . I don't think the war can be won unless the people support the effort and, in my opinion, in the last two months the government has gotten out of touch with the people. . . . In the first analysis, it is their war. They are the ones who have to win it or lose it. We can help them, we can give them equipment, we can send our men out there as advisers, but they have to win it, the people of Vietnam.

These public statements were an exception. Private pressures were not. A controversial cable dispatched during the President's last August weekend at the Cape had gone even further, indicating that the United States would not block any spontaneous military revolt against Diem. (Critics of this cable somehow assumed that a message from Kennedy could either start or stop the growing tide of discontent among the Vietnamese officer corps.) In any event, no coup followed. Kennedy was increasingly doubtful that the war could ever be won with Diem, for whom he retained great personal admiration, but he nevertheless accepted the fact that the U.S. must not bring him down and would have to make the best of his staying. His hope was to change Diem's policies and personnel, not remove him.

Kennedy remained unwilling, however, to promote or thwart any indigenous movements. He withheld all economic aid not directly related to the battlefront, including funds for Nhu's Special Forces. And he strengthened the authority of new Ambassador Henry Cabot Lodge, the least friendly to Diem and family of all the State, Defense and CIA officials in Saigon, recalling the pro-Diem CIA station chief to Washington. Lodge urged dismissal of the Nhus and an end to Diem's arbitrary actions.

But these efforts were too late—and in vain. Their tardiness reflected the President's dilemma. For eighteen months he had been skeptical of the reports from Diem's backers. But he had been equally skeptical whether U.S. threats to remove Diem, if he did not make the necessary reforms, would have worked and whether his actual removal would have helped. He blamed himself for not building more of a political-economic-social side to the U.S. effort in Vietnam to offset the impact of new repressions on the population. Now it was too late. Diem refused to listen. The only Nhu to go anywhere was Madame Nhu, who—to his great annoyance—toured this country making vitriolic attacks on Kennedy's policy. (Asked why so feminine a female would be so bitter in her attitudes, the President speculated that Madame Nhu—like a sharp-tongued American lady of note with whom he compared her—"resented getting her power through men.")

Kennedy's advisers were more deeply divided on the internal situation in Saigon than on any previous issue. The State Department, by and large, reported that the political turmoil had seriously interfered with the war effort outside of Saigon, and that one of the many coups rumored almost weekly was certain to succeed if we kept hands off. The military and the CIA, on the other hand, spoke confidently of the war's prosecution and Diem's leadership, and questioned the likelihood of finding any equally able leader with the confidence of the people who could prosecute the war as vigorously.

There were bitter disputes, with each side often trying to commit the President in the other's absence. As a result recommendations to the President differed sharply regarding the continuing or conditioning of our aid and what changes should be sought in the regime. Whichever way he turned—continuing to support Diem or interfering in his internal affairs—Kennedy foresaw the United States losing respect in the eyes of many Vietnamese. Through a series of meetings (and missions to Saigon) in September and October, he hoped to move the administration away from its total dependence on Diem without causing South Vietnam to fall or his own team to split wide open.

Finally, on November 1, 1963, as corruption, repression and disorder increased, a new effort by the Vietnamese military to take command of the government was launched and succeeded. It received no assistance from the United States, nor did this country do anything to prevent or defeat it. While all the reports of all the various plots and proposed coups had regularly reached American ears, neither the timing nor the scale of this one was known in the U.S. when it was launched (much less to Kennedy, who had previously planned for Lodge to be out of Saigon at that time reporting to Washington). The generals seized control of the government and assassinated Diem and Nhu, who had refused the offer of sanctuary in the American Embassy.

Kennedy was shaken that Diem should come to such an end after his long devotion to his country, whatever his other deficiencies, remarking that Diem's bitterest foes, the Communists, had never gone that far. An uncertain military junta took over in Saigon. The new leaders had no more deep-rooted popularity or administrative skill than their predecessors. Constant top-to-bottom changes in personnel, to be succeeded in time by still more changes, further impaired whatever momentum and morale were left in the war effort, and permitted still further Communist gains.

Obviously, then, in November, 1963, no early end to the Vietnam war was in sight. The President, while eager to make clear that our aim was to get out of Vietnam, had always been doubtful about the optimistic reports constantly filed by the military on the progress of the war. In his Senate floor speech of 1954, he had criticized French and American generals for similar "predictions of confidence which have lulled the American people." The Communists, he knew, would have no difficulty recruiting enough guerrillas to prolong the fighting for many years. The struggle could well be, he thought, this nation's severest test of endurance and patience. At times he compared it to the long struggles against

Communist guerrillas in Greece, Malaya and the Phillippines. Yet at least he had a major counterguerrilla effort under way, with a comparatively small commitment of American manpower. He was simply going to weather it out, a nasty, untidy mess to which there was no other acceptable solution. Talk of abandoning so unstable an ally and so costly a commitment "only makes it easy for the Communists," said the President. "I think we should stay."

He could show little gain in that situation to pass on to his successor, either in the military outlook or the progress toward reform. His own errors had not helped. But if asked why he had increased this nation's commitment, he might have summed up his stand with the words used by William Pitt when asked in the House of Commons in 1805 what was gained by the war against France: "We have gained everything that we would have lost if we had not fought this war." In the case of Vietnam, that was a lot.

RED CHINA AND INDIA

Behind both the Laotian and Vietnamese crises loomed the larger menace of Communist China. That nation's unconcealed, unswerving ambition to impose upon the Asian Continent a system bitterly hostile to our fundamental values and interests imposed in turn upon John Kennedy an obligation not to desert any independent government desiring our protection. In the absence of American combat troops, China's role in Laos and Vietnam seemed indirect at most. But there was nothing indirect about Red China's announced intention to take Formosa by force or—equally dangerous to the peace of the area—about Chiang Kai-shek's announced intention to reconquer the mainland from Formosa.

Chiang was often vexed with Kennedy—over the UN admission of Outer Mongolia, over the granting of a visa to an anti-Chiang lecturer, over our quiet pressure for the removal of his foraging force from Burma and over other issues. But their alliance was most severely strained in mid-1962. Chiang and most of his cohorts, with advancing age increasing their sense of urgency, observed the growing rift between the Soviets and Red Chinese, observed the mounting farm and economic difficulties on the mainland, and decided that 1962 looked like their last best chance for an invasion.

To Kennedy it looked more like the Bay of Pigs all over again. That, too, was supposed to be the last best chance to topple a Communist dictator. There, too, native discontent was supposed to have made the country ripe for an exile takeover. But there, too, the exile force was too small, its appeal to the native population was too limited, the police state control was too entrenched and the whole operation was doomed to failure unless the United States launched an all-out attack in support and thereby risked a world-wide war. This time Kennedy was not tempted for even a moment. He had no confidence in Chiang's ability to regain control of the mainland, even with American assistance. He had no desire to expand this nation's commitment beyond the defense of Formosa and the Pescadores Islands. Without giving Chiang the kind of flat rejection the Generalissimo might exploit politically, he politely informed him that the time was not ripe and that unlimited American backing would not be forthcoming.

Chiang, however, began talking freely about an invasion, hoping to embarrass the United States into action. The Communist Chinese simultaneously deployed large numbers of troops in the key coastal sectors. Whether their purposes were defensive or a new attack on Quemoy and Matsu could not be ascertained. The President, deciding once again to use his news conference for a policy declaration, asked me to excerpt from his campaign speeches those statements making clear his determination to defend Formosa and the Pescadores against attack, including any attack on the offshore islands if it threatened Formosa. His news conference statement was addressed to Chiang as well as the Communists, underlining the fact that "we are opposed to the use of force in this area. . . . The purposes of the United States in this area are peaceful and defensive." A similar message was delivered to the Chinese Communists through the ambassadorial talks in Warsaw, and tensions on both sides of the Formosan Straits soon subsided.

Within a few months, however, a new outbreak of Chinese Communist aggression caused the President new concern. Persistent Chinese incursions on India's northwestern and northeastern Himalayan frontiers reached invasion proportions on October 20, 1962, just as the discovery of Soviet missiles in Cuba reached the crisis peak in Washington. The President, despite his preoccupation with the more direct threat to this nation and hemisphere, wondered aloud which crisis would be the more significant in the long run. It was not merely because soldiers were being killed in India, as large numbers of Chinese advanced almost at will into some twelve thousand square miles of Indian territory, going beyond even the disputed areas they had long claimed. It was because India—one of the largest nations on earth, with a population greater than that of all Latin America and Africa combined—was widely admired by her fellow neutrals, substantially aided by the Soviet Union, and the only country on the Asian mainland capable of competing for political and economic leadership with the Chinese. An all-out war between the two most populous nations on earth might well rival the confrontation in the Caribbean in long-run implications.

But it was not an all-out war. The Chinese, having obtained a favorable mountain position for future aggressions, cleverly called for a cease-fire in which they would neither withdraw from the territory seized nor give a guarantee against future attacks. Khrushchev, whom Nehru had regarded as a friend and backer, informed the Prime Minister that he could not intercede for him and that the Chinese offer should be accepted. Nehru's fellow neutral Nasser suggested the Afro-Asians mediate the dispute. The Indian Prime Minister was stung. Rejecting the advice of both men, he admitted that India had been living in a dream world; and on October 26 he turned for help to the United States and John Kennedy.

His letter, the first of some fifteen which he and Kennedy exchanged over the next six months, asked for "sympathy" and "support." His kinsman and Ambassador to Washington, B. K. Nehru, explained to the President when delivering it in person that afternoon that the Prime Minister, after all these years in the neutralist pacifist camp, found it difficult to make a direct request for armaments from the United States. He was hoping, instead, that the President in his reply would offer "support" instead of "military assistance" on the basis of "sympathy" instead of an "alliance." I understand, replied the President, adding that he had no wish to take advantage of India's misfortune to coerce her into a pact. The United States would offer support out of sympathy— and our representatives could translate those terms into the military specifics. (Speaking unofficially, he added, Nehru ought to make Khrushchev "put up or shut up" on an earlier promise of MIGs and military equipment.)

Nehru's reluctance to mention military specifics was only temporary. Pleas for a vast arsenal of American armaments began to pour in. Kennedy, although not coming close to fulfilling all these unrealistic requests, promptly responded with substantial amounts of light weapons, mortars, ammunition and other items. Within a few days he dispatched a high-level survey team under Averell Harriman to report precisely how we could be most useful without driving Pakistan into Red China's arms. To the President's great satisfaction, and as the inadequacies of India's Army became apparent, the acidly anti-American Krishna Menon was out as Nehru's Minister of Defense. As younger and more pro-Western men gained strength in his government, Nehru's policy of nonalignment became at least temporarily more realistic. The United States and Great Britain (who also sent military aid) were his true friends, he said. The Chinese were never to be trusted again. The Indian people cheered all signs of U.S. aid.

As was true in the Congo, Kennedy's success in the Cuban missile crisis encouraged some to urge more direct or extensive American action. This is the place to stand against Chinese expansion in Asia, they said, with the Soviets caught in the middle and world opinion sympathetic to Nehru. But Kennedy saw no gains for India, for the United

States or for the free world in making this fight our fight in the Himalayas. In an emergency meeting at midnight, in the midst of the Cuban missile crisis, he quietly interred one excited recommendation that would have involved us directly in a war with China and never embarrassed the proposal's authors by mentioning it again.

Moreover, the improvement in America's relations with India had been accompanied by a deterioration in our relations with her neighbor and bitter rival, Pakistan. The President, in a correspondence with Pakistan President Ayub Khan that paralleled his exchange with Nehru, took pains to assure him that our military aid to India was conditioned upon its immediate use against the Chinese, that it would not be used against Pakistan and that it would not diminish the even more substantial military aid Ayub regularly received from this country. His letter suggested that Ayub privately reassure Nehru that he could safely withdraw the troops stationed at the Kashmir border—site of the most bitter dispute between the two countries—and employ them against the Communists. This might be an opportunity, the President stressed, to put the Indians in their most agreeable frame of mind for a Kashmir settlement.

Although Ayub told our Ambassador that he would be unavailable for a week to read the President's letter—simultaneously complaining that he had not been consulted—the prospects for a Kashmir settlement at first appeared better than at any previous time in the long history of that dispute. Nehru and Ayub issued a joint statement of harmonious intent, and a round of negotiations began. But progress was nil, and Pakistan's complaints about American arms in India continued to rise.

Perhaps the Pakistanis never understood, commented the President in a Cabinet Room meeting, that our alliance with them was aimed at the Communists, not at the Indians. Perhaps Ayub preferred for political reasons to have the issue of Kashmir rather than a settlement. But Galbraith's suggestion of forcing the Indians to make a generous Kashmir offer by conditioning a large aid offer upon it would not work, he said. It might only produce such violent anti-American sentiment in Pakistan that Ayub would be brought down—and his successor would surely be even more difficult to deal with. Nor were the Indians, he noticed, willing to take troops from the Pakistan border to strengthen their defenses against the Chinese. Both sides, he said, regarded the Kashmir dispute as "more important . . . than the struggle against the Communists." Indeed, the Pakistani Ambassador on a visit to the President's office launched into such an undiplomatic tirade that Kennedy coldly stood up and terminated the conversation. (His replacement brought a stunning pin for Jacqueline as a "peace offering," and the President asked her to paint Ayub a picture in return.)

The emergency phase of the Indian military aid program having ended with a cease-fire, Kennedy still faced the problem of Nehru's equally unrealistic request for long-range help. Neither full resistance to an all-out Chinese attack nor reconquest of the areas seized by the Chinese was realistically possible for the Indian Army, his special mission told him. Air defense, however, was a unique problem where we could be of help. Fear of retaliatory Chinese bomber attacks on their defenseless cities had caused the Indians to withhold the air support their army needed. Carefully and in low key—to reduce to the extent possible any adverse reactions from the Pakistanis, the Chinese, the Soviets and the sensitive Indians themselves—the President worked out with the British a joint agreement to provide air defense.

He knew the Chinese would soon threaten again, in India or elsewhere. "These Chinese are tough," he remarked in one off-the-record session. "It isn't just what they say about us but what they say about the Russians. They are in the Stalinist phase, believe in class war and the use of force, and seem prepared to sacrifice 300 million people if necessary to dominate Asia." He read all he could about the Chinese (at times enjoying streaks of quoting pertinent and impertinent ancient Chinese maxims). But since the day of his inauguration the Red Chinese—unlike the Soviets—had spewed unremitting vituperation upon him. He saw no way of persuading them to abandon their aggressive design short of a patient, persistent American presence in Asia and the Pacific. Consequently, even if Red China had not become an emotional and political issue in the United States, he said, any American initiative now toward negotiations, diplomatic recognition or UN admission would be regarded as rewarding aggression. He was prepared to use whatever means were available to prevent the seating of Red China in Nationalist China's seat at the UN.

Nevertheless he felt dissatisfied with his administration's failure to break new ground in this area, asked the State Department to consider possible new steps and did not regard as magical or permanent this country's long-standing policy of rigidity. "We are not wedded to a policy of hostility to Red China," he said.

> I would hope that . . . the normalization of relations . . . peaceful relations . . . between China and the West . . . would be brought about. We desire peace and we desire to live in amity with the Chinese people. . . . But it takes two to make peace, and I am hopeful that the Chinese will be persuaded that a peaceful existence with its neighbors represents the best hope for us all.

His efforts in Southeast Asia and his approach to the Soviets were designed to aid that persuasion. He hoped that the passage of time, an evolution among Red China's leaders, their isolation from the rest of the world, their mounting internal problems and their inability to gain through aggression would be persuasive as well. But the bulk of any new effort on his part, he thought, would require a friendlier Congress and more public understanding. In the meantime, an "open door" was to be maintained on the possibilities of improved relations. The success of his wheat sales to Russia caused him to speculate whether grain or food donations to the Chinese might be a possibility. "If it would lessen their malevolence, I'd be for it," he had said earlier. But he was persuaded that no guarantees could be obtained to prevent the reshipment of that food or grain, to assure its reaching those most in need or to enable the Chinese people to know who had sent it. "And let's face it," he said to me half in humor and half in despair, "that's a subject for the second term."

CHAPTER XXIV

❦

THE CONFRONTATION IN CUBA

O

N SEPTEMBER 6, 1962, in response to his urgent telephone request and after checking with President Kennedy, I met with Soviet Ambassador Dobrynin at the Russian Embassy. Two weeks earlier, in one of a series of get-acquainted luncheons Dobrynin held for administration officials, I had sought to dispel any Soviet assumption that the upcoming Congressional campaign would inhibit the President's response to any new pressures on Berlin. His report of that conversation, the Ambassador now told me, had resulted in a personal message from Chairman Khrushchev on which he suggested I take notes as he read in order to convey it precisely to the President:

> Nothing will be undertaken before the American Congressional elections that could complicate the international situation or aggravate the tension in the relations between our two countries ... provided there are no actions taken on the other side which would change the situation. This includes a German peace settlement and West Berlin. . . . If the necessity arises for [the Chairman to address the United Nations], this would be possible only in the second half of November. The Chairman does not wish to become involved in your internal political affairs.

The Chairman's message, I replied (as the President had suggested), seemed both hollow and tardy. The late summer shipments of Soviet personnel, arms and equipment into Cuba had already aggravated world tensions and caused turmoil in our internal political affairs. As reported in my memorandum on the conversation dictated that same afternoon:

> Dobrynin said that he would report this conversation in full to the Chairman and that he was aware himself of the political and press excitement regarding this matter. He neither contradicted nor confirmed my reference to large numbers of Soviet military personnel, electronic equipment and missile preparations. He repeated several times, however, that they had done nothing new or extraordinary in Cuba—that the events causing all the excitement had been taking place somewhat gradually and quietly over a long period of time—and that he stood by his assurances that all these steps were defensive in nature and did not represent any threat to the security of the United States.

At the time the Ambassador was speaking, forty-two Soviet medium- and intermediate-range ballistic missiles—each one capable of striking the United States with a nuclear warhead twenty or thirty times more powerful than the Hiroshima bomb—were en route to Cuba. Judging from the rapidity with which they were assembled, the planning and preparations for this move had been under way within the Soviet Union since spring and within Cuba all summer. The sites had been selected and surveyed, the protective antiaircraft missiles moved in, the roads improved and the local inhabitants evicted. Yet the reassurances given me by Dobrynin on September 6 were identical to those he gave to the Attorney General and others in the same period (presumably but not necessarily with knowledge of the actual facts). A Soviet Government statement on September 11 said flatly that its nuclear rockets were so powerful that there was no need to locate them in any other country, specifically mentioning Cuba, and that "the armaments and military equipment sent to Cuba are designed exclusively for defensive purposes" and could not threaten the United States. Khrushchev and Mikoyan told Georgi Bolshakov—the Soviet official in Washington through whom the Khrushchev letters had first arrived and who enjoyed friendly relations with several New Frontiersmen—to relay word that no missile capable of reaching the United States would be placed in Cuba. The message could not have been more precise—or more false.

The President was not lulled by these statements. (The Bolshakov message, in fact, reached him after he knew of the missiles' existence.) Over one hundred voyages to Cuban ports by Communist bloc and bloc-chartered vessels in July and August had caused him to pay close attention to the aerial photography, agent reports and other intelligence data on Cuba. But the principal concern inside the government, as reflected in my August 23 luncheon conversation with Dobrynin, had been the possibility of a new Soviet move on West Berlin. With Khrushchev's post-Sputnik offensive failing, with neither his pressures nor negotiations on Berlin getting anywhere, a new and dangerous confrontation seemed likely; and these suspicions were heightened by the report that Khrushchev had told Robert Frost, when the aged poet visited the Soviet Union in September, that democracies were "too liberal" to fight. All thought he meant Berlin; and with Berlin chiefly in mind the President had obtained a Congressional renewal of his authority to call up Reservists. "If we solve the Berlin problem without war," he said to me one evening, outlining the tack I should take with a columnist, "Cuba will look pretty small. And if there is a war, Cuba won't matter much either."

The movement of Soviet personnel and equipment into Cuba, however, had been the subject of a series of meetings and reports in the White House beginning in August. Naval ships and planes photographed every Soviet vessel bound for Cuba. Aerial reconnaissance flights covered the entire island twice monthly. A special daily intelligence report on Cuba began on August 27.

The intelligence picture was clouded by the constant rumors reported to the CIA, to the press and to some members of Congress by Cuban refugees that Soviet surface-to-surface missiles had been seen on the island. All these rumors and reports, numbering in the hundreds, were checked out. All proved to be unfounded, resulting from the inability of civilians to distinguish between offensive and defensive missiles or the wishful thinking of patriots hoping to goad the United States into an invasion of Cuba. (Those missiles later discovered were not those discussed in all these reports and were fully observable only through aerial photography.) Refugee reports of Soviet missiles on the island had, in fact, begun well before Cuba in 1960 started receiving any Soviet arms of any kind.

But these and other reports were used by Senators Keating, Capehart, Thurmond, Goldwater and others to inflame the domestic political scene and to call for an invasion, a blockade or unspecified "action." Ever since the Bay of Pigs, Cuba had been the Kennedy administration's heaviest political cross; and the approach of the 1962 Congressional elections had encouraged further exacerbation of the issue. The administration—though readying a plan of military action in the knowledge that an internal revolt, a Berlin grab or some other action might someday require it—had been stressing since early 1961 the more positive and indirect approach of isolating Castro from a developing, democratic Latin America. An Organization of American States (OAS) Conference in Punta del Este, Uruguay, in January, 1962, had declared that the present government of Cuba was incompatible with the inter-American system, excluded it from participation in the OAS, prohibited OAS members from selling it arms, and adopted resolutions for collective defense against Communist penetration of the hemisphere. The United States had placed an embargo on all exports to Cuba other than food and medicines, prohibited importers and tourists from bringing in goods of Cuban origin, and restricted the use of American ports and ships by those engaged in Cuba bloc trade. These actions, and others under way, had hurt Castro's economy, his prestige and his attempts to subvert his neighbors. But they had not removed him—and this was the political Achilles' heel at which the President's opponents aimed.

The Republican Senatorial and Congressional Campaign Committees announced that Cuba would be "the dominant issue of the 1962 campaign." The public opinion polls showed growing frustration over Communist influence on that island. Senator Keating talked of Soviet troops and then of offensive missile bases at a time when no credible, verifiable proof existed of either. His information later proved inaccurate in important respects, but his refusal to reveal his sources of information made it impossible for the CIA to check their accuracy. As the President would later comment at a news conference, "We cannot base the issue of war and peace on a rumor or report which is not substantiated, or which some member of Congress refuses to tell us where he heard it. . . . To persuade our allies to come with us, to hazard . . . the security . . . as well as the peace of the free world, we have to move with hard intelligence." Still concerned about West Berlin, he opposed an invasion of Cuba at his August 29 news conference, stressing "the totality of our obligations," but he promised "to watch what happens in Cuba with the closest attention."

Photographs taken that same day, and reported to the President on August 31, provided the first significant "hard intelligence": antiaircraft surface-to-air missiles (SAMs), missile-equipped torpedo boats for coastal defense and substantially more military personnel. But neither these pictures nor those taken on September 5 (which also revealed MIG-21 fighter aircraft) produced evidence of offensive ballistic missiles, for which in fact no recognizable equipment had yet arrived. In a public statement on September 4 revealing the August 31 findings, the President repeated that there was as yet no proof of offensive ground-to-ground missiles or other significant offensive capability. He added, however: "Were it to be otherwise, the gravest issues would arise."

With the exception of CIA Chief John McCone, who speculated that the SAM sites might be intended to protect offensive missile installations, but whose absence on a honeymoon prevented his views from reaching the President, Kennedy's intelligence and Kremlinology experts stressed that no offensive Soviet missiles had ever been stationed outside of

Soviet territory, not even in Eastern Europe, where they could be constantly guarded and supplied; that the Soviets would in all likelihood continue to limit their military assistance to Cuba to defensive weapons; and that they evidently recognized that the development of an *offensive* military base in Cuba might provoke U.S. military intervention. This distinction between offensive and defensive capabilities, while not always clear-cut, was regarded as crucial by all concerned. The presence in Cuba of Soviet weapons incapable of attacking the United States was obnoxious but not sufficiently different from the situation which had long existed in Cuba and elsewhere to justify a military response on our part.

Continued Soviet shipments and the belligerent Moscow statement of September 11, however, impelled the President to deliver an even more explicit statement at his September 13 news conference. He was still concerned about the possibility that Khrushchev hoped to provoke him into another entanglement in Cuba which would make a martyr out of Castro and wreck our Latin-American relations while the Soviets moved in on West Berlin. He refused to give in to the war hawks in the Congress and press (and a few in the Pentagon) who wanted to drag this country into a needless, irresponsible war without allies against a tiny nation which had not yet proven to be a serious threat to this country. He paid no more attention to Soviet assurances about defensive missiles than he did to refugee claims about offensive missiles—both were subject to proof and the proof as yet was not present. But he thought it important that both the American public and the Kremlin leaders understand distinctly what was and was not tolerable in the way of Soviet aid to Cuba. After a series of meetings at the White House, he had decided upon a precise warning to the Soviets not to permit their Cuban build-up to achieve serious proportions. Striking out at "loose talk" about an American invasion which could only "give a thin color of legitimacy to the Communist pretense that such a threat exists," he underlined once again the difference between offensive and defensive capabilities:

> If at any time the Communist build-up in Cuba were to endanger or interfere with our security in any way . . . or if Cuba should ever . . . become an offensive military base of significant capacity for the Soviet Union, then this country will do whatever must be done to protect its own security and that of its allies.

Answering a questioner's reference to the Moscow warning that any U.S. military action against the build-up would mean "the unleashing of war," the President replied that, regardless of any threats, he would take whatever action the situation might require, no more and no less. (The added Soviet strength then known to be on the island, he had been told, could not save Castro, should the U.S. ever have to attack, for more than an extra twenty-four hours.) He politely indicated that a Congressional resolution on the matter, while not unwelcome, was not necessary for the exercise of his authority.

When the Congress made clear that it wished to pass one anyway, he saw to it that the wording was as broad and nonbelligerent as possible, applying only to arms or actions endangering this nation's security. Khrushchev nevertheless angrily warned that the actions contemplated by the resolution would mean the beginning of war—thermonuclear war. His various statements to reporters and diplomats also spoke of continuing the dialogue on Berlin after the November elections, hinting at a summit meeting at that time.

America's allies also warned of American hysteria over Cuba. Neither Latin America nor Western Europe showed any signs of supporting— or even respecting—a blockade or other sanctions. The OAS was induced nevertheless to lend its authority to our aerial surveillance; and that surveillance soon altered the situation drastically.

DISCOVERY

On October 9 the President—whose personal authorization was required for every U-2 flight and who throughout this period had authorized all flights requested of him[1]—approved a mission over the western end of Cuba. The primary purpose of the mission was to obtain information on the actual operation of Soviet SAMs. The western end was selected because the SAMs in that area—first spotted on August 29—were believed most likely to be operational. A secondary objective, inasmuch as the September flights had surveyed previously uncovered parts of the island, was to resurvey the military build-up in that sector—specifically to check two convoy observations from inside Cuba (both delayed because of the difficulty in getting reports out) which had indicated more precisely than usual the possibility of a medium-range ballistic missile site in that location. (It was not until one day after this authorization, on October 10, that Senator Keating first asserted the presence of offensive missile bases in Cuba.)

Delayed by bad weather until October 14, the U-2 flew in the early morning hours of that cloudless Sunday high over western Cuba, moving from south to north. Processed that night, the long rolls of film were scrutinized, analyzed, compared with earlier photos, and reanalyzed throughout Monday by the extraordinarily talented photo interpreters of

[1] Missions were flown on September 5, 11, 26 and 29, and October 5 and 7. Bad weather held up flights between September 5 and 26 and made the September 11 photography unusable. Two U-2 incidents elsewhere in the world also led to a high-level re-examination of that airplane's use and some delay in flights.

the U.S. Government's intelligence network; and late that afternoon they spotted in the San Cristóbal area the first rude beginnings of a Soviet medium-range missile base.

By Monday evening, October 15, the analysts were fairly certain of their findings. Between 8 and 10 P.M., the top CIA officials were notified and they notified in turn the Defense and State intelligence chiefs and, at his home, McGeorge Bundy. Bundy immediately recognized that this was no unconfirmed refugee report or minor incident. He decided, however—and quite rightly, I believe—not to call the President but to brief him in person and in detail the next morning. (Over four months later, almost as an afterthought, the President asked why he didn't telephone him that night; and Bundy responded with a memorandum "for your memoirs":

> . . . Its validity would need to be demonstrated clearly to you and others before action could be taken. The [photographic] blow-ups and other elements of such a presentation would not be ready before morning. . . . [To] remain a secret . . . everything should go on as nearly normal as possible, in particular there should be no hastily summoned meeting Monday night. [Bundy, Rusk, McNamara and others were all at different dinner parties where reporters, foreign diplomats and other guests might become suspicious.] . . . This was not something that could be dealt with on the phone. . . . What help would it be to you to give you this piece of news and then tell you nothing could be done about it till morning? . . . You were tired [from] a strenuous campaign weekend, returning . . . at 1:40 Monday morning. So I decided that a quiet evening and a night of sleep were the best preparation you could have. . . .)

Around 9 A.M. Tuesday morning, October 16, having first received a detailed briefing from top CIA officials, Bundy broke the news to the President as he scanned the morning papers in his bedroom. Kennedy, though angry at Khrushchev's efforts to deceive him and immediately aware of their significance, took the news calmly but with an expression of surprise. He had not expected the Soviets to attempt so reckless and risky an action in a place like Cuba, and had accepted—perhaps too readily, in retrospect—the judgment of the experts that such a deployment of nuclear weapons would be wholly inconsistent with Soviet policy. Even John McCone had assumed that no missiles would be moved in until an operational network of SAMs would make their detection from the air difficult. (Why the Soviets failed to coordinate this timing is still inexplicable.) For weeks the President had been publicly discounting the wild refugee reports checked out by his intelligence experts and found to be inaccurate. He had criticized in a campaign speech the previous weekend (in Capehart's Indiana) "those self-appointed generals and admirals who want to send someone else's son to war." While he had at least conditioned all his public statements on the basis of information *then* available, some subordinate officials had flatly asserted that no offensive weapons were in Cuba.

Nevertheless the possibility was not new; he had ordered flights for this very purpose; and his pledge to act was unavoidable. He asked Bundy to arrange for two presentations of the evidence that morning—first to the President alone and then to a list of officials he requested Bundy to summon.

Shortly thereafter, upon arriving at his office, he sent for me and told me the news. He asked me to attend the 11:45 A.M. meeting in the Cabinet Room and in the meantime to review his public statements on what our reaction would be to offensive missiles in Cuba. At the time those statements were made he may well have doubted that he would ever be compelled to act on them. But at 11 A.M., as CIA Deputy Director Marshall Carter spread the enlarged U-2 photographs before him with comments by a photo interpreter, all doubts were gone. The Soviet missiles were there; their range and purpose were offensive; and they would soon be operative.

At 11:45 A.M. the meeting began in the Cabinet Room. Those summoned to that session at the personal direction of the President, or taking part in the daily meetings that then followed, were the principal members of what would later be called the Executive Committee of the National Security Council, some fourteen or fifteen men who had little in common except the President's desire for their judgment:

State: Secretary Dean Rusk, Under Secretary George Ball, Latin-American Assistant Secretary Edwin Martin, Deputy Under Secretary Alexis Johnson and Soviet expert Llewellyn Thompson. (Participating until departing for his new post as Ambassador to France the following night was Charles "Chip" Bohlen.)

Defense: Secretary Robert McNamara, Deputy Secretary Roswell Gilpatric, Assistant Secretary Paul Nitze and General Maxwell Taylor (newly appointed Chairman of the Joint Chiefs of Staff).

CIA: On the first day, Deputy Director Carter; thereafter (upon his return to Washington), Director John McCone.

Other: Attorney General Robert Kennedy, Treasury Secretary Douglas Dillon, White House aides Bundy and Sorensen. (Also sitting in on the earlier and later meetings in the

White House were the Vice President and Kenneth O'Donnell. Others—such as Dean Acheson, Adlai Stevenson and Robert Lovett—sat in from time to time; and six days later USIA Deputy Director Donald Wilson, acting for the ailing Edward R. Murrow, was officially added.)

At this meeting I saw for the first time the crucial photographs, as General Carter and his photo analysts pinpointed the evidence. Barely discernible scratches turned out to be motor pools, erector launches and missile transporters, some with missiles on them. They looked, said the President, "like little footballs on a football field," barely visible. Soviet medium-range ballistic missiles, said Carter, could reach targets eleven hundred nautical miles away. That covered Washington, Dallas, Cape Canaveral, St. Louis and all SAC bases and cities in between; and it was estimated that the whole complex of sixteen to twenty-four missiles could be operational in two weeks. The photographs revealed no signs of nuclear warheads stored in the area, but no one doubted that they were there or soon would be.

The President was somber but crisp. His first directive was for more photography. He expressed the nation's gratitude to the entire photo collection and analysis team for a remarkable job. It was later concluded that late September photography of the San Cristóbal area might have provided at least some hints of suspicious activity more than three weeks earlier, but certainly nothing sufficiently meaningful to convince the OAS, our allies and the world that actual missiles were being installed. The contrast between the October 14 and August 29 photos indicated that field-type missiles had been very quickly moved in and all but assembled since their arrival in mid-September. American reconnaissance and intelligence had done well to spot them before they were operational. But now more photographs were needed immediately, said the President. We had to be sure—we had to have the most convincing possible evidence—and we had to know what else was taking place throughout the island. Even a gigantic hoax had to be guarded against, someone said. Daily flights were ordered covering all of Cuba.

Kennedy's second directive was to request that those present set aside all other tasks to make a prompt and intensive survey of the dangers and all possible courses of action—because action was imperative. More meetings were set up, one in the State Department that afternoon and another back in the Cabinet Room with him at 6:30. Even at that initial 11:45 meeting the first rough outlines of alternatives were explored. One official said our task was to get rid of the missile complex before it became operational, either through an air strike's knocking it out or by pressuring the Soviets into taking it out. He mentioned the possibilities of an OAS inspection team or a direct approach to Castro. Another said an air strike could not be limited to the missile complex alone but would have to include storage sites, air bases and other targets, necessitating thousands of Cuban casualties and possibly an invasion. Still another spoke of adding a naval blockade combined with a warning and increased surveillance. It was agreed that the U.S.-leased Naval base at Cuba's Guantánamo Bay would have to be reinforced and all dependents evacuated. No conclusions were reached—but all the possible conclusions were grim.

The President's third directive enjoined us all to strictest secrecy until both the facts and our response could be announced. Any premature disclosure, he stressed, could precipitate a Soviet move or panic the American public before we were ready to act. A full public statement later would be essential, he said, talking in the same vein about briefing former President Eisenhower. There was discussion about declaring a national emergency and calling up Reserves. But for the present secrecy was vital; and for that reason advance consultations with the Allies were impossible. He had already given the surface impression that morning that all was well, keeping his scheduled appointments, taking Astronaut Walter Schirra and his family out in back to see Caroline's ponies, and meeting with his Panel on Mental Retardation. (Praised by the Panel's chairman for his interest, the President had responded: "Thanks for the endorsement. . . . I'm glad to get some good news.") He had also proclaimed the last week in November to be National Cultural Center Week and declared storm-struck areas of Oregon to be disaster areas.

But even as he went about his other duties, the President meditated not only on what action he would take but why the Soviets had made so drastic and dangerous a departure from their usual practice. Evidently they had hoped, with the help of the SAMs and an American preoccupation with elections, to surprise the United States in November with a completed, operational missile chain. But why—and what next? The answer could not then—or perhaps ever—be known by Americans with any certainty; but in the course of our meetings several theories, some overlapping and some inconsistent, were advanced:

Theory 1. Cold War Politics. Khrushchev believed that the American people were too timid to risk nuclear war and too concerned with legalisms to justify any distinction between our overseas missile bases and his—that once we were actually confronted with the missiles we would do nothing but protest—that we would thereby appear weak and irresolute to the world, causing our allies to doubt our word and to seek accommodations with the Soviets, and permitting increased Communist sway in Latin America in particular. This was a probe, a test of America's will to resist. If it succeeded, he could move in a more important place—in West Berlin or with new pressure on our overseas bases—with missiles staring down our throats from Cuba. A Lenin adage, said Bohlen in one of our first meetings, compared national expansion to a bayonet drive: if you strike steel, pull back; if you strike mush, keep going. Khrushchev, having invested considerable money and effort in nuclear hardware he hoped never to use in battle, at least wanted one more try at using it for blackmail purposes.

Theory 2. Diverting Trap. If the United States did respond, presumably by attacking "little" Cuba, the Allies would be divided, the UN horrified, the Latin Americans more anti-American than ever, and our forces and energies diverted while Khrushchev moved swiftly in on Berlin. (Some speculated that Khrushchev also calculated that any strong U.S. reaction would help him prove to the Stalinists and Chinese that the West was no "paper tiger.")

Theory 3. Cuban Defense. A Soviet satellite in the Western Hemisphere was so valuable to Khrushchev—in both his drive for expansion and his contest with Red China—that he could not allow it to fall; and thus, in his view, an invasion from the United States or hostile Latin-American states, which seemed inevitable if Cuba collapsed internally, had to be prevented at all costs. The Castro brothers, requesting military aid, could cite the Bay of Pigs and the constant invasion talk in Congress and the Cuban refugee community. Although they reportedly had expected no more than a firm Soviet pledge, the presence of Soviet missiles looked to them like an even tighter guarantee of their security. (It should be noted that the Soviet Union stuck throughout to this position. Mikoyan claimed in a conversation with the President weeks after it was all over that the weapons were purely defensive, that they had been justified by threats of invasion voiced by Richard Nixon and Pentagon generals, and that the Soviets intended to inform the United States of these weapons immediately after the elections to prevent the matter from affecting the American political campaign.)

Theory 4. Bargaining Barter. Well aware of Cuba's sensitive role in domestic American politics, Khrushchev intended to use these bases in a summit or UN confrontation with Kennedy as effective bargaining power—to trade them off for his kind of Berlin settlement, or for a withdrawal of American overseas bases.

Theory 5. Missile Power. The Soviets could no longer benefit from the fiction that the missile gap was in their favor. To close it with ICBMs (intercontinental ballistic missiles) and submarine-based missiles was too expensive. Providing Cuban bases for their existing MRBMs and IRBMs (medium- and intermediate-range ballistic missiles) gave them a swift and comparatively inexpensive means of adding sharply to the total number of missiles targeted on the United States, positioned to by-pass most of our missile warning system and permitting virtually no tactical warning time between their launch and their arrival on target. The fifteen-minute ground alert on which our nuclear bombers stood by on runways would no longer be sufficient. To be sure, these Cuban missiles alone, in view of all the other megatonnage the Soviets were capable of unleashing upon us, did not substantially alter the strategic balance *in fact*—unless these first installations were followed by so many more that Soviet military planners would have an increased temp-tation to launch a pre-emptive first strike. But that balance would have been substantially altered *in appearance;* and in matters of national will and world leadership, as the President said later, such appearances con-tribute to reality.

His own analysis regarded the third and fifth theories as offering likely but insufficient motives and he leaned most strongly to the first. But whichever theory was correct, it was clear that the Soviet move, if successful, would "materially . . . and politically change the balance of power" in the entire cold war, as he would later comment. Undertaken in secrecy, accompanied by duplicity, the whole effort was based on con-fronting Kennedy and the world in November with a threatening *fait accompli,* designed perhaps to be revealed by Khrushchev personally, we speculated, in a bristling UN speech, to be followed by a cocky demand for a summit on Berlin and other matters. With these somber thoughts in mind, our Tuesday morning meeting ended; and I went down the hall to my office with a sense of deep foreboding and heavy responsibility.

PLANNING A RESPONSE

My recollection of the ninety-six hours that followed is a blur of meet-ings and discussions, mornings, afternoons, evenings. The proposals varied, their proponents varied, our progress varied. In order to clear my desk, particularly of the President's campaign speeches for that week, I did not attend any of the preliminary meetings held that after-noon. One was in the Pentagon, where McNamara and the Joint Chiefs executed the President's instructions to alert our forces for any con-tingency and to be ready in a week for any military action against Cuba. The other principal meeting that afternoon was in the State Department, where Soviet motives and possible actions were discussed. Both meetings imposed extra-tight security. Also meeting that afternoon and every morning thereafter was the United States Intelligence Board, on which the State and military intelligence officers were represented with the CIA.

At 6:30 P.M. we met again with the President in the Cabinet Room, as we would regularly for the next several weeks. That Tuesday was the first of thirteen days of decision unlike any other in the Kennedy years—or, indeed, inasmuch as this was the first direct nuclear confrontation, unlike any in the history of our planet.

Much misinformation has been written about this series of meetings, about who said what, and about such terms as "hawks and doves," "think tank," "Ex Comm" and "Trollope ploy" which I never heard used at the time. With all due respect to those Cabinet and other officers sometimes credited in these accounts with shaping our deliberations when the President was absent, the best performer in this respect was the Attorney General—not because of any particular idea he advanced, not because he presided (no one did), but because of his constant prodding, questioning, eliciting arguments and alternatives and keeping the discussions concrete and moving ahead, a difficult task as different participants came in and out. Bundy and I sought to assist in this role. Indeed, one of the remarkable aspects of those meetings was a sense of complete equality. Protocol mattered little when the nation's life was at stake. Experience mattered little in a crisis which had no precedent. Even rank mattered little when secrecy prevented staff support. We were fifteen individuals on our own, representing the President and not different departments. Assistant Secretaries differed vigorously with their Secretaries; I participated much more freely than I ever had in an NSC meeting; and the absence of the President encouraged everyone to speak his mind.

It was after noting these tendencies in a Wednesday afternoon meeting, held while the President fulfilled a campaign commitment in Connecticut, that I recommended he authorize more such preparatory meetings without his presence. He agreed, and these meetings continued in George Ball's conference room on the State Department's seventh floor. But inasmuch as some or all of us met daily with the President, those meetings over which he did not preside—held chiefly while he maintained his normal schedule for the sake of appearances and to carry out other duties—were not formulating policy or even alternatives without his knowledge. And when he did preside, recognizing that lower-ranking advisers such as Thompson would not voluntarily contradict their superiors in front of the President, and that persuasive advisers such as McNamara unintentionally silenced less articulate men, he took pains to seek everyone's individual views. In sharp contrast with his first Cuban crisis, when he had conferred with a somewhat different group, he knew his men, we knew each other, and all weighed the consequences of failure.

As the week wore on, the tireless work of the aerial photographers and photo interpreters gave an even greater sense of urgency to our deliberations. More MRBM sites were discovered, for a total of six. They were no longer recognizable only, in the President's words, "to the most sophisticated expert." Their construction had proceeded at such a pace in those few days that there could be no mistaking the Soviet intention to have them operational much earlier than we had anticipated on Tuesday. The literally miles of film taken of the island—which was blanketed daily with six or seven flights—now revealed excavations for three IRBM sites as well. The 2,200-mile IRBMs, when readied in December, would be capable of reaching virtually any part of the continental United States. At these locations, too, the fields and wooded areas photographed in earlier coverage had suddenly been transformed into networks of roads, tents, equipment and construction, all completely manned and closely guarded by Soviet personnel only.

The knowledge that time was running out dominated our discussions and kept us meeting late into the night. The stepped-up U-2 flights had apparently not alerted the Soviets to our discovery. But we had to formulate and declare our position, said the President, before they knew we knew, before the matter leaked out to the public and before the missiles became operational.

Despite the fatiguing hours and initially sharp divisions, our meetings avoided any loss of temper and frequently were lightened by a grim humor. Each of us changed his mind more than once that week on the best course of action to take—not only because new facts and arguments were adduced but because, in the President's words, "whatever action we took had so many disadvantages to it and each . . . raised the prospect that it might escalate the Soviet Union into a nuclear war."

It was an agonizing prospect. In no other period during my service in the White House did I wake up in the middle of the night, reviewing the deliberations of that evening and trying to puzzle out a course of action. Not one of us at any time believed that any of the choices before us could bring anything but either prolonged danger or fighting, very possibly leading to the kind of deepening commitment of prestige and power from which neither side could withdraw without resort to nuclear weapons.

The Soviet statement of September 11 had warned that any U.S. military action against Cuba would unleash nuclear war. What would Khrushchev actually do if we bombed the missile sites—or blockaded the island—or invaded? What would we do in return, and what would his reaction be then? These were the questions we asked that week. Among the locations listed as possible targets for Soviet retaliation were West Berlin (first on everyone's list, and therefore the subject of a special subcommittee of our group established by the President); Turkey (because our exposed Jupiter missiles there were most likely to be equated with the Soviet missiles in Cuba); Iran (where the Soviets had a tactical advantage comparable to ours in the Caribbean and a long-standing desire for control); Pakistan, Scandinavia and Italy. Nor could we worry only about Soviet retaliation. Castro, not known for his steady reactions, might order an attack on Guantánamo, on Florida or on whatever planes or ships we employed. He might also order the execution of the Bay of Pigs prisoners. The news that week that Red China had attacked India made us wonder whether this was a coincidence or whether a whole round of conflagrations would include Formosa, Korea and the Indochinese peninsula. The most dire possibility of all was that the Soviets might conclude—from a similar analysis of measures and countermeasures, as seen from their point of view—that all-out war was inevitable and thereupon launch a pre-emptive nuclear strike on the United States to make certain they hit us first.

The fact that Khrushchev had already made one major miscalculation—in thinking he could get away with missiles in Cuba—increased the danger that he would make more. Our predictions of the outcome were further clouded by the Soviet Chairman's known penchant for surprise, by the difficulty of halting an escalation once started, and by the possibility that he was deliberately trying to provoke us into an attack on Cuba to facilitate his moving on Berlin (just as the Suez invasion of 1956 had confused the opposition to his suppression of Hungary). We prepared all the arguments distinguishing Cuba from West Berlin—e.g., the latter was not a site for strategic weapons, and the U.S. had suggested an internationally supervised plebiscite to determine the wishes of its citizens—but we doubted that such distinctions would impress the Soviets.

We could not even be certain they would impress our allies. Most Western Europeans cared nothing about Cuba and thought we were over-anxious about it. They had long accustomed themselves to living next door to Soviet missiles. Would they support our risking a world war, or an attack on NATO member Turkey, or a move on West Berlin, because we now had a few dozen hostile missiles nearby? And would not any disarray in the Alliance weaken both our Cuba posture and our Berlin defense? On the other hand, if we failed to respond, would that not confirm the fears of De Gaulle and others that the U.S. could not be depended upon to meet threats even farther from our shores? Failure to consult could also weaken their support; yet consultation, with the inevitable leaks, disagreements and delays, could weaken our action. The situation appeared even worse in Latin America, where nonintervention by the U.S. was a religion but a failure to intervene would bring a Castro-Communist trend.

The President asked Rusk to prepare an analysis of possible Allied reactions; and the Secretary summarized it for our Wednesday afternoon meeting in his department. He emphasized that our evidence and reasoning would have to be convincing, and that our response would have to offer the Soviets a way out, but that the above problems would still remain. When he concluded, I asked, "Are you saying in effect that if we take a strong action the Allies and Latin Americans will turn against us and if we take a weak action they will turn away from us?" "That's about it," replied Rusk. There was a moment of gloomy silence until General Taylor interjected: "And a Merry Christmas to you, too!"

The bulk of our time Tuesday through Friday was spent in George Ball's conference room canvassing all the possible courses as the President had requested, and preparing the back-up material for them: suggested time schedules or scenarios, draft messages, military estimates and predictions of Soviet and Cuban responses. Initially the possibilities seemed to divide into six categories, some of which could be combined:

1. Do nothing.

2. Bring diplomatic pressures and warnings to bear upon the Soviets. Possible forms included an appeal to the UN or OAS for an inspection team, or a direct approach to Khrushchev, possibly at a summit conference. The removal of our missile bases in Turkey in exchange for the removal of the Cuban missiles was also listed in our later discussions as a possibility which Khrushchev was likely to suggest if we didn't.

3. Undertake a secret approach to Castro, to use this means of splitting him off from the Soviets, to warn him that the alternative was his island's downfall and that the Soviets were selling him out.

4. Initiate indirect military action by means of a blockade, possibly accompanied by increased aerial surveillance and warnings. Many types of blockades were considered.

5. Conduct an air strike—pinpointed against the missiles only or against other military targets, with or without advance warning. (Other military means of directly removing the missiles were raised—bombarding them with pellets that would cause their malfunctioning without fatalities, or suddenly landing paratroopers or guerrillas—but none of these was deemed feasible.)

6. Launch an invasion—or, as one chief advocate of this course put it: "Go in there and take Cuba away from Castro."

Other related moves were considered—such as declaring a national emergency, sending a special envoy to Khrushchev or asking Congress for a declaration of war against Cuba (suggested as a means of building both Allied support and a legal basis for blockade, but deemed not essential to either). But these six choices were the center of our deliberations.

Choice No. 1—doing nothing—and choice No. 2—limiting our response to diplomatic action only—were both seriously considered. As some (but not all) Pentagon advisers pointed out to the President, we had long lived within range of Soviet missiles, we expected Khrushchev to live with our missiles nearby, and by taking this addition calmly we could prevent him from inflating its importance. All the other courses raised so many risks and drawbacks that choice No. 2 had its appeal. All of us came back to it at one discouraged moment or another; and it was advocated to the President as a preferable alternative to blockade by one of the regular members of our group in the key Thursday night meeting discussed below.

But the President had rejected this course from the outset. He was concerned less about the missiles' military implications than with their effect on the global political balance. The Soviet move had been undertaken so swiftly, so secretly and with so much deliberate deception—it was so sudden a departure from Soviet practice—that it represented a provocative change in the delicate status quo. Missiles on Soviet territory or submarines were very different from missiles in the Western Hemisphere, particularly in their political and psychological effect on Latin America. The history of Soviet intentions toward smaller nations was very different from our own. Such a step, if accepted, would be followed by more; and the President's September pledges of action clearly called this step unacceptable. While he desired to combine diplomatic moves with military action, he was not willing to let the UN debate and Khrushchev equivocate while the missiles became operational.

Various approaches to Castro (choice No. 3)—either instead of or as well as to Khrushchev—were also considered many times during the week. This course was set aside rather than dropped. The President increasingly felt that we should not avoid the fact that this was a confrontation of the great powers—that the missiles had been placed there by the Soviets, were manned and guarded by the Soviets, and would have to be removed by the Soviets in response to direct American action.

The invasion course (choice No. 6) had surprisingly few supporters. One leader outside our group whose views were conveyed to us felt that the missiles could not be tolerated, that the Soviet motivation was baffling, that a limited military action such as a blockade would seem indecisive and irritating to the world, and that an American airborne seizure of Havana and the government was the best bet. But with one possible exception, the conferees shared the President's view that invasion was a last step, not the first; that it should be prepared but held back; that an invasion—more than any other course—risked a world war, a Soviet retaliation at Berlin or elsewhere, a wreckage of our Latin-American policy and the indictment of history for our aggression.

Thus our attention soon centered on two alternatives—an air strike and a blockade—and initially more on the former. The idea of American planes suddenly and swiftly eliminating the missile complex with conventional bombs in a matter of minutes—a so-called "surgical" strike —had appeal to almost everyone first considering the matter, including President Kennedy on Tuesday and Wednesday. It would be over quickly and cleanly, remove the missiles effectively and serve as a warning to the Communists. It could be accompanied by an explanatory address to the nation and by a blockade or increased aerial surveillance to guard against future installations. The air-strike advocates in our group prepared an elaborate scenario, which provided for a Presidential announcement of the missiles' presence Saturday, calling Congress back into emergency session, and then knocking the missiles out early Sunday morning, simultaneously notifying Khrushchev of our action and recommending a summit. Cuba was to be notified at the UN shortly in advance. Leaflet warnings to Russians at the sites were also considered.

But there were grave difficulties to the air-strike alternative, which became clearer each day.

1. The "surgical" strike, like the April, 1961, overthrow of Castro by a small exile brigade, was merely a hopeful illusion—and this time it was so recognized. It could not be accomplished by a few sorties in a few minutes, as hoped, nor could it be limited to the missile sites alone. To so limit the strike, declared the Joint Chiefs firmly, would be an unacceptable risk. Castro's planes—and newly arrived Soviet MIGs and IL-28 bombers, if operative—might respond with an attack on our planes, on Guantánamo or even on the Southeastern United States. The SAMs would surely fire at our planes. Cuban batteries opposite Guantánamo might open fire. The nuclear warhead storage sites, if identified, should not remain. All or most of these targets would have to be taken out in a massive bombardment. Even then, admitted the Air Force—and this in particular influenced the President—there could be no assurance that all the missiles would have been removed or that some of them would not fire first, unleashing their nuclear warheads on American soil. The more we looked at the air strike, the clearer it became that the resultant chaos and political collapse would ultimately necessitate a U.S. invasion. Most of the air-strike advocates openly agreed that their route took us back to the invasion course, and they added Cuban military installations and invasion support targets to the list of sites to be bombed. But invasion with all its consequences was still opposed by the President.

2. The problem of advance warning was unsolvable. A sudden air strike at dawn Sunday without warning, said the Attorney General in rather impassioned tones, would be "a Pearl Harbor in reverse, and it would blacken the name of the United States in the pages of history" as a great power who attacked a small neighbor. The Suez fiasco was also cited as comparable. Latin Americans would produce new Castros in their bitterness; the Cuban people would not forgive us for decades; and

the Soviets would entertain the very dangerous notion that the United States, as they had feared all these years, was indeed capable of launching a pre-emptive first strike. But to provide advance warning raised as many difficulties as no warning at all. It would enable the Soviets to conceal the missiles and make their elimination less certain. It would invite Khrushchev to commit himself to bombing us if we carried out our attack, give him time to take the propaganda and diplomatic initiative, and stir up a host of UN, Latin-American and Allied objections which we would have to defy or let the missiles stand. Many of those originally attracted to the air-strike course had favored it in the hope that a warning would suffice, and that the Soviets would then withdraw their missiles. But no one could devise any method of warning that would not enable Khrushchev either to tie us into knots or force us into obloquy. I tried my hand, for example, at an airtight letter to be carried from the President to the Soviet Chairman by a high-level personal envoy. The letter would inform Khrushchev that only if he agreed in his conference with that courier (and such others as he called in) to order the missiles dismantled would U.S. military action be withheld while our surveillance oversaw their removal. But no matter how many references I put in to a summit, to peaceful intentions and to previous warnings and pledges, the letter still constituted the kind of ultimatum which no great power could accept, and a justification for either a pre-emptive strike against this country or our indictment in the court of history. From that point on, I veered away from the air-strike course.

3. The air strike, unlike the blockade, would directly and definitely attack Soviet military might, kill Russians as well as Cubans and thus more likely provoke a Soviet military response. Not to respond at all would be too great a humiliation for Khrushchev to bear, affecting his relations not only at home and with the Chinese but with all the Communist parties in the developing world. Any Cuban missiles operational by the time of our strike might be ordered by Khrushchev to fire their nuclear salvos into the United States before they were wiped out—or, we speculated, the local Soviet commander, under attack, might order the missiles fired on the assumption that war was on. The air-strike advocates did not shrink from the fact that a Soviet military riposte was likely. "What will the Soviets do in response?" one consultant favoring this course was asked. "I know the Soviets pretty well," he replied. "I think they'll knock out our missile bases in Turkey." "What do we do then?" "Under our NATO Treaty, we'd be obligated to knock out a base inside the Soviet Union." "What will they do then?" "Why, then we hope everyone will cool down and want to talk." It seemed rather cool in the conference room as he spoke.

On that same day, Wednesday, October 17, the President—after a brief review of the situation with aides in the morning—had flown to Connecticut to keep a campaign commitment. Cancellation would only have aroused suspicion, and Vice President Johnson also flew west to carry on his campaign tour. A day of meetings in the State Department conference room had made some progress in defining the issues; and when we recessed for dinner until 9 P.M., the Attorney General and I decided to meet the President's plane at eight. It was after nine when he arrived, to find us sitting in his car to avoid attention. I have the most vivid memory of the smiling campaigner alighting from his plane, waving casually to onlookers at the airport, and then instantly casting off that pose and taking up the burdens of crisis as he entered his car and said almost immediately to the driver, "Let's go, Bill." We promptly filled him in as we drove to the White House. I had prepared a four-page memorandum outlining the areas of agreement and disagreement, the full list of possibilities and (longest of all) the unanswered questions. With this to ponder, and for the reasons earlier mentioned, the President decided not to attend our session that night. Dropping him at the White House, the Attorney General and I returned to the State Department.

At that meeting, one of the most influential participants—who had theretofore not indicated which course he favored—read a brief paper he had prepared on his position: On the following Wednesday, after informing Macmillan, De Gaulle, Adenauer and possibly Turkey and a few Latin Americans, a limited air strike wiping out the missiles should be accompanied by a simultaneous Presidential announcement to the world and formal reference to the UN and OAS. We would expect a Soviet attack on Berlin, possibly Korea, or possibly the Turkish missile bases in response; and NATO and our armed forces should be so prepared.

This paper, another adviser pointed out, by-passed the question of warning to the Soviets and Castro. Advance warning, he said, was required if the rest of the world was not to turn against us. Moreover, if Khrushchev defied our warning or in response lied about the existence of offensive weapons, our hand would be strengthened. Others pointed out the objections to advance warning, the dangers of being trapped in a diplomatic wrangle, and the fact that no air strike could be limited and still effective. Still others repeated the objections to no warning. The original proponent, undecided on this key element, began to back away from his plan.

That discussion, and my inability the next day to draft a letter to Khrushchev that could stand the light of logic and history, turned increasing attention upon the blockade route. Most of the career diplomats in our group had initially favored the blockade course, although some had preferred waiting for Khrushchev's response to a letter before deciding which military move to make. As the consensus shifted away from any notion of trying political or diplomatic pressure before resorting to military action, and away from the "surgical" air strike as an impossibility, it shifted on Thursday toward the notion of blockade. It was by no means unanimous—the advocates of a broad air strike were still strong—but the blockade alternative was picking up important backers.

At first there had been very little support of a blockade. It sounded like Senator Capehart trying to starve Cuba out before there were even missiles on the island. It appeared almost irrelevant to the problem of the missiles, neither getting them out nor seeming justifiable to our many maritime allies who were sensitive to freedom of the seas. Blockade was a word so closely associated with Berlin that it almost guaranteed a new Berlin blockade in response. Both our allies and world opinion would then blame the U.S. and impose as a "solution" the lifting of both blockades simultaneously, thus accomplishing nothing.

Moreover, blockade had many of the drawbacks of the air-strike plan. If Soviet ships ignored it, U.S. forces would have to fire the first shot, provoking Soviet action elsewhere—by their submarines against our ships there or in other waters, by a blockade of our overseas bases or by a more serious military move against Berlin, Turkey, Iran or the other trouble spots mentioned. One view held that Khrushchev and the U.S. could both pretend that an air strike on Cuba was no affair of the Soviet Union but a blockade of Soviet ships was a direct challenge from which he could not retreat. And if Castro thought a blockade was effectively cutting him off, he might in desperation—or to involve Soviet help—attack our ships, Guantánamo or Florida.

We could not even be certain that the blockade route was open to us. Without obtaining a two-thirds vote in the OAS—which appeared dubious at best—allies and neutrals as well as adversaries might well regard it as an illegal blockade, in violation of the UN Charter and international law. If so, they might feel free to defy it. One member of the group with a shipping background warned of the complications of maritime insurance and claims in an illegal blockade.

But the greatest single drawback to the blockade, in comparison with the air strike, was time. Instead of presenting Khrushchev and the world with a *fait accompli*, it offered a prolonged and agonizing approach, uncertain in its effect, indefinite in its duration, enabling the missiles to become operational, subjecting us to counterthreats from Khrushchev, giving him a propaganda advantage, stirring fears and protests and pickets all over the world, causing Latin-American governments to fall, permitting Castro to announce that he would execute two Bay of Pigs prisoners for each day it continued, encouraging the UN or the OAS or our allies to bring pressure for talks, and in all these ways making more difficult a subsequent air strike if the missiles remained. Our own people would be frustrated and divided as tensions built. One of the air-strike advocates, a Republican, passed a note to me across the table reading:

> Ted—Have you considered the very real possibility that if we allow Cuba to complete installation and operational readiness of missile bases, the next House of Representatives is likely to have a Republican majority? This would completely paralyze our ability to react sensibly and coherently to further Soviet advances.

Despite all these disadvantages, the blockade route gained strength on Thursday as other choices faded. It was a more limited, low-key military action than the air strike. It offered Khrushchev the choice of avoiding a direct military clash by keeping his ships away. It could at least be initiated without a shot being fired or a single Soviet or Cuban citizen being killed. Thus it seemed slightly less likely to precipitate an immediate military riposte. Moreover, a naval engagement in the Caribbean, just off our own shores, was the most advantageous military confrontation the United States could have, if one were necessary. Whatever the balance of strategic and ground forces may have been, the superiority of the American Navy was unquestioned; and this superiority was world-wide, should Soviet submarines retaliate elsewhere. To avoid a military defeat, Khrushchev might well turn his ships back, causing U.S. allies to have increased confidence in our credibility and Cuba's Communists to feel they were being abandoned.

Precisely because it was a limited, low-level action, the argument ran, the blockade had the advantage of permitting a more controlled escalation on our part, gradual or rapid as the situation required. It could serve as an unmistakable but not sudden or humiliating warning to Khrushchev of what we expected from him. Its prudence, its avoidance of casualties and its avoidance of attacking Cuban soil would make it more appealing to other nations than an air strike, permitting OAS and Allied support for our initial position, and making that support more likely for whatever air-strike or other action was later necessary.

On Thursday afternoon subcommittees were set up to plot each of the major courses in detail. The blockade subcommittee first had to decide what kind of blockade it recommended. We chose to begin with the lowest level of action—also the level least likely to anger allies engaged in the Cuban trade—a blockade against offensive weapons only. Inasmuch as the President had made clear that defensive weapons were not intolerable, and inasmuch as the exclusion of all food and supplies would affect innocent Cubans most of all, this delineation helped relate the blockade route more closely to the specific problem of missiles and made the punishment more nearly fit the crime. It also avoided the difficulty of stopping submarines and planes (which would have difficulty bringing in missiles and bombers even in sections).

The next question, and one that would recur throughout the next ten days, was whether to include "POL," as the military called it— petroleum, oil and lubricants. A POL blockade, automatically turning back all tankers, would lead directly though not immediately to a collapse of the Cuban economy. Although these commodities could be justifiably related to the offensive war machine, it seemed too drastic a step for the first move, too likely to require a more belligerent response and too obviously aimed more at Castro's survival than at Khrushchev's missiles. We recommended that this be held back as a means of later tightening the blockade should escalation be required.

Our next consideration was the likely Soviet response. The probability of Soviet acquiescence in the blockade itself—turning their ships back or permitting their inspection—was "high, but not certain," in the words of one Kremlinologist; but it was predicted that they might choose to force us to fire at them first. Retaliatory action elsewhere in the world seemed almost certain. The Soviets, we estimated, would blockade Berlin—not merely against offensive weapons, which would mean little, but a general blockade, including the air routes and all civilian access as well, thus precipitating another serious military confrontation for both powers. Other blockades were listed as a possibility, as well as increased Communist threats in Bolivia, Venezuela, Guatemala, Ecuador, Haiti and elsewhere in Latin America. Inside Cuba a long and gradually tighter blockade would in time, it was predicted, produce both military and political action.

We then suggested possible U.S. responses to these Communist responses, advocating that Berlin be treated on the basis of its own previously prepared contingency plans without regard to actions elsewhere. These studies completed, we rejoined the air-strike subcommittee and the others in the conference room to compare notes.

Meanwhile, the President—with whom some of us had met both in the morning and afternoon of that Thursday—was holding a long-scheduled two-hour meeting with Soviet Foreign Minister Gromyko prior to the latter's return to Moscow from the UN. While all of us wondered whether this could possibly be the moment planned by the Soviets to confront Kennedy with their new threat, all agreed that the President should not tell Gromyko what we knew. Not only was our information incomplete after only two days, with new evidence coming in every day, but we were not yet ready to act—and Gromyko's relay of our information to Moscow would bring on all the delays, evasions, threats and other disadvantages of a diplomatic warning. Alternatively, the wily Soviet Foreign Minister might decide to announce the build-up himself from the White House steps; and Kennedy felt strongly that, to retain the initiative and public confidence, it was essential that the facts first be disclosed to the people of the United States by their President along with an announced plan of action. He was anxious as the meeting approached, but managed to smile as he welcomed Gromyko and Dobrynin to his office.

Gromyko, seated on the sofa next to the President's rocker, not only failed to mention the offensive weapons but carried on the deception that there were none. In a sense, Kennedy had hoped for this, believing it would strengthen our case with world opinion. The chief topic of conversation was Berlin, and on this Gromyko was tougher and more insistent than ever. After the U.S. election, he said, if no settlement were in sight, the Soviets would go ahead with their treaty. ("It all seemed to fit a pattern," the President said to me later, "everything coming to a head at once—the completion of the missile bases, Khrushchev coming to New York, a new drive on West Berlin. If that move is coming anyway, I'm not going to feel that a Cuban blockade provoked it.") Then the Soviet Minister turned to Cuba, not with apologies but complaints. He cited the Congressional resolution, the Reservists call-up authority, various statements to the press and other U.S. interference with what he regarded as a small nation that posed no threat. He called our restrictions on Allied shipping a blockade against trade and a violation of international law. All this could only lead to great misfortunes for mankind, he said, for his government could not sit by and observe this situation idly when aggression was planned and a threat of war was looming.

The President made no response, and Gromyko then read from his notes:

> As to Soviet assistance to Cuba, I have been instructed to make it clear, as the Soviet Government has already done, that such assistance pursued solely the purpose of contributing to the defense capabilities of Cuba and to the development of its peaceful economy . . . training by Soviet specialists of Cuban nationals in handling defensive armaments was by no means offensive. If it were otherwise, the Soviet Government would have never become involved in rendering such assistance.

Kennedy remained impassive, neither agreeing nor disagreeing with Gromyko's claim. He gave no sign of tension or anger. But to avoid misleading his adversary, he sent for and read aloud his September warning against offensive missiles in Cuba. Gromyko "must have wondered why I was reading it," he said later. "But he did not respond."

Two days earlier, the President had been informed, on the very day he had learned of the missiles, a similar deception had taken place. Chairman Khrushchev, upon receiving our new Ambassador to Moscow, Foy Kohler, had complained vigorously about reports that a new Russian fishing port in Cuba would become a submarine base. He would have held up the announcement of the port, he said, because he did not want to burden Kennedy during the campaign. He also wanted to state once again that all activity in Cuba was defensive. (The one ominous note in that otherwise genial conversation had been a sharp reference to the U.S. Jupiter bases in Turkey and Italy.)

As Gromyko arrived at 8 P.M. that Thursday evening for a black-tie dinner on the State Department's eighth floor, our group was meeting on the seventh floor (minus Rusk and Thompson, who were with Gromyko). McNamara and McCone, surprised to see a band of reporters as they drove up, replied in the affirmative when asked if they were there for the Gromyko dinner. Obviously they had been too busy to don formal wear.

In our earlier sessions that day the President had requested a 9 P.M. conference at the White House. While we had been meeting for only three days (that seemed like thirty), time was running out. Massive U.S. military movements had thus far been explained by long-planned Naval exercises in the Caribbean and an earlier announced build-up in Castro's air force. But the secret would soon be out, said the President, and the missiles would soon be operational.

The blockade course was now advocated by a majority. We were prepared to present the full range of choices and questions to the President. George Ball had earlier directed that the official cars conspicuously gathered by the front door be dispersed to avoid suspicion. With the exception of Martin, who preferred to walk, we all piled into the Attorney General's limousine, some seated on laps, for the short ride over to the White House. "It will be some story if this car is in an accident," someone quipped.

In the Oval Room on the second floor of the Mansion, the alternatives were discussed. Both the case for the blockade and the case for simply living with this threat were presented. The President had already moved from the air-strike to the blockade camp. He liked the idea of leaving Khrushchev a way out, of beginning at a low level that could then be stepped up; and the other choices had too many insuperable difficulties. Blockade, he indicated, was his tentative decision.

Work began that night on the details. State, Defense and Justice put their legal experts to work on the basis for a blockade proclamation. Defense asked the Chiefs to prepare an exact list of offensive weapons to be on the prohibited list, to consider the feasibility of blockading aircraft, to determine which Latin-American navies could join in the blockade and to consider whether any Cuban exile organizations should join as well. Also requested was a list of riot control equipment we could make available to the Latin Americans; and on the following day the Atlantic and Caribbean Commands were alerted against possible air attacks on the Panama Canal and other targets within reach of Castro. All U.S. ambassadors to Latin America who were away on leave or consultation were ordered back to their posts. At the conclusion of the Gromyko dinner after midnight, Rusk and Thompson discussed the night's decision with Ball, Martin and Johnson.

But it was not a final decision; and on Friday morning, October 19, it seemed even more remote. Preparing to leave as agreed for weekend campaigning in the Midwest and West, the President called me in, a bit disgusted. He had just met with the Joint Chiefs, who preferred an air strike or invasion; and other advisers were expressing doubts. In retrospect it is clear that this delay enabled us all to think through the blockade route much more thoroughly, but at the time the President was impatient and discouraged. He was counting on the Attorney General and me, he said, to pull the group together quickly—otherwise more delays and dissension would plague whatever decision he took. He wanted to act soon, Sunday if possible—and Bob Kennedy was to call him back when we were ready.

Our meetings that morning largely repeated the same arguments. The objections to the blockade were listed, then the objections to the air strike. Those who had not been present the previous evening or days went through the same processes the rest of us had gone through earlier. I commented somewhat ungraciously that we were not serving the President well, and that my recently healed ulcer didn't like it much either. Yet it was true that the blockade approach remained somewhat nebulous, and I agreed to write the first rough draft of a blockade speech as a means of focusing on specifics.

But back in my office, the original difficulties with the blockade route stared me in the face: How should we relate it to the missiles? How would it help get them out? What would we do if they became operational? What should we say about our surveillance, about communicating with Khrushchev? I returned to the group late that afternoon with these questions instead of a speech; and as the concrete answers were provided in our discussions, the final shape of the President's policy began to take form. It was in a sense an amalgam of the blockade–air-strike routes; and a much stronger, more satisfied consensus formed behind it. Originally I was to have drafted an air-strike speech as well, but that was now abandoned.

Friday night—fortified by my first hot meal in days, sent in a covered dish by a Washington matron to whom I appealed for help—I worked until 3 A.M. on the draft speech. Among the texts I read for background were the speeches of Wilson and Roosevelt declaring World Wars I and II. At 9 A.M. Saturday morning my draft was reviewed, amended and generally approved—and, a little after 10 A.M. our time, the President was called back to Washington.

"The President has a cold," announced Pierre Salinger to the White House pressmen who had accompanied them to Chicago. He did have a cold, but it was not a factor in his decision. Before boarding his plane, he called his wife at Glen Ora and asked her and the children to return to the White House. No other decision in his lifetime would equal this, and he wanted his family nearby. (Once the decision was made he asked Jacqueline if she would not prefer to leave Washington, as some did, and stay nearer the underground shelter to which the First Family was to be evacuated, if there was time, in case of attack. She told him no, that if an attack came she preferred to come over to his office and share whatever happened to him.)

The President's helicopter landed on the South Lawn a little after 1:30. After he had read the draft speech, we chatted in a relaxed fashion in his office before the decisive meeting scheduled for 2:30. I gave him my view of the key arguments: air strike no—because it could not be surgical but would lead to invasion, because the world would neither understand nor forget an attack without warning and because Khrushchev could outmaneuver any form of warning; and blockade yes—because it was a flexible, less aggressive beginning, least likely to precipitate war and most likely to cause the Soviets to back down.

Our meeting at 2:30 P.M. was held once again in the Oval Room upstairs. For the first time we were convened formally as the 505th meeting of the National Security Council. We arrived at different gates at different times to dampen the now growing suspicion among the press. The President asked John McCone to lead off with the latest photographic and other intelligence. Then the full ramifications of the two basic tracks were set before the President: either to begin with a blockade and move up from there as necessary or to begin with a full air strike moving in all likelihood to an invasion. The spokesman for the blockade emphasized that a "cost" would be incurred for whatever action we took, a cost in terms of Communist retaliation. The blockade route, he said, appeared most likely to secure our limited objective—the removal of the missiles—at the lowest cost. Another member presented the case for an air strike leading to Castro's overthrow as the most direct and effective means of removing the problem.

At the conclusion of the presentations there was a brief, awkward silence. It was the most difficult and dangerous decision any President could make, and only he could make it. No one else bore his burdens or had his perspective. Then Gilpatric, who was normally a man of few words in meetings with the President when the Defense Secretary was present, spoke up. "Essentially, Mr. President," he said, "this is a choice between limited action and unlimited action; and most of us think that it's better to start with limited action."

The President nodded his agreement. Before his decision became final, he wanted to talk directly with the Air Force Tactical Bombing Command to make certain that the truly limited air strike was not feasible. But he wanted to start with limited action, he said, and a blockade was the place to start. The advocates of air strike and invasion should understand, he went on, that those options were by no means ruled out for the future. The combination of approaches contained in the draft speech anticipated not only a halt of the build-up but a removal of the missiles by the Soviets—or by us. The blockade route had the advantage, however, of preserving his options and leaving some for Khrushchev, too. That was important between nuclear powers, and he wanted our action directed against the other nuclear power, not Castro. "Above all," he would say later at American University, in drawing the moral of this crisis, "while defending our own vital interests, nuclear powers must avert those confrontations which bring an adversary to a choice of either a humiliating retreat or a nuclear war." Khrushchev had launched this crisis, but a blockade might slow down the escalation instead of rushing him into some irrevocable position. It applied enough military pressure to make our will clear but not so much as to make a peaceful solution impossible. The President then reaffirmed the decision not to include at the start POL or carriers other than surface ships; and, in a major decision, he adopted the term "quarantine" as less belligerent and more applicable to an act of peaceful self-preservation than "blockade."

Then he asked about the Berlin planning. The Soviets would move there, he expected, but they probably would whatever we did; and perhaps this show of strength would make them think twice about it: "The worst course of all would be for us to do nothing." I made a mental note to add that sentence to the speech. "There isn't any good solution," he went on. "Whichever plan I choose, the ones whose plans we're not taking are the lucky ones—they'll be able to say 'I told you so' in a week or two. But this one seems the least objectionable." By the time he finished, those members of our group who had come to the meeting still advocating an air strike or invasion had been essentially won over to the course he outlined.

But bitter disagreement broke out over the diplomatic moves to accompany it.[2] The President, although opposed to proposing a summit at that time, wanted to stress the desirability of a peaceful solution, of communications between the two powers, of an approach to the UN, of persuading the world that our action was prudent and necessary. But, as one of those present pointed out, little had been done to work out the political-diplomatic side of the program without which Allied and OAS approval was doubtful. We should go to the UN first, said this adviser, before the Russians do, and have ready an acceptable resolution worded our way. With this the President agreed.

There was disagreement, however, over what our diplomatic stance should be. Earlier in the week—Wednesday morning, the day after he had personally briefed this same individual—the President had been annoyed by a somewhat ambivalent handwritten note he had received from him. On the one hand:

> The national security must come first . . . we can't negotiate with a gun at our head . . . if they won't remove the missiles and restore the status quo ante, we will have to do it ourselves— and then we will be ready to discuss bases in the context of a disarmament treaty or anything else. . . .

But on the other hand:

> To risk starting a nuclear war is bound to be divisive at best and the judgments of history seldom coincide with the tempers of the moment. . . . I feel you should have made [sic] it clear that the existence of nuclear missile bases anywhere is negotiable before we start anything. . . . I confess I have many misgivings about the proposed course of action. . . .

That note, which also proposed the high-level courier-to-Khrushchev approach, had been written in the context of the air-strike solution. On Saturday and earlier, the author of the note fully endorsed the blockade route, although casting doubt on any unilateral action we took without OAS approval. He wanted this military action accompanied, however, by suggested diplomatic actions which the President found wholly unacceptable. He wanted the President to propose the demilitarization, neutralization and guaranteed territorial integrity of Cuba, thus giving up Guantánamo, which he said was of little use to us, in exchange for the removal of all Soviet missiles on Cuba. Alternatively or subsequently, he said, we could offer to withdraw our Turkish and Italian Jupiter

2 "Any historian," the President later commented, "who walks through this mine field of charges and countercharges should proceed with some care"; and I have thus relied only on my own notes and files in recounting the passages that follow. The same is in fact true for the most part of this entire chapter.

missile bases if the Russians would withdraw their Cuban missile bases, and send UN inspection teams to all the foreign bases maintained by both sides to prevent their use in a surprise attack. He also talked of a UN-supervised standstill of military activity on both sides—thus leaving the missiles in with no blockade—and of a summit meeting, and of UN inspection teams investigating not only Cuba but possible U.S. bases for attacking Cuba. The offer of such a political program, he would later write in a follow-up memo, would avoid comparisons with the Suez invasion. The offer would not sound "soft" if properly worded, he declared. It would sound "wise," particularly when combined with U.S. military action.

There was not a hint of "appeasing the aggressor" in these plans, as some would charge, only an effort to propose a negotiating position preferable to war and acceptable to the world. Even the synopsis prepared by the air-strike "hard-liners" earlier in the week had included not only a call for a summit but a pledge that the United States was prepared to promptly withdraw all nuclear forces based in Turkey, including aircraft as well as missiles. The Joint Congressional Committee on Atomic Energy had also recommended the Jupiters' withdrawal the previous year.[3]

Now an adviser who had served in the preceding administration agreed, to the President's great interest, that the Jupiter missiles in Turkey and Italy were obsolescent and of little military value, practically forced on those countries by the previous administration.

Nevertheless several of those present joined in a sharp attack on these diplomatic proposals. The President admired the courage of their proponent in adhering to his position under fire. He agreed we should beef up the political side of the speech, and said he had long ago asked McNamara to review the overseas Jupiter missiles. But now, he felt, was no time for concessions that could break up the Alliance by confirming European suspicions that we would sacrifice their security to protect our interests in an area of no concern to them. Instead of being on the diplomatic defensive, we should be indicting the Soviet Union for its duplicity and its threat to world peace.

The remainder of the meeting was occupied with a brief discussion of the speech draft and its timing. The President wanted to speak the next evening, Sunday. Secrecy was crumbling. Premature disclosure could alter all our plans. But the State Department stressed that our ambassadors had to brief Allied and Latin-American leaders and

---

[3] The vulnerable, provocative and marginal nature of these missiles in Turkey and Italy, so strikingly revealed in this week, led to their quiet withdrawal the following year in favor of Mediterranean Polaris submarines, a far superior and less vulnerable deterrent.

noted the impossibility of reaching them all on a Sunday. The President agreed to Monday, but stated he would still speak Sunday if the story appeared certain to break. He was, moreover, going ahead regardless of Allied reaction, though he wanted them to be informed. The speech was set for 7 P.M. Monday, October 22 (known in the scenario as P hour); and another meeting was set for Sunday.

We then returned to our offices and the multiple tasks at hand. The speech was circulated and redrafted. The quarantine proclamation was prepared. An approach to the OAS, letters to heads of state, a letter to West Berlin's Mayor and a simple message of information to Khrushchev were all drafted. Eisenhower was brought by helicopter from Gettysburg for his second briefing of the week by John McCone. The Vice President was brought back from his campaign tour in Hawaii— he had caught the President's cold. The U.S. Information Agency prepared a special hookup with private medium-wave radio stations to carry twenty-four hours of broadcasts, including the President's speech in Spanish, to Cuba and to all Latin America. The State Department prepared a thorough, highly efficient scenario outlining the timing of each step by each agency. The Joint Chiefs advised all service commanders to be prepared for possible military action. They ordered Guantánamo reinforced and its dependents evacuated on Monday. Acheson, who had earlier in the week wisely suggested a special high-level emissary to brief De Gaulle and NATO, was given that assignment. Military preparations continued for all levels of action against Cuba.

On Sunday morning I incorporated all suggested changes and corrections for the speech into a fourth draft. Simultaneously, the President met with Tactical Air Command Chief Walter Sweeney, Jr. and a few others (the Attorney General driving in directly from Virginia still in his riding togs). Told there was no way of making certain all the missiles would be removed by an air attack, Kennedy confirmed that the air strike was out and the blockade was on. He met with the British Ambassador, his close friend as well as ally. O'Brien and Salinger were informed. O'Brien was to round up the bipartisan Congressional leaders all over the country with White House military aides arranging transportation. Salinger was to coordinate our information policy with his State, USIA and Pentagon counterparts.

News leaks and inquiries for the first time were a growing problem, as crisis was in the air. The movement of troops, planes and ships to Florida and the Caribbean, the unavailability of high officials, the summoning of Congressional leaders, the Saturday night and Sunday activity, the cancellation of the Presidential and Vice Presidential campaign trips and the necessity of informing a much larger circle of officials meant that our cherished hours of secrecy were numbered. Washington and New York newspapers were already speculating. Publishers were asked not to disclose anything without checking. One newspaper obtained the story Sunday evening and patriotically agreed at the personal request of the President not to print it. The direct questions of other reporters were avoided, evaded or answered incorrectly by officials who did not know the correct answers; and a few outright falsehoods were told to keep our knowledge from the Communists.

It was "the best kept secret in government history," said the President, amazed as well as pleased. For most of the week, very few people outside the fifteen regulars, most of their wives and some of their secretaries knew the facts. (Of the three girls in my office, I worked two in alternate night shifts, believing it in the interest of the third that she be kept in the dark, inasmuch as her roommate worked for Senator Keating.) Some officials typed out their own papers or wrote them out in longhand. We stopped signing the entry book at the State Department door, used various entrances to that department and the White House and kept routine appointments where possible.

At 2:30 that Sunday afternoon, October 21, the President met with the NSC once again. He reviewed the State Department's drafts of instructions to embassies and Presidential letters to allies, all to be sent out in code that night and held for delivery. He reviewed the approaches to the OAS and UN, and agreed that UN supervision and inspection of the missiles' removal would be requested. He asked Navy Chief of Staff Anderson, Jr. to describe plans and procedures for the blockade. First, said the Admiral, each approaching ship would be signaled to stop for boarding and inspection. Then, if no satisfactory response was forthcoming, a shot would be fired across her bow. Finally, if there was still no satisfactory response, a shot would be fired into her rudder to cripple but not to sink. "You're certain that can be done?" asked the President with a wry smile. "Yes, sir!" responded the Admiral. Nitze reported on Berlin planning. More aerial surveillance of Cuba was ordered.

Most of that meeting was spent in a page-by-page review of the latest speech draft. Among the issues raised at that meeting, and in my earlier and later meetings with the President, were the following:

1. Should the latest enlarged photographs be shown by the President on TV? No, he decided—both because the average viewer could discern too little for it to be intelligible and because the mere presence of pictures might contribute to panic. The desire to avoid panic also caused the President to delete all references to the missiles' megatonnage as compared with Hiroshima, and to speak of their capability of "striking," instead of "wiping out," certain cities. But to increase hemispheric unity, he did include a reference to the Canadian and Latin-American areas within their target range.

2. Should the speech admit our secret surveillance by U-2 planes, internationally sensitive since 1960 and an illegal violation of Cuban air space? Yes—deciding to make a virtue out of necessity, the President listed increased surveillance as an announced part of his response, justifying it on the basis of an earlier OAS communiqué against secret military preparations in the hemisphere, adding that "further action will be justified" if the missiles remain, and hinting at the nature of that action by urging a consideration of the hazards "in the interest of both the Cuban people and the Soviet technicians *at the sites*."

3. Would he institute the blockade without OAS approval? Yes, if we could not get it, because our national security was directly involved. But hoping to obtain OAS endorsement, he deliberately obscured this question in the speech by a call for unspecified OAS action and an announcement of the blockade and other steps "in the defense of our own security and of the entire Western Hemisphere."

4. Should his speech anticipate, and try to forestall, a retaliatory blockade around Berlin? Yes—both by emphasizing that we were not "denying the necessities of life as the Soviets attempted to do in their Berlin blockade of 1948" and by warning that we would resist "any hostile move anywhere in the world against the safety and freedom of peoples to whom we are committed—including in particular the brave people of West Berlin."

5. What should he say about diplomatic action? Nothing that would tie our hands, anything that would strengthen our stand. Saturday's discussion, which obtained some additional State Department support and refinement over the weekend, was of major help here. The President deleted from my original draft a call for a summit meeting, preferring to state simply that we were prepared to present our case

> and our own proposals for a peaceful world at any time . . .
> in the United Nations or in any other meeting that could be
> useful, without limiting our freedom of action. . . . I call upon
> Chairman Khrushchev . . . to join in an historic effort to end the
> perilous arms race and to transform the history of man. . . . We
> have in the past . . . proposed the elimination of all arms and
> military bases. . . . We are prepared to discuss . . . the possibil-
> ities of a genuinely independent Cuba.

These remarks were a far cry from the Saturday afternoon proposals, but they were more than we had for the first draft.

6. How would we explain our action to other nations long living in the shadow of missiles? The President deleted a specific reference to self-defense against armed attack under Article 51 of the UN Charter, but carefully chose his words for anyone citing that article:

We no longer live in a world where only the actual firing of weapons represents a sufficient challenge to a nation's security to constitute maximum peril. Nuclear weapons are so destructive, and ballistic missiles are so swift, that any substantially increased possibility of their use or any sudden change in their deployment may well be regarded as a definite threat to peace.

He made dozens of other changes, large and small. After each recitation of the September Soviet Government and October Gromyko assurances, he inserted the sentence: "That statement was false." References to Latin America and the hemisphere were inserted along with or in place of references to this country alone. And a direct appeal to the Cuban people was expanded considerably by one of Kennedy's top appointees in State from Puerto Rico, Arturo Morales Carrión, who understood the nuances in Spanish of references to "fatherland," "nationalist revolution betrayed" and the day when Cubans "will be truly free— free from foreign domination, free to choose their own leaders, free to select their own system, free to own their own land, free to speak and write and worship without fear or degradation."

But Kennedy struck from the speech any hint that the removal of Castro was his true aim. He did not talk of total victory or unconditional surrender, simply of the precisely defined objective of removing a specific provocation. In the same vein, he deleted references to his notification of the Soviets, to the treatment awaiting any ships attempting to run the blockade and to predictions of the blockade's effect on Castro, believing that making these matters public was inconsistent with his desire not to force Khrushchev's hand. Lesser action items proposed by the State Department—specifically, a Caribbean Security Conference and further shipping restrictions—he deleted as too weak-sounding and insignificant for a speech about nuclear war. There was no mistaking that central subject, underlined most specifically in the words: *"It shall be the policy of this nation to regard any nuclear missile launched from Cuba against any nation in the Western Hemisphere as an attack by the Soviet Union on the United States, requiring a full retaliatory response upon the Soviet Union."*

Throughout Sunday evening and most of Monday, minor changes in the text were made, each one being rushed to USIA translators and to the State Department for transmission to our embassies. The whole nation knew on Monday that a crisis was at hand—particularly after Salinger's announcement at noon that the President had obtained 7 P.M. network time for a speech of the "highest national urgency." Crowds and pickets gathered outside the White House, reporters inside. I refused all calls from newsmen, answering the telephoned questions of only one powerful Congressman ("Is it serious?" "Yes") and Ted Kennedy ("Should I give my campaign dinner speech on Cuba?" "No"). I informed Mike Feldman and Lee White in my office by giving them copies of the speech. "It's a shame," cracked White with heavy irony, gazing out the window. "They've just finished sanding that Executive Office Building." Upon hearing that Gromyko was to make an announcement on his departure for Moscow, a special monitor was arranged—but his remarks contained only the usual farewell.

For the President that Monday, October 22, was a day of conferences. By telephone he talked to former Presidents Hoover, Truman and Eisenhower. He met with our group in the morning and with the full National Security Council at 3 P.M., all Joint Chiefs of Staff present. These were taut, organizational meetings, nothing more. The group he had originally summoned six days earlier was formally established as the "Executive Committee" of the National Security Council, with a standing order to meet with the President each morning at ten. At 4 P.M. he met with the Cabinet, briefly explained what he was doing and promptly adjourned the meeting. His presentation was tense and unsmiling. There were no questions and no discussion.

Just before the Cabinet meeting he kept a long-scheduled appointment with Prime Minister Milton Obote of Uganda. He had hoped to cut it short; and Secretary Rusk, who sat in on the conference, was visibly distracted. The Prime Minister blithely talked on, debating with the President the wisdom of U.S. aid to Rhodesian schools. The President found himself drawn into the debate, enjoying the change of subject and the clash of intellects. Rusk rustled his papers, the Cabinet paced outside the windows. Finally the meeting ended and the President personally escorted Obote to the door of the White House, looking more relaxed than he had all day. (The following day the Prime Minister, informed by Kennedy's speech of the grave matter with which he had competed for time, wrote the President that his patient attention at that hour was proof of his genuine regard for the new African nations.)

Elsewhere the State Department scenario was being effectively carried out. The President's speech, now completed, served as the basic briefing document in all capitals of the world and in a series of ambassadorial meetings in the State Department. Photographs were provided as well. Soviet Ambassador Dobrynin was invited to Rusk's office at 6 P.M. Ambassador Kohler delivered the same message in Moscow a little later. U.S. custodians of nuclear weapons in Turkey and Italy were instructed to take extraordinary precautions to make certain that such weapons were fired only upon Presidential authorization. Latin-American governments were told of possible disorders and the availability of riot control equipment. Our own missions were instructed to tape their windows. Many State, Defense and White House officers went on a twenty-four-hour watch, with cots in offices and personnel working in shifts.

The only sour note of the day was the President's meeting with some twenty Congressional leaders at 5 P.M. They had been plucked from campaign tours and vacation spots all over the country, some by jet fighters and trainers. (Hale Boggs, for example, fishing in the Gulf of Mexico, was first buzzed by an Air Force plane dropping a note to him in a plastic bottle, and was finally taken by helicopter to New Orleans, traveling by jet from there to Washington.) Members of both parties campaigning for re-election gladly announced the cancellation of their speeches on the grounds that the President needed their advice.

But in some cases their advice was captious and inconsistent. Reacting to a McNamara-Rusk-McCone picture briefing the same way most of us originally did, many called the blockade irrelevant and indecisively slow, certain to irritate our friends but doing nothing about the missiles. An invasion of the island was urged instead by such powerful and diverse Democratic Senators as Russell and Fulbright (who had strongly opposed the 1961 Cuban invasion). Charles Halleck said he would support the President but wanted the record to show that he had been informed at the last minute, not consulted.

The President, seeking bipartisan unity, announced that he, the Vice President and Cabinet had canceled the rest of their campaign trips, whatever happened. An invasion could not begin immediately in any event, he said, and it was better to go slow with Khrushchev. But Russell, one of the authors of the original, more belligerent forms of the Congressional resolution, complained that more than halfway measures were required.

The President, however, was adamant. He was acting by Executive Order, Presidential proclamation and inherent powers, not under any resolution or act of the Congress. He had earlier rejected all suggestions of reconvening Congress or requesting a formal declaration of war, and he had summoned the leaders only when hard evidence and a fixed policy were ready. "My feeling is," he said later, "that if they had gone through the five-day period we had gone through—in looking at the various alternatives, advantages and disadvantages . . .—they would have come out the same way that we did."

The meeting dragged on past 6 P.M. I waited outside the door with his reading copy, angry that they should be harassing him right up to the last minute. Finally he emerged, a bit angry himself, and hustled over to his quarters to change clothes for his 7 P.M. speech. As I walked with him, he told me of the meeting, muttering, "If they want this job, they can have it—it's no great joy to me." But in a few minutes he was calm and relaxed once again. Alone back in the Cabinet Room, we reviewed the text once more; and in a few more minutes the most serious speech in his life was on the air:

Good evening, my fellow citizens:

This government, as promised, has maintained the closest surveillance of the Soviet military build-up on the island of Cuba. Within the past week, unmistakable evidence has established the fact that a series of offensive missile sites is now in preparation on that imprisoned island. The purpose of these bases can be none other than to provide a nuclear strike capability against the Western Hemisphere. . . .

This urgent transformation of Cuba into an important strategic base, by the presence of these large, long-range and clearly offensive weapons of sudden mass destruction, constitutes an explicit threat to the peace and security of all the Americas. . . .

For many years, both the Soviet Union and the United States . . . have deployed strategic nuclear weapons with great care, never upsetting the precarious status quo which insured that these weapons would not be used in the absence of some vital challenge. Our own strategic missiles have never been transferred to the territory of any other nation, under a cloak of secrecy and deception. . . . American citizens have become adjusted to living daily in the bull's-eye of Soviet missiles located inside the U.S.S.R. or in submarines. . . .

But this secret, swift and extraordinary build-up of Communist missiles, in an area well known to have a special and historical relationship to the United States and the nations of the Western Hemisphere, in violation of Soviet assurances, and in defiance of American and hemispheric policy—this sudden, clandestine decision to station strategic weapons for the first time outside of Soviet soil, is a deliberately provocative and unjustified change in the status quo which cannot be accepted by this country, if our courage and our commitments are ever to be trusted again by either friend or foe.

The 1930's taught us a clear lesson: aggressive conduct, if allowed to go unchecked and unchallenged, ultimately leads to war. This nation is opposed to war. We are also true to our word. Our unswerving objective, therefore, must be to prevent the use of these missiles against this or any other country, and to secure their withdrawal or elimination from the Western Hemisphere. . . .

We will not prematurely or unnecessarily risk the costs of world-wide nuclear war in which even the fruits of victory would be ashes in our mouth, but neither will we shrink from that risk at any time it must be faced.

He went on to outline—in careful language which would guide us all week—the initial steps to be taken, emphasizing the word "initial": quarantine, surveillance of the build-up, action if it continued, our response to any use of these missiles, the reinforcement of Guantánamo, OAS and UN action and an appeal to Khrushchev and the Cuban people.

The path we have chosen for the present is full of hazards, as all paths are, but it is the one most consistent with our character and courage as a nation and our commitments around the world. The cost of freedom is always high, but Americans have always paid it. And one path we shall never choose, and that is the path of surrender or submission.

Our goal is not the victory of might, but the vindication of right; not peace at the expense of freedom, but both peace *and* freedom, here in this hemisphere, and, we hope, around the world. God willing, that goal will be achieved.

The crisis had officially begun. Some Americans reacted with panic, most with pride. A Congressional leader telephoned the President that a group of them watching together after leaving his office now understood and supported his policy more fully. A U.S. resolution was presented to that month's Security Council President, Russia's Valerian Zorin. Briefings of diplomats and the press continued at the State Department and Pentagon. Strategic Air Command and North American Air Defense units had been put on maximum ground and air alert as the President began speaking. His remarks had been broadcast around the world by the USIA in thirty-eight languages and immediately printed and distributed in many more. The OAS would meet the next day as an "organ of consultation," and the formal proclamation of the blockade would not occur until then. After a brief chat with the President, I went home to get some sleep.

The President also went to bed early, having had no rest after lunch and only a brief swim before. Many marveled that he swam or slept at all. But throughout both the previous week and the week that followed, he had adhered to as normal a life as possible, working nights with no sense of hours, requesting the postponement of minor matters, never taking his mind off the Cuban missiles, but still eating with his family, meeting with unknowing foreign leaders and staff aides, presenting an aviation trophy, and dining the night after his speech with the Ormsby-Gores and other guests as a substitute for a previously planned gala party. "His calmness . . . [and] unfailing good humor," said the British Ambassador, were "extraordinary to behold [and] kept everybody else calm and in a good mood." The telephone interrupted him constantly during that dinner, but he always returned immediately to the lighter conversations he had begun before the interruption. His wife saw more of him during the crisis than usual, as he sought her company at meals normally devoted to business and on walks around the South Lawn.

Similarly, in our meetings and in his office during those two weeks he was calm and deliberate, his mind clear, his emotions controlled, never brooding, always in command. He retained that composure even when fatigue was overtaking us all. After one meeting during the second week he expressed concern to me that one official had overworked himself to the point of mental and physical exhaustion.

The Presidency was never lonelier than when faced with its first nuclear confrontation. John Kennedy never lost sight of what either war or surrender would do to the whole human race. His UN mission was preparing for a negotiated peace and his Joint Chiefs of Staff were preparing for war, and he intended to keep both on rein. He was determined, despite divided counsel and conflicting pressures, to take all necessary action and no unnecessary action. He could not afford to be hasty or hesitant, reckless or afraid. The odds that the Soviets would go all the way to war, he later said, seemed to him then "somewhere between one out of three and even." He spoke on the back porch on that Saturday before his speech not of his possible death but of all the innocent children of the world who had never had a chance or a voice. While at times he interjected humor into our discussions, his mood can best be illustrated by the doodles he scratched on two sheets of his yellow legal pad during one of our meetings shortly after his speech:

> serious . . . serious . . . 16-32 [missiles] within a week . . . 2200 [miles] . . . Khrushchev . . . Soviet submarines . . . submarines . . . submarines . . . blockade . . . Sunday . . . Guantanamo . . . 16-32 . . . Friday morning . . . increases risk . . . need to pursue . . . McCone . . . 1 million men . . . holding the alliance.

QUARANTINE

The Alliance held. Macmillan phoned his support, although expressing his interest in a summit talk on disarmament and an interim suspension of activity on both sides. Adenauer, Brandt and the people of West Berlin did not flinch or complain. Despite some wavering by Canada, the NATO Council and De Gaulle pledged their backing after Acheson's briefings, attaching neither reservations nor complaints on grounds of no advance consultation, and ignoring the pickets and protests flooding London and other capitals. The British press, even more than that of the French and some neutrals, was largely negative. Some questioned whether missiles were really there, and at the suggestion of Ambassador Ormsby-Gore, with whom he reviewed the pictures after Tuesday's dinner, the President released the best photographs of the evidence. Pacifist complaints, interestingly enough, were all directed at the American quarantine, with no word about the Soviet missile deception. Philosopher Bertrand Russell, for example, wired Kennedy: "Your action desperate . . . no conceivable justification," while wiring Khrushchev: "Your continued forbearance is our great hope."

But of far greater importance to Kennedy than Lord Russell was the action taken by the twenty members of the OAS in immediately and unanimously adopting a broad authorizing resolution. The President, who had been concerned about getting the necessary two-thirds vote to back his quarantine, warmly congratulated Rusk and Martin. Martin, in fact, had been one of his most thoughtful and steady advisers all week. So had Llewellyn Thompson, who along with Martin had emphasized the fundamental importance of obtaining OAS endorsement of the quarantine. Martin's concern was Latin America's inevitable resentment of any unilateral U.S. action. Thompson's interest was the added legal justification such endorsement would give to the quarantine under international and maritime law as well as the UN Charter. That was important, he said, not only to our maritime allies but to legalistic-minded decision-makers in the Kremlin.

In the UN, in Washington and in the foreign embassies, support for the U.S. position was surprisingly strong. This was due in part to the shock of Soviet perfidy, and their futile attempts to deny the photographic evidence of attempted nuclear blackmail. It was due in part to world-wide recognition that this was an East-West nuclear confrontation, not a U.S. quarrel with Cuba. It was due in part to the President's choice of a low level of force at the outset and to his forceful but restrained approach. It was due, finally, to the excellent presentations made in the UN by Ambassador Stevenson, with Schlesinger as an emergency aide and John McCloy to lend bipartisan stature.

At 4 P.M. Tuesday, October 23, and again on Thursday, October 25, flanked by photo interpreters and intelligence analysts, Stevenson made a forceful presentation to the UN Security Council. Zorin had charged that the CIA had manufactured the evidence. Then let a UN team inspect the sites, said Stevenson.

STEVENSON: All right, sir, let me ask you one simple question: Do you, Ambassador Zorin, deny that the U.S.S.R. has placed and is placing medium—and intermediate—range missiles and sites in Cuba? Yes or no. Don't wait for the translation. Yes or no.

ZORIN: I am not in an American courtroom, sir . . .

STEVENSON: You are in the court of world opinion right now!

ZORIN: . . . and therefore I do not wish to answer a question that is put to me in the fashion that a prosecutor does. In due course, sir, you will have your reply.

STEVENSON: I am prepared to wait for my answer until Hell freezes over, if that's your decision.

Still another kind of support was essential—and forthcoming. Some Americans sought to flee, to hide or to resupply their fallout shelters. The stock market dropped. But by a ratio of ten to one the telegrams received at the White House expressed confidence and support. Reminded that the public mail response in the 1958 Formosa crisis had been against risking military action, Kennedy offered no comment. But he must have inwardly taken some satisfaction with his labors over the previous two years to prepare the American people to face the facts. He mentioned only two telegrams to me, both sarcastically. One came from a right-wing leader who had long urged a tougher policy toward the insignificant Castro but now quaked at the prospects of our confronting a nuclear power. The other came from Mississippi's Governor Barnett, who "retracted" an earlier wire complaining about our military might being used in Mississippi instead of the Caribbean.

Later in the week the House Republican Campaign Committee would charge that the whole Kennedy approach appeared "brazenly false" and ineffective. Still later some would maintain that the whole crisis had been politically timed and inspired. But on Tuesday the GOP Congressional leaders, echoed by Senator Keating, called for complete support of the President.

"We cannot tell anyone to keep out of our hemisphere," young Jack Kennedy had prophetically written twenty-two years earlier in *Why England Slept*, "unless our armaments and the people behind these armaments are prepared to back up the command, even to the ultimate point of going to war." On Tuesday, October 23, 1962, the people appeared prepared—and so did the armaments. During his twenty-one months in the White House he had, among other moves, increased the number of combat-ready divisions from eleven to fifteen, increased airlift and tactical air support, accelerated the Polaris schedule to place nine instead of three missile submarines (each with sixteen missiles aboard) on active station, and increased the military personnel, fleet readiness and vessel numbers of the U.S. Navy. All these increases were now poised for action.

His attention was focused on the Navy as never before. The "quarantine" was a new form of reprisal under international law, an act of national and collective self-defense against an act of aggression under the UN and OAS charters and under the Rio Treaty of 1947. Its legality, much strengthened by the OAS endorsement, had been carefully worked out. A "Proclamation of Interdiction of the Delivery of Offensive Weapons to Cuba" was discussed in our two Executive Committee meetings on the first day after the President's speech—at 10 A.M. and 6 P.M. Tuesday—and it was then immediately issued, effective the next day. The proclamation stressed that

> force shall not be used except in case of failure or refusal to comply with directions . . . after reasonable efforts have been made to communicate them to the vessel or craft, or in case of self-defense. In any case force shall be used only to the extent necessary.

Behind this "disable, don't sink" order, its graduated timing, its exclusion for the time being of POL (which automatically let all tankers pass) and the President's personal direction of the quarantine's operation, was his determination not to let needless incidents or reckless subordinates escalate so dangerous and delicate a crisis beyond control. He had learned at the Bay of Pigs that the momentum of events and enthusiasts could take issues of peace and war out of his own hands. Naval communications permitted this operation, unlike the Bay of Pigs situation, to be run directly out of his office and the Pentagon. During his first week as President, he recalled, exiles had seized a Portuguese passenger ship in the South Atlantic which the U.S. agreed to find. The President, surprised at the time it took the Navy to locate the liner, had accepted the answer offered: "It's a big ocean." In October, 1962, it still was—and the quarantine was no automatic solution, even with a line of 16 destroyers, 3 cruisers, an antisubmarine aircraft carrier and 6 utility ships, with nearly 150 others in reserve.

Other issues were discussed in the two Tuesday meetings of the Executive Committee: what to do if a U-2 were shot down, how to keep the press and Congress informed, preparations at Berlin, preparations to invade, cancellation of the President's fall trip to Brazil and defense of the Southeastern states against a sudden air attack. Civil defense authorities in that region were alerted and planes were dispersed, the President persisting that he had earlier seen them lined up wing to wing, an easy target, on a flight to Palm Beach. (When reassured once again that these fears were unfounded, he ordered aerial photographs taken without the knowledge of the Florida bases and found, to the discomfort of the military, that our aircraft were still highly concentrated.) Under that fall's Congressional authorization, military tours of duty were extended. For the first time low-level reconnaissance flights were ordered over Cuba, flying in just over the treetops below the range of the Soviet SAMs. These pictures showed in remarkable detail more Soviet military personnel and weapons than anticipated, all Cubans excluded from missile areas and two deadly MRBMs ready to operate.

The big question was the big ocean. To us, Khrushchev appeared— in a harsh but rambling Soviet Government statement Tuesday morning rejecting the quarantine as "piracy," in two private letters to Kennedy Tuesday morning and Wednesday evening (both answered within hours after their receipt with firm restatements of our position) and in his answers to appeals from Bertrand Russell and Acting Secretary General U Thant—to have been caught off balance, to be maneuvering, to be seeking a consensus among the top Kremlin rulers, uncertain whether to admit that the missiles were there in view of the widespread denunciations of that action. The Soviets, it seemed, had counted on surprising us, on disunity in the West and on a sufficient fear of war in the United States to prevent any military response. Having proven them wrong on those counts, we wondered whether their inconsistent positions reflected a possible internal struggle. We joked around the Cabinet table about Khrushchev's apparently yielding to his hard-liners one day and his peace advocates the next, and about the fact that—because of the time differential and slowness of transmission—we worked all day to send messages they would receive upon waking up and they did exactly the same.

But the eighteen Soviet dry cargo ships still heading toward the quarantine were no joke. Five of these ships with large hatches were being watched with special care. The Executive Committee, in session most of each day, soon knew every Soviet ship by name and which of them were suspected of carrying armaments. Tuesday night, as the ships came on, the tension built. Robert Kennedy was dispatched that night to find out from the Soviet Ambassador whether any instructions had been issued to the Soviet ship captains. He learned nothing. "You fellows who thought the blockade was the most peaceful answer may find out differently pretty soon," said the President. At our Wednesday morning meeting, held just as the quarantine went into effect, some half-dozen Soviet submarines were reported to have joined these ships. Orders were prepared to sink any subs interfering with the quarantine. In the midst of the same meeting, more news arrived. The Soviet ships nearest Cuba had apparently stopped or altered their course. A feeling of relief went round the table.

The prospects of confrontation at sea were not, however, by any means over. Soviet intentions were not yet clear. The quarantine had not yet been tested. Kennedy told U Thant, in response to the Secretary General's initial appeal, that the blockade could not be suspended, that "the existing threat was created by the secret introduction of offensive weapons into Cuba, and the answer lies in their removal of such weapons." (A second U Thant proposal on Friday, negotiated through Stevenson, urging both sides to avoid unnecessary contact during the next few days, was more acceptable, Kennedy simply stating the obvious—that there would be no incidents if Soviet ships stayed away.) Khrushchev summoned a visiting American businessman to tell him that Kennedy should agree to a summit, that conflict in the Caribbean could lead to nuclear war (including the use of the offensive missiles he now admitted were in Cuba) and that Soviet submarines would sink any American vessel forcing a Soviet ship to stop.

At dawn Thursday a Soviet tanker was hailed and, on the instructions of the President—who thought it possible that the tanker had not yet received its instructions from Moscow—passed through the barrier like all nonsuspicious tankers after merely identifying itself. So was an East German passenger ship. At dawn Friday an American-made, Panama-owned, Greek-manned, Lebanese-registered freighter under charter to the Soviet Union was halted and boarded—after the Navy obtained the President's authorization. His preference had been not to intercept any Soviet ships until necessary, but to have a nonbloc ship under Soviet charter boarded to show we meant business. Inspected by an unarmed boarding party and found to be carrying only trucks and truck parts, the freighter was allowed to pass through.[4]

The real problem was not Lebanese freighters and Soviet tankers but the Soviet cargo ships and their submarine escorts. They would have to be stopped Friday, said the President, if U Thant's proposals had not altered their course by then. The Navy was eager to go far out into the ocean to intercept the key Soviet ships. The President, backed by McNamara and Ormsby-Gore and watching the tracking of each ship on a large board in the White House "Situation Room," insisted that Khrushchev be given all possible time to make and communicate an uncomfortable decision to his ships. In a sharp clash with the Navy, he made certain his will prevailed.

Gradually, rather than dramatically, the good news came in, mixed, in fact, with the "bad" news recounted above. Sixteen of the eighteen Russian ships, including all five with large hatches, were reported Wednesday to have stopped—then to be lying dead in the water or moving in uncertain circles—and, finally, Thursday and Friday to have turned around. "That's nice," observed one member of our group. "The Soviets are reacting to us for a change." U.S. planes followed them all

---

[4] One of the boarding ships, the President learned afterward, was the U.S. destroyer *Joseph P. Kennedy, Jr.* About the same time, a replica of the PT-109—then in Florida for a film story—was commandeered in a side incident involving Cuban exiles, and the President felt these coincidences would never be believed.

the way back to Soviet ports. A minimum of force had obtained a maximum gain. The value of conventional strength in the nuclear age had been underlined as never before. The quarantine, speculated the President later, "had much more power than we first thought it did because, I think, the Soviet Union was very reluctant to have us stop ships which carried . . . highly secret and sensitive material." The Soviet military, he reasoned, long obsessed with secrecy, could not risk letting their missiles, warheads and electronic equipment fall into our hands.

PERIL POINT

The dangers of a naval confrontation had not ended, but at least they had temporarily eased. The dangers posed by the missiles in Cuba, however, were increasing. More of the MRBMs—now hastily camouflaged—were becoming operational, reported McCone at the briefings which began each of our morning meetings. Work was going ahead full speed. All the MRBMs would be operational by the end of the week, with the IRBMs to be ready a month or so later. Throughout Thursday and Friday the President and Executive Committee pondered new ways of stepping up the political, economic and military pressure on the Soviets, including:

1. Tightening the blockade. The addition of missile fuel to the proscribed list already provided a reason to stop tankers, if desired. The next step would be POL, then all commodities other than food and medicine.

2. Increased low-level flights. These would provide not only improved reconnaissance but also a means of harassing the Soviets and humiliating Castro, particularly if nighttime flights with flares were added. The fear of more serious reprisal had stopped Cuban as well as Soviet attempts to down these planes. Their daily operations, moreover, would make more feasible a surprise air strike.

3. Action inside Cuba. The President authorized a leaflet drop directed at the people of Cuba, asked the USIA to prepare it, personally cleared its text and pictures (low-level photographs of the missile sites), ordered it to go ahead and then held it up temporarily. Meanwhile ways of reaching Castro directly were explored once again.

4. Air strike.

5. Invasion. Those who had favored the last two courses the previous week now renewed their advocacy.

The President refused to rush. Preparations for an invasion as well as other military contingencies were still under way. Soviet ships had turned back. Talks were going on at the U.N. But in a message to U Thant, in a White House statement and in a State Department announcement, the continued work on the missile sites was noted in the gravest tones.

The State Department press officer, in making this announcement Friday noon, went beyond the White House position by referring reporters to that passage in the President's Monday night speech which had said "further action will be justified" if work on the missiles continued. This remark, accompanied by some imprecise Congressional and press speculation, immediately touched off headlines that an invasion or air strike was imminent. For the first time, the President lost his temper. He called the Secretary of State, then the Assistant Secretary, then the press officer, Lincoln White, his voice rising and his language intensifying with each call. This was going to be a prolonged struggle, he argued, requiring caution, patience and as little public pressure on him as possible.

But in the next twenty-four hours he was to joke that White's error might have had a helpful effect. A new Khrushchev-to-Kennedy letter was received at the State Department Friday evening, October 26—long, meandering, full of polemics but in essence appearing to contain the germ of a reasonable settlement: inasmuch as his missiles were there only to defend Cuba against invasion, he would withdraw the missiles under UN inspection if the U.S. agreed not to invade. Similar talk came the same day in the UN from Zorin to U Thant and, through a highly informal channel, from Counselor of the Soviet Embassy in Washington Aleksander Fomin to the ABC-TV correspondent covering the State Department, John Scali. In Khrushchev's letter the offer was a bit vague. It seemed to vary from one paragraph to the next, and was accompanied by the usual threats and denunciations. Nevertheless it was with high hopes that the Executive Committee convened Saturday morning, October 27, to draft a reply.

In the course of that meeting our hopes quickly faded. A new Khrushchev letter came in, this time public, making no mention of the private correspondence but raising the ante: the Jupiter missiles in Turkey must be removed in exchange. In addition, we learned, Fomin and Zorin were talking about extending the UN inspection to U.S. bases. Had Khrushchev's hard-liners once again taken the lead, we speculated, or had the appearance of this same swap proposal in Washington and London newspapers encouraged the Soviets to believe we would weaken under pressure? Many Western as well as neutral leaders were, in fact, quick to endorse the new Soviet position. Still another possibility was that the second, public proposal had actually been written first.[5]

[5] While the answer to this and all other questions about internal Soviet thinking and actions will probably never be known with any certainty, the far greater length of time required to send a private, coded message made this possibility highly doubtful.

More bad news followed. A new Soviet ship was reported approaching the quarantine zone. The latest photographs showed no indications that missile site work was being held up awaiting our reply to the Friday letter. On the contrary, permanent and expensive installations of nuclear warhead storage bunkers and troop barracks were going ahead rapidly. Khrushchev's letter, said some, was designed merely to delay and deceive us until the missile installations were complete. Then came the worst news: the first shooting and fatality of the crisis, ground fire on two low-flying reconnaissance planes and the downing of a high-flying U-2 by a Soviet-operated SAM. The dead pilot, Major Rudolf Anderson, Jr., had flown the mission thirteen days earlier which first discovered the missiles.

We had talked earlier in the week of what response this nation would make should an unarmed U.S. plane—on a publicly announced mission of surveillance—be shot down, and had decided tentatively on a single retaliatory strike against a SAM site, then knocking them all out if attacks continued. Now the time had come to implement that policy, killing Soviets in the process, probably flushing Castro's planes, possibly leading to a full air strike, an invasion or further Soviet ripostes. But the President had been careful not to give blanket authority to carry out this decision to the Air Force in advance; and he preferred not to give it now. He wanted to wait one more day—for more information on what happened to our planes and for Khrushchev's final negotiating position. He called off the flare-drop flight scheduled for that night (each reconnaissance flight had to be approved individually by the President each day), because of the danger that the flares might be taken for air-to-ground fire from the planes. But he approved an announcement that all necessary measures would be taken "to insure that such missions are effective and protected," authorized fighter escorts, and ordered the fighters to respond to any MIG attack. He also urged State and Defense officials to prepare for the worst in Berlin, Turkey and Iran, where, in the face of unexpected Allied unity, the expected Soviet counterthrust had not yet occurred.

That same day, to make matters worse, an American U-2 plane over Alaska had encountered navigational difficulties and flown deep into Soviet territory, bringing up a bevy of Soviet fighters but no fire, before regaining its course. The President decided to ignore this incident unless the Soviets publicized it; but he wondered if Khrushchev would speculate that we were surveying targets for a pre-emptive nuclear strike. (Khrushchev did, in fact, write later of the danger of such a plane, "which might have been taken for a nuclear bomber . . . intruding when everything has been put into combat readiness.")

Everything was in combat readiness on both sides. The conventional and the nuclear forces of the United States were alerted world-wide. Both air-strike planes and the largest invasion force mounted since World War II were massed in Florida. Our little group seated around the Cabinet table in continuous session that Saturday felt nuclear war to be closer on that day than at any time in the nuclear age. If the Soviet ship continued coming, if the SAMs continued firing, if the missile crews continued working and if Khrushchev continued insisting on concessions with a gun at our head, then—we all believed—the Soviets must want a war and war would be unavoidable.

The President had no intention of destroying the Alliance by backing down, but he thought it all the more imperative that our position be absolutely clear. He decided to treat the latest Khrushchev message as propaganda and to concentrate on the Friday night letter. An impersonal White House statement, issued at 4:30 P.M., dismissed the Saturday letter with a reference to "inconsistent and conflicting proposals . . . involving the security of nations outside the Western Hemisphere." As soon as the present Soviet-created threat is ended, the statement read, sensible negotiations on arms limitations can proceed. A private letter to U Thant also stressed the rapidly approaching point of peril, and asked him to ascertain urgently whether the Soviet Union was willing immediately to cease work on these bases in Cuba and to render the weapons inoperable under UN verification so that various solutions could be discussed.

The most attention was given to Khrushchev's letter of the previous night. Under the President's direction, our group worked all day on draft replies. Fatigue and disagreement over the right course caused more wrangling and irritability than usual. Finally the President asked the Attorney General and me to serve as a drafting committee of two to pull together a final version. He also asked me to clear the text with Stevenson, who had skillfully advanced parallel talks at the UN. The final draft of his reply—which confined itself to the proposals made in Khrushchev's Friday letter, ignoring the Fomin and Zorin talks and any specific reference to Turkish bases—read into the Chairman's letter everything we wanted. Stevenson feared it might be too stiff. But with two minor amendments acceptable to the President, I obtained Stevenson's clearance; and the President, in the interests of both speed and psychology, released the letter publicly as it was being transmitted to Moscow shortly after 8 P.M.

> The first thing that needs to be done . . . is for work to cease on offensive missile bases in Cuba and for all weapons systems in Cuba capable of offensive use to be rendered inoperable, under effective United Nations arrangements. [Note that, instead of arguing with Mr. K. over whether his missiles and planes

were intended to be offensive, he insisted on action against those "capable of offensive use."]

As I read your letter, the key elements of your proposals— which seem generally acceptable as I understand them—are as follows:

1. You would agree to remove these weapons systems from Cuba under appropriate United Nations observation and supervision; and undertake, with suitable safeguards, to halt the further introduction of such weapons systems into Cuba.

2. We, on our part, would agree—upon the establishment of adequate arrangements through the United Nations to ensure the carrying out and continuation of these commitments—(a) to remove promptly the quarantine measures now in effect and (b) to give assurances against an invasion of Cuba. [Note that, unlike the action to be undertaken by Khrushchev, ours was conditional upon UN arrangements.]

. . . the first ingredient, let me emphasize . . . is the cessation of work on missile sites in Cuba and measures to render such weapons inoperable, under effective international guarantees. The continuation of this threat, or a prolonging of this discussion concerning Cuba by linking these problems to the broader questions of European and world security, would surely lead to an intensification of the Cuban crisis and a grave risk to the peace of the world.

At the private request of the President, a copy of the letter was delivered to the Soviet Ambassador by Robert Kennedy with a strong verbal message: The point of escalation was at hand; the United States could proceed toward peace and disarmament, or, as the Attorney General later described it, we could take "strong and overwhelming retaliatory action . . . unless [the President] received immediate notice that the missiles would be withdrawn." That message was conveyed to Moscow.

Meanwhile the Executive Committee was somewhat heatedly discussing plans for the next step. Twenty-four Air Force Reserve troop carrier squadrons were called up. Special messages to NATO, De Gaulle and Adenauer outlined the critical stage we had reached. The POL blockade, air-strike and invasion advocates differed over what to do when. An invasion, it was observed, might turn out differently than planned if the overground rockets (FROGs) spotted by our planes in the Soviet armored division now in Cuba were already equipped with nuclear warheads. In front of the White House, more than a thousand pickets mustered, some pleading for peace, some for war, one simply calling JFK a traitor.

The President would not, in my judgment, have moved immediately to either an air strike or an invasion; but the pressures for such a move on the following Tuesday were rapidly and irresistibly growing, strongly supported by a minority in our group and increasingly necessitated by a deterioration in the situation. The downing of our plane could not be ignored. Neither could the approaching ship, or the continuing work on the missile sites, or the Soviet SAMs. We stayed in session all day Saturday, and finally, shortly after 8. P.M., noting rising tempers and irritability, the President recessed the meeting for a one-hour dinner break. Pressure and fatigue, he later noted privately, might have broken the group's steady demeanor in another twenty-four or forty-eight hours. At dinner in the White House staff "mess," the Vice President, Treasury Secretary Dillon and I talked of entirely different subjects. The meeting at 9 P.M. was shorter, cooler and quieter; and with the knowledge that our meeting the next morning at 10 A.M. could be decisive—one way or the other—we adjourned for the night.

SUCCESS

Upon awakening Sunday morning, October 28, I turned on the news on my bedside radio, as I had each morning during the week. In the course of the 9 A.M. newscast a special bulletin came in from Moscow. It was a new letter from Khrushchev, his fifth since Tuesday, sent publicly in the interest of speed. Kennedy's terms were being accepted. The missiles were being withdrawn. Inspection would be permitted. The confrontation was over.

Hardly able to believe it, I reached Bundy at the White House. It was true. He had just called the President, who took the news with "tremendous satisfaction" and asked to see the message on his way to Mass. Our meeting was postponed from 10 to 11 A.M. It was a beautiful Sunday morning in Washington in every way.

With deep feelings of relief and exhilaration, we gathered in the Cabinet Room at eleven, our thirteenth consecutive day of close collaboration. Just as missiles are incomparably faster than all their predecessors, so this world-wide crisis had ended incredibly faster than all its predecessors. The talk preceding the meeting was boisterous. "What is Castro saying now?" chortled someone. Robert McNamara said he had risen early that morning to draw up a list of "steps to take short of invasion." When he heard the news, said John McCone, "I could hardly believe my ears." Waiting for the President to come in, we speculated about what would have happened

- if Kennedy had chosen the air strike over the blockade . . .
- if the OAS and other Allies had not supported us . . .

• if both our conventional and our nuclear forces had not been strengthened over the past twenty-one months . . .

• if it were not for the combined genius and courage that produced U-2 photographs and their interpretations . . .

• if a blockade had been instituted before we could prove Soviet duplicity and offensive weapons . . .

• if Kennedy and Khrushchev had not been accustomed to communicating directly with each other and had not left that channel open . . .

• if the President's speech of October 22 had not taken Khrushchev by surprise . . .

• if John F. Kennedy had not been President of the United States.

John F. Kennedy entered and we all stood up. He had, as Harold Macmillan would later say, earned his place in history by this one act alone. He had been engaged in a personal as well as national contest for world leadership and he had won. He had reassured those nations fearing we would use too much strength and those fearing we would use none at all. Cuba had been the site of his greatest failure and now of his greatest success. The hard lessons of the first Cuban crisis were applied in his steady handling of the second with a carefully measured combination of defense, diplomacy and dialogue. Yet he walked in and began the meeting without a trace of excitement or even exultation.

Earlier in his office—told by Bundy and Kaysen that his simultaneous plea to India and Pakistan to resolve their differences over Kashmir in view of the Chinese attack would surely be heeded, now that he looked "ten feet tall"—he had evenly replied: "That will wear off in about a week, and everyone will be back to thinking only of their own interests."

Displaying the same caution and precision with which he had determined for thirteen days exactly how much pressure to apply, he quickly and quietly organized the machinery to work for a UN inspection and reconnaissance effort. He called off the Sunday overflights and ordered the Navy to avoid halting any ships on that day. (The one ship previously approaching had stopped.) He asked that precautions be taken to prevent Cuban exile units from upsetting the agreement through one of their publicity-seeking raids. He laid down the line we were all to follow—no boasting, no gloating, not even a claim of victory. We had won by enabling Khrushchev to avoid complete humiliation—we should not humiliate him now. If Khrushchev wanted to boast that he had won a major concession and proved his peaceful manner, that was the loser's prerogative. Major problems of implementing the agreement still faced us. Other danger spots in the world remained. Soviet treachery was too fresh in our memory to relax our vigil now.

Rejecting the temptation of a dramatic TV appearance, he issued a brief three-paragraph statement welcoming Khrushchev's "statesman-like decision . . . an important and constructive contribution to peace." Then the President's fourth letter of the week—a conciliatory reply to the Chairman's "firm undertakings"—was drafted, discussed, approved and sent on the basis of the wire service copy of the Chairman's letter, the official text having not yet arrived through diplomatic channels.

Weeks later the President would present to each of us a little silver calendar of October, 1962, mounted on walnut, with the thirteen days of October 16 through October 28 as extra deeply engraved as they already were in our memories. But on that Sunday noon, concealing the enormous sense of relief and fatigue which swept over him, he merely thanked us briefly, called another meeting for Monday morning and rejoined his family as he had each night of the crisis.

I went down the hall to where my secretary, Gloria Sitrin, was at work as she had been day and night for almost two weeks. From her bookcase I picked up a copy of *Profiles in Courage* and read to her a part of the introductory quotation John Kennedy had selected from Burke's eulogy of Charles James Fox: "He may live long, he may do much. But here is the summit. He never can exceed what he does this day."

CHAPTER XXV

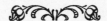

THE STRATEGY OF PEACE

THE CUBAN MISSILE CRISIS, Harold Macmillan told the House of Commons shortly after it ended, represented "one of the great turning points in history." The autumn of 1962, said President Kennedy, if not a turning point, was at least "a climactic period . . . even though its effects can't be fully perceived now. . . . Future historians looking back at 1962 may well mark this year as the time when the tide . . . began [to turn]."

Time will tell whether subsequent events—in Peking, Moscow, Dallas and elsewhere—have altered or will yet alter the accuracy of those prophecies. But in 1962-1963 little time elapsed before the impact of that crisis was affecting Soviet-American relations, Soviet-Chinese relations, the Western Alliance, domestic American politics and Castro's Cuba itself.

POSTCRISIS CUBA

The first task was to make certain all Soviet offensive weapons left Cuba. One high official warned the day after Khrushchev's letter of retreat that it might have been a fake while work continued on the missiles. Somewhat more attention was paid by the President to a letter he received from Dean Acheson which praised in superlative terms Kennedy's handling of the crisis but warned, out of his experience with Korea, that national exultation could turn to national frustration as Communist negotiators wrangled on and on. Kennedy continued our aerial reconnaissance in the absence of the UN's ability to mount a substitute, and provided formal notice to the Soviets of his action. He continued the daily, sometimes twice daily, meetings of the Executive Committee—continued the high state of readiness of American military forces in the Caribbean and elsewhere—and continued to supervise personally all releases to the press and all details of the prolonged discussions carried on at the UN by his team of negotiators. (Their views did not always reflect his caution after the earlier Soviet duplicity or his concern for Congressional relations; and he remarked to them only half in jest after one of many long sessions that "we seem to be spending as much time negotiating with you as you are negotiating with the Soviets.")

The Soviet negotiators, fearful that taunts from Red China would impair their standing in the eyes of other non-European Communists, were concerned with their relations with Cuba. Fidel Castro—who had earlier snarled that "whoever tries to inspect Cuba must come in battle array"—was stunned by Khrushchev's reversal, to which he obviously had not consented. He adamantly insisted on five new conditions of his own, and harangued and harassed the UN's U Thant when the Secretary General arrived to work out details. The baffled U Thant returned to New York, and the Soviet Union's Mikoyan flew down for similar treatment. Castro complained to him that Cuba had been betrayed, tried to give the impression that the Chinese were moving in, argued fruitlessly with him for a week, totally ignored him for ten days, and finally resumed discussions only when Mikoyan prepared to fly back to Moscow. Castro, the Armenian was reported to have said, is like a mule—hard to convince and hard to deal with.

Meanwhile, regardless of Castro's wishes, the missile bases were dismantled by Soviet technicians. The sites were destroyed and plowed over. The missiles and other equipment were crated for return to the Soviet Union. Inasmuch as Castro continued to prohibit any on-site inspection, the crates were counted and inspected by American air and sea forces in the Caribbean, and the Soviet ships transporting them were followed all the way back to their home ports.

Khrushchev at first balked at also removing the IL-28 bombers. They were too limited in range to pose much of a threat to the United States. Some of Kennedy's advisers also suggested that he let the matter drop. But Kennedy (though wondering at times whether his stand was necessary) felt he had to insist on his original vow against all offensive weapons systems, rejected a variety of Khrushchev conditions, kept the quarantine ships on station and finally announced that he would hold a news conference on November 20 to discuss future steps. Setting the hour at 6 P.M. helped signal the seriousness of his intended statement. On November 19 he prepared letters to Macmillan, Adenauer and De Gaulle, warning them that the crisis was about to heat up again, and that air strikes and extensions of the blockade were being considered. On November 19 and 20 we worked on an opening statement which would sternly insist that the IL-28's must go and call a new OAS Organ of Consultation meeting that week. On Wednesday afternoon, November 20, a few hours before the news conference was to begin, a new letter from Khrushchev arrived. The IL-28's would be withdrawn in thirty days under full inspection, and Soviet combat units (identified a few days earlier) would be withdrawn "in due course." A few hours later the President announced to the press not the calling of an OAS council but the end of the quarantine. November 22, 1962, became a Thanksgiving, in his words, with "much for which we can be grateful, as we look back to where we stood only four weeks ago."

From that date on the problem of a Soviet offensive military base in Cuba gradually and somewhat fitfully subsided. The President, at his news conference, had announced that the permanent withdrawal of all offensive weapons and the absence of any Cuban aggression would mean "peace in the Caribbean." The Soviets regarded this as an insufficient fulfillment of the no-invasion pledge, particularly when the President accompanied it by a statement that our battle against Cuban subversion and our hopes for Cuban liberation would both continue. Nor did they like his announcement that our aerial surveillance of the island, a humiliating violation of Cuban air space, would continue, with a clear indication that any fulfillment of Castro's threat to fire on such planes would be returned with whatever force was required. But the President insisted that Castro's blocking of on-site inspection and controls not only required such flights but represented a Soviet failure to make good their side of the bargain. After exasperating weeks of haggling over how to wrap the crisis up officially in the UN, it silently sank into limbo.

The problem of Castro, however, remained. However insignificant he may have been compared to nuclear missiles, the American public's continued irritation with his presence, the Cuban refugees' desperate efforts to keep the crisis alive and the Republican Party's not unnatural desire to becloud John Kennedy's triumph soon drowned the nation's sense of pride in a sea of rumors and accusations. The national unity produced by military danger could not be maintained for the follow-up negotiations. Many patriots, once they recovered from their fright, went right back to calling for a blockade of Cuba because it was Cuba. Khrushchev, in one of his letters on the IL-28's, expressed satisfaction with the election defeats of Nixon and others, who had, he said, made the most frenzied, bellicose speeches. But the number of such speeches was hardly diminished.

More than three hundred competing, bickering Cuban refugee organizations flooded the Congress and the press with wild reports of missiles

in caves, of secret submarine bases, of the potential use of MIGs and torpedo boats for offensive purposes and a supposed Kennedy promise for a
second invasion. Public antagonisms were further aggravated by the
dawdling rate at which the Soviets removed their 23,000 troops (although they had made no precise commitment on timing), by a MIG
attack on an unmarked American shrimp boat near the Cuban coast
and by the Republican charge that Kennedy's aim of "peace in the Caribbean" amounted to a guarantee of Castro. A crackdown by Federal authorities on the publicity-seeking Cuban refugee groups who conducted
hit-and-run raids on Cuban ports and shipping—damaging little other
than our efforts to persuade the Soviets to leave—fed fuel to the fire.
Success was also dimmed by a variety of charges regarding the adequacy
of U.S. intelligence, the positions taken by particular advisers, the
secrecy surrounding the Kennedy-Khrushchev letters and the "management" of news during the crisis.

Time and again Kennedy patiently explained that our full surveillance would continue; that every refugee report was being checked
out; that we had not tied our hands against Cuban subversion, sabotage
or aggression; and that we had not weakened our efforts to isolate Castro
politically and economically and end Communism in this hemisphere by
every act short of war. Time and again he emphasized that questions
of war and peace, attack and reprisal, should not be left to private organizations of exiles who had no responsibility or prospects of success (and
whom he contrasted with those Bay of Pigs veterans who were quietly
entering the American armed forces under special arrangement). "We
should keep our heads and . . . know what we have in our hands," he
said, "before we bring the United States . . . to the brink again." Finally,
he authorized McNamara to present, in an unusual public disclosure
of our reconnaissance capabilities, a comprehensive televised briefing
which traced with aerial and naval photographs the arrival, installation,
dismantling and removal of the Soviet weapons systems.

In time much of the noise about Cuba faded away. But Kennedy
never took his eye off Cuba. While he dismissed in his own mind more
firmly than before the possibility of bringing Castro down through external military action, the effort to isolate his regime continued with
increased success. Castro was hurt, though not mortally, by a lack of
trade with the free world, a lack of spare parts and consumer goods,
additional breaks in Latin-American diplomatic relations, plummeting
popularity throughout the hemisphere and rising discomfort among
hungry Cubans. "I don't accept the view that Mr. Castro is going to be
in power in five years," said the President. "I can't indicate the roads
by which there will be a change, but I have seen enough change . . .
to make me feel that time will see Cuba free again."

The newly established "Standing Group" of the National Security Council reviewed regularly the potential range of further actions against Castro, including:

1. What military action would be taken in the event of a Hungary-type revolt, a reintroduction of offensive weapons or the downing of a U-2, the latter possibility having been increased by Cuban operation of Soviet SAMs.

2. What steps could be taken to harass, disrupt and weaken Cuba politically and economically.

3. What steps could be taken to get either Castro or the Soviets out of Cuba, or to get either Cuba or Castro away from the Soviets (the possibility of enticing Fidel into becoming a Latin-American Tito with economic aid was regarded as a doubtful alternative because of his unreliability, because Congress would balk at providing the money, and because his success might encourage other Latin Americans to try the same course).

4. What steps could be taken to curb the export of arms, agents and subversion from Cuba, a principal topic at Kennedy's March conference with Central American leaders at San José, Costa Rica.

5. What steps could be taken to make clear our concept of a free post-Castro Cuba. Pushed by Murrow, action on this front was of deep interest to the President. The United States could not—by supporting one of the many rival refugee groups as a government-in-exile or otherwise—dictate the personnel or policies of a future Cuban regime. But it was important, he thought, to make clear that our objection was to subversion, to dictatorship and to a Soviet satellite, not to "the genuine Cuban revolution . . . against the tyranny and corruption of the past." He opposed an effort in the Congress to impose as the first condition to our dealing with a new Cuba its compensation of those Americans whose property had been expropriated by Castro. He stressed in a November 18, 1963, address to the Inter-American Press Association in Miami that only Cuba's role as an agent of foreign imperialism prevented normal relations.

> Once this barrier is removed, we will be ready and anxious to work with the Cuban people in pursuit of those progressive goals which a few short years ago stirred their hopes . . . [to] extend the hand of friendship and assistance.

These remarks were little noticed. But Kennedy hoped to expand on this theme in future speeches, to spell out to the Cuban people the freedoms, the hemispheric recognition and the American aid which would be forthcoming once they broke with Moscow. The Miami speech was unfortunately his last opportunity.

THE BREAKTHROUGH TO AGREEMENT

The fate of Cuba, however, was the least of the consequences of the Cuban missile crisis. That confrontation has aptly been called "the Gettysburg of the Cold War." For the first time in history, two major nuclear powers faced each other in a direct military challenge in which the prospects of a nuclear exchange were realistically assessed. Berlin, had its access been cut off, and even Laos, had there been no cease-fire, made a total of three potentially "major clashes with the Communists . . . in twenty-four months which could have escalated," said the President, adding "That is rather unhealthy in a nuclear age."

Khrushchev, it appeared, had reached the same conclusion. He had looked down the gun barrel of nuclear war and decided that that course was suicidal.

He had tried the ultimate in nuclear blackmail—dispatching not the usual missile threats, which had been issued over a hundred times since Sputnik, but the missiles themselves. That move having failed, nuclear blackmail was no longer an effective weapon in Berlin or anywhere else.

He had tested his premise that the United States lacked the will to risk all-out war in defense of its vital interests. That premise having proved wrong, he was less likely to underestimate our will again.

He had attempted a quick, easy step to catch up on the Americans in deliverable nuclear power. That step having been forced back, he implicitly accepted the superiority of our strategic forces as a fact with which he must and could live.

He had accepted—although only in Cuba, not in the Soviet Union —both a measure of inspection and an acknowledgment that the aerial camera was rapidly ending total secrecy. And he had learned, finally, that the American President was willing to exercise his strength with restraint, to seek communication and to reach accommodations that did not force upon his adversary total humiliation.

The result of all these lessons was apparently an agonizing reappraisal of policy within the Communist camp. The Soviet-Chinese split had been further widened when the Chinese—who had simultaneously and successfully attacked Russia's friend India—openly assailed Khrushchev for his weakness in Cuba. Throughout the winter of 1962-1963 the Kremlin appeared to flounder. Reports of a new power struggle were widespread. But the change which finally emerged was one not of personnel but of policy—a change not of basic purposes but of methods and manner. The taunts and threats to his leadership from the Red Chinese caused Khrushchev to reshuffle his priorities, removing conflict with the West from the top of his agenda. They also required him to prove concretely the value of coexistence and to isolate the more reckless Chinese position.

The arms race, moreover, looked very different to the Soviet Chairman than it had a few years earlier. The Kennedy acceleration of 1961 had given the United States, even earlier than planned, several times as many operational ICBMs as the Russians could deploy and every prospect of retaining that advantage for years to come. Khrushchev's submarine-based missiles were fewer in number and inferior in capability to the Polaris system. The total number of strategic aircraft available to him for a strike in the Western Hemisphere was less than half the number of missile-equipped, long-range bombers placed by Kennedy on constant ground and air alert alone. In addition to obtaining tens of thousands of nuclear warheads for tactical and strategic use, the United States had discouraged any move on Berlin by sharply increasing its number of combat-ready divisions and tactical air support wings. For Khrushchev to match all these increases in not only personnel but equipment and air transport would be enormously expensive. The slowdown in Russia's industrial, investment and agricultural growth, particularly in comparison with the new burst of growth in the United States, along with the simultaneous rise in Russian consumer demands, pressured him to forgo trying to win the arms race, to allocate more resources to his civilian economy and to avoid another crisis that would threaten its very existence.

"Mr. Khrushchev and I are in the same boat in the sense of both having this nuclear capacity and both wanting to protect our societies," said Kennedy.

> He realizes how dangerous a world we live in. If Mr. Khrushchev would concern himself with the real interests of the people of the Soviet Union . . . [their] standard of living [and] . . . security, there is no real reason why . . . [we] should not be able to live in peace.

The Soviet Chairman, in talks with Harold Wilson and Paul Spaak, and in his letters to Kennedy, seemed to be looking for a chance to live in peace, for a meaningful breakthrough in nuclear arms control that would prevent any breakthrough on nuclear arms, for a breathing spell to focus on goulash and housing and ballet instead of weapons. He removed the pressure from Berlin, saying only that he would welcome new suggestions from the West.

The Chairman, reported Mikoyan to Kennedy in late November at the White House, liked the spirit of the President's statements and felt that the United States and the Soviet Union should proceed to a point-by-point negotiation of all outstanding questions. It would be help-ful, the President replied, for the Soviets to start by devoting their efforts to the pursuit of Russian interests only instead of kindling fires all over the world. He did not forget—and did not fail to remind Khrushchev by letter and Mikoyan in person—that the missile crisis had originated in a high-level, calculated attempt by the Soviets to deceive him. The possibility of improving Soviet-American relations, he warned Mikoyan, had suffered a severe blow because of this deception. Recognizing also that their failure in Cuba might force the more militant voices in the Kremlin to try again closer to home—as in Berlin—he had no intention of relaxing his vigil. Nevertheless he recognized that the Soviet Union was probably more ready for serious negotiations with the United States in early 1963 than at any time since the close of the Second World War.

He derived little comfort from the Soviet-Chinese dispute, and thought, on the contrary, that it might increase the dangers of despera-tion in Moscow or irresponsibility in Peking. Their disagreement, he told the Congress, "is over means, not ends. A dispute over how to bury the West is no grounds for Western rejoicing." But the new fluidity in the post-Cuban Communist camp, he recognized, presented opportuni-ties which seventeen years of cold war rigidities had never made possible before.

Kennedy, too, was ready to negotiate—to apply, as Dean Rusk put it, the lessons of World War III before it could occur because it will be too late to apply them afterward. Success in Cuba had not endowed him with any smug belief that the results were due to military superiority alone, or that superiority meant omnipotence, or that the pattern in Cuba could be often repeated. Cuba, he said, was located in an area where our conventional superiority posed problems for the Communists. Secret intelligence had enabled careful planning and timing which took the initiative away from the Soviets. Our side of the dispute had been convincing, even without advance consultation, to both allies and neutrals. A crisis in Berlin or Southeast Asia would have none of those features. "You can't have too many of those," he said of the Cuban showdown in his 1962 year-end interview. "One major mistake either by Mr. Khrushchev or by us . . . can make this whole thing blow up."

Nevertheless the President recognized that the impact of Cuba was broader than its precedent. It had helped clear the air in this country about the fatal futility of total nuclear "victory" and the creative possi-bilities of agreement. It had sharpened his own interest in peaceful solu-tions. Disarmament looked more like a necessity and less like a dream. He began to look at the new arms requests for his budget in terms of their effect on ultimate arms control. His perspective, too, had changed after looking down the nuclear gun barrel. After the first Cuban crisis he had stressed to the nation's editors that "our restraint is not inexhaustible." After the second Cuban crisis, questioned by the same audience about that statement, he replied: "I hope our restraint—or sense of responsibility—will not ever come to an end."

He had often argued that fruitful disarmament negotiations could never take place at the point of a Communist gun—or as long as the Communists thought they could overtake us in the arms race or effectively break up the Alliance—or until they were convinced by a test of will that we would not yield our vital interests, whatever the risk or threat—or until the United States had some serious, specific arms control proposals with which it could take the diplomatic offensive. In 1963 those conditions finally prevailed.

But the usual suspicions, misunderstandings and bureaucratic delays seemed destined at first to frustrate his hopes of converting the new atmosphere into any solid agreements. Only two minor accords were reached—the exchange of weather and other information from space satellites, previously mentioned, and the "hot line" teletype link between Moscow and Washington to make possible quick, private communications in times of emergency.

The "hot line"—passing through Helsinki, Stockholm and London, but with no kibitzers—was not insignificant. Such a communications link (originally labeled the "purple telephone") had been under discussion since Kennedy's first months in office; and its importance had been dramatized during the Cuban missile crisis when it had taken some four hours for the transmission of each Kennedy-Khrushchev message, including time for translation, coding, decoding and normal diplomatic presentation. As indicated in the missile chapter, Khrushchev had made his final message of withdrawal public long before it had arrived in Washington as the only means of assuring its immediate delivery. A future crisis—which could be caused not only by some actual conflict but possibly by an accidental missile firing or some misleading indication of attack—might not permit either four hours or a public broadcast. Nevertheless an agreement on communication was not as important as the matters to be communicated. "If he fires his missiles at me," observed the President, "it is not going to do any good for me to have a telephone at the Kremlin . . . and ask him whether it is really true."

His chief hope for a more substantive agreement—a treaty ending nuclear tests—had foundered once again, with each side blaming the other. In response to Khrushchev's talk of new accords after the Cuban crisis, Kennedy had put the test-ban treaty first. Indeed, since the day of his inauguration, a test ban had been his principal hope for a first step toward disarmament and other pacts. He had termed the collapse of the Geneva talks in 1961 "the most disappointing event" of his first year. He had hopes that a new treaty would be the most rewarding event of his third. The time was right. Both sides had tested extensively. Neither had scored a decisive breakthrough. The American tests had not been as important as the scientists and military had predicted. And the U.S.-U.K. draft treaty to ban all testing had impressed the neutral world as a fair and effective proposal. Kennedy after Cuba thus pressed again for a treaty—and, to his surprise, Khrushchev agreed to the principle of on-site inspections apparently without reference to a Troika.

Following Khrushchev's December, 1962, letter to this effect, unofficial, off-the-record talks between spokesmen for both sides were held in this country. The Russians made what they regarded as a major concession, "two or three" on-site inspections a year of suspicious seismic disturbances inside any one nation. Kennedy had reduced our insistence on twelve to twenty such inspections to a scale of eight to ten and then seven after his scientists learned that the Soviet figure on unidentifiable underground shocks was more precise than our own. But two or three, in the light of the still incomplete science of distinguishing earthquakes (of which there were many in the U.S.S.R.) from clandestine nuclear tests, was still unacceptably low. The Soviets said heatedly that they had been led to believe that their figure would be acceptable, and that Congressional protests—stirred by press rumors that the United States was changing its position—had caused the American President to renege. They went home in January complaining bitterly that Khrushchev had risked his political prestige within the Kremlin to get their mission approved, and that he had been embarrassed in front of his critics by its failure.

The President wrote Khrushchev that he was certain that American negotiators Dean and Wiesner had never, as the Soviet Chairman charged, indicated a readiness to agree on three inspections. An honest misunderstanding, he wrote, had somehow occurred. He sent Averell Harriman to Moscow to review the full range of problems dividing the two nations. He took advantage of a visit by U.S. magazine editor Norman Cousins to Khrushchev to send word once again that he really did want a treaty. With Macmillan he made new proposals for a test ban in letters delivered by their ambassadors, although he rejected Macmillan's suggestion of a summit in the absence of any assurance of agreement.[1] He again urged the Soviets to relate the number of inspections to the number of unidentifiable seismic disturbances and to raise their figure of three in exchange for an American reduction below seven. He suggested that the reopened talks at Geneva seek agreement

[1] The Prime Minister, speculated Kennedy, since he sounded so much more optimistic than our scientists on seismic identification, might well have been the source of Khrushchev's confusion on the acceptable number of inspections.

on all other issues regarding inspection—so that numbers would mean something—and then reconsider the issue of numbers.

But the Soviets refused to consider any issues until he accepted their position on three tests. They seemed at times to back away even from three. Khrushchev was hurt and suspicious. He was no more willing to ask his Council of Ministers for a new number still unacceptable to Kennedy than the President was willing to wear down the opposition of the Joint Committee on Atomic Energy to a new number still unacceptable to Khrushchev. Deadlock prevailed once again. The three-power Geneva conferees, now a mere subcommittee of the eighteen-nation disarmament conference, were no nearer agreement than they had been throughout five fruitless years of talk. "I am not hopeful," the President said in May, 1963.

> If we don't get an agreement this year . . . I would think . . .
> the genie is out of the bottle and we will not ever get him back
> in again. . . . Personally I am haunted by the feeling that by 1970,
> unless we are successful, there may be ten nuclear powers in-
> stead of four. . . . I regard that as the greatest possible danger
> and hazard. . . . I think that we ought to stay at it.

He stayed at it. While not hopeful, he had not abandoned hope. An exploratory message from a Soviet scientist attending a private conference in London, a Khrushchev hint to Cousins and others that he hoped for a fresh signal from the United States, and a new resolution in the Senate for an atmospheric test ban—cosponsored by thirty-four Senators, ranging from Humphrey of Minnesota to Dodd of Connecticut, a former test-ban opponent—all helped keep his hopes alive. The tax cut and other legislative measures were competing for his attention, and the civil rights struggle was rising to a crescendo. But Kennedy took time in the late spring of 1963 to take three important steps in search of an agreement with the Soviets:

1. He joined with Macmillan in proposing new talks on a test-ban treaty, to be held in Khrushchev's capital and by new high-level emissaries as a sign of our earnest intention to forget past misunderstandings and reach agreement. The President had no clear evidence that agreement was possible, but he felt obligated to make this last great effort, which had been suggested by Macmillan in May. The announcement of this proposal was set for Kennedy's Commencement Address at American University on June 10. As the speech underwent its final revisions in Honolulu on June 8-9, Khrushchev sent word of his acceptance. The announcement—simultaneously made in Moscow and London— was thus one of action rather than suggestion. It was accompanied in the President's speech with hopes for the mission's success, "hopes which

must be tempered with the caution of history—but with our hopes go the hopes of all mankind."

2. To improve the atmosphere for agreement, he decided—without any recommendation from the departments or consultation with the Congress—that this nation, once its present series of tests had ended, would not be the first to resume nuclear tests in the atmosphere. That decision also was announced at American University. He rejected suggestions that he also suspend testing underground for a limited period, for he felt that, in the absence of any inspection, our atomic laboratories had to be working to avoid the dangers of secret Soviet testing underground or secret preparation to test aboveground. (Only underground tests required inspection to prevent cheating, inasmuch as our own monitoring systems could detect all others.) He was convinced that we were still ahead in nuclear development and could stay ahead without testing in the atmosphere. Nevertheless it was a bold step to take unilaterally, and he took it, he said, "to make clear our good faith and solemn convictions" on the test-ban issue, adding, however, that it was "no substitute for a formal binding treaty."

3. The final step was the American University speech itself, the first Presidential speech in eighteen years to succeed in reaching beyond the cold war. The address had originated in a Presidential decision earlier in the spring to make a speech about "peace." His motives were many. It was, first of all, an expression of his deep personal concern. He had not elaborated his views on this topic since his 1961 address to the UN. He thought it desirable to make clear his hopes for East-West agreement as a backdrop to his European trip in June. He valued in particular an April 30 letter from Norman Cousins. Cousins suggested that the exposition of a peaceful posture prior to the May meeting of the Soviet Communist Party Central Committee, even if it could not deter an expected new rash of attacks on U.S. policy, might at least make those attacks sound hollow and hypocritical outside the Communist world. That meeting had been postponed until June, and the June 10 commencement at American University appeared to be the first appropriate forum on the President's schedule.

I obtained material from Cousins, Bundy, Kaysen, my brother Tom and others, and gathered appropriate passages that had been cut from the Inaugural Address in 1961, or discarded when the Kennedy-Khrushchev TV exchange fell through in 1962, or used in previous Kennedy speeches and worthy of repetition. Unlike most foreign policy speeches —none of which was as sweeping in concept and impact as this turned out to be—official departmental positions and suggestions were not solicited. The President was determined to put forward a fundamentally new emphasis on the peaceful and the positive in our relations with the Soviets. He did not want that new policy diluted by the usual threats of destruction, boasts of nuclear stockpiles and lectures on Soviet treachery.

When he decided that the civil rights crisis necessitated his addressing the U.S. Mayors' Conference in Honolulu, on Sunday, June 9, at the close of a long Western trip, he instructed me to stay behind to complete the American University draft. He was due to deliver it Monday morning, and I was to fly out with it Saturday. It was not until Sunday evening, returning home on "Air Force One," that he applied the finishing touches. Bundy Deputy Carl Kaysen had meanwhile obtained a quick minimum clearance from the necessary Cabinet-level officials and telephoned the changes resulting from Khrushchev's acceptance.

The next morning we arrived in Washington; and the President, after stopping by the Mansion and office, proceeded to the American University campus. Soviet officials in Moscow and Washington, and weary White House correspondents on the plane back, had been briefed in advance that the speech was of major importance. That description was wholly accurate.

President Kennedy began with a commitment to genuine, lasting peace:

> Not a *Pax Americana* enforced on the world by American weapons of war . . . not merely peace for Americans, but peace for all men; not merely peace in our time but peace for all time.

The dreamers' "absolute, infinite concepts of universal peace and goodwill . . . merely invite discouragement and incredulity," he said. But a practical peace, "based not on a sudden revolution in human nature but on a gradual evolution in human institutions," was not impossible— and neither was war inevitable.

> Our problems are man-made; therefore they can be solved by man. . . . Some say that it is useless to speak of world peace . . . until the leaders of the Soviet Union adopt a more enlightened attitude. I hope they do. I believe we can help them do it. But I also believe that we must re-examine our own attitude. . . .

He challenged his listeners to look anew at the Soviet Union and the cold war, to put past conflicts and prejudices behind them and to concentrate on the common interests shared by both powers. These passages, many of them saved from the abandoned TV exchange, were also addressed to the Russian people. He quoted from a Soviet text to illustrate their "baseless" misconceptions of our military and political aims (partly because they sounded precisely like this country's traditional view of *their* aims). "It is sad to read these Soviet statements," he said,

to realize the extent of the gulf between us. But it is also a warning—a warning to the American people not to fall into the same
trap as the Soviets, not to see only a distorted and desperate view
of the other side. . . . History teaches us that enmities between
nations . . . do not last forever. . . . Among the many traits the
peoples of our two countries have in common, none is stronger
than our mutual abhorrence of war. Almost unique among the
major world powers, we have never been at war with each other.
. . . We are not here distributing blame or pointing the finger of
judgment. We must deal with the world as it is, and not as it
might have been had the history of the last eighteen years been
different. . . .

We must conduct our affairs in such a way that it becomes in
the Communists' interest to agree on a genuine peace . . . to . . .
let each nation choose its own future, so long as that choice does
not interfere with the choices of others. . . . If we cannot now end
our differences, at least we can help make the world safe for
diversity. For, in the final analysis our most basic common link
is the fact that we all inhabit this planet. We all breathe the
same air. We all cherish our children's future. And we are all
mortal.

He spoke of this nation's nonprovocative and carefully controlled
weapons, our avoidance of diplomatic threats and irritants, our hopes
for the UN's evolution into a "genuine world security system," our efforts
to keep peace within the non-Communist world, and our support of
peace and freedom among all races here at home. To lessen Allied fears,
he re-emphasized our commitments to their security before announcing
the Moscow meeting and the decision not to resume testing in the
atmosphere. These two specific proposals, far more than all the rhetoric
about peace, made the speech an important step away from war. And
it was satisfaction with these proposals that enabled him to close on a
note of hope:

The United States, as the world knows, will never start a war.
We do not want a war. We do not now expect a war. This
generation of Americans has already had enough—more than
enough—of war and hate and oppression. We shall be prepared
for war, if others wish it. We shall be alert to try to stop it. But we
shall also do our part to build a world of peace where the weak
are safe and the strong are just. We are not helpless before that
task or hopeless of its success. Confident and unafraid, we labor
on—not toward a strategy of annihilation but toward a strategy
of peace.

England's Manchester *Guardian*—in contrast to the American press, which largely underplayed the speech, and then largely forgot it after the President's TV civil rights address the following evening—called it "one of the great state papers of American history." Various Congressional Republicans called it "a soft line that can accomplish nothing . . . a shot from the hip . . . a dreadful mistake." Khrushchev, in a later conversation with Harriman, would call it "the best speech by any President since Roosevelt."

The "signal" the Soviet Chairman had awaited was loud and clear—and it was received by the Russian people as well as their leaders. The full text of the speech was published in the Soviet press. Still more striking was the fact that it was heard as well as read throughout the U.S.S.R. After fifteen years of almost uninterrupted jamming of Western broadcasts, by means of a network of over three thousand transmitters and at an annual cost of several hundred million dollars, the Soviets jammed only one paragraph of the speech when relayed by the Voice of America in Russian (that dealing with their "baseless" claims of U.S. aims)—then did not jam any of it upon rebroadcast—and then suddenly stopped jamming all Western broadcasts, including even Russian-language newscasts on foreign affairs. Equally suddenly they agreed in Vienna to the principle of inspection by the International Atomic Energy Agency to make certain that Agency's reactors were used for peaceful purposes. And equally suddenly the outlook for some kind of test-ban agreement turned from hopeless to hopeful.

The President departed on his trip to Europe. A new and major purpose was to assure the Allies—and particularly the ever-suspicious Germans—that negotiations with the Soviet Union would be in their interest, not at their expense. "Our alliance was founded to deter a new war," he said upon his arrival in Bonn. "It must now find the way to a new peace." "When Pandora opened her box and the troubles flew out," he told a German news conference, "all that was left in was Hope. In this case, if we have nuclear diffusion throughout the world, we may even lose hope." In a major policy pronouncement little noticed compared to his Berlin City Hall address, he told the Free University of Berlin that a reunited Germany could best be attained in a reunited Europe on both sides of the Wall.

He completed his trip on July 2 at NATO headquarters in Naples. Even there he avoided the customary cold war rhetoric. "The purpose of our military strength," he said, "the purpose of our partnership, is peace. . . . Negotiations for an end to nuclear tests and . . . attention to defense . . . are all complementary parts of a single strategy for peace."

That night, as we flew back to Washington, a message radioed to the plane told of a Khrushchev speech that day in East Berlin. It endorsed an atmospheric nuclear test-ban treaty.

THE TEST BAN TREATY

To underline the importance he attached to the new three-power talks, and to increase their prospects for success, the President named his favorite trouble-shooter, Under Secretary of State Averell Harriman (who had also been suggested by Macmillan), as head of the new mission to Moscow. The designation of a sub-Cabinet officer instead of an arms control expert raised some eyebrows, inasmuch as it rendered useless a scheduled Rusk visit to Moscow the same month. But the President's decision was final. After some tugging and hauling within the government, he completed a first-rate team, including Carl Kaysen from the White House, Adrian Fisher from Disarmament, John McNaughton from Defense, and William Tyler from State.

In a series of meetings before their departure, he made clear his belief (1) that this was the last clear chance to stop the diffusion of nuclear tests and poisons and to start building mutual confidence with the Russians; (2) that the delegation should keep in daily contact with him; and (3) that extreme precautions should be taken to prevent their prospects of success from being ruined by any premature leak of their position. Instead of the usual wide circulation in all interested bureaus, he made arrangements for only six top officials outside the White House (Rusk, Ball, McNamara, McCone, Thompson and Foster) to read the cables from Moscow on a hand-delivered, "for-your-eyes-only" basis.

With Macmillan's loyal help, he also arranged to have the American delegation lead for the West in the negotiations. Chief British negotiator Lord Hailsham, he observed—after Hailsham had spoken with him and the Prime Minister during Kennedy's June stopover in England—wanted to play the role of mediator between the Russians and the Americans as Roosevelt had between Churchill and Stalin. The President had more confidence in Harriman, a shrewd, no-nonsense bargainer and a former Ambassador to Moscow.

The Adenauer government still took an alarmist attitude about the whole matter. But the trip to West Germany had improved popular as well as official feeling in that country about our intentions, the President told his negotiators, "and I am willing to draw on that as much as necessary, if it's worthwhile. I don't, however, want to do what we did in the Berlin talks, getting the Germans suspicious if the Russians aren't going to agree on anything anyway." Inasmuch as even a limited test-ban treaty required a Soviet acceptance of permanent American superiority in nuclear weapons, he refused to count too heavily on the success of the Moscow meetings.

Khrushchev had set the date for July 15, significantly little more than a week after he was to meet with a delegation from Red China. Glum with the Chinese, he was all smiles with Harriman and Hailsham. The United States and United Kingdom in 1962 had formally offered a draft treaty to ban nuclear tests in all environments except underground; and, once it was clear that a comprehensive treaty with inspection was not yet negotiable, that draft served as the basis for the Western negotiators. Soviet Foreign Minister Gromyko offered a shorter, less detailed draft of his own which Harriman felt left too many questions in doubt. With these two drafts on the table, ten days of intensive negotiations began.

Each evening during the negotiations the six officials listed above met with the President to discuss details of the talks. All communications to the delegation in Moscow were cleared through Kennedy. Frequently he altered or rewrote completely the daily cable of instructions prepared in the Department of State. He confidently granted considerable leeway to the initiative of his negotiators, and they in turn demonstrated considerable skill in representing his interest. But he made certain that over-all direction remained in his hands.

Questions arose in Moscow over peaceful-use explosions (as in building a new Panama Canal) and over spelling out the right to withdraw ("something like a marriage contract with a protocol for divorce," said one observer). "Every word, every phrase, every sentence, every article was analyzed and discussed in Moscow," said Harriman; and meantime the President was analyzing and discussing them in Washington. But the four basic foreign policy issues which arose had all been initially decided before the delegation left:

1. *Was a treaty which did not ban underground tests desirable?* The President said that it was—as a step toward halting the arms race, building trust, discouraging proliferation and preventing radioactive pollution. But he added the proviso that it must not be accompanied by another unpoliced moratorium on underground testing. He had warned in 1962 that the Soviet's ability in 1961 to prepare secretly for test resumptions had placed us at a disadvantage he could not prudently accept again. The fact that we had subsequently completed all pending atmospheric tests of current importance reduced this worry considerably; but, in the absence of a comprehensive treaty with on-site inspection, the President intended to continue testing underground.

2. *Was a summit meeting to sign such a treaty desirable?* Macmillan wanted one, Kennedy didn't. The French and West Germans would be aroused by Macmillan's presence, he said. The British elections would be tied in, and his own discussions with Khrushchev would be too formal. But if a summit should prove necessary to securing Khrushchev's approval, he told Harriman, he would go to the summit.

3. *Was a simultaneous NATO-Warsaw Pact nonaggression treaty avoidable?* The two treaties had been closely linked in Khrushchev's July 2 speech, and there was apprehension that he would insist on both or neither. Kennedy was willing to explore any such pact that did not foreclose the ultimate reunification of Germany. But he and Macmillan could not speak for NATO, and he felt that Senate approval of the test ban would be difficult enough without this addition. Harriman's task was to separate the two proposals and to defer consideration of the nonaggression pact until the Allies had a position.

4. *Could future nuclear powers be induced to sign the treaty?* The President hoped—but in vain—that some form of pressure was available to the Soviets to require the Communist Chinese to sign. (He regarded the resulting isolation of the Chinese, however, as a major gain; and the Soviets may have been similarly motivated.) He also hoped—but also in vain—that an offer of American assistance with French underground testing would persuade General De Gaulle to sign. He instructed Harriman to repeat our position that the MLF was designed to prevent nuclear proliferation, not add to it, but to explore without assurances whether our standing still on that project could help the Russians with the Chinese. By arranging for official texts to be open to other governments for signature in Moscow, London and Washington, such worries as our recognizing East Germany (who signed in Moscow) and Russia's recognizing Nationalist China (who signed in Washington) could be avoided.

Once it appeared that a reasonable treaty was possible, the President was determined that no quibbling over language or sniping from his subordinates would prevent it. The force of his leadership in the daily sessions overrode all the nit-picking the skeptics could devise. He gave his final approval, clearing up one minor point at issue, in response to a telephone call from his negotiators in Moscow on the very day the treaty was concluded and initialed. It was July 25, 1963, six weeks after the American University address.

A formidable hurdle still remained—Senate approval. Congressional Republicans had consistently bombarded the President with attacks on "his fuzzy-thinking disarmament advisers" and their thinking on the test ban. Leading members of the influential Joint Atomic Energy Committee had predicted that anything other than "a reasonably foolproof test-ban agreement . . . [could be] a greater risk to the national security than an arms race," because of our need to test new weapons. Democratic Senator Henry Jackson, even before the treaty was initialed, said that he and other members of the Senate Armed Services Committee were "cautiously skeptical." Republican Senate leader Dirksen—who with Charles Halleck had earlier expressed the fear that the negotiations "may end in virtual surrender by our negotiators"—forecast that "a good many reservations would be presented." Halleck added that the absence of inspection and the possibilities of cheating made the treaty "far more tragic than no agreement at all."

The President's chief concern was that enough Southern Democrats might combine with Republicans to prevent the necessary two-thirds vote. Angered by his civil rights bill, they would be hoping to use the treaty as a bargaining counter and follow the lead of Armed Services Committee Chairman Russell, who was opposed. A popular line among other conservative Congressmen and newspapers was the charge that "a secret deal with Khrushchev" had been made during the Moscow meetings at the price of this nation's security. A Harris Poll found general public approval, but fewer than 50 percent giving "unqualified approval." Many observers predicted "the biggest Senate foreign policy battle since the struggle over . . . the League of Nations treaty after World War I."

Far more pessimistic than most of his advisers, and determined not to repeat Wilson's mistakes with the League of Nations, Kennedy had started early. He sent Rusk to brief the key committees and Foster to talk individually with every Senator while the Moscow talks were still in session. He included a bipartisan group of Senators on the delegation traveling to Moscow with Rusk for the official treaty-signing ceremony.[2]

The day after the treaty was initialed, the President took his case to the American people in one of his most effective televised addresses:

> I speak to you tonight in a spirit of hope. . . . [Since] the advent of nuclear weapons, all mankind has been struggling to escape from the darkening prospect of mass destruction on earth. . . . Yesterday a shaft of light cut into the darkness. . . .
>
> This treaty is not the millennium. . . . But it is an important first step—a step toward peace, a step toward reason, a step away from war. . . . This treaty is for all of us. It is particularly for our children and our grandchildren, and they have no lobby here in Washington. . . .
>
> According to the ancient Chinese proverb, "A journey of a thousand miles must begin with a single step.". . . Let us take that first step.

Less than two weeks later he sent a strongly worded message to the Senate officially requesting consent to ratification. He urged approval at every press conference. He endorsed it again in the opening minutes

2 Although Dirksen and Iowa's influential Hickenlooper refused to go. Also not making the trip was Adlai Stevenson, who justifiably viewed the treaty as a vindication of his 1956 campaign fight, but whom the President regretfully excluded to prevent reminders of a partisan nature.

of his TV address on the tax cut. He sent a letter of assurances to Mansfield and Dirksen. He spoke individually to key Senators on the fence. In each of these presentations he anticipated and answered with precision each argument raised in opposition.

Some argued that the treaty accomplished very little. Kennedy agreed. He repeated the words "limited" and "first step" until he was weary of saying them. He emphasized what it would not do as well as what it would. But he also warned of the perils of a continuing arms race, continuing atmospheric pollution and continuing nuclear proliferation.

Other opponents argued that the Soviets might engage in secret violations or in secret preparations for a sudden termination of the treaty. Kennedy agreed. He intended for that reason to keep our development steady, our ability to resume ready and our vigilance high—by maintaining underground testing, nuclear laboratories and a satellite detection system. Any test so small and so far away in space that it could not be detected, he pointed out, could be more easily and cheaply conducted underground without risking the consequences of violation. There are, he said, "risks inherent in any treaty, [but] the far greater risks to our security are the risks of unrestricted testing."

Still others argued that we needed atmospheric tests to develop new nuclear weapons. But we have no need for a hundred-megaton bomb, said the President; neither side needed nuclear tests to achieve an anti-missile missile; and no amount of Soviet underground or undetected testing could overtake us.

He assured the Senators that there were no secret conditions or side agreements, that the treaty could not be amended without the Senate's consent and that it would not affect our freedom to choose any weapons in any future war.[3] He took pains also to coordinate the testimony of administration witnesses on Capitol Hill. McNamara, as always, was the most impressive, and the Joint Chiefs of Staff, as always, were the most difficult. General Taylor understood the net advantages to our security in a test ban, and the President had been careful to obtain in advance the agreement in principle of Taylor's colleagues. But their agreement had assumed that a test ban, like all other disarmament proposals, was only a diplomatic pose unlikely to achieve reality. Confronted with an actual treaty limiting the development of weapons, the Chiefs began to hedge.

Repeatedly, and ultimately successfully, Kennedy and McNamara reassured them that underground testing would continue our nuclear progress, and that all the safeguards they desired would be provided. The President blocked a maneuver by the less friendly Senate Armed

[3] Eisenhower had referred vaguely to a "reservation" on this last point. A formal reservation would have required renegotiation of the treaty.

Services Subcommittee to cross-examine the Chiefs before Taylor could present their views to the Foreign Relations Committee. Taylor testified under cross-examination that "arm twisting by superiors" was not responsible for the Chiefs' position. Air Force Chief LeMay acknowledged that he would have opposed the treaty had it not already been initialed; and his Strategic Air Command General Thomas Power flatly denounced it. But the support of the other Chiefs was helpful, and the President held similar sessions with the nuclear laboratory directors to ensure their backing.

The treaty nevertheless encountered heavy attack—from nuclear scientist Edward Teller, former Atomic Energy Commission Chairman Lewis Strauss and former Chiefs of Staff Arleigh Burke, Arthur Radford and Nathan Twining. The Air Force Association, composed of military, former military and defense contractors, came out against it (and the Association's dinner was consequently shunned by the administration). Influential Senators Stennis and Goldwater as well as Russell announced their opposition. Other Senators said their mail was evenly divided; and the Senate Armed Services Preparedness Subcommittee filed a special report on the treaty's "serious military disadvantages" to the United States. The President did not want "only grudging support," he told his news conference, but "the widest possible margin in the Senate" as a demonstration of the fact "that we are as determined to achieve . . . a just peace as we are to defend freedom."

To help secure that margin, to reduce the large number of uncommitted Senators, he worked through unofficial as well as official channels. A series of telephone calls and off-the-record meetings encouraged the creation of a private "Citizens Committee for a Nuclear Test Ban," a bipartisan group of prominent leaders organized to mobilize support. The President, beginning with an off-the-record meeting in the Cabinet Room, advised them which Senators should hear from their constituents, approved their newspaper and TV advertisements, counseled them on their approach to the unconvinced, and suggested particular business and other leaders for them to contact.

In a remarkable shift of public sentiment between July and September, sentiment for the treaty became overwhelming. Dirksen's speech in support was a highlight of the debate. Goldwater's attempt to condition U.S. acceptance upon a Soviet withdrawal from Cuba found few backers.[4] When the roll was called, only 11 Democrats (all Southerners except for Lausche) and 8 Republicans (all West of the Missouri except for Mrs. Smith) were opposed, with 55 Democrats and 25 Republicans voting

4 At a news conference, after he had refuted a Goldwater assertion about a secret "deal" on Cuba as a part of the test-ban negotiations, the President was asked if he cared "to comment further on this type of attack by Senator Goldwater." "No," said the President, "not yet, not yet."

yea. The vote, said the President happily, was "a welcome culmination." No other single accomplishment in the White House ever gave him greater satisfaction. He decided to sign the official instrument of ratification in the historic and newly restored Treaty Room in the Mansion, partly because it enabled him to have the pleasure of signing it on a desk belonging to him personally.[5]

THE EMERGING DÉTENTE

Kennedy regarded the Test Ban Treaty itself, however, as more of a beginning than a culmination. It was an important beginning. After 336 nuclear explosions in the atmosphere by the United States, Great Britain and the Soviet Union, after thirteen years of almost steady accumulation of radioactive poisons in the air, those three powers had formally committed themselves to no more atmospheric tests. Over a hundred other nations signed the same pledge. While testing by France and Red China or the development of other weapons might someday outmode this gain, the genie was at least temporarily back in the bottle.

The political change in the atmosphere was even more important than the physical, in John Kennedy's view. The treaty was a symbolic "first step," a forerunner of further agreements. It facilitated a pause in the cold war in which other, more difficult problem areas could be stabilized.

On the very day the Senate approved the Test Ban Treaty, work on a new area of accommodation was under way in the White House. On the preceding day Agriculture Secretary Freeman told a Cabinet meeting that a Minnesota grain trader had just reported a possible Soviet interest in purchasing American wheat. In the only occasion I can recall when a subject spontaneously raised at a Cabinet meeting produced a valuable discussion, the President heard the views of his Secretaries of State, Defense, Commerce, Labor and Treasury, all of whom had an official interest. Other members volunteered comments. One official, for example, warned on the basis of his experience of political opposition from Polish-Americans. The President then held a much smaller session in his office to consider the problem further.

The following day, as soon as the Test Ban Treaty was approved, he departed on an extended conservation tour of the West. At his request, I gathered with Bundy's help all the pertinent information, legislation, pro-and-con arguments and intelligence estimates. The picture which emerged was encouraging. In their rush to develop heavy industry,

[5] Nor could anything have pleased me more than his decision to give me one of the pens he used in signing the official instrument of ratification. Inasmuch as I saw no hurry about getting an autographed picture from a man I saw daily, that pen is now a prized possession.

space and armaments, the Soviets had short-changed investment in agriculture. The collective farms were riddled with inefficiency—"for a closed society is not open to ideas of progress," as the President had said, "and a police state finds it cannot command the grain to grow." The original soil moisture and productivity in the "New Lands" opened by Khrushchev in Siberia and Kazakhstan had been used up, and a severe drought had held per capita food production to its lowest point in history. Large imports of grain from the West were required; and sizable purchases had already been concluded with Canada and Australia. Soviet exports were insufficient to pay for these imports along with necessary industrial supplies; and the Soviet gold reserve was being drawn down faster than their mines could replace it.

While the sale of 65 million bushels of surplus wheat would hardly make a dent in our several hundred million bushels in storage, it would bring added income and employment to American agriculture and business, benefit our balance of payments and reduce Federal storage costs. Other Western nations had sold wheat and flour to the Communist bloc for many years. France and West Germany, two of the leading "anti-Communist" nations, had in fact bought our wheat and then sold wheat flour to Red China.

The President, reviewing these findings, preferred to base his approval publicly on economic grounds. He did not share the view that "a fat Communist was a good Communist," or that the Soviets were so desperate that they would grant political concessions in return. Nor did he believe that increased economic contacts would in time make capitalists of them all. But he welcomed the opportunity to demonstrate to the Soviet leaders that the improved climate of agreement could serve the interests of both nations.

Once again, however, he did not wish to go out on a controversial limb if no agreement were possible. Llewellyn Thompson was instructed to sound out the Soviet Ambassador, and on October 5 a reply was received. The Soviets were interested—under normal commercial terms and at the world market price. They were also agreeable to the use of American ships. This comment amazed us all, inasmuch as American shipping rates were among the most expensive in the world and no such condition had been attached to our offer. But the President gladly accepted the additional stipulation; and when the Soviets later balked at our shipping rates, and a fifty-fifty compromise was effected, we speculated that Russian bureaucracy could be as confused as our own. Some political commissar, we joked, had decreed American ships to avoid problems with our longshoremen and port security restrictions, and a belatedly informed commercial commissar had then told him about high-cost American shipping.

The next problem was the Congress. The granting of export licenses to sell wheat to the Russians was not prohibited under any of the statutes limiting commercial transactions with the Communists. But Congress had added to the Agricultural Act of 1961 an amendment opposing the sale of subsidized agricultural commodities to unfriendly nations. Republican legislators were already invoking this provision as an obstacle to any sale. Kennedy decided to ignore it, and offered ample reason. It was only a nonbinding declaration of interest. It had been adopted at the height of the Berlin crisis in a wholly different climate. It had been assumed by at least some members of Congress to apply to a different kind of sale. And it made no sense when we had been selling the Russians nonsurplus agricultural commodities and dozens of other items for many years. The subsidy went not to the foreign buyer but to the American wheat farmer, regardless of where and whether the wheat was sold.

As the Republicans would later charge, the President did not "consult" the Congressional leaders, he merely informed them. Certain that the information would leak promptly once it left the Executive Branch, he scheduled his meeting with the legislators for 4 P.M., October 9, two hours before the press conference at which his decision would be announced. With Dirksen and Hickenlooper absent, only the House Republicans were negative;[6] and Kennedy's announcement that evening, long and factual, was unchanged by their opposition. Asked immediately whether he feared "political repercussions," he replied matter-of-factly, "I suppose there will be some who will disagree with this decision. That is true about most decisions. But I have considered it very carefully and I think it is very much in the interest of the United States. . . ."

The next day, beginning with a comprehensive report to the Congress, he set the wheels in motion for obtaining public support. He sought help from several of the same civic and religious leaders who had helped on the test ban. He armed friendly members of Congress with speeches and statistics. He persuaded Polish-language newspapers in Chicago and elsewhere to endorse his decision. Told at the next pre-press conference breakfast that Nixon had attacked it, he expressed his belief that the American people preferred his view to Nixon's (adding that they had so demonstrated in 1960—"a somewhat *thin* answer," Walter Heller observed afterward).

In time he overcame attempted Congressional restrictions, attempted longshoreman boycotts, Soviet haggling about freight rates, disagreements between Agriculture and State, disagreements between Labor and Commerce, disputes over financing and a host of other obstacles. The

6 Congresswoman Frances Bolton of Ohio startled the President by suddenly asking, "Mr. President, aren't we at war?"

export licenses were granted, the wheat was sold, and the President hoped that more trade in nonstrategic goods would follow.

Still other agreements were in the air: new interest in serious first-stage disarmament measures, prospects for breaks in the Berlin Wall and near-accord on a new Soviet-American civil air agreement and consular treaty. Even a ban on underground testing, the President believed, would come when science outmoded the argument of three versus seven inspections.

Added to the list of agreements actually concluded was a ban on nuclear weapons in outer space, a measure with no immediate military consequences for either nation but a sign, nevertheless, of easing tensions. Dubious over its enforceability as well as the desirability of sending it to the Senate, the President agreed instead that both nations simply pledge their support of a UN resolution of October 17 against placing weapons of mass destruction in orbit or on celestial bodies. "There is not an agreement . . . [and] no way we can verify . . . Soviet intentions," he said. "But we are glad to hear the intention."

Addressing the United Nations General Assembly on September 20, and commenting on the improved outlook for peace since his address some twenty-four months earlier, he called—again on his own initiative, with only a minimum of checking with his space and foreign policy officers—for increased U.S.-Soviet space cooperation, including specifically a joint expedition to the moon. Both powers having forsworn any territorial rights in outer space, he said, why engage in costly duplication?

The Soviets were still negative. Perhaps they understood better than those Congressmen attacking the proposal that a cooperative approach would just as effectively bar a Soviet militarization or monopoly of outer space, and a Soviet claim to pre-eminence in science, as an American first-place finish in the space race. Our effort in that race, Kennedy reassured the Congress, "permits us now to offer increased cooperation with no suspicion anywhere that we speak from weakness."

His UN speech listed other areas in which he hoped early agreement could be reached:

> . . . measures which prevent war by accident or miscalculation . . . safeguards against surprise attack, including observation posts at key points . . . further measures to curb the nuclear arms race, by controlling the transfer of nuclear weapons, converting fissionable materials to peaceful purposes and banning underground testing, with adequate inspection and enforcement . . . agreement on a freer flow of information and people from East to West and West to East.

The speech was built on the foundations laid at American University. It defined the real and major differences between the Soviets and ourselves, differences which "set limits to agreement and . . . forbid the relaxation of our vigilance." But it also called for "further agreements . . . which spring from our mutual interest in avoiding mutual destruction," for "a new approach to the Cold War" on both sides, and for changes in the UN Charter to enable "the conventions of peace [to] . . . pull abreast and then ahead of the inventions of war. . . . But peace," he said, in a near-paraphrase of Judge Learned Hand's discourse on liberty,

> does not rest in charters and covenants alone. It lies in the hearts and minds of all people. And if it is cast out there, then no act, no pact, no treaty, no organization can hope to preserve it. . . . So let us not rest all our hopes on parchment and on paper. Let us strive to build . . . a desire for peace . . . in the hearts and minds of all of our people.

Four days later he set out to help build that desire in the hearts and minds of his own people. As already mentioned, the stated subject of that five-day, eleven-state tour was conservation. Increasingly, however, his extemporaneous interpolations related the strength of our resources to the maintenance of freedom and peace. (The foreign policy topics to which he devoted his major addresses at the close of the tour had already been planned before he left Washington, however, and were not, as some speculated, the results of his findings while en route.) Many of his talks were in the heart of right-wing territory. Yet he struck boldly at those who yearned for a return to isolationism or offered oversimplified answers to world problems. The Test Ban Treaty, he found, elicited far greater applause than support of a local dam or mineral.

> Look at the true destructive power of the atom today, and what we and the Soviet Union could do to each other in the world in an hour. . . . I passed over yesterday the Little Big Horn where General Custer was slain—a massacre which has lived in history —four or five hundred men. We are talking about three hundred million men and women in twenty-four hours. . . . That is why I support the Test Ban Treaty . . . because we have a chance to avoid being burned.

Four weeks later he carried the same message to New England and the University of Maine.

> While maintaining our readiness for war, let us exhaust every avenue for peace. . . . Let us not waste the present pause by

either a needless renewal of tensions or a needless relaxation of vigilance.[7]

Two weeks later he told a Democratic rally in Philadelphia that America was "stronger than ever before, and the possibilities of peace brighter . . . than ever before."

Each time the response was enthusiastic. The President had once remarked that he would gladly forfeit his re-election, if necessary, for the sake of the Test Ban Treaty. But in the autumn of 1963 he saw that its approval had helped register a new national consensus—that "peace" was an issue in his favor—and that his posture of maintaining both strength and goodwill had been embraced by the American people. (A Gallup Poll revealed that, for the first time, the Democrats were regarded by the public as the "peace party," best able to keep this country out of war.)

Kennedy did not minimize the problems that remained—particularly Red China and Southeast Asia. Nor did he claim that the Soviets had undergone a fundamental change of heart. Conflicts of interest as well as ideology would persist—and a local conflict in a peripheral area could still drag both powers into a suddenly escalating fight. But the events of the past twelve months—since he had declared the Cuban quarantine—had shown the Soviets more willing to accept at least tacitly both this nation's superiority in strategic power and our restraint in exercising it. Despite an autumn incident on the *Autobahn,* they seemed more interested in effective agreements, less interested in military expansion, more interested in normal relations, less interested in belligerent speeches. West Berlin remained free, and the dangers of another direct nuclear confrontation were more remote than ever.

The breathing spell had become a pause, the pause was becoming a *détente* and no one could foresee what further changes lay ahead. With the gradual rise in the living standard, education and outside contacts of the Russian people—with the gradual economic and political erosion of the barriers which kept Eastern Europe dependent on the Soviets and separated from the West—no European accommodation looked impossible in the long run. Kennedy's stand in the Cuban missile crisis, said a European political leader in my office, may well be like the Greek stand against the Persians at Salamis in 400 B.C.—not only a great turning point in history, but the start of a true Golden Age.

In November President Kennedy, at the height of his confidence, pursued further his theme of peace through strength—with the release of a statement to American women on their role in the quest for peace,

---

7 This equal emphasis on vigilance and strength caused the Soviet Ambassador to inquire whether it was possible that the same speech-writer had worked on the American University and University of Maine addresses. He had.

with an address to New York's Protestant Council on understanding the emerging peoples, with a strongly worded and successful protest to the Soviets over their detention of an American professor, and with a series of speeches in New York and in Florida. On November 20 he transmitted an optimistic report to the Congress on our participation in the United Nations. On November 21 he started another tour into the heartland of the opposition, this time in Texas. That evening, in Houston, he talked of "an America that is both powerful and peaceful, with a people that are both prosperous and just." The next morning, in Fort Worth, he expressed confidence that "because we are stronger . . . our chances for security, our chances for peace, are better than they have been in the past." That afternoon, in Dallas, he was shot dead.

EPILOGUE

JOHN FITZGERALD KENNEDY had no fear or premonition of dying. Having narrowly survived death in the war and in the hospital, having tragically suffered the death of a brother and a sister, having been told as a young man that his adrenal deficiency might well cut short his years, he did not need to be reminded that the life he loved was a precious, impermanent gift, not to be wasted for a moment. But neither could he ever again be worried or frightened by the presence of death amidst life. "I know nothing can happen to him," his father once said. "I've stood by his deathbed four times. Each time I said good-bye to him, and he always came back."

John Kennedy could speak of death like all other subjects, candidly, objectively and at times humorously. The possibility of his own assassination he regarded as simply one more way in which his plans for the future might be thwarted. Yet he rarely mentioned death in a personal way and, to my knowledge, never spoke seriously about his own, once he recovered his health. He looked forward to a long life, never talking, for example, about arrangements for his burial or a memorial. He had a will drawn up, to be sure, but that was an act of prudence, not premonition; and asking Ted Reardon and me to witness it on June 18, 1954, he had made it the occasion for a joke: "It's legal for you to do this— because I can assure you there's nothing in here for either of you." Two years later, driving me home one evening at high speed, he humorously speculated on whom the Nebraska headlines would feature if we were killed together in a crash.

He had no morbid fascination with the subject of death. When his wife and daughter stopped by his White House desk with a dead bird Caroline wanted to bury, he preferred not to look at it. (Dead animals, in fact, appalled him. He did not like to hunt, was upset about the deer he had shot at the LBJ ranch, and often dangerously swerved his car to avoid running over a rabbit or dog, alive or dead, in the middle of the road.)

During the Berlin and Cuban missile crises, he expressed concern not over the possibilities of his death but over the terrible tragedy that might befall his children and all the children of the world. Even then he was not moody or melancholy about the subject; although his own letters to the next-of-kin of those killed in Vietnam, he admitted, constituted one of his most difficult tasks. Perhaps he came closest to revealing his inner thoughts when the Irish Ambassador presented a Wexford cup in honor of little John's christening with a poem:

> *. . . When the storms break for him*
> *May the trees shake for him*
> *Their blossoms down;*
> *And in the night that he is troubled*
> *May a friend wake for him*
> *So that his time be doubled;*
> *And at the end of all loving and love*
> *May the Man above*
> *Give him a crown.*

The President, moving toward the microphone for his remarks of acceptance, whispered to the Ambassador: "I wish that was for me."

Another poem—one of his favorites, which he often asked Jacqueline to recite—was Alan Seeger's "I Have a Rendezvous with Death." He was moved by the fact that Seeger had been cut down in the brilliance of his youth. "It is," he once said at a war memorial, "against the law of nature for parents to bury their children . . . a son with all of his life before him." "The poignancy of men dying young always moved my husband," said Jacqueline, "possibly because of his brother Joe." And possibly he lived each day of his own life to the utmost because he did not know when his own rendezvous with death might come.

Simply accepting death as an inevitable fact of life, and simply recognizing assassination as an unavoidable hazard of the Presidency, he refused to worry about his personal safety—not with any bravado or braggadocio but with an almost fatalistic unconcern for danger. He had preferred the risks of a dangerous back operation to the frustrations of life on crutches. He had preferred the risks of flying in poor planes and poor weather to the frustrations of holding back his campaign. And he preferred the risks of less protection in the Presidency to the frustrations of cutting off public contact.

He mentioned more than once—but almost in passing—that no absolute protection was possible, that a determined assassin could always find a way, and that a sniper from a high window or rooftop seemed to him the least preventable. Occasionally he would read one of the dozens of written threats on his life that he received almost every week in the White House. But he regarded assassination as the Secret Service's worry, not his. "Jim Rowley," he quipped, "is most efficient. He has never lost a President."

He paid little attention to warnings from racist and rightist groups that his safety could not be guaranteed in their areas. He went to Caracas where Nixon had been endangered by rioters, he stood overlooking the Berlin Wall within Communist gunshot, he traveled more than 200,000 miles in a dozen foreign countries where anti-American fanatics or publicity-seeking terrorists could always be found, he waded into uncontrolled crowds of handshakers at home and abroad, he advocated policies he knew would provoke venom and violence from their opponents, and he traveled in an open car in Dallas, Texas, where the Lyndon Johnsons and Adlai Stevenson had been manhandled by extremists—not to prove his courage or to show defiance but because it was his job. "A man does what he must," he had written in *Profiles in Courage*, "in spite of personal consequences, in spite of . . . dangers—and that is the basis of all human morality." Life for him had always been dangerous and uncertain, but he was too interested in its opportunities and obligations to be intimidated by its risks.

His trip to Texas, like his mission in life, was a journey of reconciliation—to harmonize the warring factions of Texas Democrats, to dispel the myths of the right wing in one of its strongest citadels, and to broaden the base for his own re-election in 1964. Just before he boarded his helicopter on the South Lawn—November 21, 1963, 10:45 A.M.—I ran out with some suggestions he had requested for "Texas humor." I never saw him again.

I must ask to be excused from repeating the details of that tragedy. How and why it happened are of little consequence compared to what it stopped. No amount of argument or investigation can alter the fact that Jack Kennedy was assassinated. His assassin was assassinated. His assassin's assassin, as of this writing, has been condemned to be executed. Some blame leftists, some blame rightists, some blame Dallas or the security forces, some blame us all. John Kennedy would have said it is too late to be blaming anyone—and he would have had compassion for his assassin and compassion for us all.

He would not have condemned the entire city of Dallas. Certainly the warmth of its welcome that day was genuine and impressive. Yet we can never be certain whether the fumes of hate and malice which too often polluted the atmosphere of that city might not have further distorted the already twisted perspective of one of its inhabitants.

He would not have condemned the Dallas police, the FBI and the Secret Service. Certainly there were limitations on their ability to guard an active, strong-willed President in a free society, and certainly to this President his agents were deeply devoted. Yet we can never be certain what prevented a more alert coordination of all the known facts on the Kennedy route and the potential Kennedy assassin.

He would not, finally, have doubted the conclusions of guilt pronounced by the Warren Commission. Certainly the members and staff of that Commission deserve the highest praise for their painstaking investigation and report. Yet, in the Commission's own words, "because of the difficulty of proving negatives to a certainty, the possibility of others being involved . . . cannot be established categorically"; and thus we can never be absolutely certain whether some other hand might not have coached, coaxed or coerced the hand of President Kennedy's killer.

Personally I accept the conclusion that no plot or political motive was involved, despite the fact that this makes the deed all the more difficult to accept. For a man as controversial yet beloved as John Kennedy to be killed for no real reason or cause denies us even the slight satisfaction of drawing some meaning or moral from his death. We can say only that he died as he would have wanted to die—at the center of action, being applauded by his friends and assaulted by his foes, carrying his message of reason and progress to the enemy and fulfilling his duty as party leader.

He regarded Dallas' reputation for extremism as a good reason to include it on his schedule, not a good reason to avoid it. For, with all his deep commitments, Kennedy was fanatical on only one subject: his opposition to fanatics, foreign as well as domestic, Negro as well as white, on the Left as well as the Right. He was against violence in foreign relations and in human relations. He asked his countrymen to live peacefully with each other and with the world. Mental illness and crime, racial and religious hatred, economic discontent and class warfare, ignorance and fear of this world's complex burdens, malice and madness in the individual and society—these are the causes contributing to the atmosphere of violence in which a President may be assassinated—and these are the very evils which John Kennedy strove most often to root out.

On the morning of November 22, as he glanced at a full-page, black-bordered advertisement in the Dallas *News* accusing him of a series of pro-Communist attitudes and actions, he said to his wife, shaking his head: "We're really in 'nut country' now." He spoke contemptuously of oil millionaires who paid little taxes, sounding as angry, she thought, as he had been one night in Newport when a wealthy Republican had complained about the minimum wage. But John Kennedy never stayed angry long. He had traveled to Dallas to tell its citizens that "ignorance . . . can handicap this country's security," and that "the righteousness of our cause must always underlie our strength. For as was written long ago: 'Except the Lord keep the city, the watchman waketh but in vain.'" On November 22, 1963, in the city of Dallas, Texas, the watchman woke but in vain.

I must also ask to be excused from repeating here in detail the re-action of his staff, his countrymen and the world during those dark days in November—November, a favorite Kennedy month, the month of his election victories and his children's birthdays and the Thanks-giving reunions at the Cape. "The only two dates that most people re-member where they were," the President once said, "are Pearl Harbor and the death of Franklin Roosevelt." None of us will forget where we were when we first learned, disbelieved and learned again of the death of John Kennedy. No one will forget how his widow, eyewitness to the lowest level of human brutality, maintained the highest level of human nobility. No one will forget how low the flags seemed at half-mast on that crisp New England kind of day when they buried him at Arlington Cemetery.

The intellectual who had written in 1960 that Kennedy, like his elec-tion opponent, was not "a man at whose funeral strangers would cry" was proven wrong. The name of a familiar Irish ballad, which I saw on a hand-lettered sign as we departed the previous summer from Shannon, summed up the feelings of many: "Johnny, I hardly knew ye." An era had suddenly ended, the world had suddenly changed and the brightest light of our time had suddenly been snuffed out by mindless, sense-less evil.

"There is a time to be born and a time to die," according to the passage he liked to quote from Ecclesiastes; but this was not John Kennedy's time to die. He had so much more to do and to give that no religion or philosophy can rationalize his premature death as though it served some purpose; and no biographer can assess his truncated life as though it had been completed.

He had written that his brother Joe's life, though denied its future promise, nevertheless had a "completeness . . . the completeness of perfection." He cited the words of Solomon: "Having fulfilled his course in a short time, he fulfilled long years." All this could be said of Jack Kennedy, too. But that is not enough. Joe's death, he observed, "seems to have cut into the natural order of things." So did Jack's. Upon his inauguration, he had vowed only to begin—but he had only begun. He was given so little time.

If one extraordinary quality stood out among the many, it was the quality of continuing growth. In November, 1963, he had learned more about the uses and limitations of power, about the men on whom he could depend, about the adversaries and evils he faced, and about the tools and techniques of policy. He had undertaken large tasks still to be completed and foreseen future plans still to be initiated. He had, in the words of his favorite Frost poem, "promises to keep and miles to go before I sleep." With all his accomplishments in the past, he seemed destined to accomplish still more in the future.

"What made it so unfortunate . . . about Kathleen and Joe," he once said, was that "everything was moving in their direction. [For] somebody . . . who is miserable anyway, whose health is bad . . . that's one thing. But for someone who is living at their peak, then to get cut off— that's the shock." That was the shock of November, 1963. Jack Kennedy was living at his peak. Almost everything seemed to be moving in his direction—abroad after the Cuban missile crisis and Test Ban Treaty, at home with the tax and civil rights bills, in office with a more complete mastery of the Executive Branch. He was healthier and happier than he had ever been, neither wearied nor disillusioned by his burdens, more respected and beloved than before, still growing, still striving, confidently looking forward to five more years of progress in the Presidency—and then suddenly to get "cut off." The world's loss is the loss of what might have been.

On the night of November 21, lavishing praise on Texas Congressman Albert Thomas, he had quoted the Scriptures once again: "Your old men shall dream dreams, your young men shall see visions . . . [and] where there is no vision, the people perish." Jack Kennedy was old enough to dream dreams, and still young enough to see visions. Of what could he have been dreaming as he smiled and waved to the people of Dallas on November 22?

On this most successful trip, he might well have been thinking of future trips, including an early one planned for the impoverished areas of eastern Kentucky for which he had initiated a crash assistance effort. He was planning for early 1964 a tour of Asia—including Japan, India, Pakistan, the Philippines and Indonesia. He looked foward to an official "state visit" to Italy with his wife. He had assured his happily harassed cousin in County Wexford, Ireland, that "we promise to come only every ten years," but he had later pledged at Limerick to "come back to Erin in the springtime." Most intriguing of all was the prospect of touring the Soviet Union at the invitation of Nikita Khrushchev, an invitation often repeated in the Chairman's letters and other messages. The test ban and other signs of accommodation had now made that trip possible; and a Berlin solution, or even a continuation of relaxed tensions, would have made that trip definite.

More immediate problems were on his mind as well. He was to have lunch back home on Sunday with Ambassador Lodge to discuss his most vexing worry, Vietnam. On his last full day in Washington, November 20, at breakfast with the legislative leaders, he had reviewed progress on the tax, civil rights and education bills, and spoken out strongly against attempts to curb his foreign aid funds and wheat sales to the Soviet Union. A host of Kennedy bills—on conservation, mass transit, youth employment and other priorities—clogged the legislative calendars and committees. The leaders were optimistic that all would pass that Congress, if not that session; and the President said they could stay all year, if necessary. "I am looking forward to the end of this Congress," he had told his last news conference like a prospective parent,

> but . . . this is going to be an eighteenth-month delivery. . . . By the time this Congress goes home . . . next summer—in the fields of education, mental health, taxes, civil rights—this is going to be a record. . . . However dark it looks now, I think that "Westward, look, the land is bright."

It looked bright in Dallas. The controversial nature of his program did not seem to have dimmed the enthusiasm of his reception—and Dallas had voted more strongly against Kennedy in 1960 than any other big city. Perhaps that encouraged him to think, as he rode through the streets, about his new proposals for 1964. He had started us working on that program more than a month earlier; and foremost among the new items was a comprehensive, coordinated attack on poverty.

More likely he was thinking of 1964 in terms of the campaign, for this was a barely disguised campaign trip. There was no doubting the fact that he would be a candidate for re-election, despite his smiling evasions of the question in public. And there was no doubt in his own mind that he would win, despite defections over the issue of civil rights. He expected to carry at least all the states he had carried when religion was a handicap in 1960—with the possible exception of a few more Southern states—and to carry as well California, Ohio, Wisconsin and others. In his two state-wide races in Massachusetts, he had moved from a squeaker to a landslide, and he hoped to duplicate that pattern nationally. The growing urban majorities, the civil rights movement and his new "peace" commitment might even have led to a fundamental realignment of political forces and a new and stronger majority party.

But he was taking no state for granted. He thought most states would be "a hard, close fight." On November 13 he had devoted the longest (three and a half hours) meeting of 1963 to preliminary planning with his political team of the 1964 convention and campaign. He favored a reapportionment of convention delegates to reflect actual

Democratic strength, a liberalizing influence comparable in importance and timing to Roosevelt's abolition of the two-thirds rule in 1936. We reviewed at that same meeting plans for convention films, loyalty pledges and state campaign organizations.

He had already flatly committed himself to a restaging of the televised debates with his opponent and was looking forward to them. He cautioned us not to talk to the press regarding prospective Republican nominees, fearful that our indication of a favorite might encourage the Republicans to turn elsewhere. Within the confines of the White House he predicted—and fervently hoped—that Barry Goldwater would be nominated. For Rockefeller to be named, he said, "would be too good to be true—but he doesn't have a chance." Romney or some dark horse, he felt, had a chance and would be tougher to beat than Goldwater, whom he liked personally but who stood diametrically opposed to him on every major issue. "This campaign," said the President with relish, "may be among the most interesting as well as pleasurable campaigns that have taken place in a long time." Defeating Goldwater, he thought, would halt the growth of the radical right and provide him with a renewed and more powerful mandate.

He expected his second term, like that of Theodore Roosevelt, to be more productive of domestic legislation than the first, with a more responsive, responsible Congress and a less distracting, distressing foreign scene. He did not deliberately defer controversial proposals until that term—with the exception of a few in need of more study, such as new patent and pension fund regulations, new tax treatment for foundations and the adoption of the metric system of measurement. But he believed that the second term would see far-reaching breakthroughs to meet the modern problems of automation, transportation, urbanization, cultural opportunity and economic growth. He anticipated that an increased stabilization of the arms race and an easing of East-West tensions would enable him to devote a larger share of expenditure increases to domestic and particularly urban needs. This trend was already reflected in his forward Budget planning for 1964.

Even more important were his long-range goals in foreign affairs—a Decade of Development to put the poorer nations on their feet, an Atlantic Partnership with Western Europe as an equal and increasingly more intimate partner, a United Nations made stronger as national sovereignty became weaker and, most importantly, an evolving *détente* with the Soviet Union and the eventual reunification of Europe. He had learned so much from the first and second Cuban crises, from his travels and talks with foreign leaders, from his successes and failures. He knew better than he had even a year earlier how to stay out of traps, how not to antagonize Germans, and how to stay on top of international nuclear politics. He expected, before the end of his second term, to be dealing with new leaders in England, France, Russia and China, and to be dealing with a world in which no nation or bloc of nations could maintain a meaningful nuclear superiority or retain a camera-free secrecy. New arms limitations, new science and space cooperation, new approaches on Berlin, and increased trade and contacts with Eastern Europe were all on the future agenda. And the one major foreign policy issue deliberately postponed to the second term was, as earlier mentioned, Red China.

After the second term . . . well, I do not believe he was thinking about that in Dallas that day. I do not believe he thought about it much at all. Certainly he would not have permitted any constitutional movement to enable him to seek a third term. As a Congressman he had supported the two-term limitation—the only specific restriction on the Presidency, to my knowledge, for which he ever voted. He had supported it, he once told me, not out of fear of dictatorship or as a reflection on Roosevelt, but out of the conviction which he retained in the White House that no President should be expected to extend his political and physical reserves beyond an eight-year period. "I think eight years are enough for any man," he repeated as President, adding that he saw no reason why the second term had to be any less influential than the first.

After the second term, what? I have an idea he would have groomed his own successor as Democratic standard-bearer, but I have no idea whom he would have picked, and I don't think he did either. He would have remained active and influential in the party—ex-Presidents, he said, in some ways have more influence than they did when they were Presidents. He would have written his memoirs. He would have spent time at his library.

But none of these outlets would have been sufficient for a man of his exceptional energies at the age of fifty-one. Occasionally he speculated about what it would be like, jokingly asking a former President of the UN General Assembly how it felt to be an ex-President, discussing with Truman his altered role, remarking on inauguration night what an adjustment it must have been for Eisenhower to wake that morning as President and leave that afternoon a private citizen. But he did not worry about it, and he told his wife not to worry about it. "Those things have a way of taking care of themselves when the time comes," he said.

Citing John Quincy Adams' role in the House after leaving the White House, he commented on the implausibility of saying "that at fifty-one there would not be something left to do." He might have purchased, published or edited a newspaper, as he once contemplated when still in the Senate, or become a syndicated columnist. He might have been Secretary of State in some subsequent Democratic administration. He might have been president of a university. When I told him that Bundy had been mentioned as a possible new president of Yale (but said he wasn't interested), Kennedy dead-panned: "I wish somebody would offer *me* the presidency of Yale!"

Necessarily on the list of possibilities was a return to his first love, the United States Senate. His wife, remembering his contentment in that body, once asked Ted Kennedy at dinner whether he would give back Jack's seat when the time came, and Teddy loyally said that of course he would. But the President was upset, and sternly told Jacqueline later never to do that to Teddy and not to worry about his future.

On November 22 his future merged with his past, and we will never know what might have been. His own inner drive, as well as the swift pace of our times, had enabled him to do more in the White House in three years than many had done in eight—to live a fuller life in forty-six years than most men do in eighty. But that only makes all the greater our loss of the years he was denied.

How, then, will history judge him? It is too early to say. I am too close to say. But history will surely record that his achievements exceeded his years. In an eloquent letter to President Kennedy on nuclear testing, Prime Minister Macmillan once wrote: "It is not the things one did in one's life that one regrets, but rather the opportunities missed." It can be said of John Kennedy that he missed very few opportunities.

In less than three years he presided over a new era in American race relations, a new era in American-Soviet relations, a new era in our Latin-American relations, a new era in fiscal and economic policy and a new era in space exploration. His Presidency helped launch the longest and strongest period of economic expansion in our peacetime history, the largest and swiftest build-up of our defensive strength in peacetime history, and new and enlarged roles for the Federal Government in higher education, mental affliction, civil rights and the conservation of human and natural resources.

Some moves were dramatic, such as the Cuban missile crisis and the Test Ban Treaty and the Peace Corps and the Alliance for Progress. Some were small day-by-day efforts on Berlin or Southeast Asia, where no real progress could be claimed, or on school dropouts or National Parks. Some were simply holding our own—no nation slipped into the Communist orbit, no nuclear war raised havoc on our planet, no new recession set back our economy. But generally Kennedy was not content to hold his own. His efforts were devoted to turning the country around, starting it in new directions, getting it moving again. "He believed," said his wife, "that one man can make a difference and that every man should try." He left the nation a whole new set of basic premises—on freedom now instead of someday for the American Negro

—on dampening down instead of "winning" the cold war—on the unthinkability instead of the inevitability of nuclear war—on cutting taxes in times of deficit—on battling poverty in times of prosperity— on trade, transportation and a host of other subjects.

For the most part, on November 22, these problems had not been solved and these projects had not been completed. Even most of those completed will impress historians a generation from now only if this generation makes the most of them.

But I suspect that history will remember John Kennedy for what he started as well as for what he completed. The forces he released in this world will be felt for generations to come. The standards he set, the goals he outlined and the talented men he attracted to politics and public service will influence his country's course for at least a decade.

People will remember not only what he did but what he stood for— and this, too, may help the historians assess his Presidency. He stood for excellence in an era of indifference—for hope in an era of doubt— for placing public service ahead of private interests—for reconciliation between East and West, black and white, labor and management. He had confidence in man and gave men confidence in the future.

The public complacency plaguing his efforts was partly due to a sense of hopelessness—that wars and recessions and poverty and political mediocrity could not be avoided, and that all the problems of the modern world were too complex to be understood, let alone unraveled. I believe that John Kennedy believed that his role as President was to initiate an era of hope—hope for a life of decency and equality, hope for a world of reason and peace, hope for the American destiny.

It will not be easy for historians to compare John Kennedy with his predecessors and successors, for he was unique in his imprint upon the office: the first to be elected at so young an age, the first from the Catholic faith, the first to take office in an age of mutual nuclear capabilities, the first to reach literally for the moon and beyond, the first to prevent a new recession or inflation in modern peacetime, the first to pronounce that all racial segregation and discrimination must be abolished as a matter of right, the first to meet our adversaries in a potentially nuclear confrontation, the first to take a solid step toward nuclear arms control—and the first to die at so young an age.

He was not the first President to take on Big Steel, nor was he the first to send a controversial treaty to the Senate, nor was he the first to meet state defiance with Federal forces, nor was he the first to seek reform in a coordinate branch of government. But he may well have been the first to win all those encounters. Indeed, all his life he was a winner until November, 1963. In battle he became a hero. In literature he won a Pulitzer Prize. In politics he reached the Presidency. His Inaugural, his wife, his children, his policies, his conduct of crises, all reflected his pursuit of excellence.

History and posterity must decide. Customarily they reserve the mantle of greatness for those who win great wars, not those who prevent them. But in my unobjective view I think it will be difficult to measure John Kennedy by any ordinary historical yardstick. For he was an extraordinary man, an extraordinary politician and an extraordinary President. Just as no chart on the history of weapons could accurately reflect the advent of the atom, so it is my belief that no scale of good and bad Presidents can rate John Fitzgerald Kennedy. A mind so free of fear and myth and prejudice, so opposed to cant and clichés, so unwilling to feign or be fooled, to accept or reflect mediocrity, is rare in our world— and even rarer in American politics. Without demeaning any of the great men who have held the Presidency in this century, I do not see how John Kennedy could be ranked below any one of them.

His untimely and violent death will affect the judgment of historians, and the danger is that it will relegate his greatness to legend. Even though he was himself almost a legendary figure in life, Kennedy was a constant critic of the myth. It would be an ironic twist of fate if his martyrdom should now make a myth of the mortal man.

In my view, the man was greater than the legend. His life, not his death, created his greatness. In November, 1963, some saw it for the first time. Others realized that they had too casually accepted it. Others mourned that they had not previously admitted it to themselves. But the greatness was there, and it may well loom even larger as the passage of years lends perspective.

One of the doctors at the Parkland Hospital in Dallas, observing John Kennedy's six-foot frame on the operating table, was later heard to remark: "I had never seen the President before. He was a big man, bigger than I thought."

He was a big man—much bigger than anyone thought—and all of us are better for having lived in the days of Kennedy.

APPENDIX A

❦❦❦

Selective Legislative Accomplishments of the Eighty-sixth and Eighty-seventh Congresses

1. The Nuclear Test Ban Treaty (required Senate approval only)
2. The Civil Rights Act
3. The Tax Reduction Act
4. The Trade Expansion Act
5. The Peace Corps
6. The Mental Health and Mental Retardation Acts
7. The Higher Education and Medical Education Acts
8. The depressed communities Area Redevelopment Act
9. The Manpower Development and Retraining Act
10. The authority and funds for
    a. A full-scale outer space effort, focused on a manned moon land-ing in the 1960's
    b. The largest and fastest military build-up in our peacetime history
    c. New tools for foreign policy: the Disarmament Administration, a revamped Foreign Aid Agency, an independent Food-for-Peace program and a UN bond issue
    d. The Alliance for Progress with Latin America
    e. More assistance to health, education and conservation than had been voted by any two Congresses in history
    f. A redoubled effort to find an economical means of converting salt water to fresh
    g. The world's largest atomic power plant at Hanford, Washington
11. Modernization of New Deal–Fair Deal measures:
    a. The most comprehensive housing and urban renewal program in history, including the first major provisions for middle-income housing, private low-income housing, public mass transit and protection of urban open spaces

    b. The first major increase in minimum wage coverage since the original 1938 act, raising it to $1.25 an hour

    c. The most far-reaching revision of the public welfare laws since the original 1935 act, a $300 million modernization which emphasized rehabilitation instead of relief

    d. A revival of Food Stamps for the needy, plus increased food distribution to the impoverished and expanded school lunch and school milk distribution

    e. The most comprehensive farm legislation since 1938, expanding marketing orders, farm credit, crop insurance, soil conservation and rural electrification

    f. The first accelerated public works program for areas of unemployment since the New Deal

    g. The first major amendments to the food and drug safety laws since 1938

    h. The first full-scale modernization and expansion of the vocational education laws since 1946

    i. A temporary antirecession supplement to unemployment compensation

    j. The first significant package of anticrime bills since 1934, plus a new act on juvenile delinquency

    k. The first major additions to our National Park System since 1946, the provision of a fund for future acquisitions, and the preservation of wilderness areas

    l. A doubling of the water pollution prevention program, plus the first major attack on air pollution

    m. The most far-reaching tax reforms since the New Deal, including new investment tax credit

    n. Major expansions and improvements in Social Security (including retirement at age sixty-two for men), library services, hospital construction, family farm assistance and reclamation

12. The Twenty-fourth Amendment to the Constitution, outlawing poll taxes (required ratification by states instead of the President's signature)

13. The Community Health Facilities Act

14. The Communications Satellite Act

15. The Educational Television Act

NOTE: This listing is restricted to measures advanced as well as initiated by John F. Kennedy and thus omits the War on Poverty Bill of 1964. While he was not present to sign approximately one out of six of the measures listed above—including such important measures as civil rights and tax reduction—and while President Johnson skillfully facilitated their passage, the Democratic and Republican leaders of both houses have stated publicly that these measures, too, would have passed the Eighty-seventh Congress had Kennedy lived and—in view of his role in formulating and forwarding them—properly belong in his record.

APPENDIX B

Selected Milestones in the Presidency
of John F. Kennedy

1961

January	Inaugurated
February	Proposes measures to end recession and gold outflow
March	Launches Alliance for Progress
April	Takes responsibility for Bay of Pigs landing
May	Pledges U.S. space team on moon before 1970
June	Meets Khrushchev in Vienna
July	Augments combat troop strength to meet Berlin crisis
August	Denounces Soviet breach of nuclear test moratorium
September	Challenges Soviets to "peace race" at UN
October	Calls for national program to combat mental retardation
November	Grants exclusive interview for publication in Russian newspaper *Izvestia*
December	Renews American commitment to Vietnamese independence

1962

January	Calls for new Trade Expansion Act
February	Proposes U.S.-Soviet space cooperation following Glenn orbital flight
March	Announces resumption of nuclear testing in absence of treaty
April	Seeks rescission of steel price increase
May	Increases economic stimulants in wake of stock market slide
June	Announces Geneva Conference agreement on neutral Laos
July	Outlines Atlantic Partnership in "Declaration of Interdependence"
August	Pledges 1963 reduction of taxes to boost economy
September	Sends troops to fulfill court order of desegregation at University of Mississippi

October   Imposes quarantine to force withdrawal of Soviet missiles in Cuba and rushes aid to India under attack from Red China
November   Issues Executive Order against racial discrimination in Federal housing
December   Concludes Nassau agreement on NATO nuclear fleet with British Prime Minister Macmillan

1963

January   Hails reunification of Congo through U.S.-supported UN effort
February   Initiates series of policy reviews following De Gaulle's block of European unification
March   Confers with all Central American heads of government on combating Cuban subversion
April   Takes first of a series of actions to prevent a nationwide rail strike
May   Seeks end to racial strife and discrimination in Birmingham, Alabama
June   Speaks at American University on test ban and peace, to nation on civil rights, to Berliners and other Europeans on U.S. commitment
July   Announces conclusion of nuclear Test Ban Treaty
August   Meets with leaders of Washington march supporting his civil rights proposals
September   Calls at UN for further U.S.-Soviet cooperation, including joint moon mission
October   Authorizes negotiations for sale of American wheat to Soviet Union
November   Initiates emergency assistance program for destitute areas of eastern Kentucky

Acknowledgments

It is not possible to list all those who helped make this book possible. I owe a debt of thanks to all who generously made available to me their files, scrapbooks or other materials, including Richard Neustadt, UN Ambassador Arthur Goldberg, Florence Mahoney, Bill Donoghue, Henry Kosinski, James McGregor Burns, *Time* magazine, *Look* magazine, CBS Radio and Television, ABC Television and NBC Television; to Dr. Wayne Grover and Alan Gorham of the National Archives for their invaluable assistance with my files; to all those whose accommodations were so helpfully made available, including Dean Don K. Price and the Harvard Graduate School of Public Administration, Master Richard Gill and Leverett House, and Ambassador Matthew McCloskey; and especially to all those who gave their time and talent to make helpful suggestions on the manuscript, including the Messrs. Neustadt, Goldberg and Gill previously mentioned and Charles Bartlett, Charles Daly, Douglas Dillon, Myer Feldman, Roswell Gilpatric, Kermit Gordon, Walter Heller, Sidney Hyman, Burke Marshall, Paul Samuelson, Richard Scannon, Stephen Smith, Thomas Sorensen, Dr. Janet Travell, Lee White, Theodore White, Jerome Wiesner, The Most Reverend John J. Wright, Bishop of Pittsburgh, and Adam Yarmolinsky.

My work could not have been completed without the tireless assistance of Carl Kaysen, who coordinated these comments and added valuable ones of his own.

Special thanks for their cooperation are due to Mrs. John F. Kennedy, Senator Robert Kennedy and Senator Edward Kennedy.

All errors of fact and judgment, of course, are the sole responsibility of the author.

I am grateful to Irish National Television for permission to use my favorite picture of the President, taken from a film showing him standing at attention at the graveside ceremonies at Arbor Hill, Dublin.

The task of deciphering my illegible pen fell principally, as it has for more than ten years, to Gloria Sitrin; and she was joined in this effort by

Rebecca Cooley, Christine Petrone, Rose Franco, Sue Vogelsinger, David Sitrin, Toi Bachelder, Valerie Cooley, Christine Camp, Mary Connolly and Stella Thompson.

While authors and editors are natural enemies, I freely confess that this book would have been poorer and later without the suggestions, encouragements and deadlines I received from Evan Thomas at Harper & Row. It was in fact his encouragement, along with that of Joe Alsop, Joe Kraft, Lipman Redman and William Marin, that persuaded me to undertake this project.

Finally, the forbearance and understanding of my wife, Sara, and my three sons, Eric, Stephen and Philip, were indispensable during the long days and nights this book was written over the last eighteen months. Fortunately they shared my deep feelings about the man whose memory kept me going.

T.C.S.

Hyannis Port, Massachusetts
August, 1965

INDEX

Abel, Rudolf, 517
Academic Advisory Committee, 388, 406
Acheson, Dean, 255, 256, 270, 271, 288, 334, 391, 571, 583, 584, 589, 590, 598, 675, 705, 719
Adams, John Quincy, 67, 289, 755
Adams, Sherman, 232, 238, 261, 262, 281
Adenauer, Konrad, 331, 541, 554, 559, 569, 570, 572, 578, 581, 584, 596-597, 598, 686, 705, 715, 720, 734
Adoula, Premier, 533, 638
Adzhubei, Aleksei, 515, 517, 552, 556, 598, 613n.
Adzhubei, Mrs. Aleksei (Khrushchev), 556
AFL-CIO, 52-53, 438, 439
Africa, 646, 662
"Africa for Africans," 538, 539
Agar, H. S., 62, 67
Agency for International Development, see AID
agriculture, 237, 741, 742
Agriculture Act (1961), 742
AID, 288, 350, 452, 530-531, 532, 534, 539
Air Force, 612
Air Force Academy, 605
Air Force Association, 739
"Air Force One," 367, 520, 601, 731
air strike (Cuba), 684, 685, 686, 687, 691, 692, 693-694, 696, 713, 714, 715, 716
Alabama, 478, 479, 488-493
Alabama National Guard, 493, 502
Alabama, University of, 488-493
Albert, Carl, 355, 356
Algeria, 65, 228, 547, 571, 638
Allen, George, 204
Alliance for Progress, 533-540
Alphand, Hervé, 559, 561
Alsop, Joseph, 66, 165, 272, 315, 379
Alsop, Stewart, 315
American Bar Association Journal, 67
American Medical Association, 343-344, 439
American Nazi Party, 504
American Presidency, The, 392
Anderson, George, 608, 698
Anderson, Marian, 240

Anderson, Rudolf, Jr., 713
Angola, 533, 538
Annapolis, 55, 370
anti-missile missile, 621
Arab League, 540
Area Redevelopment Act, 404
Aristotle, 367
Armco, 456
armed forces Reserves, 480
"Armenian Radio," 556n., 613n.
arms inspection, 518, 519, 728, 730, 733
Article VI, 110-111
Arvey, Jake, 53, 115
As We Remember Joe, 375
Asia Magazine, 581
ASNE, 144, 189
Atlanta (Ga.), 479
Atlántico (ship), 299
Attwood, 279
Australia, 647, 741
Austria, 548, 600
Autobahn (East Germany), 584, 587, 594, 598, 600, 745
Autobiography (Franklin), 100
Autobiography (Poling), 192
automation, 402, 441, 488
Ayub Khan, 664

B-26, 299
B-70, 390
Bacon, Robert, 2
Badeau, John, 54, 279
Baer, Howard, 101
Bailey, John, 82-83, 84, 87, 89, 117, 120, 171, 211
Bailey, Peter James, 190
"Bailey Memorandum," 82-83, 127, 146, 217
Baker, Robert, 165
balance of payments, 405-412, 563, 570
Baldwin, James, 503
Ball, George, 236, 260, 280, 282, 287, 288, 289, 323, 395, 411, 566, 674, 679, 682, 691, 692, 734
Baltimore Sun, 316
Baring, Walter S., 260-261
Barkley, Alben W., 118
Barnes, Donald, 581
Barnett, Ross, 483-484, 486, 487-488, 707